THE LATER MEDIEVAL CITY

A History of Urban Society in Europe
General Editor: Robert Tittler

This major series investigates the variety, functions and character of the cities of Europe, and the changing lifestyles of their inhabitants, since early medieval times. Strong in outline and rich in detail, each volume will synthesise the present state of scholarship on the often controversial issues involved; and each will offer interpretations based on the author's own research. The books will be necessary reading for students of urban and social history, and enjoyable and informative for non-specialists as well.

ALREADY PUBLISHED

The Growth of the Medieval City
From Late Antiquity to the Early Fourteenth Century
David Nicholas

The Later Medieval City
1300–1500
David Nicholas

The Early Modern City, 1450–1750
Christopher R. Friedrichs

The Later Medieval City 1300–1500

DAVID NICHOLAS

Longman
London and New York

Addison Wesley Longman Limited
Edinburgh Gate
Harlow
Essex CM20 2JE
United Kingdom
and Associated Companies throughout the world

Published in the United States of America
by Addison Wesley Longman Inc., New York

First published 1997

ISBN   0 582 01318 6   CSD
ISBN   0 582 01317 8   PPR

British Library Cataloguing-in-Publication Data

A catalogue record for this book is available from the British Library

Library of Congress Cataloging-in-Publication Data

Nicholas, David, 1939–
    The later medieval city, 1300–1500 / David Nicholas.
        p.   cm. — (A history of urban society in Europe)
    Includes bibliographical references and index.
    ISBN 0–582–01318–6 (CSD). — ISBN 0–582–01317–8 (PPR)
    1. Cities and towns, Medieval—Europe.   I. Title.   II. Series.
HT115.N55   1997
307.76′094′0902—dc20   96–27175
                                                                    CIP

Set by 35 in 10.5/12pt Bembo

Transferred to digital print on demand 2002
Printed and bound by Antony Rowe Ltd, Eastbourne

Contents

Contents

Contents

List of Maps and Plans

MAPS

CITY PLANS

Editor's Preface

The four volumes of this series are designed to provide a descriptive and interpretive introduction to European Urban Society from the Middle Ages to the present century. The series emerged from a concern that the rapidly burgeoning interest in European Urban History had begun to outstrip the materials available to teach it effectively. It is my hope that these volumes will provide the best possible resource for that purpose, for the serious general reader, and for the historian or history student who requires a scholarly and accessible guide to the issues at hand. Every effort has been made to ensure volumes which are well-written and clear as well as scholarly: authors were selected on the basis of their writing ability as well as their scholarship.

If there is a bias to the project, it is that some considerable degree of comprehension be achieved in geographic coverage as well as subject matter, and that comparisons to non-European urban societies be incorporated where appropriate. The series will thus not simply dwell on the familiar examples of urban life in the great cities of Europe, but also in the less familiar and more remote. Though we aim to consider the wide and general themes implicit in the subject at hand, we also hope not to lose sight of the common men and women who occupied the dwellings, plied their trades and walked the streets.

This undertaking did not come about by random chance, nor was it by any means conceived solely by the series editor. Well before individual authors were commissioned, extensive efforts were undertaken to survey the requirements of scholars active in research and teaching European Urban History in all periods. I am grateful to Charles Tilly, Miriam Chrisman, William Hubbard, Janet Roebuck, Maryanne Kowaleski, Derk Visser, Josef Konvitz, Michael P. Weber, Laurie Nussdorfer, Penelope

Corfield and Tony Sutcliffe, as well as of the authors themselves, whose comments and concerns have been extremely valuable in shaping the series.

Robert Tittler, Montreal

Acknowledgements

This book owes much to the support and encouragement of my long-suffering wife and to past and present professional colleagues, particularly Beth Carney, Richard Golden, Alan Grubb, Pam Mack, Steve Marks, Ed Moïse, Denis Paz and Bob Waller. The debt is especially great to Tom Kuehn, who read the entire manuscript and suggested emendations from the perspective of a profound student of urbanisation in medieval Italy. I am also grateful to the University of Georgia Library for permitting me the unrestricted use of collections there. The manuscript also owes a great deal to the careful critique that it received from Professor Robert Tittler, the general editor of the series in which it appears.

Dedication

The Later Medieval City and its predecessor, *The Growth of the Medieval City*, are dedicated in affection and esteem to Bryce Lyon, who suggested in 1964 that I write a comparative history of urbanisation in the Middle Ages and has been waiting patiently ever since.

CHAPTER ONE

The Medieval City at the Turn of the Fourteenth Century[1]

Cities, markets and trade before 1200

During the three centuries after the millennium the European city developed as a type and in a regional pattern that would remain essentially fixed politically until the rise of national capitals in the modern period, and economically until the Industrial Revolution, albeit with some important structural changes in the late Middle Ages. The concentration of cities in 1600, with northern Italy, the German Rhineland and the Baltic, and the Low Countries as the major foci and London and Paris overshadowing the urban development of the other centres of England and France, was almost exactly the same then as in 1300. The only exceptions were the growth during the sixteenth century of Madrid and Amsterdam from small places, Antwerp from a major city to a great city, the late medieval growth of Munich and particularly Nuremberg, and the decline of the lesser Italian centres.

The cities of early medieval Europe had developed on a Roman base with a structure of bishoprics superimposed on it. The episcopal organisation was principally late Roman, although in England it came in the seventh century and in Germany east of the Rhine it was Carolingian. Virtually all of these pre-urban nuclei housed a bishop, who was often the secular town lord, other priests and a smaller number of monks. Some housed a lay prince and his entourage in addition to or instead of the bishop. The demand market created by these wealthy consumers attracted some long-distance trade in luxury goods that catered to the

1   This chapter summarises the conclusions of the companion volume of the current publication, David Nicholas, *The Growth of the Medieval City: From Late Antiquity to the Early Fourteenth Century* (London: Longman, 1997). Readers who wish for a more complete explanation of theses or description of events are referred to that book.

ecclesiastical and lay princely courts, as well as artisans and local merchants. The capital base of these settlements was thus created by long-distance trade, almost entirely importing luxury goods. The population base, by contrast, was created by local trade and artisanry, providing utilitarian goods for the residents of the court but also for the traders who catered to them. There is little evidence in the north before the late tenth century of specifically urban elites or governments. In Italy, by contrast, which had stronger ties to Roman patterns of urbanisation, the official and landholding character of the urban elites remained strong, and the organs of civil government developed more quickly than in northern Europe. Evidence of local and long-distance trade centring in the cities of the north, and of mainly local trade around those of Italy, increases in the tenth century and quickens substantially in the eleventh.

While the tenth-century city was primarily ecclesiastical and political, and was almost exclusively a consumer of goods and services, its essential character changed in the eleventh and particularly twelfth centuries. It became an economic agglomeration that not only consumed, but also produced exportable industrial goods and provided important services of reconsignment of basic necessities as well as of luxuries. The major urban industries that produced for more than a site-based constituency at this stage involved working imported wool into fine cloth. This in turn necessitated importing wool and dyes from a wide supply area. Once the network for these exchanges had been created, first by direct contact between northern and Mediterranean merchants and more systematically by the Champagne fairs in the twelfth century, more goods joined textiles in long-distance trade. Some new towns were founded that eventually became major cities, but most urban plantations remained villages in an economic sense, as the available market for urban services eventually became saturated.

The growth of trade in raw materials and in luxuries from the east, and the interregional trade in fine woollens made in the cities naturally led to the increasing importance of merchants in urban society, but there is still little evidence of artisans except as producers for the courts of bishop and prince. As the cities became less seigniorial and their social structures more complex, their lords, who were more bound to the rural world, gave them charters that granted a limited right to manage their own internal affairs, usually through a council chosen by the citizenry. Particularly in France the grant of liberties sometimes came through the formation of a sworn association of the inhabitants, called a commune, which negotiated with the lord. If the first city government grew out of the lord's court, as happened in the Low Countries and Germany, the magistrates were usually called *scabini* (French *échevins*,

German *Schöffen*, Flemish *schepenen*). If it evolved from the sworn association of the commune, the councillors were more often called 'sworn persons' (*jurés*). In England, where the communal movement was much weaker than on the continent, they were 'aldermen', officers of the ward associations that comprised the city. Citizens were originally all members of the sworn association of the community or all landholders, but citizenship became increasingly restricted, particularly in the thirteenth century. Although we cannot say much about urban government in the north in the twelfth century beyond the fact that councils led it, in Italy the cities were already developing specialised services, several boards within what had initially been a single city council composed of consuls, and an independent financial competence.

The cities became focal points of more or less clearly defined local regions. This process went furthest in Italy, where the bishop as lord of the town and its surrounding countryside (*contado*) frequently led warfare with rival cities and developed a strength in the rural regions that was passing to the city governments even as early as the late eleventh century. During the twelfth and particularly thirteenth centuries the Italian city governments subjugated the *contado*. This process also aided the cities' efforts to control the local nobles who held both rural castles and towers in the cities and used both to wage warfare against their families' enemies. Control of the *contado* often took the form of economic exploitation in the thirteenth century, as some cities taxed the rural communities more heavily than the city, tried to hinder immigration, and forced peasants of the *contado* to provide grain at below-market prices to the by then overpopulated areas within their walls.

Although commercial wealth was becoming more important, social status and often political rights such as control of the municipal councils continued as before to be tied to landownership, most strongly in Italy but also in most north European cities. The norm in the eleventh century was for landowning families to use their city residences and contacts to expand into commerce, but the reverse process more often occurred in the twelfth and particularly thirteenth centuries, as persons who gained wealth through trade bought land in the city and then increasingly in the rural environs as a means of gaining social status and political influence. Immigration to the cities quickened, and some newcomers benefited through the urban charters by gaining legal emancipation from the bonds of serfdom, although this element of citizenship was not as universally applicable as was once thought. Many of the leaders of the older German cities, indeed, were descended from families of ministerials, the serfs who had elevated their standing by serving the local bishop or secular lord through controlling his castle or particularly his mint. By 1200 this landowning elite had made itself into a patriciate. It was by no means closed, but it controlled the burgeoning offices of city government. The earliest guilds in the cities were utterly unlike those that we commonly associate with the medieval city. Initially they were composed almost entirely of merchants and/or of landowners – the evolution of guilds of landowners into guilds of merchants can be documented most convincingly in England – but most cities of Italy and some in the north also had craft organisations by the twelfth century. Particularly in England and the Low Countries the merchant guilds are often hard to distinguish from the formal city governments. This bond becomes even more symbiotic in the thirteenth century. The merchant guilds that controlled Saint-Omer and Ghent are particularly famous.

Except in England, whose cities declined after the Norman conquest of 1066, urban populations expanded tremendously during the central Middle Ages, in many cases doubling between 1000 and 1200 and doubling again during the thirteenth century. This growth was accompanied by a progressive enclosure within the main wall of the city of suburban settlements that had developed outside the late Roman and early medieval walls. With the expansion of their walls, the cities became important as military strong points for their princes but also became better able to resist them. As the walls were extended, the first walls became internal but were not torn down, creating fortified sectors within the cities. Urban populations became more diverse, with a large artisan population producing for a market that was increasingly driven by the establishment of intercity networks of trade. Craftsmanship was less centred than before on the demand generated by princely courts.

With the physical expansion of the central Middle Ages, the centre of gravity within the cities shifted. While a single market had generally sufficed through the tenth century, multiple markets with specialised functions developed in the eleventh and twelfth centuries to handle the trade generated by the burgeoning resident population. Although local conditions determined the shape and location of the new markets, the main market of many cities was an open space just outside the earliest fortification, at its intersection with the first suburb to be walled. The street plans, often inchoate in the early Middle Ages except for the planned *burhs* of King Alfred of Wessex, became more regular in the areas enclosed later, some of which suggest genuine urban planning. This process culminated in the thirteenth century in the attempts of several Italian cities to use property vacated by confiscation during the political quarrels to straighten and widen streets and establish an imposing city centre dominated by public buildings.

The thirteenth century until about 1270

The thirteenth century witnessed the intensification of these trends. Whether any place except Rome and Córdoba was a true city in 1000 depends upon one's definition, but by 1200 a network of genuine cities was in place upon which most of Europe's exportable industry and a substantial part of its trade had become centred. The chief poles of urbanisation and certainly of city independence from territorial lords were more clearly now northern Italy and Flanders and adjacent northwestern France, but Germany also had substantial cities that would grow with the deterioration of the emperors' power in the thirteenth century. The English provincial cities, after a period of decay following the Norman conquest in the eleventh century, began growing through their role in the increasingly profitable Flemish trade, although London stagnated economically. Paris and London and its suburb Westminster were becoming the chief residences of the kings of France and England.

The fairs of Champagne reached their height in the thirteenth century as the major foci of exchange between north Italy and Flanders. But regional fairs were also scheduled to permit merchants to travel to the international clearing houses in Champagne, where banking facilities were increasingly centred. For with the tremendous expansion of international trade came a need to arrange transactions on credit, accompanied by the reciprocal development of mutually dependent trading regions.

The cities were still governed in the thirteenth century by fractious elites that were dominated by landowners who had subsidiary interests in commerce. Although commerce became increasingly important in the wealth of the landowners who dominated the councils in both northern and southern Europe during the thirteenth century, only after 1270 were many persons of purely merchant background who did not also own large amounts of land in the city councils. In Germany councils (*Räte*) were formed between roughly 1190 and 1220, evidently with the aid of the emperors, who hoped thereby to break the power of the older body of urban rulers, the *Schöffen*. In fact, the *Räte* and *Schöffen* usually shared functions, and the same families served on both boards. Membership of these oligarchical councils was often determined by heredity or cooption according to terms of the city's charter. Thus some councils, which had begun as elites of perhaps one hundred persons, as at Rouen, gradually narrowed to a few persons who perpetuated city government in their own families. Accusations of corruption inevitably followed. In the thirteenth century membership of city councils in northern Europe was generally based on membership of a merchant guild or lineage, never on membership of an artisan organisation. In Italy it was usually by geographical sector of the city rather than an occupational affiliation. Among the major cities of the north, only London, whose council of aldermen consisted of the law-men of the wards, had geographical representation.

In places, particularly in France, whose government resulted from a sworn association breaking away from the territorial government of the town lord, the structure of multiple councils is less often found. The officeholding elite was usually distinguished legally from the rest of the population, although all were considered citizens. They imitated the nobility, including by perpetrating vendettas, and a few families managed to marry into noble lineages. Although the councillors' social position and political privilege was still determined more by their possession of land, their wealth was being increasingly generated by trade. Although the feuds of the leading citizens made the cities dangerous and occasionally prompted intervention by the still powerful lords, in northern and southern Europe alike, they had a collective consciousness of their standing and strenuously resisted any effort of artisan organisations to penetrate the inner circles of city government. The ruling elites were always family-based and thus shared many characteristics of the landed nobility.

The northern regimes of councils seem to have used the Italian consuls of the twelfth century as their model. Yet conciliar government took different routes in north and south during the thirteenth century. One or two councils controlled most northern cities. In principle they rotated annually, although in some cities informal schemes were developed to return individuals of the proper family to office after a stated interval, during which others in the elite shared power. The change was accompanied in many cities by the council, particularly when it had consisted of *scabini* and as such was basically judicial in character, taking on administrative functions. The growth of public administration and finance is thus an important development in the history of the European cities during the thirteenth century. Some northern cities had mayors or burgomasters in the thirteenth century, particularly the French communes and the cities that were influenced by their law. Burgomasters are found in some German cities as early as 1174, and they were generally stronger figures than the French and English mayors, who were chiefly ceremonial officials.

In the cities of northern Italy, however, the consuls themselves, who were caught up in the endemic factionalism that would plague Italian urban politics throughout the medieval period, yielded in the early thirteenth century to the control of a single police official, the *podestà* or rector. The *podestà* was restricted in turn, particularly after *popolo-*

dominated governments came to power in and after 1250, by the development of a myriad of councils that rotated several times during the year. This was in contrast to the annual rotation that was customary in the north and was perhaps an attempt to keep any faction in the murderous feuding from monopolising power. For both the *podestà* and the councils the electoral procedures were extremely complex; it was either done by lot or involved several drawings and scrutinies.

The Italian cities in the thirteenth century were no longer communes with a single legal personality, as was becoming the case in northern Europe, but rather comprised various societies, consortia, 'regions', parish organisations, and the *popolo*. Most north Italian cities had a merchant association, similar to the northern merchant guilds, that controlled sales and the market and tried to control the crafts. Each of these had its own officials that in some degree pre-empted the separate officials of the communal government.

The *popolo* is a characteristic feature of Italian city government in the thirteenth century that has no equivalent in northern Europe. The *popolo* was not the 'people' in the modern sense of the word; it is closer to the present meaning of 'citizenry'. Although most *popolani* were merchants, along with some craftsmen, the leaders were landowners who were being excluded from the offices of the commune by the elite that controlled the consulate and the office of *podestà*. Some knights were in the *popolo*. The *popolo* was a state within a state, beginning as a personal organisation that linked diverse social groups within the commune that had the goal of limiting violence. They developed variously from tower societies and from other military organisations that were based on the gates and regions of the city. The *popolo* was thus a territorial organisation, with officials chosen by district within the city, not at first a guild-based organisation. It opposed the 'magnates', but some magnates were also in the *popolo*, and some wealthy merchants were seeking magnate status by buying land in the *contado*, acquiring castles and having themselves dubbed knights.

Popoli were being formed in the north Italian cities by the early thirteenth century, but they generally achieved power only in the cities of Tuscany and a few of the larger cities of other regions that were not firmly controlled by lords. The *popolo* was also caught up in the political fighting involving pope and emperor, which produced the Guelf (papal) and Ghibelline (imperial) parties, and family factions that adopted one side because their hereditary enemies took the other. Once in power in the Tuscan cities, starting with Florence's famous 'first *popolo*' in 1250, the *popolo* governments generally absorbed some of the other anti-magnate military societies but did not end them entirely. The *popolo* had its own officials who functioned alongside the earlier councils of the city but gradually limited them. They particularly restricted the *podestà*, who was associated with the earlier magnate regime.

The *popolo* governments divided the Italian cities into district-based military companies under 'standard-bearers'. They had a council of elders who eventually would become the major council of the city, although it remained technically a council of the *popolo* rather than of the commune. The *popolo* governments are also associated with a more intense exploitation of the *contado*, inflicting punitive taxation on it and turning it more overtly into a source of food and industrial raw materials than before. In the meantime they fostered industry in the cities that could be exported as the city elites expanded their trade. The *popolo* governments also multiplied the councils and are generally associated with Guelf, anti-imperial regimes, although they did not completely exclude Ghibellines from major offices until after 1270. Their focus was against magnates rather than specifically Ghibellines; but the Ghibellines tended to become more identified with rural landholding than the Guelfs in the thirteenth century. Thus the Ghibelline = magnate equation had more validity after 1270 than before and eventually contributed to their total exclusion from the government at Florence and less completely elsewhere.

The thirteenth century thus witnessed considerable turmoil, but it was less often of merchant versus artisan than of rival factions within the elite. Even analysing these conflicts in terms of old or landowning elements versus new or commercial interests is too neat to fit what was actually occurring. Local issues of patronage were frequently tied to the fighting, as was the church. In Italy the birth of the Guelf and Ghibelline political factions is connected less to a political programme or ideology than to questions of religious institutions and the desire of the popes to remain independent in central Italy. Also involved were the aspirations of the north Italian cities to consolidate the gains that they had achieved at the expense of their bishops and the German emperors during the twelfth century. The Guelf party became the official political party of the Florentine state. It formed its own organisation in 1267, complete with treasury, and was wealthy enough to be loaning money to the city government soon after. The Guelf party became one of the numerous corporations, including the *popolo*, that tried to govern the Italian cities.

The matter of borrowing by the cities leads to a discussion of their finances. Most Italian cities had a common treasury of some sort by the twelfth century, if for no other reason than to collect the money owed to the town lord, but we can say little else with certainty before the thirteenth century. Except for the communes the English and French cities had little independence in financial matters, but those of Germany and Italy enjoyed considerably more. In the Low Countries the cities were more or less on their own financially, with disastrous results, although this is clearest after 1270. Most cities used both direct and indirect taxation. In the north direct taxation was used at this time mainly for emergencies and indirect for the normal expenses of running the government; the reverse was true in some Italian cities. The basis of direct taxation was the taxpayer's personal declaration of his assets (*estimo*), usually orally before city officials but sometimes in writing.

Indirect taxation came most often in the form of excises on the consumption of goods that passed through the city's gates; for the cities had to import virtually all of their food and industrial raw materials. Since the northern cities had small bureaucracies – those of the Italian cities seem bloated by comparison – they usually left collection of these levies to tax farmers, which naturally led to abuses. This is not true of England, where the kings made the cities responsible for enforcing royal legislation but deprived them of the tax base that would have made it possible for them to do so effectively. Although Louis IX in 1262 required the French communes to present annual accounts to the royal treasury, this was not enforced until much later. Only after 1270 do many municipal accounts survive, and we cannot be certain how widespread comprehensive, annual written records were before this time. Some northern cities and virtually all those in Italy were already borrowing heavily in the thirteenth century; Venice established the basis of a funded public debt.

The influx of artisans had an impact on social geography in the cities. In the early stages of urban development the relatively few artisans had congregated together into the same streets – sometimes named after the craft – or at least neighbourhoods, but as population grew in the thirteenth century this became impossible. Immigrants tended to live initially on the peripheries of the cities but would move inside when the opportunity presented itself. Except for some artisan suburbs such as the weavers' and fullers' districts of Ghent, which were on the outskirts of the central city, and those where sanitation or noise was an issue, as in the case of the tanners and smiths, most crafts were dispersed through the city. Most city neighbourhoods had a mixture of rich and poor sectors, often interspersed, but the dispersal of interests throughout the city led to most city councils being chosen, insofar as they were not purely hereditary, on the basis of quarter or neighbourhood rather than professional affiliation. Choosing city councils on the basis of guild affiliation was rare before 1270 and only became common after 1325.

For the first time, however, manufacturing became an important generator of wealth in the thirteenth century, although artisans would only gain political representation even partly commensurate with this higher standing in the city's economy in the fourteenth. The immediate impact of the growth of urban industry was that artisans streamed to the cities, creating the enormous population boom that by the end of the century was straining resources. Citizenship, which had been a concomitant of membership in the sworn association of the city or was inherited from one's parents, became tied increasingly to the possession of land, which deprived some newcomers of the ability to participate in the political process. As the cities developed more services and councils, another common test of citizenship was paying taxes to the city.

Most cities except in Flanders and England had some legally recognised artisan guilds before 1270; they had existed in England in the twelfth century but became less numerous in the thirteenth. The earliest to organise were usually foodmongers and leather- and clothworkers. Each of these groups included both poorer elements, who rendered the basic services and/or made the goods, and a richer elite that engaged in the more 'socially respectable' side, wholesale merchandising of the goods produced by themselves and their guild brothers and distribution of raw materials, including but not exclusively to other members of the guild. An upwardly mobile artisan could easily expand within the trade by investing in the raw materials from which members of his craft made goods. Butchers not only cut meat for sale; they also bought and sold live animals and bought rural land on which to pasture them, both of which were activities that elevated their standing.

During the thirteenth century the gap widened, however, between the purely craft and the merchant elements within the individual guilds. Since the merchants who controlled the guild offices did not want their sale markets compromised by allegations of poor quality, thirteenth-century guild statutes, particularly for clothmakers, are extremely precise. The guild exercised quality control through inspectors. Sales had to be done at the city hall or the guildhall, depending on the particular conditions in the city, and then only after the goods had been inspected to make certain that they met the standards.

The city governments in the thirteenth century, as later, used craft organisations to control the artisans – indeed, sometimes the city rather than the practitioners of the trade appointed the guild officers. Some northern cities, such as Metz, had composite guilds on the Italian model, linking related or sometimes totally diverse trades under one umbrella organisation. The most common in the thirteenth century were drapers' guilds, which included the various clothmaking specialities under the control of merchant drapers who sold the finished product. Some guilds were already gaining monopoly privileges over the labour market in some cities, requiring newcomers who wished to practise the trade to join the guild. This was frowned upon by the authorities, however, and implementation of this key element of the guilds' agenda did not generally come until later.

The Italian cities too had craft organisations, and some achieved political recognition during the thirteenth century; but those few were even more strongly mercantile than the few craft guilds of northern Europe. The oldest and most politically respected guilds of Florence, whose membership contained a large magnate element, were the cloth importers, the moneychangers and bankers, and the mercers of Por Santa Maria street, which gave its name to their guild. They were joined in the early thirteenth century by the wool guild. As in southern France but not in regions of Europe farther north, some Italian occupational guilds evolved out of devotional confraternities to which an occupational component was added later. While composite guilds that included artisans as well as merchants were still somewhat unusual in the north, they were already the rule in Italy. As in the north the crafts enforced city regulations upon their members and normally had to submit their statutes to the city for ratification. By 1270 most Italian cities had as many separate craft organisations as the northern cities would have half a century later, but most of them were not guaranteed representation on the important city councils. They were more successful than the northerners in enforcing the principle that one had to be a member of the guild or at least submit to its jurisdiction in order to work in the city, but in Italy too the city government tried to break up cartels.

During the thirteenth century town lords continued to have important financial rights in virtually all cities, and some administrative personnel in most. Their demand markets for luxuries heightened as more goods became available in international trade. In Germany the town lords were generally weaker than in the west. The cities in the Rhineland, though not elsewhere, managed to limit their rights significantly, but this process would only culminate later. Where the town lord was strong, such as in England and Aquitaine, urban factions were frequently linked to political programmes that originated among the nobles, who in their turn developed parties in the major cities. London is a particularly flagrant case of this.

Lay town lords generally held their ground more effectively in the thirteenth century than did the bishops. The early power that the churches had in the cities was virtually ended by 1270. The Italian bishops had lost their governmental control to the communes in the early twelfth century and were concentrating on their rural holdings. This happened in northern Europe during the thirteenth century. But the bishops continued to be important landowners in the city, and the regalian rights that they had held, notably coinage, gave advantages to their ministerials, who still dominated city councils. In cities where the bishop was not powerful, most conflicts between lay and religious authorities were over whether the cities could tax church property, access on streets that went through church immunity districts, and particularly over the right of sanctuary, which the church extended to persons accused of crime who could flee to church property before being apprehended by the civil authorities.

The relationship between city and countryside in northern Europe during the thirteenth century was much closer than was once thought, albeit less symbiotic than in Italy. A 'ban mile' became a part of the corporate area of the city, subject to the same jurisdiction as the territory inside the walls. In cases such as Toulouse, where the city government controlled a larger area than this, the town lord generally cooperated or even fostered the endeavour, hoping to use the city magistrates to help control the rural areas. Thus the greater power of territorial lords in northern Europe in the thirteenth century prevented most cities from encroaching on broader areas until later. The reverse was happening in Italy, where the lords were being restricted by urban encroachments on the *contado*.

The cities of northern Europe derived considerable benefit from princely grants of privilege that gave them control of markets within their environs. Usually this gave the city power either over a region or over the marketing of a specific valuable or strategic commodity, such as the wine that made the fortune of Bordeaux. Such 'staples' were often also on the sale of food from the environs, at least in the north, where the cities lacked extensive *contadi* of the sort that fed the Italian cities at least into the thirteenth century. However, during the thirteenth century, all large cities had to develop facilities for importing grain from a considerable distance. Such municipal interference with the market mechanism often meant that peasants of the environs would be undersold; but it also led to the rise of economic regions with few large cities but grain surpluses, such as Sicily and Sardinia, Picardy and the German and Slavic East. The cities drew an increasing proportion of their food from distant sources in the thirteenth century.

The need to attract foreign goods and capital had been leading princes for centuries to grant to foreign nationals the right to have enclaves in the cities that they could use as trading posts. Often these persons were allowed to use their own law rather than be subject to the law of the host city. Particularly as the thirteenth century wore on the princes of northern Europe extended commercial privileges to Italian merchants in return for loans. In the period before the cities became powerful this does not seem to have caused much conflict; but in the thirteenth century it provoked resentment on the part of native merchants. Their domestic trade was guaranteed, not only for local exchange but also as sellers of goods that they imported through the privileged foreign communities, but they were unable to branch into exporting unless the foreigners were restricted.

The cities also began developing the notion of public space and buildings during the thirteenth century. Before 1200 most conclaves of city councils or other public meetings met in a Roman ruin or increasingly the square in front of the cathedral. The councils met in the town lord's palace or in one of the members' homes. But in the thirteenth century most cities built one or more halls, with separate buildings used for guildhalls, particularly Cloth Halls. Some city halls were differentiated internally for different bureaux. These halls were usually on or near the main market, sometimes – particularly in Italy – with a symbolic distance separating it from the cathedral, the headquarters of the erstwhile town lord, the bishop. Public squares were cleared and sometimes subjected to detailed building codes. Streets were widened when possible, and access to them protected by statute.

Despite the obvious features that distinguish the Italian cities from those of the north, recent research has shown some broad parallels. The Italian cities were much larger than those of northern Europe – places that were small centres in the urban world of thirteenth-century Italy would have been major cities in terms of size in the north. The Italian cities had control over a *contado* even before 1200, sophisticated financial bureaux, and conciliar government. They were also much more faction-ridden than those of the north, which in themselves were hardly models of public order. Extended family alliances were the base of officeholding and patronage in both Italy and the north. In both, but more often in Italy, surrogate families that had a biological family at their base but included clients also developed as political pressure organisations. In the north there was a clearer separation than in Italy between landed nobility and municipal elite, although some city people owned land both within and beyond the walls and tried to penetrate the nobility. In Italy from the early Middle Ages and perhaps even from antiquity the wealth of most families that filled offices in the cities came more from landownership than from trade. This may in turn be because, except for Venice, Pisa and Genoa, the wealth and population base of most Italian cities was in local, agrarian trade before 1200. To a great extent this continued to be true even in the thirteenth century, when Florence became the major exception to that generalisation; and Florence was also the most plagued by political conflicts.

During the thirteenth century control over eastern dyes and edible spices that were being sold to the northerners at the fairs of Champagne also came to form the base of much of the great wealth of the Italian cities. Before 1200 only the coastal emporia had been more trade-oriented than the leading northern cities. At precisely the time when the northern textile industries, which were now mainly centred on the cities, became so dependent on supplies from Italy that any interruption of supplies from the Mediterranean would be catastrophic, Italian financiers became indispensable to northern princes. While most northern cities developed a stronger industrial component than before, in Italy this happened only in Florence, where native woolworking took its place alongside the traditional speciality in Tuscan cities, finishing undressed cloth that had been purchased from northerners at the Champagne fairs.

The crisis of the turn of the fourteenth century

After 1270 important changes fundamentally altered the economic organisation of Europe and transformed the political and social structures of its major cities. The changes were at least as profound in terms of urban structures as those occurring during the years after the plague of 1348–9. Population expansion peaked in the wake of an ecological crisis that was prompted in part by overcropping, in part by a worsening climate that shortened the growing season. Food production diminished and prices rose, as marginal farmland fell out of cultivation. Severe weather-based shortages began in the 1290s. They were followed by plagues that struck the malnourished population. Perhaps 10 per cent of the population of northern Europe died in the catastrophic famine of 1315 and plague of 1316, and the problem was much worse in the cities than in the rural areas. Peasants streamed into the cities; but since the cities' markets had peaked and started to decline, they could no longer absorb the migrants.

Many cities thus began restricting free immigration for the first time in the late thirteenth century. Craft guilds also instituted restrictions on admitting persons who were not sons of masters, in some cases by raising entry fees to the guild, in others by limiting access to the guild to sons who were born after the father had become a master, and by restricting the rights of daughters to inherit their fathers' freedom in the guild. Many trades that previously had not been organised formed their own guilds in the half-century after 1270 to hinder access to the labour market. Unemployment was not helped by the attempts of some cities to attract skilled craftsmen while excluding the unskilled. At many places, such as Florence and Bruges, extentions of the walls that were planned in the late thirteenth century were either not completed for many years or simply enclosed vacant areas, which were expected to fill but did not in view of the falling populations. The situation was especially severe in northern Italy, which had more large cities than any other region.

The European cities became somewhat more industrial in this half-century. Industry certainly became more specialised, as regulations of quality proliferated, as higher-quality wool and dyes were used in the clothmaking process, and as more goods were coming onto the market. This threw the urban economies into greater dependence on long-distance trade; conditions had been stable but at a lower level at an earlier stage when most of the food and industrial goods had been imported from the immediate environs of the city and a circumscribed area around it. This in turn meant that trade disruptions could cause starvation and unemployment in the cities if supplies of food or industrial raw materials were cut off.

City populations became more diverse during this half-century, which actually made them more interdependent. The market for city goods and services became more directed than before toward other cities whose specialities were complementary, and less toward peasant and noble markets. But while the great metropolises had highly individual characteristics, there was a broad similarity in social structure among the middle-range cities. All of them had a large percentage of inhabitants who were food purveyors, construction workers, merchants and makers of commonly used utilitarian goods; the variable was in the number of craftsmen who produced high-quality goods, principally although not exclusively for export. For the majority of urban craftsmen most of their customers for ordinary consumer goods were within the city itself. As incomes of the urban wealthy rose, they became increasingly consumers of goods whose principal market had previously been outside the cities.

While before 1270 most evidence of economic reorientation among the urban elites involves landowners who were turning toward commerce, the reverse process now becomes strongly documented for the first time, as commercial families invested in land for security and social respectability. The extent of burgess landownership in the environs of the home city varied, but in most places it was significant enough for city governments to use the fact that under terms of their charter their burgesses were subject to the jurisdiction of the town court alone to gain juridical footholds in the rural areas. But while social prestige was determined by landholding and officeholding, most wealth continued to be in long-distance trade, which underwent important modifications at this time that would condition the nature of urban life and economy in the fourteenth and fifteenth centuries. The trend that we have observed in 'craft' guilds of the central Middle Ages continued, with a merchant element dominating those who remained purely artisans. But the enhanced opportunities for trade, both local and long-distance, meant that successful businessmen had several specialities, trading in different commodities, some connected and some widely disparate, thereby enhancing opportunities for wealth and minimising the risk of losing everything in the event of the total collapse of one area of endeavour.

Of critical importance in reorienting the trade of western Europe during this half-century is the fact that merchant convoys began sailing directly from the Mediterranean to the north European ports from 1278, and the rhythm of this trade quickened after 1310. Larger ships were now used, which permitted the shipment of both bulk goods and the traditional luxuries over great distances. The fairs of Champagne, which had been the commercial and financial nerve centres of Europe during the thirteenth century, declined in favour of the ports that were frequented by the Italian merchants. New banking centres developed: Bruges, on which so much of the trade of northern Europe with the south was now centred; Avignon, the capital of the popes; Paris; and London. Cities such as Arras that had been mainly dependent on the Champagne banking network declined. Genoa and Venice now became bitter rivals, and Florence rose as a banking centre, in a major shift that began during the thirteenth century and culminated in the early fourteenth.

Just as the volume and value of goods exchanged between distant regions increased tremendously, the plentiful supply of coin that had fuelled the economic revival of the central Middle Ages began to diminish in the 1290s, and the decline became rapid by the 1320s. This meant that while long-distance trade through the fairs had involved payment in specie and by commercial instruments, creating a balance-of-payments problem for kings but no serious problems for the city merchants, now it was necessary for regions to develop reciprocal trading arrangements so that goods could be exported and imported in rough balance. Thus England, for example, exported wool to the Italians in exchange for spices and dyes, and it exported both wool and cloth to regions of the northwest in exchange for wine, dyes, and bulk raw materials. The economies of the cities of France and England thus became more subject to royal regulation than before and more dependent on imported goods from the Mediterranean that passed through the Italian cities.

A critical part of this change is the reorientation of the Flemish and English economies after the commercial rupture of 1270 between the two. After that time few Flemish merchants visited England directly but instead bought wool from English exporters or the Italians. The English government began establishing staples or official depots for the sale of wool on the continent, beginning with a short-lived staple at Saint-Omer in 1313. The cities of the German Hanse began exporting the plentiful grain from the German and Slavic East, as well as forest products from Russia and Scandinavia, in return for cloth. They gained important trading concessions in Flanders and England, making themselves indispensable for the products that they brought but also causing friction with local merchants, whose ability to move into the export trade was being hindered.

These changes caused structural modifications in the internal government and society of many cities. London, which had declined in the early thirteenth century as the eastern ports expanded through their domination of the Flemish trade, grew again after 1270 as the point of entry for Cahorsin and particularly Italian merchants, many of whom were also moneylenders. The growth of foreign trade stimulated the supply sector, and craftsmen flocked to London. This led numerous crafts of the city to organise for the first time and prompted the city government to require the crafts to register their apprentices, since citizenship could be acquired through apprenticeship as well as through purchase and heredity. Since London lacked a merchant guild, power came to rest during this half-century with guilds of specialists that had a large merchant element, mainly in the luxury and food crafts. The best examples are the pepperers (who would eventually become the grocers), who imported dyes and spices from the Mediterranean and exported wool and who were thus bound to the king's staple politics, and the drapers, who imported Flemish cloth. Other guilds that had once been purely artisan, such as the fishmongers, also branched into exporting and thereby gained political recognition.

As the merchants gained control of the older guilds, smaller organisations dominated the 'craft' movement. Those that had a substantial artisan element, which are comparable to the Italian 'middle guilds', often split into separate organisations in the late Middle Ages, and it was at that stage that the guild-based urban governments were established. Between 1270 and 1325, however, power was passing to guilds that were dominated by merchants. The city council in London was composed of ward representatives, as was generally true in Italy. But after the king granted a charter in 1319 in response to agitation against foreign merchants, the foreigners had to use English and primarily London merchants as intermediaries to sell their goods in the counties. The aldermen and the mayor were to serve a single uninterrupted term in office, foreigners were forbidden to trade retail, and election by guild or mistery was instituted to replace election by ward, although this change had little practical impact for another half-century. In London the period after 1270 thus witnessed the consolidation of a merchant-dominated political regime under the guise of a guild organisation.

While London had at most 100,000 inhabitants at the turn of the fourteenth century, when a noticeable downturn began despite the heavy immigration, Paris probably had two to three times that number. The French kings had less trouble in controlling Paris than the English did with London, even though London was much smaller. Paris did, however, share with London the development of citizenship as an exclusive status that was tied to mastership – not journeyman status – in the occupational guilds. In both cities patronage of the royal court was important in generating capital. The French kings developed the status 'bourgeois of the king' to gain juridical footholds in the seigniorial towns, which were less numerous and sizeable in England, and began designating specific merchants who purveyed to the court as 'butcher [or whatever the trade] of the king'. As in virtually all major cities, great wealth could be made in only one way in Paris: wholesale trade in goods that the city or its exterior demand markets required.

Most large cities in France and the adjacent Low Countries experienced some agitation to broaden the basis of officeholding during this period. These were suppressed by royal intervention in France but were more successful in the Low Countries. Rouen's commercial privileges on the Seine were subordinated to those of Paris. The city's twelfth-century charter, the 'Establishments of Rouen', had created a self-perpetuating aristocracy of 100 'peers' that had declined to twenty-five by 1291. Following tax riots in the 1280s and disturbances from 1315 over allegations of corruption, this body was replaced by a new peerage of thirty-six members chosen for three-year terms by district of the city. Severe fiscal constraints and accountability were imposed on the mayor and the new peers.

The French kings also began to limit the autonomy of their communes during this period. Most were either terminated or placed under strict royal control. As in Rouen, old lineages that had constituted a relatively broad aristocracy in the much smaller towns to which the charters had been granted in the twelfth century had now died out. This meant that the oligarchy was smaller in cities that were much larger. High royal taxation, the lack of a tax base that could have paid the taxes and lackadaisical enforcement of the requirement that municipal accounts should be audited led to disorders, each of which resulted in royal intervention. The communes were so unpopular even among their own citizens by this time that the king felt safe in asking for a referendum at

Provins in 1320 on whether the commune should be be continued: the vote was 11.4: 1 against it in the city proper.

The cities of the Low Countries and northwestern France, which had a large textile-industrial component, saw more development toward a guild-based regime during this half-century. Craftsmen were admitted to the government in most of them by 1325. But – and this distinction is critical – they served on city councils as individuals, since the governing aristocracy was no longer restricted officially to the old lineages. They did not serve as representatives of their guilds. Only in Germany and in Italy did some composite guilds obtain the right to a certain number of seats in city councils this early.

The Flemish cities were hurt by the trade rupture with England from 1270, for other customers had taken up the slack for English wool before peace was re-established. This ended Flanders' near-monopoly on export-grade textiles made with English wool. As competition increased, unemployment loomed, and city governments restricted artisans when they tried to organise into anything more potentially dangerous than a devotional fraternity. The governments of such places as Valenciennes and Ghent were narrowly based and behaved capriciously. Allegations of fiscal mismanagement had a considerable impact; the cities were keeping written accounts by the 1260s, and these records show that the governments were borrowing heavily, in part to defray the expenses of their increasingly sophisticated administrations, in part to pay indemnities that the princes assessed after unsuccessful rebellions. The cities were increasingly using indirect taxes on consumer goods, which hurt the workers more than the aristocracy in proportion to their incomes.

As hostility between the French kings and the Flemish counts developed in the 1290s, political parties developed in the Flemish cities, the Lilies and Claws. With the Lilies supporting the French (the fleur-de-lis), and the Claws the Flemish lion, they have superficial similarities to the Guelfs and Ghibellines in Italy. These were not social conflicts, since lineages and commoners alike had members in both parties. After the famous battle of Courtrai against the French in 1302 the craft guilds were permitted to organise, and some craftsmen entered city government for a few years. However, after 1312, when the lineages returned, few guildsmen are found again until the 1330s. A city council of two boards of thirteen *schepenen* ruled Ghent after 1301, compared to three such boards earlier.

Following the agitation in Flanders, revolutionary developments began at Saint-Omer between 1305 and 1316 – with a similarity to Flanders in that guildsmen were allowed into the magistracy but few actually served – and in Liège. There the crafts initially had more success than in Flanders, with guaranteed seats on the city council after 1313. But from 1330 a twenty-four member council divided between 'greater' and 'lesser' persons was established, chosen by geographical sector of the city. And while the crafts gained some measure of political recognition, if not representation, in Flanders and the prince-bishopric of Liège, in Brussels during these years control was confirmed to seven multi-family lineages, each of which provided one *échevin* in a regime that lasted until 1421.

Since most cities of Germany were geared mainly toward local markets in the late thirteenth century, and some already had guild representatives on the councils before 1270, changes there were less revolutionary than in France and the Low Countries. The weakness of the imperial government and of many princely regimes had already allowed many German cities considerable local autonomy before 1270. Some city lords were still locally powerful in 1270, but scarcely any still were by 1330; financial embarrassment forced them to pawn and eventually to sell their remaining seigniorial rights in the cities to the local governments. The only partial exceptions are the bishops of the Rhineland, but even they saw their judicial powers strictly limited. Throughout the Rhineland the guilds of the mint associates, descendants of the ministerials who had operated the prince's coinage, became the dominant element of the council against whom the artisans were reacting. Cologne's archbishop became more often a political enemy of the city than its lord during this period. After 1321 Cologne was governed by a small council as heir of the thirteenth-century council, the *Schöffen* and the Rich Club of merchants who had controlled access to public office since 1179–80, and a general consultative council of eighty-two parish representatives.

Still, virtually all large German cities experienced craft revolts during this half-century. The early ones, between 1301 and 1310, were unsuccessful, and some were linked, as in Italy and the west, to party formations outside the city. New outbursts after 1327 meant that by the 1330s most larger cities of Germany allowed at least some token representation on the council for the larger, wealthier or more prestigious crafts. When guilds were allowed on the councils, they were generally composite groups, with a merchant element such as the drapers dominating clothmakers within the same organisation. Magdeburg gives an excellent example of how this occurred. After 1330 the city was ruled by a council of representatives of five great guilds, all of them mercantile, which had had seats on the city council since 1293. They were now joined by eight 'common' guilds that included more craftsmen, but some of them did highly skilled or necessary work and had a large merchant component, such as the goldsmiths and butchers. Erfurt had given ten merchant-dominated guilds guaranteed seats on the city council alongside fourteen from the lineages by 1284. This did mean some broadening of political participation, but it was more often giving more influence to newer families and to merchants at the expense of older lineages and landholders than to genuine craftsmen. On balance, however, although most German cities continued to be governed by councils, the changes during this half-century amounted to making lineage restrictions less strict rather than giving political rights to craftsmen.

The changes in Italy were spectacular but in some senses more organically tied to developments before 1270. In Milan and most of the smaller centres of the north local potentates were beginning to make themselves town lords, often using ancient offices or sometimes offices within the *popolo* organisation as a springboard to supreme power. Venice changed in a peculiar revolution: in 1297 the council was 'closed' with the inscription of the names of about 1,100 persons – double the number previously eligible for office – in a 'Golden Book'. Those in the Golden Book were considered nobles who were eligible for membership in the Great Council. In the beginning this represented a wider participation beyond the older lineages, but it became difficult for newcomers to penetrate the elite after a revolution was aborted in 1310. Venice was most unusual in making its governing elite a legally closed class. A committee of ten, which would eventually become the real executive and secret police power, normally functioned after 1316.

In Tuscany the main change was that the *popolo* councils were now chosen by a combination of district of the city and guild affiliation rather than purely by district, as earlier. At Florence the captain of the *popolo* began yielding to trade-based regimes as the city became more industrial and the societies less military, although lineage-based feuding was perhaps at its most severe at the turn of the fourteenth century. Conflicts became endemic after 1280, when the Guelfs tried to exclude the repatriated Ghibellines from the *popolo* and from political power. From 1282 Florence was governed by a 'second *popolo*' through a college of fourteen 'good men' and six 'priors', one from each district of the city. The priors were also chosen from the trade organisations, which now included five 'middle guilds' alongside the seven greater guilds. The priors served for two months and met regularly with the rectors of the twelve guilds.

In 1293 the *popolo* of Florence issued 'Ordinances of Justice' which brought seven 'lesser guilds' into the government, added a seventh prior called the 'standard-bearer of justice' who would be rotated among the six districts at two-month intervals, required the priors to be guildsmen who actually practised a profession, and declared 152 families 'magnate' and hence ineligible for all offices of the guilds or the *popolo*. The priors and the standard-bearer became the *Signoria*, the chief executive organ of Florence. The magnates had to post bond for their good behaviour. The twenty-one guilds and six districts provided priors who were chosen by a complicated procedure. While the middle guilds were predominantly merchant, the seven lesser guilds were mainly but not exclusively artisan.

The regime of twenty-one guilds established in 1293, each of them composites of several different trades but still disenfranchising numerous groups who are attested in the city at the turn of the fourteenth century, continued to rule Florence until 1378. The twenty-one political guilds had 7,000–8,000 members in the early fourteenth century, which is not especially narrow in a population of perhaps 20,000–25,000 heads of households. But few of them were ever priors; for although officers were technically chosen by lot, the drawings were rigged. Between 1282 and 1293, when the constitution was finalised, the major guilds furnished 90 per cent of the priors, and nearly half came from the Calimala and moneychangers' guilds. The priors were technically officers of the *popolo* but were in fact a city council. Magnates could still hold some lesser offices and enjoy patronage, and elsewhere in Tuscany their exclusion was less complete than in Florence. They remained an extremely wealthy and influential group. Guildsmen did not have much power in fact in Italy, but they had more in law there than in most northern cities.

Although control by the *popolo* through the priors was technically fixed, the family infighting involving Guelfs and Ghibellines, most often under such names as Whites and Blacks, so racked Italian urban society and government that after 1310 *balie* (*ad hoc* commissions designated by the *Signoria*) often suspended normal electoral procedures and named new priors directly. The *balie* were ended in 1328 in favour of a complex four-step electoral procedure involving scrutiny and power of veto vested in the incumbent *Signoria*, the captains of the Guelf party and officers of the *Mercanzia* (an organisation of the five greater guilds, first mentioned in 1308). The *balie*, however, would become an important part of Florentine political life again later.

At Siena the Nine, who took power in 1287, are the equivalent of the priors of Florence. They provided more continuity than did the priors, but many of the same principles of choice by lot and scrutiny apply to them. A major difference is that while the *popolo* that governed Florence developed a guild basis during the half-century after 1270, the Nine of Siena, although technically officials of the *popolo*, avoided this. The families eligible to serve on the Nine were a broadly based aristocracy of Guelf *popolani*, aged 30 or more, citizens for ten years, and taxpayers. They served two-month terms, as did the priors, but in strict isolation in the city hall. Far from being dictators, they could issue no new ordinances unless they had been approved by a two-thirds majority of the Council of the Bell, a district-based assembly of more than three hundred members. Although Siena was officially Guelf, the party label was much less important than in Florence. As virtually everywhere, this regime at Siena severely limited both the *podestà* and the captain of the *popolo*.

Thus in Italy this half-century saw the consolidation of the rule of groups within the commune variously called *popolo*, Guelf or Ghibelline party. The conflicts had less impact than one would expect on the formal structure of the permanent institutions of government, which were broadly similar in the cities of Tuscany but more varied in Lombardy and the coastal metropolises. Family competition for offices and power was strong everywhere, overshadowing the formal government of the city whether through a *popolo* or not. Disorder was so endemic and these *popolo*-based regimes were so weak by 1325 that the way was opened for strongmen to seize power in the next period.

Both the tax bases and the level of taxation in the Italian cities were considerably higher at this time than was true of the north. Despite this, Italian sources do not have the vociferous complaints about peculation by city officials that so disturbed the northern centres at the turn of the fourteenth century. Part of the reason is that the various treasuries were so independent that no one was sure who was doing what. Although around 1300 the cities were trying to centralise their finances, individual corporations still had their own treasuries and financed some activities on behalf of the commune. All Italian cities were taxed mercilessly by the wasteful regime of huge and undifferentiated councils. The tax burden grew tremendously in the thirteenth century and did not diminish with the onset of population decline around 1300. There was thus an even greater temptation to shift the burden to the *contado*. The Italian cities relied mainly on direct taxation until around 1250, particularly for the *contado*, basing it, as before, on the taxpayer's declaration of his own assets, but now more often actually collecting it.

The decades at the turn of the fourteenth century thus witnessed severe disorder in cities virtually everywhere but ended in the consolidation of regimes whose composition would be changed later in northern Europe, mainly by giving certain guilds and groups of guilds the statutory right to seats on the councils. Later modifications of the formal conciliar structure in Italy were even less significant, although the councils in many cities would yield in fact if not in name to locally-based despotisms. The governmental changes evolved against a backdrop of growing regional interdependence for both luxuries and basic raw materials that fostered trade, just as a severe shortage of coin was making trading relations more genuinely reciprocal than before. The cities were producing a much greater variety and a higher quality of exportable industrial goods than before. More and finer goods were being conveyed to distant places by city merchants, who developed sophisticated business techniques. In the coming chapters we shall explore the continuing evolution of these trends into a mature urban system.

CHAPTER TWO

Cities in Crisis: the Economic and Demographic Realignments of Urban Europe in the Later Middle Ages

Changes in long-distance trade

We have noted that by 1325 long-distance trade had quickened and diversified in volume. Local markets were much expanded, while many long-distance traders, and even some more modest merchants and artisans, handled their business in foreign parts by written messages. The spread of partnerships and branches into overseas locales, which were linked to the home office and to partners in different cities by correspondence, is perhaps the most important change in commercial technique associated with the late Middle Ages. In 1357, seventeen Florentine companies established the *Scarsella dei mercanti fiorentini* [*Purse of the Florentine Merchants*], a weekly courier service between Florence and Avignon over Genoa. Companies other than the founders could also use the service, but their messages went to the end of the queue. Elsewhere private individuals offered courier services between cities, but this was more expensive, for each voyage to a distant location had to be negotiated individually with the correspondent. Municipal governments frequently and regularly sent messengers to other cities with whose merchants trade was significant, often with 'letters for their market'. Thus more news was being spread about topics such as political events, changes in fashion, what was likely to be produced locally in surplus in a given year and thus have low prices, and what was scarce and thus a good risk for importers. All of this made possible more rational business calculation and fostered regional interdependence.[1]

---

1   Favier, *De l'or et des épices*, 85–8; Municipal Archive of Ghent, ser. 400, 9, fo. 246r.

In northern Europe, the decline of the Champagne fairs centred this change on the Bruges market, the Frankfurt fairs and Nuremberg. Grain, once unusual in long-distance commerce, was now exported by the Hanse cities from the German and Slavic east to the overpopulated west. Items once considered luxuries were now necessities. The most common industrial operations required goods that had to be imported, often from a considerable distance. City populations had always been dependent on grain imports. As the cities became more (if rarely predominantly) industrial, they depended on their governments and their merchant leaders to secure and protect the sources of industrial raw materials.

The late Middle Ages witnessed important changes in business techniques. Long-distance merchants of the early Middle Ages had been wanderers who accompanied their goods to market. Most full-time merchants were 'marginals' such as Jews and Syrians. Many domain agents of landlords, ministerials and transporters also sold goods as a secondary interest. A third group consisted of local merchants who specialised in food and agricultural products that had an industrial application. With minimal government control over the market, the second and third groups were the political and economic elite of most cities before the mid-thirteenth century. By 1320, however, many cities were controlled by guilds that included some craftsmen who were also merchants (especially those dealing in food products), and merchant-craftsmen who sold on a regional rather than interregional market. This group, of less total wealth than the older families, was pushing long-distance traders out of local retail sales to some degree. For example, while in the thirteenth century the cloth cutters had monopolised importing luxury textiles and selling the locally manufactured product, some weavers entered the cloth cutting trade in the fourteenth and fifteenth centuries. The older cloth cutting unions became 'political guilds' or even social clubs.[2]

Industry and the urban market

The fact that guilds controlled city governments does not mean that manufacturing became the basis of urban wealth. Industrial technology did not change much in the late Middle Ages. The Arsenal (shipyard) of Venice was similar to a factory, mass-producing goods with standard specifications. Individual construction guilds that worked in the Arsenal had their own statutes and were highly skilled and well paid.[3] As in the west, industrial production in the Muslim cities was mainly in the house-

---

2 Analysis based on Irsigler, 'Kaufmannstypen', 385–93.
3 Dante Alighieri used the Arsenal as an example of crowded conditions in Hell. Mackenney, *Tradesmen and Traders*, 11; Lane, *Venice*, 163.

hold unit except for trades producing for the ruler or the army – for example, the arsenal, royal textile workshops and the sugar factories of Egypt.[4] Some metalworking in the European cities was conducted in large work places by the sixteenth century; but most other urban industrial production, even if strictly regulated by the city or a guild, was conducted in the household, in which large-scale mechanisation was unfeasible. Most goods were produced in the family, supplemented by journeymen and apprentices as needed. Demography and its concomitant, the supply-demand nexus, were the basic determinants of production levels: for the more people, the more shops and the more was produced within each shop. As heavy migration provided the towns with more cheap labour than their economies could absorb in a period of contraction in all but the most skilled trades, there was no motive to mechanise.

Wage figures have been used to determine standards of living, but there are so many variables that they must be used with extreme caution. In some trades the master sold his product and did not get a wage. In others the wages paid to masters varied considerably, depending on the skill required and market demand, while unskilled workers were paid a daily wage at roughly the same rate across trades. The fact that our best wage figures are for construction workers also distorts our perception, for they tended to have high wages when they worked, but they were employed irregularly. Nominal wages (the wage expressed simply in amount of coin) were remarkably stable during this period, despite the fall in prices at the end of the fourteenth century. But real wages (wages seen in terms of their purchasing power, i.e. the nominal wage adjusted for inflation) in most cities seem to have risen quickly until the mid-fourteenth century. There was a sudden jump immediately after the plagues, followed by a decline. Such broad figures conceal as much as they reveal. Seasonal drops in wages were quite severe, as were supply-generated variations in food prices. Comparing nominal wages to wheat prices in Florence suggests that real wages rose by about 50 per cent between 1348 and 1360, then held high until a decline began in 1370. Since nominal wages were generally steady, the difference was caused by the fluctuation of wheat prices, which were kept low by population decline.[5] At Ghent real wages rose sharply in the 1350s and 1360s, stabilised somewhat in the 1370s while remaining high, then dropped dramatically with the onset of civil war in 1379.[6]

Increased demand for goods provoked a wage rise in the fifteenth

4 Hourani, *History of the Arab Peoples*, 112.
5 Goldthwaite, *Building of Renaissance Florence*, 317–42.
6 Nicholas, *Metamorphosis*, 120–34.

century. By 1440 wages in the French cities had reached levels higher than ever before except immediately after 1348, and grain prices dropped. At Rouen real wages were then triple those of 1320–30. A master mason of Tours around 1450 earned 50 per cent more than his ancestor of 1380–1420. In the Burgundian Netherlands the period from 1433 to 1467, the maturity of Count Philip 'the Good', saw real wages in the cities at their peak.[7]

The movement of prices and wages contributed to a 'golden age of the family shop, but not of the enterprise', the larger operation that paid wages to workers. Those who owned their shops and thus had steady work did well; those who were employed by others did not. Small operators were dependent also on suppliers of raw materials, who as merchants controlled the market and gave work, paying the manufacturer a wage unless he had direct access to the market. Capital accumulation was hard under these circumstances, although some managed it, through diversification of endeavour rather than concentration on one product or type of work.[8]

Diversification of urban textile production

The textile industry that had been so instrumental in the rise of the northern cities underwent important structural modifications. Changes occurred in the geography of woollen clothmaking. Mixed-fabric textiles were entering the international market for the first time. Coarse cloth had always been made in the rural areas, but even in the late thirteenth century medium-grade rural cloth was competing with that of the cities. The cities too were making more diverse grades, particularly mixtures of wool with cotton or linen. Worsteds were made at Norwich along with traditional broadcloths, but the city also sold abroad fabrics produced in rural Norfolk.[9] Changing fashions promoted the large-scale manufacture of lighter and mixed fabrics. A new market for underwear stimulated production of linen and tirtey, a mixture of wool and linen. Cologne's export market for tirtey in France and the Low Countries was less affected than traditional woollens by depression in the fifteenth century. Tirtey weavers were subject to the wool weavers' guild, paying one-quarter their entry fee, but until 1429 many weavers made both types, for the difference between heavier woollens and tirteys was in the quality of wool used; the technology was the same for both.

7 Rossiaud, 'Crises', 491.
8 Chevalier, *Bonnes villes*, 151–62.
9 The name 'worsted' comes from the village of Worstead, northeast of Norwich. Lobel, *Atlas* 2: 15.

The expanding use of cotton and fustian also gave employment to weavers that cushioned the decline of the older specialities.[10]

Traditional woollens were also affected, but here the guilds limited change. In 1340 war drove drapers from Aubenton, 60 km north of Reims, into the city, where they were immediately received into the guild. The archbishop issued a new statute governing the manufacture of the lighter types of cloth in which Aubenton had specialised. Thus 'new drapery' came to Reims from Aubenton.[11] Rouen's development was similar initially but did not lead to more diversified production. Until the mid-fourteenth century Rouen's entire product was luxury woollens, but the influx of refugees who complained to the king that local people were preventing them from working led in 1373 to a royal ordinance giving newcomers the right to work in the city and suburbs for ten years, on condition that their work be of good quality and not imitate the specialities of the old guild. In 1402 the bailiff subjected these 'external drapers' to the same industrial regulations required in 'great drapery', but relations between the two now equal branches of drapery were hostile.[12]

Some older centres stubbornly concentrated even more than before on the luxury market, in effect abandoning production of the cheaper grades to the small centres. At Florence, where one-third of the population was probably involved in clothmaking by 1330, the industry became so concentrated on luxuries for export that there were complaints by the late fourteenth century that Florentine cloth could not be found on the local market. Florence had been unusual among the Italian cities in having a significant textile industry early, but into the thirteenth century it was mainly refining unfinished cloth brought from the north. Giovanni Villani's famous complaint that Florence had about three hundred workshops producing 100,000 pieces of cloth around 1300 but only two hundred shops producing 70,000–80,000 pieces by 1338 misses an important point: the value of the cloth had doubled, because Florence had recently begun using fine English wool. Florence's economic expansion after 1350 thus came through banking connections with Rome and papal Avignon and in court markets for luxury woollens and silks.[13] Silkworking became the export speciality of several cities, particularly Lucca, which had already been famed for its silk in the thirteenth century. Genoa, which never had a major export trade in woollens, exported

10 Irsigler, *Wirtschaftliche Stellung Köln*, 18–20.
11 Desportes, *Reims*, 348–50.
12 Mollat, *Histoire de Rouen*, 103–4.
13 Goldthwaite, *Building of Renaissance Florence*, 34–6, 42–4; Luzzatto, *Economic History of Italy*, 97, 106.

considerable quantities of silk; but until the city began introducing silkworms in its environs in the mid-fifteenth century, its weavers were finishers of raw silk imported by merchants.[14]

The large cities of Flanders and Brabant, which originally had produced a variety of cloths for export, abandoned the cheaper grades to the villages and small towns and concentrated on one or two luxury textiles. The Flemish cities relentlessly suppressed rural textile industries that they considered imitations of these specialities, but the domestic market for cloth also explains much industrial protectionism: Ghent and Ypres forbade the sale on the local market of any cloth of whatever grade not produced locally, thus giving an immense captive market to local craftspeople. Except for the greatest industrial centres, however, the protectionist measures were limited. Virtually all cities imported large amounts of cloth from other cities. The city government of Metz protected the interests of the merchant drapers, who sold both local and imported cloth, but was hostile to the turbulent weavers. From 1380 wholesale purchases of foreign or domestic cloth had to be made four times yearly in 'display areas'. Exporting local wool through the city market was encouraged, and the government actually benefited from taxing imported cloth.[15] Bruges had an important textile industry but permitted the sale of foreign cloth, which was an important part of its commercial prosperity. The open market could have an adverse impact on local industry, particularly in cities where the crafts had little political influence. Production of linen and fustian declined at Barcelona in the fifteenth century as a result of competition on the local market from foreign imports, which was made possible by royal guarantees of free trade in Barcelona to Italian, German and Savoyard merchants.[16]

Industry and the international market

Thus the merchant elite that directed the wealthier and more prestigious crafts was supplying a regional as well as a long-distance market, making a wider range of consumer goods available locally and controlling access to them through staples or other regional privileges. The late medieval city was a centre of regional exchanges and re-export. The city market was large and wealthy enough to make it profitable to import exotic goods for sale there, but this in turn made these commodities available to peasants and others within the city's economic region who

---

14   Heers, *Gênes. Civilisation*, 184–91.
15   Schneider, *Ville de Metz*, 240–1.
16   Carrère, *Barcelone*, 370.

bought in its market. From here it was an easy step for urban merchants to sell these goods in the markets of the small centres, which became dependent on the large cities for luxuries and some necessities that had to be imported from a great distance. Thus, although most attention has been given to the importance of locally produced industrial goods in the export trade of the cities, they also re-exported large quantities of raw materials that they initially had imported. Gdánsk is a particularly good example. The city received metals coming downstream along the Vistula; rye from Prussia, wood from Masovia, and goods from the Black Sea region that were obtained through Kraków. Gdánsk established colonies in Lithuania to get wax, amber and furs, which were in high demand in western Europe, and traded these exportable raw materials in the Lübeck–Bruges–England network. This also gave merchants of Gdánsk access to locally produced goods such as English, Flemish and Brabantine cloth, and also commodities that came to Bruges from the south, such as salt and southern French wine.[17]

Although rural and village industries were growing, the smaller places had to get their products into the international markets through the great cities. Many German centres became dependent on the Frankfurt fairs and the Hanse cities, adding to the wealth that the carrying trade was providing for their merchants. The new international emporia attracted wealthy merchants who had no interest in promoting the interests of craftsmen and lesser traders of their home cities, but rather benefited from fostering industry in the environs.

Whilst in the early Middle Ages a place that could convert the products of its region into manufactured goods could expand into a major city, so many specialised products were available by the fourteenth century that no place could become great from only one. Expansion required a combination of advantages that were generally acquired only over a long history. Export now required gaining access to a complex mechanism of international trading. Thus in the late Middle Ages the export depot was the large city that had existed for several centuries, over time developing central facilities, capital and international ties. These cities usually subordinated the independent trade of the places where the goods were actually extracted or made, thus preventing them from growing into major cities. For example, Cologne controlled the Rhenish trade in wire, and copper workers were the most rapidly growing metal craft there in the fifteenth century. Yet the device for drawing wire was invented at Iserlohn, and the first wire factory was built nearby.[18]

17 Favier, *De l'or et des épices*, 27–8.
18 Irsigler, *Wirtschaftliche Stellung Köln*, 52, 118; Peeters, 'De-industrialization in Brabant', 165; van der Wee, 'Structural changes', 222.

The cloth produced by the smaller Flemish communities passed into the international market through German and Italian firms headquartered at Bruges. Tuscan merchant houses such as Alberti and Datini bought immense amounts of cloth in the small towns of the Leie river valley in southern Flanders, putting out raw wool to local labourers, then exporting it through Bruges to the Mediterranean. Poperinge, the largest of the secondary Flemish centres, sold light woollens in the Slavic east. Before the mid-fifteenth century the city's drapers agreed to sell their entire product through the Hanse offices in Bruges, evidently at the Germans' initiative.[19] The decaying textile industry of Saint-Omer became dependent on the Germans: a text of 1389 says that 'when they arrived, the bell of the hall was sounded, all cloths had to be taken to the hall, and for three days no one else could buy'. The Germans eventually demanded that the cloth be taken to the fairs of Antwerp and Bergen-op-Zoom and even Utrecht, saving them a trip to the manufacturing site.[20]

Accordingly, the most prosperous 'crafts' were actually those that engaged in long-distance importing. The politically powerful drapers of London controlled the sale of imported cloth, particularly from Flanders. The magistrates of Ghent forbade dyers to buy dyes with the intent of reselling them and tried to keep them from branching into wool sales. Their efforts were fruitless, and prominent dyers not only controlled sales of the imported colours to their guild brothers but also brokered supplies of dyes and alum that went to the smaller Flemish cities.[21]

Access to international goods and capital markets was a key to Cologne's success. Cologne's government was not industrial-protectionist. Foreign cloth sales were a monopoly of the patrician brotherhood of 'cloth cutters under the Gaddemen'. Cologne marketed the cloth of its environs, much of which was made according to Cologne specifications. Much of the cloth cutters' trade came from merchants of Brabant and the Meuse towns, who stopped to get a safe conduct for the Frankfurt fairs. Businessmen of Cologne also sold considerable quantities of English cloth, especially through the fairs but also by direct ties to Venice and throughout Germany. In the opposite direction Cologne sent fustian from southern Germany and northern Italy toward England and the Low Countries. There was no specialisation for, to diversify risks in a time when travel was dangerous, the cloth cutters also handled wine, fish and other goods. This receptivity to foreign products hurt native textile production in Cologne, but the cloth cutters' international ties

19   Nicholas, *Town and Countryside*, 194–5, 212–15.
20   Derville, *Histoire de Saint-Omer*, 84–5.
21   Nicholas, *Metamorphosis*, 165–8.

gave opportunities for expansion to other industries. Cologne gained control of the regional metal trade in this way.[22]

Bruges, which like Cologne was dominated by merchants but also had a substantial artisanate, was also more concerned with staple rights than with industrial protectionism. Its merchants sold the cheaper grades of cloth made in the Flemish villages to the Italians and Germans and accordingly resisted the harsh industrial protectionism of Ghent and Ypres.[23] Barcelona made no effort to hinder the sale of cloth from rural Catalonia, for its merchants were cloth sellers who did not care who made the material that they sold. Artisans were hostile to rural imports from overseas, although not to imports from the rest of Catalonia. The drapery of Barcelona and of the villages was responding to the same demand, and only through Barcelona could rural products be marketed in distant places. The welfare of Catalonia thus became linked to the prosperity of its metropolis.[24]

The Frankfurt fairs, which grew especially after 1330, were critical to the success of the new trading regime. After the civil wars in the 1420s ended the direct trade of Cologne's merchants with the southeast, goods were exchanged at the fairs through merchants of Nuremberg, which became Cologne's most important trading partner within Germany. The importance of the fairs did not preclude direct ties: Cologners visited Italy but also bought Italian goods at Frankfurt. Although they used Bruges for English cloth, they also operated directly in England, using London and increasingly abandoning the provincial cloth centres after 1420.[25]

The schedules of the fairs and the arrival of the galleys set the rhythm of commercial life. Most long-distance wholesalers handled a wide variety of luxury and common goods and had partners in other trading cities. Jacobus de Magalassio of Montpellier, for example, had trading partnerships with merchants of Narbonne, Alès, Aurillac, Béziers and in Montpellier itself. Short-term partnerships dominated in north Germany, while family-based companies might persist for several generations in Italy, southern Germany and the Rhineland. One partner

22 The Gaddemen were cloth shops near the archbishop's mint that eventually became the guildhall of the weavers of the Oversburg quarter. Irsigler, *Wirtschaftliche Stellung Köln*, 43–4, 60–87, 323; Howell, *Women, Production, and Patriarchy*, 102–3.

23 Interestingly, Bruges was even more eager than they to enforce monopolies claimed by artisans of Bruges outside the clothing trades, specifically the victuallers, who insisted that their guilds license all brewers, butchers and bakers who could practise in the rural communities and restrict their numbers. Nicholas, *Medieval Flanders*, 277, 336; Nicholas, *Town and Countryside*, 196–9.

24 Carrère, *Barcelone*, 407–9.

25 Hirschfelder, *Kölner Handelsbeziehungen*, 467–80.

usually went abroad with the goods, using innkeepers in the fair cities and in Bruges as partners in everything but name, despite local statutes forbidding the practice. The south German firms left considerable discretion to factors (employees who lived semi-permanently overseas).[26]

In addition to the international emporia, most cities had at least one or two fairs, during which the normal rules of the market were suspended, including the monopolies of particular groups on sales. At Paris shops had to be closed on fair days and all business transacted at the Halles. Parisians were also forbidden in theory to sell in their shops on days when 'common places of their commerce' (the Halles) were open, meaning Wednesday, Friday and Saturday. Given the difficulty of carting everything to the Halles, some artisans began boycotting them and openly advising customers to visit their shops on days when the Halles were closed. Thus they tended to use the Halles for goods that remained unsold at the regional fairs.[27]

The growth of interregional trade in the fourteenth and particularly fifteenth century gave a wider market to goods of modest value, such as combs, purses and cooking pots. Mercers' guilds, which handled imported goods that did not fall under one of the major staple monopolies such as cloth and grain, grew in virtually all cities. Ghent had about 110 mercers in 1357, 324 in 1485. They originally sold from prefabricated booths on the Grain Market but were confined to the larger Friday Market and adjacent streets by 1338.[28] At Chartres the mercers had stalls outside the cathedral in the beginning but by 1294 had relocated to quarters nearby, adjacent to the cloister but outside its jurisdiction. The new hall was the required location for sale by mercers, spicers, glove makers and knife makers of Chartres and its banlieue.[29]

As population pressure eased and living standards rose in the late Middle Ages, the intercity market in manufactured items became as important as the farm-to-city market in food. Although some medium-sized places gave short-term competition to the larger cities of their environs, the size advantage of the latter eventually prevailed. Some large cities also compensated for the decline of their textile industries by branching into areas of manufacturing that, in contrast to textiles, emphasised quality and skill rather than division of labour. This is true of the market in paintings, the 'arts and crafts sectors of the textile industry' such as embroidery and carpet weaving, curtains and bedspreads;

26 Reyerson, *Montpellier*, 19, 40.
27 Cazelles, *Paris*, 389–90; Favier, *Paris 1380–1500*, 271–7.
28 Nicholas, *Metamorphosis*, 266–7. Their guildhall, interestingly, remained in an alley leading off the Grain Market.
29 Billot, *Chartres*, 135.

now-fashionable clothing such as hats, hose, shoes, gloves, silks, fur, lace and ribbons; cloth finishing; salt and sugar refining; and services such as new forms of entertainment and literature. At Mechelen altar screens and leather wall decorations became local specialities. The braziers' guild included makers of pots, kettles and eventually guns. It had become so large by 1444 that it was subdivided into several independent crafts. Such diversification was easier in the large cities, with their large labour base, than in the smaller ones.[30]

Foreigners and foreign trade

Virtually all cities had colonies of foreigners who handled moneylending and some foreign trade and sometimes brought a new speciality to the local market. The Flemings at Westminster made eyeglasses and felt hats.[31] Florentine exiles, including Michele di Lando, one of the leaders of the Ciompi rebellion of 1378, helped the woollen industry of Lucca in the 1380s.[32] Foreigners were most conspicuous and numerous in ports and political capitals. The popes' move to Avignon made it a banking centre and attracted numerous foreigners. Six hundred Florentine merchants were expelled from the city in 1376.[33] All major Italian cities had colonies overseas that were governed from the home city. Barcelona established 'consulates' in the leading ports of Europe and the East, each enjoying privileges from the local government.[34] Although in most cities the foreigners were concentrated in a single area or street, German merchants dominated two entire quarters at Novgorod, the Foreign Quarter (the famous Peterhof), which had outstripped the Gotland quarter by the fourteenth century. Since most of Russia's trade with the west passed through Novgorod, the Germans had a virtual stranglehold on the export economy. The Peterhof had its own court to judge cases involving Germans against Novgoroders, although the mayor of the city sat in on important cases.[35]

Foreigners from distant areas were most conspicuous, particularly when a different language was involved. They tended to congregate in the same streets, which were often named after them.[36] The nature of the foreign community might change with altered circumstances. Most Florentines surveyed in Rome in 1377 were of modest means; many had come to

30 van der Wee, *Rise and Decline of Urban Industries*, 324–32.
31 Rosser, 'London and Westminster', 54.
32 Meek, *Lucca 1369–1400*, 39–41.
33 Guillemain, *Cour pontificale d'Avignon*, 607–10.
34 Carrère, *Barcelone*, 121.
35 Langer, 'Medieval Russian town', 17.
36 Geremek, *Margins of Society*, 68.

the city in 1367, thinking that Pope Urban V's return to the city signalled more jobs. But by the early fifteenth century the Florentines in Rome were bankers of the popes and controlled the city's foreign markets.[37]

Natives resented the foreigners, who generally had privileges that local merchants and craftsmen did not enjoy. Some governments issued identity cards to their citizens to avoid conflict over who enjoyed the franchise, which was especially important for toll exemption in places with reciprocal arrangements. More often those who wished to have proof of their citizenship simply paid the town clerk for a statement; but the fact that they could do this shows that the cities were keeping current lists of citizens.[38] Foreigners seem to have been prone to violence, but some of this was undoubtedly due to hostility toward them. The Flemings at London and Winchester were notorious brawlers but were also abused. A Flemish colony is attested at Winchester in the twelfth century, and the largest concentration of foreigners there in the fifteenth century still came from the Burgundian Low Countries. Most of them lived in the city centre, where they were nearly one-fifth of the taxpayers in 1515. The more prosperous of them were tailors and brewers, while most of the poorer Flemings were textile workers.[39]

THE INTERNATIONAL EMPORIA

Bruges

Foreign colonies were attracted by advantages offered them by princes who sought their capital and interregional connections and hoped to centralise toll collection. At Bruges the Flemish counts gave extraterritorial jurisdiction first to the Germans in 1280, then to others. The 'Easterlings', including the Dutch and the merchants of the Hanse, were the largest ethnic group at Bruges. Until declining sharply in favour of the Florentines in the 1380s, the Luccans were the largest Italian community, dealing mainly in silks. The foreigners' halls were on the Buerze square, near the main market and the moneychangers. As much as one-tenth of the population of Bruges in the late fourteenth century may have consisted of foreign traders, their families and personnel. The English wool staple was intermittently at Bruges after 1297; and although the English fixed the staple at Calais in 1363, Bruges bankers continued to handle payments and acquired some wool stocks at Calais whose actual

---

37   Esch, 'Führungsgruppen Rom', 292–7.
38   Carrère, *Barcelone*, 23; Dilcher, 'Bürgerbegriff', 78.
39   Keene, *Medieval Winchester*, 301, 381.

possession was transferred at Bruges. Merchants of Nuremberg and the Italian cities picked up English wool at Bruges, paying for it through Italian brokers there who had offices at Calais. Bruges thus became the link between the Hanse merchants who brought grain and forest products from the Baltic regions, the English, merchants of the various Italian cities and increasingly the Castilians. Bruges even re-exported Baltic grain to Barcelona, where it was called 'Flemish' grain.[40]

Barcelona

While Bruges was the dominant North Sea port and banking centre, Barcelona controlled the trade of the western Mediterranean. In 1339 the king of Aragon granted a tax on most goods entering and leaving the port by sea. The money was used to build a merchant loge in a vacant area near the shore, the old centre of business and moneychanging. It became the headquarters of the 'Consulate of the Sea' and the commercial and information centre of the city. The area was colonnaded, with places assigned to merchants. Brokers called 'couriers of the ear' transmitted oral agreements between buyers and sellers. Arrangements were finalised before a notary or moneychanger, many of whom had tables at the loge. From 1272 the city council had nominated two Consuls of the Sea, one each from the estates of 'honourables' and merchants, and an appeals judge who was always a merchant. The Barcelonese appointed consulates of the sea in the other Catalan towns. After 1394 a Council of Merchants set wages and tax rates on merchandise, initially only on exports. By 1405 the tolls had been extended to imports and applied throughout Catalonia, not just in the city. The Consuls of the Sea and their two 'Defenders' for practical purposes took over the administration, finance and defence of Barcelona.[41]

Nuremberg

Nuremberg's dominance of the interregional economy in south Germany paralleled that of Bruges in the North Sea area and Barcelona in the western Mediterranean. Nuremberg benefited from imperial patronage; the Golden Bull of 1356 designated it as the site of the first imperial diet

40 Wolff, 'Structures sociales', 91–2; van Houtte and van Uytven, 'Nijverheid en handel', 89–90; Meek, *Lucca 1369–1400*, 42; Pfeiffer, *Nürnberg*, 95; Nicholas, 'English trade', 29–32; Carrère, *Barcelone*, 340. The Luccans were also the most numerous foreign group at Paris, with more than thirty families in the city in 1400. As at Bruges they intermarried with local merchant families, becoming citizens of Paris and entering royal service. Favier, *Paris 1380–1500*, 63–6.
41 Vicens Vives, *Economic History of Spain*, 218–19; Carrère, *Barcelone*, 37–8, 49–60.

of each reign. But Nuremberg remains the classic case of a city whose staple on land routes established its prosperity, just as Bruges' staple on goods entering Flemish waters ensured its commercial hegemony. Seven main roads crossed at Nuremberg, many of them diversions of older routes. Several were toll-free; ninety smaller towns were in Nuremberg's toll-free zone by 1332. Since the Pegnitz at Nuremberg was not navigable, and the nearest usable river centres were Regensburg and Bamberg, they became in effect Nuremberg's river ports.

Nuremberg controlled the overland flow of north European goods into Bavaria, which lacked major cities except for the political capital of Munich, and from there across the Brenner to Venice and back with Mediterranean goods. From this base Nuremberg merchants developed a triangular trade based on Hungary, Venice and Bohemia, bringing metals west and re-exporting western items such as Flemish and English cloth into eastern Europe. They were active at the Frankfurt fairs, travelling in city-funded convoys, and by 1400 they were trading at the fairs of Bergen-op-Zoom and Antwerp.

The Nurembergers naturally expanded into finance, beginning with moneychanging operations in rural Franconia. In 1346 they became the first north Europeans outside Bruges to use the bill of exchange. As a reward for Nuremberg's refusal to support the Hanse blockade of Flanders in 1358, the Flemish authorities gave the Stromer firm of Nuremberg a charter at Bruges in 1362. As partners of the Bruges broker Arnold Poltus, the Stromer went into papal banking, transferring funds to Rome through Lombard and Tuscan banks. They obtained commercial privileges in Poland in the 1360s, and in 1373 Lübeck and Nuremberg made a toll union that gave Nuremberg access to the Baltic. Nuremberg also exported forest products and metals from the nearby mountains. In 1390 Ulrich Stromer established the first paper mill in Germany near Nuremberg, and other paper and wire mills were soon established along the Pegnitz and Fischbach. Yet these industrial operations only became important for Nuremberg after it had risen to greatness through trade and finance.[42]

The growth of capital cities

Princes became less mobile in the late Middle Ages as the need to oversee increasingly complex administrations required their presence in a single place. Their courts generated demand for technical specialists and

---

42 Bischoff, 'Stadtherrschaft im ostfränkischen Städtedreieck', 104; Du Boulay, *Germany*, 119; Pfeiffer, *Nürnberg*, 47–8, 53–4, 94–9; van Houtte and van Uytven, 'Nijverheid en handel', 91.

enormous quantities of food and luxury products that helped to solidify their cities' prosperity. The dukes of Bavaria were heavily in debt to citizens of their capital, Munich, not only to wealthy patricians, but also to persons such as bakers and butchers, who sold goods or provided services to the court.[43] The easy availability of luxuries and the fact that Paris enjoyed rights of purveyance throughout France contributed to such a sharp decline of Paris' industry in the late Middle Ages that it became an almost purely consumer city. The number of master weavers at Paris declined from 360 around 1300 to sixteen by 1372. By 1391 the metropolitan area including the suburbs contained fewer than 100 households supported by textiles. Paris' clothing industry was only resurrected after 1450, and then with speciality dyers and silkmakers.[44]

Although Kraków had become the capital of the previously weak and generally itinerant Polish kings by 1400, Prague (Plan 8) is our best example of the growth of a national capital in the late Middle Ages. On the Moldau, it is surrounded by mountains, and all roads in the region led to it. There were four separate jurisdictions reflecting ethnic elements. As at Kraków, where the castle precinct on the Wawel hill remained technically distinct from the colonial city established in 1257, the Old Town of Prague, the original German city around the castle precinct, was joined by a colonial city of merchants and craftsmen planned by Duke Wenceslas I shortly after 1230. It was expanded after 1257 to include a second plantation, the 'Little Side', on the left bank of the river. The native Czechs were removed to make way for German colonists, who built a market square and adopted the law of Magdeburg. These cities were linked by a bridge. The third city of Prague was on the other side of Hradcany castle, on the left bank of the river. The fourth, the 'New City', was begun in 1348 by the Bohemian king, the emperor Charles IV, and a new wall was built around all four. The 'New City' had regularly-spaced squares and churches that were also aligned with public buildings in the older city, roughly evenly spaced from them. In 1344 the bishop became an archbishop and was given the right to crown the king. In the same year the king and archbishop began a new cathedral. The royal complex was rebuilt, and a university was founded. A new 'Caroline Bridge' was built across the Moldau in 1357 and was the terminus for the Luxembourg–Aachen–Frankfurt–Nuremberg–Prague road. Prague grew so rapidly that even after the plagues it had some 40,000 inhabitants.[45]

43 Patze, 'Landesherrliche Residenzen', 17–19.
44 Favier, *Paris 1380–1500*, 312–17.
45 Knoll, 'Urban development of medieval Poland', 97–9; Braunfels, *Urban Design*, 279–85; Patze, 'Landesherrliche Residenzen', 27–35.

Other capitals were less successful. Duke Rudolf IV of Habsburg made Vienna his capital, obtaining an archbishopric in 1358 and founding a new university in 1365. He evidently hoped to expand Vienna to rival Prague, but he did not undertake a planned expansion of the city.[46] Tours became the residence of the French kings during the English occupation of Paris in the 1420s, but not even the royal presence could make a major centre of Tours, which suffered disadvantages of site that would have prevented it from developing a strong economy even if the kings had not returned to Paris. The court was only intermittently present; and despite the kings' use of tax incentives to attract artisans, particularly armourers and silkworkers, Tours' growth remained 'soft', lacking a base in the regional economy. When the kings returned to Paris, the boom collapsed.[47]

Ports and outports

As interregional trade grew, interior cities tried to gain extraterritorial rights in smaller places that became their outports. Inland Florence was vulnerable despite its financial markets and accordingly tried to make Pisa a client city, finally succeeding in 1406. Siena tried to gain a port by taking Talamone.[48] As Bruges' natural links with the North Sea silted over, the city founded outports at Damme in 1180, then at Sluis in 1290. After 1323 most goods entering Flemish waters were unloaded and passed customs at Sluis, then were taken to Bruges for clearance through the halls. Bruges mercilessly suppressed local industry and brokerage in Damme and Sluis. In the fifteenth century Bruges gradually gave up trying to keep its canals open and brought goods overland from Sluis.[49] Delft in 1389 began a canal that linked the city with the Meuse and kept extraterritorial jurisdiction on it. Delfshaven, the new harbour town, was as dependent on Delft as Damme and Sluis were on Bruges. Lübeck acquired extensive privileges at Travemünde, which was necessary for its access to the sea by 1223.[50]

Staples

Princes created and maintained the prosperity of some centres by granting staples, which required foreigners to deposit their goods in the staple

46   Patze, 'Landesherrliche Residenzen', 35–43.
47   Chevalier, *Tours*, 114–19, 143–7, 156–61, 213–42, 256–70, 366–77.
48   Brucker, *Renaissance Florence*, 86–7; Bowsky, *Siena Under the Nine*, 164–72.
49   van Houtte and van Uytven, 'Nijverheid en handel', 87.
50   Nicholas, *Stad en Platteland*, 101; Raiser, *Städtische Territorialpolitik*, 61–6.

city, pay a toll, and arrange through local people to sell on the local market and in the region where the staple applied. This drove prices up outside the staple city but created business for the favoured locality. The staples guaranteed supplies for the city and a controlled commodity for re-export. Food could only be re-exported from most cities after the residents had had an interval, often three days, to make their purchases.[51] A staple thus gave the cities control of a regional market, assured them the business of peasants of their environs, facilitated the work of the prince's toll collectors and gave jobs to city people. In 1332 Louis of Bavaria, admitting that he had been violating custom by allowing 'guests' to take salt through Munich, required that all salt coming through Bavaria along the Yser pass through Munich and be unloaded there, either to be processed and sold locally or re-exported by local merchants or their guests. Munich's status as ducal residence and its salt staple were the most important elements of its prosperity.[52]

By 1323 and probably earlier Ghent had a staple on grain coming down the Scheldt and Leie rivers from France. This monopoly was fed by more localised staples, which enabled smaller cities to centralise sales on their markets, then direct the surplus for resale. Lille, for example, required all grain harvested in its castellany to be offered for sale on the city market, then re-exported the surplus to Douai and thence to Ghent.[53] The grain remained at Ghent for at least three days to give local merchants first right of refusal, then was re-exported downriver toward Brabant, passing other tolls en route. The price of French grain was 50 per cent higher at Antwerp than at Ghent in the 1380s. Ghent extended this monopoly in the fifteenth century to trade on the interior streams of Flanders, taking military action to prevent communities south of the city from building canals to divert grain coming from France. By mid-century Ghent claimed the right to bring to the city all grain entering Flanders except through Bruges. The grain staple brought enough income to the city to diminish the impact of the decline of its textiles.[54]

Staple privileges enabled Kraków to develop into the commercial metropolis of the Polish interior during the late Middle Ages. The great merchant families and ruling elite were almost exclusively of German ancestry. Most of them had only come to Kraków after 1257 and, reminiscent of the 'new' patriciate of Barcelona in the thirteenth century, remained commercially active. Even among craftsmen there were probably

---

51   Gouron, *Métiers en Languedoc*, 293–5.
52   Möncke, *Quellen*, 179–81.
53   Trenard, *Histoire de Lille*, 244.
54   Nicholas, 'Scheldt trade', 256–8; Nicholas, *Metamorphosis*, 125; Nicholas, *Medieval Flanders*, 361–2.

as many Germans as Slavs. Kraków had acquired four great commercial privileges before 1400, all of them over transient trade, for the city's industrial capacity remained small: between 1390 and 1405, foreigners, mainly Flemings and Brabantines, accounted for roughly twice the number of pieces of cloth exchanged on the local market as merchants of Kraków. A monopoly that was initially granted in 1306 on the trade in Hungarian copper had been extended by 1372 into a general staple on all Hungarian imports. Kraków exported salt from the rich deposits in the Carpathians; the surrounding regions had little salt. In 1368 King Casimir the Great gave the city a formal monopoly over salt exports to Mazovia, Russia, Silesia, Lithuania and Lublin. Although neighbouring princes resisted this and tried to obtain salt from other sources, they were generally unsuccessful. Most salt in these areas and in Hungary came through Kraków and was sold directly in the foreign markets by merchants of Kraków. Finally, all foreigners entering the area were diverted onto roads that led to Kraków, giving the city a stranglehold on trade in all directions. Kraków often closed the road from Warsaw to Ruthenia, thus controlling the passage of most goods from west to east.[55]

Probably no urban agricultural staple was more oppressive for the environs than that of Dordrecht. In 1299 the count of Holland ordered that all wood, oats and wine coming downstream on the Merwede and Lek and all salt going upstream on the Meuse should pass through Dordrecht and be sold on its market. From 1337 all German vessels going upstream on the Meuse had to be unloaded at Dordrecht and the cargoes sold there. This restriction was extended to other foreigners in 1344. From 1355 all river trade in South Holland had to come to Dordrecht. The city then attempted to expand this from a transit staple to a grain staple. In 1438 it tried unsuccessfully to force all grain harvested in South Holland onto the Dordrecht market, even demanding that this occur within three days of harvest. This was extended to dairy products in 1442. The count annulled this ordinance each time Dordrecht issued it, but the pressure of the city on the agricultural economy was constant.[56]

In England the county towns were the statutory markets of their districts, and many of them built a solid regional prosperity on this basis. They enjoyed the sole right to sell foreign imports in their shires. Some, such as Lincoln, had difficulty enforcing this, but its commerce revived from 1326 when 'home staples' were established in Newcastle, York,

55 Knoll, 'Urban development of medieval Poland', 92–5; Carter, *Trade and Urban Development in Poland*, 55–6, 69–70, 91–2; Malowist, 'Trade of Eastern Europe', 55–6.
56 Nicholas, *Stad en Platteland*, 61–7.

Lincoln, Norwich, London, Winchester, Exeter and Bristol: all wool, hides, skins, tin and perhaps timber had to pass through the staple communities. Each staple had a mayor distinct from the city government and usually chosen from merchants of the region; one merchant of Boston was mayor of the staple at Lincoln.[57]

However, the local privileges of the county towns of England pale beside those of London. A staple was usually but not always in the city that had the monopoly. All English wool exports had to be sold at the staple, which was generally on the continent after 1313, except in cases where a specific exemption to export directly was given, most often to Italians. The company of the staple, a fluctuating group of merchants who loaned money to the crown in return for the privilege of controlling the country's most valuable export, was composed mainly although not exclusively of Londoners and contributed mightily to London's growing prosperity at the expense of the county towns. Establishment of the staple meant that increasing amounts of wool went through London en route to the continent. This accelerated the trend that had begun in the transitional phase of the late thirteenth century, but with the difference that the wool now went to the staple, where English merchants had control, rather than being sold directly to the Italians in England in return for spices, and then exported directly. Whenever the Italians were given licences to export directly from Southampton, bypassing the staple, London interests suffered and petitioned the king for redress. London was exporting about half of England's wool by 1320, much of it through the pepperers, who sold it to the Italians in return for spices and dyes, the distribution of which they controlled in the shires. The staple permitted the London merchant guilds to branch away from their earlier orientation of being solely middlemen for the Italians and gave them a share of the lucrative export trade.[58]

There were limits to the efficacy of the staples. Cities that specialised solely in exporting the products of an agrarian hinterland were hurt by the devastation of the rural areas. Bordeaux's prosperity depended solely on its monopoly on the sale of wine produced in the Gironde valley. As armies ravaged the area from the 1330s, wine tonnage on the river declined in 1336 to 22 per cent of its 1335 level. The reduced figure of 1336–7 was still 16,577 tons, but it dropped to 5,923 in 1349, recovering then to an annual average of 30,000 tons between 1356 and 1369. The resumption of the war in 1369 started a sharp decline that was permanent. The long-term averages are shocking: annual exports declined

57 Hill, *Medieval Lincoln*, 248–51.
58 Nightingale, *Medieval Mercantile Community*, 3, 132–3.

from 83,165 tons between 1303 and 1337 to 11,483 between 1369 and 1381 and 11,000 tons between 1401 and 1440.[59]

The food markets

Even when no formal staple existed, the cities had to ensure their food supplies. Given the agrarian depression, the cities could easily be starved out, even though, paradoxically, grain prices were generally low. The Muslim city rulers were the most successful in this regard. The state, not individual merchants, controlled the import and supply of strategic but scarce material, such as wood, metals and grain. The emirs and other public officials regulated the grain supply and had a big bureaucracy to control sale and distribution in the towns. The sultans and emirs forced merchants to buy grain above cost from them, then suffer the hatred of local populations over the high prices. But these urban grain merchants were not really market-based independent importers, as in the west.[60]

In the west city people had to buy their food on the market. The only partial exceptions were those who had rural estates, and people in that economic bracket also bought more luxurious foods that had to be imported. Even in the largest cities the most active local market was in agricultural goods, especially grain, followed by wine, animals, leather, wool and hemp. Although the largest cities had food markets that were open every day, particularly for perishables, most limited sales of specific commodities to a few days a week, so that the market space could be used for more than one purpose. Most food sales at Leicester occurred on the Monday, Wednesday and particularly the Saturday market (the most recent of them, on the site of the present marketplace). York had a corn market, stock market and fish market at the Ouse and Foss bridges, and a Thursday market for poultry, game, salt, spices, pottery, herring and dairy goods.[61] The larger cities had less success than the smaller ones in centralising food sales. Paris was too large to accommodate all food purchasers at a single location. The Halles were open on Friday and Saturday, and shops elsewhere had to remain closed on those days. But an ordinance of 1351 noted twenty-four grain measurers at the Halles, eighteen on the Place de Grève and twelve in the Jewry on the Île de la Cité.[62]

59 Renouard, *Bordeaux sous les rois d'Angleterre*, 358–66, 411, 423–8.
60 Lapidus, *Muslim Cities*, 51–2, 66.
61 Simmons, *Leicester*, 37; Tillott, *City of York*, 98.
62 Cazelles, *Paris*, 388–9; Favier, *Paris 1380–1500*, 258, 285–6, 330; Thompson, *Paris Under English Rule*, 54.

This could occur through normal market mechanisms. London's great size hampered the growth of secondary cities in its region. London merchants rather than natives actually controlled the grain trade in some villages of the Thames valley, which severely limited their economic potential. This in turn meant that the grain of the region went to the metropolis and was not siphoned off by regional centres. Much of London's grain came from northern Kent, but the Londoners also bought on rural and small town markets. In the thirteenth century Wallingford, which was further away from London and upstream on the Thames, lost prosperity to Henley in Oxfordshire, where London grainmongers had storehouses and wharves. London obtained mainly wheat, the most expensive grain, from these places, which were about 100 km from the city but were accessible by water. Cheaper grain came by cart from areas closer to London. Other small towns and villages specialised in livestock for London.[63]

But shortages often forced governments to take extraordinary measures. Florence built Orsanmichele in 1336, a loge open on all sides that served as a market and granary. This meant enclosing the market square, and the grain market was thus moved behind the city hall. After 1388 it was linked with the other two markets by wide streets, along which buildings had to be of uniform specifications. In 1411 London acquired a covered site that had been used as a dairy market in the fourteenth century and converted it to an arcaded granary and market building, called the Leadenhall because of its roof.[64] Magistrates surveyed private stocks of food and even ordered their sale to prevent hoarding, but most households were in no position to stockpile enough to get them through a shortage caused by a war emergency or by a poor harvest. Statutes at Ghent from 1338 prohibited hoarding, which was defined in 1343 as keeping more than six months' supply. Yet professional merchants could keep large stocks, for in 1350 they were forbidden to put out more than 5 per cent of their total supplies for sale at a single time, so that hoarders would not be able to buy in quantity.[65] The six *jurats* of Valencia bought grain and employed an overseer of the grain supply. The city loaned money to grain merchants and guaranteed its suppliers aid that varied according to the exporting region, generally high in periods of scarcity and for grain brought from distant areas. The government itself sometimes arranged for the transport of grain, operating in 1422 through 'the factor of the city in Sicily'.[66]

63 Keene, 'Small towns and the metropolis', 230–3.
64 Schofield, *Medieval London Houses*, 19–21.
65 Trautz, 'Versorgung', 176, 273; Nicholas, *Metamorphosis*, 243.
66 Guiral-Hadziiossif, *Valence*, 250–9.

Some cities sold grain directly to their populations but did not try to drive out other suppliers. The magistrates of Barcelona dealt with middlemen who contracted with the city to deliver a certain quantity of grain by a given date and also guaranteed free sales to private grainmongers.[67] The Italian cities were still vulnerable to interruptions in the grain supply. Venice, with a constant overseas supply, maintained public granaries and made no effort to restrict or control grain entering the city.[68] On the mainland, however, overregulation of the *contado* had contributed to a depression, while warfare made it dangerous to count on supplies from more distant places. Siena had a municipal grain office that maintained granaries at key points in the city and *contado*.[69] In normal periods the *contado* of Orvieto produced enough food to feed the city, but in 1346 the city had such a severe grain shortage that the council freed from tax all persons from outside the *contado* – characteristically not the *contadini* themselves – who would bring grain to Orvieto. Notaries stationed at the city gates recorded grain going to the mills. Residents of city and *contado* had to provide written declarations of grain stocks in their possession.[70]

The cities also regulated the market in prepared foods. The English Assizes of Bread and Ale imposed weight and quantity restrictions, and municipal regulations had the same impact in most continental cities. Some had an excruciating precision. From 1348 the tin cups and bottles used in taverns at Cologne had to have a standard size attested by the city's seal and were to be filled to a marked line.[71] Some regulations ignored the facts of supply and demand and caused real hardship. When the royal court or armies came to York, there was concern that provision might be inadequate, but the city government preferred to allow foodmongers to exhaust their stocks rather than raise prices.[72]

Most cities tried to stop regrating (purchase in order to resell at a higher price after the market had closed) and forestalling (interrupting goods en route to market, a practice forbidden by royal statute in England around 1285). The Florentine Ordinances of Justice of 1293 forbade price cartels, and this was supplemented by various statutes of the *podestà* and the captain of the *popolo* against monopolies, particularly of foodmongers. A baker was hanged for trying to corner the market in 1347, probably to set an example.[73] Virtually all cities forbade their

67 Carrère, *Barcelone*, 327–31.
68 Mackenney, *Tradesmen and Traders*, 12.
69 Bowsky, *Siena Under the Nine*, 202–9.
70 Carpentier, *Ville devant la Peste*, 46, 79.
71 Irsigler, *Wirtschaftliche Stellung Köln*, 115.
72 Tillott, *City of York*, 99.
73 De Roover, 'Labour conditions in Florence', 289–90.

residents to buy food on village markets within a given radius of the city walls. Lübeck in 1350 also prohibited burgesses from employing their 'own' shepherds, an effort to force those who owned land to bring its products to the grain hall rather than consuming them. Erfurt exiled persons who bought grain, hops or woad 'in front of the town'.[74] But some large cities so desperately needed food, and their markets were so crowded, that they had to regulate rather than forbid these practices. The king licensed regrators at Paris, permitting petty foodmongers to escape the fixed prices at the Halles and sell in shops and on the open street and vary prices as they saw fit. Montpellier was more typical. In 1205 someone present at the close of a market could ask a buyer to sell him part of what he had purchased in return for the same price that the original buyer had given the seller. Persons buying for their own households were exempt, and citizens were not bound to do it for foreigners. Thus the local consumers were protected from non-citizen regrators and from hoarding.[75] The fine line between saving and hoarding is illustrated by a survey of grain stocks during a military emergency at Strasbourg in 1444. One-third of the inner-city residents had no grain at all, while only 12.18 per cent of the residents of the banlieue had none. The five central districts had 53.45 per cent of the residents and 73.33 per cent of the food reserves. The establishments with storage facilities in the old city centre, the grain markets and religious houses with rural estates had more food than did those on the peripheries and in the suburbs.[76]

Grain merchants were always among the richest citizens, and taken together with persons in the food and beverage trades they constituted the largest population group in most cities that were not dominated by an export industry. Even at textile-industrial Ghent two-thirds of the 131 citizens declared liable for a forced loan in 1327, who also farmed excises from the city, at some point leased the tax of the gates, which included food. In 1356–7 11.05 per cent of the militia came from the food and drink trades, while those in transport and loading (including shippers who brought grain to the city) were another 9.56 per cent; and this does not include the petty hawkers and specialists outside the guilds, such as the recent migrants whom the government in 1383 allowed, over the objection of the bakers' guild, to bake and sell bread on St Veerle square.[77]

74 Sprandel, *Quellen zur Hanse-Geschichte*, 42; Möncke, *Quellen*, 202–3.
75 Cazelles, *Paris*, 387; Gouron, *Métiers en Languedoc*, 294, 298.
76 Möncke, *Quellen*, 312–16, with table, 316. Similar conclusions are suggested for Nuremberg in 1449–50; Möncke, *Quellen*, 317–19.
77 Nicholas, 'Structures du peuplement', 515–16; Nicholas, *Metamorphosis*, 21, 252.

The dynamic and mechanism of the local market

In addition to special markets for the main imports, general Market Halls, which had been built in the larger cities in the thirteenth century, are found virtually everywhere in northern Europe in the fourteenth. That of Mainz, the oldest in western Germany, existed by 1311 as a storage depot, but from 1317 the city collected tolls on goods sold there. Only wholesale transactions were handled at the Market Hall. Although in the fourteenth century some wholesale trade was still handled in merchants' and patricians' homes, inns and the guildhalls, by the fifteenth the Hall handled wholesale trade, while the archbishop's officials supervised retail trade on markets and in shops.[78] The main commercial building of Kraków was the Drapers' Hall. Originally built as four aisles of sale booths covered by a single roof but without a common wall, it yielded between 1380 and 1400 to a new stone Drapers' Hall on the main square of the city.[79] The government of Brussels gradually acquired most 'economic' public buildings from the dukes of Brabant, beginning with the crane and public weight in 1291, although the duke kept the Grain Hall until 1460. In 1360 citizens were forbidden to weigh merchandise of more than 25 pounds at home. The city had three butcheries, the fish market, and Cloth, Wool and Bread Halls, in which stalls were made available at ground rent or on term of lease. The city issued regulations and appointed inspectors for smaller markets for coal, cheese and vegetables.[80]

Most cities required that all transactions, large and small, involving imported goods should be handled through brokers or through the halls, so that fees could be collected and fraud prevented. Brussels had a wine staple in the Fullers' Street, a fair indication in itself of the breakdown of professional-social geography in the northern cities, where sworn brokers handled exchanges. The free market in the cities was hampered by a 'multiplication of intermediaries'. Members of local trade organisations, such as the merchant guild in the English cities and the Merchants of the Water in Paris, escaped much of this bother, but foreigners were subjected to it. They could only sell on public markets through the brokers in the cities of Languedoc, and some trades required outsiders' merchandise to pass inspection by the trade leaders.[81] Around 1460 at the Place de Grève in Paris there were six master wine measurers, twenty-four brokers for horse sales, and even twenty-seven sworn log-counters.[82] The number of brokers varied with the complexity of the city's trade

---

78 Falck, *Mainz in seiner Blütezeit*, 103–4.
79 Carter, *Trade and Urban Development in Poland*, 68.
80 Martens, *Histoire de Bruxelles*, 109–15.
81 Martens, *Histoire de Bruxelles*, 115; Gouron, *Métiers en Languedoc*, 296–7.
82 Favier, *Paris 1380–1500*, 277–9.

network. Bruges had 355 in 1341, while Arles had 42 (35 of them Jews) in 1307, involved mainly in the three staple items of the city's economy: grain, wool and hides.[83]

Brokerage requirements were often petty. Cologne forbade the menials who brought wood into the city on carts to buy or sell directly from their wagons, thus guaranteeing the monopoly of the local halls and brokers.[84] Although victuallers from the villages were encouraged to come to York, evidently to keep prices down by preventing the local foodmongers from getting monopolies, the city tried to confine foreigners to wholesale trade in the fifteenth century. In 1417 they were ordered to sell wine, spices and dyes only to citizens, not to other foreigners, and in 1459 they were ordered to lodge at a single inn.[85]

Brokers were officers of the city government, not of the trade organisations. They posted bond and swore not to take more than the lawful brokerage fees, nor buy on their own accounts nor accept gratuities. To avoid conflicts of interest, brokers were usually also forbidden to act as intermediaries for goods manufactured by their own trades.[86] Brokerage requirements did not apply to local craftsmen selling their own manufactures, such as bakers and cobblers, unless they were selling something that could otherwise be exported from the city.

Innkeepers, who often stored their customers' goods, did brokerage for foreigners and thus posted bond, could not normally be merchants. Nuremberg forbade citizen hosteller-brokers to become the partners of their foreign guests in transactions outside the city. They had to surrender goods that were leaving the city to wagoners and carters, who were paid a separate fee.[87] After 1372 Cologne required foreign merchants to lodge with innkeepers. They were wholesalers who could not compete with local retailers: they had to sell their goods in the same containers that had housed them when they were brought into the city. In 1439 an act of Parliament required foreigners arriving at English ports to provide their innkeepers' names, and the innkeepers had to file reports twice a year with the Exchequer.[88]

The emirs of the Muslim cities exercised a degree of control over their central markets that was unknown in the west. They owned the choicest properties in the city (in addition to their own palaces, the

---

83 Stouff, *Arles*, 257.
84 Schultheiss, *Satzungen*, 164.
85 Tillott, *City of York*, 105.
86 Gouron, *Métiers en Languedoc*, 301–2.
87 Schultheiss, *Satzungen*, 106–7, 143. These clauses were specifically directed at 'woman or man'.
88 Le Goff, 'Town as an agent of civilisation', 77; Keutgen, *Urkunden*, no. 247, pp. 343–4.

rulers controlled the baths, markets and bazaars) and rented or granted them out. They even forced profitable trades to move to their properties: in 1292 at Damascus the emir moved the silk merchants from the previous market to one that he owned. Another emir did this to the cloth merchants in 1326. The *madina* was the nerve centre of all great cities, although it was not always centrally located. The main mosque was usually on the *madina*, as the cathedrals were in the west. Nearby were the house of the chief *qadi* and schools and the shops of merchants catering to the schools and the mosques. Also in the *madina*, but separate from the mosque, was the *suq*, the central marketplace. The great merchants often lived in side streets off the *suk*, and the artisans in their residential quarters were further away. By the fifteenth century the *suqs* had multistorey buildings built around courtyards. The ground floor was used for storage, while the upper floors had hostels for foreign merchants, which were called *funduqs* in the Magrib (whence the Italian *fondaco*, meaning a loge for and under the jurisdiction of foreign merchants).[89]

THE DEMOGRAPHIC DISASTERS OF THE LATER MIDDLE AGES

The increased sophistication of commercial techniques and the growth in the volume and range of goods available on local markets was played out against a population decline that was clear everywhere by 1320. It was accelerated markedly by the series of epidemics that began with the 'Black Death' of 1347–9 and continued with plagues in 1357–8, 1361–3, 1371, 1373–4, 1382–3 and 1400. The cycle then slowed. Although not all regions were affected each time, qualitative amelioration occurred in the face of massive diminution of the size of the potential market.

Italy

The plague entered Europe through Italy, beginning at Genoa in late 1347 and reaching Florence by the following March. Given the density of population in the Italian cities, mortality was worse than in the north. Chroniclers report that hundreds of persons died daily in the summer of 1348. Florence declined from about 90,000 souls in 1338 to fewer than 40,000 in 1427. It was an older population that remained, since the plagues were more severe among the young, and this in turn hampered replenishment. Population rose after 1427 and the age pyramid

89   Lapidus, *Muslim Cities*, 59–60; Hourani, *History of the Arab Peoples*, 122–5, 134.

normalised. Venice lost three-fifths of its inhabitants during the Black Death. It had a population of about 120,000 in 1300 but reached this level again only around 1500. Mortality at Siena was at least 50 per cent, with death rates worst among the clergy and the poor. Lucca declined from some 15,000 persons in 1331 to 10,000 by 1369. At Orvieto one or two elders were replaced at each meeting in May 1348. On 30 May the city established an emergency magistracy of seven, four of whom had died by 7 August. By late June the number of eligible candidates was down so far that the council of the *popolo* was reduced from one hundred to sixty members.[90]

The authorities were powerless. The government of Orvieto forbade citizens to travel to Pisa and Lucca. It ordered linen cloth and used woollens to be burned, not resold. Residents were forbidden to visit the homes of the dead, accompany family convoys to the cemetery or have public mourning. At Florence a public crier circulated reciting sanitation ordinances that had been in effect since 1321. The captain of the *popolo* on 3 April 1348 forbade contact with Genoese and Pisans and selling the personal effects of plague victims. The priors on 11 April chose eight 'wise men' as a committee of public health. In October the elders of Orvieto, in a complete reversal of earlier policies, tried to encourage immigration by giving newcomers ten years' tax immunity and freedom from military service; yet the situation was so bad that no one took advantage of this offer until 1356. High mortality produced many orphans and confused inheritances. On 18 December the councils ordered the captain of the *popolo* to ask parish officials to compile lists of orphans in their districts who had not been assigned guardians by testament or by the captain's judge, who would then appoint their nearest relatives as guardians.[91]

The north

In the north virtually all cities lost between one-quarter and one-half of their populations. London may have declined from 100,000 in 1300 to 60,000 in the late fourteenth century. London's population, which was already much reduced from its early fourteenth-century height, probably declined by some 40 per cent in the single plague year 1348–9.[92]

90 Klapisch-Zuber, *Women, Family, and Ritual*, 16, 29; Lane, *Venice*, 18–20; Bowsky, *Siena under the Nine*, 19–20; Bowsky, 'Black Death at Siena', 14; Meek, *Lucca 1369–1400*, 23–5; Carpentier, *Ville devant la Peste*, 127.
91 Carpentier, *Ville devant la Peste*, 126–8, 134, 145–8, 207.
92 Swanson, *Medieval Artisans*, 2; Nightingale, *Medieval Mercantile Community*, 194–5.

Paris sustained enormous losses beginning in August 1348. A chronicler claimed that 500 bodies were buried daily at the chief hospital. Other authors place total mortality between 50,000 and 80,000, figures that are plausible if the population was 200,000 in 1328. Before 1348 the two butcheries of Sts Marcel and Genevieve had housed 120 butchers, but only thirty-five remained in 1377. There were 136 reformed prostitutes in the hospice of Filles Dieu in 1346, 112 at Easter 1348, 104 in October 1348 and forty in October 1349. The problem was exacerbated by war and the burning of the suburbs, which were virtually abandoned between 1358 and 1360. The population of Paris may have dropped to one-third of its pre-1348 level by 1360, as habitation was concentrated within the old walls. Contrary to the general rule elsewhere, Paris then recovered rapidly until civil strife became severe around 1405.[93] Reims evidently lost more than one-quarter of its population. Montpellier declined from 30,000 inhabitants before the plagues to 13,000 by 1480. At Barcelona four out of five councillors and nearly the entire Council of One Hundred died during the Black Death.[94]

The plague took longer to reach Germany, but it conforms to this dismal picture. Twelve of thirty-four master bakers of Hamburg died in 1350, eighteen of forty butchers, twenty-one of thirty-seven city employees, six of their thirteen replacements and sixteen of twenty-one members of the city council. Of these 145 persons, seventy-two survived the year 1350–1. The yield on Hamburg's inheritance tax was twelve times the normal in 1350, eight times the normal in 1351 and 1353. Population may have dropped from 10,000 to 4,000 in one year. Bremen suffered a total mortality of 7,500–8,000, including unidentifiable bodies. No more than fifteen of the fifty city councillors survived. At Lübeck eleven out of thirty councillors died in 1350.[95]

The fact that the plagues returned at intervals of between three and ten years throughout the rest of the fourteenth century before slowing somewhat in the fifteenth is critical for our understanding of long-range demographic trends in the cities. In the Low Countries the plague of 1368–9 was a worse killer than that of 1348–9. The epidemic of 1374–5 was also catastrophic; more than 40 per cent of the tenancies changed hands at Canterbury that year, three times the normal rate. Death rates were highest among women and newborns in the 'plague of the children' of 1361. This contributed to a youthful age structure and made

93 Cazelles, *Paris*, 24, 149–56; Favier, *Paris 1380–1500*, 346.
94 Desportes, *Reims*, 544–9, 572–5; Faber and Lochard, *Montpellier*, 192; Reyerson, 'Women in business', 136; Bisson, *Crown of Aragon*, 165.
95 Reinecke, 'Bevölkerungsprobleme der Hansestädte', 267–9.

long-term replenishment of population more difficult after 1375, by which time the children who had perished in 1361 would otherwise have been marrying.[96] Most late fourteenth-century councillors of Hamburg were under age thirty when first elected.[97] The pepperers of London had established their fraternity of St Antonin in 1345. One-third of the twenty-one founders died during the plague, but the organisation conducted business as usual; for most of those who died were middle aged, while many of the thirteen who joined during 1349–50 were young enough to be called by diminutive names.[98] At Rochester about half of those who died in 1348 were succeeded by widows or children, but the families had lost so many members by 1361 that considerable property thereafter went to collateral lines or even outsiders.[99]

Immigration and replenishment

The demographic disasters of the fourteenth century provoked fundamental changes in urban morphology. Even in periods of ordinary mortality no premodern city could maintain itself by natural reproduction alone. A burgomaster of Hamburg in the late fifteenth century had thirty-six children from three marriages, but his family was extinct in the male line after three generations.[100] Medieval cities thus could not exist without heavy immigration. While some cities may still have been overpopulated even after 1350, there was an immediate manpower shortage after each plague.

Wages and prices rose sharply, by one-third in a single year at Reims, and this enticed peasants to leave their villages. The years immediately after the Black Death were sharply inflationary. Demand for luxuries was high, as people spent inherited money. Coin supplies rose as money hoarded in the early 1340s was released. Prices in London almost doubled between 1346 and 1352. The City issued statutes regulating prices and wages for each craft whose masters petitioned the aldermen to do so. There was an acute labour shortage, especially for skilled labour.[101] But over the long term more grain was being produced than was needed for the reduced demand, and thus stable or declining food prices, which

---

96 The number of children per male testator at Genoa in 1343 was 3.18; in 1348 it was 0.68, rising to 1.17 in 1358–61. Heers, *Gênes. Civilisation*, 44.
97 Reinecke, 'Bevölkerungsprobleme der Hansestädte', 266.
98 Nightingale, *Medieval Mercantile Community*, 196–8.
99 Butcher, 'English urban society', 94–9.
100 Dyer, *Standards of Living*, 188.
101 Nightingale, *Medieval Mercantile Community*, 200–1.

were a boon to the urban poor, drove many small farmers into the cities. However, as markets stabilised, and guild masters tried to ensure the best situations for themselves and their descendants, there was little work for the newcomers, many of whom were unskilled. Furthermore, since mortality was higher in the cities than in the rural areas, the migrants stood a greater chance of being caught by the next plague than if they had stayed on the farm. The cycle of demographic decline thus deepened.

Fragmentary indices suggest massive migration both to and from the cities after 1350. Most rents at Exeter declined only slightly in 1348–9, suggesting that population losses were rapidly replenished through migration. A rise in admissions to the freedom of the city, few of which were by succession, caused court profits to double in a single year.[102] Trier had at least 12,000 persons in 1339; although a chronicler claimed that Trier lost half its population in the Black Death and the Jewish pogrom of the same year, tax lists suggest recovery by 1375 to perhaps 10,000, which remained Trier's highest population before 1500.[103] Public order in London broke down in the wake of a massive influx of immigrants in 1349–50, attracted by the demand for labour and the large number of pillageable houses whose occupants had died.[104] Immigration to Barcelona was so heavy that in 1359 the king of Aragon authorised a new wall that nearly doubled the previous area.[105] At Périgueux 82 per cent of those who entered the city between 1346 and 1350 did not remain, and two-thirds of the patronymics had a life span in the city of less than twenty years.[106]

City populations were also swollen with war refugees. The refugee problem in Reims was severe, for all villagers within three leagues of the city, who were taxed for the upkeep of its walls, had the right to seek asylum there. Refugees were one-quarter of the population of the parishes of Sts Hilaire and Pierre in February 1422 and may have been as much as half in the poorer areas. About two-thirds had come from within three leagues. Some dwellings, particularly garrets in the city walls, had as many as eighteen inhabitants.[107] Paris sustained frequent plagues

---

102 Rowe and Draisey, *Exeter Receivers' Accounts*, xxi–xxii.
103 Matheus, *Trier*, 16–18, 20–1. Matheus calculates this figure from a list of bakers from 1339 and assumes that a baker could serve about 239–62 persons. Although he finds corroboration at Freiburg, Ghent had 324 bakers in 1357 and a total population of 50,000, a ratio of 1:154. Nicholas, *Metamorphosis*, 37, 250.
104 Nightingale, *Medieval Mercantile Community*, 200.
105 Carrère, *Barcelone*, 671–4.
106 Le Goff, 'L'Apogée', 332.
107 Rossiaud, 'Crises', 438; Desportes, *Reims*, 578–81.

but suffered most from the Burgundian–Armagnac strife of the early fifteenth century and the subsequent English occupation. The city may have lost half its population between 1410 and 1423; although 200,000 persons are alleged to have been in Paris in 1418 as the Burgundians advanced on the city, this figure probably included more refugees than permanent inhabitants.[108]

Thus both the rate and the character of immigration to the cities changed. Most immigrants to Florence in the thirteenth century, far from being displaced serfs, were prosperous peasants who sought the advantages of the city.[109] Recent immigrants to Perugia in 1285 had an average taxable wealth 2.4 times that of the entire city, but by the 1330s the immigrants fell considerably below the city average. The growth of poor immigration to Perugia corresponds to the rise of its woollen industry, which gave them jobs.[110] Throughout Europe economic displacement was a more common cause of migration to cities in the fourteenth century than in the thirteenth, although the mobile demographic situation also gave opportunities to some newcomers. Immigration from the rural areas remained heavy as long as they were depressed, declining somewhat as the agrarian crisis eased in the mid-fifteenth century.[111]

We usually cannot say much about the occupational profile of immigrants unless they had to enter a guild when they became citizens. The expansion of ironworking at Cologne was accompanied by immigration of ironworkers from neighbouring principalities. They kept ties to their natal villages: 600 scythes were confiscated in Paris in 1471 from the innkeeper of Johann von Kroenenberg, a citizen of Cologne who had bought them from Cronenbourg smiths.[112] Craftsmen constituted 36.86 per cent of the newcomers to Hamburg between 1370 and 1387, declining to 20.29 per cent between 1461 and 1500 after most guilds set a maximum number of masters. The number of new citizens who did not belong to a trade, mainly merchants, shippers and brewers (who did not have their own guild at Hamburg) remained constant at around 55 per cent between 1370 and 1500. Merchant immigration thus took in a larger percentage of the total after 1400 than before, as the crafts declined, helping to explain the consolidation of political power by merchants in the Hanse towns in the fifteenth century.[113] Local conditions

---

108 *Parisian Journal*, 113–14, 131–2; Rossiaud, 'Crises', 423; Favier, *Paris 1380–1500*, 53–6.
109 Plesner, *L'émigration de la campagne*, 116–28, 162–75.
110 Blanshei, *Perugia*, 42–3.
111 Holt, 'Gloucester', 158.
112 Irsigler, *Wirtschaftliche Stellung Köln*, 169.
113 Reinecke, 'Bevölkerungsprobleme der Hansestädte', 281–3.

seem to have determined whether the authorities were receptive to new citizens and whether immigrants found citizenship a sufficiently desirable status to be worth acquiring. Comparing numbers of admissions to the freedom of the city with poll tax populations in 1377 suggests that York was relatively open to craftsmen, Norwich less so, and Hull, Lynn and Exeter admitted few.[114]

Over time immigrants thus became a substantial and in some cities a dominant element of the population. Many of them were marginals, at least initially, and were regarded with suspicion. Although all cities had a large non-citizen population, Nuremberg in 1382 required such residents to find citizens to vouch for them.[115] Particularly in the skilled crafts, especially those in which the local guild controlled employment, recipient cities might demand proof of proper training from the guild, and the government of the city of previous residence might be asked to certify good behaviour.[116]

Heavy mortality and migration extinguished many families: 78 per cent of the family names disappeared at Albi between 1343 and 1357 and 93 per cent at Châlons-sur-Saone between 1361 and 1381. The elites were most likely to persist. Those of Cologne and Arras are famous, and eighty-four families of Périgueux lasted from the twelfth century into the fifteenth.[117] But at Canterbury the ruling elite changed completely. Of 188 tenancies held by the priory, only thirty-four were held by the same family in 1366 as in 1351, and only eight of those had held them before 1348. But the losses were made up by migration from the country; the total population of Canterbury did not decline, and the priory did not have to lower rents to attract tenants.[118]

The increase through immigration was more significant in the larger cities, which had a larger catchment area than the smaller centres. So many immigrants came to London from the East Midlands that the London dialect came to resemble that of East Anglia rather than that of the home counties.[119] Lübeck probably lost at least one-third of its population, or 6,000–7,000 persons, in the Black Death, but this was compensated by immigration. Between 1317 and 1349 an annual average of 175 new citizens enrolled in the city, and this does not count those who remained 'inhabitants'. In the five years between 1350 and 1355 the average was 266. When families are included, this would have

114 Goldberg, *Women, Work and Life Cycle*, Table 2.4, pp. 54–7.
115 Schultheiss, *Satzungen*, 277.
116 Stoob, *Urkunden*, 281.
117 Chevalier, *Bonnes villes*, 32–5; Le Goff, 'L'Apogée', 332.
118 Butcher, 'English urban society', 95–9.
119 Hilton, *English and French Towns*, 64.

been enough within a decade to bring the population almost back to its pre-1348 level.[120]

It is usually difficult to say how long the new residents had been physically present in the city before taking citizenship. The guilds' efforts to restrict mastership to sons of masters did not mean that journeymen would not emigrate to the city but only that they would not become citizens. Many undoubtedly came as single youths and became citizens when they married and/or bought houses.[121] In many cities citizenship was given when an outsider married a burgess, although the importance of this route declined after 1400 as more towns gave up entry fees.[122] Other cities, however, tried to restrict immigration, particularly those that were being swamped by war refugees, although probably nowhere on the continent was citizenship as restricted or tied to guild membership as in England.

Amiens, for example, had a low entry fee in the fifteenth century that encouraged citizenship, yet actually admitted a number of newcomers comparable to Douai and Valenciennes, which charged six times as much. Saint-Omer, which was only slightly larger than Amiens, admitted far more new burgesses than Amiens between 1400 and 1469. The difference is that since many artisans received mastership and citizenship simultaneously at Amiens, unskilled labourers were not admitted to citizenship, and the lower fee encouraged skilled craftsmen to come. Valenciennes and Douai admitted the unskilled in principle but charged such high entry fees that few could afford it.[123]

Late medieval cities had demographic and occupational characteristics that differentiated them from the rural areas. About one-fifth of the economically active population of the cities was involved in food and drink manufacture and preparation, over half in leather or metal crafts, textiles, clothing and mercery. The percentage of urban adults who married was low, but mean household size was larger than in the villages; there was an inverse correlation between community size and percentage of persons married; young adult children still lived in the parental homes in the rural areas, but they were largely gone from urban households. The cities, particularly their wealthier central sections, had many more servants per household than the rural areas, and many cities had a low sex ratio (women outnumbered men), suggesting heavy

---

120 von Brandt, 'Lübeck', 220–1.
121 Reinecke, 'Bevölkerungsprobleme der Hansestädte', 281.
122 Maschke, 'Unterschichten', 404–6.
123 Desportes, 'Nouveaux bourgeois', 28–40. Registers of freedmen in the English cities were much more likely in the early fifteenth century than previously to list the newcomers' professions; Swanson, *Medieval Artisans*, 4.

migration of rural women to the town. The sex ratio is the least generally applicable of these charactics. Cities as diverse as Ghent and Bury St Edmunds had more males, due perhaps to the textile-shipping character of the one and the clerical supremacy in the other.[124]

Citizenship and xenophobia in the later medieval city

Thus, although the cities were losing population, they were considerably less free than earlier in bestowing citizenship; for citizens had privileges that mere residents lacked, notably rights of political participation and guild membership. The exceptions were only partial, as cities offered inducements to specialists such as silkworkers or silversmiths.[125] When the freedom of the city was restricted, as in England, this contributed to closing the municipal oligarchy. When guild membership and citizenship were conditions of each other, the fact that increasing numbers of guilds had the right to demand that only guild members practise a given trade in effect put an economic ceiling over the heads of many immigrants. In many cities, however, marriage to the daughter or widow of a master gave newcomers access to mastership. At Frankfurt 32 per cent of new burgesses between 1371 and 1380 married a master's daughter, 17 per cent a widow.[126]

Citizenship was normally tied to residence and sometimes to landownership. By 1330 the normal prerequisite at Frankfurt was an entry fee and possession or purchase of urban land in the city worth 10 marks. When an exception was made, the beneficiary was usually given a year and a day to acquire the property. The city also required citizens to pay a yearly rent of 1/2 mark, usually by buying an annuity on a piece of land owned by the city.[127] Nuremberg tried to keep newcomers out of the central city by its land use policy. From 1382 it had three categories of citizens that were tied to net worth and property holdings of houses and land. Full citizens lived in the inner cities of St Sebald or St Lorenz. A newcomer who had property worth 200 fl paid an entry fee of 10 fl, but he could only move into one of the inner cities when the council allowed it and he could buy a house worth 50 fl. A second category consisted of master artisans or tradesmen who had under 200 fl. They had to live for a minimum of five years in the fortified suburbs and pay an entry fee of 60 Heller, corresponding to about six days' wages. A

124 Goldberg, 'Urban identity', 194–213; Nicholas, *Metamorphosis*, 30; Gottfried, *Bury St. Edmunds*, 47–8.
125 Gouron, *Métiers en Languedoc*, 187.
126 Bechtold, *Zunftbürgerschaft und Patriziat*, 79; Maschke, 'Soziale Gruppen', 130.
127 Dilcher, 'Bürgerbegriff', 76.

third group consisted of 'day labourers', who paid a 30-Heller fee, lived in the suburbs and were not considered citizens. From 1386 they had to swear only to work for a daily wage, and not to undertake independent craftsmanship. There were only 436 of them in 1393, and the category was ended around 1430. Between 1382 and 1500 some 1,710 full citizens were allowed into the inner city, and 17,983 craftsmen, day labourers and persons in other trades entered the suburbs.[128]

Virtually all cities had residence requirements for citizenship. The notion that 'town air makes a person free' no longer had an even limited application. Serfs were discouraged everywhere and forbidden in many places from entering the cities.[129] Citizens of Barcelona were expected to rent or own a permanent residence in the city, live on their own resources, pay municipal taxes, buy grain when the city offered it, either provide or hire service on the walls, and participate in parish festivals. In doubtful cases concerning citizenship the authorities would inquire of neighbours and parish curates. Citizens thus identified had to give the name of a personal surety and agree to surrender their identity cards if they left the city.[130] Some cities were less rigid. Bordeaux granted freedom after residence of one month and a day. Ghent required only that newcomers register with the aldermen within three days of entering the city and charged no fee. Citizenship was also easy to acquire at Reims, most often by birth, marriage to a citizen or continuous residence, even in rented housing.[131]

Purchasing citizenship when the father had held it amounted to validating a hereditary right, but. some cities required it. Lille charged 4s 2d for sons to assume the father's citizenship, but for outsiders it was 60s, even in the thirteenth century, when town populations were reaching their high point and the cities had to discourage immigration. Lille was unusual in keeping this same fee, which coinage depreciation had made much less onerous in real terms by the fifteenth century. By 1470 it represented 7.5 days of work for a master carpenter. Other cities required sons to take the oath within a year of reaching their majority or within a year and a day of marriage, when the new taxable household was established. If they failed to attend to this formality, they had to pay the higher fee as outsiders. The cities were also becoming more rigid about continuous residence. Lille required outsiders to live for three years

---

128 Isenmann, *Deutsche Stadt*, 96–7. This is similar to the restriction of landownership in the central city of Constance to lineages enjoying *Salmannenrecht*. Bechtold, *Zunftbürgerschaft und Patriziat*, 112–14.

129 Stoob, *Urkunden*, 285–6.

130 Carrère, *Barcelone*, 23–4.

131 Lodge, *Gascony Under English Rule*, 164; Nicholas, *Metamorphosis*, 39; Desportes, *Reims*, 183–7.

in the city before becoming citizens, then have four more years of continuous residence before the status became final. But although an earlier requirement that newcomers buy land in the city was ended in 1372, thereafter Lille required outsiders who applied for citizenship to be married and undergo an inquest into their status, condition, and morals. The single entry fee for all yielded to a scale ranging from 10 livres for the richest to one livre for the poor. Most purchasers of citizenship at Lille were thus long-term residents of the city who were subject to the fiscal and military exactions and wanted to gain the privileges of citizenship.[132]

Citizenship or freedom of the borough was most restrictive in England. It could be acquired by patrimony/inheritance from the father, apprenticeship, and 'redemption' (purchase), as we have seen. In both York and London records of admission to the freedom by patrimony only begin in the late fourteenth century, probably because earlier, before so many workers migrated to the city, inherited status was known in most cases. Freedom of the borough still went hand in hand with membership in the merchant guild in places that had them. Many cities had initially excluded craftsmen, particularly clothworkers, from the freedom: weavers were first admitted at Norwich in 1317, York in 1319, Colchester by 1327, and Leicester in 1334.[133]

In places without a merchant guild the right to buy and sell on the city market and to enjoy toll exemption was limited to burgesses, but in such cases anyone born in the 'liberty of the borough' could claim citizenship. The freedom conferred the right to trade retail, the right to vote and run for public office, and participation in a monopoly on the sale of commodities such as wool and cloth. Thus it was sought mainly by the merchant elites of the crafts. Victuallers, who imported their products, needed to buy the freedom; relatively few weavers did. This changed after 1350 as more guilds gained the right to exclude non-members from the work place, but the freedom was still chiefly of benefit to and affordable by the elite. At Exeter, where the guilds were powerful but not numerous, only 21 per cent of the heads of households belonged to the freedom in 1377. By contrast, between one-quarter and one-half of the population of York enjoyed the freedom in the late fourteenth century, but the guilds were more numerous and the economy more diversified there.[134]

Although initially the guilds' attraction had been to free persons, they

132 Desportes, 'Bourgeoisie de Lille', 541–9.
133 Rigby, 'Urban oligarchy', 71.
134 Britnell, *Colchester*, 24, 36; Kermode, 'Merchants', 8; Kowaleski, 'Commercial dominance', 200–2; Kowaleski, 'Women's work in Exeter', 146 and 159 n. 5; Swanson, *Medieval Artisans*, 108–10; Goldberg, *Women, Work and Life Cycle*, 52.

were so aristocratic by the late fourteenth century that in 1387 the government of London closed both apprenticeship and the freedom of the city to villeins. This deprived peasants of the right to trade in the city; the leaders of the 1381 rebellion, who came from the upper reaches of the peasantry and the small towns, thus demanded the freedom. The cities were jealous of their privileges: Londoners who opposed John of Northampton in 1382 objected to his allowing victuallers from outside to sell their goods throughout the city. Non-citizens probably outnumbered the freemen in London by three to one in the late fourteenth century.[135]

URBAN DECLINE IN THE FIFTEENTH CENTURY

The cities suffered massive population losses in the wake of the first plagues, then stabilised or in some cases even grew after about 1375. Even when absolute numbers declined, the cities' share in the total productive capacity and population increased; for although the epidemics were less severe in the villages, the rural areas suffered more from wars and lost a considerable proportion of their population through migration to the cities.

But from the 1420s the examples of urban decline outnumber those of rise, particularly in England. Immigration to Constance between 1400 and 1420, stimulated by the church council that met there between 1414 and 1418, was nearly double that of 1375–1400, but the high point was reached in a period of civil conflict after the council had left. Between 1420 and 1430 Constance received more than four hundred newcomers, with a large majority in the food trades and most of the rest in crafts. Constance enrolled nearly twice as many new burgesses as taxpayers between 1375 and 1450 and thus was left with a population of persons whose ability to support themselves was precarious after the artificial stimulus of the council was removed.[136]

Migration did not always make up for plague losses, and warfare in the fifteenth century exacerbated the problem. Dijon had 2,156 heads of households in 1385. By March 1386, 58 had died, but 333 newcomers had enrolled. The mortality rate of 2.7 per cent is low for a preindustrial population even in a normal year, but immigration more than replaced losses through death. During the plague year of 1400–1, however, 2,013 households were reduced by 298 deaths and 97 departures, which were

135 Platt, *English Medieval Town*, 117–18; Britnell, *Commercialisation of English Society*, 224–5; Hanawalt, *Growing Up in Medieval London*, 35.
136 Bechtold, *Zunftbürgerschaft und Patriziat*, 47–50.

not made up by 101 new households. Plague-induced mortality was nearly quintuple the normal death rate. In the normal year 1406–7, 114 died or left the city, while 91 new households are recorded. The two-decade trend was thus for immigration to Dijon to be strong, but not enough to make up for the plagues and some emigration. Population declined by one-fifth between 1385 and 1407 and continued to drop even after the plague threat had receded.[137]

The Dijon example suggests that French urban populations may have declined in the fifteenth century due to inadequate replacement. The number of Christian households at Arles declined from 2,194 to 910 between 1319 and 1438, and replenishment was low. The number of heirs per deceased person was 1.81 between 1351 and 1375, 1.75 in the 1390s and 1.03 between 1471 and 1475. Of the places for which such sources are available only Toulouse, at 1.0, had a lower rate of survival of heirs than Arles. Yet the problem was high mortality, not fecundity: most parents had several children, but 42 per cent of testators between 1391 and 1475 died without children surviving them. Given the heavy mortality and low replacement rates, immigration had to be extremely high if a city were not to lose absolute numbers.[138]

Thus cities reacted to their population losses in diverse ways. Those that attracted war refugees had more people than they could handle. In 1444 roughly one-third of the 26,000 persons living within the walls of Strasbourg had fled there from the rural environs.[139] The newcomers were not welcomed. Some banded together with people from the same or nearby villages on their own volition, but sometimes it was stipulated by the authorities. Arezzo in 1327 required newcomers to live in neighbourhoods with others from their natal villages. In northern cities immigrants were sometimes required to have guarantors or sponsors, and they often chose people who had preceded them to the city from the same village.[140]

Other cities tried to attract productive newcomers but differentiated between potential settlers. Mainz in 1436 offered nobles and knights ten years' freedom from the normal obligation of joining a craft as a condition of citizenship and from all direct taxes. Those who wished to practise a trade had to join the appropriate guild, but the city appointed a special commission to facilitate their admission and determine the entry

---

137 Dubois, 'Mortalité à Dijon', 333–40.
138 Stouff, *Arles*, 124–37. Inadequate replacement rates among the resident population also explains demographic decline at Bury St Edmunds. Gottfried, *Bury St. Edmunds*, 52–71.
139 Schulz, *Handwerksgesellen und Lohnarbeiter*, 28–31 after Dollinger, 'Population de Strasbourg', 521.
140 Balestracci, 'Immigrazione e morfologia urbana', 89–90.

fee. The magistrates also agreed 'that if any man or woman who previously resided in the city wishes to return, he or she should appear in
person before the four men deputised for this purpose; and they should
be pleasant to such persons and agree with them concerning their
residence'.[141]

The rise and decline of urban regions

Immigration and natural replacement were not enough to restore the
populations of most cities of northern Europe to their pre-plague levels,
but the decline was sharpest in Italy, whose level of urbanisation was
comparable to that of the north by 1400. The table illustrates the change
dramatically:

Number of inhabitants	*c. 1300*	*c. 1420*
80,000+	Milan, Venice, Florence	Milan, Venice
40–80,000	Bologna, Verona, Brescia, Cremona, Siena, Pisa, Palermo	Genoa
20–40,000	Padua, Pavia, Mantua, Piacenza, Parma, Lucca, Bologna, Rome, Perugia, Naples	Florence, Verona, Brescia, Ferrara, Bologna, Perugia, Palermo, Rome, Naples
10–20,000	Ferrara, Modena, Vicenza, Arezzo, Viterbo, Melfi	Padua, Pavia, Parma, Siena, Piacenza

Rome and Naples remained relatively stable, but the others experienced massive decline. During the fifteenth century the middle-sized
cities declined sharply, while the largest centres remained stationary or
grew. Overall urbanisation thus declined in Italy, but the dominance of
the great metropolises of Milan, Genoa and Venice was accentuated, with
Florence, Perugia, Bologna, Naples, and Rome in a second order.[142]

141 Keutgen, *Urkunden*, 449–50.
142 Ginatempo and Sandri, *L'Italia delle città*, tables, 224–39.

The demographic changes of the fourteenth century altered the relative standing of the cities and of entire urban regions. Commercial and industrial shifts also produced important mutations. The decline of the Flemish urban textile industry in the fourteenth century is well known, and the causes of the malaise are complicated. Craftsmen emigrated in the wake of nearly constant civil discord, initially to neighbouring Brabant and, after the 1380s, to England.[143] Textile production in Ghent had been declining since the early fourteenth century and more sharply in the 1350s, when the weavers were disenfranchised for their role in the rebellion of the 1340s, and many emigrated. The city lost markets that it did not recover when more settled conditions returned.[144] Although the Flemish cities did not diversify their textile production to meet the demand for new products, they remained important producers of goods and deliverers of services. Bruges, which never had the textile capacity of Ghent or Ypres, flourished through its staple. Ghent's population reached a nadir by 1385 that was only half the level of 1357, which was in itself much lower than before 1315, but most of the decline was in the textile sector. The city's staple on grain entering Flanders from France created an immense source of wealth if not of jobs and put pressure on rural Flanders and the smaller towns. The city's shippers also controlled the export southward of peat that was extracted from the bogs of northeastern Flanders. Other sectors of the city's economy grew as shipping intensified: new houses were constructed, public works were expanded and some new industries developed, particularly hop beer.[145]

The signs of decline at Bruges were more real than was apparent until the 1470s, but Barcelona, so similar in many respects to the Flemish port, became a horror story of decline in the fifteenth century. Its economy was essentially stable between 1380 and 1420, then declined modestly for a decade and sharply after 1430. Shipping suffered from naval wars. Immigrants had been assimilated easily in the fourteenth century, but their numbers rose disproportionately as hostilities in southwestern France worsened. Slaves also made up an increasing percentage of the labour force. The government of Barcelona tried to resuscitate the textile industry and halt the haemorrhage of money due to trade imbalance. They provided subventions and loans, obtained raw materials when artisans could not get them through normal channels, recruited specialists abroad

---

143 Nicholas, *Medieval Flanders*, 279 and literature cited.
144 Brabantine textiles, which had initially competed successfully with the Flemish, were not spared. Mechelen's production of 24,000 cloths made it roughly equal to Ypres in 1332, but it had declined to 8,000 by 1370. Leuven made 14,000 textiles before 1350, barely 6,000 by 1400. Nicholas, *Metamorphosis*, 136–42, 154–6; Nicholas, *Medieval Flanders*, 276–8; van Houtte and van Uytven, 'Nijverheid en handel', 105.
145 Nicholas, *Metamorphosis*, 38, 289–91.

and bought new manufactured products, notably silk, tapestries and fustians so that their producers would be guaranteed a market. After 1438 the magistrates in desperation turned to textile protectionism, forbidding the import of Flemish cloth. But nothing could halt Barcelona's catastrophic decay.[146]

Urban decline in later medieval England?

The upsurge of clothmaking in England contributed to the prosperity of some cities, but most of the cloth that was England's major industrial export in the late Middle Ages was produced in the small towns. The growth of the smaller market towns may have balanced the decay of the major cities to a degree. Yet the decline of wool exports that paralleled the rise of clothmaking hurt the places, mainly in the east Midlands and the northeast (Lincoln, Stamford, Northampton, Boston and Lynn) that had grown great by shipping wool to the continent. Boston declined from fourth in wealth among English cities in 1334 to twenty-second in the 1520s. Lincoln went from fifth in size in 1377 to tenth in 1524, but by then it was twentieth· in wealth. Lincoln's decline, caused in part by the silting of the Trent and its dependence on declining Boston as its port, was so marked that in 1390 the guildhall was pulled down as a hindrance to traffic.[147]

Most large centres experienced growth in the late fourteenth century. The cities had been overpopulated for their potential markets before 1348, but the first wave of population decline had balanced their populations with available resources by about 1370. Continued population decline thereafter meant that the English towns had a real shortage of people by the early fifteenth century. The available labour in the cities was inadequate to meet regional demand: in 1381 York had to allow women to work as smiths and carpenters, which were traditionally male preserves.[148] But this in turn meant that the cities offered plenty of work for immigrants.

Decline set in around 1430, most severely in northern England. A few cities had petitioned to have their fee farms reduced on grounds of poverty in the early fifteenth century, and the requests were numerous from the 1430s.[149] The declining supplies of coin since the 1390s had hurt the merchants of London first, but their domination of the overseas

146 Carrère, *Barcelone*, 663–70, 728, 806, 837.
147 Dyer, *Decline and Growth*, 20–3; Hill, *Medieval Lincoln*, 254.
148 Dyer, *Decline and Growth*, 14–17.
149 Keene, *Winchester*, 92–4, 105.

trade meant that they could continue to trade for goods rather than coin·more easily than could the provincials. Before the fifteenth century the London grocers, who handled the importing of Italian spices and dyes in the provinces and the exporting of English wool, had based most of their distributive system on the merchants of the provincial towns; but after 1400 they more often dealt directly with their rural suppliers through itinerant traders, bypassing the smaller towns. The loss of the business of the London grocers was an element in the declining prosperity of some cloth cities of the interior, such as Coventry.[150]

The problems of Hull, Lynn, Yarmouth and Boston reflected England's trade vicissitudes with the Hanse. Income from the market and fair at Boston, which had specialised in the German trade, declined by more than two-thirds between 1428 and 1435 and stayed at a low level.[151] York had grown in the early fourteenth century as a virtual capital during the kings' Scottish campaigns. It flourished in the 1330s and 1340s on the business of the great wool merchants, then to the end of the fourteenth century on cloth exports. Overseas trade increased greatly from the early fourteenth century, and York was a home staple town from 1326. Its merchants were also active at the Calais wool staple and in English expansion into the Baltic trade. While foreign merchants controlled York's long-distance trade at the beginning of the fourteenth century, natives dominated by the 1330s. The population was about 8,000 at the end of the Scottish wars, rising to 11,000 in 1377 and 13,000 by 1400, despite the plagues. Enrolments of new freemen, a much smaller number than the rise in population, doubled between the second and last quarters of the century. Yet the city declined in the fifteenth century, as relations with the Hanse deteriorated and York's cloth industry suffered from competition with the clothiers of rural Yorkshire.[152]

Most cities that grew in the fourteenth century were already regionally dominant by the late thirteenth century, with the strong base in local and overseas trade needed to surmount the crises. Bristol was second only to London in wine imports in the late thirteenth century. By 1350 it controlled the distribution of English cloth, mainly from the Cotswolds, to Gascony and Ireland. Clothworking then developed in Bristol itself and its suburbs. In contrast to the situation in London, most merchants in Bristol were natives who were part of the permanent population base.[153]

150 Nightingale, *Medieval Mercantile Community*, 364–7.
151 Goldberg, *Women, Work and Life Cycle*, 73–9; Palliser, 'Urban decay revisited', 13–17; Britnell, *Commercialisation of English Society*, 157.
152 Tillott, *City of York*, 84–5, 100–5.
153 Lobel, *Atlas* 2: 9–10.

Some cities in the interior grew as economic power shifted from areas producing grain to those specialising in wool and cloth. Based on the tax records of 1377 and the 1520s, Exeter grew from twenty-third to sixth among English cities, and Norwich, Canterbury, Worcester and Newcastle did better than the national trend. But most of the ten top towns of 1377 had a smaller population by 1524.[154] Colchester grew after 1350 as its cloth filled some of the vacuum left by the decline of Flemish textiles in England. The high point of trading was in the late 1390s, but the volume had dropped by nearly half by 1420 in the wake of interruptions in the Baltic and Gascon trade. Colchester's German trade never recovered from the Hanse–English war of 1468, and the depression affected all Colchester's overseas markets. Population declined by one-third between 1400 and 1524.[155] Coventry, England's closest equivalent to the cloth towns of the continent, was the chief city of the west Midlands by 1377. Unusual among English medieval cities, Coventry grew through industry rather than trade, for its distribution of goods was blocked by the spheres of influence of Leicester and Northampton. Like other English cities, Coventry probably reached its height in the 1430s, then declined gradually until 1500 and sharply thereafter. Coventry prospered as long as its textiles did well in international markets; when they declined, the city was ruined.[156]

Much of the problem seems to have been an issue that did not affect many continental cities, probably because their rural environs were so dangerous after the 1330s: the depopulation of the suburbs combined with the high taxes in the cities due to monopolies and public services made the cities so expensive that the more substantial citizens were withdrawing to the countryside. In the 1450s even among such wealthy tradesmen as the grocers and mercers of London numerous freemen were living in the suburbs of Southwark and Westminster to avoid taxation in the city, then coming into the city to work. Aided by guild fines, the mayor and aldermen threatened such people with loss of the freedom, and the practice, after reaching a height in the 1440s, declined in the 1450s.[157] The cities' tax bases suffered. Rural men came to the cities for long enough to become enfranchised but then left, using burgess standing as a way to sell manufactured goods on rural markets. The declining urban economies were unable to support the expensive ceremonies, pageants and plays that were such an important cultural contribution of

154 Dyer, *Decline and Growth*, 40.
155 Britnell, *Colchester*, 54–7, 157–70.
156 Phythian-Adams, *Coventry*, 26–35.
157 Nightingale, *Medieval Mercantile Community*, 481.

the late medieval cities. The financial obligations of officeholding were so onerous that prominent people were evading municipal and guild offices, although except at York most known examples are from the end of the fifteenth century.[158]

Nevertheless there is evidence of growth in the English cities that cannot be overlooked. Gloucester in 1447 petitioned the crown for tax relief on grounds that many houses were abandoned due to recent epidemics. Yet a survey of the town in 1455 shows 700 holdings, of which forty-eight were new and only six were 'ruined' or 'decayed'. Remissions of taxes were most numerous when the kings, most conspicuously Richard III, needed to buy support. Although most economic indices are down at York after 1425, four enormous guildhalls were built there in the late fourteenth and fifteenth centuries, financed by the city corporation but with substantial private donations. They included the Merchant Adventurers' Hall, the Merchant Tailors' Hall and the modern Guildhall, then called the 'common hall'. York Minster was completed and at least seven churches were expanded in the fifteenth century. One of them, Holy Trinity Hall, is the largest parish church in England. Most other evidence of construction of city halls is from the sixteenth century.[159]

While most large English cities declined, London grew rapidly. The seat of government was in its suburb of Westminster.[160] London expanded also because the demand of its market attracted a diversity of goods and services, and its communications network was so good that foreign merchants could be assured of their goods reaching a wide market in the interior. London was the leading English port by the 1430s, surpassing Southampton and those of the northeast that had specialised in the Hanse trade. Southampton had been a real threat to London's control of the Italian trade during much of the fourteenth century, but by the mid-fifteenth century merchants of Southampton and Bristol were buying the livery of the London grocers' company to give them more business opportunities overseas. At Southampton John Payne, a London grocer from a Southampton family, led a political faction against the Italians in the 1450s.[161] Other English cities rarely drew migrants from more than forty miles away, and more than half the

---

158 Phythian-Adams, 'Urban decay', 180 ff.
159 Dyer, *Decline and Growth*, 46; Palliser, 'Urban decay revisited', 4–5; Dobson, 'Urban decline', 275–7, 282; Tittler, 'Late medieval urban prosperity', 553–4; Kermode, 'Merchants', 32–3.
160 Rosser, *Medieval Westminster*, 36.
161 Nightingale, *Medieval Mercantile Community*, 506–31.

migrants to York, Norwich and Leicester whose places of origin can be determined came from within twenty miles. The catchment area of London and Westminster was sixty miles, and 11.3 per cent of London's immigrants and 23 per cent of Westminster's came from one hundred miles or more away. Thus while most immigrants from the countryside had earlier gone to the nearest large city, they were going to London by the late fifteenth century. The growth of the metropolis to 60,000 souls by 1500 thus prevented normal population replenishment in the county towns.[162]

Although English wool exports were declining in favour of cloth, London's share in the wool trade rose. The fifteen collectors of the wool customs under Richard II included seven who were lord mayors of London at some time, three mayors of the staple at Westminster, two mayors of the staple at Calais, while nine represented the city in Parliament, and at least ten were aldermen. The city government loaned to the crown and repaid itself from customs receipts of the port of London, almost always by assignment from royal customs on wool. Official and private business were closely intertwined, and public office was used for private gain that now would be considered illegitimate. Such leaders of the city as Nicholas Brembre and John Philpot rotated the major city and customs offices among themselves informally, assuring continued business with the crown.[163]

While the English cities generally declined in the fifteenth century, those of Scotland were growing. The Germans called Edinburgh, followed at some distance by Aberdeen, Perth and Dundee, the 'four great towns of Scotland'. Scotland had a Court of the Parliament of the Four Burghs to handle questions concerning burgess standing and trade; it met annually at Edinburgh from 1454. In the 1370s the four burghs paid 58 per cent of Scotland's customs revenue, most of it from wool and woolfells (sheep skins with fleece still attached). The share of these four had risen to 81 per cent by 1500, and by then it came from more commodities. Although the crafts of Aberdeen were troubling the authorities enough for weaver 'conspiracies' to be forbidden in 1398, Parliament forbade craftsmen to choose deans (guild presidents). An act of 1469 provided that members of the city councils would choose their own successors. Edinburgh was outstripping the other three in the fifteenth century. It was the national capital by 1437, and King James III (1460– 88) borrowed large sums from the city's wool merchants. Purveyance

---

162 Britnell, *Colchester*, 157; Rosser, *Medieval Westminster*, 186; Keene, *Winchester*, 375– 7.
163 Coleman, 'Collectors of customs', 182–7.

to the royal court contributed largely to a commercial boom in the late fifteenth century, and James may have accorded formal recognition to the city's craft guilds. Yet even with the late medieval growth the Scottish cities were much smaller than the English. They did have merchant guilds: Aberdeen's had sixty-three members in 1445 and Perth's more than one hundred, including many craftsmen.[164]

Although the population of most cities declined in the late Middle Ages, the decline was relatively less than that of the rural areas. The greatest cities of Europe around 1300 were Paris with 200,000 inhabitants, Granada with 150,000, followed by Venice with 110,000, Genoa and Milan with 100,000 each, Florence with 95,000, Seville with 90,000, Ghent with 75,000, Cologne with 55,000, and Naples, Barcelona, Palermo and Siena with 50,000 each. The other major Italian cities had populations of 25,000–40,000. Bruges, London, Ferrara, Montpellier, Lisbon, Perugia, Saint-Omer and Rouen all had between 25,000 and 35,000 souls. During the fourteenth century Paris, Bruges and perhaps London grew, but the others lost population while gaining relative to their rural environs.

A considerably larger proportion of Europe's population thus lived in cities by 1450 than in 1300. The large cities, with greater attractive power, larger employment markets and better facilities for poor relief, recovered more rapidly than did the middle group, many of which dwindled into small towns. Even omitting the smallest centres as not genuinely urban, city populations declined no more than 5–10 per cent in the long term, as against 27–35 per cent for the rural population. Taking 5,000 souls as the minimum for an 'urban' place, the population of Europe grew from 9.5 per cent urban in 1300 to 11.9 per cent in 1800. Within this period the most important time is the fourteenth century, when the urbanisation index rose in western and central Europe from 9.5 per cent to 12.5 per cent, declining to 10.3 per cent in the fifteenth century. The fourteenth century figures are the more striking in that Spain and Italy lost urban population but gained in the index, for rural losses were even higher. The pronounced shift toward the Atlantic from the Mediterranean that is so conspicuous in early modern Europe thus began in the fourteenth century. Numerous individual cities declined even as their regions grew in level of urbanisation. In France, for example, the urban index was slightly higher in 1400 than 1300; yet of thirty-eight cities for which there are usable statistics for

---

164 Lynch, 'Towns and townspeople', 175–84; Fradenburg, *City, Marriage, Tournament*, 8, 22, 29–30; Grant, *Independence and Nationhood*, 85.

both periods, twenty-six declined in total population, two were stable, and ten grew.[165]

Given these circumstances and the always symbiotic relationship between the cities and the rural environs that generated them, it is important to examine in more detail the economic and increasingly the political bonds of city and countryside in late medieval Europe.

165 Discussion based on Bairoch, *Population of European Cities*, 173, 253–4, 259–60, 276–9. Bairoch gives a shockingly low urbanisation figure for the United Kingdom, below even Switzerland, Poland and Russia; but his data are distorted by the inclusion of Scotland and Ireland, neither of which had large cities in the fifteenth century apart from Edinburgh and Dublin.

CHAPTER THREE

The City and the Region: City-states and the Symbiosis of the Rural and Urban Economies

The cities' share of the diminished population of late medieval Europe increased even as they declined in absolute numbers of inhabitants. Despite the massive population losses from the plagues Europe still had more people than its agriculture could feed properly until the 1370s. Yet rural overpopulation combined with structural problems caused peasants to migrate to the cities. This tilt in the demographic balance entailed important modifications in town–countryside relations.

Decline of the suburbs

While lack of an adequate tax base and peculation had been the major problems of urban finance in the thirteenth century, the issues in the fourteenth were the waves of refugees who were streaming into the cities, insecurity on the roads and particularly the need to spend immense amounts on fortifications. Some cities reverted to their earlier situation of being citadels whose main economic functions were providing their inhabitants with necessities.

Most cities in Italy, the Low Countries and Germany had expanded their walls to enclose suburbs. In France, however, the relative peace of the thirteenth century had lulled many governments into abandoning work on their walls, leaving their suburbs unprotected. Papal Avignon was the only French city that had fortified large suburbs before 1340. The devastation of the Hundred Years' War was the more complete because so many cities were unprepared. To meet the wartime emergency Tours, Paris, Auxonne and Grenoble hastily erected brick walls that were of little use. Although work was begun on the new wall of

Reims in 1209, the only permanent structures in 1337 were gates; the rest was an earth rampart and a moat.[1] Paris's wall was still that of Philip Augustus, who had expanded it to include suburbs that were admittedly sparsely inhabited. By 1300 there were at least fifty streets outside this wall. The new wall of Paris was begun in the late 1350s and completed by King Charles V (1364–80). It was really a series of fortresses that narrowed the trace of Philip Augustus' wall on the south but extended it on the north. It was between eight and ten metres high and more than three metres thick.[2]

Gates were kept locked and their keys entrusted to officials. Ghent used its gates as arsenals for firearms but rented them to citizens during peacetime. In 1368 Ghent fined a mercer who was living in a gate on the west end for having torn down a portion of the wall that ran through his home. The city council of Burgos met in the gate of Santa Maria, while the Carretas gate, which opened onto the main town square, had a balcony from which the council members presided over festivals. Some English city gates, such as Newgate in Bristol, were used as prisons. London's seven gates were enormous. Two of them (Newgate and Ludgate) contained prisons, and the others were residences. While Geoffrey Chaucer was royal controller of the wool custom, he enjoyed life lease of an apartment above Aldgate. The gates also continued to be critical elements of the cities' market and control apparatus. In 1407 a fishmonger who sat on the council of Cologne and held the keys to one city gate opened it too early, threw spoiled fish into the Rhine and sold fish packed in baskets earlier in the day than was allowed. He was placed under house arrest, ejected from the council and lost his trade for six years.[3]

As walls were strengthened, moats were widened, towers added at intervals along the circuit, and previously inhabited areas under the walls yielded to swamps; for many cities, needing to clear the suburbs of anything that could give shelter to an enemy, denuded them of vegetation and buildings. Citizens remained outside at their peril. At Saint-Omer the suburb of the rue Boulnizienne had 294 houses in 1346 but 56 in 1413 when the English burned the settlement. Wolves killed fourteen people within the walls of Paris in the last week of September 1440. The towns feared having fortifications in their environs. Virtually all cities

---

1 Guillemain, *Cour pontificale d'Avignon*, 505–7; Desportes, *Reims*, 526–9.
2 Thompson, *Paris Under English Rule*, 78–9; Rossiaud, 'Crises', 424–5; Geremek, *Margins of Society*, 67; Guillemain, *Cour pontificale d'Avignon*, 505–7; Cazelles, *Paris*, 25, 205–6, 346–7.
3 Municipal Archive of Ghent, ser. 400, IX, fo. 318r; Huiskes, *Beschlüsse Köln*, 75; Lobel, *Atlas 2*: 13; Hanawalt, *Growing Up in Medieval London*, 24; Howard, *Chaucer*, 207; Ladero Quesnada, 'Fortifications Castille', 159.

in the Netherlands obtained the count's permission to forbid fortresses in the ban mile. Part of Philip Augustus' wall on the left bank in Paris was sacrificed in 1356–7 to keep the English from using outbuildings that had been erected on it. Troyes destroyed most of the Croncels suburb, including houses and tannery mills. As the market increased for products made by environmentally hazardous processes such as leatherworking and linen bleaching, their sites were often moved inside the city but near the walls. The destruction of suburban water mills hampered drainage from the inner-city canals.

The decline of the suburbs occurred in the wake of population decline from plagues and warfare. The Nine of Siena had started an extension of the walls in the early fourteenth century but never finished it. A new quarter of Santa Maria was planned and regular plots laid out. Although Santa Maria had ninety houses by 1330, it was abandoned by 1385, for with so much property available in the city, there was no reason to settle in the suburbs. At Reims the bourgs around the Chacre gate had become 'dirty' quarters for the butchers and tanners but were abandoned after 1356. The suburbs, particularly the bourg of Vesle, were especially hurt by the declining textile industry and wartime devastation. By 1400 the bourgs had at most one-fifth of the population of the urban agglomeration.[4]

Even after conditions became more peaceful around 1450 the pattern continued of decay in the suburbs and, in some places, of areas within the walls nearest the peripheries, compared with a more active city centre. This contrasted with the suburban vitality of the early medieval cities. Although the suburbs had been industrial throughout the thirteenth century, efforts now were made to keep the ban mile (the area nearest to the wall) agricultural even in places whose suburbs were still inhabited. Ypres was the only city in the Low Countries that tried to get craftsmen to live outside the walls, although others achieved the same end by not extending their fortifications. In 1412 Haarlem forbade burgesses to buy or sell food or manufactured goods from or to anyone who lived within 300 rods of the city. The ban mile was to be depopulated; except for the houses of millers and shipwrights, structures built during the last two years were to be destroyed.[5] Rennes still had numerous gardens and generally low tax assessments in its suburbs in 1455. The old Roman city centre, although much smaller, had nearly one-fifth of the habitations, but all of the public buildings and squares

---

4 Balestracci, 'Development to crisis', 206–8; Derville, *Histoire de Saint-Omer*, 81, 84; *Parisian Journal*, 332; Nicholas, *Stad en Platteland*, 86–7; Guillerme, *Age of Water*, 118–24, 140–4; Desportes, *Reims*, 570–2, 593.
5 Nicholas, *Stad en Platteland*, 86–7.

except the smaller parish churches and fourteen of the seventeen taverns were there. The central quarters were generally prosperous, although with some pockets of poverty, but the suburbs were poor.[6]

Since many English cities lacked complete walls, and civil conflict was less severe there than on the continent, the depopulation of the suburbs that was so marked in France does not apply to them. Gloucester developed a 'Newland' on the north by 1375, with two leper hospitals and a new royal palace. Norwich had only a ditch and gates until 1297. By 1344 a wall surrounded by a deep moat enclosed a square mile; but the inhabited area sprawled outside the walls, while there were many open spaces inside them. Norwich had as large an area as London but one-quarter of London's population. It grew along the Wensum, with its densest population around the market and both sides of the central part of the river. Norwich had five bridges, the most of any medieval English city but considerably behind most on the continent.[7]

City plans and social geography in the later Middle Ages

The English cities shared the continental pattern of decline of areas within but near the walls; for this, in contrast to the devastation of the suburbs, was a function not of warfare but of plague, population decline and structural decay. Colchester had vacant spaces inside the walls but residences outside them. Winchester had eighty-one persons per square acre in the centre, but areas nearer the walls were abandoned or given over to gardening. The decline in occupied street frontage in Winchester between 1300 and 1417 is striking, turning the city into basically a single-street settlement. The main street, the High, had many more shops in 1300 than in 1148, due both to population growth and concentration of shops and stalls there. After 1348 the High lost some habitation, but the withdrawal of settlement from the side streets perpendicular to it, where many wealthy persons whose businesses were on the main street resided, was catastrophic. While in 1300 most of them had built-up frontages extending back to the walls, only the areas nearest the High still had much habitation in 1417. By then shops were found only in the High and St Giles Hill. Even the fullers and tanners, whose occupations usually relegated them to the peripheries, lived nearer the centre, as clothmaking replaced wool trading as a source of wealth.[8]

As homeowners tried to pay off their debts by selling annuity rents

---

6 Leguay, *Réseau urbain Bretagne*, 124–31.
7 Lobel, *Atlas* 2: 8, 10–12.
8 Britnell, *Colchester*, 1–10; Dyer, *Standards of Living*, 189; Keene, *Medieval Winchester*, 130–1, 139–54, 417–18, figures, 153–4.

or mortgages on their properties, many tenements were encumbered beyond their real value. Ten per cent of the houses in Macon were dangerously burdened in 1386, and one-third of those in Toulouse in 1391. Speculators demolished houses to make room for more elegant buildings. Between 1420 and 1440 one-third of the houses at the wealthy Notre-Dame Bridge in Paris were abandoned. In the Île de la Cité 255 residences were abandoned in 1360. One-third of Lille was deserted in 1370. Particularly in France city officials, preoccupied with defending walls with insufficient resources, let the abandoned quarters atrophy. Some Florentine palaces remained unfinished because the builder ran out of money and were sold within a generation by the heirs.[9] Flimsy construction and perils from fire and water were thus compounded by debt-induced depopulation that left substantial parts of many cities with large numbers of abandoned houses. While earlier houses had often remained in the same family for several decades, in fifteenth-century Paris the average time of occupancy of a house by the same family even in the rich quarters was only eleven years. Fewer than one-fifth of the taxpayers in the quarter of St Jacob of Bruges in 1394–6 had paid there in 1382–3, a fact indicating both heavy mortality and high mobility of fortune and location.[10]

Prominent families were concentrated around the main markets and increasingly in the side streets leading off them. In some places this is simply the persistence of a long tradition. At Genoa 892 houses within the walls were owned by magnates in 1462–3, 3,997 by *popolari*. No nobles lived in the bourgs of Santo Tommaso or Santo Stefano, on the northern and southern peripheries respectively. Few lived in Porta Nova (near the wall on the side of the city toward the mountain) and Piazza Lunga (the marina). But in the central quarter that included the cathedral almost half the houses were noble, declining to one-third in the areas just off the centre.[11]

But the general rule that the centres were wealthier than the peripheries conceals considerable variation within neighbourhoods, particularly as some of the elite moved into space that had been vacated outside the centres. Many of the largest properties in the central cities were rented out to several families, especially cellars and back yards. At Lübeck perhaps one-quarter of the population lived in such accommodation. The central cities thus housed both the richest and some of the poorest inhabitants.[12] The merchant families of Lübeck moved away from the

9 Rossiaud, 'Crises', 437; Goldthwaite, *Building of Renaissance Florence*, 103–5.
10 Rossiaud, 'Crises', 436; Nicholas, 'Social mobility', 94.
11 Heers, *Gênes. Civilisation*, 53.
12 Maschke, 'Unterschichten', 376; Haverkamp, 'Topografia e relazioni soziali', 45–6.

harbour areas, which were now given over to port facilities and houses for dockers, and lived in the Königsstraat-Kobert and the former ministerial quarter around the church of St Egidius.[13] At Reims rich and poor were mixed immediately around the markets, but most of the rich lived a short distance away in side streets and at crossroads. Wealth declined farther from the centre, and the wall area was filled with barns, small houses and gardens.[14]

As the central cities had been occupied early by churches, public buildings and the homes of the elite, immigrants – particularly craftsmen – had initially lived mainly in suburbs. Now, with the suburbs depopulated, they more often moved into vacated areas inside the walls. Most non-citizen residents of Duderstadt in 1379 had houses near the gates. Changes of residence within the city became more common. At Winchester this was generally within the same street as or at least in the vicinity of a larger house. Some poorer citizens were also moving to modest houses near the walls, as back-yard shacks in the central cities were torn down and their inhabitants moved into the suburbs. At Siena in the fifteenth century some immigrant potters settled in areas just inside the wall where their trade had traditionally been located. When an artisan changed residence, it was usually to another part of town where his trade was strong. Siena tried to hinder land speculation by requiring newcomers who bought vacant land to build a house on it. Many were unable to afford this and thus lived in rented housing. In 1428 about one-fifth of the population of Pisa consisted of recent immigrants, but they lived throughout the city – not, as in the early fourteenth century, going to suburbs that had been planned for them.[15]

Despite the mobility of the population and the mixture of rich and poor in the same quarters and even streets, notable differences in wealth remained between different sectors of the cities. In some places they became even sharper. Large cities were multinuclear and thus might have several 'good' neighbourhoods, while smaller cities more often had a single wealthy centre and poorer suburbs. Sometimes a wall or river would separate rich from poor quarters. Florence was initially divided into sixths (later quarters) for purposes of administration, then subdivided into parishes. Except for Oltrarno, across the river from the central city, the sixths were not sharply distinguished in wealth, but the parishes within them were more likely to have a distinct character, either aristocratic or

---

13 Leguay, 'Propriété et marché de l'immobilier', 176–7; Fehring and Hammel, 'Topographie der Stadt Lübeck', 175.

14 Rossiaud, 'Crises', 500; Desportes, *Reims*, 482–5, 570–2.

15 Keene, *Medieval Winchester*, 235; Rossiaud, 'Crises', 500; Fahlbusch, 'Duderstadt', 194–212; Balestracci, 'Immigrazione e morfologia urbana', 95–8, 105.

craft. At Perugia each of the five gates that furnished members of the council had sectors drawn from the three divisions (old city, bourg and suburb). The differences in wealth were not vast between the gates, for each had both rich areas, mainly the city precincts, and areas of medium and little wealth.[16]

The peripheries became depopulated, but the population density of many central cities also fell as the wealthy bought land that had been vacated during the plagues. They demolished shacks and built more opulent residences. Contrary to the earlier pattern, few cities except Prague expanded now by incorporating new nuclei of settlement. Depopulation made room in the cities for larger homes for the urban and sometimes rural elites and for larger public buildings, particularly city halls and guildhalls. Montpellier built a new city hall in 1364 behind the cathedral of Notre-Dame des Tables because the area was dirty and filled with abandoned buildings. The consuls converted an existing building into a new merchant loge in 1377, then replaced it after 1447 with a new structure on the corner across from the church.[17] Political upheavals continued to make space for newcomers by devastating substantial areas within the walls. The northeastern quarter of Santa Pace at Orvieto declined after its richest inhabitants, the Ghibelline nobles, were exiled in 1313 and their houses were destroyed. Cardinal Albornoz built his palace on deserted land there in 1354.[18] In the late Middle Ages the patricians of Constance gradually abandoned the markets and commercial arteries of the old centre for more spacious quarters in the suburbs. The great guilds built new halls on land thus vacated in the city centre after 1430.[19]

The elite of Montpellier bought abandoned houses, then demolished them and built palaces, some of them in stone. This made street plans less regular, especially in once-suburban areas that had initially had regular designs. Rear courtyards that did not alter the line of street frontage also became common.[20] Paris is our best example of this concentration of landed property. The city may have had as many as 24,000 empty houses in 1423, most with two or three storeys. This represents a population loss of roughly half. As landowners sold properties, rents declined to 90 per cent of their normal value in the 1420s. The restored royal government in 1438 gave owners of dilapidated buildings the choice of repairing or demolishing them. The social geography of Paris was thus transformed between 1420 and 1450. During the absence of the king and

16   Raveggi, 'Aristocratici in città', 75–9; Blanshei, *Perugia*, 44.
17   Faber and Lochard, *Montpellier*, 212–15.
18   Waley, *Mediaeval Orvieto*, 25, 81.
19   Bechtold, *Zunftbürgerschaft und Patriziat*, 77–88.
20   Faber and Lochard, *Montpellier*, 253.

many nobles, lesser bureaucrats bought vacant houses, especially around the Louvre and the Hôtel Saint-Pol. Officials and lawyers became so numerous in the left bank streets west of the rue Saint-Jacques that they constituted an intellectual quarter, distinct from the 'Latin' quarter of clerks on the east. Paris in the fifteenth century thus experienced 'an urbanism of notables'. An English colony developed around the Hôtel des Tournelles, the chief residence of the duke of Bedford. The aristocrats tried to be near the king's residences, while avoiding the busiest streets and the left bank.[21]

Market squares were enlarged and became more specialised in function. Cologne (Plan 1) had had a single square divided into segments by buildings for centuries. Smaller speciality markets were added, each with a Master who was appointed by the council to oversee city regulations. Other large cities now evolved toward the Cologne type of large differentiated market square and subsidiary markets. The market square at Reims was split between two parishes. The boundary was marked by a double range of houses between the cloth market on the east and the grain market on the west. The passage between them linked Minters Street to the Spicery. Each main division of the market had areas designated for particular goods; even on the grain market grain sales were permitted only on the northern extremity. The horse market was at the end of Minters Street on the site occupied now by the city hall; the wool market, where sheep may also have been sold, was east of it.[22]

The Italian cities were still extending their defences beyond the inhabited area in the fourteenth century, but often with a trench and wooden palisade rather than a wall. Genoa was unusual in having continuous walls enclosing most of the population. Although Italian cities continued to have a higher population density than the northern even after the plagues, Genoa was unusually compact. Its wall of 1346 doubled its enclosed area to 110 ha. Bruges (Plan 7), which had a population comparable to Genoa's, had 400 ha within the walls, which included considerable vacant space. Genoa shows little evidence of street planning by the authorities. All building was subordinated to defence, not comfort. The churches and hospitals did plan some initially suburban quarters, such as the Borgo Santo Stefano. It developed around the Benedictine abbey of that name east of the city and sheltered pilgrims and immigrants, particularly clothworkers.[23]

21 Thompson, *Paris Under English Rule*, 141–2; Favier, *Paris 1380–1500*, 59–61, 103–18, 179.
22 Desportes, *Reims*, 371–8.
23 Heers, *Gênes. Civilisation*, 51–2; Heers, *Fortifications*, 255–68.

Florence (Plan 6) also underwent important modifications as population decline left land vacant, as confiscations had done earlier. A new cathedral was begun in 1296, the city hall (the Palace of the Priors or Palazzo Vecchio) in 1299. But while the focus of earlier urban renewal had been secular civic building, now it was private palaces that the wealthy built on vacated sites. Before 1350 most private building improvements were internal remodellings of existing structures. As towers and loges went out of fashion in the fourteenth century, shops were eliminated from the patrician residences. In contrast to the north, they became strictly residential in Italy, with the plan emphasising the main entrance. Large internal courtyards became social centres, and their outbuildings were cleared away. Most early Renaissance palaces were centrally located, but often in small side streets that they dominated rather than on the main square. By the late fourteenth and fifteenth centuries more were being built in the outskirts, as the city centre again became congested.[24]

The late Middle Ages thus witnessed a radical change in the nature of the suburbs. In most cities the internal areas nearest the walls were either semi-deserted, occupied by persons in environmentally hazardous occupations, or given over to the palaces and gardens of the elite. Nearer the city centre were increasingly elaborate residences and some public buildings such as guildhalls, made possible by the purchase of vacated tenements and the consolidation of holdings. The centres themselves were dominated by market squares, city halls and churches, many of which were being enlarged.

Trade and occupational groupings

The fact that so much urban property fell vacant after the plagues complicates the picture of residential–occupational groupings. As the guilds developed merchant elites, professional affiliation meant less in terms of prestige, which increased one's chances of living near the centre, than did two other criteria: whether the trade had a merchant element and one's position within the guild.

Some city governments still required a degree of residential segregation by trade. The ruling lineages of Brussels, fearing the revolutionary tendencies of the weavers and fullers, in 1306 forbade them to live within the walls. They thus lived around the gates and outside the walls, mainly on the south. The new city wall of 1357 bent around the textile

24 Goldthwaite, *Building of Renaissance Florence*, 2–22; Raveggi, 'Aristocratici in città', 82.

quarter, leaving room for anticipated continued growth.[25] In other cities, mainly those that exported large quantities of manufactured items, the power of the craft organisations affected occupational concentrations. In virtually all cities that lacked prominent export industries the highest tax groups were in the streets around the cathedral, but the other parishes had a more even distribution of wealth. Highly regulated or taxed groups also tended to live together. More than half the merchants and brokers of wine of Paris lived in the rue de la Mortellerie alone, and many others were around the place de Grève.[26]

Although occupational segregation was never absolute in the cities of the north, it was rare for groups that were potentially antagonistic, such as weavers and fullers, to live near one another. The exceptions are places such as Winchester that had either declined or had not yet reached a stage where the craft population was large enough to develop coherent organisations that vied for power.[27] At Ghent most drapers were enrolled in the weavers' guild and employed fullers for wages. The two trades competed for political power. They were of nearly equal strength in the parish of St John in the central city, but from there they diverged: large numbers of weavers lived in the abbey village of St Peter south of the town and in an adjacent suburb that came under city control in the thirteenth century, while the rest of the fullers were in the parish of St James, within the wall but on the north side of town, away from the weavers.[28]

The circumstances surrounding the introduction of a particular trade into a city could affect social geography. Textile workers tended to be on the peripheries, for clothmaking was not originally an urban occupation. In cities where the textile industry was brought by migrating labourers, they often lived in a single area, where their descendants remained.[29] The tendency for related occupational groups to congregate, however, was relaxed in the late Middle Ages as more land became available for purchase. Individuals, particularly the merchant elites of the crafts, bought choice property nearer the city centre and at some distance from the main concentrations of their trades. As leatherworking revived with the growth of animal husbandry in the rural economy, nearly 60 per cent of the population of some streets in a new quarter of Freiburg in 1416 were tanners.[30] Tanners and other occupations where

25   Dickstein-Bernard, 'Activité économique', 60–1; Martens, *Histoire de Bruxelles*, 102.
26   Favier, *Paris 1380–1500*, 104.
27   Keene, *Medieval Winchester*, 302.
28   Nicholas, 'Structures', 512–13.
29   Denecke, 'Sozialtopographie', 178–9.
30   Portmann, *Bürgerschaft im mittelalterlichen Freiburg*, 150–2.

sanitary considerations were important were usually suburban or near the moat, particularly on the downwind side of the city (usually the east). Other environmental and neighbourhood concerns could dictate use of space. In 1452 Frankfurt required the coopers to move into a suburb because of complaints about their noise.[31]

The late medieval cities also display some gender segregation. Unattached women at York tended to live in close proximity to one another in cheap tenements on the outskirts, often church-owned, where turnover rates were high. This 'spinster clustering' is related to heavy female migration. While single and independent women lived mainly on the peripheries, domestic servants lived in the centre, where more jobs were available.[32]

Outside Mediterranean France streets were rarely given over entirely to a single trade. Particularly in the city centres, streets that earlier had been named after trades often had few practitioners by the fourteenth century. Only one currier lived in the rue de la Courroierie in Paris in 1300.[33] The more fluid land market of the late Middle Ages thus quickened the breakdown of some older trade units, but also created concentrations where none had existed previously. The butchers of Ghent, who gained heredity of mastership in 1302, began buying property shortly thereafter in the Drabstraat, across a bridge from the meat hall. By the 1380s all residents of this street were butchers except for a few tailors and brewers, and virtually all of them were in-laws of butchers.[34] Arles had some streets named after guilds, but except for the butchers and fishmongers and, to a lesser extent, the shoemakers there was no strict localisation of trades.[35]

Jeremy Goldberg's description of the evolution of the social geography of late medieval York is paradigmatic for a medium-sized city whose social geography shifted in response to an economic downturn. Dyers and tanners, both of whom required water for their industrial processes, were in North Street in 1381; but while the tanners stayed there, the dyers had moved south into St John's and St Denys Walmgate by 1500, staying at all times on the left bank of the Ouse. The fullers were the only textile craft that was concentrated. The butchers in both periods were mainly in the Shambles, with a smaller group across Ouse Bridge. The Shambles was also an area of mercers and tailors. Most

31 Haverkamp, 'Topografia e relazioni sociali', 48.
32 Goldberg, *Women, Work and Life Cycle*, 299–300, 313–15.
33 Cazelles, *Paris*, 91–2.
34 Nicholas, *Metamorphosis*, 84, 88–9.
35 Stouff, *Arles*, 301.

bakers were in several nuclei around Ousegate, but some were also on the peripheries. The stalls for freshwater fish were at Ouse Bridge, while saltwater fish were sold on both sides of Foss Bridge. The other trades – merchants, drapers and mercers – became more concentrated in a single commercial quarter around Fossgate, the site of the merchant guildhall. The lower-status occupations of tailor and weaver were moving out of this central area by 1500. The commercial quarter was clearly defined throughout the period but was shrinking in the fifteenth century. The heavy industries, such as metal, were near the walls; but apart from pewter and brick, few industries were expanding in the fifteenth century. The textile quarters of York declined with the industry.[36]

That these patterns are confirmed by Paris (Plan 2), the metropolis of northern Europe, suggests general validity. Shops of foodmongers, soapmakers, haberdashers and taverns were found throughout the city. Although smaller artisans frequently used their homes as workshops, and moneychangers often did so, the moneychangers of Paris had loges on the Grand Pont, where they could be controlled, but resided elsewhere. The drapers were mainly in the rue de la Vieille-Draperie, while the butchers and skinners were on the modern place du Chatelet, well within the central city. The furriers, whose trade used the same raw material as the butchers and tanners, were on the other side of the Seine, north of the drapers. The armourers and other ironworkers were north of the Chatelet, east of the rue Saint-Denis. We have noted the concentration of aristocratic habitation around the palaces. Although wealthy and poorer houses were mingled in the area of the Halles, some aristocratic homes were clustered on the outskirts of the central section of the right bank. The abbey of Cluny bought several old houses near its Hôtel in 1334, then rased them and built new ones, which it rented to artisans. The result was a characteristic mixed-use pattern, with artisan houses with shop fronts mingling with the aristocracy. Recent immigrants tended to live in streets bearing the names of their home areas, such as rue de Normandie and the rue des Lombards. The wealthy were still on the Île de la Cité, but there were also areas of poorer habitation in the City along the Seine and on the right bank on both sides of the wall and beyond it. The Grève and the parish of St Paul were the poorest and most totally artisan quarters.[37]

---

36 Goldberg, *Women, Work and Life Cycle*, maps, 66–7 and comment pp. 68–71; Tillott, *City of York*, 89.
37 Ackerman and Rosenfeld, 'Social stratification', 42–5; Le Goff, 'L'Apogée', 362.

The urban land market

As high death rates released considerable land from claims by heirs, townspeople diversified their investments, combining the quick return of the money market with the security and social prestige associated with landowning. Land was immovable property, but the house on it was often considered a chattel and thus not subject to the kin-based restrictions on alienation that sometimes bound immovables. Thus the market in houses quickened, while land became concentrated in a few old families.[38]

The larger the city and the more differentiated its social structure, the higher the percentage of renters was likely to be. By 1309 fewer than one-third of the inhabitants of Reims owned urban land, and almost half of them were in the two richest central parishes. Most lived in rented houses or apartments. Most who owned real property at all either owned their residences and nothing else or were big owners. At Arras most of the richest proprietors had fewer than ten houses; even the Crespin family had only twenty-two, the Hucquedieu twelve. The wealthy burgesses poured money into their residences, converting them to stone, enclosing gardens and decorating the façades. Most wealthy citizens of Reims sank more money into land than into their businesses, with social prestige the main motive, for the majority of these properties were not rented out. Since most rich Rémois were interested in prestigious properties, slum landlordship was left to the middle-wealth group, who bought land for its economic as well as its social return. Statistics from Rennes confirm the Reims evidence. Of the inhabitants questioned by tax commissioners in 1455, more than 73 per cent had an entire house, 14 per cent had three and only 2 per cent had four or more.[39]

Many Italian cities required lords of suburban land to sell to newcomers at prices set by the city surveyors. Combined with continued city expansion in the early fourteenth century and higher plague mortality rates than in the north, this gave more opportunity to recent migrants in Italy to own homes than in the north. In the north prices of urban real estate were so high – the price of an average house in Ghent in the 1490s was the equivalent of almost two years' wages for a skilled labourer – that virtually all journeymen lived in rented housing. By contrast, at Pisa in 1427 the majority even of the recent immigrants owned

---

38 Denecke, 'Sozialtopographie', 186; Leguay, 'Propriété et marché de l'immobilier', 193.

39 Desportes, *Reims*, 249–75, 471–81; Leguay, 'Propriété et marché de l'immobilier', 175–6.

houses, while fewer than one-third lived in houses owned by others. At Livorno the percentages of owners and renters were roughly equal, while at Siena in the fifteenth century some 43 per cent of immigrant labourers owned a house or some other immovable property.[40]

As the rich accumulated land for investment, and most inhabitants lived in rented housing except in Italy, a profitable market in rents developed. We have noted that the fixed ground rents on urban land that were granted by the charters were much lower than the term rentals at which the properties were leased. When the person owing ground rent to another party then rented out a portion of the property to a third person, the result was a rent in the modern sense. The person paying ground rent, not the person paying term rent, was usually considered the owner. By the thirteenth century the lord of a tenement held at ground rent could not prevent its sale. As long as the rent was paid, its holder had no other interest in the property.[41]

Urban landowners were surprisingly slow to abandon leases in perpetuity or for a certain number of lifetimes in favour of short-term rents, most often by the year. More did so after the onset of the plagues, but as demand lessened in the early fifteenth century, terms of between twenty and forty years became common.[42] The ground rents owed on land could be bought and sold apart from the land itself. Property could also be encumbered by annuities that were sold for a lump sum; a payment usually one-tenth to one-twentieth of the purchase price would be owed for the purchaser's life, the seller's life, or in perpetuity. This amounted to securing a loan in the form of a 'second mortgage'. There was some speculation in these rents as investments, which created heavy indebtedness on some urban properties.[43]

Most of the few rental figures that survive are for such a long term that they are difficult to correlate with other trends in the local economy. Although there is usually a rough correlation between sale values and rents on the same property, values were low but demand for rented housing high in the poorer parts of the cities. At Ghent the surveyors assumed a 1:20 ratio of legitimate rent to purchase value when adjudicating disputes, but actual cases diverged from this norm. Rents tended to rise when there was high demand, as immigrants streamed into the cities; they were lower when demand was low and the city was in effect 'overbuilt', for instance, between a plague and the entrance of a new

40   Balestracci, 'Immigrazione e morfologia urbana', 99.
41   Roux, 'Coût de logement', 246–7; Britnell, *Commercialisation of English Society*, 149.
42   Keene, 'Property market in English towns', 209–11; Rosser, *Medieval Westminster*, 44, 53, 66–74; Keene, *Medieval Winchester*, 191–2.
43   Rubin, *Charity and Community*, 223; Keene, *Medieval Winchester*, 188.

wave of immigrants. Ghent shows a clear correlation between years of low prices and low rentals; for when property became cheap because it was easily available, fewer persons rented, and landlords had to offer inducements to get tenants. The long-term trend in land and house rents and prices was sharply upward.[44] The real value of both houses and rents nearly doubled between 1280 and 1340. A master craftsman of Rome could buy a house with one upper storey with one year's salary in 1280, but required two years' salary to do so in 1340.[45] Demand generally exceeded supply of rented housing in the student quarter on the left bank at Paris, so it was expensive there, but generally not elsewhere. After 1440, when Paris began to recover from the English occupation, the typical master artisan used 15–20 per cent of his income for rent. Sale prices on houses between 1400 and 1420 averaged two to three years' salary for a skilled artisan and were rarely more than the equivalent of five years' wages.[46]

As locally based industry grew, the value of business property predictably increased. For the fourteenth century scattered indications at Ghent suggest that the value of most business property was not high except for breweries; bakeries had a low median price, but bathhouses and mills, the only other types of business property for which there is much information, were low. The determinants of price were size of the property and section of the city in which it was located, not the use to which it was put. However, more complete figures for the late fifteenth century show that industrial property was worth at least twice as much as residences. Inns had a predictably high value, followed by breweries, then mills and tanneries. Shops, bathhouses and bakeries were lower. The difference, both in values and in the number of sources stating price, shows the increasing heredity of the guilds and the workers' need to acquire capital before becoming independent masters and shopowners.[47]

Land values were declining in the English cities with the exception of London. At York, where the declining textile industry dragged the entire urban economy with it, rents were so low that trade gave a better yield than investment in immovable property. Rents also declined at Winchester, especially on the most valuable houses. Land values in real terms were one-third as high in central Winchester in 1417 as in 1110.[48]

44 Nicholas, *Metamorphosis*, 97–107.
45 Hubert, *Espace urbain*, 354–5.
46 Roux, 'Coût de logement', 245, 253–6.
47 Nicholas, *Metamorphosis*, 106–7; Boone, *Immobiliënmarkt*, 170.
48 Swanson, *Medieval Artisans*, 160; Keene, *Medieval Winchester*, 243; Keene, 'Property market in English towns', 104–5.

Most private citizens had only one piece of real property. Even wealthier persons who had extensive investments in land or houses had to use at least one of their properties as a residence and/or place of business and thus could not view land solely as an investment. Even so, by the late fourteenth century the wealthier private landlords had rental incomes comparable to all but the greatest institutions, such as the cathedral. The real value of the land of churches and other town lords declined rapidly in the thirteenth century, then recovered somewhat as they bought vacant properties after the plagues. City corporations became substantial landlords in the late Middle Ages, particularly on the continent but also in England from the late fourteenth century. At Ghent the income from city-owned land was about 3 per cent of the municipal budget in the 1360s and 1370s.[49]

CITY AND REGION: RURAL LANDOWNERSHIP BY BURGESSES AND URBAN POLITICAL SUPREMACY

Although most burgesses and town corporations concentrated their land investment in the city, they were expanding their rural interests in the late Middle Ages. The onset of large land investment by townsmen in the thirteenth century came in a period of high farm prices, and in some cases was on the initiative of the cities themselves. The Tuscan and Flemish examples show that land investment on the part of citizens was not the result of a lack of interest in commerce, but of a new business strategy that included land and farming along with commerce.[50]

The Italian cities of the interior continued to dominate their *contadi*. The fact that citizens did not pay tax on food brought from their *contado* estates into the city for domestic consumption was a powerful inducement to invest in rural land and also diminished the tax bases of the villages. The cities needed grain from the villages, although most also had to import from greater distances. Lucca came closer to being fed by its *contado* than did Florence, but even in good years it still had to import. There were grain shortages in fifteen years between 1369 and 1392. Exporting grain was forbidden during scarcities, but the city lacked the bureaucracy to enforce this. The communes had forced the farmers of the *contado* to accept low grain prices in the thirteenth century, but they were less able to do this in the chaotic conditions of the fourteenth, and there was no way for them to control prices on the

---

49 Nicholas, 'Governance', 252; Keene, *Medieval Winchester*, 204, 208, 214, 231; Keene, 'Property market in English towns', 214.
50 Barel, *Ville médiévale*, 313–19.

enormous amounts of grain that they imported from more distant areas. Thus high grain prices in the Italian cities contributed to their political turmoil. High taxes were more often the issue in the north, where grain prices were lower and town lords were more powerful than in Italy.[51]

Genoa, like all Italian port cities except Naples, was on the edge of a mountain range and thus had trouble establishing power over a *contado*. It had direct control over only a small territory, scattered and not well situated strategically. In contrast to Venice and Florence, it was unable to extend its frontiers even in the fifteenth century. Genoa was more exclusively turned toward the Mediterranean than any other great city, for Barcelona and even Venice had better overland access, and Naples was a political capital. Genoa thus obtained much of its food from the coastal islands and the eastern Mediterranean, which meant that supplies were at great risk. Genoa needed to control the Riviera coast and the Apennine passes, but its success was mixed. The Riviera had independent lordships and towns, and the mountains were the sources of vital wool and woad and trade routes to the interior. Rivalries over rural territory were extended into the city, for lords had property in both. The Fieschi, whose power was in the Apennines and who evidently hoped to make themselves lords of Genoa, were especially bothersome.[52]

Although Venice was the nominal overlord of Dubrovnik and kept a consul there to safeguard its interests, the city only tried to conquer a *contado* on the Italian mainland to ensure supplies in the years after 1402. To counter the threat from the Carrara family seigniory over Padua, Venice annexed Vicenza, Verona and Padua between 1404 and 1406. The new mainland empire brought tribute that helped finance Venice's eastern policy. The change brought no significant alterations in the central organs of the state. The Venetians never admitted representatives of the mainland communities to the councils, which made their wishes known by maintaining lobbyists in Venice. A small number of *contado* aristocrats were awarded noble status at Venice, which brought them membership as individuals in the council but did nothing for their home communities. Venice did grant economic privileges to subject cities. The Senate appointed only Venetians as officials in the mainland communities, which had considerable benefit in creating new jobs for impoverished Venetian nobles.[53]

51 Meek, *Lucca 1369–1400*, 97–8.
52 Heers, *Gênes. Civilisation*, 14, 23–5, 46, 397–402.
53 Although the Venetians exterminated the Carrara, they tried to build on the achievements of the Scaligeri of Verona; Lane, *Venice*, 226–34; Law, 'Venetian mainland state', 167. On the Dubrovnik connection, see Krekic, 'Dubrovnik', 190. On the Venetian nobility and its need for jobs in the government, see Chapter 6.

The *contado* was not spared the general increase in tax burden that affected all urban areas in the late Middle Ages. By the 1380s Florence was taxing the seigniories of the local magnates, such as the counts Ubaldini and Guidi, despite earlier treaties in which the city pledged to respect the traditional exemptions of the lords.[54] Actual oppression of the *contado* seems to have diminished, however, as the depopulated cities had to offer inducements not only to get newcomers to migrate to the city but also to maintain population and food production in the environs. The *contado* villages of Lucca petitioned for a reduction in the number of households on which they were assessed as soon as the city regained its autonomy from Pisa in 1369. More in Italy than in the north, the rural depression of the late Middle Ages hurt the cities, which were dependent on their environs not only for grain, but also for taxes.[55] The case of Siena shows the difficulty of arriving at a balanced assessment. The city abolished the individual gabelles on its *contado* in 1291 and substituted a general '*contado* gabelle' of 24,000 *lire* yearly, which had risen to 60,000 by 1333, or 53 per cent of the Biccherna budget. Some *contado* communities tried to escape the tax burden by claiming insolvency, and scholars thus once thought that Siena ruthlessly exploited its *contado*. Yet so many exemptions were given that *contado* receipts were never as much as 10 per cent of the Biccherna budget after 1338. Many levies, notably the hearth tax, were assessed more heavily on citizens than on *contadini*. The *contado* villages also collected taxes for their own administration and defence, but many of their richest inhabitants gained freedom from local taxes by purchasing Sienese citizenship.[56]

Yet the fragmentary evidence permits different interpretations. David Herlihy argued that the *contado* of Pistoia paid direct taxes at six times the city's rate in 1280s and paid 57 per cent of the total in 1427. Florence's *contado* contributed nearly half of the commune's ordinary revenue, totally apart from the fact that resources were siphoned into the city by rural land investment by burgesses. At Lucca the direct tax, the *estimo* or *lira*, was discontinued for the city but was kept in principle for the *contado*, although many *contado* communities petitioned for exemption from it. Until 1388 the communities of the *contado* of Lucca had quotas of salt for purchase, while the city did not, but this was not applied rigorously. City records show a concern with the welfare of the *contado*. When the wine tax was imposed on the *contado* of Lucca in 1388, gabelles were raised in the city, and the forced purchase of salt was extended there. The *estimo* of 1397 did not apply to the *contado*.

---

54 Becker, 'Florentine territorial state', 112–13.
55 Meek, *Lucca 1369–1400*, 77–8, 84–9.
56 Bowsky, *Finances Siena*, 225–31, 239–54.

Whether there was deliberate exploitation of the *contado* at Lucca is thus problematical.[57]

Lombardy under the lords of Milan was more a federation than a centralised state, even under the powerful rule of Giangaleazzo Visconti (d. 1402). Venice increased taxation and fixed policy at Padua, generally without harming Paduan interests, although Padua was forced to permit toll-free entry to Venetian manufactures. But elsewhere in Italy some large cities became overlords of others whose size and economic potential were not significantly inferior to the conqueror. Florence controlled Pisa from 1406 and Pistoia from 1351, in each case preferring to use local persons who were loyal to Florence but occasionally sending Florentines to the dependent community. The agreement of 1351 that gave Florence the seigniory over Pistoia for fifteen years left Pistoia the right to some local autonomy as long as the Pistoiese chose Guelfs and were ruled by a *popolo*. Although the captain had to be a Florentine, the Pistoiese chose their own *podestàs* until 1398, which meant that civil justice and many criminal cases were handled locally. The worsening of Pistoia's feuding – the Panciatichi, whom the Florentines supported, and their rivals the San Giovani divided the city in 1376 into the companies of San Paolo and San Giovanni, each with its own administration – led to the final Florentine conquest in 1406.[58]

Florence's domination over Pisa has given rise to divergent interpretations. The traditional view has been that Florence ruthlessly suppressed Pisa and neglected its interests. The *catasto* of 1428–9 shows substantial population decline and widespread poverty, but recent work has suggested that Florence taxed Pisa heavily only because it feared for Pisa's safety and spent the money defending it. Florence offered tax exemptions and rent-free housing to attract foreign merchants to Pisa. Pisa may actually have revived economically in the early period of Florentine control, following decline in the late fourteenth century. From 1419 goods going between Florence and the sea, including those intended for re-export, were not to be taxed in Pisa unless they changed hands. Several Florentine firms also opened offices in Pisa. It is possible, however, that Pisa's statistically demonstrable economic revival may actually have benefited Florentines rather than Pisans. There was heavy investment by Florentines in Pisan *contado* land, particularly by the Medici and their political allies. Florence's handling of Pisan industry and guilds also suggests self-interest. Florence supervised the guilds of Pisa closely and extended this control in the 1420s to the Consuls of the Sea. It

57 Herlihy, *Women, Family*, 303; Meek, *Lucca 1369–1400*, 106–10.
58 Herlihy, *Pistoia*, 204–5, 228–9.

protected its own woollen industry by limiting Pisa to producing for home sale only; yet the Pisan cloth industry was already moribund before the Florentines came. Some Pisan guilds received special encouragement from Florence. The leather industry and its guilds, which had been Pisa's largest in the thirteenth century, revived in the fifteenth.[59]

Pisa's own rule over Lucca between 1342 and 1369 confirms this general picture. Pisa gained custody of the citadel and gates, but most of the changes were in personnel. Lucca continued to be governed by a college of ten elders, a General Council and the Councils of Fifty and Twenty. Pisa sent rectors and vicars directly from Pisa and oversaw the local election of other officials. The *podestà* of Lucca was a Pisan. Pisa also selected the chancellor of the elders, who kept minutes of their meetings, handled their petitions and correspondence, undertook diplomatic missions and spied on the elders as needed. The government of Pisa did not encourage judicial appeals from Lucca but did keep the right to approve new ordinances issued there. Pisa supported Lucca's efforts through tax incentives to repopulate its *contado* and repatriate exiles. The fact that Lucca specialised in silks while Pisa made leather and woollen cloth helped relations, but Pisa also did not interfere in those areas of Lucca's economy where competing interests existed nor subordinate the guilds of Lucca to those of Pisa. Lucca owed large sums of money to Pisa, but most of it was spent in Lucca and not actually sent to Pisa. Pisan rule became more oppressive after 1362, when Pisa demanded that Lucca pay one-quarter of the expenses of its war with Florence.[60]

Cities founding towns

An interesting aspect of urban domination of the *contado* in fourteenth-century Italy is the foundation of new towns by the great cities. Between 1299 and 1350 Florence founded five, three in the upper Arno valley and two in the Apennines. Florentine planners used orthogonal plans everywhere; these towns still have straight streets that intersect at right angles and a central square at the intersection of the two main arteries. They were planned for 300–500 families or up to 2,500 persons. They were intended as fortresses, but they also collected produce, acted as local administrative capitals and guarded the main routes. The Florentine new towns were founded to provide defence against the still powerful magnates: the captain of the *popolo* first proposed founding towns in

---

59   Mallett, 'Pisa and Florence', 404–5, 413–15, 420–1, 432–9.
60   Discussion based on Meek, *Lucca Under Pisan Rule*, 9, 17–29, 33–5, 53–81, 105–6.

1285 'to frustrate the schemes of the exiled citizens' [Ghibellines]. The Florentines attracted settlers, particularly dependants of enemy nobles, and excluded magnates from residing in these towns. Some persons were forcibly resettled, but there seems to have been little resistance to Florence, especially since the settlers usually received five to ten years of tax exemption. The new communities were expected to defend themselves. They also served travellers going to and from Florence. Many members of the Florentine hostellers' guild actually lived at Scarperia and Firenzuola; these two towns, the earliest of the five, were founded on opposite slopes of the Apennines on a new road between Florence and Bologna that ran east of the strongholds of the Ubaldini, who preyed on traders. Overnight stops between Florence and Bologna were always made at one or both of them.

Most plans of new towns in northern Europe were more flexible than the Italian. Bern, for example, grew along an axis of the main market square in three planned stages. The plantations in southern France during the thirteenth century were laid out in a neo-Roman model of four streets intersecting at right angles. Since the width and shape of the market determined the spacing between parallel streets, one axis usually had larger plots than the other, so that expansion left the originally central market near the periphery of settlement. This never happened in the Florentine plantations, which were designed for a specific group of settlers, so no provisions were made in the original plan for growth. Expansion had to come outside the wall. Florentine new towns never oriented blocks at right angles to the main streets, as happened elsewhere in Italy; the central axis dominated as a main street. Most Florentine new towns were thus more than twice as long as they were wide. Most cities are at the intersection of routes, either multiple land routes or land and water, unless they exist solely as stopping places for travellers or for defence, both of which were primary motives for the Florentine foundations. Such places, lacking multidimensional access, rarely expand into genuine cities, and the Florentine foundations did not.[61]

Town–countryside relations in the north

Paris and London so dominated their environs that they depressed the commercial economy of the surrounding areas without combining this with political lordship. In the late fourteenth century London had three times the population of the next largest city of England. The metropolis

61 Discussion based on Friedman, *Florentine New Towns*, 5–6, 31, 40–6, 51, 54–7, 72, 168–71.

together with twenty-five county or other provincial centres accounted for 7–8 per cent of the total population of England in 1377; of this, London had 2–3 per cent and all other towns with 1,000 or more inhabitants 4–5 per cent. The eleven counties surrounding London contained about 140 'towns' in the legal sense, 23 per cent of the total in England. London alone had 6 per cent of the population of this region in 1377. Canterbury, Oxford, Southampton and Winchester, the other large towns of this area, added only another 3 per cent. Even more than population, wealth was concentrated in London. The city's valuation for the poll tax of 1377 was 43 per cent of the total for the 140 towns in the region.[62]

Some English cities were given county status in the late Middle Ages, starting with Bristol in 1373 because Bristol's suburban territory was in two shires, Gloucestershire and Somerset, creating jurisdictional problems. York then became a county in 1396, Newcastle in 1400, Norwich in 1404 and Lincoln in 1409. As counties they had a sheriff whose selection was handled with some degree of citizen participation and a council chosen by the mayor and sheriff with the consent of the 'community'. Incorporation, which was conveyed by county status, strengthened the city's corporate capacity to hold land and was often followed by integration of the suburbs into the city. Norwich's charter gave county status 'with hamlets and suburbs', but the city was never able to control its environs.[63]

On the continent, some northern cities were able in the fourteenth and fifteenth centuries to subjugate their rural environs to almost as great a degree as the Italians. Metz had one of the largest city-states north of the Alps and may serve as our paradigm. By 1323 the city government was enforcing its market ordinances in a 'country of Metz', the area within a radius of two to three leagues (14–21 km) of the walls. The villagers enjoyed toll exemption west of the Mosel and benefited from the high prices of the city market. The master *échevin* of Metz was the judicial 'head' (appeals judge) of the villages of the bishop's domain, which in turn used the legal customs of Metz. *Echevins* of Metz often sat on rural courts in cases that involved residents of the city. The city extended its right to protect burgesses into a right of jurisdiction over their rural properties. Since many of these were held at ground rent from the abbeys of Metz, the city government became protector of the monasteries. The load of cases involving burgesses of Metz with foreigners was so onerous that the three *mairies* of Metz split the rural areas among themselves. In 1347 Metz established a regional military organisation, setting up garrisons,

62   Keene, 'Small towns and the metropolis', 226–7.
63   Rigby, 'Urban oligarchy', 78–80; Tillott, *City of York*, 69; Lobel, *Atlas* 2: 11, 15.

subjecting peasants to military service, controlling the trade in strategic materials, overseeing roads and executing some robber barons. Yet the city was curiously reluctant to impose taxes on the peasants of the 'country' to help defray defence costs until 1393 and 1404, when it imposed hearth taxes.

Paralleling the expansion of the jurisdiction of the city government into the rural areas, patrician families of Metz held large amounts of rural land, especially vineyards. Many obtained portions of seigniories and advocacies. They had more success avoiding the fragmentation of their estates than did the nobles. When they bought isolated noble properties, they tried to regroup them into coherent seigniories, usually using allodial or ground rent land as a nucleus. They invested considerable sums improving the properties to make them suitable for grain agriculture or animal husbandry. When it was impossible to consolidate estates, they remained simple rentiers.[64]

Prague tried to subjugate other cities in Bohemia, to the point where some of them joined the nobles in a feud against Prague in 1419. During the Hussite wars Prague appointed officials in the smaller towns and the rural areas, judged cases on appeal and called the other towns Prague's 'subjects'.[65] Nuremberg also controlled its environs, but by subtler means. It never translated its various privileges into corporate jurisdiction over a rural state. In the 1360s the emperor Charles IV, needing the financial backing of the cities, supported Nuremberg in its running quarrel with his burgrave. As the threat to traders from robber barons became more serious, the militia of Nuremberg began seizing noble castles. In 1370 the emperor conceded that no market or court could be erected within a mile of Nuremberg, and that building a fortress required the consent of the city council. The city court took jurisdiction over rural lands that its burgesses had acquired from nobles, often by foreclosure. In 1439, 1441, and 1446 the city organised its dependent villages into captaincies. Nuremberg felt itself so regionally powerful and beyond the need of allies that it refused to join the Swabian League until 1384 and even helped Charles IV in a military expedition against Ulm.[66]

The situation at Metz and Nuremberg is paralleled by the Flemish cities. In addition to their right to enforce monopoly privileges for textile manufacture in the villages, the cities developed a broader right to tax and control the militia in the rural areas. The 'Three Cities' of Ghent,

64 Discussion based on Schneider, *Ville de Metz*, 336, 384, 393–4, 413–15, 424–35, 441, 446–7.
65 Kejr, 'Städtischen Stände', 198–202.
66 Bischoff, 'Stadtherrschaft im ostfränkischen Städtedreieck', 100; Pfeiffer, *Nürnberg*, 41, 77–8, 98, 115.

Bruges and Ypres had a recognised corporate existence with the right to consult with the count and bind the rural areas to any decisions. They were judicial 'heads' of the rural villages and had numerous 'external burgesses'. In the period 1323–8 Bruges led a rebellion in western Flanders, took over the count's administration, staffed garrisons and appointed officials. Such was Ghent's supremacy in Flanders during the 1340s and 1380s that it came close to forming a city-state. Between 1338 and 1349 Ghent led the other cities in seizing the government of Flanders during the rebellion led by the famous James van Artevelde. In 1343 the Three Cities formally divided Flanders into quarters ruled by themselves. They controlled the coinage, audited accounts, and assessed and collected taxes. Parties loyal to Ghent controlled the magistracies of Ypres and at times Bruges, and delegations from Ghent installed the aldermen there, but at all times local persons occupied the major seats in the city government. The control of Ghent over the rest of Flanders diminished after van Artevelde fell from power in 1345, but only in 1349 was the count restored.[67]

Although the Burgundian regime in the fifteenth century kept firmer control over the cities, the frequent absence of the princes meant that the cities still controlled rural Flanders much of the time. After 1395 the 'Franc' (castle district) of Bruges met regularly with the Three Cities in conclaves known as the 'Four Members'. The aldermen of the large cities summoned assemblies of the subordinate magistracies within 'their castle districts'. They continued to assess and collect taxes, meeting frequently with the prince or his representative. As the Four Members they feuded constantly among themselves but maintained a façade of cooperation in relations with the rural areas and smaller towns. Particularly in the fifteenth century, and more in the northern Netherlands than in Flanders, the right of the chief city to tax the rural areas amounted to exploitation. By 1500 two-thirds of Dordrecht's share of taxes owed to the counts of Holland was paid by Geertruidenberg and the forty villages of South Holland.[68]

The same situation is found in the other Low Country principalities. Valenciennes was judicial head of about three hundred towns and villages, roughly half the rural communities of Hainault, and dominated its countryside. It had the right to tear down the castles and houses of persons who injured citizens.[69] By the late Middle Ages the aldermen of Brussels, Leuven and Liège could simultaneously be magistrates of smaller

67 Nicholas, *Town and Countryside*, 161–72, 175–200; Nicholas, *Medieval Flanders*, 211–24.
68 Nicholas, *Medieval Flanders*, 332–8; Nicholas, *Stad en Platteland*, 105.
69 Platelle, *Histoire de Valenciennes*, 65–7.

cities in their spheres of influence. Brussels developed more extensive rights over a rural territory than did any individual Flemish city. There was so much emigration by wealthy townsfolk to the villages that in 1383 *échevins* were warned to live in the city at least during their terms in office. Brusselers with rural land were exempt from tax at the gates on their merchandise. The Brusselers' privileges in the environs were translated into a state. In 1291 the duke granted that only obligations in documents issued by the *échevins* were guaranteed automatic implementation; thus peasants had to have their contracts concluded at Brussels if they wanted to be sure of enforcement. The 'franchise' of Brussels, extending for one league around the walls, was legally part of the city. In 1295 the duke allowed the *échevins* to tax and regulate the manufacture and sale of beer and, shortly afterwards, wine in a second, broader circle around the city. Here the villagers were at first subject only to the taxes, but not to the *échevins* in judicial matters. Initially, they did not have citizenship of Brussels as individuals, but by 1400 the villages within Brussels' second zone had been incorporated into the 'liberty' of the city. Lands of burgesses were exempt from the count's tax on land transfers throughout the franchise. Judicial fines were as much as three times as high inside the extended walls as outside. From 1423 the city began requiring craftsmen in the franchise to join the parent city guild, adding that 'city and franchise constitute a single juridical corporation'. Although the villagers benefited from the fact that the municipal *Chaussée* maintained roads throughout the franchise, they did not enjoy the protection of the walls, as the gates were closed at night.[70]

City people were buying rural land in every region of Europe north of the Alps. In 1335 rural property predominated in 45 per cent of fortunes in the bourg of Toulouse and in three-quarters of those worth more than 1,000 livres, although this was an extreme case. In 1440 residents of Tours owned 72 per cent of the land along the Loire near the city. Most of these properties were not compact, and few included jurisdictional rights. Some were rented, others given in sharecropping arrangements, and still others were farmed directly by the townsmen through hired employees.[71] At Reims rural property made up a much lower percentage of the total assets of the urban elite than at Toulouse. While only 8.7 per cent of the persons in the lowest tax bracket owned rural land, this rose to 87 per cent for those owning 2,000–3,000 livres; yet even in this top group rural property represented only 15 per cent of the total wealth. Although some Rémois held fiefs, they had trouble

---

70   van Uytven, 'Stadsgeschiedenis', 267; Martens, *Histoire de Bruxelles*, 105–9.
71   Desportes, *Reims*, 258; Chevalier, *Tours*, 119–26.

buying seigniories with rights of jurisdiction. Thus most invested in peasant properties of medium value. Their lands in the banlieue of the city were considerably larger than the average peasant tenement.[72]

The Flemish burgesses fit the pattern observed at Metz, Toulouse and Reims of massive rural land investment in the late Middle Ages. Their investment in peat bogs increased through most of the fourteenth century, then slowed in the 1380s as the bogs were exhausted. During the fourteenth century they acquired fiefs and land held at ground rent and consolidated estates into viable farming units. Although they used their properties mainly for rents rather than food, they fostered diversified agricultural regimes and increased productivity. Particularly in periods of strife they took rents in kind from their rural estates, bypassing the food guilds' monopolies on the market of Ghent. They bought enormous annuities from farmers and small towns in need of ready cash. The councils of Ghent used the rural lands of burgesses, which were taxed with the city rather than with the districts in which they were located, to gain jurisdictional footholds.[73]

In northern Germany, where the larger cities were largely independent *de facto*, they usually began by securing an area immediately around the walls where a considerable amount of land was owned by citizens. Then in a second phase the corporate and individual interests were extended, and jurisdictional rights were acquired from lords and princes, often by city churches, corporations and private citizens. Urban churches and abbeys had always had rights in the countryside, including those of jurisdiction; and as city governments became protectors and patrons of the churches in the late Middle Ages, as the Italian cities had done earlier, this provided them with jurisdictional footholds that provided a base for expansion. The city governments also bought rural land. South German cities as a rule seized larger areas outside the walls than did those in the north, even the great Hanse cities, and managed to make their territories more coherent and jurisdictionally unified than did the northern centres.[74]

Taken as a group the cities of western Germany gained less control over their rural environs than did the Flemish. The Rhenish cities saw expansion into the countryside as a counterweight to powerful lords and robber barons. Basel, which only really became a major city in the

---

72 Desportes, *Reims*, 249–61.
73 Nicholas, *Town and Countryside*, 267–329. Burgesses of Reims and Cologne also bought rural land to get grain, including grain rents, for their own consumption; Desportes, *Reims*, 256; Irsigler, 'Getreidehandel und städtische Versorgungspolitik', 581.
74 Rösener, 'Aspekte der Stadt–Land Beziehungen', 669–73.

fifteenth century, tried to secure a rural state as a counterweight to Habsburg power. In 1400 Basel purchased three villages from its bishop, then systematically tried to buy out the rights of other lords to the south. The city built forts and exercised blood justice through bailiffs, all of them from aristocratic families of Basel. Later Basel collected taxes more rigidly and integrated a domain more fully into overall city policy.[75]

Cities that were oriented mainly toward long-distance commerce, such as those of the German Hanse, did not make great efforts to secure a rural hinterland. Some obtained rights along roads and waterways but not coherent territories. They did not tax the rural areas or force peasants to serve in the militia. Even in southern Germany the largest city-state, Nuremberg, contained only 80 sq km. The lands under city control were scattered, in contrast to the Swiss and Italian examples. By contrast, cities in which artisans controlled the magistracy were very concerned with securing the local market and the food supply. They tried to get control of a well-rounded and unitary territory. They encouraged agriculture, collected taxes in the countryside and forced peasants of the environs to buy and sell on the city market.[76]

Zürich was less military and more commercial than most Swiss cities and had a strong pro-Habsburg party. Whereas it was initially oriented toward long-distance commerce, the guilds gained influence at Zürich after 1336. Markets became regional, centred on the demand for salt, wine and grain in Constance, Ravensburg and Basel. Zürich acquired most of its territory of about 25 kilometres around the town and on both shores of Lake Zürich between 1384 and 1415, all but one major acquisition by purchase. The first rural territories were along the borders of seigniories owned by townspeople, particularly knights who were external burgesses, many of whom eventually sold their properties to the city. The city then expanded into more distant areas but was less successful. Zürich lost most of its rural jurisdictions in the 'Old Zürich War' of 1439–46 but regained them with the help of the Swiss Confederation. Once it had acquired most of its territory, the craft-dominated government of Zürich regulated rural agriculture and industry. By 1470 the city was trying to prohibit artisan work in the country, while favouring the use of manufactured goods of Zürich. From 1431 all agricultural products and animals had to be offered for sale first at Zürich or a place in its jurisdiction that enjoyed a market charter; buying through middlemen was forbidden. The city regulated fields and forests, forbidding farmers to turn unneeded land into pasture, since the

75 Kümmell, *Bäuerliche Gesellschaft und städtische Herrschaft*, 83–104, 123–7.
76 Raiser, *Städtische Territorialpolitik*, 9–14, 26–32.

city wanted a supply of cheap grain, even if the farmers could benefit by diversifying into crops that brought higher prices. Zürich thus kept grain prices artifically low and depressed both the farm economy and rural industry.

By contrast, Lübeck, which was dominated by merchants except between 1408 and 1416, did not prohibit manufacturing in its dependent territories. Lübeck acquired numerous properties between 1359 and 1400 along the major land routes and the Elbe. By 1470 Lübeck owned twenty-one villages along with Travemünde and Mölln. Lübeck in 1350 agreed with the counts of Lauenburg on a military defence zone between Mölln and Lake Ratzeburg, an area where several land routes crossed. By 1359 the dukes of Holstein had been forced to pawn the castle and bailiff's office of Mölln to Lübeck. In 1375 Lübeck gained the land of Stormarn by pawn, thereby improving the security of the roads to Hamburg. The territorial acquisitions of the Hanse cities concentrated on strategic routes. This meant for Lübeck the land and water routes through Lauenburg. For Hamburg it meant the Elbe, for Bremen the Weser. Göttingen similarly had acquired three nearby villages and much of the adjacent Göttinger forest by 1380, which gave protection on the east; when Göttingen acquired the village of Roringen soon afterwards, this gave the city control of the road leading into the Harz. Since Lübeck did not tax its new territories, the cost of keeping peace exceeded the city's income from the lands. Merchant families and a few rich guildsmen were buying rural land. There are some spectacular cases. Although citizens of Lübeck as a group gained more rural land than did Hamburgers, the von dem Berge family of Hamburg, one of the oldest families of the city eligible for election to the council, acquired thirteen villages near the city in the thirteenth and fourteenth centuries, some in outright ownership, others in fief. Most purchases that included jurisdictional rights, however, came during and just after the political expansion of the city into the rural areas. Most nobles were not able to redeem lands once pawned to burgesses. Townsmen's investments in land and people thus spared the city the need to incorporate these territories into the town area.[77]

Some cities gained extraterritorial jurisdiction over persons who enjoyed citizenship but resided outside the city. Such 'external burgesses' (*bourgeois forains, Pfahlbürger, buitenpoorters*) were already complicating city–country relations in the thirteenth century. They included nobles,

---

77 Discussion based on Raiser, *Städtische Territorialpolitik*, 32–4, 53–61, 73–96, 104–13, 116–19, 129–31, 136–47, 149–50; Rösener, 'Aspekte der Stadt-Land Beziehungen', 669–74.

peasants and sometimes burgesses of small towns that were in the sphere of influence of a major city. The status gave them the legal protection of citizenship and some tax advantages. The practice of country people becoming external burgesses of cities became much more common in the late Middle Ages in Germany and the Low Countries. External burgesses of Brussels owed military service to the city rather than the count. They had to live in Brussels for three periods of at least six weeks per year, but the city permitted them to commute this obligation for a fee after 1377. Those of Flanders had to maintain their 'principal' residence in the city, but this gave them the right to be taxed with the cities, which were underassessed, rather than with rural Flanders. Non-noble external burgesses generally had to live in the cities for three forty-day periods annually. Ghent in particular used its external burgesses as a militia. The Flemish counts disliked external citizenship and gradually restricted the status in the fifteenth century.[78]

Not all cities welcomed external burgesses, for they could lead the municipal government into unwanted involvements. Nuremberg required external burgesses to reside in the city periodically, but this was poorly enforced. Frankfurt required its external burgesses to spend winters in the city with their wives and families.[79] Most external burgesses were prosperous persons from nearby communities. Zürich and Constance gave external citizenship to entire villages, which caused problems of jurisdiction unless, as sometimes occurred, their lords also became burgesses.

Noble external burgesses received military advantages from citizenship, the protection of the city's court and free access to its market. Zürich took in several hundred external burgesses in the second half of the fourteenth century. Many of the nobles made treaties for a term of years with Zürich, becoming citizens during that time with all obligations and rights of the status. They gave the city free access to their castles; such treaties often preceded the incorporation of the property in question into Zürich's territory. Some Rhineland cities, especially Cologne and Aachen, also received military service from the petty princes of the eastern Low Countries by giving them money fiefs: Cologne gave at least seventeen in the thirteenth century, thirty-one in the fourteenth. An agreement of 1261 between the city and Duke Waleran of Luxembourg gave citizenship to Waleran and his heirs and a heritable money fief. In return they were to defend citizens of Cologne who were in their lands – probably a reference to other external burgesses – and would

78 Martens, *Histoire de Bruxelles*, 100–1; Nicholas, *Medieval Flanders*, 212, 331, 363–8; Nicholas, *Town and Countryside*, 235–49.
79 Schultheiss, *Satzungen*, 59–60; Keutgen, *Urkunden*, 509–10.

aid Cologne with nine knights and fifteen squires when required. Waleran received a heritable fief of 100 marcs. Cologne also promised to aid the duke with 25 men if he were attacked.[80]

The northern cities and their nobles

The cities' relations with the nobles of their environs in northern Europe were transformed in the late Middle Ages, becoming more similar to the Italian situation. Wealthy urban families of Flanders entered the nobility through marriage and by purchasing seigniories. Noble families moved into the cities for part of the year, building and often fortifying houses. As in England, knighthood cannot be equated with nobility in Flanders, but it was a preliminary stage; countless burgesses obtained knighthood. Many of the political leaders of Bruges, including some guild deans, were knights, even in the conflicts of 1302. The urban knighthood of Ghent was probably even larger than that of Bruges and included the descendants of James van Artevelde, who is often portrayed as a 'democratic' reformer.[81]

Although most townspeople sought knighthood principally for social reasons, there were solid economic advantages to the status, particularly when knighthood conferred nobility. In the late fifteenth century nobles were exempt from direct taxes in Castile and France, and their status entitled them to special consideration everywhere. The debtor lists of the Holzschuh firm of Nuremberg were arranged under three headings – noble, clergy, and burgesses – because these statuses conferred different privileges, and the firm thus had to use different techniques to collect bad debts.[82] Yet the movement of merchant families into the nobility shows in itself that the older noble lines that had dominated the primitive cities were losing their importance virtually everywhere. Although country-based nobles had second residences and owned rents in the cities, the nobles who dominated the municipal elites were actually 'nobles of the robe', who gained their status through service in city or royal courts.

Although nobles were increasingly living in the cities, turbulent barons created problems everywhere, especially in Germany. The situation was probably worse in the fifteenth century than in the fourteenth; for as the power of urban militias declined, the cities hired nobles of their environs as soldiers. The use of *condottieri* by the Italian cities is notorious.

80 Dilcher, 'Bürgerbegriff', 96–7; Bechtold, *Zunftbürgerschaft und Patriziat*, 50; Raiser, *Städtische Territorialpolitik*, 67–73; Lyon, 'Communes feudal system', 247–8.
81 Nicholas, *Town and Countryside*, 250–66.
82 Pfeiffer, *Nürnberg*, 53.

Cologne frequently required its resident nobles to pledge good behaviour or get their citizen-relatives to vouch for them. In an inconclusive case of 1401, however, the issue was whether Geert Leerse, who had been declared a public enemy, had actually been in the city's service as a mercenary at some past time.[83]

Aspects of economic symbiosis

City governments always needed to keep their rural environs pacified and productive, but this cannot be dismissed simply as urban exploitation of the farms and small towns. Cologne's export trade benefited the industries of its hinterland. The city's dyeing industry stimulated the growth of dyes, especially woad, which was exported to the Low Countries and England. Clothworkers of Aalst, in eastern Flanders, obtained their supplies of alum, which was produced only in the Mediterranean and exported through Bruges, from merchants of Ghent. In 1343 King Peter III authorised two drapers of Barcelona to open dyeing shops throughout Aragon and Valencia.[84] The power of the city thus helped to industrialise the rural economy.

The leather and hide trades were an important aspect of town–country linkage that had a strong impact on urban occupational structures. Some leather clothing was coming back into fashion, and many objects that are now made of glass or metal, such as bottles, buckets and helmets, were made of leather in the Middle Ages. The expansion of animal husbandry as farmland fell vacant after the plagues made more leather goods available. In most cities leatherworkers were outnumbered only by victuallers and clothworkers. In Exeter they were about 15 per cent of the households and in Oxford 13 per cent in 1381. Most leatherworkers bought hides and skins from butchers, a fact that helps to explain the power of the butchers in most cities. Statutes required butchers either to slaughter animals inside the city or to bring the hides into the city along with the carcasses for meat. In smaller places such as Exeter, where guild monopolies were less developed than in some larger cities, many butchers from the environs also sold hides and skins regularly enough to make it worth their while to rent stalls in the city's meat market. Some had regular customers in the town and made deliveries. Exeter also developed an important regional trade in hides; many purchasers preferred to buy at Exeter rather than closer to the point of origin in the villages. Urban tanners also circulated through the coun-

83   Huiskes, *Beschlüsse Köln*, 51–6, 66.
84   Irsigler, *Wirtschaftliche Stellung Köln*, 89–93; Nicholas, *Town and Countryside*, 116; Carrère, *Barcelone*, 432.

tryside, buying undressed hides on village markets and selling finished leather goods there later.[85]

Gloucester too shows the intimate interaction of a county town with its environs. It was a market for farm products and fish from the Severn, but it also had a lucrative grain trade, exporting the surplus of its shire, especially to Bordeaux, which had put such pressure on the local farmers to produce wine that the grain supply was inadequate.[86] Merchants of Gloucester imported continental luxuries for sale to the county aristocracy, especially wine, spices and other luxury foods. Yet the municipal government made no attempt to create a captive market for the city's craftsmen or foodmongers. Village brewers and bakers sold on the market at Gloucester, finding it cheaper to buy licences permitting them to trade in the city than to pay toll. Although Gloucester lost substantial population during the plagues, growing ties with Gloucestershire led to such massive immigration that the city seems actually to have grown economically from the 1370s.[87]

The political posture of the cities: urban regions and urban leagues

Urban leagues became more influential after 1330. The Hanse was the most powerful of them, including at its height more than eighty cities of the Rhineland, Saxony and the Baltic coast. The Hanse had a diet (assembly) that passed resolutions, but they were not binding on the membership, and the league always had problems agreeing on a common course of action. The Hansards established offices in Bruges, Novgorod, Bergen and the Steelyard in London. As the Italian cities made increasing amounts of their own cloth, using the north for wool but not for the manufactured textiles, the Hanse merchants exported to the east finished cloth from Flanders and England. The Hanse was able to blockade Flanders between 1358 and 1360, finally forcing the Flemish counts to agree to all their demands. England lost a trade war with the Hanse in 1468.[88]

The urban leagues had overlapping memberships. A few interior cities of the Hanse were also members of the Saxon League, although the

---

85   These arguments have been developed for Exeter and Southampton in Kowaleski, 'Hide and leather trade', 57–67. They have an obvious implication that should be explored for other cities.

86   In a reversal of policy, Bordeaux in 1408 and 1416 refused to export wine from its upcountry that had not come to the city accompanied by a load of grain. Renouard, *Bordeaux sous les rois d'Angleterre*, 424, 432–3.

87   Holt, 'Gloucester', 141–5, 157.

88   Nicholas, *Evolution*, 423.

interests of the two were dissimilar; for the trade of the Saxon towns, especially Brunswick, was severely dependent on exporting cloth to Flanders for finishing, while the coastal Hanse cities exported grain and forest products to Flanders and imported cloth. The Saxon towns appeared as a group at the Hanse diet for the first time in 1412 and regularly thereafter, sometimes represented by Brunswick. Both leagues had a loose organisation, few but increasingly frequent meetings, subgroups led by their three or four largest cities and internecine rivalries. But the Hanse was formed to promote economic interests, while the Saxon League was political, to alleviate dangers from the nobles of the environs. Most economic interests of the individual Saxon towns and even of the League itself were handled within the Hanse, of which its more prominent cities were also members. As in Flanders, the municipal accounts show intense diplomatic activity between member cities even apart from the diet meetings, which were normally annual in the fifteenth century.

The members of the Saxon League paid their contributions to Magdeburg, Brunswick and Göttingen, which thus served as regional capitals that could represent the smaller places of their districts in the League diets. Like most 'urban' leagues, the Saxon League had a rural element, for it made treaties with lords to enforce the public peace. For more than a century after 1382 the League was a continuing alliance that was renewed periodically. Major comprehensive meetings were often triennial and were never at intervals of more than ten years. When the League undertook defensive or retaliatory measures, the members were not to make a separate peace with the enemy. The cities agreed to provide mutual assistance in the event that any member city council was threatened by discord from within. Both the Saxon League and the Hanse tried to stop a tax-inspired rebellion at Brunswick between 1374 and 1380, but the leagues' real influence was minimal.[89]

Despite the disorders of the late Middle Ages, there is less evidence of urban leagues in France than in Germany. In the early 1380s Tarascon, Arles, Aix, Marseilles and Nice allied briefly. The estates of Languedoc were a sort of urban league, since they were dominated by over 120 cities and towns in the fourteenth century and excluded the rural areas.[90] Fear that the emperor was going to pawn them to his creditors prompted ten 'common imperial cities', later called the Décapole, to form an Alsatian urban league in 1354. The Décapole included all the major cities of the region except the largest, Strasbourg, which became

89 Discussion based on Puhle, *Politik der Stadt Braunschweig*, 22–3, 28–36, 39–40, 43–9, 65–9, 101, 197–8, 237–50, 208.
90 Stouff, *Arles*, 102; Barel, *Ville médiévale*, 378–80.

an imperial free city in 1358. The Décapole had a common treasury that assessed an annual tax based on the wealth of the member cities. Members owed militia service to the grand bailiff of the League.[91]

Just as the English boroughs sent two representatives to Parliament and French assemblies of estates included the burgesses, urban involvement increased in the German imperial diets. The towns also made regional treaties concerning the public peace: in 1331 the emperor confirmed a peace negotiated by princes, lords and twenty-two imperial cities in Bavaria and Swabia. A chronicler claims that in September 1344 Louis summoned 'all princes and cities and towns of all Germany to a public parliament' at Frankfurt. The cities were presented with decisions that had been made a week earlier in Cologne by the electors and other princes, then asked for advice. The towns only had a right of assent at this point.[92]

From the last quarter of the fourteenth century the imperial cities were usually called to assemblies of estates. The mark of standing as an imperial city from that time was summons to the imperial diets; princely towns were not, although they might send representatives to local diets called by their princes.[93] In the confusion over the imperial throne in 1410–11 Emperor Sigismund tried to ally with the Rhenish urban league, reversing his predecessors' hostility to urban associations. In 1415 he proposed a peace based on regional agreements between towns and lords of four districts, but the Swabian cities objected that this would mean higher taxes. Delegates from seventy-two cities and towns were at the imperial diet at Nuremberg in 1422 and resumed negotiations with the emperor for a general urban league, but no consensus was reached. After the 1420s the cities became disenchanted with Sigismund as he intervened frequently in local disputes. He allied with the ruling patricians, enforcing death sentences issued by the local council against rebels at Breslau as being offenders against the crown. He restored patrician regimes, abolished guilds, levied fines and at various times pronounced the imperial ban on Lübeck, Rostock, Bremen, Wismar, Stettin, Constance and Halberstadt.[94]

Imperial cities and good towns

The imperial cities became much more powerful after the early fourteenth century. Although they were supposedly held directly by the emperor

91 Dollinger, *Histoire de l'Alsace*, 144–5.
92 Engel, 'Frühe Ständische Aktivitäten', 35–9.
93 Rabe, 'Stadt und Stadtherrschaft', 307–8.
94 Berthold, 'Städte und Reichsreform', 67–102.

without any intermediate lord, many places whose lords were ecclesiastics, such as Constance, Worms, Speyer and Mainz, were imperial
cities. The status of imperial city could not be transferred. At the
petition of Frankfurt, the emperor in 1332 declared that its rights as an
imperial city did not extend to the country towns that enjoyed Frankfurt's law. The emperors themselves in the fourteenth century pawned
entire imperial cities or their rights in them, but they remained imperial
cities nonetheless. Ending this practice was a major goal of such unions
as the Swabian League.[95] 'Free cities' were not sharply differentiated
from the imperial cities. The emperor in 1349 referred to all cities that
were directly under him as 'free cities', not just those that had formerly
been episcopal. But 'free city' in the late fourteenth century referred
increasingly to a specific group, mainly the Rhenish episcopal cities.
Some free cities claimed exemption from military obligations owed by
the imperial cities. In the fifteenth century free cities were exempt in
principle from imperial taxes, but many that were not called 'free' paid
no tax in fact.[96]

The imperial and free cities were unlike the French 'good towns'
(*bonnes villes*), which the kings were distinguishing from other types of
settlement in the late Middle Ages. The 'good towns', like the English
boroughs, had the right to send delegates to national assemblies to represent their individual communities, not simply as representatives of an
'estate' of burgesses. After 1358 regional urban leagues of these 'ambas-
sadors' attempted to concert action, but regional assemblies organised
on an 'estate' basis continued to meet regularly enough to establish a
local custom of what was meant by a 'good town'. The notion of 'good
towns' became so entrenched that it survived the decline of the assemblies, and the kings continued to consult 'good towns' individually and
in groups.

The 'good towns' were being called 'capitals' even in the fourteenth
century. The new royal courts were being held in them, while only
local assizes were held in the small towns. The administrative map
of modern France was created through the 'good towns' of the late
Middle Ages. Their walls and militia provided refuge from armies for
local populations. By the fifteenth century the term 'good towns' was
being used consistently for cities with a completely enclosed, uninterrupted system of fortifications and the resources needed to defend them,
specifically to withstand a siege.

Although the kings tried to use the 'good towns', they were more

---

95 Keutgen, *Urkunden*, no. 399, p. 498; Sydow, 'Reichsstadt', 299; Rabe, 'Stadt und
    Stadtherrschaft', 301–6.
96 Möncke, 'Freie Stadt', 87–90.

often opponents of the crown than its allies until after 1420. The tax burden was substantial, and the role of municipal officials in collecting them was a contributing element in the tax revolts of 1379–82. Royal interventions in local elections had been common even in the fourteenth century, and in the fifteenth the cities were increasingly dominated by royal officers. Louis XI exempted cities that maintained their own fortifications from the *taille*, whose stated purpose was to pay for the army. The cities' power over the rural areas whose administrative capitals they were becoming was paradoxically increased by the loss of the extended suburbs during the wars of the late Middle Ages, which created a separation of city from countryside that had not existed previously.[97]

The Italian cities had always dominated their rural environs, but in the Middle Ages some of the larger northern cities also extended their jurisdiction beyond their walls. In areas where powerful lords blocked this expansion the cities operated through regional peace associations or urban leagues. Links between urban and rural market mechanisms became stronger everywhere, even if at times under compulsion from the cities. The older urban merchant elites were buying rural property and intermarrying with the landed aristocracy. This paralleled a loss of political power in the cities by these lineages to the rising merchant element within the more powerful crafts. We thus turn to changes in the cities brought about by the victory of the crafts, which come in two phases, before and after about 1370–80.

97   Discussion based on Chevalier, *Bonnes villes*, 13, 44–61, 94–5, 100–3, 176–80.

CHAPTER FOUR

City Governments and Urban Conflict: Patricians and Political Guilds

By the 1320s most Italian cities were controlled by councils whose membership was allocated among occupational guilds, often with geographical sectors of the city also being guaranteed representation. Some northern cities had a version of this regime by the 1320s, and virtually all did by the 1370s. Power was centred in the council, and most change involved efforts of wealthy newer families to dent the monopoly of the older lineages, often using guild membership as a criterion of political participation. The guilds had both internal and external hierarchies of honour and influence. The more prestigious and politically powerful guilds, which filled most seats on the councils, were those of merchants, notaries and judges and importers and exporters. Joining them were guilds that had a substantial merchant element that controlled the affairs of the trade and gave work to the craftspeople in the guild. The lower-ranked trades, consisting solely of craftspeople, had little representation on the councils.

CITY LORDS AND MUNICIPAL GOVERNMENTS IN THE LATER MIDDLE AGES

Ecclesiastical lordship and immunity

City lords, particularly prelates, remained powerful enough to contest power with city councils. Hildesheim had a population of 5,000 with fifty ecclesiastical institutions, many of them occupying desirable properties. Gloucester, which was only slightly larger than Hildesheim, had three hospitals, one abbey, two priories, and eleven parish churches, most of which had chantries with priests and parish guilds. These institutions collected ground rents on more than half the houses in the city. In 1540

72 per cent of the taxable property at Chartres was in the hands of the church.[1] Rodez was still divided in the fourteenth century between the hilltop City ruled by the bishop and the count's Bourg downhill, which was more commercial. Each was fortified. Although there was nothing unusual about a city having discrete nuclei, at Rodez they still had separate governments, laws, weights and measures. There was a main gate between the two, which was locked at night, but in places the border was marked only with stones, the residues of a ditch that had existed earlier. Some properties and their outbuildings were on both sides, and many workers lived and worked in separate sectors. The two settlements even recognised different overlords: the City rendered homage to Edward III of England after 1360, but the Bourg refused.[2]

Church properties, including those rented to laypeople, were immunity districts outside the control of the city authorities. Even in Paris the bishop retained the right to judge all cases on his scattered properties except for rape and murder. Seventeen religious institutions and organisations, including the bishop, had justice over all civil actions and many criminal cases.[3] Criminals were still escaping prosecution by fleeing to consecrated ground, but the secular jurisdiction of most churches was weakening seriously in the late Middle Ages. In France most cases involving laypeople could be appealed to a royal court after 1330. Yet problems continued. The bailiff of Ypres was excommunicated in 1386 for apprehending three murderers in a church. In 1436 a beggar struck a child in the church of the Innocents at Paris. The mother tried to hit him on the head but instead scratched his face, thereby drawing blood. For this she was imprisoned for twenty-two days, during which time the bishop of Paris refused to reconsecrate the church unless he was paid a fine.[4]

The ecclesiastical immunities were significant gaps not only in the legal jurisdiction of the cities but also in their efforts to regulate the economy. Although sanctuary for escaped felons in the churches of London was limited to forty days, Exeter paid men to snare fugitives who tried to leave the church of St John the Baptist. There was violence against the churches in York over the archbishop's refusal to contribute to the upkeep of the walls. The city also fought St Mary's abbey over its estate at Bootham. After the city had tried to starve out Bootham by stopping its supplies along the Ouse in 1354, Bootham was given to

1   Schwarz, 'Stadt und Kirche', 63–73; Holt, 'Gloucester', 155; Billot, *Chartres*, 200.
2   Wroe, *A Fool and His Money*, 39–41, 69–70.
3   Thompson, *Paris Under English Rule*, 49–50; Cazelles, *Paris*, 177–8, 226–31.
4   Nicholas, 'Crime and punishment', 331–2; Nicholas, *Medieval Flanders*, 296–7, 355–6; *Journal Paris*, 310–11.

the city in return for a pledge to stop this and not to arrest the monks except for felony and trespass.[5] The dean and chapter of Lincoln had stalls for merchants in the close, which attracted those who wanted to avoid the city's stallage fees. Municipal officials were accused of hindering operations in the close in 1382, and the city in turn accused the dean and chapter of harbouring felons fleeing from the city's jurisdiction. Citizens who were elected mayor or bailiff were also fleeing into the close to avoid service.[6] Some London retailers gained sanctuary from debt prosecution by buying or renting tenements in the Westminster Abbey precinct. Debts contracted in Ghent were unenforceable in the abbey village of St Peter, across a canal from the city.[7]

In general, however, prelates were less successful in maintaining themselves than were temporal princes. Most bishops had to build new residences outside their cities. The archbishop still controlled important public services at Mainz, but financial pressures forced him to accept a payment from the townspeople in 1325 in return for his pledge that he would not again interrupt these services for financial reasons. While the archbishop's court had jurisdiction over most criminal cases, the city court judged property questions that did not involve clergy or church estates directly.[8] The bishop of Constance was an exception to the general pattern of weakness of ecclesiastical town lords. Bishop Johann Windlock tried to rule after 1351 through the *Amman* and bailiff, both of them ministerials, and dispense with the burgomaster and council. Although he was assassinated in 1356, the next year the emperor restored rights that the bishop had not enjoyed since the early fourteenth century. An alliance of guildsmen against the bishop was unable to dislodge him until the period of the famous church council in the fifteenth century.[9]

Lay lords

The problem of conflicting jurisdictions was not confined to the ecclesiastical immunities. Even in the powerful Flemish cities the count continued to confirm elections to the councils. An electoral college of eight, four each chosen by the count and by the outgoing councils, chose the two city councils of Ghent on the basis of political 'members' [on the

5   Hollaender and Kellaway, *Studies in London History*, 81; Rowe and Draisey, *Exeter Receivers' Accounts*, 28; Tillott, *City of York*, 68–9.
6   Hill, *Medieval Lincoln*, 264–7.
7   Rosser, 'London and Westminster', 50; Rosser, *Medieval Westminster*, 226–37; Nicholas, 'Governance', 242.
8   Patze, 'Landesherrliche Residenzen', 19–20; Falck, *Mainz in seiner Blütezeit*, 149, 163–5.
9   Bechtold, *Zunftbürgerschaft und Patriziat*, 124–9.

members, see below] and within the members by affiliation with specific guilds. The count of Holland chose the *Gerecht* of Leiden, the executive arm of the government, from a slate submitted by the *Vroedschap* (City Fathers), a broad council that consisted of former magistrates. In Maastricht the two lords, the bishop of Liège and the duke of Brabant, jointly named the town government.[10]

In France the monarch intervened in the governance of the cities, usually installing his own officials alongside locally elected magistrates, whose election he had the right to confirm, and encouraging appeals to the royal court from the city councils. When the king wanted to compel a town to adopt a particular course of action, he might send the same letter simultaneously to the *échevins* and to royal officials there and/or to the lords of the various immunity jurisdictions. Even at Reims the royal court by 1334 was recognising the archbishop's *échevins* not as a seigniorial court, but as a city court with the right to appeal directly to the king. By 1345 a crime committed against an *échevin* was made a plea of the crown.[11]

The king was the lord of most English cities. The royal government encroached on the role of the city magistrates to such an extent that many records that were kept locally on the continent were centralised in England. In 1339 the magistrates of Exeter sent messengers to London to seek records concerning a pending legal action.[12] The kings were not benevolent lords, although they did not suppress municipal institutions to the extent that the French did. They generally became involved only to raise money and ensure defence. After a French raid in 1338 devastated Southampton, Edward III blamed the city for neglecting its defences, seized its franchises and appointed two 'keepers of the borough' to take charge of the repair. After the crisis passed, the city's liberties were restored.[13] The inhabitants of Gloucester so disliked the royal castle that they turned the Bareland, a vacant lot between the fortress and the town that was supposed to be used for military manoeuvres, into a cesspit by dumping ordure there. The stink made life so unbearable for the inhabitants of the castle that an inquiry was held in the critical year 1381.[14] The king's hand always weighed heavily on the government of London. The king's butler became the *de facto* coroner, although the city technically had a separate coroner. Both had

---

10   Nicholas, 'Governance', 235; Howell, *Women, Production, and Patriarchy*, 53; Alberts, *Middeleeuwse stad*, 47.
11   Chevalier, 'Bonnes villes', 110–28; Desportes, *Reims*, 505–16.
12   Rowe and Draisey, *Exeter Receivers' Accounts*, 28.
13   Platt, *Medieval Southampton*, 111–16.
14   Holt, 'Gloucester', 154.

chamberlains; the king's obtained wine for the royal household and collected the customs dues on it, while the city chamberlain enrolled apprenticeships and admissions to the freedom and kept the city records. The city chose its own mayor, but the king evidently appointed the successor of an incumbent who died in office.[15]

The Bohemian towns were also subject to strict royal control. The prince appointed municipal judges until the fifteenth century. Although the cities had a voice in choosing members of their councils, the king could quash an election by refusing to install them. Although the councils handled ordinary administration, changes of statutes or economic regulations could only be done through the king. The Bohemian kings evidently hoped to use the cities against the nobles. In 1337 King John established a Court of the Royal Cities, with a judge responsible to his under chamberlain. Both officials made regular circuits in the towns. The under chamberlain became a sort of general factotum for urban affairs, especially concerning finance, and was disliked by town governments.[16]

The Wittelsbach dukes of Bavaria appointed judges as chief officials of the cities, which only gradually gained the right to choose them. In the largest cities the judge was eventually replaced by the chamberlain and later the burgomaster. The dukes kept Munich under tight control, although it did have its own council.[17] The prince's overlordship yielded to council and burgomaster in most imperial cities. The first step was generally the transfer of high and blood justice from the imperial bailiff to the *Schultheiss*, who was usually a citizen of the town where he was serving. Municipal governments tried to buy this office to keep the emperors from pawning it, but with limited success. In 1329 Louis of Bavaria permitted Frankfurt to buy out all imperial incomes in or around the city, specifically mentioning tolls, weights, the king's right to tax Jews, taxes on imports, excises and the office of *Schultheiss*, and this was not untypical. Yet only in 1372 was Frankfurt able permanently to acquire the *Schultheiss* position.[18]

The cities exercised an attraction for princes from the mid-thirteenth century, but this placed the lords in potential conflict with the increasingly independent towns. Although Munich was the preferred residence of the Wittelsbach dukes of Bavaria, the citizens fought them almost

---

15 Richard II named the famous Richard Whittington mayor to fill an unexpired term in 1397. Whittington then was chosen on his own in 1406 and 1419. Hollaender and Kellaway, *Studies in London History*, 75–9; Barron, 'Richard Whittington', 205.
16 Kejr, 'Königliches Städtewesen in Böhmen', 79–83.
17 Störmer, 'Stadt und Stadtherr im wittelsbachischen Altbayern', 261–2; Bischoff, 'Stadtherrschaft im ostfränkischen Städtedreieck', 98–104.
18 Rabe, 'Stadt und Stadtherrschaft', 310–14; Dilcher, 'Bürgerbegriff', 70; Keutgen, *Urkunden*, no. 393, pp. 493–4.

constantly between 1377 and 1403. Finally the duke forced the city to build a new wall linking his palace to the main city wall, thus giving security to his personnel even if there was an uprising outside. Yet luxury goods were so important for the opulent late-medieval courts that even when town lords had to withdraw, they were so dependent on the trade and capital nexus that they could not move very far away. When the bishop of Passau was forced out of the city, he built a palace just across the Danube.[19]

CITY GOVERNMENT WITH GUILD PARTICIPATION, c. 1330–c. 1370

Hierarchy and composition of the councils

When the city had more than one council, or separate boards of *jurés* and *échevins*, one either reduced the other to largely ceremonial functions or they shared responsibilities. Except for London, which was dominated by crafts with a strong merchant element, most English cities remained under merchant guilds. Groups of crafts shared power in those of Italy and southern France. Single occupational guilds rarely had a guarantee of certain seats on the magistracy until after 1370, but groups of guilds often did, and the trades that were more oriented toward commerce had many more seats than did those that were more strictly artisanal. In Germany, the Low Countries and northern France wealthy craftsmen served on city councils as individuals rather than as representatives of their guilds during this phase. At Nuremberg, for example, the small council from 1348–9 had thirty-four members from the lineages and eight craftsmen, but the latter were always big businessmen or industrialists.[20]

Still, there is an undeniable movement toward broader participation for the middle class of substantial guild masters, if not for the wage-earners whom they employed. Conflicts over the composition of the magistracy generally pitted groups of outsiders calling themselves the 'people' against the entrenched aristocracy, but in most cases the reality behind the rhetoric was new money against old, not poor against rich. Philip VI settled disturbances at Montauban in 1328 by ruling that the ten new consuls should be coopted by the retiring group but that five each should be burgesses and 'populars'.[21]

19 Patze, 'Landesherrliche Residenzen', 17–20.
20 Pfeiffer, *Nürnberg*, 92.
21 Mollat and Wolff, *Popular Revolutions*, 65.

Italy

The councils of the turbulent Italian cities underwent only minor modifications in the middle years of the fourteenth century. But while in the north the guild revolutions modified or abolished old magistracies, the norm in Italy was to institute a new council without abolishing its predecessor, merely taking away its real policy-making functions. Thus below the priorate or the elders the Italian cities had large councils with largely honorific or patronage functions that have few northern equivalents.[22]

The *Signoria* at Florence consisted of the standard-bearer of justice, who served a six-month term, and eight priors, who served for two months. The priors represented guilds that were grouped into greater, middle and lesser. Below the *Signoria* two councils, of the commune and of the *popolo*, with a total membership of some five hundred members, rotated every six months. They acted as a legislative assembly below the essentially administrative priors. Other legislative bodies were the sixteen standard-bearers of the militia companies, who were organised on a neighbourhood basis; the captains of the Guelf party; and the guild consuls. Factional struggles were so severe after 1328 that the duke of Athens, Walter of Brienne, became war captain briefly in 1343. After his departure three separate committees nominated candidates for the scrutiny: the captains and priors of the Guelf party, the incumbent priors and the Five of the *Mercanzia* and the consuls of the major guilds, each group supplemented with parish representatives. The chronicler Villani claimed that 3,346 persons were nominated, which would represent about three-quarters of the total population of the twenty-one politically capable guilds. The change of 1343 also provided that each priorate would contain two *popolani grassi* (members of the *popolo* who were affiliated with one of the seven greater guilds), three from the five middle guilds, and three from the nine minor guilds. Numerous new families thus entered the priorate before 1348, and the high mortality during the plagues necessitated new scrutinies in 1348 and 1352. The nominating board became so large that it could not conceivably have served a narrow oligarchy. Although the entry of new families into offices was slowed in the 1360s and 1370s, the Florentine elite by 1378 consisted largely of persons whose families had not held office before 1348. The major change in Florentine government during these decades was not in the formal institutional structure of the city but in the growing power of the Guelf party. Although the elite kept tighter control of offices after

22 Meek, *Lucca*, 8–9.

1382, the requirement of rotation meant that virtually all members of the elite could eventually hold office.[23]

The Nine of Siena fell in 1355, when the emperor visited the city. Although chroniclers suggest that the old order was overthrown completely, families from the Nine continued to be chosen for city offices. The change was due to the discontent of newly rich Sienese at being excluded from government by the narrow rules of eligibility, together with allegations of corruption and the government's inability to deal with the violence that had been worsening after 1348. The new government after 1355 perpetuated Siena's tradition of a mixed regime. There were two councils of twelve: the 'governors and administrators of the republic', who were *popolani*, and twelve nobles who had to be from different families. In the General Council of the Commune the *popolani* had 250 seats, the nobles 150. The captain and standard-bearer of justice were appointed by the General Council from the *popolani*.[24]

The eight-member priorate at Florence and the Nine at Siena are typical of the Italian city councils that actually directed policy. They were drawn by lot from purses containing names of candidates whose eligibility had been determined by a rigid strutiny that took both property and ancestry into account. Sometimes a complex electoral process would be used, rather than drawing by lot. The nine elders of Lucca were elected by the previous college and a council of thirty-six, supplemented by six persons designated from each of the three districts of the city. The elders were divided into six colleges, each holding office for two months. The contents of the purses were renewed at intervals, often of two years.[25] These councils are somewhat smaller than most north European boards of aldermen, *Schöffen*, councillors and peers, but they were supplemented by larger general councils.

Flanders

The larger Flemish cities had multiple councils. In normal periods Ghent was ruled by the Law Aldermen (*schepenen*), who issued statutes and ratified guild regulations, set overall city policy and conducted diplomacy, recorded contracts and heard appeals from subordinate jurisdictions. A revolving committee of three Law Aldermen was present at all

---

23 Brucker, *Florentine Politics and Society*, 160; Brucker, *Civic World*, 14; Brucker, *Renaissance Florence*, 134–6; Najemy, *Corporatism and Consensus*, 131–49, 158–9, 164–79, 190–7; Herlihy, 'Rulers of Florence', 198–9.
24 The nobles tried to restore the Nine in Siena in September 1368 and held the city hall for twenty-two days. Bowsky, *Siena Under the Nine*, 301–6; Mollat and Wolff, *Popular Revolutions*, 135–6.
25 Meek, *Lucca 1369–1400*, 8–11.

times in the city hall to handle routine business. The Estate Aldermen recorded all property left to minors and supervised their guardians. They were also justices of the peace, handling uncontested cases of violence and settling of feuds between warring parties whenever they actually reached the courts. During emergencies captains were chosen from the parishes, but one captain usually overshadowed the others and seized real power from the Law Aldermen; James van Artevelde is the most famous example.

After 1302 craftsmen could serve in the city government on the same basis as scions of the patrician lineages, but after 1312 the older families occupied most seats on the councils. The weavers or the fullers, or occasionally both, usually occupied some seats. The locally based trades that individually had political recognition had corporate organisation as the 'Small Guilds' by 1317. When they began they were similar to the 'minor arts' of Florence, but their numbers had grown from a score in 1317 to sixty-three in 1332, finally becoming fixed at fifty-nine by 1357. But until 1361 they never sat on the councils in a fixed ratio to other artisan groups.[26]

France

Most French cities continued to be dominated by older lineages, despite modest gains by the guildsmen. The fact that city councillors were generally unsalaried at this time meant that persons who could not live off their investments could not afford the time required for municipal service. Political careers were prestigious but sometimes costly. There was some compensation, particularly in tax farming, which aldermanic families often did in years when they were not occupying seats on the council. In addition, the small group who controlled offices often received tax remission and were awarded public works contracts. The city governments were becoming large-scale consumers of goods that were provided by members of the municipal aristocracy, such as wine and ale and building material.

Royal officials increasingly restricted the municipal *échevins*, particularly after 1356. Most of the Loire cities limited the powers of their lords but saw this translated into dependence on the king. General assemblies of citizens, rarely including over two hundred persons, developed more practical importance by the 1350s, for such decisions as extraordinary taxation for defence had to be taken in a general assembly under the

26 Nicholas, 'Governance', 235–9; Nicholas, *Van Arteveldes*, 5; Nicholas, *Metamorphosis*, 4–8.

presidency of the royal captain. *Élus* who were chosen by clergy and burgesses oversaw the funds. As war and insecurity continued, the councils of *élus* became permanent financial boards. Over time some seats on the council of *élus* were reserved for particular groups: at Troyes one for the abbot of Saint-Rémi or Nicaise, two for the canons of Notre-Dame, two for the *échevins* of the archbishop, while others were chosen from the general population. The royal military captains who had been installed in the good towns during the crisis continued to function in peacetime. The captain was often absentee, represented by a lieutenant, who, after 1376, was generally a native of the city chosen in its general assembly. The assembly's authority was enhanced as the real power of the *échevins* yielded to the *élus*.[27] The general assemblies of the French cities have some similarity to the broader Italian councils below the priors.

Germany

Most serious conflict over the occupational composition of city councils in northern Europe during these decades occurred in Germany. Although disorders were sometimes serious in the cities of France and the Low Countries, the issues were more often foreign policy, wars and finances. The magistracies that were in place by the 1330s sufficed for another generation. In Germany, however, some cities experienced guild revolutions in the 1330s that were similar to what the western cities had undergone around the turn of the century.

Patrician regimes stayed in power in the Hanse cities and some in central and southern Germany (Breslau, Leipzig and Regensburg) that exported metals. Craft organisations were more successful in the southwest. At Ravensburg in 1346 and Speyer in 1350 the patricians formed a corporation with the same rights as the legally recognised occupational guilds. At the other extreme, Magdeburg denied the patricians corporate recognition after 1330 and forced them to register as individuals in guilds. A third form was the mixed regime in which patricians and crafts shared power.[28]

The crafts were unable to penetrate the governments of the Hanse cities until the late fourteenth century. In some strongly merchant cities of the interior and those with a powerful and still-resident town lord, their rebellions failed utterly. Regensburg did not have a guild revolution. Conflicts that erupted between 1330 and 1334 were between factions of the patriciate, the ministerials who had controlled the town to

---

27 Desportes, *Reims*, 505–16, 563–70. For comparison, see Valous, *Patriciat Lyonnais*, 41–5.
28 Mollat and Wolff, *Popular Revolutions*, 74–5.

that point versus the newer merchant families. In Mainz the patrician Emrich zum Rebstock led a guild revolution in 1332 and represented the 'community' on the twenty-two-member council that resulted from it. But in Mainz as in Magdeburg the real conflict was not between patriciate and craftsmen who could form trades, but between the non-patrician merchants and the lineages. Only the latter had the three essential privileges that could be obtained only from the archbishop: cutting cloth, holding fiefs and exchanging money. The lineages, who were living largely on the incomes from rural properties, thus recovered their position rapidly, and the city was so exhausted by internal conflicts that it was unable to preserve its liberty.[29]

The government of Nuremberg also remained patrician. A guild rebellion inspired by a rival of the emperor Charles IV in 1348 installed a new council dominated by craftsmen but with a few patricians. Charles quickly isolated Nuremberg, was reconciled with his opponents, permitted the exiled patricians of Nuremberg to form a government in absentia, and forbade 'guilds and unions'. From 1370 eight non-voting representatives of the crafts chosen by the emperor were added to the council in a consultative capacity.[30]

German city governments whose composition had been broadened in the early fourteenth century underwent only minor adjustments. In a refinement of an arrangement of 1318, Munich by 1365 had two bur-gomasters, a fourteen-member inner council and a thirty-one-member outer council. A Great Council had 145 members in 1365; newer families of merchants and merchant-artisans began exercising a political role there. At Speyer the settlement of 1330 was adjusted in 1349, when the mint associates were given representation on the council as a single guild. They and each of the fourteen other guilds that were already in the magistracy were to have two representatives on a thirty-member council. A Large Council of ninety – the incumbent council and its two predecessors – made the weightiest decisions. The two previous councils provided most municipal officers, including the two burgomasters.[31]

Two guild-based revolutions

Although most German cities in which the crafts would ever have a significant political role had admitted them earlier to the magistracy,

29 Bosl, 'Regensburg', 194–7; Maschke, *Städte und Menschen*, 187–8.
30 Mollat and Wolff, *Popular Revolutions*, 73; Pfeiffer, *Nürnberg*, 73–5. Charles IV was not always an opponent of the guilds in the imperial cities. What bothered him about the Nuremberg crafts was their alliance with his rivals, the Wittelsbachs of Bavaria.
31 Gleba, *Gemeinde*, 137–9; Maschke, *Städte und Menschen*, 124–5.

agitation during the 1330s brought partially craft regimes to power in Zürich and Strasbourg. The revolution at Zürich was unusual because of the great role played by one man, Rudolf Brun, a knight who in 1336 became burgomaster for life in a new regime of patricians and corporations. A council of twenty-six was established, rotating every six months. Thirteen came from the patrician 'constabulary' (*Konstaffel*), defined as persons who had to keep a horse for professional reasons and had to let the city use it in an emergency: knights, nobles, landowners, wholesale merchants, textile magnates, moneychangers, goldsmiths and salt dealers. The other thirteen came from crafts or groups of crafts. Each had a banner, and most included several occupations. Each group had to defend a segment of the city wall during emergencies. Brun and six electors from the retiring council chose the thirteen new patrician councillors. Corporations elected their own, but the burgomaster intervened in cases of disagreement. This arrangement enabled parties to develop, favouring the Habsburgs and the Swiss Confederation respectively. In 1373 it was modified to weaken the burgomaster.[32]

Strasbourg, too, was rigidly aristocratic, with a faction-ridden patrician council of twenty-four. In 1332 a disturbance erupted between the most influential noble lineages, the Zorn and Mullenheim, at a banquet of the Round Table – in itself an interesting manifestation of noble consciousness among townspeople. The merchant patricians joined the guildsmen to expel these two and change the constitution. As at Zürich the old patrician lines and the nobles were linked in a 'constabulary'. An Old Council of twenty-five (eight knights and esquires, fourteen patrician burghers and three masters chosen for life) was joined by a New Council of twenty-five guildsmen. The guilds' leader, the *Ammeister*, replaced the four burgomasters and soon became the most influential officeholder, although the office was often held by patricians until 1349. While the trades had previously had purely occupational-economic functions, now they were also political and military. New agitation in 1349 led by the renegade patrician Klaus Zorn gave representatives to four new guilds, and the *Ammeister* was to come thereafter from the crafts. In 1362 the richest guilds, including the goldsmiths and cloth cutters, and others that were previously considered part of the constabulary were ranged with the other guilds, and it was decreed that anyone who worked for a living rather than living off his property had to serve in the militia with the guilds. The patricians gradually lost power.[33]

32 Maschke, *Städte und Menschen*, 184; Burghartz, *Leib, Ehre und Gut*, 32–3; Mollat and Wolff, *Popular Revolutions*, 70–2.
33 Dollinger, *Histoire de l'Alsace*, 146–7; Schulz, *Handwerksgesellen und Lohnarbeiter*, 15–24; Maschke, *Städte und Menschen*, 184; Mollat and Wolff, *Popular Revolutions*, 67–70.

Functions, power and influence

Most city councils on the continent except in France had the power to legislate, subject to confirmation by the prince and with the proviso that they should not violate the city's fundamental charter. At Ghent by the mid-fourteenth century the regulations of one board of aldermen were considered binding unless repealed by their successors. The *échevins* of Brussels legislated in consultation with various groups of their own choosing, including the administrators of the Common Guild and, after 1360, often the craft deans. Their ordinances were promulgated by the duke's *amman* on the parapet of the city hall.[34] From 1298 the German cities, too, were permitted to issue statutes as long as they did not contravene imperial law. The council of Riga issued police regulations annually by reading them aloud in a public assembly in front of the city hall. These assemblies, called *Burspraken* (Latin *colloquia*), were held for police matters and statutes in most cities of the Baltic and Scandinavia that used the law of Lübeck. Every six months Cologne, whose statutes were not assumed to be given in perpetuity, promulgated 'Morning Speeches' (*Morgensprachen*), reissuing or modifying earlier statutes about fighting fires, mummery, street-cleaning, carrying lanterns at night and court terms.[35]

The royal takeover of justice in the French 'good towns' deprived their *échevins* of the legislative function that they had exercised earlier. The *échevins* were confined to defence, public order and taxation. Even justice became problematical, as the status 'burgess of the king' was given to encourage appeals from the city consuls to the king. Some French city governments even lacked power to enforce the laws. When the king wanted to give police power to a 'good town', as at Tours in the 1460s, he might face opposition from local lords. Specific royal legislation for individual towns gives a confused picture of the extent to which the cities could police themselves, even on such civil matters as weights, measures and contracts.[36]

The 'revolutions' of the middle decades of the fourteenth century were thus very conservative. Only the wealthiest and least 'mechanical' guilds gained access to the city councils. In most German cities that permitted craft representation, the councils were chosen formally on a

---

34 Nicholas, 'Governance', 237; Martens, *Histoire de Bruxelles*, 125.
35 Pfeiffer, *Nürnberg*, 33–4; von Bunge, *Riga*, 126; Sprandel, *Quellen zur Hanse-Geschichte*, 29–30; Huiskes, *Beschlüsse Köln*, 60–1, 141. In England the 'Morning Speeches' were guild assemblies that, as at Leicester and Southampton, sometimes became the city council or court; Hilton, *English and French Towns*, 93.
36 Faber and Lochard, *Montpellier*, 182; Chevalier, *Bonnes villes*, 201–2, 220–4.

guild basis during this period, before it became the norm elsewhere in northern Europe. In determining the number of seats on the magistracy the prestige of a guild as well as the number of members was important. Lines were blurred between merchant-crafts and purely artisanal work, and a single guild might contain not only merchants and craftsmen but craftsmen who sold more than what they made themselves and people who made different things. Distinctions between groups of guilds were already widening. The guild hierarchy varied between cities, depending on local conditions. Wine merchants were high in status everywhere, for they either controlled vineyards or imported a highly valued commodity. At Basel they and the grocers enjoyed high standing, while the weavers and fishmongers were held in low esteem. At Strasbourg the shippers, grocers, butchers, innkeepers, drapers, and grain merchants were prestigious, with gardeners and masons at the bottom of the hierarchy.[37] The guild revolution at Augsburg in 1368 gave two representatives to each guild that was 'great and honourable', including tailors, cloth wholesalers, weavers, merchants, grocers, weavers, and such trades as bakers, butchers and shoemakers, which had a long history in the city. The other trades were given one delegate. Constance after 1371 had a Great Council of 140, of whom the guilds chose seventy. Most guilds had a single representative, but the merchants, grocers and butchers each chose six, the tanners four, and the goldsmiths, furriers, linen weavers and wool weavers two each. Basel had four 'gentleman guilds' of merchants, mint associates, grocers and wine merchants. Among the leather trades at Leipzig in 1349 the tanners and cobblers even exercised court jurisdiction over butchers and shoe restorers.[38]

Given the hierarchies among the guilds and the fact that in scarcely any city were the older landed lineages excluded from power, it would be a mistake to wax overly sanguine about the democratic character of the early craft regimes. In some the guildsmen had fewer than half the seats or formed an organisation that was an adjunct to the inner council. In Speyer the patricians simply became a guild with the same number of seats as the others. As this practice became more common after 1350, it blurred the distinction between lineages and crafts.[39] When the patricians were given half the seats on the town council, it was easy for them to get another vote to form a majority. Even when they only had a minority of seats on the council, they were more successful in obtaining other offices, especially judgeships and burgomasterships.

37 Maschke, *Städte und Menschen*, 176–80.
38 Maschke, 'Mittelschichten', 14–15; Maschke, *Städte und Menschen*, 14–15, 175–83.
39 Maschke, *Städte und Menschen*, 190.

Several city constitutions even required the burgomaster to be a patrician. Augsburg had an overwhelming majority of guildsmen on the councils from 1368, but one of the two burgomasters had to be a patrician. In addition, ninety-four of the guilds' burgomasters at Augsburg between 1368 and 1548 were from the guild of long-distance merchants, thirty-two from the salt refiners who were also wholesalers, and fourteen each from the grocers and weavers. Many of them were patricians who had joined a guild so that they could sell on the city market. The picture is similar in Speyer, Regensburg, Constance and Frankfurt. Wine importing and shipping were good guilds for patricians, since they were service and commercial businesses that did not involve working with the hands and thus entail derogation of standing. Thus even under guild regimes the wealthy guilds that patricians could join dominated, and few artisans became politically prominent.[40]

The question thus naturally arises of the real power exercised by each group under the new regimes. Burgomasters generally presided over meetings of the council. In Germany they held many executive powers that had previously been performed by the imperial *Schultheiss*.[41] The mayors played a more important role in administration in England than was usual on the continent, even in Germany. They often came to the office with some background in other municipal offices, particularly finance. At least ten of the sixteen mayors of Exeter between 1304 and 1354, and seven of the eight who served after 1335, had been city receivers at some point. After 1348 the mayor had to be a £5 freeholder and have been a city steward for at least one year.[42]

The complexities of diplomacy and law and the ornate language and conventions required the education, expertise and polish of the patricians. Demands on time also played a part, for few craftsmen could afford to spend much time on unpaid city service. Even attending council meetings was a burden.[43] At Cologne before 1396 the inner council normally met on Monday, Wednesday and Friday mornings, the Great Council on Monday and Friday. Members received a fixed payment per diem for ordinary meetings and up to ten payments yearly in wine for extraordinary sessions, but these could hardly compensate for the loss of one's trade.[44] A statute of 1370 at Osnabrück provided that no incumbent member of the council could practise his craft. Thus the only

40 Maschke, *Städte und Menschen*, 193–8, 203–5, 219.
41 Rabe, 'Stadt und Stadtherrschaft', 311–13; Schultheiss, *Satzungen*, 302; Pfeiffer, *Nürnberg*, 34–5.
42 Rowe and Draisey, *Exeter Receivers' Accounts*, x.
43 Kowaleski, 'Commercial dominance', 198.
44 Huiskes, *Beschlüsse Köln*, xxvi.

craftsmen who could serve were those who were rich enough to live for a year off their investments or older men who had passed the trade on to their sons. In Speyer, Augsburg and many English cities, many who were elected tried to escape service, and attendance at meetings was low. This meant that for practical purposes the craftsmen had to abandon the time-consuming burgomastership and diplomacy to the rentiers or merchants.[45]

Thus with rare exceptions, usually due to a strong personality, most guild representatives on the city councils were really merchants, rentiers or financiers in all but name. Although public participation was much broader by 1360 than in 1270, patricians held more leading offices in towns under guild regimes than a literal reading of the sources suggests. The ruling 'type' in the early guild regimes – and to a considerable extent those after 1370 – was the merchant and to a lesser degree the rentier, not the craftsman. Hence discontent continued even after the guilds came to power.[46]

THE URBAN REBELLIONS OF THE FOURTEENTH CENTURY: THE FIRST PHASE

Several major cities experienced disturbances in the mid-fourteenth century, but most specifically urban rebellions with coherent political programmes occurred before 1330. The later ones were often part of territorial uprisings that were not specifically urban and had national political goals rather than a change either in the form or the personnel of city government. Rarely can an analysis based on social class struggles withstand careful analysis. The rebels of Rouen of 1382 crowned a draper their king, turning the uprising into a festival, but when a democratic movement triumphed at Besançon in 1450, its leader, a goldsmith, sold the confiscated property of aristocrats to indemnify the archbishop for his damages. Most revolts were led by solidly middle-class persons, such as butchers in Paris and Lyon and notaries and scribes in Lyon and Metz.[47]

Family alliances were important in virtually all of the urban rebellions. Groups that had previously been excluded were often admitted to the government, but only briefly. Common aspects included resentment over escalating royal taxation and personal dislike of the city's rulers, but without reference to the offices that they were holding. Most urban

---

45   Wensky, 'Osnabrücker Gilden', 372; Maschke, *Städte und Menschen*, 236–7.
46   Maschke, *Städte und Menschen*, 251, 263–4.
47   Rossiaud, 'Crises', 518–22.

revolts were led by newly rich men, either persons new to the city or members of older lineages who had stayed in trade while others invested in land and who thus did not have political power commensurate with their economic position.[48]

Discontent over high food prices was an issue in some urban uprisings. The city rulers provided considerable sums for poor relief and tried to keep grain prices low, if only through an instinct for self-preservation. But they were paternalistic, keeping control of the government vested in a small oligarchy. Thus even when the poor participated in the urban rebellions, the issues were usually the individuals in the magistracy, not government policy, which did not change much after any of the uprisings. Poverty was more often involved in rural than in urban rebellions.

The Flemish rebellion of 1338–49 and its aftermath

The rebellion of the Flemish cities led by James van Artevelde of Ghent has been called a worker revolt against an oligarchical regime. Van Artevelde himself has become a hero to the socialist movement in Belgium. In fact, his rebellion was the most thoroughly political of the great urban uprisings of the fourteenth century, and that of his son Philip in 1382 was the most thoroughly family-based.

As hostilities mounted between the English and French in the late 1330s, the two used embargoes to force the Flemings to choose sides. In 1338 a regime of parish captains was set up, chief of whom was James van Artevelde. He was a broker and landowner who had ties to the brewers and whose family was friendly toward the weavers, who had been excluded from the government of Ghent since 1320. Van Artevelde kept the regime of aldermen in place. Although he opened officeholding to masters of all guilds, including the weavers, he never supported the journeymen of any guild against the aristocratic masters and indeed adjudicated wage quarrels in the masters' favour. He married his children into noble families and invested heavily in rural land. He consolidated the legal control of Ghent over eastern Flanders and that of the 'Three Cities' over the entire county, and he made Ghent the informal master of Bruges and Ypres. His power began to wane after 1342, and in 1345 he was assassinated by personal enemies. Neither his rise nor his fall changed the governing institutions of the city. The extraordinary regime of captains was only ended when Ghent capitulated to the Flemish count in 1349. Several thousand persons were banished, most but not all of them clothworkers or textile merchants. For the next decade Ghent was ruled

---

48   Rotz, 'Urban uprisings', 218.

by a coalition of the count's allies, mainly the fullers, who resented the more prosperous weavers, fishmongers, shippers and butchers.[49]

The Paris rebellion of 1358

In 1357, with King John II held captive by the English, the government of Paris was seized by Etienne Marcel, provost of the merchants and purveyor of goods to the royal *argenterie*. Marcel's family's feuds in the city are also relevant: he was descended from royal officials on his mother's side, from moneychangers and drapers on his father's. His second wife was the daughter of Pierre des Essars, a businessman and moneylender of Rouen who had obtained a patent of nobility in 1320. Marcel alienated his in-laws in 1349 when he opted to take his wife's dowry rather than accepting the des Essars inheritance, which he considered too risky. Far from being a revolutionary, Marcel was leading the Paris militia for the king as late as the spring of 1356. But in January 1357 Marcel organised a general strike in response to the government's devaluation of the coin and summoned the population to take arms. A month later he organised a mass meeting and led several thousand people into the royal palace. The Dauphin was forced to wear the emblem of the provost of the merchants. But the prince escaped Paris and proclaimed himself regent. After disturbances in Arras, Toulouse, Rouen and Amiens, Marcel tried to gain support at an assembly of delegates of communes. He began a new city wall by enclosing most of the suburbs on the right bank of the Seine, later called the wall of Charles V. To prevent revolution Marcel put chains across the streets, had a twenty-four-hour guard circulating and closed the gates at night.

Marcel's movement was compromised by its association with the Jacquerie, the brief but bloody peasant rebellion of the summer of 1358, but the Parisians were not the only townspeople to join the Jacques. Amiens and Montdidier sent troops to help the peasants and razed nearby castles. In Laon and Amiens the hood worn by the rebels of Paris was adopted to show solidarity with them. A guild regime was installed at Amiens after the count of Saint-Pol seized the city for the king, but King Charles V restored the old order's privileges when disorders continued. Marcel only allied with the peasants after they threatened to blockade the consumer-city capital and cut Paris' contact with supporters of his rebellion in the northern towns, but this action tainted his regime irretrievably. His fate was sealed when King Charles the Bad of Navarre, whom Marcel had invited to Paris and made captain general as it became

---

49 Nicholas, *Medieval Flanders*, 217–24, 243, summarising Nicholas, *van Arteveldes*, 19–71.

clear that the Dauphin was hostile, invited English troops to occupy it. They were expelled in a riot. The issues, which were murky at best and were always political and military, were now lost in mob violence. Marcel was killed on 31 July in street fighting by a mob that feared the re-entry of the English; its leaders were his in-laws, the des Essars. His regime had no more lasting impact on the government of Paris than van Artevelde's did at Ghent.[50]

Rome

The theatrical rebellions of Cola di Rienzi at Rome were hardly typical, for their goal was to force the local aristocracy to permit the town lord to return. Rienzi was inspired by the political ideas of Petrarch. A public assembly in 1347 proclaimed him tribune with unlimited power. The Orsini and Colonna, the noble families whose feuds had upset the city for centuries, fled to their rural estates. Rienzi pursued criminals into noble immunities, occupied castles and punished former government officials for peculation. He imposed a special tax on the nobles and took away their tolls, which had been causing food prices to rise. Classically-inspired ceremonies culminated in his receipt of a crown on 15 August. But the nobles counterattacked, and Rienzi was ejected from Rome in riots in December. After lobbying for several years at the imperial and papal courts, where he received the title of senator, Rienzi re-entered Rome in 1355 with a German guard and arrested his leading opponents; but on 8 October the *popolo* set fire to the capital, and Rienzi was killed. Papal government was quickly restored.[51]

THE URBAN REBELLIONS OF THE FOURTEENTH CENTURY: THE SECOND PHASE

The most severe urban rebellions of the late Middle Ages occurred between 1370 and 1420. Millennarian doctrines accompanied some of them, as preachers inflamed the poor with visions of the equality of all before God. Yet most rioters were not poor; and despite a high incidence of poverty, high wages, low prices, and an increased volume of consumer goods meant that standards of living were undeniably higher for most in 1380 than their ancestors had known before 1348.[52]

---

50 Cazelles, 'Jacquerie', 77–9; Cazelles, *Paris*, 218–21, 283–7, 301–6, 310–44; Petit-Dutaillis, *French Communes*, 128–9; Mollat and Wolff, *Popular Revolutions*, 118–26.
51 Mollat and Wolff, *Popular Revolutions*, 98–104.
52 Mollat, *Poor*, 211.

The urban side of the English 'Peasants' Revolt' of 1381

Although the English 'Peasants' Revolt' of 1381 began as a tax rebellion and had its chief impact in the rural areas and the small towns, there was an urban component. The rebels occupied London briefly, helped by three aldermen from the food guilds, but the city government did not take the rebel side. Rebels returning from London destroyed the property of some burgesses at Canterbury. Personal rivalries had more impact on local revolts than ideology or institutions. The armourer Henry Bongay, a new man who had not penetrated the elite of officeholders, incited villagers outside Canterbury to make disturbances in the town. Residents of the monastic boroughs of St Albans and Bury St Edmunds used the troubles to extract concessions from the abbots.[53]

The disturbances of 1381 at York exacerbated existing conflicts between the partisans of the mayor Simon de Quixlay, and his predecessor, the mercer John de Gisburne, who had been expelled in a riot. Both sides distributed liveries to their party affiliates, and gang violence racked the city and environs through most of 1382. De Quixlay was re-elected in 1383, but Gisburne never held office again, although he continued to live in York. The fact that the city leaders before 1381 were tainted by involvement with the royal government, particularly as collectors of the hated poll taxes, helped their opponents. Thus the issue was less the size of the council or particular programmes than replacing incumbent officeholders with new people.[54]

The French tax rebellions, 1380–3

Royal taxation had increased substantially in France since the onset of war with England in 1337 and particularly since 1356. The wars had forced the French cities to build expensive fortifications, and their resources were strained to accommodate numerous refugees. In 1380 King Charles V on his deathbed abolished the *taille* (the direct tax) but not the *aides* (excises). The regents of his young successor reimposed the *taille* in January 1382, to take effect in March at a rate even higher than before. Revolts erupted in twenty-seven French cities and towns between 1380 and 1383. The issue in each case was taxation, and the result was the restriction of even the limited autonomy that the cities

---

53 Mollat and Wolff, *Popular Revolutions*, 184–208; Butcher, 'English urban society', 84–5, 106–10.
54 Dobson, 'Risings in York, Beverley and Scarborough', 119–30, 139–40.

involved had enjoyed. The disturbances evidently were not concerted, despite the similar grievances.[55]

The most famous uprisings were the revolt of the 'Maillotins' (mallet wielders) at Paris and the 'Harelle' at Rouen. Disturbances in Rouen began on 24 February 1382. The drapers were the largest single group involved, but it was a general rebellion. There was no programme except pillaging abbeys, churches and the homes of rich citizens. The royal government had restored order and executed the leaders by the end of March. The bells that had summoned the population to rebellion were removed from the belfry. Chains that had been used to bar the streets were removed, and the arms of burgesses taken to the royal castle. The city paid a heavy indemnity, and the king seized the local government.

Disorders in Paris were complicated by the false rumour that Charles V had abolished the *aides* as well as the *taille*. The provost of the merchants then demanded that the *aides* be abolished in fact. The king briefly acceded, then restored the *aides*. Riots erupted in November when the provost restored to their families some Jewish children whom the Christians had seized to baptise them. New disturbances began on 1 March 1382, a week after those in Rouen: a grocer refused to let the collector take the excise by seizing her fruit, and the incident escalated into a tax riot. The mob went to the new Châtelet, where lead mallets had been stored for use against the English, then opened the prison. While there were only two deaths in Rouen, there were thirty in Paris. Many master artisans and guild militias, comprehending the implications of the mass movement, fought the rebels. Resistance spread through Normandy and the Paris basin but was broken by the royal government.

To this point the French rebellions were over taxes, but they became linked to developments in Flanders in late 1382. Ghent had led a political rebellion against Count Louis of Male since 1379 and forced him into exile in 1382. Louis sought help in France, specifically from his son-in-law, Duke Philip of Burgundy. When the royal government levied an aid to help Louis against the Flemish cities, which the French now considered allies, new disturbances began in Rouen in August. The rebels at Paris swore oaths on mallets, which had become a symbol, not to pay the tax and to riot and murder the provost of the merchants. When the king returned from Flanders in January 1383, retaliation was brief and effective. One hundred leaders were executed. Paris lost its *échevinage*, seal and the office of provost of the merchants, which was joined to the provostship of Paris. Except for religious ceremonies, occupational guilds could only meet in the presence of the provost or his men.

---

55   Mollat, *Poor*, 212–13; Hilton, *English and French Towns*, 139.

Other cities in northern France that joined the rebellion lost heavily. Orléans was fined and its leaders arrested and some executed. No one could leave town for any reason, and those who had fled were ordered to return within three days or suffer banishment. Amiens lost its guild-based 'masters of the banners', subdivisions of the militia where ·the troubles had erupted. Their powers were given to the government of the town, which was under royal control. The magistracy could only be rotated with royal authorisation, which had to be sought separately each time. At Rouen there were executions, banishments with property confiscated, and fines to regain liberty. Charles VI seemed less inclined to pursue the matter at Rouen than did his local subordinates, who ignored two royal orders to cease confiscations in 1383. He remitted half of the indemnity that they imposed, but the city's finances were still heavily encumbered.[56]

The Flemish rebellion of 1379–85

A quarrel between Bruges and Ghent over canal rights precipitated a civil war that engulfed Flanders in the summer of 1379. By late 1381 the Flemish count had nearly closed the circle around his largest city. Although a substantial party in the city led by butchers and shippers wanted to sue for peace, a revolutionary party led by the weavers came to power, and Philip van Artevelde, James's youngest son, became captain. After using his first month in power to avenge his family's wrongs (see Chapter 8), van Artevelde galvanised the city into action, seized Bruges in a surprise attack in May, expelled the count, and allied with the English as the weavers had traditionally urged. The count appealed to the French, who in November slaughtered the Flemish army. Although some artisans of Ghent were implicated in the rebellion, dossiers of confiscated property show that the driving force behind the rebellion was defence of the city's commercial privileges. Although the weavers supported Philip van Artevelde, the influence of the textile guilds had been declining since the 1350s, and chroniclers state that his elevation to power was opposed by half the population. He made no institutional change in the city's government nor in the basis of representation on the councils. The memory of his father was important in his rise, but family interests rather than public policy were Philip's overriding concern. His and his father's rebellions were political, not social; and the

---

56 Discussion of the French rebellions of 1380–3 based on Mirot, *Insurrections urbaines*, 13, 40–1, 47–9, 76, 85, 90–1, 98–106, 149, 163–5, 196–205; Mollat and Wolff, *Popular Revolutions*, 167–76; Favier, *Paris 1380–1500*, 131–41; Petit-Dutaillis, *French Communes*, 128.

only economic motivation was the need to ensure supplies of wool from England and grain from France. Philip van Artevelde's cause had far more revolutionary consequences in France than in Flanders.[57]

The Ciompi uprising at Florence

Although the elite of Florence was more open after 1343 than before, the city's large industrial proletariat was suffering from the fluctuating demand for cloth. Real wages rose and grain prices were low, but many workers were not continuously employed. Political life remained chaotic, and the merchant elite was displaying deep fissures. During the 1360s the Guelf party, dominated by houses of both magnate and *popolano* extraction, began systematically to use Ghibelline ancestry as an excuse to keep unwelcome persons out of office. Some targets of party wrath were 'new men', but others were Guelfs of ancient lineage such as Salvestro dei Medici. The 'War of the Eight Saints' against the pope was popular, but a papal interdict limited the grain and English wool that could reach Florence. Violence began when the Guelf party instituted a reign of terror in the spring of 1378. On 1 May Salvestro dei Medici became standard-bearer of justice. He tried to moderate the proscriptions, but on 14 June the party captains accused a dyer and tanner of being Ghibelline. When Salvestro offered to resign on 18 June, the party hierarchy plotted to overthrow the regime. The war party used crowds of *popolani minuti* to political advantage. During the summer the clothworkers tried to escape the control of the wool guild, which had raised the matriculation fee in the spring, to raise wages and to gain rights in government.

The Ciompi [wool carders] violence began on 20 July. The *podestà*'s palace was seized, grain stocks plundered and the archives of the courts, the fiscal departments and the wool guild burned. A reform programme was elaborated on 21–22 July and presented to the priors in the name of the minor guilds and *popolo minuto* [lesser *popolo*]. The Ciompi wanted a guild of the *popolo minuto* to be created; some Guelfs to be rehabilitated; amnesty for those involved in the June disorders; a reform of the penal system; suspension of arrest for debt; and no forced loans for six months. They demanded cheap grain and production quotas on woollen cloth, and scrutinies for the *Signoria* open to all guilds, with guildsmen nominated by their districts. Only citizens who actually practised their trades could hold office. Relief from the gabelles was not a major part of the Ciompi programme, although they were unpopular, probably

---

57   Nicholas, *Medieval Flanders*, 227–31, summarising Nicholas, *van Arteveldes*, 120–87.

because they had stabilised after the 1360s, and the rates, although much higher than in the 1330s, were now considered customary.[58] The priors capitulated, and the wool carder Michele di Lando became standard-bearer of justice. The new government was actually a guild regime broadened by three new textile guilds (the Ciompi, dyers and doublet makers), all of them numerically large. Authority was vested in a *balia* recruited from the lesser guildsmen and shopkeepers, but not, as has been maintained, the unemployed. The three new guilds had 13,000 members, but barely one-sixth of them met the property qualification for office.

The *balia* ruled for six weeks but faced mounting difficulties. Shops were still not reopening in August, as employers fled to the *contado*. Although grain prices were stable and no scarcity can be demonstrated, by 9 August the *balia* had to order that all grain owned in the *contado* by Florentines should be brought into the city, and on 30 August ordered free distribution of grain to the indigent. A revision of the *estimo* was ordered in late August, and a forced loan was declared, violating the regime's pledge. In late August the *popolo minuto* formed its own organisation at a mass meeting, chose eight 'Saints of the People of God' as leaders and marched on the *Signoria*. They claimed that Salvestro dei Medici and Michele di Lando had betrayed then and demanded a moratorium on debts and liquidation of the public debt. On 31 August the other guilds ejected the radicals from government. The wool merchants closed their shops to prevent the rebels from working. The old order was restored; dei Medici and di Lando were exiled, although they had abandoned the rebels, and 160 were executed during the next five years. On 2 September 1378 the 'Eight Guards' became a police force and were formally joined to the *Signoria* in 1382. The Ciompi guild was suppressed immediately, and the dyers and doublet makers were ended in 1382.

The Ciompi rebellion was the work of the *popolo minuto*, a group consisting of the less skilled clothworkers, including apprentices and journeymen in all trades and shop owners in the less prestigious crafts, such as burlers (cloth finishers) and shearers; journeymen, apprentices and assistants in other craft guilds, and the poorest craftsmen in such low-status occupations as carpentry; menials such as carters and peddlers; and the marginal population of vagabonds, beggars, prostitutes and criminals. These groups were too diverse and unorganised to be generally effective politically, although their capacity for violence made them dangerous. Out-of-power factions could and in 1397, 1400 and 1412 did get elements of the *popolo minuto* to riot.[59] Although this was the most intellectually

---

58 De la Roncière, 'Indirect taxes at Florence', 190–2.
59 Analysis of Brucker, 'Florentine popolo minuto', 156–7, 170–2, 177.

radical and agenda-driven urban revolt of the fourteenth century, most of the rebels were not ordinary labourers, but were small shopkeepers, some with investments in the public debt, and were led by aristocrats such as Salvestro dei Medici. Michele di Lando was exiled to Volterra, became captain of the *popolo*, and died a wealthy wool merchant of Modena. Even the common name for the uprising is inaccurate, for the majority of the 'Ciompi' rebels seem to have come from the building trades rather than textiles.[60]

Political life in Florence after 1378 disintegrated into factions. After 1382 the basis of service remained guild affiliation, but the oligarchs controlled actual nomination and selection more tightly. *Balie* frequently usurped the power of the priors and councils. Fewer guildsmen passed the scrutiny in 1382 than before 1378. Numerous 'new' men were admitted in 1382, but their families quickly became part of the 'establishment', and the choices came from an increasingly narrow group.[61]

The rebellious merchant oligarchy of London

The great rebellions of the 1380s did little to alter the governing institutions of the cities. Richard II's London illustrates how most of the strife was caused by rivalries within the merchant elites. The oligarchy came mainly from five misteries (guilds): vintners, grocers, mercers, goldsmiths and fishmongers, who had the political power in London that the butchers had in most continental cities. The fact that the leaders vying for power came from guilds of fishmongers and grocers has led some to see 'class conflicts' over food between the merchants and the small retailers and craftsmen, who were led by the draper John of Northampton. In fact the London guilds were so diverse that the real issue was wool policy, not the price of food.

The rivalry of John of Northampton and the grocer Nicholas Brembre seems to have been due to personal dislike, which over time led to different political factions supporting the two. Brembre had considerable real property and like most of the London aristocracy loaned money to the king. As a grocer, he traded iron, wine, woad and especially wool. The grocers firmly supported the Calais wool staple and resented the privileges that Edward III had given to foreigners to trade in the realm. Northampton's wealth also came mainly from real property, especially in Dowgate Ward, where he was alderman. He acquired most of it by

60 Summary of events based on Mollat and Wolff, *Popular Revolutions*, 133–6, 145–60; Brucker, *Civic World*, 39–46; Brucker, *Renaissance Florence*, 67; Mackenney, *Tradesmen and Traders*, 30–1; Cohn, 'Florentine insurrections', 148–51.
61 Najemy, *Corporatism and Consensus*, 226–7, 246, 263–300.

marrying a rich widow. He was thus less affluent than Brembre and loaned much less to the crown. The fishmongers and grocers held over half the aldermanic seats in the 1370s and they were entering the wool trade, which was the basis of prosperity of the drapers, who were losing council seats. The drapers' affluence was based on their monopoly of cloth sales in the city and control of the import of Flemish cloth into England. They had no interest in the Calais staple and actually tried to evade it. Since Flemish cloth exports were declining, the drapers needed to control the market in English cloth by getting the court of aldermen to pass legislation that favoured them. The drapers had been trying to gain control over the clothmaking crafts of London in the 1360s, but in 1364 the crown gave the fullers and weavers the right to elect their own surveyors. Thus the drapers focused on controlling the Common Council of London.[62]

The Common Council had been elected by ward since 1319. Northampton's group wanted election by mistery, which would limit the number of grocers and fishmongers, and he persuaded the 'Good Parliament' of 1376 to make this change. When John of Gaunt regained control after Edward III's death, the Common Council purged Northampton's allies. The Stapler government under Brembre as mayor fixed ward boundaries so that fishmongers and grocers would be returned. In fact, while some small trades were not represented when elections were held by wards, others were excluded when election was by mistery; the two modes of election were equally undemocratic in practice. The pool of candidates was affected so minimally that in 1384 the mayor ended the interval of a year between terms of service as an alderman, and annual elections were even abolished in 1394.

Just as the Ciompi rebels tried to keep grain prices low in Florence in 1378, much of the agitation in London in the 1370s and 1380s was directed against the fishmongers. John of Northampton returned to power in 1381 with a campaign accusing the fishmongers of keeping food prices high. Northampton's propaganda also included the grocers as food merchants, but they were not 'grocers' in the modern sense; rather, they were 'grossers' who controlled goods that were weighed at the great beam, notably spices, dyes and wool. The royal government secured Northampton's re-election in 1382, probably because his attack on the

---

62 The drapers of Barcelona are similar in this respect to those of London. Although most were small operators in the early fourteenth century, they had considerable capital by 1400. They not only sold locally-produced cloth but also imported foreign cloth, which they bought undressed and had prepared for re-export at Barcelona. Beginning as promotors of local Barcelona industry, they were competing with it by the mid-fifteenth century through imports, and they opposed the protectionism that the cloth preparers were demanding. Carrère, *Barcelone*, 513–22.

fishmongers was so popular that the king did not want to alienate London. The fishmongers were being sued in Parliament at the time for monopolising the sale of fish to keep the price high, refusing to let pleas concerning their mistery be handled except in their guild court, and falsifying the size of baskets in which fish were sold. After Parliament forbade all victuallers to hold judicial office in any city or town – not only London – and opened wholesale and retail trade in food to all foreigners who were not enemies of the king, the king dropped John of Northampton in 1383. The statute was repealed during Brembre's mayoralty in 1388, but the fishmongers were even then put specifically under the authority of the city government. Brembre was killed by the 'Merciless Parliament' because he supported the king; the group that he represented continued to control London. In 1392 Richard II used the allegation that city officials were corrupt as a pretext for seizing the government, but the real reason was that London supported his opponents. The city only regained its liberties in the next reign.[63]

Crafts and politics in the German cities

Several German cities had craft-based rebellions in the 1370s and 1380s. As in France, the issues were high taxes and official corruption. In the late fourteenth and fifteenth centuries the butchers gained considerable power in many cities. They were the spokesmen of the crafts of Hamburg in requesting a tax reduction in 1374. They were deeply involved in a rebellion against the merchant oligarchy at Lübeck in 1384. Butchers held their stalls in the Meat Hall for life, but the properties were owned by the city, and the council selected the new stallholder when a butcher died. In 1384 the butchers, led by Heinrich Paternostermaker, the son of a rich exporter of amber rosaries, plotted to seize the city hall, but the council discovered it. The butchers' guild was dissolved and nineteen were executed. This rising has been used as an example of rebellion by downwardly mobile craftsmen, but in fact the butchers and their allies were well-to-do artisans and merchants.[64]

Given that the crafts had their own aristocracies, the older view that the efforts of the German guilds to enter city governments were a revolutionary movement of artisans against the lineages has been weakened seriously. A decade of conflict at Brunswick ended in 1386, when seats

---

63 Discussion based on Bird, *Turbulent London*, 1–17, 38–41, 63–84, 90, 99–104, 110–12, as recently modified by Nightingale, 'Capitalists, crafts', 5–7, 11–14, 17–22, 25–6, 33; Nightingale, *Medieval Mercantile Community*, 205–6, 228–91.
64 Mollat and Wolff, *Popular Revolutions*, 209–10; Rotz, 'Urban uprisings', 219–26; Gleba, *Gemeinde*, 201–2.

on the council were allotted to each of the city's five districts (*Weichbilde*) and occupational groups. Yet, when actual service on the council is considered rather than apportionment of seats per group, the old lineages still outweighed the crafts. The rebels were persons of substance, not the poor. The only distinction was one found elsewhere: the older elite was more oriented toward landholding, the new one more toward trade and finance.[65] The motif of old versus new money rather than crafts versus merchants or merchants versus landowners also appears at Constance. Agitation began in 1370 in a feud of several patricians who had been excluded from the council by their rivals. The guilds joined the dissatisfied aristocrats to break the monopoly of the inner circle. In a second rising in 1389 the textile wholesalers, mercers and wine merchants were ejected from the council and allied with the lineages.[66]

Cologne had escaped the guild agitation that had gripped most cities of its size after 1270. It was governed by its *Schöffen*, a Great Council, and the Rich Club. The weavers briefly ended this regime in 1370, installing a Great Council of fifty members who were chosen from the guilds rather than from parishes as previously. However, the lineages returned the next year, and the Great Council was reduced to thirty-one merchants, with no representation for the guilds. But the patricians' new regime was overthrown in 1396 by an alliance of the weavers, some other crafts and the newer merchant families who were outside the elite. A single council of forty-nine members was elected from twenty-two *Gaffeln*, which were composite political units. The merchants originally had four *Gaffeln*, later raised to five, while the approximately forty craft organisations were grouped into the others. The merchant *Gaffeln* were arranged by geographical area within the city, while the crafts were arranged by occupation, incorporating all persons in the same trade or groups of trades throughout the city. Eleven *Gaffeln* chose two councillors each, the weavers four, while ten chose one each. These thirty-six councillors elected the other thirteen. During the fifteenth century the link between *Gaffel* membership and occupation became even more tenuous. Patricians could enrol in the guilds, and the council continued to have a largely aristocratic cast. Certain groups were ineligible for election: the archbishop's *Schöffen*, grain and salt measurers, city officials, and market officials such as moneychangers, brokers and innkeepers. The council had almost total power except for blood justice; but it could only conclude alliances, declare war, sell annuity rents and contract expenses of more than 1,000 Gulden in conjunction with the Forty-Four,

---

65   Mörke, 'Beispiel der Stadt Braunschweig', 149.
66   Bechtold, *Zunftbürgerschaft und Patriziat*, 130–1.

consisting of two persons chosen yearly from each *Gaffel*. The council frequently consulted the Forty-Four on other matters, particularly in making guild regulations. As happened in London, Cologne was thus dominated by merchants under the guise of a craft regime, but the basis for election to the city council was professional affiliation rather than district of residence.[67]

The example of Cologne seems to have inspired guild agitation over council membership elsewhere. After 1396 the burgomaster and council of Vienna, which had previously been chosen by the Inner Council, were elected by the entire citizenry. The landowners, merchants and artisans each chose six of the eighteen councillors. Yet few craftsmen served on the council, evidently because of the demands on their time. Trier was governed after 1365 by a council of twenty-four, consisting of the ten *Schöffen*, four representatives of the New St Jacob Brotherhood and ten from the four greater guilds (weavers, butchers, bakers and tanners). The *Schöffen* families continued to dominate the city, and in 1396, exactly one week after the rule of the lineages was ended in Cologne, a new regime gave the greater guilds the same ten seats, but they were joined by two each from the furriers, mercers, tailors and coopers and one smith, shipper, carpenter, roofer and stonemason. Although the size of the council was unchanged, the *Schöffen* had to enrol in a guild to sit on it.[68]

THE FIFTEENTH-CENTURY REBELLIONS

Urban rebellions continued in the fifteenth century, but except in Paris they were more peaceful than the fourteenth-century disturbances. Virtually all had political or factional rather than economic causes.

Germany

The Hanse cities were controlled by merchants who were not even nominally enrolled in craft organisations. Others German centres were under merchant control, but through regimes based on guilds that were dominated internally by merchants. A third type divided power between the older landowning families and merchants who were ostensibly grouped into trade guilds. Yet the Hanse cities had relatively broad

---

67 Huiskes, *Beschlüsse Köln*, xi–xix; Howell, *Women, Production, and Patriarchy*, 105–7; Irsigler, *Wirtschaftliche Stellung Köln*, 258; Maschke, *Städte und Menschen*, 227.
68 Csendes, 'Stadtherr und bürgerliche Führungsschicht', 254; Huiskes, *Beschlüsse Köln*, xxvi; Matheus, *Trier*, 93–7, 104–15, 133, 154.

oligarchies; at least three-quarters of the political opposition came from the top quarter of the taxable population. The only common element in the disturbances there was the lack of mass participation.[69]

The government of Lübeck was heavily in debt by 1403, when the brewers, as leaders of the trades, summoned a guild assembly that did not initially include merchants. They demanded written accounts and a moratorium on new taxes. In 1406 the 'community' (*Gemeinde*, a term that in the German cities meant a group similar to the *popolo* in Italy)[70] established a committee of sixty to function alongside the council to control finances. The conflict worsened when fifteen council members left the city in 1408. They would be called the 'old council' for the next eight years. The Sixty remained bound to the community; they could not act independently without new instructions. After the Sixty divided the city into four districts, each under a captain, similar committees appeared in Rostock and Wismar in 1409 and in Hamburg in 1410. But the exiles had Lübeck placed under the imperial ban and excluded from meetings of the Hanse. When the Danes began imprisoning merchants of Lübeck in 1416, the Sixty had to capitulate. By 1417 the Hanse had forced the rival councils of Rostock, Wismar and Hamburg to disband.

The result was orderly. The councils agreed to obtain the consent of the citizenry on 'major matters' and to keep the city's records in German rather than Latin. Each year an assembly was to choose six electors from the merchants and rentiers and six from the brewers and other artisans. These twelve chose twelve councillors, who were also to be divided evenly between the two colleges. The old council became a sort of honorary outer council. But the artisan element is deceptive. Only a few councillors were genuine craftsmen, and they were rich. Fourteen of the ninety-four whose names survive were in the aristocratic Circle Society, and fifty-two were merchants. Twenty-five were artisans but from distinguished trades that included five brewers, four goldsmiths and two amberworkers. Several were relatives of former council members.[71]

Disturbances in other German cities led to greater participation by guildsmen, although no more than at Lübeck did this mean genuine craftsmen. After the elite that had ruled Mainz since 1333 was narrowed

69   Rotz, 'Urban uprisings', 231–2.
70   For example, the community of Munich consisted only of citizens who owned a house or land or paid a substantial tax of half a pound. Persons who participated in community meetings without satisfying these qualifications were punished. Gleba, *Gemeinde*, 149–51.
71   Gleba, *Gemeinde*, 204–23; Maschke, *Städte und Menschen*, 183–4; Rotz, 'Urban uprisings', 227–30.

further in 1411 by a requirement that all newly elected councillors should pay 50 gulden, the guilds barred the councillors who had purported to represent them from the guild assemblies and presented an agenda to the council. Their demands were essentially political, not social or economic. All money was to be used for the benefit of the community. All citizens, including councillors, were subject to the town watch. Weighty matters such as war and taxes had to be approved by the whole community and guilds. The guilds' demands were not met, and the crafts continued to negotiate as a body against their own representatives, the 'new council'. Some lineages left Mainz, fearful of being forced to pay the municipal debt. More agitation in 1428–9 installed a Council of Thirty-Five, chosen by cooption, not through the guilds; but although the elections in 1429 produced seven councillors from the lineages against twenty-eight from the guilds, all but one of the guildsmen were from the upper guild hierarchy. In 1437 a council of twenty-eight, half each from the lineages and the community, replaced the Thirty-Five. Two burgomasters appointed all other officers and held keys to the gates and bells. Yet so many lineages had left the city since 1411 that they had trouble finding enough persons to fill their guaranteed seats on the council. Thus they obtained financial guarantees, including liability for only part of the city debt and exemption from the obligation to join a guild, which had been a major demand of the trades. The citizen members of the council had to be guildsmen. This was changed in 1444 to a complex electoral arrangement in which the lineages were excluded completely from the council. When vacancies occurred, each guild was to nominate one councillor, but the remaining members of the council would choose the successor. No guild or group of guilds had the right to seats on the council.[72]

Metz and Brussels

In 1405 a revolution started in parish assemblies led by butchers briefly ended the old order of lineage control at Metz. Most patricians left the city. The old institutions were kept at first, with patricians being replaced with burgesses as their terms expired, but in November the government was reorganised. The old magistracies were retained, including the Thirteen, but twenty-one *élus* (one per parish) were chosen to participate in important decisions and to control justice and finance. Counts were to be chosen in the parishes, and members of the six lineages were ineligible. The most radical measure was to annul sales from

---

72 Gleba, *Gemeinde*, 52–83.

the domain of the city and all leases of public revenue during the previous thirty years. But the new regime fell on 14 May 1406 when a patrician who had stayed inside opened the gates to those who had left. The *élus* were suppressed, and the old order was restored.[73]

The changes at Brussels were permanent but slight. While the presence of a princely court usually stimulated a city's economy, it could also involve its leaders in palace intrigues. Some *échevins* of Brussels held offices from the duke and city simultaneously until the practice was forbidden in 1418. The lineages that controlled the city pursued vicious vendettas. In 1421 a guild insurrection led by the duke's younger brother and rival reformed the government to include the guilds in a subordinate role. They were grouped into nine 'nations' that rotated city offices by a regular scheme. The seven *échevin* posts were still reserved for the lineages. They chose six 'councillors' from the nations from a list submitted by the *jurés* of the guilds. Each group chose a burgomaster and two receivers. The *jurés* became a second consultative body, but they could only meet in the presence of the burgomasters and six councillors of the nations. Brussels thus had three 'members': the law, consisting of the councillors, *échevins*, burgomasters and receivers; the guild *jurés*; and the chiefs of the ten militia captaincies into which the city was divided.[74]

Paris

The bloodiest urban disorders of the fifteenth century occurred in Paris. Paris' truncated city government had been suppressed in 1383. The royal court provided much of Paris's prosperity, but the chaos surrounding King Charles VI's descent into madness split the city. Disorder mounted from the 1390s, as retainers of the dukes of Orléans and particularly Burgundy flouted the legal conventions of the city.[75] Duke John 'the Fearless' of Burgundy controlled Paris between 1411 and 1413 with the militia of the butchers' guild, a hereditary group that was outside the older merchant power structure. In 1413 the king yielded to agitation and dismissed several officials, but disorders continued. Riots tore the city between April and July, as the butcher Caboche ruled the city. After he fled, the restored government violated a promised amnesty and took out its rage on the butchers and their Burgundian allies. Suspicions were so rampant by 1417 that a statute required bridegrooms to pay for

73 Schneider, *Metz*, 493–501.
74 Martens, *Histoire de Bruxelles*, 142–7; Favresse, *Régime démocratique à Bruxelles*, 161–284.
75 Prevenier, 'Violence against women', 269–76.

sergeants at their nuptials to make sure 'that nobody plots anything'. Although the Orléanists ruled the city itself, the Burgundians still controlled the environs. As the English closed in on Paris, the Burgundians were let in through a gate on the night of 28–29 May 1418. The Dauphin withdrew, and six hundred of his adherents were killed. There were more massacres in August. The Burgundians gave tokens to the leaders of their constabularies to distribute to known partisans in their jurisdictions. They were then to go about asking for tokens. Those who could not produce them were to be killed. This was blind violence, without political programme. But then one of the most serious plagues of the fifteenth century struck the city, and in 1419 the English occupation restored order to the depopulated capital. The carnage may have cost as many as two thousand lives.[76]

Barcelona

Barcelona's generally peaceful political party troubles have been misinterpreted as economic or social in character. Five councillors who functioned as an executive, chosen from the estate of *honrats* (patrician-rentiers), shared power with a council of one hundred *jurés*. From 1387 four estates were represented in the Council of One Hundred: *honrats*, merchants, *artistes* (persons from the liberal arts and trades requiring a large capital) and artisans in the sense of handworker. A council of thirty, chosen from the full Council of One Hundred and rotated every three months, handled most ordinary business. Conflicts erupted in 1433. The Biga (beams) party was composed mainly of the *honrat* families that had ruled the city since the thirteenth century, and their allies, who included some craftsmen and numerous lawyers. The only common bond of adherents of the Busca (thorns) party was opposition to the Biga. They included both radical and moderate elements. In 1433 the Consul of the Sea refused to march behind the *honrats* in a procession, and most of the Council of One Hundred sided with him. For the next twenty years the Biga tried to govern with minimal involvement of either deliberative council, for they had the majority of the executive councillors. A temporary Busca victory in 1453 meant monetary devaluation and general trade growth, but the Biga returned in 1462, joined now by the clothworkers who also wanted cloth imports restricted. Some *honrats* were involved in importing foreign textiles, while others were not and joined the Busca because they wanted industrial

76 Favier, *Paris 1380–1500*, 149–71; *Journal Paris*, 122–3.

protectionism. Family alliances and neighbourhood bonds transcended economic lines in determining political affiliations.[77]

CITY GOVERNMENT AND CITY COUNCILS UNDER CRAFT CONTROL, c. 1370–c. 1500

Urban government and the composition of city councils thus changed surprisingly little as a direct result of the revolutionary agitation. In some places the excesses of the rebels so frightened the middle class that the authorities had little trouble in restoring the old regime. In others the merchant-dominated crafts gained more representation on the city councils, but often they were still outweighed by the older lineages. Even where this was not the case, the limited victory of this merchant group amounted to power-sharing within the elite between older and newer families. The political position and representation of persons who actually practised a craft were scarcely altered by the outcome of the revolutionary movements.

This is particularly true in France, where the 'good towns' were relatively unaffected by guild agitation. Perhaps because most of them amounted to large market towns with little industry, they lacked the degree of occupational differentiation found elsewhere. The craft guilds had little power except in northernmost France, in the textile centres that were influenced by or dependent on the Flemish market. Money-changers and goldsmiths were powerful at Beauvais, woad merchants at Amiens. At Abbeville 'woad mayors' set fines for industrial infractions and were present when the entire population filed past the assembled *échevins* and swore to pay their taxes. Sixty-four guild chiefs, called 'mayors with banners' – four for each of sixteen crafts – also joined the mayor and *échevins* in tax collection.[78] General assemblies were more important in the French cities than in Germany, but their real power declined in the fifteenth century in the face of royal involvement in municipal affairs. At Rouen the assembly, usually with between 150 and 400 persons in attendance, proposed candidates for office to the bailiff, most of them from old families. The assembly heard royal letters read, nominated councillors, voted taxes, and discussed municipal affairs.[79]

Most French cities welcomed royal control. Many functions of their ancient *échevinages* were taken over by royal officials. After the tax

77 Carrère, *Barcelone*, 687–96, 748–52, 771; MacKay, *Spain*, 182–3; Heers, *Parties and Political Life*, 235–43.
78 Petit-Dutaillis, *French Communes*, 107.
79 Desportes, *Reims*, 651–60; Mollat, *Histoire de Rouen*, 123–4.

rebellions of 1380–3 most French cities were governed by tightly constituted oligarchies, usually of lawyers and officeholders and less often of
merchants than in France's neighbours. Rarely did occupational guilds
have guaranteed seats on a French city council. Tours, for example, experienced none of the jurisdictional conflicts between *échevins* and royal
officers that are found in the northern French cities. From 1356 it and
most 'good towns' of the Loire valley developed administrations under
élus and syndics. The number of *élus* declined from six to three, with
each division of this composite settlement (Tours, Chateauneuf and City
(the area within the late Roman fortification)) having its own officials
until after 1385. By 1389 the two *élus* chosen by the laity had supplanted
the larger group and become a permanent administration, representing
the whole community, including the clergy. The only organ superior
to them was the general assembly, which consisted of about forty persons in most years and never more than one hundred. This body also
nominated the receiver and minor officers. The *élus* were in fact coopted,
but after 1449 one was a merchant and the other a barrister. There were
no representatives of guilds as such. The city government maintained
walls, bridges, roads and quays, but not police, and they were always
under royal captains and bailiffs, as was true of most 'good towns'. Only
the provost and officers of the bailiwick could legislate, but most of
them were from great city families who could represent Tours' interests
effectively with the bailiff. Thus, although most 'good towns' had little
administrative autonomy in theory, their domination of the bailiwick
gave them considerable real power.[80]

Outside France and England, most large cities of the north were moving toward a regime in which certain guilds or groups of guilds were
guaranteed seats on the city councils. The ossified guild regimes that are
associated with the late Middle Ages thus are features of the second stage
of the guilds' gaining political power, not of the so-called 'guild revolutions' of the early fourteenth century. Although most offices were controlled by an elite of merchants who were guild members, the rigidity
of the rotation schemes meant that a few craftsmen were able to serve,
but only in cities with a strong industrial base. Realising the political power that could come from trading from within a guild, in 1393
Metz prohibited the wine trade to anyone who did not *own* – not rent
– at least 3 *journaux* of vineyard and have two horses worth 20 florins
each. This ordinance was directed at the butchers, leatherworkers, chandlers, spice dealers and even barbers, in whose shops wine was sold.[81]

80 Chevalier, *Tours*, 82–95.
81 Schneider, *Metz*, 492.

Enforced rotation and restriction of the elite

No medieval city council was chosen directly by the people. They were picked by electoral colleges or by lot from bags or lists of eligible persons. The election of the council of Osnabrück was described in 1348: when the bell was sounded, the sixteen aldermen of the previous year went before the 'commonalty' and threw three dice. This procedure enabled them to choose two electors, who would swear to choose sixteen other electors, with each district of the city having a fixed number. The sixteen chose yet another sixteen electors on the same geographical basis, and this group in turn chose the sixteen new aldermen, likewise by district.[82] The repeated choices of different electors served the same function as the scrutiny in the Italian cities: it excluded persons who were considered undesirable by the previous council.

The basis of eligibility for the council was either territorial divisions such as quarter or ward, or socioprofessional groups called by various names ('tribes' in Alsace, 'members' in Flanders, 'ladders' in Languedoc, 'estates' in the cities of the Rhône). The *Gaffeln* of Cologne were also composite guilds that were constructed broadly along occupational lines. The tripartite division of political society was common everywhere. The citizenry of Valencia was divided into three 'hands': the patriciate was the 'major hand'. The 'middle hand' included merchants, notaries and masters of honourable guilds, while the masters in less prestigious guilds and the craftsmen were the 'minor hand'.[83] A royal arbitration at Lynn in 1412 was accepted by twenty-three 'powerful', eighty-one 'middle class' and fifty 'lower class who did not enjoy the freedom of the borough'.[84]

The earliest city councils, insofar as they were not chosen by cooption, were usually named by parish or other geographical district, but there is a movement away from this towards nomination by guilds or members (groups of guilds) in the late Middle Ages. Although the role of the guilds in the major Italian cities is justly famous, they played no part in political life in the smaller Italian centres; the elders of Lucca, for example, were chosen from geographical 'thirds' without regard to their occupation.[85] In some cities, most conspicuously London and Norwich, the issue of whether guild affiliation or district of residence would constitute the basis of composition of the city council was divisive. A motion was passed by the assembly of Norwich in 1369 to change the method of choosing the bailiffs, treasurers and members of the Council

---

82 Keutgen, *Urkunden*, no. 171, pp. 229–30.
83 Guiral-Hadziiossif, *Valence*, 394.
84 Owen, *Making of King's Lynn*, 391–3.
85 Meek, *Lucca 1369–1400*, 185.

of Twenty-Four from ward electors to guaranteeing representation for the crafts. It was never implemented, however, evidently foundering on the opposition of commoners who felt that they had more political voice in the wards than through the aristocratic guilds.[86]

Some cities combined parish and occupational representation. In Florence the politically recognised guilds rotated offices but with a guarantee of two priors per quarter. At Valencia elections to the council were held twice a year on the basis of district and professional affiliation combined. Four councillors for each of the twelve parishes were chosen on Quinquagesima, four per guild on Pentecost. By the end of the fifteenth century this meant 160 councillors. In addition, there were four jurist councillors, six knight councillors for the city and two knights for the towns of the municipal territory. The executive consisted of six *jurats*, including two nobles after 1329, who were named by the king from a slate presented by the council. Ostensibly to keep the same families from monopolising elections, Valencia switched in 1412 to choosing the parish councillors by a complex system of lot through an electoral college of thirty. In 1418 the king limited eligibility to married men aged at least twenty-five who had resided continuously in Valencia for at least twenty years. The executive was no longer to be chosen by the outgoing *jurats*, but from a list of candidates who were chosen with the agreement of the king's representative. Re-election to office was permitted from 1418. Thus Valencia was governed by a tight family-based oligarchy between 1418 and 1525. Craftspeople could serve on the councils, but not as *jurats*, and they served as individuals, not as members of their corporations.[87]

Even when the guilds were composites, it was rare for a single craft organisation, as opposed to a merchant guild, to control a city government. They were more successful when large groups were joined into members or scales. Ghent came as close as any medieval city to control by a single guild, the weavers, but they only managed it by allying with the 'Small Guilds'. A text of 1340 uses the term 'members' for the weavers, fullers and Small Guilds, which then shared power. After 1361 the twenty-six seats on the two boards of aldermen were apportioned among three political members: five numbered seats per bench for the weavers and the lesser clothmaking trades that were their dependants; five for the fifty-nine Small Guilds, all of them except the shippers engaged in small-scale local merchandising and service occupations; and three for the landowners. Each member had an overdean, an official

---

86 McRee, 'Peacemaking', 838–9.
87 Guiral-Hadziiossif, *Valence*, 394–5, 426–9.

of considerable political influence, in addition to the deans of the individual guilds that joined to form a single political member. Within the Small Guilds some large and powerful trades such as the shippers, butchers and brewers had seats guaranteed. Others rotated by groups, such as the six construction trades, which were called collectively the 'Guilds of the Square'. Ghent also had a Great Council, consisting of the deans of the individual Small Guilds and dependent textile trades, ten landowners, and the overdeans of the Small Guilds and the weavers. It was an important check on the aldermen in the fifteenth century. Voting was by political member. By 1369 Ghent had a three-person receivership, one for each member. The three members even divided clerkships and positions on the police force. Most of the members did not change composition after their initial formation. Thus in the fifteenth century occupational groups with growing markets and numbers that had not been strong in the mid-fourteenth often found themselves without a political voice.

The other Flemish and eastern Low Country cities had similar arrangements. Dinant, which was as famous for copper work as Ghent and Ypres were for woollens, had three members after 1348: landowners, coppersmiths and nine 'common' guilds. The landowners and coppersmiths each had nine *jurés* on the council, while the commons had twelve. The landowners always chose the *échevins*. Ypres had four members: four crafts were joined to the landowners, while the fullers were a separate member. Bruges had nine, seven of them consisting of trades that at Ghent were linked in the member of the Small Guilds; for Bruges, with a more diversified economy than Ghent, was less dominated than the larger city by textiles and the weavers.[88]

The changes in government after the 1360s thus accompanied the move to oblige workers in trades that enjoyed political privileges to enrol in the guilds. Within the guilds a wealthy elite was developing that exercised power largely independently of the membership at large.[89] The genuine crafts were sometimes strongly represented in councils and offices immediately after a revolution, then declined in favour of richer persons, as old families returned and new ones were coopted and intermarried into the elite.

Through the mid-fourteenth century most guilds linked persons of the same or similar socioeconomic level or orientation. Their political role was secondary. This was changing as more cities based representation on

---

88 Nicholas, *Medieval Flanders*, 243–4, 309, 373; Nicholas, *Metamorphosis*, 5–10; van Uytven, 'Stadsgeschiedenis', 234–5; Boone, *Gent en de Bourgondische hertogen*, 33–48.
89 Schulz, *Handwerksgesellen und Lohnarbeiter*, 27.

the council on guild affiliation. The guilds jockeyed for power. When individual or composite guilds obtained recognition, they guarded their privileges ferociously and excluded from power those who were too small to organise at the time the formal guild structure was cast in stone. Although 196 non-textile trades have been identified in Ghent, only fifty-three of them were in the political member of the Small Guilds; the rest were excluded from the government.[90] In the smaller centres more effort was made than in the larger cities to enrol every citizen in a guild. At Überlingen, which had only seven recognised guilds, the guild masters had the duty of assigning new citizens to one of them, depending on their professions.[91]

As the guilds became more closed to outsiders, city councils whose members were chosen by a rigid application of guild rights to certain seats became even more impenetrable than the thirteenth-century patriciates had been. Some cities applied the break that was required between terms in office to close relatives as well as the individual, but this was commoner in Italy than in the north. Even in the thirteenth century the French jurist Philippe de Beaumanoir noted complaints that the town elites became self-perpetuating because 'some of them are mayor or assessor or treasurer one year, and the next year they have their brothers or their nephews or their near relatives appointed, so that for ten or twelve years all the rich have the administrative positions of the towns and afterwards when the common people want to have an accounting they defend themselves by saying that they have given an accounting to each other'.[92] In the fifteenth century the tendency for magistrates to return to office and for family members to succeed one another was accentuated as the distance between the council and the rest of the citizens widened. Between 1360 and 1369, of the thirty councillors chosen annually at Speyer, 23.8 per cent were chosen only once and 15.4 per cent twice, the other 60.8 per cent were chosen three times or more. Between 1470 and 1502 the number chosen three or more times had risen to 73.6 per cent; and the group was more exclusive in the fifteenth century, since the council was reduced in 1432 from thirty to twenty-four members.[93]

The requirement that councillors be chosen from specific members or guilds entailed a broader rotation in the Flemish cities, but the raw numbers conceal important distinctions. More than one-third of the councillors of Ghent of the fifteenth century served only once, and

90 Nicholas, *Medieval Flanders*, 309.
91 Eitel, *Oberschwäbischen Reichsstädte*, 34.
92 Beaumanoir, *Coutumes de Beauvaisis*, 545.
93 Maschke, *Städte und Menschen*, 132–5.

two-thirds held no more than three positions; but the third who served more than three years held two-thirds of the positions, and the 17 per cent who served more than five years held 44.9 per cent of the offices.[94] The councils of Lübeck had 152 members from 104 families between 1300 and 1408, 130 members from ninety-four families between 1416 and 1530, a statistically insignificant difference. The ruling group always consisted of between forty and fifty extended families or 120 to 150 nuclear families; but it was not static, for some 20 per cent per generation died out or left the city.[95] The oligarchical tendency was even stronger with burgomasters than with the councils. Between 1452 and 1519 only seventeen persons were burgomasters of Trier; the weaver Heinric Ecken served eight times.[96]

The numbers in the ruling group varied but had three characteristics everywhere: wealth, antiquity of lineage and 'maturity'. Avignon required a fortune of 1,000 florins in immovable property for council membership. Becoming a *jurat* of Bordeaux required an income of 1,000 livres or 200 livres in annuity rents; in some years this equalled one-seventh of the entire income of the commune. The *échevins* of Valenciennes had to own a horse. Property qualifications were just as high in Italy. To be eligible for the scrutiny that would choose the priors, the 'good men' who advised them and the standard-bearers of justice of Florence, the candidate had to be a *popolano*, enrolled in a trade organisation but not actually practising the craft, and from about 1406 they had to own shares of the public debt.[97] Paris, Lille, Le Puy and Lyon required native birth for membership of the council, but this was hard to enforce in view of the tumults and mobility of the age. Other options included residence for a specified number of years or marriage to a native woman. Tax liability was critical. Toulouse required five years on the fiscal lists for service on the council, Avignon ten.[98]

The landowners or older lineages were usually defined either as a separate member or formed their own guild. Patrician social clubs sometimes had guaranteed seats on the council. Often the patricians had to join guilds nominally, but their great wealth enabled them to dominate these organisations and thus control the city council through them. In 1386 the council of Constance ordered the guilds not to accept members of the old lineages as members in the future, evidently fearing that

94 Nicholas, *Medieval Flanders*, 373, after W. Blockmans.
95 von Brandt, 'Lübeck', 231–2.
96 Matheus, *Trier*, 115.
97 Renouard, *Bordeaux sous les rois d'Angleterre*, 452; Platelle, *Histoire de Valenciennes*, 62; Herlihy, 'Rulers of Florence', 198.
98 Rossiaud, 'Crises', 509–10.

patricians would simply take over the crafts.[99] In most cities the lineages were guaranteed a certain number of seats on the city council or administrative offices such as the burgomastership; but as the patricians entered other guilds or moved to their rural properties, some cities had trouble recruiting enough to occupy the requisite number of places. In 1422 the patricians of Strasbourg were given one-third of the places on the council, compared with half earlier, but they had trouble filling them even after 1471, when the government, reversing a decision of ninety years earlier, permitted guildsmen to leave their trades and enrol in a noble club. Commissions of Thirteen, Fifteen and Twenty-One, named for life, rather than the council really controlled the city administration.[100]

England remains an exception in allowing only a minimal political role to craft organisations, even those that were dominated by merchants. The guilds were represented on the Council of Forty-Eight after York changed the basis of representation from ward to guild, but only thirteen craftsmen, including five dyers and three goldsmiths, were mayors between 1364 and 1500, and the sheriffs were generally merchants. Although most disturbances at York were caused by the aldermen's factional rivalries, many rioters came from prominent crafts. This was particularly likely when the issue was of special concern to their trades, such as when the butchers objected to a toll at the Shambles.[101]

Some English city councils were enlarged in the fifteenth century, but others contracted. At Norwich in 1415 a new council of Sixty was placed beside the older council of Twenty-Four. Elsewhere pressure from below enlarged existing councils, but did not create new ones. The council of Exeter doubled in size between 1435 and 1455 but then reverted to the older form. As in Italy the occasion for the change was usually not a question of principle or guild structure, but a specific grievance. When that had been resolved, there was no impetus to keep the reform.[102] York had three deliberative bodies by the late fourteenth century: twelve aldermen, twenty-four 'good men' and forty-eight representatives of the community who were called mainly for political purposes and to ratify decisions. New aldermen and the twenty-four were coopted by the mayor and remaining aldermen, but the choice of the twenty-four was limited to those who had previously been sheriffs. Like the aldermen, they served until death or discharge. The council met frequently but irregularly. Attendance was low, usually about half

99 Eitel, *Oberschwäbische Reichsstädte*, 87–90; Bechtold, *Zunftbürgerschaft und Patriziat*, 132–3.
100 Rapp, 'Sozialpolitische Entwicklung', 149–53.
101 Swanson, *Medieval Artisans*, 121–4.
102 Rigby, 'Urban oligarchy', 72–4.

the membership. Virtually all aldermen and members of Parliament and most councillors were merchants. The representatives of the community came mainly from the crafts. Elections to offices were tightly controlled. London's system of having the mayor chosen by his predecessor and aldermen from two candidates nominated in an assembly was widely imitated. At York from 1392 the retiring mayor nominated two or three aldermen from whom the entire group of burgesses elected his successor.[103]

At Salisbury the oligarchy was neither monolithic nor impenetrable, despite the control of the merchant guild rather than craft organisations. Salisbury was larger and more independent than most episcopal cities, with regular meetings of the merchant guild (the Guild of St George), which amounted to the body of the freeholders. The mayor and two councils, of twenty-four and forty-eight members, met more frequently and handled elections to most offices. The Forty-Eight were responsible for keeping order and collecting fines and taxes; many persons were fined for refusing to serve on this body. Most administrative officers of Salisbury came from the Twenty-Four, including the mayor, four aldermen, two reeves, two sergeants, one assessor and the delegates to Parliament. Most of the mayors were mercers, drapers and grocers, but a carpenter served in 1417 and an ironmonger between 1420 and 1423.[104]

A similar picture is found among the Italian urban oligarchies. Although control was tight, eligibility requirements were broad enough to make participation possible to persons who could afford to be away from their businesses. The shorter terms of office in the Italian cities, most often two months instead of the year that was common in the north, would have facilitated public participation by craftsmen if the scrutinies had not required a two-thirds vote for election. At Florence, in a population of about 120,000, there were about 24,000 eligible males over the age of 30 between 1328 and 1342, but only 675 actually served. The oligarchy was tightest in the 1330s, then was relaxed. The population of Florence declined sharply after 1348 but not the number of persons in high government office, which was a good career. After 1406 eligible candidates had to own shares of the public debt, which, with the overall decline in population, reduced the number of eligible males to about 5,200. Even so, it was hard to find candidates who passed the scrutiny. Eight hundred drawings were required in 1428, one thousand in 1454 to fill 156 seats in the major offices. Large extended families, often with collateral branches, provided nearly half the officeholders.[105] Aristocratic factions jockeyed for influence and manipulated the councils.

103 Tillott, *City of York*, 77–80; Rigby, 'Urban oligarchy', 81.
104 Analysis of Carr, 'Urban patriciate Salisbury', 118–26.
105 Herlihy, 'Rulers of Florence', 203–10.

The inner circle of power brokers in Florence consisted of about seventy men who were constantly at the city hall wheeling and dealing. Although the scrutiny lists for the *Signoria* had 6,354 names in 1433, only one-third of them actually held office. The ratio of those eligible to those nominated for the scrutiny declined from 1:10 in 1391 to 1:5 in 1411. This gave an appearance of broadening the regime, but the increase came mainly from the older and larger families in the greater guilds. The Strozzi family had seventy-four members who were eligible in 1411. As corporatism declined in Florence in the fifteenth century, political life became more centred around patron–client relations. Most of those from outside the old families who actually served were their clients.[106]

The requirement of rotation led to the development of an informal *cursus honorum*. The councillors of Cologne had to be out of office for three years between terms but could hold other offices in the interim. The three-year rotation is also found in administrative and judicial offices, including the two burgomasters. The *Rentmeister*, who handled finances and city buildings and was second in dignity to the burgomaster, was generally a former burgomaster. He served a two-year term, and the normal rotation here became six years instead of three.[107] In 1447 a royal charter made official what had become normal practice at Colchester: the bailiffs, justices of the peace, coroners and claviers, who held the keys to the chests where city records were kept, had to be chosen from present or former aldermen. Most of the constables and receivers of Salisbury used the expertise gained in those positions to move into higher offices. All but three of York's eighty-five mayors in the fifteenth century had previous experience as sheriff and/or chamberlain. The mayoralty required expertise and the leisure to serve. The tradition of mayors holding numerous offices previously was so ingrained that most mayors were at least in their forties.[108]

The movement towards despotism in Italy

The formal institutions of government in the Italian cities did not change significantly in form in the late fourteenth and fifteenth centuries. The issue became not changing republican institutions or the composition of city councils but rather their informal subversion by powerful families.

Venice faced no serious threats after its war with Genoa ended in 1381. Thirty families who had risen to prominence in that conflict were added to the hereditary membership of the Great Council. Population

106 Brucker, *Civic World*, 251–6; Brucker, *Renaissance Florence*, 97–101.
107 Huiskes, *Beschlüsse Köln*, xx–xxi.
108 Carr, 'Urban patriciate Salisbury', 122, 125–6; Kermode, 'Formation of oligarchies', 92–3, 96–8; Tillott, *City of York*, 70–1.

decline since 1348 meant that the Venetian nobility, which was already larger than most municipal elites, became even broader. For the next 250 years the doges came from newer families (the *corti*, 'short'); previous doges had been *lunghi*, descended from tribunes who had governed the lagoons before the election of the first doge. Nobles continued to monopolise all councils and offices except for the grand chancellorship, a position amounting to civic secretary that was reserved for *cittadini originarii*, old but non-noble families. The main governmental change was the growth of the power of the Senate, which absorbed the Forty in the fourteenth century, but the Senate in turn lost some authority to special commissions given emergency powers by the Great Council.[109]

Genoa was also dominated by its aristocracy, but with a stronger landed element than in Venice and a division of offices among Whites and Blacks. The doge, since 1339 the chief of the 'popular' party, was the only official not chosen by a complex electoral scheme. Holders of lesser offices and a 'Great Council' of 300–600 citizens chose the new doge by casting white and black balls. The doge presided over all councils and could exercise enormous informal influence, particularly in the militia. He had a personal guard, and the captains of the *popolo* and of the Palace Square were always his kin or protégés. He had powers of appointment and enriched his family and clients by awarding them contracts. He was such a military power that Genoa never recruited *condottieri*. By the fifteenth century the doge was always either a Fregoso or Adorno. The council of the eight elders, which rotated every four months, was the chief magistracy. It or delegations of between three and five members met virtually daily, and nothing could be decided without its participation. Three other councils – Finance, Sea and the *Officium Gazarie*, which ruled commerce and the Black Sea colonies – often met with the elders. During emergencies Genoa also gave supreme power to *balie*.[110]

The formal structure and institutions of Florence's government also changed very little between 1382 and 1411. The extreme Guelfs returned from exile after the fall of the Ciompi regime. The lesser guilds were reduced from three to two members of the *Signoria* in 1387. Actual control was in the hands of *balie*, but the formal council organisation was retained, amounting to a *Signoria* of fifty-four members and ninety-six in the advisory colleges each year. Continuity was an obvious problem, given the large number of offices and the rapidity of rotation.[111]

Although the Tuscan cities and the great ports of Venice and Genoa had traditionally enjoyed republican and conciliar forms of government,

109 Lane, *Venice*, 196–201; Romano, *Patricians*, 28–9.
110 Heers, *Gênes. Civilisation*, 403–7.
111 Brucker, *Civic World*, 64–99; Brucker, *Renaissance Florence*, 133–5.

powerful lords had long ruled the smaller Italian communities, which had weaker commercial and industrial sectors and thus had strong ties to the rural economy and nobility. Some *signori* were descended from landed families who had been officials of the bishops who had been the first lords of the cities, then had expanded into personal rule and excluded the bishop from practical authority. Others began as *popolani*. The Della Scala of Verona were captains of the *popolo* and guild rectors who then established personal lordship in 1298. The Este of Ferrara also subverted the 'popular' institutions to which they owed their rise. The breakdown of public order and the choking proliferation of bureaux and councils strengthened the appeal of giving power to a single individual.[112] In Lucca the Guinigi family, who had the largest merchant company in the city and built a clientele by land purchases, loans and marriage alliances, established a despotism in 1392 that lasted until 1430, when the republican councils were restored. The Italian cities thus moved in the fifteenth century toward one-person or one-family rule that subverted republican institutions.[113]

Members of the Della Torre ['Of the Tower'] family held important offices in the *popolo* of Milan in the thirteenth century. Although Milan was commercial and industrial, it also had powerful nobles with rural ties who were able to resist the *popolo*. In 1277 the archbishop of Milan, Ottone Visconti ['Viscounts'], was declared lord of the city. Azzone Visconti was made imperial vicar of the city in 1299, a distinction confirmed by Milan's Council of Nine Hundred in 1330. The brothers Bernabò and Galeazzo Visconti ruled separately at Milan and Pavia respectively after 1359. Giangaleazzo Visconti, Galeazzo's son, captured his uncle Bernabò and two of his sons by a ruse in 1385 and quickly took power in Milan, where he was welcomed as a liberator by the Great Council of the city, which recognised his dominion. Giangaleazzo was a prince on the European scale; his first wife was a daughter of King John II of France, whose need for cash forced him to accept a son-in-law who was in at least some sense a townsman. Giangaleazzo was given the title of count of Vertus in Champagne.

This most powerful of the Visconti kept his chief residence at Pavia but paid considerable attention to affairs in Milan, his major centre of power. He preserved the form of acting through the ordinary city government which, obviously at his behest, prohibited unauthorised guild conclaves within a month of his entry in 1385. The prince appointed all

---

112 Castagnetti, 'Città della Marca Veronese', 75; Heers, *Parties and Political Life*, 117–32.
113 Meek, *Lucca 1369–1400*, 182–4, 194–9, 229–30, 237–8, 245–6, 257–64, 281–3, 333–43; Bratschel, 'Lucca 1430–94', 19–20.

major communal officials, including the *podestà*, whose remaining functions were mainly judicial and in law enforcement. Giangaleazzo appointed an Office of Provisions, a council that rotated every two months. In 1384 he ended municipal collection of excises and the *estimo* at Pavia and simply took over all revenues of the city. He gradually extended this system to Milan and the other cities of what had been his uncle's part of the Visconti domain. In 1386 he established an 'Office of the Notes' at Milan, which opened all correspondence brought into or sent outside the city. There are no records of how this censorship system actually functioned. In 1395 he bought the title 'duke of Milan' from the emperor.

Giangaleazzo Visconti is best known and was most feared as a conqueror. He seized Verona, Padua and Pisa and their dependencies. He fought several wars with Florence from 1390 and was on the verge of conquering Milan's great rival when he died unexpectedly in 1402. His overweening power provoked a coalition of cities against his successors. The largely absentee last Visconti, Filippo Maria, married his daughter to Francesco Sforza, a *condottiere* who became so powerful that he threatened the stability of the regime. In 1450 Sforza had himself proclaimed duke of Milan.[114]

Most urban despots of late medieval Italy, like Giangaleazzo Visconti, preserved the form of traditional communal institutions while stripping them of substance. The Este marquesses of Ferrara, whose rule was unchallenged by the 1330s, suppressed the municipal statutes of 1287, which set up a great council of 200 and a lesser one of forty, and appointed a council of twelve 'Wise Men'. After a period of inactivity in the late fourteenth century the Wise Men – who became the 'Senate' in the classically inclined fifteenth century – resumed considerable day-to-day administration. They set policy towards the *contado*, controlled the police, assessed and collected taxes, issued economic regulations, funded the new university of Ferrara and hired grammar teachers for pre-university studies. Most of the Wise Men were businessmen who were not personally close to the marquis. Their presiding officer, the Judge, was usually noble and provided their link to the Este court.[115]

The rise of the Medici in Florence is often taken as the prototype of the peaceful rise of an aristocratic family from the chaos of faction. Reacting to the threat from Giangalezzo Visconti, the Florentine government, through its chancellors, espoused an ideology of 'civic humanism', lauding republican forms of government over despotic. The city faced another challenge between 1411 and 1414 with the effort of Ladislas

---

114 Martines, *Power and Imagination*, 94–110, 140–8; Bueno da Mesquita, *Giangaleazzo Visconti*, 6–11, 31–4, 46, 50, 52, 54–7, 121–36, 173.
115 Dean, 'Commune and despot', 186–95.

of Naples to extend his rule northward. Although the great Florentine families shared power by rotating offices and controlling the scrutinies, this did not diminish their internal rivalries. The Albizzi family initially seemed the most likely to establish personal rule. Financial problems mounted in a period of economic stagnation and frequent conflict with Milan. Florence extended its *contado* and acquired formal lordship over Pisa, Siena and Pistoia, but it found conquest easier than administration of the fruits of victory.

The resources of the regime were strained by wars, which were alleviated somewhat by an alliance of Florence with Venice against Milan in 1425. But dissatisfaction over the conduct of the war weakened the Albizzi, and complaints of rigged tax assessments were only partially allayed by the imposition of the Albizzi-backed *catasto* in 1427 (see Chapter 5). In 1429 accusations of corruption led to the creation of Defenders of the Law whose powers amounted to a mandate to purge the regime. By 1430 the Medici controlled the councils. Although Cosimo dei Medici was exiled briefly in 1433, he returned the next year, and his partisans, who controlled the major offices, banished the Albizzi.

The Medici consolidated their control by careful manipulation. When they came to power, the Florentines had been using the same basic electoral system for more than a century. The scrutiny, which certified citizens' qualifications for specific offices, was to occur every five years. Once a person's name was drawn by lot from the bags, he had to serve unless there was some technical disqualification, such as tax debts, having held the same office too recently or being related to other officeholders. The scrutiny was thus more important than the actual drawing from the bags. But the scrutinies were carefully manipulated. The Medici used the *balia*, which the *Signoria* had approved in general assemblies of the citizens, to exercise extraordinary powers, particularly to exile their opponents and their adherents, starting with the Albizzi in 1434.

The regime of Cosimo dei Medici (ruled 1434–64) also used *accoppiatori* ['Couplers'] to draw the ballots by hand from the bags for the more important offices, which in effect gave them actual power to appoint the *Signoria*. Secretaries handled the lesser offices. Whenever opponents of the Medici managed to slip through and become vocal on the *Signoria*, as happened in the early 1450s, the ruling family tried to have the bags closed, so that the Couplers could not see whose names they were drawing. This system was ended briefly in 1455, and Florence returned to the earlier system of scrutinies and election by lot; but after 1458 the imposition of a new *catasto*, which was very popular among the *popolo minuto*, permitted Cosimo to consolidate his authority. A general assembly (*parlamento*) gave authority to a new *balia*, which conducted a new scrutiny. The *parlamento* also gave extraordinary powers to the priors, who proceeded to arrest and exile opponents of the regime, the first time since 1434 that many had been exiled.

Florence had a separate police power, the Eight of the Guard, who were chosen separately by the *Signoria* and the Couplers after 1434. In 1444 the *balia* took over election of the Eight, and this continued with a few interruptions to be the rule. In 1458 the Eight themselves were given powers of *balia* for two years. From this point they were regularly called the 'Eight of the Guard and of the *Balia*'. The similarities to the police powers of the Ten at Venice are clear. A new Council of One Hundred was also given extensive powers, and the Couplers again elected the *Signoria*, rather than having it chosen by lot. Symbolically, in 1459 and 1463 the Couplers added names to the purses not in the Palace of the *Signoria* but rather in Cosimo's palace.[116]

Yet Cosimo was not a dictator. He was a much less obtrusive ruler than his contemporaries, the Sforza dukes of Milan. Cosimo operated behind the scenes, always controlling the scrutinies but only holding office himself twice. Cosimo used his family's banking interests and his own money to extend his and his city's influence in Italy and overseas. Cosimo did make his family's palace a sumptuous establishment and received foreign dignitaries as the actual lord of Florence. On the surface little had changed except that the extent of factional infighting had perceptibly diminished. Conciliar elections were regularly held and continued to give patronage to the elite. Cosimo's grandson Lorenzo 'the Magnificent' (ruled 1469–92) played the prince and was less than beloved save among the humanist intellectuals whom he patronised. In 1471 he reduced the number of lesser guilds from fourteen to five, limited the powers of the *podestà* and abolished the office of captain of the *popolo*.[117]

Despite factional discord in most cities, their governing institutions were changed mainly by making their oligarchies more rigid and lineage-based, particularly after 1360. Although guilds, merchant or ostensibly craft, gave access to civic life virtually everywhere, the cities were governed by commercial elites whose members invested their profits in land and to a lesser extent industry. To this point we have considered only the social composition of the urban magistracies in the late Middle Ages. We must now consider what city governments actually did and how well they accomplished the increasingly complex tasks that their rulers undertook.

116 Discussion based on Rubinstein, *Government of Florence Under the Medici*, 4–7, 23–4, 34–5, 49–51, 88, 108–12, 121–35.
117 Kent, *Rise of the Medici*, 211–351; Brucker, *Civic World*, 396–500; Brucker, *Renaissance Florence*, 119–21; Favier, *De l'or et des épices*, 352.

CHAPTER FIVE

Public Administration and Finance in the Later Medieval Cities

The Italian cities had been overgoverned for centuries. After Pistoia passed into Florentine control in 1351 its government included at least thirty-seven separate bureaux. By the 1430s the tax burden per capita was triple the amount of the 1330s, as municipal income stabilised while population declined sharply.[1] The much smaller northern cities were underfinanced and undergoverned when measured by this standard. They did not provide the range of services of their Italian counterparts. They may have been just as intensely regulated as the Italian cities but had fewer paid officials, relying more on the guilds to handle industrial policing that in Italy was a function of the municipal government.

However, urban government in northern Europe became so complex in the late Middle Ages that the councils could only direct policy, not control administration directly. By the fifteenth century the large cities had numerous officials and commissions to handle peace-keeping, record-keeping and finance. Annual rotation of city councils did not mean discontinuity of policy, for political leaders tended to return to office, and there was considerably more continuity at the lower levels of the city bureaucracy, where most of the work was done. City councillors were chosen for various reasons involving social position and/or wealth, but salaried functionaries were paid for their skill and education.

Guild involvement in city government brought close regulation of production standards and work practices, which necessitated larger staffs. In 1340 Reims had only two clerks, two sergeants, one procurator and several gendarmes, although royal officials must be added to this number. From 1357–8 Nuremberg had forty-six market police who enforced regulations concerning food, drink and manufacturing. By the early

1   Herlihy, *Pistoia*, 231–9.

fourteenth century the mayor and each alderman of London had his own clerk. The three chief bureaucrats were the chamberlain, who handled accounts and kept some other records; the common clerk, who handled most non-financial and legal documents; and the common sergeant-at-law, who kept legal documents. He seems to have developed out of the office of city prosecutor in the late thirteenth century.[2]

The English cities, which were under strong royal control, had less developed administrations than those of the continent. York had three bailiffs, who were replaced by two sheriffs when the city achieved county status in 1396. The bailiffs held the royal commission of the peace, paid the city farm, enforced market regulations including the assizes of bread and ale, empanelled jurors and collected court fines. The farm included ground rents, tolls, stall rents in the markets and other incomes from city property. Originally chosen by their own predecessors, the sheriffs in the fifteenth century were nominated by the mayor, aldermen and councillors, who then presented their names to the commonalty. Most were merchants, and most fifteenth-century aldermen and eventually mayors had served as sheriffs earlier in their careers. The three chamberlains, who handled city finances, had a broader occupational distribution than the mayor and aldermen; about half each came from merchants and the crafts. York also had three coroners and miscellaneous bridge-masters, gatekeepers and even minstrels. The recorder is first known from 1385 and a common clerk from 1317. The courts of York are typical in becoming more complex and handling a much wider variety of types of action. The sheriffs' court met on Tuesday, Thursday and Saturday for pleas of debt, trespass, account and detinue (unlawfully detaining personal property), and infractions of the statute of labourers. The mayor's court was held for common pleas every Monday in the guildhall.[3]

The larger German cities had chanceries with permanent personnel by the second quarter of the thirteenth century, and virtually all cities were transacting their most important business in writing by 1300. The city hall of Nuremberg was designed in 1332 to include space for an archive.[4] The magistrates of Brussels posted written ordinances in an antechamber that was open to the public in the city hall, and citizens were expected to go there for information.[5]

Some clerks were simply scribes, but others had legal training from a university or cathedral school. In addition to a clerk and an attorney,

2   Lobel, *Atlas* 2: 15; Pfeiffer, *Nürnberg*, 36; Williams, *Medieval London*, 94–5.
3   Tillott, *City of York*, 71–80.
4   Bischoff, 'Stadtherrschaft im ostfränkischen Städtedreieck', 101.
5   Martens, *Histoire de Bruxelles*, 124.

Lübeck had several secretaries of the city council, most of whom were at least Masters of Arts by the late fourteenth century. The syndic (the city attorney when this role was distinct from that of the secretaries) normally had the Doctor of Laws degree by the mid-fifteenth century.[6] The city secretary also became extremely important in the growing Dutch cities, as the aldermen gradually confined themselves to justice and the burgomasters to administration after 1450.[7]

The duties of the city clerk are described in detail in the Augsburg municipal code of 1276.

> He should copy the city taxes and everything that the council prohibits the citizens and community to do, and everything that the town has to do, whether with letters or in other things. . . . He should also write all letters for both the city and of the citizens on real parchment, not on paper. He should pass no judgement on the court nor on the council, and his opinion can have no force. . . . And when the Small Council is chosen at Candlemas, he is not to be present but remain outside the chamber and write down the names of those chosen. . . . He should also keep the city law book and no other book belonging to the city, and should read this book to the court and the Council whenever requested. Otherwise no one should read or show it unless one or both burgomasters is present, and no one, including the clerk, may transcribe it.[8]

Caught between the increasing litigiousness of their citizens and princely encroachments, the city governments required expert legal advice. City councillors knew local customary law but rarely the 'bookish' or 'commented' Roman law that princes on the continent were trying to impose on them in the late Middle Ages. Even in such a large city as Ghent there were no jurists as aldermen in most years between 1384 and 1468, and only in eleven years were there two or more. There was only one jurist at the court of Liège in the entire Middle Ages.[9]

The chief clerk was sometimes the city attorney, but the offices were increasingly being distinguished in the late fourteenth century. Nuremberg hired one Master Erhard as city clerk and attorney for the term 1363–70 to give legal counsel to magistrates and burgesses. In cases of conflict between two citizens, he had the option of advising only the one

---

6 Wriedt, 'Amtsträger', 228.
7 Marsilje, *Financiële Beleid Leiden*, 310–11.
8 Quoted by Peters, *Literatur in der Stadt*, 232, 252.
9 van Caenegem, *Law, History*, 128–9.

who had the better right. In his capacity as clerk he was given two apprentices, one of whom was to be in the accounting chamber when Erhard was absent. He received special payments for extra work and was entitled to a wedding gift if he decided to 'change his ways and take a wife'.[10]

As university education spread, the government of most cities included many more advocates and masters in the fifteenth century than in the fourteenth. Most clerks came from the prosperous middle ranks of the citizenry, while jurists employed by the cities, many of them ecclesiastical pluralists, were more often from the lesser nobility. They were well paid, and many had private practices in addition to their municipal employment. In southern France the city lawyers often used their legal expertise as an avenue into the moneylending business. At Ghent the city attorney's wage was second only to those of the overdeans of the three political members. The council often consulted the attorneys before making important decisions and sent them on diplomatic missions. The Flemish cities normally sent the attorney with a subcommittee of the council to meetings of the four members of Flanders but used simple messengers for ordinary business. The English cities often sent lawyers to Parliament, but they were not much involved in the municipal councils until later.[11]

Jurists were especially important in the provincial capitals of France and in university cities and seats of local parlements. Although barristers generally could not serve on city councils before 1300, jurists gained entry through their guilds as council membership came to depend on guild affiliation. The council of Cahors had a professor of laws by 1292, that of Toulouse by 1318, and the practice quickly became more common. After 1380 about one-fifth of the *capitouls* of Toulouse were jurists. During the fifteenth century lawyers worked their way into most town governments of the French Midi and dominated them by the early sixteenth.[12]

The cities maintained impressive systems of public works. Street paving and work on the walls and the increasingly numerous and opulent public buildings usually accounted for 15–25 per cent of the city expenditure at Ghent during peacetime. Reims levied a tax for street paving and maintained a permanent road crew. Keeping the streets in repair was so important that the Rémois acquired the right to quarry paving stone within a four-league radius of the city on condition of indemnifying the

10 Schultheiss, *Satzungen*, 244–5.
11 Gouron, *Science du droit*, 58–61; Nicholas, 'Governance', 249; Kowaleski, 'Commercial dominance', 197.
12 Stouff, *Arles*, 177; Gouron, *Science du droit*, 62.

owners. Some cities centralised their public works. Those of Trier were originally under the rent master, but by 1406 there was a separate building master. Building masters or municipal surveyors kept records of property boundaries and adjudicated disputes. They also appraised the sale or rental value of property. The city surveyors were usually taken from the building trades; at Ghent one of them was always a carpenter.[13]

Most cities had public works done by the local construction guilds and therefore had to delegate supervisory functions to guildsmen. Bruges called the dozen or so guildsmen whose technical expertise was needed 'city masters' and used them on mills, buildings, streets and bridges. They were the elite of their guilds; two master masons controlled four-fifths of the masonry contracts entered into by the city in the late four-teenth century. The council leased specified tasks to such persons for a term or for life and paid them a salary. The 'city masters' controlled most of the piece work handled by their trades, generally purveying the raw materials needed for the job. Public works at Bruges provided menial jobs for many but great profits for only a few. And since there was not enough work even for the city to occupy a master for an entire year, they stayed in private business. They received the most important contracts from foreigners, churches and princes and for buildings else-where in Flanders. The famous town hall of Damme, Bruges' outport, was built by masters of Bruges.[14]

The city masters included such officers as apothecaries and physi-cians, who examined injuries that were the subject of cases in the mun-icipal court. Nuremberg maintained one apothecary and five physicians by 1377. Augsburg hired a city physician in 1362, but they were unusual in northern Germany until the end of the fifteenth century. Ghent had several surgeons, one of whom continued in city service even although he was found guilty of five assaults between 1357 and 1378.[15] Such persons could move easily into commerce and rise into the municipal elite. The firm of the Paris contractor Guillaume Cirasse worked for the duke of Berry, renowned for his building and artistic patronage, and made repairs on the parlement buildings. Cirasse became provost of the merchants in 1417.[16]

The first corporate properties owned by the cities had been land and public buildings such as city halls, but in the late Middle Ages most of the larger centres bought industrial property to ensure the supply of

13 Nicholas, 'Governance', 245, 252; Desportes, *Reims*, 489; Matheus, *Trier*, 160–2.
14 Sosson, *Travaux publics*, 161–78, 189–201.
15 Möncke, *Quellen*, 224–5; Wriedt, 'Amtsträger', 228; Pfeiffer, *Nürnberg*, 35; Nicholas, *Domestic Life*, 49–50; Nicholas, 'Governance', 249.
16 *Parisian Journal*, 78.

needed materials. Virtually all cities owned mills. Some leased them to entrepreneurs, but others operated them directly. Kraków bought the village of Grzegorzowice in 1388 and exploited its quarry directly. Bruges built a brick factory at Ramskapelle, in its ban mile, in 1331. Production was sufficient for most of the city's needs until after 1416. Nijmegen, Arnhem and Gouda in the Netherlands also had brick factories. Hamburg owned three building tile plants. Municipally-owned factories also sold to a wider public as well as to the city government, but efforts to realise a profit from these operations generally failed. Brunswick's municipally-owned industries accounted for 17 per cent of the city's gross receipt between 1403 and 1423, with the mills twice as lucrative as the tile works, but maintenance expenses nearly balanced this out. At Hildesheim the profits of the mills covered the deficit in the tile works.[17]

Parishes, quarters and urban militias in the later Middle Ages

Cities were organised into parishes or civil subdivisions, variously called thirds, quarters, sixths, constabularies or wards, for purposes of administration and defence. In the late Middle Ages as earlier the communal identity of many citizens, particularly of the lower orders, seems to have been focused more on these districts than on the city as a whole. This sense is even stronger outside Europe than in the west. Novgorod was divided into five *kontsi* in late Middle Ages. Each had its own assembly that acted independently of the city government. Representatives of the *kontsi* met in a city assembly held by the archbishop in his compound. Each sector had its own powerful aldermen who were in charge of their internal administrations. All corporate acts of Novgorod had to be approved by each quarter. The quarters of the Muslim cities continued in the late Middle Ages as before to be marked by solidarity, generally homogeneous and family- or ethnic-based. Some but not all had their own gates. They had their own markets, apart from the main bazaars. As in the west, factional quarrels within the quarters were common. The districts had sheiks as spokespersons, corresponding to the aldermen of the *kontsi*; but while in Russia they were selected within the quarter, in Syria and Egypt the emir's government appointed them, although some of them identified more with the people of the quarter and helped them evade the strictures of the government. They apportioned and collected taxes and were police officials.[18]

17 Carter, *Trade and Urban Development in Poland*, 68; Sosson, *Travaux publics*, 70–9; Diermeier and Fouquet, 'Eigenbetriebe Städte', 258–72; Nicholas, *Stad en Platteland*, 71.
18 Dejevsky, 'Novgorod', 344; Lapidus, *Muslim Cities*, 85–7, 92–3; Hourani, *History of the Arab Peoples*, 123.

The citizens of Nuremberg swore obedience to their quartermasters. In other cities the gates were focal points both for quarters and militia organisations. From 1442 Vienna was divided into four quarters, each with an arsenal in a tower gate at the entrance of the city. Guilds mustered their members within the quarters. The changing demographic patterns of the late Middle Ages required some alteration to keep the districts roughly equal in terms of wealth and population. Lucca had five ancient districts centred on the town gates as the basis for elections and taxes, but in 1370 they were reorganised into thirds.[19]

London had twenty-five wards from 1394, each with an alderman and subordinate officials, a beadle, sergeants, and constables. The ward administration handled routine matters and defence, police and sanitation. The aldermen held biennial courts, the 'wardmotes'. Aldermen were originally elected directly at the wardmote, but by the fourteenth century they were chosen by ward representatives meeting at the guildhall. From 1376 the mayor was elected by the aldermen and the 'commons' (actually the wealthier of them in council). The six wards of York, whose courts handled much of the city's business, were also militia units. Their constables levied contributions to repair the walls and in 1482 were made responsible for closing the gates. In the fifteenth century two aldermen and a varying number of wardens were assigned permanently to each ward. The parishes of York also had organisations, with two or three constables to keep the peace.[20]

Paris had sixteen quarters, each under a *quartenier* who was responsible to the provost of the merchants. The quarters were divided into tithe groups. The 128 *dizainiers*, who amounted to ward captains in charge of one or two streets, reported to the *quarteniers*. They were unpaid and unpopular neighbourhood officials who supervised the watch. The occupational guilds rotated the night watch every three weeks but organised it by the quarter and recruited it in the *dizaine*. The *dizainiers* were well placed to know political opinions. The Orléanist occupation of Paris foundered on the Burgundian sympathies of most *dizainiers*. The assemblies of Languedoil in 1317 had placed royal captains at the head of the city militias, and this had spread to Paris by 1359, where mounted royal guards supplemented and commanded the guild contingents. Their duties included making certain that the guildsmen were at their posts. The 'knight of the watch' in 1418 was a Burgundian partisan who was preceded on his circuit by a troop of musicians, whose noise would obviously warn miscreants and give them time to escape. Elsewhere the guild

---

19 Schultheiss, *Satzungen*, 58; Hummelberger, 'Bewaffnung der Bürgerschaft', 195; Meek, *Lucca*, 6–7.
20 Robertson, *Chaucer's London*, 69–70; Tillott, *City of York*, 76–7.

masters supervised the guards directly, but a royal officer commanded the militia on expeditions outside the city. The military responsibilities of the crafts of Paris were confirmed in an ordinance of 1467 that divided them into twenty-five banners, most of which were either large individual guilds or groups of related guilds. While previously the watch had been arranged by neighbourhood, the 1467 ordinance substituted a guild watch that included sixty-one separate trades. All males aged 16–60, masters and journeymen alike, were to register, and those who were not in guilds, including rich persons and jurists, were assigned to a banner and required to serve.[21]

Citizens who were subject to the militia were frequently divided into tax groups, with more elaborate weaponry required of the wealthier townspeople, since the cities did not provide weapons except for specialists such as archers, who were not in the constabularies. All citizens were supposed to own arms for defence of the town but were generally forbidden to carry them on the street. This was difficult to enforce and contributed to violence. Although elaborate weaponry reflected prestige, doing night watch was a burden that the elite tried to shift to the guild militias.[22] By the fourteenth century the untrained citizen militias were hopelessly inadequate, and during wartime most cities had to rely on mercenary troops.[23] Vienna started hiring entire contingents in 1368, drawn mainly from farm labourers from the environs. By the mid-fifteenth century the city was supplementing the citizen watch with mercenaries and ordering masters whose journeymen did military service for the city to hold their jobs open for them.[24]

CITY FINANCES: NORTHERN EUROPE

Financial administration and municipal accounts

Stimulated by the imperatives of defence and public works, city finances became much more sophisticated in the late Middle Ages. Maintaining the walls and bridges accounted for some 65 per cent of Tours' expenses during the war years of the early fifteenth century. Even at Rouen, which was less affected by the wars than other cities of Normandy,

21 Thompson, *Paris Under English Rule*, 85, 98–105, 151; Cazelles, *Paris*, 187–92; *Journal Bourgeois Paris*, 98–9; Favier, *Paris 1380–1500*, 245, 433; Chevalier, *Bonnes villes*, 122–3.
22 Chevalier, *Bonnes villes*, 121–2; Wensky, 'Osnabrücker Gilden', 372; Renkhoff, *Wiesbaden*, 137.
23 The first Nuremberg ordinance concerning mercenaries was issued shortly after 1335. Schultheiss, *Satzungen*, 248–51.
24 Hummelberger, 'Bewaffnung der Bürgerschaft', 193–4.

about one-quarter of the yearly budget was spent on the wall. The excises voted by the Estates General in 1356–8 initially went to the crown, but in 1367 the government left one-quarter of the *aides* to the 'good towns' to help with defence. Cities that required more money received the king's permission to levy a supplementary aid. *Ad hoc* royal grants also were made to cities that were in special need: in 1358–9 Tours was given one-quarter of the profit of the local mint.[25] Totally apart from military needs, princely taxation became a serious burden. The Burgundian counts of Flanders demanded huge aids from their cities. From the 1390s the princes of Arles were demanding virtually annual aids, which the cities raised by levying excises. Arles paid only four 'free gifts' to the French king between 1310 and 1389, then six between 1390 and 1399 and twenty-six between 1400 and 1449.[26]

The fiscal machinery, once established to pay for defence and princely subsidies, was kept for civilian purposes. As the cities became more involved in charity and poor relief, regulating the economy, cultural patronage and particularly public works, defence needs 'gave birth to public finance, which in its turn was the origin of municipal administration'.[27] The murage grants that were ostensibly given to the English to maintain their fortifications were similar to the excises levied in the cities of the continent, and like them were used as ordinary income. Exeter collected murage in 1341–2 on all merchandise that landed at Topsham and entered the city through the gates. The percentage of the total municipal receipt that these items represented was roughly what the city spent on walls, streets, and bridges, which of course were considerably smaller than on the continent.[28]

Virtually all cities were keeping written accounts by 1350, most of them in the vernacular language. In the small places an alderman or burgomaster might be the treasurer, but the larger ones had one or more separate receivers. At Brussels the two receivers had the assistance of a financial expert, usually a merchant banker, who loaned the city money as needed and invested its assets. He received a salary, but he had so much freedom of action that he amounted to a city banker. In most German cities at least one receiver was from the lineages. In Basel the president of the Seven, who handled the treasury, had to be a knight. Under the Constitution of 1321 two of Rouen's four receivers were peers.[29] Pisa

25 Glénisson and Higounet, 'Comptes villes françaises', 47–9; Mollat, *Histoire de Rouen*, 100–1.
26 Stouff, *Arles*, 173; Appendix 2, 714.
27 Leguay, *Réseau urbain Bretagne*, 81–4; Curry, 'Towns at war', 148–56.
28 The murage account of 1341–2 is printed in Appendix by Rowe and Draisey, *Exeter Receivers' Accounts*, 93, and comment, xviii.
29 Maschke, *Städte und Menschen*, 206–28; Mollat, *Histoire de Rouen*, 97.

had eight treasurers (serving the commune, the noble association, and each of the principal courts). Lübeck had several separate treasuries at the end of the fourteenth century, not all of which were controlled by the two chamberlains, the chief financial officers. The Rent Office was the central financial bureau at Cologne, handling both collection and disbursement of funds. It was also called the Wednesday Chamber when it heard financial actions. From 1394, however, expenses were separated from the Wednesday Chamber into a second office, the Saturday Chamber, to manage the municipal debt and rents. In 1417 a Friday Rent Chamber was instituted for the new excise on tapped wine.[30]

The chief receivers were political appointees and generally rotated out of office after a year or two. They were rich, and some loaned money to the city, a practice that became the norm in the fifteenth century. Not surprisingly, many eligible persons tried to avoid this office. It was the single municipal office in which there was little repetition or re-election, particularly in the fifteenth century. But since knowledge of finances was specialised, most cities left the clerks in place for years at a time. Cities with several financial bureaux tended to have a permanent cadre of officials but rotated them between offices: a clerk might handle direct taxes one year, then indirect, then tolls, then debt administration.[31]

Few cities used double-entry book-keeping, which permitted an examination of the total financial situation of the town by studying receipts and disbursements simultaneously. Since so much of the city's income came from farming excises, there could be no budget at the beginning of the fiscal year. Only past experience could give the authorities an idea of what to expect. Most cities realised considerable income from judicial fines, but they are difficult to trace, for fines were often kept in a treasury separate from the main receipts. At Zürich they accounted on average for over one-third of the city's extraordinary income in the late fourteenth century. Fines were often handed over directly to the city building inspector to defray the expenses of the fortifications.[32]

Constance also shows the complexity of municipal finances. Receipts and disbursements were rigidly separated. There were distinct administrations for direct taxes, excises and the wine tax, reporting to the general treasurer. The receivers handled most other income, but the hall

30 Irsigler, 'Industrial production', 275.
31 Nicholas, 'Governance', 242–5, summarising van Werveke, *Gentse Stadsfinanciën*; Nicholas, *Medieval Flanders*, 374–5; Nicholas, *Metamorphosis*, 226–30; de Roover, 'Comptes communaux', 86–102; Martens, *Histoire de Bruxelles*, 126; Kirchgässner, 'Rechnungswesens der Reichsstädte', 247; Irsigler, 'Industrial production', 275.
32 Burghartz, *Leib, Ehre und Gut*, 89–96.

lord accounted for tolls and fees at the Merchant Hall, the building master for the income of the public buildings. The general treasurer handled receipts from loans, repayments and sometimes the salt office, the lard office, the linen trade and the coin. The Accounting Office collected incomes that were not accounted for elsewhere and issued the Ground Rent Book, Debt Book, Book of Punishments, and a total income ledger. From 1450 the tax lords and accounting officers were the same persons, but they still had separate administrations, which were even lodged in different buildings.[33]

More coordination is clear after about 1430. The comprehensive accounts that were presented to the auditors usually list receipts and expenses separately but in a single document. Most cities recorded receipts in a very summary fashion but distinguished fixed from movable receipts. Some compiled accounts by the week, with marginal notations marking expenses that were contracted over a longer period. Expenses of public revenue, which were the auditors' main concern, are given in much greater detail. They are usually arranged chronologically within categories, such as public works, diplomacy and charitable donations.[34]

Sources of municipal income: direct taxation

The tax burden increased significantly everywhere in the late Middle Ages. Most cities divided their populations into wealth groups and fixed liability to direct taxes highest for the rich, reducing it for the poorer citizens. The totally indigent were generally exempted altogether. Exemptions could also be found on the other end of the scale for clergy, nobles and officials of the town lord or the king. Particularly in Castile and France this was a substantial group. Some guilds also received tax breaks in France. In 1447 the furriers, cordwainers and tailors of Nantes were freed from the *taille* and other exactions because they provisioned the duke's court. Since horses and armour were so expensive, the fifty-member cavalry of Rouen received tax exemption.[35] The violent tax rebellions were provoked by direct taxes, not indirect, which may be why most patrician regimes favoured indirect taxes.

---

33 Feger, 'Konstanz und Basel', 226; Isenmann, *Deutsche Stadt*, 179.
34 Isenmann, *Deutsche Stadt*, 179; Marsilje, *Financiële Beleid Leiden*, 108–11; Glénisson and Higounet, 'Comptes villes françaises', 39; Sprandel, *Quellen zur Hanse-Geschichte*, 62; Barel, *Ville médiévale*, 281–2; Desportes, *Reims*, 516–23; van Uytven, 'Stadsgeschidenis', 241; Rausch, 'Rechnungswesen', 194–6; Kirchgässner, 'Rechnungswesens der Reichsstädte', 250.
35 Leguay, *Réseau urbain Bretagne*, 91–2; Mollat, *Histoire de Rouen*, 101.

Liability to direct taxation was a mark of citizenship. Most cities maintained a territorial rather than personal basis for the land tax. Thus the rural possessions of citizens were generally not taxed by the city, but possessions of non-citizens in the city were. Movables, immovables and annuity rents were taxed. The head of the household paid the property tax for spouse and/or dependent children. The clergy and their personnel had immunity from public taxation, but in practice they were required to pay on land.[36]

The finances of most English cities were much less sophisticated than on the continent. They derived a much larger part of their income from fines for 'trading offences', specifically those involving the royal assizes of bread and ale, than did most cities of the continent, certainly the larger ones. Exeter's income came from rents on property inside and outside the city and particularly from 'issues of the city' including bagavel and brithgavel (taxes on persons not holding the freedom who sold bread and ale respectively). Judicial profits also were substantial, including fines in the mayor's court, false measures, amercements of bakers and the confiscated property of felons, waifs and vagrants. The city also collected customs at its port of Topsham by royal grant and rented grazing land in the town meadow.[37] As late as 1378 most of Winchester's income still came from dues and entry fees to the merchant guild or to the franchise of the city. Four pairs of 'aldermen and lawmen', representing the 'houses' of the merchant guild rather than the city aldermen, accounted for these incomes annually, deducted their expenses and rendered the balance to the mayor. Other payments, such as gifts to visiting dignitaries, were collected separately by citizens appointed for the purpose, and the aldermen of the wards collected murage. The English cities used direct taxes to pay the fee farm and parliamentary taxes, collecting the money by parishes on the basis of assessments that remained unchanged for generations.[38]

The German cities were the only ones in the north that used much direct taxation during the Middle Ages. In some it was the main source of income. There is no discernible pattern. Basel used mainly indirect taxes, while nearby Constance preferred direct taxation. Cologne, after using direct taxes earlier, gave them up after 1371 and financed the government with indirect taxes, fines, use charges and rents on city property,

---

36 Dilcher, 'Bürgerbegriff', 84; Schuler, 'Goslar', 443–4; Pfeiffer, *Nürnberg*, 34–5; Schultheiss, *Satzungen*, 310; Sprandel, *Quellen zur Hanse-Geschichte*, 68; Erler, *Bürgerrecht und Steuerpflicht*, 44.

37 Rowe and Draisey, *Exeter Receivers' Accounts*, ix–xxix.

38 Dyer, *Standards of Living*, 209; Keene, *Medieval Winchester*, 80–1; Tillott, *City of York*, 65–7; Dobson, 'Urban decline', 277.

the protection fee levied on the Jews and admissions to the freedom of the city.[39]

Some cities still used oral personal estimates of taxable wealth, but most switched to written declarations in this period. While most Italian cities had given up self-declaration in favour of official assessment by the early fourteenth century, most German cities only did this in the modern period. The Munich tax ordinance of 1374 permitted the collectors to discuss the matter with anyone whose declaration seemed too low, but in the last analysis they had to accept the person's oath. In some cities, starting with Stendhal in 1285, then Hamburg and Munich in 1377, the council had the right to buy property for the assessed value if the owner persisted in a declaration that they considered too low.[40]

The procedure is described in a Frankfurt tax ordinance of 1370:

> Be it known that a tax [*bedde*] has come to our lords [the city government], and they then chose lords to collect the tax. First they should perambulate the houses and lanes, coming to all, and they are to have those to whom they come swear to the saints that they will be responsible for their taxes without delay and bring them within the next two weeks after they swear to the tax house where the lords are, both from the upper and lower city.

Thus the oath preceded payment. At Basel in 1446 the oath was accompanied by a declaration of taxable property:

> And our lords of the Council and the masters of the rents chose three persons in each parish, who were to circulate in the city ... from house to house and write the names of all people in the city fourteen years of age and older, both men and women, clergy and lay, male and female servants alike, and ask them under oath what they have, then tell them, according to their property, what they owe for the tax and where and on what day and in what house they should go to make payment.

At Nuremberg the population was divided into captaincies based on streets. Messengers in red city uniforms went through the streets beating on windows with hazelnut branches, telling the occupants to come to the city hall to take the oath when the bell sounded. The roll was called, and the names of those who swore were marked in the book. Persons who failed to appear or refused to take the oath were summoned

39   Feger, 'Konstanz und Basel', 233; Irsigler, 'Industrial production', 272.
40   Erler, *Bürgerrecht und Steuerpflicht*, 72, 84–5, 97–8.

in writing to the city hall. The procedure took five days, one for each captaincy. The money went into two *Losungen* or treasuries under control of the lineages, which handled expenditure.[41]

Sources of municipal income: indirect taxation

Most cities in France and the Low Countries were financed by indirect taxes that were payable by all, rich and poor, although some cities exempted clergy, university students and nobles. Although most southern French cities were moving toward direct taxation, indirect levies were preferred in the north. In 1337, when the king demanded a flat-rate aid, the *échevins* of Paris, reversing the preference of their predecessors in 1293, asked that it be replaced by a sales tax. Indirect taxes were normal at Rouen except in 1356, when the city had to borrow to pay its share of the king's ransom.[42]

The issue of direct and indirect taxation became blurred in France along with the distinction between municipal and royal revenues. Some towns persuaded the king to agree to return a share of the taxes collected locally to them. From the late fourteenth century the royal government generally saw the wisdom in allowing the cities to take *aides* each year to avoid the unpopular *taille*. This began with a tax on wine, then spread to other goods, mainly foods, always at a much lower rate than the taxes that the king demanded for himself. By 1370 the basic structure of urban finance was in place, based on indirect taxes on consumption. Only in the southwest was the *taille* much used thereafter except for emergencies. Indirect taxes thus accounted for two-thirds of the receipts in most French cities, while 'ordinary receipts' (rents and domain revenues) were insignificant. The wine tax was the most lucrative, often comprising over 80 per cent of municipal income, and salt was also taxed heavily. But the cities administered direct taxes ordered by the royal government and kept whatever surplus was collected over their quotas. Only the larger cities used extensive borrowing and/or annuity rents.[43]

Taxation in the Middle Ages was rather 'progressive'. The poorest citizens were not liable for most direct taxation. Although indirect taxes on food and common goods struck the lower classes more severely than did direct taxation, rates were much higher on luxury items, particularly

41   Erler, *Bürgerrecht und Steuerpflicht*, 58, 65–6, and sources quoted 64–5, 72.
42   Cazelles, *Paris*, 253–4; Mollat, *Histoire de Rouen*, 101.
43   Rossiaud, 'Crises', 432–3; Desportes, *Reims*, 587–94, 657–60; Chevalier, *Bonnes villes*, 210–17.

wine, than on staples.[44] Wine was taxed twice at Trier and Cologne, at the gates and again when it was tapped. Ghent used this double tax during a fiscal emergency in 1356. Most of Cologne's excises were based on weights and measures, but some were on value of the goods.[45]

The excises were generally leased at the beginning of the fiscal year to syndicates of brokers who specialised in the types of goods coming under the tax that they farmed. Cologne collected the wine tax directly, for it accounted for about 15 per cent of the city's income. Guild corporations generally did not farm the excises in the north, and indeed it is not always possible to deduce the tax farmer's guild affiliation from the excise that he leased. Most city governments, and in England a royal statute of 1318, forbade officers of the city or borough who were responsible for the excises of wine or food from trading in these commodities during their term of office, but such rules were ineffective.[46]

Tax farmers and collectors were notoriously disliked, among other reasons because they controlled the supply of the goods being taxed. During the hard winter of 1421 the anonymous Paris chronicler related that

At Candlemas [2 February], for poor people's comfort, Satan's children were raised up again – imposts that is, and fourths and *maltôtes*. They were organized by idle men who could no longer find anything to live on and who squeezed everything so tight that all goods stopped coming into Paris, partly because of the currency and partly because of the subsidies. All prices therefore rose, so that at Easter a good ox cost two hundred francs or more. . . . And all day and all night there were such groans and lamentations all over Paris because of this scarcity, such miserable weepings and lamentations as never, I believe, did the prophet Jeremiah make when the city of Jerusalem was destroyed and the children of Israel were led away captive into Babylon.[47]

The governments generally leased the excises at a public auction. The person who was awarded the contract usually paid a year's rental in advance, in effect making a loan on his anticipated profits. Curiously, the excises do not seem to have been particularly lucrative, and the cities sometimes had trouble finding takers. When political circumstances

44 For a Marxist interpretation of the preference of aristocratic regimes for indirect taxation, in my opinion completely at variance with the facts, see Barel, *Ville médiévale*, 283.

45 Huiskes, *Beschlüsse Köln*, 170; Matheus, *Trier*, 177; Nicholas, *Metamorphosis*, 226; Irsigler, 'Industrial production', 242, 273; Marsilje, *Financiële Beleid Leiden*, 133–4.

46 Swanson, *Medieval Artisans*, 24–5.

47 *Journal Paris*, 157.

such as war prevented the leaseholder from making a reasonable profit, the city might defer payment or provide subsidies and rebates, but damages from bad harvests and climate changes were the risk of the tax farmer. There was no limit on renewal of the leases.[48]

The indirect taxes in most cities were of two types: the excises on food, drink and most other raw materials imported into the city being the most lucrative. They were assessed at the city gates: the street widens outside each of the six gates of London, probably from carts crowding around awaiting clearance to pass through.[49] Sales and use taxes on the marketplaces, the Cloth Halls, the crane, the fish market and the Meat Hall, which were regalian rights that had been renounced to the city by the prince, were much less profitable. But the two types combined accounted for at least 80 per cent of the income of both Ghent and Bruges in most years. The Flemish cities also realised some income from the land tax, but at Ghent this provided less than 4 per cent of the budget in most years. More important were 'issue' taxes on the property of persons who ceased to be taxable by the city. These included emigrants and persons entering holy orders, but 'issue' was most often a death duty, which in plague years amounted to a sizeable segment of the city's budget. It was 14.29 per cent of the municipal receipt in 1368–9, the year of Ghent's most severe fourteenth-century plague.[50]

Municipal indebtedness

Demands on the cities were outstripping their tax bases in the late Middle Ages, forcing most to operate at a deficit. The irresponsible city financing of the thirteenth century was succeeded by a much more conservative approach in the early fourteenth. Ghent borrowed from the Lombards of Paris early in the fourteenth century but did little public borrowing thereafter except early in the Hundred Years' War. The city met emergencies by levying forced loans on its wealthier citizens and by selling annuity rents. But Ghent's new-found solvency broke down in the wake of the high demands of the Flemish counts, particularly the Burgundian regime after 1385. The city ran a chronic deficit in the fifteenth century, with an income of 3,078 pounds and debits of 3,608 pounds in 1439–40. Punitive fines levied by the count after 1453 forced Ghent to levy surcharges and rents and eventually to collect some direct taxes.

48 Irsigler, 'Industrial production', 242, 273–4; Leguay, *Réseau urbain Bretagne*, 149–51; Meek, 'Public policy', 46.
49 Schofield, *Medieval London Houses*, 7.
50 Nicholas, 'Governance', 252.

Yet the finances of Ghent were healthier than those of Bruges, despite the commercial prosperity of Flanders' chief port. Like Ghent, Bruges borrowed much less often during the fourteenth century than earlier. In extreme need Bruges borrowed from Italians, most of them representatives of merchant banking houses based at Bruges. Bruges did levy forced loans, but until late in the century it used life and perpetual rents less than Ghent. But the pressure of Burgundian taxation became insupportable. In 1407 Bruges commuted its obligations to the prince in return for one-seventh of the city's total receipt each year, but by 1413 the count was demanding advances on these payments. Bruges' accounts were balanced only four times between 1435 and 1467. The Flemish cities thus became permanently indebted during the fifteenth century. They consolidated their debts, consisting mainly of perpetual and life rents, often listing them as a separate item at the end of the account after the balance for the year.[51]

Most cities tried to avoid becoming debtors of their own citizens, but the urban rich saw the forced loans and annuity rents, in which a sum was paid in return for an annual payment for the rest of the buyer's life, as sources of investment. Burgesses of Trier, Frankfurt and Mainz arranged loans through the goldsmiths, and the cities sold one other's rents. The annuity rents sold by the cities were thus very close to municipal bond issues. In crisis periods the rates on these rents were extremely favourable for investors. For tax purposes no distinction was made in Flanders to account for the age of the purchaser. Augsburg used a primitive actuarial scheme in 1457, when the councils restricted the sale of life rents to persons aged 40 and above, and to one life. The rate for 40-year-olds was 1:10; for older persons and the sick, the *pawmeister* set whatever rate he thought appropriate.[52]

War expenses and the uncertain tax base forced many French cities, like their neighbours in Flanders, into serious debt in the fifteenth century. By 1467 Saint-Omer had an annual deficit of 2,500 *livres* and a floating debt of 5,000–6,000 *livres* on an annual budget of 20,000 *livres*. The *échevins*, realising that the *taille* was resented, instead sold life annuities, often at low rates. The rates on the excises more than trebled during the fourteenth century to make up the difference. By 1473 interest on the rents absorbed over half the total income of the city, and the government was selling new rents to pay for the old ones! In 1473 the duke authorised partial bankruptcy and instituted a municipal lottery. Repayment of rents and the accumulated interest involved 79 per cent of the

51 Nicholas, *Medieval Flanders*, 244–5, 329–32, 374–5 and literature cited.
52 Matheus, *Trier*, 66; Keutgen, *Urkunden*, no. 210, pp. 265–6.

municipal expenditure of Arles in 1448, 86 per cent in 1449 and at Rouen 70 per cent for the century as a whole.[53]

Expenses, audits and responsibility

Virtually all city accounts were audited, at least by the city council, but sometimes also by the lord, the king or a committee of citizens. Given the time needed to compile a finished account from preliminary drafts and expense vouchers, new governments had to audit the accounts of their predecessors. At Rouen the new mayor and receivers were to present accounts within eight days of taking office. The incoming mayor was to seize the property of his predecessor within thirty days if he had not turned in his accounts.[54]

Audits often found discrepancies that suggest that the picture given by the formal city records is somewhat sanitised. Although overt corruption was punished when caught, all cities gave 'presents' that were really ill-disguised bribes to officials of the central court. Chartres spent an average of 28 per cent of its budget in the fifteenth century on presents and gratuities for the king and other dignitaries. The figure approached 60 per cent in years when the king or queen made a formal entry into the city. Ghent usually spent 4–10 per cent of its income for such purposes in the fourteenth century, and the figure rose in the fifteenth. Gifts to dignitaries were a severe drain on York's shaky finances. Many of the 'gifts and presents' in the English city accounts were payments to the itinerant justices.[55]

The unofficial perquisites of high office caused financial trouble for many cities. They spent large amounts on banquets and celebrations, some of which were public, though others amounted to private parties for magistrates and notables. Although the wealthy members of the city council were usually either unpaid or received a modest salary, they were reimbursed for daily expenses and uniforms, and they received costly presents and comestibles during public functions. Members of the councils often farmed the more lucrative excises in years when they were rotated off the magistracy. Given the possibilities for corruption, the excise

---

53 Bruges had had a lottery since 1439. Nicholas, *Medieval Flanders*, 374; Derville, *Histoire de Saint-Omer*, 78–9, 91; Stouff, *Arles*, 316; Mollat, *Histoire de Rouen*, 124–5.

54 Mollat, *Histoire de Rouen*, 116–17. In practice the narrow elite rarely called a predecessor government to account.

55 Billot, *Chartres*, 149–50; Prevenier, 'Comptes communaux en Flandre', 111–45; Nicholas, 'Governance', 253; Blockmans, 'Comptes urbains', 287–338; Chédeville, *Histoire de Chartres*, 150; Tillott, *City of York*, 57–9; Rowe and Draisey, *Exeter Receivers' Accounts*, xxvii–xxviii.

farmers had to post enormous bonds. Trier changed to direct administration of the excises in the fifteenth century to prevent such abuses.[56]

Most cities did not have large budgets for wages, but the amounts rose in the fifteenth century. Valenciennes paid wages to forty-six people in 1435–6, including clerks, bell-ringers, gendarmes and a man responsible for burying dead animals. Ghent, which was much larger and had a more complex administration, had between 123 and 138 persons in the city government in the period 1354–76, but roughly one-third of them were unpaid aldermen and excise farmers. In these decades wages reached a high of 9.29 per cent of municipal expenditure in 1372, a low of 4.25 per cent in 1360. Wages were only 2 per cent of Lille's municipal expenditure in 1465.[57]

CITY FINANCES: THE SOUTH

The Italian cities were much wealthier than the northern and had more sophisticated financial institutions. Their incomes were rising despite the severe population decline. Florence had an income of 370,000 *lire* in 1316, 390,000 in 1317, 930,000 in 1336–8, 1.5 million in 1362 and nearly 2 million in 1424. Even accounting for monetary devaluation, the city was smaller but its government considerably wealthier in the fifteenth century than in the fourteenth. Similar figures have been calculated for other Italian cities. Although taxes were rising in the northern cities, none even approached these rates. The municipal receipts of Milan and Venice in 1423 were comparable to those of the national monarchies of Castile, France and England.[58]

As in the north, we cannot evaluate the success of any city in balancing its budget, for there were many sources of income and exemptions and omissions in the records. Comparing the tax structures of north and south is also made more difficult by the fact that 'gabelles' in the north were always indirect, while in Italy the term included both direct and indirect taxes. Direct gabelles were assessed on persons who were no longer taxed with the *contado* communities from which they had emigrated, and on certain salaries. But administration of the gabelles was similar to the excises in the northern cities. After 1323 Siena farmed all gabelles, both direct and indirect. As in the north, frequent discounts were granted to tax farmers who claimed that unusual circumstances,

56 Matheus, *Trier*, 170–2.
57 Platelle, *Histoire de Valenciennes*, 65; Schulz, *Handwerksgesellen und Lohnarbeiter*, 372–4; Nicholas, 'Governance', 253–5; Trenard, *Histoire de Lille*, 229–31.
58 Herlihy, 'Tuscan urban finance', 386; Barel, *Ville médiévale*, 436.

such as war, prevented them from collecting as much as they had anti-cipated. A 'gabelle of the gates', corresponding to the 'excise of the gates' in the north, was very important in all Italian cities, especially Florence. It was paid on goods entering and leaving the city except food and drinks, which were taxed separately. The gabelle on wine was high, as in the north. Siena even had a 'gabelle of contracts', amounting to a brokerage fee, which was hard to enforce since so many sales and rentals were not recorded. Gabelles as a whole were increasing as a percentage of the total city income in the late fourteenth century.[59]

Most Italian cities used both direct and indirect taxes. The *estimo*, a tax on income from land, accounted for only 10 per cent of the receipts of Florence in the fourteenth century, half that in the dependent towns of Prato and Pistoia. The *estimo* was abolished for the city of Florence in 1315, but it was kept as the base of *contado* taxation. Although the agrarian depression diminished revenues from it, Florence's territory contained some medium-sized cities that kept total receipts at a reason-able level.[60] At Genoa three colleges of assessors decided who would be inscribed on the registers of the *avaria mobili*, the most lucrative direct taxes, then set the amount owed by each. The bases by which the tax was calculated were not entirely consistent. The assessors did check in advance the respective shares owed by nobles and *popolari*; but the noble *alberghi* of Spinola and Fieschi were exempt from the *avaria*, as were others who had made special arrangements with the city on grounds of recent migration, poverty or economic incentive. The favoured guilds of silk weavers and seamen also received tax reductions. Except for the Spinola and Fieschi the nobles as a group were not privileged; indeed, since most who defaulted were *popolari*, a greater tax burden was thrust on the nobles.[61]

Siena too relied more heavily on direct taxes (*dazi*) than did most Italian cities in the fourteenth century. The Nine (1287–1355) levied at least eighteen. Rates varied from 20 per cent to less than 1 per cent, probably because some were based on the *lira* assessment of rentals and income, others on market or sale price, and still others on movables or immovables. The assessment rate also depended on what other taxes were being collected at the same time. In 1323 the council of Siena agreed to the principle of maintaining several systems of taxation, so that persons who were burdened by one would be relieved in another. But direct taxes lost importance in the late fourteenth century.[62]

59   Bowsky, *Finances Siena*, 114–65.
60   Bowsky, *Finances Siena*, 87–97.
61   Heers, *Gênes. Civilisation*, 97–9.
62   Bowsky, *Finances Siena*, 279–86, 98–113.

The Tuscan cities farmed most indirect taxes before the Black Death. Lucca collected the more lucrative excises directly and farmed the others, which probably explains why the tax farmers of Lucca were mainly 'new men' from the *contado* or the middling wealth group of the non-merchant element of the city. The bakers' guild of Siena farmed the tax on bread between 1297 and 1314, and the butchers, although generally out of favour with the city government after 1318, also leased some excises.[63]

The termination of the *estimo* in 1315 had forced the city to raise excises to compensate. The gabelles included the levies on consumption, together with profits from the state monopoly on salt, taxes on the sale of assets such as shares of the *Monte* (the public debt), and excises at the gates on imports and exports. The variety of Florentine taxation is mind-boggling. Villani lists thirty different indirect taxes, and his list is incomplete. Rents were taxed, as were the profits of pawnbrokers and fines for breach of peace. Florence, like Orvieto earlier, had a primitive value added tax. Foods were taxed at different stages of production: when the crop was gathered, when it was sold wholesale, when it was processed and finally when it was sold retail. In times of need the *Signoria* tacked on additional gabelles, but most were short-lived. The rates on food clearly had an impact on the cost of living. Except for some short-term increases, the gabelle on wheat, which was assessed at the gates, was generally steady, perhaps reflecting the generally low grain prices. Taxes on oil and livestock rose, particularly between 1327 and 1364, but then dropped, although these were still much higher than they had been early in the century. Taxes at the gates on oil rose 500 per cent between 1328 and 1380, on pigs 700 per cent between 1333 and 1380, and on eggs 500 per cent between 1320 and 1380. The wine tax levied at the gates underwent a sixfold increase between 1335 and 1349, then declined after 1360 to a rate that was still five times higher than before 1336. A separate tax on wine was calculated as a percentage of sale price; it rose from 6.25 per cent in 1299 to 66 per cent in 1359. Even when the *estimo* was reinstituted in 1338 it accounted for only one-third of the receipt from the gabelle of the gates alone, and it had declined to less than 20 per cent by 1375.[64]

Throughout the first half of the fourteenth century Florence sold the excises to tax farmers at annual auctions. The system did not work well, in part because the farmers had to borrow to pay the lump sum at the beginning of the fiscal year, and some of them lost money. From the

63 Meek, 'Public policy', 42, 60–9; Bowsky, *Siena Under the Nine*, 209–12.
64 Discussion based on de la Roncière, 'Indirect taxes at Florence', 144–57, 177–82; see also Larner, *Age of Dante and Petrarch*, 218.

1340s the city could not find takers for some taxes, which forced the commune to go over gradually to direct administration of most of them after 1350. Despite the rising rates of the gabelles, the income from the individual taxes remained stable, for fewer goods passed the tolls as rates were raised, and many people were able to bypass the market mechanism by consuming products brought from their rural estates.[65]

Thus the Tuscan cities realised less than one might expect from the excises. The grain tax yielded only 1.41 per cent of the income of Florence by 1338, but 21 per cent at Prato and 17.10 per cent at Pistoia.[66] In 1371 Lucca consolidated several indirect taxes, which were pledged in advance to repay loans, into a single 10 per cent tax on salt. The salt gabelle was used mainly to pay interest on the rapidly growing city debt. The city also realised considerable income from indirect taxes on other items, particularly the customs levy on food, and from sales taxes on transfers of real property.[67]

Most Italian cities used long-term forced loans to a greater extent than in the north, perhaps because of the great wealth of their leading political families, although the forced loans did not strike only the wealthy, as in the north. The excises were inadequate by the late fourteenth century to pay off the enormous debts that had been generated by constant warfare and bloated bureaucracies. Lucca levied a general *estimo* in 1397, with half of each taxpayer's property made the basis for the tax. Technically this was considered a forced loan, not a direct tax, to be repaid as soon as the emergency had passed. The public debt remained large, but except during crises it did not grow much after the 1390s, generally remaining about the size of the annual income of the city.[68] The loans were repaid at interest and were good sources of investment – Siena paid 10 per cent – and the interest on them was a serious burden on the city. The income from certain *dazi* or gabelles might be assigned for such repayment.

Deficit financing was raised to a fine art at Florence and Venice. Venice had had a public debt based on forced loans since the early thirteenth century. In 1363 the city government gave up the pretence of eventually paying off the debt when it started using the ordinary income of the city in good years to buy shares of the debt. Government securities were thus bought and sold. The system was not oppressive before the war of Chioggia (1378–81), but then the rates were raised and interest payments suspended. This led gradually to the reimposition

65 Herlihy and Klapisch-Zuber, *Tuscans*, 2; Molho, *Florentine Public Finances*, 22–53.
66 Herlihy, 'Tuscan urban finance', 399–400.
67 Meek, *Lucca 1369–1400*, 50–7.
68 Meek, *Lucca 1369–1400*, 69–76.

of direct taxes. A permanent income tax, the tithe, was established in 1403.[69] The forced loans at Florence were really direct taxes under another name, for they were assessed only in the city, roughly in proportion to taxable wealth, with the iassessment determined by boards in each *gonfalone*. Although they were theoretically loans to be repaid, the government defaulted on them or frequently suspended repayment.[70]

The forced loans at Florence were causing such discontent in the late fourteenth century that the Ciompi regime appointed assessors to devise a rate for a new *estimo*. It was repealed in 1381, and city finances reverted to forced loans and deficit financing. In 1427, following a financial crisis set off by the war with Milan that resulted in the highest level of forced loans in the republic's history, the long campaign to institute a *catasto*, a direct tax based on ability to pay and levied on both movable and immovable property in both city and *contado*, was finally successful. The assessment, based on information provided by the heads of households, exempted the family residence and personal furnishings, giving relief to the poor while leading the wealthy to invest in art works, furnishings and other items of conspicuous consumption within the house. The records of this and subsequent *catasti* have given scholars immense resources for studying wealth and family structures. The *catasto* was ended in 1434, to be restored permanently in 1458: although the Florentines feared arbitrary taxation, the notion of individual privilege and negotiation was so fundamental to their political culture that they also disliked the more rational *catasto*.[71] Venice used a *catasto* based on principles of assessment that are so similar that Florence almost certainly borrowed some details. Yet, although the *catasto* improved public finance, it did not end reliance on forced loans and deficit financing, although the loans were distributed more equitably after 1427 on the basis of the improved assessment data. It is not even clear whether the poor or the rich benefited more from the *catasto*.[72]

The Italian cities consolidated their considerable obligations into funded debts (*Monti*) earlier than the northern cities, beginning with that of Florence in 1345, which combined the city's liabilities from the numerous forced loans and paid 5 per cent interest. The funded debt of Lucca paid 10 per cent interest initially, 5 per cent after 1378. The

69 Luzzatto, *Economic History of Italy*, 124–6.
70 Bowsky, *Finances Siena*, 166–88, 196–9, 275–6, 285–90; Herlihy and Klapisch-Zuber, *Tuscans*, 3–4; Molho, *Florentine Public Finances*, 74–87; Kent, *Neighbours and Neighbourhood*, 20.
71 Kent, *Neighbours and Neighbourhood*, 25, 48–66.
72 Discussion in Brucker, *Civic World*, 55, 481–5; Molho, *Florentine Public Finances*, 63; Herlihy and Klapisch-Zuber, *Tuscans*, 8–10; Klapisch-Zuber, *Women, Family, and Ritual*, 13.

Ciompi regime abolished the *Monte* and interest-bearing loans briefly, thinking correctly that the rich benefited; but they had to restore the *Monte*, for they did not understand that the lesser guildsmen with small investments also had an interest in it.[73] Governments placed high taxes on the transfer of *Monte* shares, but they remained subjects of fiscal speculation. Although Lucca did allow assignments on debt shares, it was unusual in permitting alienation only to the state after 1378.[74] Genoa sold shares in its funded debt, the *compera*, in amounts varying with particular needs. Each time the commune borrowed, a new *compera* was created or those already existing were increased. In 1407 Genoa linked the *compere* in a municipal bank, the Casa San Giorgio, which was the strongest financial institution of western Europe in the fifteenth century. The directors of San Giorgio were great merchants and nobles involved in international trade. The city gradually entrusted the bank with its finances, including tax collection and disbursement.[75]

Taxes were higher in the cities of the late Middle Ages than the tangible benefits of municipal expenditure warranted. But although the cities were experimenting with tax bases, and means of money-raising and accounting were often inchoate, financial abuses of the sort associated with thirteenth-century city governments are rare after 1330. Most cities had an income sufficient for their ordinary expenses, but that income was hopelessly inadequate to pay for wars and ruinous princely taxation. The municipal elites were wealthy aristocrats who were very conscious of their privileges, but they do not appear to have been dishonest. We must now examine the composition, status and perquisites of the ruling elites of the late medieval cities.

---

73 Herlihy, 'Tuscan urban finance', 400; Bowsky, *Finances Siena*, 275, 295; Brucker, *Civic World*, 53.
74 Meek, *Lucca 1369–1400*, 50, 65–6.
75 Heers, *Gênes. Civilisation*, 101–18.

CHAPTER SIX

The Elites of the Later Medieval Cities

The older lineages continued to dominate city councils in the late Middle Ages, but 'old' is a relative term. The urban elite included several groups by the late fourteenth century.

The ministerial elite

A ministerial elite of knightly and/or landowning families dominated the colleges of *scabini*. Landowners controlled many governments even in commercial cities, particularly in Germany. The ambiguous legal standing of the ministerials continued to cause problems in the Low Countries, although not in Germany. They were initially serfs, and as late as 1300 the city council of Koblenz contained seven unfree ministerials. In the fourteenth century many magistrates of Liège paid rents to rural lords in recognition of their servile status. Most of Nuremberg's aristocracy of about thirty families were long-distance and wholesale merchants, but many were descended from imperial ministerials. Others, such as the Holzschuh and Välzner, were non-ministerial warriors or landholders of the Nuremberg area. Only a few were of purely merchant origin. The old groups were best able to preserve their control in places such as Saint-Omer, where commerce provided little new wealth in the fourteenth century.[1]

The older merchant elite

A group of merchant families was sharing power with the older lineages by the early fourteenth century and thereafter identified with them

---

1 Gonthier, *Cris de haine*, 63 n. 20; Bischoff, 'Stadtherrschaft im ostfränkischen Städtedreieck', 104; Pfeiffer, *Nürnberg*, 35; Derville, *Histoire de Saint-Omer*, 90; van Uytven, 'Stadsgeschiedenis', 227.

against newcomers. They dominated the colleges of *jurés* and the city councils properly so called. As contact between the major centres increased in the late Middle Ages, merchant elites in most cities included a few who had originated in neighbouring places where their families sat on the councils. Members of wealthy urban families frequently emigrated, either because they were excluded by their kin from leadership in their families' businesses or simply to seek greater opportunities elsewhere. Some patricians of Nuremberg came from neighbouring communities. Lübeck had four great burgomasters in the period after 1370, none of them native-born.[2] A branch of the Adorno family of Genoa, which had business interests in the market of Bruges, settled in the northern port and became burgomasters in the fifteenth century.

Contemporaries called the ministerial elite 'lineages', while the newer and mainly merchant group were 'honourable persons'. 'Honourable persons', the wealthy merchants and members of 'free trades' who were eligible for membership of the council but were neither ministerial patricians nor craftsmen, did not work with their hands but rather lived off their investments. Dortmund's Honourables arose during the struggles against the emperor's decree of 1332 that limited council membership to the old lineages. Ancestry was as important to both groups as to the rural nobles; economic orientation was secondary. One-third of the memoir of Werner Overstolz of Cologne deals with his kinspeople, and much of the rest discusses alterations of his coat of arms and contains an excursus on the Roman origins of the Cologne lineages.[3] Norwich required craftsmen to renounce their trades to become mayor or enter the Common Council. The Bremen constitution of 1330 required councillors to conduct themselves 'in a gentlemanly manner' and not to work during their terms of office.[4]

Although lineage became important to this group, it was also defined on the more fluctuating bases of wealth and the ability to avoid working with one's hands. It was thus more permeable than the ministerial aristocracy. The high mortality of the late Middle Ages made it more difficult than before to keep property intact. Although some top families were able to entail estates, it was unusual although not unheard of for the same property to stay in the family for more than three generations.[5] The average number of male heirs per family reaching adulthood

---

2 Reinecke, 'Bevölkerungsprobleme der Hansestädte', 266, 272–3.
3 Bischoff, 'Stadtherrschaft im ostfränkischen Städtedreieck', 104; Du Boulay, *Germany*, 141; Herborn, 'Bürgerliches Selbstverständnis', 502–6.
4 Hilton, *English and French Towns*, 102; Maschke, *Städte und Menschen*, 231, 258.
5 Two houses bought in 1348 and 1362 by Peter Mangold of Constance were owned by Konrad Mangold in 1448, although the family was occupying neither. Bechtold, *Zunftbürgerschaft und Patriziat*, 34.

was never higher than two and in the fifteenth century closer to one.[6] Since movable property was chattel and hence subject to inheritance division, most businesses were ended with each generation unless the merchant had enough money to make cash bequests and/or set up various heirs in business. Relatively few grandsons of merchants making wills are proven; thus businesses rarely lasted more than two generations in the fourteenth and fifteenth centuries, an even shorter time than landed property generally remained in the same family.[7] Even in London few families stayed in the city longer than three or four generations.

Inheritance customs contributed to the ability of families to preserve property and cohesion across generations. At Reims the individual could dispose freely only of what he had acquired personally, not inherited property. All kin, not simply the nearest relative, had a right of first refusal on immovable property before outsiders could buy it. Thus until the plagues, estates tended to remain in the same family and helped the lineages perpetuate their influence.[8] Other inheritance regimes permitted easier alienation of family property through sale, marriage settlement or bequest. Flanders had partible inheritance without distinction of age or gender, and the result was a rapid combination and recombination of fortunes. The political elite there, although narrow, was more open than in regions where daughters or younger sons could be disadvantaged. Although the Italian cities normally excluded females from inheritance beyond the dowry, Florence and other Tuscan cities had partible inheritance among sons, resulting in great mobility of fortunes among the merchant elite.[9]

In cities that permitted disposal by testament only of acquisitions, estates would be kept reasonably intact for the children, with some rights of common property and jointure for a surviving spouse, even if uses and marriage portions could alienate other assets. Preserving the family property, which was obviously a more serious concern for the elite than for others, thus made marriages critical. Italian fathers used their daughters' dowries to compete for appropriate sons-in-law, leading to a family structure in which older men married younger women with dowries that were so big that their brothers could have no property until they inherited the father's estate.[10] Reacting to the increasing size of dowries, the Venetian Senate, filled with people who were being ruined by this

6   Platt, *English Medieval Town*, 119.
7   Kermode, 'Merchants', 16.
8   Desportes, *Reims*, 249–67.
9   Nicholas, 'Poverty and primacy', 37–8; Goldthwaite, *Building of Renaissance Florence*, 63.
10   Herlihy, *Medieval Households*, 153–5.

practice, in 1420 narrowly passed a statute limiting the size of marriage settlements. It proved impossible to enforce.[11]

While lineage preservation among the newer elites was hindered by partible inheritance and in Italy by competition over dowries, the ministerials of northern Europe were plagued by a diminishing pool of acceptable marriage partners. The patrician lineages that were guaranteed seats on French and German city councils in the early fourteenth century sometimes lacked personnel to fill them by the fifteenth. Augsburg had fifty-one patrician families in 1368, eight in 1538. Two-thirds of the old families of Reims were gone by 1400, and the decline was especially marked after 1360 due to losses during the plagues. Of some thirty families that were present when the commune of Lyon originated, only six remained into the fifteenth century, and three of them were gone by 1500. Intermarriage with noble families raised the patricians' prestige but weakened their real power in the city.[12]

The memoir of Werner Overstolz, a scion of one of the most ancient houses of Cologne, illustrates the problem of lineage preservation among the ministerial elite, which was worse than with the merchant lineages. The Overstolze of the Rheingasse had been in the city in the twelfth century and by the late thirteenth were entrenched on all three policy-making boards: council, *Schöffen* and Rich Club. Although other branches of the family married into the rural nobility, Johann, father of the author of the memoir, was the first of the Rheingasse branch to achieve knighthood. He was exiled after the revolution of 1396 but was back by 1399, serving the new government on diplomatic missions but not on the council. He became a justice of the city court in 1419. His son Werner, who was also a knight, was *Schöffe* in 1421 and succeeded his father as judge in 1423. Although Johann had been an uncontroversial judge, Werner tried to extend the competence of the *Schöffen*, the bastion of the older families, against the council, which was dominated by the families that had come to power in 1396. He was imprisoned briefly in late 1423, then left Cologne until 1429. He seems to have lived exclusively on income from rents, for there are no references to him or his father being in trade outside the city. Werner's grandfather Werner had three children. Johann, father of Werner the younger, had sixteen children, most of whom died young. Werner the younger was the only one of his sons who reached adulthood who married. Since Werner's two older sons joined the Teutonic Order, he left all his property in and around Cologne to his youngest son Wynant and finally

11 Chojnacki, 'Marriage legislation', 165, 177.
12 Maschke, *Städte und Menschen*, 78; Valous, *Patriciat Lyonnais*, 93; Desportes, *Reims*, 614–25.

joined the Order himself and left public life. He died in 1451, followed by Wynant at age 15 in 1453. With Wynant their branch of the Overstolz in the Rheingasse became extinguished.[13]

A sense of class

Naturally the older and newer patriciates interacted and intermarried. Numerous examples illustrate the artificiality of making too fine a distinction between the older and newer elites. At Trier non-ministerial families were *Schöffen* by the end of the thirteenth century. They controlled the city by 1400, as the older families died out or entered the clergy. The old elite of Rouen lived mainly on income from rents and left government to the commercial aristocracy, but this group also sought the classic marks of prestige, often using municipal office as a springboard to the nobility. Jacques Le Lieur, a wine and salt merchant, was mayor in 1357 and was ennobled in 1364. The Alorge family of salt, alum and wine merchants built a solid base in the city, including investment in immovable property, rents and tax farming, culminating in the mayoralty in 1348, then moved into rural land investment. Guillaume Alorge was ennobled in 1394.[14]

The older and newer officeholding groups felt more community of interest with each other than with the merchant craftsmen. Marriage into the older lineages became more a social than a political issue. Both groups were distinguishing themselves from others by the notion of families being eligible for membership of the council. In 1405 the hereditary burgesses of Vienna appear as a corporation that included both those currently eligible for the council and the ancient lineages, many of them knightly and going back to the thirteenth century. The Coin Book of Albrecht von Eberstorf defined a hereditary burgess as one 'who does not trade as a merchant or engage in other trade'.[15] The question was generally whether the old patriciates were open to persons who were newly rich from commerce and thus whether one could join a patrician lineage without giving up one's previous trade. Constance permitted continuation of the trade, but at Ravensburg and at Strasbourg after 1472 the lineages could only be entered by giving up trade and living on income from rents as a person of 'leisure'. In 1383 the lineages closed the patriciate at Augsburg; on the demand of the guilds, which wanted to keep the patricians from gaining political power by joining their organisations and controlling the city council through them, the patriciate was

13 Memoir discussed by Herborn, 'Bürgerliches Selbstverständnis', 490–7.
14 Matheus, *Trier*, 185; Mollat, *Histoire de Rouen*, 110–11.
15 Author's translation. Csendes, 'Stadtherr und bürgerliche Führungsschicht', 254.

closed at Ulm and Basel. As patriciates lost power, social climbers tried to join them, but not politically ambitious wealthy people. The patriciate of Augsburg, which had declined to thirteen families, tried to coopt four rich merchant-guild families in 1478, but they refused to join.[16] The ruling elite adopted titles: after 1330 the members of the council at Speyer were to be called Lords (*Herren*), a title elsewhere used only for nobles and clergy, and in Speyer until 1304 for the mint associates. Other German city governments followed suit.[17] The title 'Herr' was used for all eminent persons at Strasbourg, including heads of guilds. In 1309 the emperor Henry VII refused to consider a petition from the *Herren* of Strasbourg until they changed the form to 'burgesses'.[18] The mayor and aldermen of London were variously styled 'worshipful', 'gracious', 'sire' or 'lord', although this title was later reserved for the mayor. Public officials everywhere wore uniforms furnished by the city, with the finest cloth used for mayor and council members, coarser grades for the lesser officials.[19]

The city governments insisted on deference to such lords. Honour, like lineage, was important to the urban elite. The Cologne burgomaster Goedart van dem Wasservasse complained to the council in 1444 that when the magistracy was rotated the previous year Herr Herman Scherftgin had insulted him with words touching his honour. The councillors urged him to let it pass, since they had heard the words and nonetheless chosen Goedart burgomaster.[20] In a *Bursprake* of 1350 the 'lords of the council' of Lübeck ordered everyone to be 'courteous and well behaved, night and day, in church, on the markets, and in the streets. If it is found that anyone makes a disturbance, the lords will judge it in an exemplary fashion'. They ordered everyone to keep a courteous countenance toward 'lords and princes, to knights and squires and priests, in the countryside and in the towns', or be fined. A *Bursprake* of Wismar in 1419 intoned that 'no one may speak ill of princes, lords, virgins or other honourable people, clerical and lay'.[21]

The newer merchant/craft elite

Wealthy craftsmen who began to trade as merchants and tried to gain political power by using guild affiliation as a test were the newest element

16 Maschke, *Städte und Menschen*, 252–3, 262.
17 Maschke, *Städte und Menschen*, 131.
18 Le Goff, 'L'Apogée', 345.
19 Thrupp, *Merchant Class*, 171–18. See in general Mollat and Wolff, *Popular Revolutions*, 26.
20 Huiskes, *Beschlüsse Köln*, 197.
21 Sprandel, *Quellen zur Hanse-Geschichte*, 34, 38.

of the urban elite. Even in the more industrial guilds a small group, often those who filled the guild magistracies, sold the raw materials of the trade to guild members, to the point of monopoly in some cases.[22] The gap between these merchant-craftsmen and the older merchant families was greater in most cities than that between the older merchant houses and the ministerial lineages. This group gained influence in places whose industry was growing, such as Leiden, and in cities where the older merchant houses moved toward the nobility, as happened at Cologne after 1396.[23] The road to power of the merchant-oriented guild elites was to have membership on city councils based on guild affiliation, with individual guilds or groups of trades having guaranteed seats. This group thus entered city governments by controlling their crafts. Even in largely industrial cities landowning and commercial wealth, rather than craftsmanship, determined prestige within and between guilds. This craft elite shared power in most places except the Hanse cities by the late fourteenth century. Some persons in this group were political revolutionaries. Robert de Saint-Yon, a butcher with interests in finance and the wine trade, was one of the leaders in the butchers' terror in Paris in 1413.[24]

The merchant guildsmen were the most mobile element of the urban elite and initially had the least consciousness of lineage, but they too were becoming status- and lineage-conscious by 1450. In the fourteenth century most craftsmen marketed their own wares, even in clothmaking, which was the most interregional of the major industries. But by 1450, as access to the fairs and princely courts determined the success of local markets, professional merchants dominated the local economy and lost their guild ties. At Cologne there were still some merchant–craft combinations in fustian and yarn work, especially by married couples when the man functioned as merchant and the woman as craftsperson.[25]

A few well-documented cases show how poor people could gain fortune and status through the guilds. Jan Sloesgin of Cologne was born in 1389 at Nijmegen in the Netherlands and was thus a mature man when he went to Cologne in 1415. He entered the *Gaffel* of Windech, the corporation of traders with England, which suggests wealth before he came to Cologne. In 1417 he took a house for ten years for the enormous ground rent of 42 gulden, then in 1426 bought another for 700 gulden. By 1425 he was in the corporation of mint associates and loaned money to the city. In the 1430s he was buying rural land. In addition to his English business, he traded at Deventer, Antwerp and

22 Mackenney, *Tradesmen and Traders*, 16–17.
23 Howell, *Women, Production, and Patriarchy*, 108.
24 *Parisian Journal*, 78.
25 Irsigler, *Wirtschaftliche Stellung Köln*, 320.

the Frankfurt fairs. Sloesgin married in 1416 and had twelve children, of whom nine died unmarried. His son and his brother Andreas founded a company, with business throughout Upper Germany and Thuringia, and Michael Sloesgin traded in Venice. The Sloesgins gained political influence in the second half of the fifteenth century, after an economic rise in the first half.[26]

Christoffel Zipp of Constance illustrates the progression from money-lending to politics. A wealthy merchant, moneylender and money-changer of relatively recent lineage, Zipp's net worth increased by 40 per cent between 1418 and 1433, making him one of the four richest men of the city. Thereafter he concentrated on politics as a representative of the aristocratic wine guild – he never joined the patrician Cat Society – and spent less time on his business. Zipp's business links had extended throughout southern Germany, but successive recensions of his children's property after he died in 1435 show a gradual limitation to the region of Lake Constance. Illustrating the trend that descendants of persons who made their fortunes in smaller towns were leaving for the large cities, where capital and trade were becoming more concentrated, Zipp's son had left Constance for Zürich by 1450.[27]

Patrician clubs

Some patriciates tried to hinder mobility into their ranks by forming a fraternity or social club, a drinking society named after the device on its coat of arms, that was closed to outsiders. The 'urban knights' (*caballeros villanos*) of Burgos formed two devotional fraternities, Our Lady of Gamonal in 1285 and the Real Hermandad in 1338. Our Lady had ninety-nine members in 1305, most of whom listed trades, including all the *alcaldes* of the city. By the sixteenth century this was known as the confraternity of merchants. The more aristocratic Real Hermandad required its members to possess horses and weapons for cavalry combat. There were 171 members in 1338, probably representing 2–3 per cent of a total population of 6,500–8,000. Entry fees to the brotherhood were raised astronomically after 1348. All members of the Real Hermandad lived on four streets around the centrally located cathedral.[28]

In the north such clubs are generally found only when the older

26 Herborn, 'Bürgerliches Selbstverständnis', 498–500; Hirschfelder, *Kölner Handelsbeziehungen*, 56, 65, 303, 383, 439, 464. The chronicle of Burkard Zink of Augsburg contains his autobiography, which details his rise from draper's apprentice to fustian trader. Maschke, 'Der wirtschaftliche Aufstieg des Burkard Zink (1396+–1474/5) in Augsburg'. In *Städte und Menschen*, 420–47.

27 Bechtold, *Zunftbürgerschaft und Patriziat*, 38–45.

28 Ruiz, *Burgos and Castile*, 17–20.

patriciate had lost most political power but hoped to maintain its social exclusivity. Those of Germany are the best known. The 'Lineage Halls' (*Geschlechterstuben*) had great prestige for merchants, who wanted membership even at the cost of political influence. In Ravensburg in 1444 persons who wanted to join the patrician society *zum Esel*, 'whether cloth wholesalers or other' – showing where the money was – had to surrender their trades. Far from being a private regulation, this was an ordinance issued by the burgomaster, council and guild deans. Social distinctions were sharpest in the few cities that combined a guild regime with a closed patriciate. At Ravensburg the merchants established their own society *zum Ballen* that excluded both craftsmen and the patrician members of *zum Esel*. At Augsburg the 'Augmenters of Society' were the non-patrician upper group of guildsmen who formed their own club in reaction to the closing of the patriciate.[29]

The patrician societies of the Hanse cities became amanuenses for the city government. The Circle Society of Lübeck had fifty-two members in 1429; in 1483 only one member of the council was not a member. Frankfurt had several patrician associations. The most eminent was the Old Limburg Society, which in 1407 had sixty members from twenty-nine families, though one-quarter of them were from the Weiss family. In places where the lineages shared power on the council with merchant-guildsmen, 'Gentlemen's Chambers' were formed to help maintain patrician power on the council, although sometimes they simply isolated the lineages. Membership in such clubs was generally hereditary for the oldest son, but other sons could enter for a fee.[30]

The social clubs are not the same as the political guilds into which the patricians were joined when they were guaranteed seats on the magistracy. The political guilds chose officers just as the crafts did. Their rights were vaguer when their organisations were purely social and only 'guild-like', such as *zum Esel* at Ravensburg. When patricians had guaranteed seats, they sat together in council sessions in the first bench after the burgomaster and voted before the guildsmen but had few other real perquisites.[31] The social aspect of the patrician clubs was not lost on the authorities and was imitated by guildsmen. A statute of 1420 ordered the 'new patricians' of guild origin at Constance to relinquish membership in patrician social clubs, specifically the Cat Society and drinking halls, and to return to the guilds to which their ancestors had belonged, on the grounds that the guilds were being weakened by their departure. The drinking halls founded by guildsmen were also prohibited to rival

---

29 Maschke, *Städte und Menschen*, 254–9.
30 Maschke, 'Soziale Gruppen'. 138–40.
31 Eitel, *Oberschwäbischen Reichsstädte*, 37–47; quote, 44.

the 'official' guildhalls, which also served as social centres. The old lineages were forbidden to hold dances with restricted invitation lists in the town hall except on special occasions, as when a visiting dignitary was being entertained. Murals illustrating the Last Judgement were to be hung on all walls of the council chamber bearing the inscription 'The Council Hall is a Council Hall and not a dance hall'. The effort to bar guildsmen from the Cat Society troubled the city for a decade. In 1430 the emperor permitted guildsmen to join the society, thus facilitating mobility into the patriciate and weakening the efforts of the guilds to keep their own elites from joining the lineages.[32]

Lineages and nobility

The ministerial elite had been linked to the territorial nobility from the beginning, but large numbers of older merchant families were entering it in the late Middle Ages. Hostility to the nobles persisted in some places where their vendettas endangered public safety. Bad experiences with robber barons caused some German cities to exclude nobles from citizenship, but this was unusual. The social rapprochement of the city elites with the nobility is perceptible virtually everywhere. Most ministerials living in and around Duderstadt in the fourteenth century became citizens. The Breton nobles generally spent part of each year in town houses, and some older noble lines became influential in municipal politics, such as the Chauvin at Nantes and the Brullon at Rennes. At Metz, where landowning and the sale of farm products had always been the basis of the city rulers' wealth, some patricians simply broke their ties with the town, moved to their rural estates, and entered the service of nobles of the region.[33]

Wars and the easier availability of consumer goods in the cities led many nobles to move there. After recovering Poitiers from the English in 1369, King Charles V gave patents of nobility in 1372 to the mayor, *échevins* and councillors, the first collective example of ennoblement in France. The merchant families of Bordeaux were also entering the nobility by marrying their daughters with generous dowries to impecunious aristocrats. Although nobles were forbidden citizenship after disturbances between nobles and townsmen in 1375, the regulation was so preposterous that in 1392 the nobles were even readmitted to the *jurade*.[34]

32   Bechtold, *Zunftbürgerschaft und Patriziat*, 134–5, 144–8.
33   Fahlbusch, 'Duderstadt', 194–212; Leguay, *Réseau urbain Bretagne*, 307–8; Schneider, *Ville de Metz*, 452–7.
34   Dez, *Poitiers*, ch. 4; Renouard, *Bordeaux sous les rois d'Angleterre*, 346; Robertson, *English Administration*, 124–34.

Many English burgesses moved into the squirearchy in the late Middle Ages. London and Westminster of course had many royal officials who were called gentlemen or esquires, and most county towns had some resident gentry. Lawyers, a rapidly rising element in local politics in the fifteenth century, moved toward the gentry, intermarrying with county families and frequently moving to the country after a career in town. This was done for reasons of social prestige; the rental values of rural land were too small to make them much of an inducement from an economic standpoint. At Gloucester the business of rentier, which occupied much of the elite as a sideline, was much more profitable on city properties than on rural.[35]

Statutes acknowledged rural–urban equivalencies. The English sumptuary law of 1363 permitted merchants and master craftsmen with chattels worth £500 and more to dress like gentry with incomes of £100 per year; those with chattels of £1,000 could dress like esquires with £200 per year.[36] Although large-scale landholding was a *sine qua non* of gentleman status, most families did not have a conscious strategy of ennoblement. Most who bought rural land had no intention of leaving the city completely. They bought rural land slowly and piecemeal as a good investment, as it became available. Many administered their rural lands and rents from the town. The reverse movement sometimes occurred; some small landholders, such as Stephen Bramdene of Winchester, used a rural base as a starting point for making a fortune in the city.[37]

Some townsmen, especially merchants, entered royal service, although except for Londoners this was less common than in France. Mayors and aldermen were considered the urban equivalent of esquires. By the end of the fifteenth century the king often visited a city to dub the mayor a knight. The term 'gentleman' only comes into general use in the fifteenth century, although 'esquire' was used earlier. Much of the apparent growth of the urban gentry in the fifteenth century comes simply from applying these status designations to groups that already existed. Such men as William Spayne of Boston (1360s and 70s), Richard de Morton of Canterbury (1330s–40s) and the de la Poles of Hull would have been 'gentlemen' had they lived in the fifteenth century.[38]

In Flanders, as the nobility ceded economic power to the townsmen, wealthy burgesses of Ghent and Bruges were purchasing titles of knighthood as a first step into the nobility. The inquest after the Flemish civil war in 1328 shows that many magistrates and leading businessmen of

35   Holt, 'Gloucester', 151–3.
36   Hilton, *English and French Towns*, 117.
37   Keene, *Winchester*, 227–8; Horrox, 'Urban gentry', 27.
38   Horrox, 'Urban gentry', 22–37.

Bruges were already knights, and the numbers were probably even larger in Ghent. The townsmen bought seigniories and intermarried with noble families. The land purchases were evidently purely for social reasons in view of the low rents on rural land. Some townsmen moved to their rural estates, and nobles bought town houses and spent part of the year in them. Service to the Flemish counts, particularly under the Burgundian dynasty in the fifteenth century, also gained access to the nobility for townsmen. By the fifteenth century the distinctions separating citizen from noble, such as the prohibition against burgesses buying fiefs, were dead in Flanders. Socially the urban elites were very close to the lesser nobility throughout the Burgundian Netherlands, but the country-based nobles generally did not participate actively in city politics except during crises.[39]

The nobility of the robe in France

Although municipal officeholding was a mark of prestige everywhere, it followed rather than caused status elevation except in France. There the urban elites were so heavily legal-official by the late fifteenth century that Marxist historians have spoken of 'treason' of the merchants for failing to invest in industry, spending their money on things that ideologues of economic determinism consider inappropriate. The titled nobles and royal officeholders distanced themselves from the municipal 'nobility of the robe' (the judicial aristocracy that controlled city governments) which, in turn, was shutting itself off from the merchants.[40]

The separation of an 'honourable elite' began around 1380 in the French cities. Officeholding required money; but once attained, it generated income through contracts and tax farming. The 'bourgeoisie of the robe' was still very active in commerce and industry. Officeholders made business partnerships in city provisioning with their kin who remained merchants. While elsewhere many wealthy citizens avoided officeholding as not worth the bother, it could be the capstone of a successful merchant career in France, and even in other regions the perquisites of office cannot be overlooked in assessing the entirety of a family's fortune. Fees were very lucrative, even for honest public servants. The ability to buy or lease offices was the key to many families' fortunes, and few French merchants could rival local officeholders and lawyers in wealth.[41]

39 Nicholas, *Town and Countryside*, 250–66; de Win, 'Lesser nobility', 105–7.
40 Chevalier, *Bonnes villes*, 129, 133, 143–9.
41 Chevalier, *Bonnes villes*, 130, 135–41.

The Italian urban nobilities

The urban elites in the major centres of Italy were wealthy merchants, although virtually all of them also owned land. By this time magnate status was essentially political rather than genealogical except at Venice. The frequent rotation of offices in the Italian cities meant that much less prestige was attached to council membership *per se* than in the north. Rather, the elites were defined by their wealth, informal influence and clienteles. This is not to say that officeholding was insignificant. Some Italians, including the famous Gregorio Dati, thought public office a nuisance, an attitude that he shared with some northern merchants, especially in England. But other Italians were proud of their offices and listed their various positions in their family records (*ricordanze*) as among the accomplishments for which they wanted to be remembered. Most of them in doing so emphasised their respect for the law and their concern with the public good that superseded individual interests. When the magistracy was renewed at Florence, the city chroniclers recited the family accomplishments of the incoming officials; family and city identity were intertwined for them.[42]

The merchant elites were no less eager to preserve their social position for their descendants than were the landowners. The most famous example is the patriciate of Venice, whose names were enshrined in the Golden Book of 1297. Status was initially inherited through the father, permitting many Venetian nobles to marry the daughters of rich commoners without prejudice to the children's status. In 1422, however, the Great Council made nobility bilateral by denying membership to sons of noble fathers by non-noble mothers. The Great Council had about 2,500 members in 1500.[43]

Yet, although there were no legal differences in rank within the nobility at Venice, differences in wealth gave rise to conspicuous consumption, clothing codes and different types of acceptable behaviour. Contemporary documents distinguish three groups of nobles: the 'old houses' of pre-twelfth-century lineage; the 'new houses', which had been noble only since the twelfth and thirteenth centuries and in some cases later; and 'ducal houses', those of the 'new houses' who controlled the dogeship. The old houses were more endogamous than the others, but they were losing economic power, while the ducal houses were the richest of the new houses and were trying to cut themselves off from the rest. The ducal and old houses did not intermarry much; there was

---

42 Bec, *Marchands écrivains*, 281–4.
43 Lane, *Venice*, 252–3; Chojnacki, 'Marriage legislation', 167.

more intermarriage by the new houses with both ducal and old houses, in the former case motivated by economic considerations, in the latter by social prestige, and in all cases contributing to the willingness of fathers to pay enormous dowries.[44]

Genoa was unusual among the Italian cities in the extent to which its nobility was city-based, with little rural land, for the mountains around the city hindered Genoa's expansion into a *contado*. Although it was relatively easy to become a noble at Genoa by entering a 'noble' *albergo*, the 'landed nobility' was virtually closed, for they scarcely ever sold their rural properties. Levels of wealth distinguished the strata of the Genoese elite more than antiquity of lineage. The most powerful bankers in the late Middle Ages were the Centurioni brothers, Filippo and Federigo, new men who led a family enterprise and whose various kin managed their overseas offices. The main distinction between this echelon and merchants such as the Grimaldi brothers was their lesser degree of overseas involvement.

The Genoese *alberghi* were open to all. The magnate–*popolano* distinction referred more to political affiliation, with offices rigidly divided according to formulas, than to antiquity of ancestry. Thus many Genoese nobles were of recent and modest origin, since all that one had to do to become a noble was to be inscribed in one of the roughly forty noble *alberghi*. Among the *alberghi* there were great differences in wealth. Nobility also extended to the clients of the older families, who continued to hold most offices. The cohesion of the *albergo* came from the fact that its members lived in the same quarter of the city – a tendency perceptible but less sharp elsewhere among party affiliates – and had their own churches and regular meetings. Each *albergo* had 'governors' elected by all members, who represented it to the town government. From 1363 the *popolari* had *alberghi*, divided into merchants and artisans, each of which chose half the officers allotted to the *popolari* in the city government. Like the noble *alberghi*, the *popolari* included diverse groups ranging from rich bankers to poor artisans but were dominated by the wealthy. Half the officers of the commune were thus noble, with one-quarter each being merchants and craftsmen. Although this guaranteed the crafts some representation, the result was similar to the pattern elsewhere, particularly since the nobles were such a diverse group.[45]

44 Chojnacki, 'Marriage legislation', 172–7.
45 Discussion based on Heers, *Gênes. Civilisation*, 368–78, 383–92. The patronage networks in the Florentine *gonfaloni* were used skilfully by the Medici faction. Kent, *Neighbours and Neighbourhood*, 2–5, 93–4.

THE REPLENISHMENT OF PATRICIAN FORTUNES: STRATEGIES OF PERPETUATION

Status and wealth

The municipal aristocracies were defined by family consciousness, land-owning and officeholding. Particularly as the newly rich, guild-based merchants gained political power, the cities were plutocracies. Municipal offices were almost always monopolised by members of the top tax groups. Tax registers must be used with caution as indices even of wealth and certainly of status, but all that have survived show that a small number of persons held most of the taxable wealth, with the wealth pyramid broadening considerably at the bottom. In 1325, 936 heads of household were liable for the *estime* in the bourg of Toulouse (many were too poor to be taxed): 7 per cent of them held 61 per cent of the registered property, while 51 per cent held 6 per cent. Other cities had an even more skewed distribution of resources.[46]

There was a general but not absolute correlation between landown-ership and total wealth in the cities. Arles, a city in marked decline by the fifteenth century, shows a pattern of property ownership that is somewhat less concentrated at the top than at Toulouse. In 1437 7.5 per cent of the landowners there owned nearly 40 per cent of the pro-perties, while 54 per cent held 15 per cent. In the middle range 21 per cent held 17 per cent of the properties; above this, another 21 per cent owned 44 per cent. Shifting the sample base to total wealth, thirty-seven of the fifty richest Arlésiens were 'noble' or 'bourgeois', the older landed families. Only 36 per cent were on both lists; the Jews, notaries and apothecaries had more urban fortunes, while the nobles and labourers were more rural than urban.[47]

Although virtually all those in the governing elites were wealthy, some rich persons did not enter politics. Gaps between rich and poor were widening, accentuating the conspicuous consumption associated with high rank. The imbalances were sharper in industrial places that had numerous poor craftsmen. The 1327 subsidy records show very few rich people at York, but later records show the numbers of both rich and poor rising at the expense of the middle group as capital became concentrated. At Augsburg the number of taxpayers grew by 61 per cent between 1396 and 1461; and since the poorest were exempt, this

46 Mollat and Wolff, *Popular Revolutions*, 22–3.
47 Stouff, *Arles*, 341–6.

suggests growing prosperity of the upper-middle class and the rich, whose numbers grew by 116 per cent.[48]

Although persons of high status were almost always wealthy, not all wealthy persons enjoyed elevated social rank. Klaus Bechtold has used the records of Constance to make an important critique of the modern tendency to equate property structure, which can be gleaned from tax registers, with social structure, which includes intangible considerations of status. Its tax records make late medieval Constance appear a wealthier place than it actually was. During the fifteenth century the taxable immovable property of the poorest persons at Constance virtually disappeared, but the ratio of movable and immovable remained stable in the property of the wealthy. The poorer taxpayers were more bound to the economy of the city than the rich, who received income from long-distance trade and could invest in immovable property and business outside the town and to some extent escape taxes. When the patriciate of Constance was reformed in the 1420s, the Cat Society built a new hall. The fifty-eight contributors to the building fund, many of them social-climbing guildsmen, accounted for 30 per cent of the taxable wealth of Constance in 1425, but eleven of the fifty-eight paid no tax at all to the city. Family relations explain some discrepancies, such as only fathers contributing to the society while the entire family was taxed. The contributors to the Cat Society Hall were spread among the top four tax classes, not just the highest. There is thus no necessary correlation between wealth, as shown in the tax rolls, and status, shown in the desire to contribute to the Cat Society.[49]

The traditional bases of wealth of the older lineages were becoming less lucrative in the complex economic world of late medieval Europe. The raw tax figures often conceal the fact that while the lineages were prestigious, wealth was concentrated in the two merchant levels of the civic aristocracy. The handful of wealthiest persons were often from the lineages, but there were not many of them. At Reims, for example, the middle class was growing relatively in the fifteenth century, while the numbers of the extreme rich and poor declined.[50] Some lineages left the cities, lost their fortunes or failed biologically. Others adapted to the changing circumstances.

Venice illustrates most graphically the lack of linkage between membership of a closed patriciate and wealth. The *estimo* of 1379 shows ninety-one nobles with fortunes over 10,000 *lire*, but 817 were under 300 *lire*. As a group the taxable *popolani* were almost as wealthy as the

48 Maschke, *Städte und Menschen*, 69–70; Tillott, *City of York*, 110.
49 Bechtold, *Zunftbürgerschaft und Patriziat*, 11, 17–31.
50 Desportes, *Reims*, 684–95.

nobles.[51] Although the Venetian patriciate was wealthier as a group than the commoners, many were so poor that they did not even meet the minimum property qualification for officeholding. The *estimo* records suggest a division of wealth within the patriciate corresponding to the wealth pyramid common for all of taxpaying urban society in the north: 'fewer than one-tenth of the lineages controlled over half the wealth of the entire patriciate, while over 70 per cent had less than one-fifth'.[52]

Officeholding

The extensive and wasteful network of public offices at Venice became a kind of welfare system for impoverished nobles. Thirty commoners were admitted to the nobility in 1381, but in 1403 the council rejected a proposal to admit one *popolano* family whenever a noble lineage died out. This made the elite a closed group, with no opportunity for outsiders to penetrate the elite and share the graft. Many jobs were created simply to give an income to a particular noble. Although it was illegal to seek office, which was supposed to be done by lot and rotation, nobles in fact electioneered and influenced nominating committees and electors. Thirty-eight persons were banished in 1432 for coming into the electoral conclave with gold balls concealed in their sleeves to stuff in the urns from which names would be chosen. The larger families controlled most offices through broad networks of clients. Yet while some Venetians sought office for its perquisites, salaries and emoluments, others, mainly those whose income from business was greater than the salaries that officials received, tried to avoid public service, disregarding statutes forbidding this. While in the north most persons with political ambitions spent the first part of their careers making a fortune, then entered government in their maturity, Venetian patricians were likely to hold office during their twenties, then stop to concentrate on business.[53] Thus the councils in the Italian city-states were often dominated by young men, while in the north municipal politics was largely the domain of the middle aged.

In Florence too officeholding was more a matter of social prestige than wealth. There was little correlation between wealth and the number of offices held. Gene Brucker has seen a change in 'style of politics'

---

51   Romano, *Patricians*, 33.
52   Queller, 'Venetian family', 187–8.
53   Argument of Queller, *Venetian Patriciate*, esp. 29–113, 122–3, 146–60. See also Romano, *Patricians*, esp. 49, 155.

from a primarily corporate and collegial framework that was based firmly on the guilds, in which decisions were made by a group with a firm institutional base, to government by *balie* that were dominated by an elite group who held real power. This was linked to a change in the Florentine aristocracy at the turn of the fifteenth century. Of the city's seven leading business families in 1380, only the Albizzi and Strozzi were still much involved in trade, banking and industry by the 1430s. The Pitti had declined, the Alberti were in exile, and the others had been forced out of the economic elite through political misfortune. The Medici, who would consolidate a seigniory after 1434, were the great powers, rivalled only by the Pazzi, a new family who had risen rapidly in the early fifteenth century.[54] Yet this example may be extreme, for the wealth pyramid in Florence was especially pointed, and these families were at the top. The *catasto* of 1427 shows that the richest 1 per cent of the households (about 100 families) controlled one-quarter of the property value in Florence and one-sixth in Tuscany. While 78 per cent of the families had no share in the *Monte* (the funded debt), 2 per cent (about 200 families) controlled 60 per cent of it. Fifty-three families named Strozzi controlled 2.6 per cent of the taxable property; sixty Bardi families controlled 2.1 per cent, thirty-one Medici 1.9 per cent, eighteen Alberti and twenty-four Albizzi 1 per cent each, and twenty-eight Peruzzi 1.1 per cent. These families together had about 10 per cent of the taxable property in the city.[55]

Wealth was thus an important constituent of status, but not all kinds of wealth were respectable and could be gained without loss of social standing. The fact that the craft organisations that controlled city governments in the late Middle Ages were actually led by merchants rather than artisans made it possible for those persons from even the ministerial aristocracy who wanted political careers to enrol in guilds without losing status. Even in such a 'mechanical' craft as ironmongering a small top group within the guild gained control of the raw materials and sold to their craft brothers. At Cologne 95 per cent of the lead trade was being handled by 1460–9 by eleven merchants. In the 1460s the top four had 49 per cent and the top two 36 per cent; in the 1450s, by contrast, the top four had 74 per cent, the top two 47 per cent. Johann von Binge was the sixth greatest lead importer in the 1450s, but by the 1470s he had cornered 66 per cent of the market by buying out his competitors.[56]

54 Brucker, *Civic World*, 262–71, 283; Brucker, *Renaissance Florence*, 85.
55 Herlihy and Klapisch-Zuber, *Tuscans*, 100–1.
56 Irsigler, *Wirtschaftliche Stellung Köln*, 126–9.

The money market and social status

Although artisanry was closed to the elite for social reasons, moneylending on a large scale was not. The fact that princes were waging ruinous wars and going into debt for expensive luxuries in the late Middle Ages gave city financiers a golden opportunity. Many landowners (the first political member) of Ghent were also moneylenders and brokers (in the third member). There was no prestige in petty usury or pawnbroking, which were done casually and in many cases by women. In most smaller cities the moneychangers still came from the oldest and richest families, but they were a declining group in some cities with a stable or diminishing international market. Ghent, for example, had a small number of moneychangers. Some were from old families, but the most prestigious moneychangers were not politically active. Much of their prosperity came from dual involvements in hostelry and brokerage. One of the most prominent was a woman, and their numbers declined in the fifteenth century as the Burgundian counts centralised operations in a municipal exchange. At Bruges too women were active as moneychangers, but the profession was so risky that it was hard to remain active for more than a generation or two. Bankers and moneychangers replaced drapers as the city elite of Lille, the site of the Burgundian Chamber of Accounts, but actual moneychanging was a minor part of their activity by the fifteenth century; instead they loaned, invested, handled orphans' property and issued life rents for the Burgundian counts.[57]

During the late Middle Ages the lineages had a respectable source of income that was previously unavailable on such a large scale: they invested immense reserves in rents sold by their own and other cities. Although investment in rents rather than industry has been claimed as a mark of diminished interest in moneymaking among the old patrician lines, this is based on an exaggerated notion of the intrinsic importance of industry and craftsmanship in the late medieval cities. The trade in rents was an important investment of commercially gained capital, one with social prestige, and relatively safe. At Lübeck, which had a large rent market, one-sixty-sixth of the purchasers bought one-seventh of the capital value of the rents. The lineages of Metz controlled the money supply of the region. The wealthy of Reims bought life rents on communities north of the city, for opportunities for investment to the east were blocked by the financial power of Metz, to the west by Arras.[58]

Large-scale moneylending was thus a powerful instrument of elite

57 Nicholas, *Metamorphosis*, 126–7; Murray, 'Family, marriage and moneychanging', 114–25; Trenard, *Histoire de Lille*, 240.
58 von Brandt, 'Lübeck', 234–5; Desportes, *Reims*, 449.

preservation. Konrad Gross of Nuremberg, the son of 'Rich Heinz', obtained immovable property by sharp business methods and by paying the debts of abbeys in exchange for land. He had a fulling mill and an iron foundry and loaned money to the emperor. In 1338–9 he bought the office of *Schultheiss* and the toll of Mainz, then the mint of Nuremberg; thus he gained the most important rights that the prince still exercised inside the wall. King Louis of Bavaria was often Gross's guest at his palatial residence in Nuremberg, later called the Plobenhof. The value of the immovable property of Konrad Mangold, a member of one of the oldest lineages of Constance, declined slightly between 1418 and 1448, but his movable property doubled in value, mainly from low-risk interest-bearing loans to abbeys, nobles and town governments, including Constance itself. Given the borrowers, the loans had a political dimension. Furthermore, since Mangold's business took up so little of his time, moneylending gave him avenues for influence and offices, including the burgomastership. There is no evidence that he was ever in retail commerce. The most famous moneylenders of the period are Jacques Coeur of Bourges and Simon de Mirabello of Ghent, son of an Italian moneylender who married a natural sister of the Flemish count and eventually became regent of Flanders in the 1340s.[59]

Thus, although the elite of virtually all trades consisted of merchants, they were also increasingly characterised by an element of moneylending and workgiving. Apart from money operations and marriage into distinguished lineages, the route to social advancement continued to be long-distance trade in luxuries or wholesale items, or the learned professions. Mass production of craft goods was based on small shops. In an economy that was dominated by credit in goods and money, this was feasible only by putting out raw materials. Individual craftsmen fell into debt to merchant entrepreneurs, often their guild brothers, who made possible sales over a wide area that were impossible for small craftsmen. This is especially observable at Cologne in the leather and iron trades. The iron staple that the government of Cologne managed to enforce at the end of the fifteenth century would probably not have been viable if Cologne entrepreneurs had not been able to pay directly for foreign iron and let their artisan customers pay them by credit, with payment due when the finished goods were sold.[60]

Although the very oldest, generally ministerial, urban families still disdained wholesale trade, few of them were left. Most long-distance trade was done by patricians. Of 335 Cologne merchants who are known to

59   Pfeiffer, *Nürnberg*, 41–3; Bechtold, *Zunftbürgerschaft und Patriziat*, 32–4.
60   Irsigler, *Wirtschaftliche Stellung Köln*, 321–2.

have traded at the Frankfurt fairs in the fifteenth century, 134 were members of the city council at some point, and many were burgomasters or rentmasters. Interurban leagues of merchants continued to unite long-distance merchants of both the ministerial and older merchant groups. The Great Company of Ravensburg, founded in 1380, had eighty partners from many south German cities. The St Gallen-based Diesback-Watt Society had twenty-three partners including in addition to the St Gallener three from Basel, two from Nuremberg, and one woman of Breslau.[61]

Many patricians entered the wine trade. Much of its appeal was that since it was seasonal and hard coin was in short supply, the trade was largely dependent on credit. The patricians largely monopolised the lucrative wine market of Cologne for a generation after the Wine Brotherhood became a closed corporation after 1372. After the new regime of 1396 opened the brotherhood to all citizens, the patricians' share declined in favour of the merchants on the council. Thus in the fifteenth century as in the fourteenth, the groups controlling the council controlled the wine trade. Most of the leading wine importers of the second half of the fifteenth century were members of the five merchant *Gaffeln*. Of the wine dealers who were in craft organisations within the *Gaffeln*, most were brewers and coopers, with a scattering of weavers, cloth cutters, shoemakers and others.[62] The status of other occupations was ambiguous. Cloth cutting began as artisanry but became retail trade in cloth, and patrician cloth cutters are found in most cities. The trade was forbidden only in cases where the patricians had social clubs with rigid rules for members.[63]

The patriciate of Lyon illustrates these themes. The group was defined by urban landowning; few invested in rural land before 1400, and only the greatest families held fiefs. Only a dozen families gave up trade completely for royal service, but many of them had members in royal service while others kept up the family business. The patriciate gradually narrowed until it was a virtually closed corporation by 1400. Since Lyon had little industry, the patriciate was entirely merchant, with side interests in deposit but not investment banking. The most important were drapers, then spicers and to some extent furriers. As Lyon became more prosperous through its international fairs and royal patronage in the fifteenth century, notaries became important, and barristers entered the consulate in large numbers after 1430, intermarrying with or replacing some older patrician families. The newer commercial

61   Maschke, *Städte und Menschen*, 61–6.
62   Irsigler, *Wirtschaftliche Stellung Köln*, 246–59.
63   Eitel, *Oberschwäbische Reichsstädte*, 135.

elements, by contrast, showed little interest in assuming the burdens of city government.[64]

In the burgeoning capitals in particular moneylending and purveyance to the princely court became linked with municipal officeholding in a pattern of patronage. Adam Fraunceys and John Peyl were immigrants to London who became mercers and mayors. Both sold wool and wine to the royal Wardrobe. Fraunceys loaned money to the crown and entered politics in London. Most big lenders to the crown were appointed collectors of customs to repay them. In Fraunceys' case this led to a political career in the 1350s as member of Parliament for London and member of royal inquisitorial commissions. After being imprisoned briefly in the late 1340s over a loan dispute, Peyl stayed out of moneylending until after he became an alderman of London in 1369. Both Peyl and Fraunceys were used on sensitive commercial-diplomatic missions in the late 1360s and 1370s.[65]

Richard Whittington's career is unusual but illustrates the possibilities open to a rich London merchant, particularly one who provisioned the royal court. Born in Gloucestershire, the third son of a knight who died in debt, Whittington was in London by 1379. He became a mercer, then a wool exporter and royal financier. His breakthrough came between 1392 and 1394, when he sold nearly £3,500 worth of goods to the Wardrobe, including velvets and cloths of gold. He continued purveying cloth and precious stones to the Wardrobe of Henry IV but became less active as a mercer as his loans to the crown increased. It is hard to say how profitable loaning money to the crown was *per se*, but it definitely brought political influence. The king appointed Whittington mayor of London in 1397 to fill an unexpired term. He was then chosen on his own in 1406 and 1419. He was also mayor at different times of both the Westminster and Calais staples. Whittington was Master of the Mercers' Company three times. Though he was less active in the mistery after 1409, he never joined another company, and the mercers gave a lavish celebration on his last election as mayor. He owned little property outside London. Most of it was in Gloucestershire, his home county, although he made no claim on the estate of his own family there, and in Dorset, where his wife had family and interests. His most valuable property was in London. Yet for a man of his status, his London properties were not large. He kept most of his capital liquid, moving it around in different investments, including works of art. He died a childless widower in 1423. His will established almshouses

---

64 Valous, *Patriciat Lyonnais*, 48–90.
65 O'Connor, 'Royal service by two London merchants', 18–33.

and a college for secular priests attached to the church of St Michael in Paternoster Row, the street of his residence, all administered by the Mercers' Company.[66]

The elites of the Muslim cities form an interesting contrast to the situation that we have described for western Europe. The Syrian and Egyptian cities lacked a 'class' organisation in the western sense. The rulers were a group apart, followed by the religious leaders and intellectuals, who in some texts were put on an approximate plane with other leaders, including rich merchants. The *ulama*, who were the social and religious elite of the Islamic cities, consisted of judges, jurists, and teachers called *qadi*. They controlled marriages, wills, guardianship and matters relating to honesty (including over prices and wages). They were much involved with the emir's bureaucracy, but some also came from the lower social orders, and not all of them supported the regime. Long-distance merchants were urban notables in something closer to the western sense, but they were more linked to the state than in the west. They were importers of eastern luxury goods and controlled the spice, gold and grain trade with the interior of Africa and Asia. The European carrying trade was handled mainly by Italians. Banking and moneylending in the Muslim cities were mainly in the hands of spice merchants. They and other merchants also loaned to the state. The government protected merchants, who still travelled with their own goods to a greater extent than in the west. Nevertheless the repression of the market mechanism by the emirs deprived this group of any chance to exert political influence; and social respectability came even more from involvement with the government and religion than in the west.[67]

Ancestry, high political office and patronage, landownership, wealth in wholesale commerce or money management, both of them 'respectable' and non-manual ways of generating income, were the characteristics of the urban elites of the late Middle Ages. As the merchant elite of the guilds accumulated capital through trade, sometimes starting from artisanry, they invested it in ways that elevated their social status. We turn now to the groups in the medieval cities below the elite, the middle and lower social orders.

---

66 Barron, 'Richard Whittington', 198–215, 233–4 sees Whittington as a cold and formal man who became conservative after his patron and probably friend Richard II died, followed by his wife. He bought little property after 1402, simply living well on his existing investments. The story of 'Dick Whittington's Cat' is Elizabethan.

67 Lapidus, *Muslim Cities*, 79–85, 107–13, 130–41; Hourani, *History of the Arab Peoples*, 111, 117–30.

CHAPTER SEVEN

Occupational Guilds, the Middle and Lower Orders, and Poverty in the Later Medieval City

In this chapter we shall consider industrial organisation and productive relationships; guild organisations, regulations and hierarchies; and the impact of the increasing industrialisation of the cities on politics. We shall also consider poverty, which chiefly concerns those on the margins of the guilds and outside them, and poor relief.

The occupational structure

Guild records are an imperfect guide to the extent of occupational differentiation, for many trades did not have legally recognised organisations. The larger cities supported more specialists than the smaller, and specialisation was greatest in areas that had a strong export trade. However, the more highly specialised occupations, with only a few practitioners, were usually not organised or at most were a subgroup with separate rules within a composite guild. A royal decree in 1364 ordered the trades of London to choose sworn masters, but many small crafts never did so. London had some precision specialists. The textile trades had over twenty subspecialities, and the clothiers had specialists such as wimplers and camisers.[1]

The Master Book of Nuremberg of 1363 shows about 1,200 masters distributed among fifty professions, and an enumeration of 1370 adds several others. Bakers, butchers, tailors and shoemakers were one-quarter of the total. Another quarter were in metalworking, Nuremberg's major industrial export, but these trades were strongly differentiated. The

1   Veale, 'London craftsmen', 141–6.

leatherworking trades had about two hundred masters. Woollen textiles, which were so strong in the western cities and Cologne, numbered only seventy masters, many of them living in the suburbs. Curiously, only seventy were in the construction trades.[2] Ghent had sixty-one guilds, eight of them textile-related. Militia figures from 1358 suggest that 13,383 masters were living in the city, 7,488 of them (55.95 per cent) textile workers. The rest of the occupational breakdown of the city workforce gives 11.1 per cent in victualling, 9.6 per cent in transport and loading, 5.6 per cent in construction, 5.1 per cent in clothing, 5.0 per cent in fur and leather. The other trades were very small. Distinguishing the occupations by function yields 76.9 per cent in industry and crafts, 12.5 per cent in trade and 10.6 per cent in services.[3]

The smaller centres had more self-contained occupational structures than the large industrial cities, which exported manufactured items but had to import basic goods and sometimes skills. Records show 163 occupations at Winchester, or 151 if exporters and importers are excluded. About half the inhabitants were in the business of feeding and clothing the residents of the city and environs. Leatherworkers, who accounted for about half the number of victuallers, were next but were declining with the erosion of the fur trade. The only other large groups were in construction, clerical/legal, and metal.[4] Similarly, no single trade dominated Tours. In the mid-fifteenth century one-quarter of the workforce was involved in making cloth and clothing, one-fifth in leatherworking and hides, one-tenth in victualling, 17.7 per cent in construction and 10.9 per cent in metalwork (the latter figures were unusually high at Tours due to the presence of the royal court).[5]

The locally based trades were less specialised and apt to be linked in composite guilds for purposes of political participation. Lille, a political capital with an expanding textile production, had fifty-seven organised guilds in the late fifteenth century. Valenciennes had thirty-eight guilds in 1357, ten of them of woollen textile workers, while one was for linen weavers.[6] The degree of specialisation could be ridiculous. Venice had two bakers' guilds: *forneri*, owners of ovens who baked dough that had already been kneaded by the customer, and the confectioners (*pistori*), who kneaded the dough as well as baking it. Ghent had bread bakers, pastry bakers who were part of the spicers' guild and baked condiments that the spicers sold, and bakers outside both guilds who could sell on

2 Pfeiffer, *Nürnberg*, 99.
3 Nicholas, *Metamorphosis*, 19–21.
4 Keene, *Medieval Winchester*, 250–1.
5 Chevalier, *Tours*, 132–43.
6 Trenard, *Histoire de Lille*, 243; Platelle, *Histoire de Valenciennes*, 71.

specific markets in the city.[7] Often the sole purpose of the specialisation was to keep a less prestigious group from rising in the hierarchy. Among the cordwainers of Nantes persons who were authorised to make 'great shoes' (high-quality boots) were distinguished from simple shoemakers who could only make small sheepskin shoes or slippers and could not become *jurés* of the guild.[8]

While some cities grouped trades functionally, guilds that were not large enough to sustain a full complement of officers were linked in peculiar combinations, even in the large cities. At Cologne the saddlers were in the same *Gaffel* as the artists, escutcheon makers and glassblowers, probably because they often decorated their saddles.[9] Smiths and marshals did virtually identical work but were separate crafts at York until the city government forced them to merge in the mid-fifteenth century. Potters and founders both worked in bronze but were separated. Pewterers and braziers were in the same guild in fifteenth-century Coventry, despite the different techniques, and some men practised both trades. York had potters, pewterers and founders, but the main distinction seems to have been that they lived on opposite sides of the Ouse. The procedure of combination and separation worked in many ways. Norwich grouped the small crafts into 'misteries', while the York government permitted even such tiny guilds as saucemakers and bowstring makers to stay independent.[10]

Some composite guilds, such as the twenty-one of Florence, were purely political creations. Statutes of 1330 list forty-six professions grouped into eight guilds at Pistoia. Some groupings were arbitrary, but others joined practitioners of related trades: butchers, leatherworkers and furriers were together, as were the ironworkers and iron merchants.[11] Although the textile trades had separate organisations and minute industrial regulations, they sometimes had a single organisation for political purposes, dominated by the largest or most politically powerful craft, often the weavers. Construction trades were also likely to be composites, despite the large number of persons involved. At Ghent a comprehensive guild embraced all the building trades, but they retained their separate organisations. The Art of Stone and Wood Masters of Florence, incorporating virtually all construction crafts, was the largest of the twenty-one political guilds and included perhaps 20 per cent of their total membership in 1391. In 1355 Siena merged all artisans into

7   Mackenney, *Tradesmen and Traders*, 63; Nicholas, *Metamorphosis*, 252–3.
8   Leguay, *Réseau urbain Bretagne*, 269.
9   Irsigler, *Wirtschaftliche Stellung Köln*, 230.
10   Swanson, 'Artisans in the urban economy', 43–7.
11   Herlihy, *Pistoia*, 172–3.

twelve guilds, of which one was for construction, but they kept their own internal structures and separated again in the fifteenth century. Especially in Italy organising trades into composite political guilds benefited the dominant groups within them. The guild of doctors and druggists at Florence included painters, who in turn included subgroups ranging from artists to mattress-workers to box makers. The only masters in the wool guild were the *lanaioli*, who imported the wool and dyes. Other masters of the workshops, such as dyers and shearers, who had their own guilds in northern Europe, were 'underlings' (*sottoposti*) in the Italian guilds, although they in fact employed workers in their shops, and some of them were wealthy enough to be in the top tax brackets.[12]

Jeremy Goldberg has divided the occupational groups of late medieval York and other English cities into twelve categories: victuals, leather, textiles, clothing, merchants excluding grocers, metal, construction except for wrights and sawyers, who are separated, transport, armament, chandlers, and others excluding yeomen and gentlemen. Comparing these twelve as percentages of the population at York, various smaller towns, and Northampton, Oxford and Worcester as shown by the poll tax records of 1377–81 shows common elements despite the structural diversity of the cities. Victualling was the largest except in the port of Lynn, which had larger numbers in maritime occupations and transport than the others, and the textile town of Wakefield. Leather, textiles, clothing and metal were comparable, accounting for 10–15 per cent of the population in each. The food trades involved a lower percentage of the population in the larger towns. Leather tended to be high in the large places. Nowhere were more than 15 per cent of the population in construction, which was a low-status line of work except for the great contractors, but this may be distorted by the fact that tax records under-report the poorer groups.[13] These figures are generally congruent with Valenciennes, where 30.3 per cent of new burgesses in the second half of the fourteenth century were in textiles, 15.9 per cent in leather, 11.7 per cent in commerce and transport, 6.7 per cent in metalwork, 4.6 per cent in woodworking, 9.1 per cent in construction, 3 per cent in service occupations, 10.3 per cent in victualling, and a scattering in agriculture.[14]

Much depended on local conditions, especially for skilled trades; the stonecutters had guilds in Venice, Genoa and Rome, but not in Mantua, Modena and Bologna, where stone was unavailable. Venice had a guild

---

12 Larner, *Age of Dante and Petrarch*, 196.
13 Goldberg, *Women, Work and Life Cycle*, 45–7, 60–3.
14 Platelle, *Histoire de Valenciennes*, 72.

of kilnmen by the thirteenth century, but the Po valley towns did not have them until the sixteenth century. The roofers usually had their own organisation in the northern cities, and Ghent distinguished straw roofers from tile roofers. Yet in Italy the roofers as a unit had their own guild only at Lucca in the fifteenth century, and in other Italian cities they were a subgroup within the wallers' guild. At Pisa the masons' and woodworkers' guilds had become so small in the early fifteenth century that they merged, but they had grown enough again by 1477 to warrant separating once more. Venice had more than two hundred separate guilds, but they were grouped into composites, and some had subdivisions. The drapers, who put out work to artisans, were the only legally recognised wool guild. The hemp spinners had great and subordinate arts, while the furriers had new and old arts. The glassmakers, whose product was renowned, had numerous specialised trades. Sawyers were in the house carpenters' guild but had their own statutes. The warden of the metalworkers was chosen from the smiths, cauldronmakers and armourers. The painters' guild had separate branches for painters of shields, saddles, chests, pictures and furniture.[15]

Trades and sworn guilds

Sworn craft guilds on the west European model developed late in Poland, where the cities were under the influence of German law, and they were weaker and less tumultuous than those in the west. Guilds did not exist in either the Russian or Islamic cities. The weavers of Warsaw rose against the local merchant oligarchy in 1333, the bakers in 1375. The crafts of Kraków had twelve of twenty-four seats on the city council, although in practice the great merchants dominated. Novgorod had an association of overseas merchants, the St John's Hundred, but neither a comprehensive merchant guild nor craft organisations.[16] The industrial organisation of the Muslim centres was probably hampered by the domination of the cities by the *qadi*, but even more by the fact that they remained principally consumer cities. With a few exceptions such as luxury woodworking and marble in Aleppo and bowl- and glassmaking in Damascus, large-scale manufacturing did not develop except in the state factories of Mamluk Egypt; most manufactured goods were imported from Constantinople and the cities of western Europe. Perhaps

15 Epstein, *Wage Labor and Guilds*, 228; Mackenney, *Tradesmen and Traders*, 4–5; Romano, *Patricians*, 67–71.
16 Knoll, 'Urban development of medieval Poland', 77, 91; Birnbaum, 'Kiev, Novgorod, Moscow', 35.

paradoxically, although the markets of the Muslim centres were more thoroughly supervised by the centrally-appointed *muhtasibs* than were those of the west, they were also less organised. An *'arif* was chosen from among the practitioners of each trade as a supervisor, but by the *muhtasib*, not by the other tradespeople. There is thus no equivalent in the Muslim world of either industrial regulation or industrial policing through occupational organisations.[17]

The occupational guilds of the west were a characteristic outgrowth of virtually ubiquitous household units of production. Yet, although the late medieval cities abounded in occupational and social organisations of diverse types and functions, substantial parts of Europe lacked sworn guilds. Arles and Tarascon had trade-based charitable confraternities but not craft organisations. They did not exist at Canterbury and Leicester until the modern period. Lynn in 1389 had forty-three social and religious guilds – more than London – but no craft guilds. The only guilds that are known at Lincoln before the Reformation are tailors, sailors, weavers, mercers and tilers. The Gascon towns generally lacked merchant guilds, and craft guilds were unusual. Except for a few small guilds, such as goldsmiths and barbers, Bordeaux had none until the period of Louis XI (1461–83).[18]

The northern type of 'sworn guild' only reached Montpellier and Nîmes in the late fifteenth century. In 1484 the king declared Narbonne a 'sworn city' and made all the craft organisations into sworn guilds. In Languedoc industrial regulations were issued initially by the city consuls, then by the king in the fifteenth century. They applied to all persons in the town and sometimes in the region who were practising the trade in question, rather than to corporate guilds. Few trades were 'free' in the sense used in the north, with the right to control their internal affairs and regulate economic activity. But the absence of sworn guilds did not mean that the crafts were unorganised, unregulated or without political influence.[19]

Metz represented an intermediate stage in the early fourteenth century but then moved decisively toward the southern model. In 1327 the ten older trades, called the Franc-Métier, were granted a single statute that gave their Grand Master extensive authority, but the city council, the Thirteen, abolished his office in 1336 and forbade the Franc-Métier to receive new corporations. After the Thirteen suppressed the Franc-Métier in 1360, no trade organisation of Metz had independence. Each

17 Lapidus, *Muslim Cities*, 18–20, 96–100; Hourani, *Arab Peoples*, 134.
18 Hilton, *English and French Towns*, 68–9; Hill, *Medieval Lincoln*, 327; Lodge, *Gascony under English Rule*, 152–3.
19 Gouron, *Métiers en Languedoc*, 281, 154, 369.

of the Thirteen exercised personal surveillance over five or six trades, presiding over their elections and reporting the results to the entire Thirteen for ratification. The courts of the trade organisations, which had been trying to get civil and criminal jurisdiction over craftsmen, were limited to those concerning professional credentials and standards. After 1366 the guild courts had to have the Thirteen confirm their decisions even in these matters. Fines for industrial infractions went directly to the city, not to the craft organisation. The Thirteen had to authorise any guild assembly. In response to violations of this statute, in 1382 the Thirteen suppressed the confraternities and religious ceremonies and limited the crafts to a single meeting each year, at which they would elect a master and six *jurés*. Statutes were then issued for each trade of the city.[20]

Confraternities and occupational associations

Although most occupational organisations originated in charitable associations, most in northern Europe did not establish formal confraternities until after the association had become a trade group and issued craft ordinances. Although the 'brotherhood' and the 'mistery' often had the same membership, they were distinct in members' minds. Confraternities spent lavishly on funerals of brethren and the great social event of the year, the guild procession or banquet. The confraternity was also a peace association: brothers often promised not to sue or prosecute one another before an external party, and some pledged to attend public meetings unarmed.[21]

The evidence that charitable fraternities eventually gave birth to trade guilds is strongest in southern France. Only Toulouse and Albi, in western Languedoc, where confraternities appeared after the occupational guilds, followed the northern pattern. Elsewhere the confraternity assumed corporate attributes, owning property and holding courts. It was inconceivable to be a member of the guild without belonging to its confraternity. Belonging to two confraternities was forbidden; persons who changed professions changed confraternities. Journeymen participated in the confraternity and paid dues, usually at a lower rate than masters. If the master paid for his journeyman, he was entitled to deduct the cost from the employee's wage.[22]

Even when a confraternity was not the origin of the occupational

20 Schneider, *Metz*, 236–7, 469, 472–3, 476–9, 482–4.
21 Swanson, *Medieval Artisans*, 111; Rossiaud, 'Crises', 524–8.
22 Gouron, *Métiers en Languedoc*, 263–4.

association, most occupational guilds founded brotherhoods in the late Middle Ages. At Rennes in 1340 the confraternity of the Assumption was kept by the bakers, St Anne by thread makers, Notre-Dame in September by the drapers and fullers, St Martin by the purse makers and legging makers, St Philip and St James by the mercers, St Michael by the parchment makers, Holy Sacrament by the butchers and Notre-Dame de la Conception by the cordwainers.[23] Since city authorities often used the guilds to police and tax the members, the craftsmen founded separate fraternities for social or religious functions. By the fifteenth century Rouen and its suburbs had 130 fraternities, Avignon 100, Marseilles forty, Aix-en-Provence and Arles thirty, in each case far more than the number of occupational guilds.[24]

Most brotherhoods were attached to a church or cloister. Some became linked to brotherhoods of journeymen. Most journeymen brotherhoods, like the parish fraternities, were primarily burial and devotional organisations in the beginning. They are found mainly in the less prestigious guilds where the wealth spread among the members was not extreme. The confraternity of the tailors of Paris and Saint-Denis was called 'confraternity of the Trinity of journeymen tailors and clothiers', and all masters and journeymen paid dues.[25]

The journeyman brotherhoods provided little charity. Some would only care for sick journeymen whose masters refused to do so, a clear indication that this was normally considered the masters' obligation. The journeymen weavers of Basel had a brotherhood in the local hospital by 1340, the greytawyers (workers in grey leather) and furriers in 1398. In 1404 the Strasbourg tanners established a brotherhood in the cathedral to provide anniversary masses for themselves and their heirs. Although most foundations were small, the journeymen bakers of Strasbourg maintained an entire chapel in the hospital.[26]

Many fraternities were more parish- than guild-based. The growth of confraternities in the Italian cities may be tied to the large numbers of urban parishes; Florence at the turn of the fourteenth century had about fifty parish churches, Venice seventy. Fifty-one new confraternities were founded in Florence in the fourteenth century and another eighty-seven in the fifteenth. Venice had forty-five new ones between 1360 and 1476. The subversive potential of these organisations was not lost on the authorities. In the 1370s the *Signoria* of Florence was appointing captains of the religious confraternities and was putting the city treasury

23   Leguay, *Réseau urbain Bretagne*, 34.
24   Hilton, *English and French Towns*, 72–4.
25   Geremek, *Salariat*, 111–13.
26   Schulz, *Handwerksgesellen und Lohnarbeiter*, 184–9, 199.

in charge of their funds. By the early fifteenth century the confraternities were expressly forbidden all political activity. From 1415 organising a new one required the consent of the *Signoria*.[27]

Some older parish confraternities in northern Europe became surrogates for the sworn association of the entire citizenry. Reims had only two parish confraternities, those of St Julien and Madeleine, in the late fourteenth century, neither of which was associated with the churches. The interparish confraternity of Saint-Pierre-aux-Clercs, founded in 1172 and reorganised in 1348, was open to all inhabitants of the city. Although it had an annual banquet, it was primarily a funeral association, arranging masses and candles for the dead. It did not distribute alms regularly. By the late fourteenth century it had a more complex financial organisation, with procurators who rendered accounts to nine masters of the confraternity.[28] The brotherhood of St Jacob of Cologne was confined to woad merchants whose members had a monopoly of the trade in the city until 1396. This organisation had much the same membership as the cloth cutters' guild. Yet the proceedings of the brotherhood that survive between 1308 and 1347 show more social/charitable than economic activity, although the fraternity's court handled commercial disputes between brothers.[29]

The vitality of parish guilds in England may reflect the weakness of craft organisations there. England follows the southern pattern of artisan associations originating in charitable fraternities. The reason is probably that while misteries, which were craft organisations, had to submit their ordinances to the city authorities for ratification, and fines imposed by a mistery went to the municipal chamberlain, a fraternity was not under these restrictions even if it was closely associated with a professional group or was part of a mistery.[30] The London companies of the salters, brewers and whittawyers (workers in white leather) are examples. The transition between confraternity and occupational guild is illustrated by the skinners, most of whom lived along Walbrook below Cheap and attended the Church of St John Walbrook. In 1327 they were given a royal charter for a fraternity of Corpus Christi housed there; the charter also included professional regulations and standards. The fraternity became a liveried company in 1393. The journeymen skinners originally belonged to two different fraternities that were merged into a single Fraternity of Our Lady's Assumption in the parent church in 1397.

27 Goldthwaite, *Wealth and the Demand for Art in Italy*, 105–6, 116–19; Becker, 'Florentine territorial state', 111–12.
28 Desportes, *Reims*, 336–8.
29 Irsigler, *Wirtschaftliche Stellung Köln*, 89–90.
30 Nightingale, *Medieval Mercantile Community*, 177–8.

Corpus Christi, like all liveried companies, became aristocratic, enrolling nobles and other non-skinners.[31]

The grocers are also a good example, and in their case the fraternity broadened a professional nucleus into a genuine company. In 1345 twenty-one pepperers of the Sopers Lane neighbourhood, by no means all pepperers of London, founded a fraternity dedicated to St Antonin. Initially those who were in the pepperers' mistery, which had been founded in 1316, but were not in the fraternity could attend the group banquet without wearing its livery. However, the fraternity also admitted persons who were not pepperers, particularly spicers and apothecaries, then tried to extend its control over the entire mistery by legislation that restricted the practice of the 'grocery' trade to members of the fraternity. There is no documentation of the fraternity between 1359 and 1372; but when it re-emerged, the man who had been warden of the fraternity in 1359 was the warden of the newly established grocers' company in 1372–3. By 1386 the grocers were strong enough to decree unilaterally that 'every man who keeps a shop of spicery should be under the government of the said masters', thus extending control of the company over the entire retail trade, including non-members. Interestingly, although official records mention a company in 1372, the organisation only received a charter of incorporation in 1429, when it was made necessary by the members' purchase of property for the construction of a hall.[32]

In 1389 the English government required all guilds to report. Exactly what was meant by 'guild' is unclear. London had forty, only nine of which were associated with crafts. One of Lincoln's twenty-eight guilds had a craft tie, seven of Norwich's nineteen and none of Bury's eighteen.[33] Twenty-one guilds of Lynn returned certificates. All were religious fraternities, many founded since 1348. They evidently modelled their practices on Trinity Guild (Great Guild), the merchant organisation. The Great Guild, far from being narrowly aristocratic, had a wide membership. It distributed food to the poor and had funerals and anniversary masses and regular devotions. The hall of the Great Guild was being used for meetings of the city government by 1313. Today it houses the municipal archive and museum.[34]

The English and French municipal guilds were also important in fostering cultural life and a sense of civic identity, particularly in the fif-

31 Robertson, *Chaucer's London*, 84–5.
32 Nightingale, *Medieval Mercantile Community*, 178–81, 215–22, 301 including quote, 427.
33 Hilton, *English and French Towns*, 72–3.
34 Owen, *Making of King's Lynn*, 60–2, 385, 420.

teenth century. The most aristocratic of Paris was the Great Confraternity of Notre-Dame, whose membership in 1400 included the dukes of Burgundy, Berry and Orléans.[35] The confraternity of the Passion at Nantes was performing plays by 1371, one of the oldest in Europe to do this.[36] In many English cities the originally merchant guild was being reconstituted as a civic devotional guild. A hint of this is found in a scandal at York in 1306, when a religious guild with fifty-four members – significantly, York would have fifty-six craft guilds with ordinances in the late Middle Ages – was dissolved on grounds of manipulating the city government and forcing artisans to pay extra fees to join. Many members of the guild were victuallers.[37] Leicester's Corpus Christi guild was established in 1343 at the church of St Martin by wealthy founders. It did not become a municipal fraternity, but it became closely associated with the pre-existing merchant guild. By 1495 the Corpus Christi guildhall was being used as the city hall.[38]

The guilds of Coventry are especially notable. Holy Trinity and Corpus Christi originally came from the two territorial jurisdictions of the town. Corpus Christi was the younger; its main functions by 1500 were a civic procession and two banquets. Corpus Christi guild at one time contained nearly all middling to prosperous citizens but had become more aristocratic by the early sixteenth century. By 1515 it had 282 members, still comprising about 40 per cent of the resident masters of the city. The most prominent citizens, however, normally changed membership from Corpus Christi to Trinity, the senior and much smaller and more aristocratic guild, at a particular stage. A year or two before election as mayor, a man would become master of Corpus Christi and as such the leader of the ex-sheriffs and other civic officers. Membership in Trinity required rank of sheriff; the entry fee was £5, too much for the humbler men in Corpus Christi.[39]

The Italian cities also had numerous religious organisations. The government of Siena was associated with the confraternity of Virgin Mary, to which most members of the Nine belonged. The government sponsored processions and celebrations and celebrations in Mary's honour.[40] Venice distinguished six *scuole* [confraternities] *grande*, often reserved for non-noble *cittadini* and not bound to a trade, from *scuole piccole*, which were founded by the guilds but with membership not restricted to them.

35 Thompson, *Paris Under English Rule*, 176.
36 Leguay, *Réseau urbain Bretagne*, 344.
37 Swanson, *Medieval Artisans*, 111, 120.
38 Simmons, *Leicester*, 49–50.
39 Phythian-Adams, *Coventry*, chs 7–8.
40 Bowsky, *Siena Under the Nine*, 265, 274–7.

These were social and charitable clubs that lacked the tie to occupational groups that is usually found with northern confraternities apart from those with a strong grounding in a parish. Florence, which despite its strong industry lacked the rigid guild structure of the northern cities, did not have guild confraternities until the fifteenth century. As in the north, the location of the church to which the confraternity was attached tended to determine its membership; but socially most in Italy were more mixed.[41]

The guilds and city administration

The organisations of the guilds that included only a single craft or related crafts were relatively simple. All practitioners of the trade, or all members of the guild in places that did not require guild membership as a condition of working, chose a dean or master and a sworn council whose size varied with the number of members. This council usually constituted the guild court. The officers were usually chosen in an annual meeting of the entire membership, often coinciding with the rotation of the city magistracy. The composite guilds were much more complicated. When the separate professions had their own organisations that simply reported to the umbrella group, problems were not serious except that there was an increased tendency toward monopoly. The wool guild of Florence was so powerful that it was able to prevent the subordinate crafts, such as the dyers and fullers, from organising, although some of them were able to hold offices in the guild, particularly the dyers.[42]

English guilds continued to be somewhat different from those of the continent, and London was an exceptional case within England. It lacked a merchant guild; the merchants were spread over several wealthy guilds, which gained prestige as they became more oriented toward trade than manufacture. In the fifteenth century the craft guilds gained a voice in the government, and in the sixteenth they became liveried Companies, membership in which was a prerequisite of citizenship. The liveried companies were aristocratic, often led by wardens as chief officers, each of whom chose his own successor.[43] In the county towns one or two guilds were usually reserved for merchants and drapers, with other trades organised into craft guilds that might or might not have a voice in government. Only York had a large number of independent craft organisations. The weavers were strong early in Oxford, but as clothmaking in England became a more rural occupation, their numbers were vastly diminished by 1275, and by 1457 they and the fullers had formed a

41 Mackenney, *Tradesmen and Traders*, 5, 53–61, 68–9; Romano, *Patricians*, 7–8, 81.
42 Brucker, *Renaissance Florence*, 61–5.
43 Imray, 'Mercers' Company', 176–7.

single guild. The tailors are the only Oxford craft for which medieval records survive, although others probably had them. The university had its own trade guilds.[44]

The city governments rarely opposed guild officials in their dealings with their own members. The guilds were municipally sanctioned corporations. In 1401 a mason sitting on the city council of Cologne was expelled for disrespect toward a communication from the masons and carpenters.[45] The borough protected the guilds and shared fines levied by the guild supervisors. Even in the north, where the guilds issued their own industrial regulations, the city governments reviewed them. Guild deans represented the city government with their constituencies, and their appointments were generally subject to confirmation by the council. Some cities paid their wages.[46]

Venice had established a *Guistizia Vecchia* [Old Justice] in 1173 to standardise weights and measures, but in the thirteenth century it also supervised the Arts and approved their statutes. A New Justice branched off from it in 1261 to regulate the food and wine trades and taverns. The *Ternaria*, although still subordinate to the Old Justice, handled the oil trade. The silk industry was under the Old Justice in the thirteenth century, but the woollen manufacture of Venice was under separate 'Provisors of the Commune'.[47] The fact that Venice had such open guilds, from which appeals could be made to the Old Justice, may explain much of the city's political stability, even though the crafts had no political role.[48]

The guilds at Florence and Bologna were more exclusive; and although appeal was possible from Florentine guild courts to the *Mercanzia*, it was unusual. The guilds issued statutes and handled litigation between members. Most guild courts depended on the city government to enforce punitive ordinances, but the wool guild of Florence had its own prison and police. Both communal and guild statutes in Florence forbade the 'underlings' to organise against their masters. The statute of the *podestà* of 1325 forbade all wool workers, including specifically dyers and several less skilled groups, to form 'colleges' or 'bodies' apart from the wool guild. Workers of all guilds were forbidden to hold assemblies or found brotherhoods, including those of a religious or charitable nature, without the approval of one of the twenty-one 'official' guilds, which

---

44   Swanson, *Medieval Artisans*, 6; Salter, *Medieval Oxford*, 60–5.
45   Huiskes, *Beschlusse Köln*, 56.
46   Britnell, *Commercialisation of English Society*, 175; Platt, *English Medieval Town*, 140; Guiral-Hadziiossif, *Valence*, 378.
47   Mackenney, *Tradesmen and Traders*, 9; Bowsky, *Siena Under the Nine*, 212–14.
48   Mackenney, *Tradesmen and Traders*, 34.

did permit some. The authorities were watchful. The *podestà* in 1345 arrested Ciuto Brandini and his two sons for trying to organise a brotherhood, for which consuls and captains had been chosen and dues collected. His activities can hardly have been secret, since he was accused of having held large meetings at two leading churches. The wool carders and combers organised a work stoppage and demanded his release, but to no effect. He was executed.[49]

The guild courts

The guild courts handled industrial infractions and conflicts between guild brothers over professional matters. The courts were an important way in which city governments relied on the guilds to enforce order and policy. Some of them also adjudicated civil or even criminal cases arising between members of the guild. Legal actions lower than felony between members of the pepperers' fraternity of London were to be arbitrated by the two wardens of the organisation; if any brother took such a case to the public court, the rest of the membership was bound to go there and oppose him. The pepperers' court could also register credit transactions among pepperers without involving the city courts.[50] Guild statutes, not those of the city government, made the guild a peace association and punished assaults and vile language against guild members, particularly the officers. Composites, such as the Small Guilds of Ghent, had separate courts for the individual trades but also a general court for the entire unit that handled cases arising between persons in different parts of the composite guild or member. Thus at Ghent a case between two butchers was handled at the court of the butchers' guild; one between a butcher and a brewer would be handled at the court of the dean of the Small Guilds; but one between a butcher and a weaver would be tried in a city court, since they were in different members. The overdean ruled in collective cases between individual small guilds and occasionally arbitrated difficult cases that the individual guild courts felt unable to determine.[51] At Coventry the crafts handled their own internal affairs, but relations between the crafts were handled by the city government.[52]

The French cities were unusual in the weakness of their guild courts. The rebellions between 1380 and 1383 were catastrophic for guild lib-

---

49 De Roover, 'Labour conditions in Florence', 292–4; Larner, *Age of Dante and Petrarch*, 201.

50 Nightingale, *Medieval Mercantile Community*, 179.

51 Nicholas, *Medieval Flanders*, 311.

52 Phythian-Adams, *Coventry*, ch. 7.

erties. The trades of Paris lost their corporate existence. Their property was confiscated, meetings were forbidden without the provost's consent, and they lost jurisdiction over professional infractions. Their elected masters and *jurés* were replaced with 'visitors' appointed by the provost. Although the old privileges were recovered gradually in the next years, the guilds could only denounce violations, not punish them. The guardian of the *prévoté* of the merchants decided industrial conflicts, although appeal could be made to the parlement against his decisions. The butchers had a strong guild organisation, as did merchant associations and craft groups with a strong merchant component. The drapers, spicers, goldsmiths, merchants, furriers and butchers – the 'Six Corporations' of the modern period – had places of honour at the entry of Henry VI in 1431.[53]

Prestige and status

Some occupations were considered honourable, while others were not. This distinction existed not only between merchants and craftspeople, but also between different forms of artisanry. In the French Midi and Italy the 'arts' were higher than 'crafts', and those that emphasised commerce rather than manual labour were more highly regarded. Some Italian cities, notably Florence, recognised a legal cleavage between major and lesser guilds, with the greater having more council seats.[54] Barcelona distinguished between the 'estate of the artists', which included the drapers and notaries, and the 'estate of manual labourers', to which all clothworkers belonged. Both had less prestige than the long-distance merchants.[55]

Several criteria determined the status of trades:

1. The antiquity of the guild;
2. Its strategic value to the survival of the community, such as through food procurement or production;
3. Whether the local market was large;
4. Whether the local market was captive;
5. Whether the guild controlled the supply of raw materials that its craft manufactured into consumer goods;
6. Whether the guild's product could be exported outside the city;
7. Whether the trade was unhygienic;

53 Favier, *Paris 1380–1500*, 251–6.
54 This was not invariable; Venice lacked a division between greater and lesser guilds such as Florence had, or between masters and *sottoposti* who took work. Mackenney, *Tradesmen and Traders*, 8.
55 Carrère, *Barcelone*, 508.

8. Whether it offered access to wholesale trading or control of strategic commodities.

Rising mobility was clearly in trade, which was less regimented than industry, and in guilds with an export market.

The rank order of the guilds in civic processions is a key to their standing. It was not invariable and combined elements of prestige with size of membership, particularly in places that were still giving corporate recognition to new trades. Direct access to the market was thus important, and guilds that sold finished products had higher rank than those whose members merely laboured. In 1392 the council of Valencia fixed the order in which the twenty-four guilds would appear during royal entries. The butchers led, followed by the silkworkers, tanners, tawyers, cutlers, drum makers, bakers, mat makers, weavers, fishmongers, smiths, millers, animal brokers, carpenters. The list ended with tailors, silversmiths (both of which were among the most prestigious trades elsewhere), curriers and cloth preparers. By 1459 there were twenty-nine recognised trades, with butchers still at the top, followed by tawyers, lacemakers, masons, manual labourers, tanners, and the others in roughly the same order except for some new trades.[56]

Of power and influence: the victualling guilds

Victualling trades were always in the political elites of the small towns, and their influence grew in the late Middle Ages in the larger ones. They were flexible, and crossing trades was easy. The bakers were generally the least influential food guild. In some places they were in the same organisation as the millers, and there was considerable mobility between the two crafts virtually everywhere. The English authorities tried without much success to keep bakers from owning inns or mills.[57] In England many bakers were wealthy, but as on the continent their control of the bread supply was by no means exclusive. Much food preparation was casual, part-time and/or done in the home. While in cities of the continent where guild organisations were strong bakers were allowed to buy their grain before the market was open to private citizens, the reverse was generally true in England. There bakers were forbidden to buy until a given hour of the day, since it was assumed that most citizens would bake their own bread. When the bakers were an officially recognised craft, they were very powerful politically, but in most cities hucksters who sold bread, much of it baked in private homes,

---

56   Guiral-Hadziiossif, *Valence*, 376–7.
57   Swanson, *Medieval Artisans*, 13–14.

outnumbered the master bakers.[58] The bakers had a tighter monopoly at Nuremberg, where an eight-member board chosen by the bakers controlled weights and measures, forbade mixing grains in the same loaf, subjected bakers within two miles of the city to the ordinance, and forbade citizens to import bread.[59]

The bakers' guilds were especially prone to having a few big operators, separated by an enormous gulf from the others, because the prominent ones gained control of grain imports and sold to their fellows. At Constance three bakers owned nearly 60 per cent of the total property in the guild. There was a substantial middle range (30 per cent of the property was in the hands of 25 per cent of the guild members), but 40 per cent of the bakers were tax-exempt because of poverty. The butchers' wealth was even more concentrated. The city had forty-eight butchers in 1428, but the total wealth of the guild was in fourteen hands, and over half of that was the property of a single man, Conrat Zillikofen. Characteristically, most of his wealth came not from selling meat retail, where profits were small, but rather the trade in live animals and hides.[60] In contrast to the butchers, who sold meat in stalls in the municipally-regulated Meat Hall rather than from their homes, most bakers sold directly from ground-floor shops in their residences and thus were more dispersed throughout the city.[61]

The extent to which a guild was able to limit access to membership also increased its prestige and political influence. The butchers were among the earliest guilds to gain this privilege. Even though they were not particularly rich as a group, since wealth tended to be concentrated at the top of the trade, they were politically powerful. The fact that they could have dangerous knives made them potentially extremely dangerous. At Reims butchers were often *échevins*, while the bakers, who were both more numerous and wealthier, were not; for theirs was a less hereditary and thus less prestigious guild.[62]

Meat formed a larger part of the urban diet in the late Middle Ages than later. The butchers controlled local sales through their stalls and sold animal by-products, such as hides, to other tradespeople whose standing was lower than theirs in most cities. The powerful butchers of Freiburg-im-Breisgau had two groups: a higher-status element who bought animals and sold animal by-products, and the tripers, sausage

58 Swanson, *Medieval Artisans*, 9–11.
59 Schultheiss, *Satzungen*, 35–6.
60 Bechtold, *Zunftbürgerschaft und Patriziat*, 57–60.
61 Portmann, *Bürgerschaft im mittelalterlichen Freiburg*, 138–9; Nicholas, *Metamorphosis*, 251.
62 Desportes, *Reims*, 359–60.

makers who actually killed the animals and used the cheaper cuts and intestines.[63] Basel distinguished ordinary butchers from butchers *en gros*, who swore to offer a fixed number of fattened oxen for sale continuously through the year, securing the meat supply in months of scarcity; this meant, of course, that they had to see that the animals were sheltered and fed in the winter and thus were raising them.[64]

The butchers were usually linked closely to the fishmongers, sometimes sharing facilities with them, and some cities permitted simultaneous enrolment in the two guilds. But the fishmongers, although often the more numerous, had little political influence. London and Winchester, where the fishmongers were more socially prominent than the butchers, are most unusual. Most cities had a handful of rich fishmongers, but the others were poor. Nearly half the fishmongers at Constance were tax-exempt because of poverty.[65] In England outside London the fishmongers were the largest but probably the most disorganised food trade. Fresh- and salt-water fishmongers had different organisations at York; but the fresh-water fishmongers were more prosperous, since salt-water fish were an international trade that was dominated by members of the merchant guild. The tie of large-scale merchant activity to the fish trade, so prominent in London, thus appears also in the larger county centres.[66]

Wool and clothworkers

The importance of a guild's activity in the economic structure of the city also determined its prestige. Thus trades that had low status in one place were higher in others. Weavers, who tended to be poor except in cities where drapers were enrolled in weavers' guilds, were ill-represented in city councils in proportion to their numbers in most cities and were considered a revolutionary element. They were high only in places with a big cloth export, where they sometimes exercised influence and had seats on the council disproportionate to their numbers. The Cologne weavers had such strict control over the textile industry that they were able to prevent the dyers from forming a guild. Cloth was often dyed in the weaver's shop by journeymen who worked for a wage.[67] The weavers of Ghent had five of thirteen seats on each of the two city councils, even though Ghent's economy was based much less on textiles

---

63 Portmann, *Bürgerschaft im mittelalterlichen Freiburg*, 138–9.
64 Schulz, *Handwerksgesellen und Lohnarbeiter*, 415–16.
65 Bechtold, *Zunftbürgerschaft und Patriziat*, 55–7.
66 Swanson, *Medieval Artisans*, 18–20.
67 Irsigler, *Wirtschaftliche Stellung Köln*, 93.

after 1350 than before. They had two seats at Augsburg and Frankfurt, the highest number possible. Despite this, their rank in processions was often lower, for in addition to a rich aristocracy of cloth merchants all weavers' guilds had many poor members who actually worked at the looms.[68]

Fullers, whose work was dirty and unskilled, rarely enjoyed high prestige. At Ghent they were disenfranchised in city politics after 1360 and were employed by the weaver/drapers, who paid them a wage set by the city government. But there are exceptions to any generalisation. Even at Ghent a few fullers became drapers and even employed weavers.[69] The fullers were the most politically prominent textile craft after the dyers in Winchester. Cloth was sold there in 1394–5 by sixty-one persons whose professional affiliation is known: fifteen were fullers, nine dyers, eight weavers, and the rest included construction and leatherworkers and victuallers. In the fifteenth century the fullers were accused more frequently than any other group of having cloth woven outside the city liberty. The use of the fulling mill may have enhanced the dignity of the trade, for several fullers of Winchester owned mills in the suburbs and through the Itchen valley.[70]

The dyers had low status because of the dirtiness of their work in the cities of southern France that lacked substantial textile exports; but they were the richest textile group *per capita* in the northern cities, for dyeing required the greatest expertise and capital investment of the textile trades. Although drapers were always politically prominent, the dyers were the first clothworkers to have mayors and bailiffs at Winchester.[71] All trades had a gulf between independent masters and those who did not own their shops and had to work for those who did; but with the dyers this was exaggerated by the fact that many became dye merchants and sold to the humbler members of their own trades and to dyers in smaller communities who depended on them for access to international markets. Ghent had a separate organisation for 'blue dyers', who were more highly skilled than other dyers. This was a trade with many women, although generally only as labourers rather than masters.[72]

Tailors, whose occupation was not distinguished in many places from that of cloth cutters or wholesalers, almost always enjoyed high status. Demand was rising, and changes in fashion in the late Middle Ages gave

---

68   Maschke, *Städte und Menschen*, 13–14, 18.
69   Nicholas, *Metamorphosis*, 157–62.
70   Keene, *Medieval Winchester*, 304–10.
71   Keene, *Medieval Winchester*, 303.
72   Swanson, *Medieval Artisans*, 42–3; Nicholas, *Metamorphosis*, 163–8; Platt, *English Medieval Town*, 140.

them a big market. Their profits depended more on the sale of cut cloth and on the quality of the cloth used than on their own labour. Some specialised in making particular garments. By the sixteenth century they were recognised as merchant tailors at York, a standing gained at the expense of the skinners and drapers, the former because the tailors fringed and made fur clothes.[73] The skinners, who were fur importers, declined sharply in most English cities in the late Middle Ages, for by 1400 the London merchants had taken over the skin trade.[74] At Cologne, however, the furriers and skinners were prosperous and had high standing. They benefited from the growing market for leather goods in the late Middle Ages; more importantly, in contrast to leatherworkers, they were almost always fur traders. The fraternity of the furriers was an aristocratic club containing many merchants.[75]

The leatherworking trades

Although the market for leather was growing in the late Middle Ages, most leatherworkers did not have high social standing, for their occupations were dirty and odiferous. The tanners were frequently forced to live and work in the unfashionable peripheries of the cities. Others depended on merchants in other guilds for their raw materials and to sell their finished goods. Tanners and saddlers were more important in the French cities, which had a large rural component, than in places with a strong industrial export or foreign trade. The questions of relation to the market and whether one was primarily a labourer or a merchant were critical.[76] The tanners dominated the leather trades in most cities by controlling the supplies of leather needed by cordwainers, shoemakers, glove makers and saddlers, even though some of them were larger groups than the tanners. The cordwainers and tanners were often in the same guild in the early Middle Ages but separated later. The tanners of Ghent were a smaller group than the cordwainers but were able to prevent the other leatherworkers from having direct access to leather in bulk lots. They were required to buy their hides at the municipal Meat Hall immediately after the animals were slaughtered. Many tanners married into butcher families. The shoemakers and belt makers accused the tanners of not bringing enough leather to the market to permit the other trades to fill their customers' orders.[77]

---

73 Swanson, *Medieval Artisans*, 45–8.
74 Swanson, *Medieval Artisans*, 62.
75 Irsigler, *Wirtschaftliche Stellung Köln*, 233.
76 Chevalier, *Bonnes villes*, 83–4; Maschke, 'Mittelschichten', 17.
77 Nicholas, *Metamorphosis*, 256–7, 276–80.

In England the growing market for specialised leather goods caused some decline in the number and prestige of tanners in the fifteenth century, since the tanners simply made the leather from hides. Parchment makers and tanners had a similar relation to the merchant guild as the weavers and fullers. As the tanners lost control of their sources of raw materials, they forfeited status. The English cordwainers claimed the right to tan hides until they were forbidden to do so by royal statute after 1389. In compensation those of York got the right to search for illicitly tanned leather, including in tanners' homes. By 1400 the tanners and cordwainers were about equally powerful in York, although the tanners had been stronger initially. The change in the tanners' situation is especially marked in Norwich: they were the largest leather-working occupation in the late thirteenth and early fourteenth centuries, but they then dropped so sharply that no tanner held city office in the fifteenth century.[78] They were a depressed group at Cologne, for they depended on merchants outside their own guild for hides.[79]

The case of the tanners within the leather trades suggests that numbers and even assets cannot alone explain a guild's standing. Individual wealth and economic orientation, which might transcend the guild structure, were at least as important as corporate affiliation, particularly as new speciality trades that had no political representation developed in the fifteenth century. At Constance the goldsmiths, butchers, mercers, tanners, wine tappers and bakers all had high per capita wealth, although with a substantial gap between the merchant upper level and the majority who actually practised the craft. The smiths, shoemakers and coopers constituted a small middle group. All other crafts were a long way behind these. If the total picture is corrected by factoring out the guilds whose total wealth is distorted by a very few rich, the middle group within each guild looks stronger, but the total rank order of fortune of the guilds remains almost the same. The guild hierarchy of Constance thus had the merchant-oriented guilds at the top, then the food guilds not far below – indeed, some foodmongers surpassed many merchants in wealth. A bigger gap distinguished this group from a middle group of fishmongers, coopers and shoemakers; in its turn this group was sharply distinguished from the bottom: vineyard workers, tailors, shippers, shearers, smiths, carpenters, weavers and furriers.[80] Wealth averages are thus misleading, for most nominally craft groups had extremes of wealth and poverty. Of eleven tanners living in Tanner Lane at Basel in 1453, the three lowest paid tax of 10, 43 and 50 gulden, the three

---

78 Swanson, *Medieval Artisans*, 53–60, 65; Kowaleski, 'Hide and leather trade', 66–7.
79 Irsigler, *Wirtschaftliche Stellung Köln*, 220.
80 Bechtold, *Zunftbürgerschaft und Patriziat*, 72–3, 153.

greatest 800, 950 and 1,000. Five cobblers living adjacent to each other paid 10, 21, 50, 100 and 300 gulden.[81]

Shippers and supplying the local market

Involvement in wholesale and long-distance trade lent prestige to a craft. This included importing goods and controlling local markets in strategic commodities as well as sales. The fact that the elite in so many guilds were retailers of the raw materials used by the guild probably explains why crafts were so concerned with controlling technological innovations and limiting the number of journeymen and apprentices but rarely took corporate action against the monopoly of the supply of raw materials by the rich.[82]

Thus the nature of the local export trade often determined the relative position and status of guilds. Shippers were poor in the French and south German cities (at Speyer they were grouped with masons and carpenters in a guild that chose one council member), but they were rich and powerful in Flanders and in the Hanse cities. In Ghent the 'free shippers', who monopolised the grain staple along the Leie and Scheldt rivers, were distinguished from the 'unfree', who could only navigate the canal that linked Ghent with Damme and the Bruges market. They were given heredity of mastership by 1436. They also transported peat from northeastern Flanders to the city and invested heavily in the bogs themselves. Thus they had ample opportunities to branch into trade and were by far the largest and one of the most powerful and distinguished of the Small Guilds.[83] Shippers were also prominent in the Hanse cities, but there is more evidence there of newcomers entering the elite by making careers in shipping. Typically from Friesland or Holland, skippers made partnerships with financiers of a port city, then became citizens of the partners' home communities. Simon von Utrecht from Haarlem was captain for a Hamburg merchant in 1399, became a citizen in 1400, led a naval expedition against pirates the next year, then entered politics, becoming a councillor in 1426 and burgomaster in 1432.[84]

The brewers

The brewers came increasingly to fit the pattern of long-distance trade. Most beer was brewed from miscellaneous combinations of spices until

---

81   Maschke, 'Unterschichten', 379.
82   Sosson, *Travaux publics*, 147–50.
83   Nicholas, *Metamorphosis*, 236–44.
84   Reinecke, 'Bevölkerungsprobleme der Hansestädte', 289.

the thirteenth century, when hops, which were grown in substantial quantity only in northern Germany, first entered the export market and became the essential ingredient of good beer. The only strenuous objections came from the old city families who had controlled the supply of brewing spices. Although the brewers were not generally organised into guilds when their trade was largely domestic, their numbers grew rapidly, and they formed guilds when brewing became an export trade. But the chief beneficiaries were characteristically not the producers of the beer but rather those who imported it and/or sold it locally. The increasing profit of beer exports for the north German cities gave some merchant brewers access to the aristocracy. German beer imports so saturated the Dutch market that the native guild of brewers at Dordrecht ceased to exist in the fourteenth century.[85] The brewers of Lille, however, were extremely powerful in the fifteenth century. The city had fifteen breweries, most belonging to a master who handed over actual operations to a journeyman who was hired for a long term. Some were owned by persons who were not brewers, as many brewers concentrated on importing hops and left actual production of beer to employees.[86] Yet although beer was the chief industrial export of the Hanse cities, it remained a household industry there, with little putting-out or capitalist organisation.[87]

In England brewing remained more often a second occupation for persons whose main occupation was another craft, including many women who brewed as a sideline. Hops only reached London after the 1420s, and then in response to demand from the Flemish colony there for better beer. There were so few full-time brewers in York that they did not form a guild, although York was unusual for its size in the large number of its craft organisations. In 1450–1, 221 persons were fined in York for violating the assize of ale; only seven of them had entered the freedom of the city as brewers. In England the older monopolies lasted longer than on the continent, hindering the growth of good native brewing. As late as 1471 Norwich brewers were forbidden to use hops. The only English city where brewers and vintners were numerous was Oxford, perhaps reflecting the domination of its economy by semi-transient scholars.[88]

Winchester, however, displays the pattern characteristic of the continent by the late fourteenth century. Actual brewing, which was a skilled

---

85 van Vollenhoven, *Ambachten en neringen*, Appendix 1.
86 Trenard, *Histoire de Lille*, 255.
87 Maschke, *Städte und Menschen*, 13–14, 18; von Brandt, 'Lübeck', 236; Uitz, *Women*, 59; Pitz, 'Wirtschaftliche und soziale Probleme', 167–8.
88 Swanson, 'Artisans in the urban economy', 51; Swanson, *Medieval Artisans*, 21–5; Goldberg, 'Women in town life', 116–17; Schofield, *Medieval London Houses*, 53.

occupation, was becoming distinguished from tapping or selling in ale-houses, much of it done by women. About one-quarter of the brewers were women, most of them acting as their husbands' successors, but their numbers declined in the fifteenth century. Although brewers were about four times as numerous as tapsters until 1380, the two groups were roughly equal by 1410. Thereafter the tapsters became more numerous, as a distinction developed between the manufacturer who imported hops and the casual seller. There were sixty-three brewers in 1380, eleven in 1501. Brewing was moving away from the household unit of production as large enterprises were established, particularly along river-fronts or canals; for hop beer could be stored longer than ale.[89]

Imports also gave other specialities access to power. The chandlers were small but influential at York, in part due to their investing in wax, which made better candles than tallow. Some rose into the merchant class as spicers or apothecaries, even though York lacked composite guilds of the sort that often grouped wax workers with spicers. Barber-chirurgians, who had low standing almost everywhere, rose by becoming chandlers, a progression possible because wax was used in salves.[90] Coopers were not usually a high-status trade except in the Hanse ports, where the demand for barrels for herring and beer made them essential. As Reims gained importance as a regional wine market in the fifteenth century, the coopers became more prominent there.[91]

The construction trades

Construction workers, with a low level of skill and a large element of migrant labour, did not enjoy high prestige as a group. Their standing was high in places that were dominated by a single church, such as Durham and Westminster, where building was the only significant basic industry.[92] They were well paid, especially on public works projects for city governments, but the work was not steady. Construction workers could not move easily into long-distance trade, the avenue of money and prestige.

The carpenters were generally the most powerful construction workers in northern Europe, where most building was in wood, and the reversion of farmland to brush and forest renewed supplies in the late Middle Ages. Some carpenters were contractors in the modern sense, undertaking projects and hiring joiners, masons and other specialists either by

89 Keene, *Medieval Winchester*, 265–6; Keene, 'Continuity and development', 9.
90 Swanson, *Medieval Artisans*, 98–100.
91 Rotz, 'Urban uprisings', 221; Desportes, *Reims*, 693–4.
92 Rosser, *Medieval Westminster*, 150–5, 162.

the job, a term of days or as subcontractors. Yet despite the building boom most carpenters, except 'city masters' who contracted to undertake public works, were poor and outside the municipal elites. Apart from city halls, most surviving building accounts in the north before the sixteenth century are for renovation and repair of old buildings, not new constructions.[93]

The masons were skilled, and some became prosperous, but even in the late Middle Ages they were a partly itinerant group and did not strike firm roots locally. Carpenters were normally hired by the cities to direct work even on stone bridges, then hired masons as labourers, and the masons resented it.[94] There are exceptions. Masons enjoyed high standing at Durham. York had a city mason, and masons performed plays in the Corpus Christi pageants at York, Beverley and Norwich. The London guildhall was rebuilt between 1411 and 1430 by the mason John Croxton, who acted as general contractor. Rural land investment meant that artisans of all crafts had stocks of food, which gave them access to regional merchant networking and higher status. The York mason Hugh Grantham branched into the grain trade and owned cattle and sheep. He was owed substantial sums of money at his death in 1410, mainly for barley. Peter Mapeltoun of Winchester was simultaneously a mason and innkeeper; others were shipowners, carvers or brewers.[95]

GUILD ORGANISATION AND POLITICS

Officers

Guilds had meetings up to four times a year, but most often they had a single annual meeting and banquet on the festival day of the guild's patron saint, or sometimes on a holiday or when the city council was rotated. They usually met in the church of the patron saint, in individual homes, or in the guildhall. During the fifteenth century virtually all major guilds that did not own halls acquired them; the fishmongers of London owned three halls and the other twenty-five guilds one each, most of them built or rebuilt in the fifteenth century.[96] The meetings had an elaborate ceremonial. Only masters and their wives participated in most northern guilds, but journeymen were admitted to some Italian conclaves. New masters were admitted at these meetings; fines were

93 Keene, *Winchester*, 172; Swanson, *Medieval Artisans*, 83–4.
94 Boyer, 'Working at the bridge', 218–19.
95 Swanson, 'Artisans in the urban economy', 49; Bonney, *Durham*, 156; Swanson, *Medieval Artisans*, 90–2; Schofield, *Medieval London Houses*, 14–17.
96 Schofield, *Medieval London Houses*, 44.

assessed for industrial violations; ordinances were issued subject to promulgation by the city council, and new officials were installed.[97]

The internal hierarchies of the occupational guilds became more rigid in the late Middle Ages. As the guilds became more politically influential, persons who were ambitious for public office often took the route of guild politics, particularly in the larger cities. The majority of guilds had an elected council that handled most business, including the guild's dealings with outsiders, and acted as the guild court. Crafts that were disenfranchised in a guild-based regime, such as the fullers of Ghent after 1360, were exceptions to this. They had 'directors' who were generally not fullers, appointed by the city councils, but they still had a guild whose courts were staffed by fullers and performed the same functions as in politically recognised crafts.[98]

At Florence, for example, each of the twenty-one politically recognised 'arts' had a council of 'consuls', varying in number from three to twelve. There was almost always an age qualification (usually 25 or 30), and frequently one of wealth. Their terms of office were reduced from six months to four in 1328. The exiting consuls had to render accounts to their successors. Decisions in most had to be taken by a two-thirds majority. The consuls in turn had advisors called priors, who rotated weekly. They had no executive power but were involved in finances and industrial policing and discussed matters that the consuls would eventually ratify. Guilds also had other officers, such as the chamberlain, who handled finances, and the notary.[99]

The council advised the guild chief, variously called provost, *juré*, visitor, abbot, master or dean. Although in some places the lineages or city governments chose him, the master was more often elected either by the membership or by the guild council. He generally had to practise the craft, and he was the guild's representative on the city council.[100] At Venice, where the guilds had no political voice, the *gastaldo* (warden) was the chief of the craft, elected annually by the members or sometimes appointed by the city government. The term was normally one year, although some guilds permitted re-election. The guild elites were more open than those that controlled the city government and usually included some genuine working craftsmen. Yet either through lack of interest or through unwillingness to spend the time, most stayed out of guild politics, for it required time away from one's own profession, just

97 Goldthwaite, *Building of Renaissance Florence*, 252; Leguay, *Réseau urbain Bretagne*, 266; Clune, *Medieval Gild System*, 107–8.
98 Nicholas, *Metamorphosis*, 157, 162.
99 Doren, *Arti Fiorentine* 1: 231–49.
100 Eitel, *Oberschwäbischen Reichsstädte*, 26–7, 30–2.

as municipal service did. Even the prestigious grocers' company of London had to use duress to get people to serve as officers. The two wardens who were chosen in 1417 were not even in the grocers' livery until 1424. In 1418 the company agreed that wardens could not be required to serve again before a seven-year lapse. Some guilds had statutes against those who refused to accept office.[101]

Recognising the dangers of family faction, many guilds forbade the simultaneous service on the same council of fathers, sons, brothers, and even those related by marriage. But the frequent rotation and the presence of multiple councils permitted some families to dominate. A member of the Borlin family of butchers was on the council and/or burgomaster of Speyer for more than a century after 1379.[102] Between 1389 and 1515, 104 men and their immediate relatives, many of whom appear in the city building accounts in connection with public works contracts, filled two-thirds of the consulships in the masons' guild at Florence. Although requirements for rotation of offices within the same guild were less strict than for the city magistracies, a small minority held most important guild offices at Bruges. The top guild offices in Coventry were the province of a virtual gerontocracy, but the situation was more fluid in the lesser offices; it was rare to hold one more than once. Career politicians from craft families usually began in one of the prominent guilds, although such cases as Arnoud van der Varent, the carpenter who was overdean of the Small Guilds of Ghent between 1360 and 1377, are unusual. The rulers of guilds with the right to a council seat were thus a subgroup of the political elite that ran the city.[103]

Industrial regulations and inspections through the guilds

All manufacture of goods and delivery of services was strictly regulated in the medieval cities. Some of it was done by guilds, with the city council reserving the right to confirm or deny. Some city councils regulated industrial quality directly, usually with the technical advice of leading practitioners of the trade. The more highly differentiated and specialised the guild structure and the more independent of the city council the guilds were, the more minute the regulations tended to be.

For items that were bought locally, particularly food, protection of the consumer was all-important. The northern French cities appointed

101 Leguay, *Réseau urbain Bretagne*, 267; Mackenney, *Tradesmen and Traders*, 22; Nightingale, *Medieval Mercantile Community*, 378.
102 Maschke, 'Soziale Gruppen', 130.
103 Goldthwaite, *Building of Renaissance Florence*, 272–86; Nicholas, *Medieval Flanders*, 243–4; Sosson, *Travaux publics*, 155–60; Phythian-Adams, *Coventry*, ch. 7.

inspectors for the food guilds. The textile and leather guilds generally appointed their own overseers, but the other guilds were only forced to do this in the fifteenth century. They had seals to signify their approval. At Venice the craft inspectors could visit workshops at least twice a year. The guilds relied on spies and secret denunciations for information about industrial infractions. Penalties for violations were usually money fines. Goods that did not meet specifications were seized and sometimes given to charity if at all usable. The wool guild of Florence hired a non-citizen inspector for a salary and a share of the fines. He had six guards and secret informers. He could fine 'underlings' for poor work, abusing the masters, and for more serious crimes, including debts to the guild that could never be repaid. In severe cases he had the right of mutilation and even capital punishment.[104] The government of Paris strictly regulated four 'bound guilds': goldsmiths, chirurgiens-barbers, apothecaries and locksmiths. All were trades in which there would be great peril if the consumer was defrauded. This distinction was unknown in Languedoc before 1400 and was rare as such thereafter, but all these trades except locksmiths were strictly regulated by royal agents.[105]

While earlier industrial regulations were broad and dealt with matters of general concern, the later statutes were much more exact. As late as 1293 both the leather and cloth trades of Toulouse were given a single statute, encompassing all subspecialities; between 1464 and 1467 the *capitouls* issued regulations for more than seventy distinct corporations, more than twice the number documentable in the town at the end of the thirteenth century.[106] Just as for food, quality control was needed for export items to ensure that the reputation of the trade was not compromised, but this often became a subterfuge for keeping persons out of the guild.

The growing differentiation of labour and subdivision of guilds after 1350 contributed to minute regulations, particularly in the ironworking and leather guilds. The knife makers of Cologne were the most important subdivision of the ironmongers' guild in the fourteenth century, yielding during the fifteenth to the pot- and pansmiths. The locksmiths were also important, working at times in tandem with the shrine makers. Cologne had separate organisations for cordwainers, belt makers, ordinary shoemakers, makers of children's shoes and wooden shoes, cobblers who repaired old shoes, and those who worked pig, horse and deer hide into horse coverings. The furriers too had numerous subspecialities,

104 Larner, *Age of Dante and Petrarch*, 196.
105 Doren, *Arti Fiorentine* 2: 141–51; Mackenney, *Tradesmen and Traders*, 22–6; Desportes, 'Police des métiers', 334–5; Gouron, *Métiers en Languedoc*, 284–5.
106 Gouron, *Métiers en Languedoc*, 284.

depending on the type of animal, and several had separate offices within the guild until 1495.[107]
The textile industry was also diversified, requiring the skills of numerous specialists. Regulations proliferated particularly from the late thirteenth century, when the less skilled processes such as spinning were put out to rural workers who could not demand the high wages required by the urban guilds. Rural competition was particularly serious in the case of Ypres, whose drapers relied heavily on villagers for labour. Ghent from 1297 forbade the sale of cloth not woven and fulled in the city or its ban mile. Winchester likewise forbade having cloth woven or fulled outside the city liberty.[108] The goal was to keep work in the city while not damaging the profitable business that the city had with the artisans of the environs.

The technical specifications of each process, number of threads of what specific wool or other material, the mix of dyes and the like were laid down with excruciating exactness. The cities also tried to protect the integrity of their markets, where tolls were taken and the seals attesting quality were apposed. Nuremberg forbade selling cloth without the city seal and limited sales of specific grades to the Cloth Hall on Friday and Saturday, but direct sales were permitted on other days. Burgesses of Nuremberg were permitted to sell cloth fulled elsewhere as long as it bore the seal of the place where it was fulled, but not unfulled cloth.[109]

Although the drapers were merchant-entrepreneurs, their hold on local textile industries was stronger in the northern cities than in Italy, for the lesser craftsmen needed them as agents to market their goods at the fairs and international emporia. Although at Florence some shop owners amounted to subcontractors working for a merchant in the wool guild and were paid on a piece work basis, most production was still centred on small family shops.[110] Precapitalist organisation is found more in the silk industry, which at Genoa was run entirely by the merchant putting out raw silk to entrepreneurs who owned one or more shops and hired workers, delivering the thread to their homes where they worked it into cloth. The woollen industry at Genoa was similar. The weavers depended on merchant drapers who paid them by the piece, often in kind rather than money even in the fifteenth century. The drapers in turn obtained their wool from the same long-distance merchants who sold their cloth overseas. They contracted with these

107 Irsigler, *Wirtschaftliche Stellung Köln*, 165–8, 224–6, 230, 233.
108 Nicholas, *Town and Countryside*, 90–6, 110; Keene, *Medieval Winchester*, 301.
109 Schultheiss, *Satzungen*, 92–3.
110 Mackenney, *Tradesmen and Traders*, 30–1; Brucker, *Renaissance Florence*, 61.

entrepreneurs to deliver a certain number of pieces of cloth of a specific type at a given time and place. The draper paid rent on shops and the workers' wages, while the merchant paid the wages of those who were not part of the household or clientele of the draper. The entrepreneur recovered the sums that he had advanced for wool and wages. All other profit was divided equally except that the cloth merchant received two-thirds of the yield on cloth that he sold personally; thus the draper was to try to sell as much as he could from his shop on the local market but depended on the entrepreneurs for distribution outside the city.[111]

In the late Middle Ages speciality trades in some cities moved away from producing goods from raw materials and concentrated on final finishing of goods made elsewhere, as the city merchants gained control of the export markets of villages and the environs. The sword polishers of Cologne are a conspicuous case in point. Many woollen cloths were ordered by Cologne merchants in neighbouring towns and villages, then finished for sale by Cologne cloth cutters on a wage or piece work basis. This is especially true of dyeing, which was done often on undressed foreign cloth in the establishments of master weavers.[112] Some industrial protectionism was regional rather than strictly urban. Valencia encouraged silkworkers to emigrate from Genoa in the fifteenth century, then adopted protectionist measures against Genoese silk. Once established in the city, silk making was expanded to the rural environs, as city merchants hired jobs done and marketed the finished product.[113] As more specialised processes became centred in the cities while less skilled work was done in the rural areas, the extreme occupational differentiation in the cities led to greater economic integration of the larger cities with their rural environs.

City governments had always regulated industry through craft organisations. Even in Languedoc, where 'sworn guilds' with the power to regulate themselves were unusual before the fifteenth century, the city governments relied on craft elites to enforce economic regulations. They appointed officials variously called *bayles*, *majorals* and consuls in the thirteenth century, evidently with the same functions as the 'chiefs of the misteries' of Provence. They normally practised the trade that they supervised. Most trades had four *bayles*; professions that were practised in different parts of the city and some small trades sometimes had more. The number of *bayles* tended to increase as the trade became less accessible to newcomers and powers of the general assembly of the trade

111 Heers, *Gênes. Civilisation*, 180–91.
112 Irsigler, *Wirtschaftliche Stellung Köln*, 165, 322.
113 Guiral-Hadziiossif, *Valence*, 383–6.

declined. The consuls gradually placed the treasuries of the craft confraternities under the *bayles*. The *bayle* also controlled the corporate seal of the city that was required for all sales. In some trades he could judge civil and even criminal actions between members.[114]

Restrictions on mastership

An important element of the prestige of guilds was the extent to which they could restrict access to mastership and thus make themselves more exclusive and lineage-based. While occupational organisations of the central Middle Ages had generally been open to qualified outsiders, the late medieval guilds were closing. Given the ubiquity of family-based enterprises, the guilds amounted to associations of families that practised the same or similar trades. The tendency to hereditary succession of mastership existed in most guilds, but it was rarely unbreachable except for a few politically prominent guilds, most conspicuously the butchers. This did not mean that only masters could work, for trained journeymen provided much of the labour force.[115]

Rules for mastership thus ossified. Some guilds developed criteria of wealth. The richer guilds of Cologne required masters to have a coat of mail, an iron helmet and a crossbow.[116] Masterworks, which few guilds had required earlier, became more common as tests of professional competence in Languedoc in the fifteenth century. As late as 1500 only five guilds of Lille required a masterwork, including the smiths and barbers. In other cases the master simply certified his apprentice, whose work had doubtless been observed by most masters in the guild, or enfranchised his sons. The masterwork was rare in the Upper Rhine cities before the late fourteenth century, but the saddlers and shoemakers of the region used it by 1464. It became general in Paris in the fifteenth century. It required not only technical competence, but also enough money to buy the raw material.[117]

Higher entry fees were a more severe hindrance than masterworks. Virtually all guilds had lower entry fees for sons of masters than for outsiders, and the gap between the two became extreme in the fifteenth century. Some guilds permitted only one son to matriculate at the lower

114 Gouron, *Métiers en Languedoc*, 201–20, 234, 249–54, 320–63.
115 Chevalier, *Tours*, 410–12; Geremek, *Salariat*, 49; Leguay, *Réseau urbain Bretagne*, 268.
116 Irsigler, *Wirtschaftliche Stellung Köln*, 160.
117 Gouron, *Métiers en Languedoc*, 368–9; Trenard, *Histoire de Lille*, 301; Schulz, *Handwerksgesellen und Lohnarbeiter*, 297; Geremek, *Salariat*, 45–9; Favier, *Paris 1380–1500*, 267.

insiders' rate or permitted automatic emancipation only to sons born after the father had become a master. From the fifteenth century in the upper Swabian towns the eldest brother, in buying the guild for himself, did so for his younger brothers also.[118] Others, particularly trades in decline, asked the city council to limit the number of masters who were permitted in each craft, which could exclude sons of incumbent masters as well as outsiders.[119] In such cases the younger son(s) would be apprenticed in a different trade, generally a more recently developed speciality, often one lacking the right to a formal guild, or a guild of less skilled technique or lower prestige. Some English crafts required an 'upset' fee in addition to the purchase of freedom when a new master opened his own shop, but sons of freemen were exempt from it.[120]

The practical impact of entry fees on mobility can easily be exaggerated, however. Although they were raised sharply in nominal terms in the fifteenth century, much of the increase was a response to inflation. The charter of the bakers of Basel of 1256 established a fee of 38s., which had risen to 5 pounds in 1404; this corresponds closely to the extent of debasement of the silver penny of Basel, granted that this is not the same thing as the cost of living. The bakers wanted to raise the rate again in 1404, but the council forced them to lower it, because the change would make entry impossible for poor entrants, especially since there were now other separate fees for militia duty and the upkeep of the guildhall.[121]

Only a master could own his own shop, hire journeymen and train apprentices. Yet, although the master craftsmen constituted a solid middle class in most cities, many masters were poor. Some masters who did not inherit shops from their fathers could not afford to buy them, particularly after they had paid the guild's entry fees, provided a banquet for the members and bought presents for the guild officials, raw materials, and/or tools. Such persons became wage employees of other masters. This was especially common in the construction trades, where only the simplest tasks could be done by a single worker in the shop. Yet since most guilds paid masters at twice the piece or time rate of journeymen, there was an additional motive for the masters to limit access to mastership; they could get cheaper and often highly skilled labour from journeymen and apprentices.[122]

118 Eitel, *Oberschwäbischen Reichsstädte*, 25.
119 Pitz, 'Wirtschaftliche und soziale Probleme', 163.
120 Swanson, *Medieval Artisans*, 118–19.
121 Schulz, *Handwerksgesellen und Lohnarbeiter*, 211–13.
122 Geremek, *Salariat*, 66; Nicholas, *Metamorphosis*, 289; Schulz, *Handwerksgesellen und Lohnarbeiter*, 256; Mollat, *Poor*, 234 ff.

Although the hereditary rights of the trades hindered the freedom of the labour market, most guild monopolies were stricter in theory than in practice. The butchers of Ghent and Bruges in 1302 were granted hereditary mastership in the male line. No one could hold a stall in one of the Meat Halls who was not in the guild. Yet in some cities bakers were allowed to keep pigs and feed them on grain wastes. At Ghent they rather than the butchers controlled the trade in pigs with the local churches, since the butchers' monopoly extended only to the central city and not to the abbey villages. Nor could the butchers stop burgesses from raising and slaughtering animals for their own tables. When the bakers of Ghent tried to stop recent migrants to the city from baking and selling bread on the square in front of the castle of the Flemish count in 1383, the aldermen confirmed only the bakers' guild's monopoly on large breads, permitting the newcomers to bake smaller sizes.[123]

Furthermore, although kinsmen tended to be in the same or related trades, family tradition was not absolute. Some guilds permitted dual matriculation to those with the appropriate hereditary qualifications. William de Paeu of Ghent was simultaneously a 'baker and boatman' in 1390. Jan van der Eeken began as a shearer, then became a practising brewer without surrendering mastership in the shearers' guild. The van Hijfte family had members who were bakers, brewers and barristers. By the 1380s the brewers of Ghent automatically admitted to mastership only those sons who were born after the father had become a master. They limited the number of outsiders to three annually in 1422 and to one in 1443. Yet of 187 family names in a list of masters of 1363, only 67 were still in the guild by 1394. Thus guild lists show that reality was much less rigid than the letter of the law.[124] The coopers of Bruges charged outsiders an entry fee 19 per cent higher than that exacted from the sons of masters until 1477, 56 per cent thereafter. Yet only 145 (21 per cent) of 668 new masters enrolled in the guild between 1375 and 1500 were masters' sons. Fathers, in order to guarantee their sons' futures, would pay the higher entry fees to gain admission to a different guild if needed.[125]

The Great Charter of Ghent of 1297 allowed 'each burgess of Ghent [to] choose within three days of every 15 August [the beginning of the fiscal year] what business he wants to pursue during the coming year'.

123 Desportes, *Reims*, 358; Nicholas, *Metamorphosis*, 252–6; Nicholas, *Medieval Flanders*, 202.
124 Nicholas, *Domestic Life*, 183–6; Nicholas, *Metamorphosis*, 282–6.
125 Sosson, 'Körperschaften', 81–90; Sosson, 'Tonneliers de Bruges', 457–78; Sosson, *Travaux publics*, 136–41.

It was thus possible to change professions annually except in trades that forbade dual matriculation. This helps to explain how some craftsmen could expand into commerce: although wool workers were forbidden to buy or sell wool wholesale, they could buy it one year and have it made into cloth the next simply by declaring a different profession for that year.[126]

The Breton guilds prohibited enrolment in more than one trade, including related professions such as baker and miller. With this exception, crossing professions and dual matriculation were easy in most French cities, particularly in the south. In Languedoc multiple professions could not be exercised simultaneously, but one could move easily between crafts in the 'mechanical arts'. Many artisans of Arles practised several professions, because virtually all trades there were of the sort, including butchering and low-grade weaving, that skilled amateurs could learn. There were neither sworn guilds nor restrictions on the labour market at Lyon, and the porous craft hierarchy permitted people to pass from one trade to another or to accumulate membership in several. Drapers, spicers and mercers often doubled as moneychangers or bankers. From the beginning of the fourteenth century, and commonly in the fifteenth, artisans could belong to more than one guild at Metz.[127] Although double guild membership was unusual in Germany, Ravensburg allowed it when someone practising one trade inherited another from his father or acquired it by marrying the widow or daughter of a member of a different guild, a practice that was restricted by many guilds but common in those that were not rigidly regulated.[128]

The Italian cities also permitted crossing professions, and Florence at least was open to non-indigenous craftsmen. Florentines could also be in two guilds at once, paying a lower fee for the one that was not actually being practised. Most entrepreneurs were in several guilds simultaneously, combining banking, trading as a merchant, owning cloth shops and other property in and outside the city. Lawyers might be in trading and banking. Thus the guilds were generally not mutually exclusive. In the construction trades, while at Venice the activities of stonecutters and wallers were kept distinct, Florence even permitted crossovers between carpenters and stonecutters, and both stonecutters and goldsmiths worked in bronze. Persons who did not actually practise the trade could easily

---

126 Nicholas, *Metamorphosis*, 143.
127 Leguay, *Réseau urbain Bretagne*, 269; Gouron, *Métiers en Languedoc*, 282; Stouff, *Arles*, 293–4; Valous, *Patriciat Lyonnais*, 50, 91; Schneider, *Metz*, 235–6.
128 Eitel, *Oberschwäbischen Reichsstädte*, 25. After 1389 the bakers of Osnabrück required a masterwork from an outsider who acquired the trade by marrying a master's daughter. Wensky, 'Osnabrücker Gilden', 377.

enrol in a guild for political purposes in Florence, a practice frowned on elsewhere.[129]

A royal statute of 1363 ordered English artisans to confine themselves to one craft, but municipal authorities enforced it erratically. Not until the early fifteenth century did Colchester try to restrict entry into the guilds and hinder crossovers, such as by prohibiting weavers from fulling their own cloth. Three hostellers at York in 1381 are called mercers in other sources. John Stubbs was described in his will of 1450 and in the Register of Freemen as a barber; but the inventory of his property shows him as an innkeeper with an establishment that included a brewery.[130] English evidence thus supports the thesis that heredity of profession was the authorities' desire but not a social reality. Even among the London aldermen, whose wealth and social position would suggest more continuity, only two-thirds were followed by their sons in the same profession. Family succession was rare for more than a generation or two. Special privileges for masters' sons begin only in 1448, when the entry fee due from sons of freemen born after the fathers had been enfranchised was raised. Emancipation by patrimony became more common thereafter. Of 806 artisans' sons who enrolled in the freedom of York between 1387 and 1534, 415 kept the father's trade while 184 moved into a branch of artisanry different from the father's. When the tools of the craft were expensive, as with the potters, founders and goldsmiths, son tended to follow father. The trades that were least attractive to sons were those of carpenter, smith, mason, currier and other leatherworkers, for these crafts had low status. Fifty-nine became merchants or chapmen: six were butchers, five dyers, four each tanners and girdlers, each of which was a trade that gave access to raw materials and accordingly conveyed the possibility of expansion into trade as a merchant.[131]

Apprenticeship and the household unit of production

Apprenticeship has been misunderstood. All young persons who were to become masters had to be trained in the craft. But although standards of professional competence were becoming higher in the late Middle Ages than before, this did not mean that masters normally apprenticed

129 Doren, *Arti Fiorentine* 1: 158–9; Brucker, *Renaissance Florence*, 57; Goldthwaite, *Building of Renaissance Florence*, 256–72.
130 Hilton, *English and French Towns*, 102; Britnell, *Colchester*, ch. 12, 16; Swanson, 'Artisans in the urban economy', 50.
131 Thrupp, *Merchant Class*, 205; Imray, 'Mercers' Company', 159–62; Swanson, *Medieval Artisans*, 165–87.

their children to other masters in the same trade. Rather, they trained them personally. In cities without formal craft statutes or without a strong differentiation between masters and others, apprenticeship as a formal status was pointless. It was sometimes required as a condition of mastership when a craft first became regulated, as with the fullers of Colchester in 1418. For weavers, cloth preparers and shearers Barcelona required apprenticeship only for newcomers to the city. Fullers and dyers there had no apprenticeship requirement at all; they simply had to show proof of their professional competence.[132]

Except in Languedoc, where, by the fourteenth century, one generally had to complete apprenticeship before becoming a master, formal apprenticeship was usual on the continent only for persons who were leaving their father's profession and particularly for orphans. Most guilds made special provision to apprentice the orphans of masters, who could not be trained by their parent. Surviving lists of apprentice matriculations cannot possibly account for the total number of persons needed to provide the number of masters that the guilds are known to have had. Of 1,047 freemen recorded in the London mercers' records between 1391 and 1464, only 509, most of them wealthy, are known to have taken apprentices. Furthermore, roughly half the apprentices named did not complete their training.[133]

The age at which apprenticeship began was raised from the early teens into the late teens or even the early twenties in the fifteenth century. As the onset of apprenticeship came later, so the status became more select. In the fifteenth century the apothecaries of Nantes were forbidden to take 'low and vile people' as apprentices, and the mercers of Rennes excluded bastards.[134] Apprenticeship became the normal avenue for young persons of the home counties to gain access to the freedom of London in the late Middle Ages. Many apprentices worked for masters who were originally from their home villages, sometimes their kinsmen. This degree of intimacy explains some spectacular rises within both the family and the city. Andrew Aubrey was probably the apprentice of the pepperer Thomas de Enfield, who willed property to him; Aubrey then married Enfield's widow. He eventually became mayor of London.[135]

The length of apprenticeship varied between guilds, but everywhere the terms lengthened in the fifteenth century; the girdlers of York went from four years in 1307 to seven years in 1417. Curiously, there was rarely

132 Britnell, *Colchester*, ch. 16; Carrère, *Barcelona*, 476–7.
133 Imray, 'Mercers' Company', 159–68, 171.
134 Tillott, *City of York*, 92–3; Leguay, *Réseau urbain Bretagne*, 267.
135 Nightingale, *Medieval Mercantile Community*, 186.

a correlation between level of skill required and length of apprenticeship. The fee that the apprentice or his family had to pay to the master also rose in the fifteenth century. The master had to provide food and lodging, and often shoes and clothing. Masters in the Breton cities were expected to register their apprentices with the authorities within a week of concluding the contract, often accompanied by a payment and registration in the guild confraternity.[136]

The crafts regulated the number of journeymen and apprentices, usually one or at most two, whom a master could employ simultaneously. The apprenticeship relation presupposed the household unit: some guilds of York allowed bachelors to have two apprentices, while married men, whose wives were presumed to be helping them, were limited to one.[137] As apprentices became older, they competed with journeymen for jobs. Cologne in the late fourteenth century restricted apprenticeship to masters' sons and prohibited using an apprentice as a journeyman, thus showing that the two groups were likely to be peers in age and professional competence.[138] Troubles erupted in Paris in 1325 when workers claimed that the masters were using more apprentices than allowed, diminishing the need for journeymen; the masters in turn accused the journeymen of beginning work late, having stoppages and refusing to work at night, which in itself was often forbidden by guild statutes.[139] Even though apprentice fees were raised substantially in the fifteenth century, some masters preferred to pay the higher rates, which they passed on to the apprentice or his parents, to avoid having to pay the wages that hiring outsiders would have forced on them; for once the apprentice was taken on, he could be used for whatever labour the master wished as long as his status was not diminished.[140]

Although in Tours most boys who were admitted to apprenticeship eventually became masters,[141] this cannot be generalised. The coverlet weavers of Ghent distinguished between apprentices and sons of masters; and of eighty-nine apprentices received in the guild between 1370 and 1396, only twelve had patronymics previously found in the trade. Only three of the eighty-nine became masters, at intervals of four, seven and nine years from the onset of apprenticeship. Of seventy apprentices enrolled in the painters' guild of Tournai between 1440 and 1480, only

---

136 Nicholas, 'Child and adolescent labour', 1114–26; Reyerson, 'Adolescent apprentice/worker', 355–7; Schulz, *Handwerksgesellen und Lohnarbeiter*, 248–9; Gouron, *Métiers en Languedoc*, 267–77; Leguay, *Réseau urbain Bretagne*, 267.
137 Tillott, *City of York*, 94.
138 Schultheiss, *Satzungen*, 294.
139 Mollat and Wolff, *Popular Revolutions*, 96.
140 Nightingale, *Medieval Mercantile Community*, 479.
141 Chevalier, *Tours*, 410–12.

twenty became masters.[142] Thus most apprentices became and remained journeymen, not masters, after completing their training.

Solidarity and identity: masters, journeymen, the labour market and the extension of household production

For all its usefulness, the notion of 'household shop' must also be nuanced. At Cologne each 24 July a weaver could choose whether to do 'his own work' for the coming year or work for another master. From 1449 every Cologner, whether in the wool guild or not, could employ wage-earning weavers at three looms; and relatives who did not live in the same house could also have three looms in operation. Thus a single family with adult children could become a syndicate employing weavers.[143] Such regulations help to explain the concentration of industrial production and capital in a few hands within the guilds. A statute of Frankfurt of 1432 established how many pieces of cloth could be exhibited at the fair, ranging from eleven masters who produced thirty-six each to forty-nine who produced four each. This was probably the total productive capacity of the smaller establishments but not of the larger. One hundred and thirty-three masters were making 1680 pieces; of these, 8.3 per cent of the masters at the top produced 23.57 per cent of the cloth, while the 36.8 per cent at the bottom produced 11.7 per cent. The two top groups included 24.8 per cent of the masters and sold 55 per cent of the cloth.[144]

Although the guilds are often compared to trade unions, modern unions try to raise workers' wages, while the medieval guilds, dominated by masters, tried to keep them low. Efforts to raise wages came from journeymen, who were either outside the guilds or on their margins. The fact that wages were considerably higher in the cities than in their rural environs contributed to migration to the cities but also meant a surplus of qualified labour seeking employment in such extended 'household shops'. Masters of all building trades at Bruges had roughly comparable salaries; journeymen, however, received half the masters' wages, and the difference was not always due to different degrees of qualification. Apprentices in turn were paid half the wage of the journeymen. Salaries thus made it harder for the lower levels to become masters and caused masters with large enough operations to employ others to limit the numbers of new masters who could be received.[145] It also caused

142 Nicholas, *Metamorphosis*, 171–5; Sosson, 'Körperschaften', 81–90.
143 Irsigler, *Wirtschaftliche Stellung Köln*, 50.
144 Maschke, *Städte und Menschen*, 21.
145 Sosson, *Travaux publics*, 225–8.

work-givers to seek outside sources of labour when they were not bound by a guild monopoly. Most construction workers employed at the cathedral of Milan in 1386–7 and the Charterhouse of Parma in 1396 came from villages of the environs, not from the city artisanate.[146]

Employers valued the abundant supply of cheap labour. The earliest *Bursprake* of Lübeck announced an exile of a year and a day for any servant who ran away from the master during the period of service. In the north masters were generally prohibited in the fourteenth century from hiring the journeymen of other masters during the term of contract, suggesting that the journeymen were being taken on at a cheap rate, then kept as wages rose. This restriction spread to Languedoc in the fifteenth century as more crafts there became 'sworn' guilds of the northern type.[147]

Although journeymen were an important element of the workforce, few masters stopped actually practising their crafts. Journeymen were employed in only half to two-thirds of the trades in the towns of the upper and middle Rhine. They were most numerous in export trades and in new crafts, such as printing, that did not have guild organisations. They were also relatively strong among the bakers, tailors, cobblers and smiths. But they were rare in transport, textiles and agriculture, trades in which most employees were married and lived independently.[148]

Since hiring other masters was expensive, and apprentices might compete with their own sons, craftsmen who needed labour increasingly hired journeymen for a long term or even employees who were completely outside the guild. Messengers, secretaries, even carters of merchants sometimes rose into positions of responsibility. They were often paid well and could eventually save enough money or make themselves sufficiently indispensable by their skills to work their way into a partnership. Some started their own businesses by getting orders from the previous employer's clients or impressing his customers with their business acumen. This commercial support personnel included some four hundred persons in Cologne, skilled and unskilled – about 5 per cent of the working male population.[149] Apprentices as well as journeymen were placed into positions of responsibility. English county families apprenticed their sons to members of London merchant companies, for they gave good training for running a business in the provinces, and the young men also gained the opportunity to make their own investments and build up business contacts both in London and overseas. Stephen Sewell began

146 Braunstein, 'Salaires', 126.
147 Sprandel, *Quellen zur Hanse-Geschichte*, 40; Gouron, *Métiers en Languedoc*, 262.
148 Schulz, *Handwerksgesellen und Lohnarbeiter*, 46–8; Isenmann, *Deutsche Stadt*, 327.
149 Maschke, *Städte und Menschen*, 381–3.

as the apprentice of the London grocer Geoffrey Crimmelford, then became his agent in Bruges and Middelburg.[150]

Given the gulf between the wealthy and poor masters within each guild, it is unwise to make too great a distinction between journeymen and masters in the more proletarian occupations. So many masters were wage-earners, working the wool bought and 'put out' to them by the drapers, that they amounted to journeymen. The bakers and millers in the south German cities also illustrate this problem. The millers were often subordinated to other groups, generally the bakers, although they were in the smiths' guild in Basel and the cabinetmakers' guild in Freiburg-im-Breisgau. A conflict arose in Colmar in the 1350s over the bakers' attempt to demand a gift from the millers. This rivalry, however, also involved the journeymen, for in some cities the millers' journeymen were paid by the bakers; the millers won the allegiance of the journeymen by promising them higher wages than the bakers were willing to pay. A Speyer ordinance of 1343 had treated master and journeyman millers the same way, but by 1410 the council had to confirm a single brotherhood for the journeyman bakers and millers, distinct from the guilds that housed the masters. Thus both weaver and miller journeymen were dragged into a conflict between two groups of masters in the fourteenth century, then developed more community of interest with one another in the late fourteenth and early fifteenth centuries than with the masters of their trades.[151]

Interurban unions of practitioners of the same trade were common, showing a sense of professional identity that transcended the loyalty felt toward the city of residence. The master bakers from eight middle Rhine towns allied in 1352 and renewed the bond periodically into the fifteenth century. In 1457 the tailors of twenty cities and towns made a union and had meetings concerning wages, justice and the problems of itinerant journeymen. In 1352 the master bakers of the cities of the middle Rhine and Main formed a single association, and the master smiths did so in 1383. The master cutlers of southern Germany were grouped into four confraternities from the mid-fourteenth century, centred on Augsburg, Basel, Heidelberg and Munich.[152]

In most cities only journeymen groups who could normally live in their own households, supporting themselves on wages, were the construction workers and weavers. The wages paid to journeymen varied considerably even within the same guild, depending on age and training.

150 Nightingale, *Medieval Mercantile Community*, 340.
151 Schulz, *Handwerksgesellen und Lohnarbeiter*, 65–8.
152 Schulz, *Handwerksgesellen und Lohnarbeiter*, 78; Maschke, 'Soziale Gruppen', 133; Mollat and Wolff, *Popular Revolutions*, 248.

Journeymen bakers and smiths were relatively well paid, cloth cutters and tailors less so. While apprentices had long terms of employment, most journeymen were hired for one year or less. Construction workers were paid by the length of time worked, but weavers were paid by the piece of work. Shorter-term hires were most commonly for one week or even a day or by the job. The peak working season was summer, when wages were about one-third higher than in winter. Wage figures are distorted by the tendency to pay short-term workers and piece workers a higher wage than those hired for a month or year, but the latter often got supplementary payments in food and/or lodging, together with greater job security. The fact that servants and journeymen often received part of their compensation in lodging and maintenance makes it impossible to read too much into their wage figures. The wage schedule for construction workers at Speyer in 1342 gave masters and apprentices in skilled trades after the third year double the wage of junior apprentices and mortar makers. Those at the bottom of the scale, the stone and mortar carters, were paid only 40 per cent of a master's wage. The employer, however, could decide whether to pay these rates and have the worker bring his own food or to deduct 40 to 50 per cent of the wage for food. Statistics for Frankfurt in 1425 have the food cost at one-quarter to one-third of the total wage.[153]

Church bells sounded the beginning of the working day, at dawn or one hour later in all trades. Work ended at curfew, when lights were extinguished as Compline was sounded. The change of seasons meant that this happened at different times of the day. The maximum working day was normally 16–17 hours in the summer, 11 hours in winter. Some trades obtained permission to work before daybreak. Night work by candlelight was forbidden, but there was much evasion. Shorter working days in the winter worked well for trades that had to be conducted outside or depended on raw materials that came by the galleys, which could only sail in the summer. Exceptions were made in cases of hardship, for example when the glove makers of Paris protested in 1467 that they had only a few working hours in winter, when demand for their product was highest.[154]

Workers appeared at the construction site or at the local work market, a designated open area where masters would hire them as needed. The use of a central hiring place for journeymen is found mainly in textiles and construction. In cities where one industry predominated, the 'hiring place' was usually the main square. Saint-Omer had a Weavers'

153 Maschke, *Städte und Menschen*, 391–8; Carrère, *Barcelone*, 479–80; Diermeier, 'Condizioni materiali', 103; Geremek, *Salariat*, 37–9, 85–6.
154 Geremek, *Salariat*, 78–9; Mollat, *Poor*, 211 ff.

Square and Fullers' Bridge for this purpose.[155] Paris had several labour markets. The fullers used two, a street intersection and the square before St Gervais, while construction workers sought work at the Place de Grève, and smaller groups met in front of churches or the houses of individual masters. Those without work were required to go to the hiring square daily or be fined, to assure labour to those needing it. Street porters, the least skilled of labourers and the type of work most in demand by immigrants who were shut out of more skilled trades, had the strictest organisation. They had to queue up at the Place de Grève at the beginning of the work day, divide into groups led by a *juré* of the guild (the rank order of the groups changed weekly) and await customers. Those who had not yet worked on a given day were placed ahead of those coming back for a second job. In principle those who did not work one day went to the head of the line the next day, but this was impossible to enforce. Masters had precedence in the line over journeymen and natives over foreigners.[156]

Journeyman brotherhoods

Particularly in the larger cities that drew migrants from a great distance, journeymen were a major element of the population. Apprentices and domestics may have made up 20 per cent of Cologne's population in the fifteenth century. Extrapolations from a muster of 1431 for a sector in the St Lorenz city at Nuremberg suggest that, depending on the size of the household, journeymen constituted between 13 and 17 per cent of the population between the two walls, between 5 and 7 per cent outside. Between the walls 55.5 per cent of households had no journeymen or servants, 25.8 per cent had one, and 10.7 per cent had two. Outside the walls 84.6 per cent of the households had no journeymen or servants, 7.9 per cent had one, and 4.0 per cent had two. Figures from Nördlingen are slightly lower, from Dresden much lower; the percentage of servants/journeymen and maids was high in the larger cities and in commercial-industrial rather than agricultural centres.[157]

As a substantial element of the population without political voice and at high economic risk, journeymen, who tended to be in the more prestigious crafts, began forming brotherhoods, occasionally in the fourteenth century and more commonly in the fifteenth. Not all of these brotherhoods were directed against masters in the craft. The journeymen

155 Derville, *Saint-Omer*, 59.
156 Geremek, *Salariat*, 127–30.
157 Howell, *Women, Production, and Patriarchy*, 114; Schulz, *Handwerksgesellen und Lohnarbeiter*, 37; Maschke, *Städte und Menschen*, 386–8.

often organised against unskilled and migrant labour, which was completely outside the guild structure and could be hired more cheaply than natives of the city, whose wages were regulated by guild statutes. The journeymen of Paris tried to get legislation forcing the masters not to hire non-Parisians while natives were willing to work. Confraternities of journeymen developed especially early in the building trades, which were flooded with unskilled and wandering workers.[158]

Journeyman organisations were more common in France and particularly in Germany than in England, where they were confined to the larger cities before the sixteenth century. During the 1440s the journeymen or bachelors of the London grocers developed their own organisation within the company.[159] The less structured conditions in the Italian crafts militated against journeyman organisations there, but in Spain they developed as in the north. Efforts were made to prevent them from organising for higher wages in Barcelona as early as 1419.[160] The authorities were suspicious of journeyman brotherhoods, particularly in cities where craft guilds dominated by masters controlled the city council. In 1303 the 'servant workmen in cordwainery' of London were forbidden to hold meetings to the detriment of the trade. Plots to strike are mentioned in London in 1350 and 1387. In April 1381 some journeymen spurriers of London were accused of having maintained an illegal fraternity for nine years, whose purposes included preventing cheaper workers from outside London from competing for jobs in the city. The journeymen carpenters faced a similar accusation in 1339.[161] Associations of journeymen coopers are found in 1321 at Lübeck, Hamburg, Wismar, Rostock and Stralsund. In 1329 the journeymen curriers of Breslau struck for higher wages, and the employers responded with a lockout, pledging not to hire any of the journeymen for a year, showing clearly that they could tap other sources of labour. Lübeck in 1350 forbade 'unions and guilds except those permitted from time immemorial by the council'.[162]

The masters sometimes allowed journeymen into their guilds or the confraternities simply to keep them from forming separate organisations. The shearers of Paris gave their journeymen membership and a vote in 1412, but three years later the journeymen formed their own organisation anyway. Journeymen were given the right of representation in

---

158 Schulz, *Handwerksgesellen und Lohnarbeiter*, 27; Geremek, *Salariat*, 116; Leguay, *Réseau urbain Bretagne*, 271.

159 Nightingale, *Medieval Mercantile Community*, 478.

160 Clune, *Medieval Gild System*, 179; Swanson, *Medieval Artisans*, 115; Vicens Vives, *Economic History of Spain*, 192.

161 Clune, *Medieval Gild System*, 175; Hilton, *English and French Towns*, 146–7.

162 Sprandel, *Quellen zur Hanse-Geschichte*, 40.

the Paris guilds of bucklers, fullers, tawyers, curriers and pin makers in the fourteenth century.[163] In 1343 the council of Speyer, complaining of violence by immigrant workers who were not affiliated to guilds, decreed that criminal deeds by mint associates, members of politically recognised guilds, city employees and Jews who were citizens would be punished by a fine, but all others would receive corporal punishment. Exception was made for millers and their journeymen who lived in the city, shoe repairers, barbers, drapers and weaver journeymen if these groups restricted their associations to persons who actually practised their craft. The authorities were thus trying to keep the journeymen in the guilds.[164] Agitation continued. In 1383 the master smiths of nine cities of the Middle Rhine united against the independent organisation of journeymen. They rejected the demand that the journeymen should have their own court and be able to judge masters. At Zürich in 1412 the journeyman smiths elected their own 'king'. In the 1420s the city was the site of several conclaves of an interurban organisation of journeymen shoemakers.[165]

Some journeyman associations were charitable confraternities, but others were genuine employee federations. There was little 'class' solidarity among journeymen until the fifteenth century; their loyalty was to their trades, rather than across professions with others in comparable situations of employment. Masters and journeymen were usually on the same side on issues of taxation and political representation but split on economic concerns within the guild.[166] The journeymen weavers left Speyer as a group in 1351 until their demands for higher wages were met. A wage conflict erupted in 1365 at Freiburg-im-Breisgau between the master drapers and a brotherhood of journeymen weavers whose members claimed that their organisation was purely charitable. The city council permitted the fraternity to meet only in the presence of guild officials, but they conceded the journeymen's right to refuse to work for wages that the masters offered if they so chose. Trouble between journeymen and their guild masters grew after 1380, becoming very serious between 1400 and 1425.[167]

The journeyman associations were often interurban in the fifteenth century. In 1404 a fraternity of migrant journeymen furriers, some from as far away as Bohemia, was established at Strasbourg. In 1407 the shoemakers of the Upper Rhine cities formed an organisation and eventually

163 Geremek, *Salariat*, 113.
164 Schulz, *Handwerksgesellen und Lohnarbeiter*, 67.
165 Schulz, *Handwerksgesellen und Lohnarbeiter*, 71–6.
166 Hilton, *English and French Towns*, 145, 149.
167 Schulz, *Handwerksgesellen und Lohnarbeiter*, 63–9.

made contact with colleagues in the cities of the Middle Rhine and Lake Constance. Their home towns presented a united front against them, but there were new conflicts in 1410–11 and 1420 and 1425. In a case of 1411 that shows the journeymen's dislike of the masters but also a sense that quality of workmanship should be maintained, the journeymen bakers of the Rhenish communities between Basel and Strasbourg met in Breisach and agreed not to work for any baker's widow who married a man who had not been trained in the craft or for millers who baked. The master and journeymen ropemakers of the Upper Rhine made a common rule in 1389. When they convened in 1421 at Basel, the journeymen were so violent that the council arrested them and informed their colleagues in neighbouring centres of this fact. In 1426 they met at Schaffhausen to renew their ordinance of 1389. References multiply to noctural disturbances, games, tourneys and drinking associations.[168]

The Rhenish cities tried to develop a common policy toward the journeymen. Several agreed in advance to a general ordinance issued at a meeting at Strasbourg in 1436, then confirmed in 1465. The ordinance prohibited associations of masters or journeymen without the consent of the local city council. Journeymen had to swear obedience to the council, take a separate oath to this Rhenish Journeyman Ordinance and swear before the local guild master to obey the statutes of the local guild within eight days of finding work for a master in the town. The journeymen were subordinated to the regular guild courts. They were to have no drinking halls, 'common association' or corporately rented houses. They could have religious brotherhoods, but only after informing the guild, and these associations would meet only in the presence of one or two masters. They could also care for sick journeymen, but burial processions, which sometimes became disorderly, were to be permitted only on church festival days. No more than three journeymen could simultaneously wear marked clothing. Shoes are not mentioned, although in 1431 Freiburg had had a problem with journeymen shoemakers and tailors wearing shoes coloured white and red, which the council had forbidden. No journeyman who refused to submit to this ordinance or was expelled for violating it would be received or given work in any city that accepted it.[169]

By the mid-fifteenth century the city governments of the Upper Rhine, which initially had frowned on the interurban leagues of both masters and journeymen, were insisting that innovations had to be

---

168 Schulz, *Handwerksgesellen und Lohnarbeiter*, 71, 78–81; Mollat and Wolff, *Popular Revolutions*, 248–9; Czacharowski, 'Soziale Schichten', 128–9; Möncke, *Quellen*, 166–7, 324–8.
169 Schulz, *Handwerksgesellen und Lohnarbeiter*, 81–7, 89–97.

cleared with the regional associations before being applied locally. The masters normally collected the wages paid for a job, then paid the journeymen after deducting a proportion for themselves. Responding to a complaint from the journeymen linen weavers in 1453 that the masters were now taking a higher proportion for themselves, the city council of Colmar ordered the old rates to be restored until 'the master artisan weavers in all these lands between Strasbourg and Basel agree on another wage'.[170]

The problem of poverty

Few journeymen thus enjoyed secure employment. Although some received decent wages, the intermittent nature of their working schedules, and the fact that the guild structure in effect put a ceiling over their heads, meant that most of them could not live well. Together with the totally indigent, many females who had no professional training, some servants, orphans whose relatives would not or could not care for them, the physically disabled, and recent migrants with few employable skills, they constituted an impoverished underclass of late medieval urban society that tax records suggest included as many as half the inhabitants of most large cities by the fifteenth century.

Economic poverty can rarely be measured statistically before the fourteenth century. The sources often use 'poor' to refer to the person's general condition; condemned criminals might be called 'poor', and early medieval sources defined 'poor' in biblical terms as those with physical handicaps and/or lacking protectors, such as the sick and unattached women and orphans.[171]

Even in the thirteenth century there is considerable evidence of economic or structural poverty, in the sense of persons who can neither grow their own food nor buy it on the market. The 'poor' of Siena were defined in 1289 as having a direct tax assessment below 2 lire. On this basis one-fifth of the taxpayers were paupers, mainly water carriers, washerwomen and street cleaners. In the famine year of 1302 15,000 persons, about one-third of the population, were assessed as paupers.[172] In Perugia 30 per cent of the households in 1285 had no taxable property. One-third of the population of Carcassonne was 'tax-poor' in 1304. In Paris the 'lesser persons' [*menus*] constituted 42 per cent of the taxpayers in 1297, 47 per cent in 1298. In Reims the *menus* made up

---

170 Schulz, *Handwerksgesellen und Lohnarbeiter*, 394–6.
171 Maschke, *Städte und Menschen*, 34.
172 Waley, *Siena*, 25–6.

40–60 per cent of the population around 1300. Indigents and beggars receiving public assistance accounted for about 10 per cent of the population of Orvieto and its *contado* in 1292. Those without land but living on what they earned constituted 20 per cent and were tax-exempt. Another 5–10 per cent had small plots and paid taxes but were clearly poor. This suggests a rate of structural poverty of 35–40 per cent.[173]

Evidence grows after 1300. Tax records suggest that in most places between one-third and one-half of the citizenry were too poor to pay direct taxes. Florence had 25 per cent poor in 1330, a year of high prices following a famine in 1328–9. During the famine of 1347 more than half the population had to be helped, and four thousand still starved. The poverty rate was 33 per cent at Arles in 1462, over half at Toulouse, 15–20 per cent at Nantes and 60 per cent at Périgueux.[174] Successive tax records at Rouen show nearly 50 per cent poverty and severe depopulation as the wars with the English reached their climax around 1420. Beggars sought alms in the cathedral in such numbers that in some years the chapter clergy chased them out with dogs.[175]

The situation worsened over time. Dijon gave tax exemption to 83 per cent of its households in 1397. Thereafter the city distinguished 'miserable' persons (the working poor) from beggars. By 1431 58 per cent were miserable, 27 per cent mendicant, while in 1433 the percentages were 54 and 34.[176] Tax records of Lübeck about 1460 suggest a rise of some 10 per cent since 1380 in the combined percentages of indigent and those who were not professionally independent or did not enjoy citizenship, such as journeymen and servants.[177]

But tax poverty and indigence are not the same. Some tax records indicate the minimum income needed for a given level of taxation; others simply designate potential payers as 'poor' without saying what it means. Some are internally inconsistent. Bequests of pennies to the poor cannot indicate a level of poverty; read literally, some would make an entire city population poor. Most taxation was based on the hearth and records show that some heads of households who were tax-exempt on grounds of poverty still owned or rented land or houses. This places into a less dire perspective the 55.2 per cent of the households of Toulouse that 'had nothing' in 1398.[178]

---

173 Rossiaud, 'Crises', 410; Mollat, *Poor*, 174–6; Britnell, 'England and northern Italy', 181–2.
174 Mollat and Wolff, *Popular Revolutions*, 107; Mollat, *Poor*, 236.
175 Mollat, *Histoire de Rouen*, 137.
176 Mollat, *Poor*, 234.
177 Maschke, *Städte und Menschen*, 17–18.
178 Rossiaud, 'Crises', 489; Leguay, *Réseau urbain Bretagne*, 288. See criticism of sources by Nicholas, *Medieval Flanders*, 367–70, and by Maschke, *Städte und Menschen*, 424–9.

The centrally located parish of St Nicholas of Ghent contained the grain market and the homes of the richest merchants but also numerous poor. The number of persons receiving assistance from its Holy Ghost Table was high in the early fourteenth century, dropped sharply in the 1350s, remained stable during most of the 1360s, then declined by one-third during the 1370s, probably reflecting severe mortality in the plague of 1368–9. Combined with fragmentary evidence from other parishes, the St Nicholas figures suggest that no more than 1,000 persons out of a population of 35,000 (roughly 3 per cent) received charity in the late fourteenth century. Yet tax records of the fifteenth century suggest a poverty rate of 40 per cent. While the earlier figures must be supplemented by charity provided by the guildhalls and by family members, the example shows that numerous persons who paid no property tax could feed themselves.[179]

The lower economic levels were hit more severely in proportion to their income by indirect taxes, which applied to food and drink, than by direct. The fact that grain prices fluctuated so severely by the season, usually being at their highest in the cold months when wages were low and some forms of employment were unavailable, meant that many people were temporarily unable to buy food.[180] Journeymen were especially vulnerable, for their wages were lower than those of masters, and they were hired only when the master had more work than he could complete himself. Wage figures for construction workers at Bruges suggest that journeymen would have had to work almost continuously – and few did – to buy enough grain to support a family of four.[181] Seventy-four per cent of new immigrants to Göttingen between 1330 and 1360 had no skills. Most cities show a long-term rise in nominal wages in the late Middle Ages. Master craftsmen were much better off in the fifteenth century than before 1348. Skilled workers in strategic occupations had no trouble staying above the poverty line. Even an unskilled construction worker at Florence could feed two persons at the prevailing wage if he worked 260 days per year, but few did. Piece-work wages at York were high enough in textiles for a master weaver who was continuously employed to live reasonably well. But the wage scale benefited the masters who could count on more-or-less continuous employment, not the journeymen or unskilled labourers.[182] Structural considerations thus explain why vagabondage rose when wages were high in the late medieval cities;

---

179 Nicholas, *Metamorphosis*, 52–8.
180 Cipolla, *Before the Industrial Revolution*, 29.
181 Sosson, *Travaux publics*, 230–1.
182 Mollat, *Poor*, 244; Goldthwaite, *Building of Renaissance Florence*, 342–50; Swanson, *Medieval Artisans*, 34.

for high wages pitted the working employed, particularly the masters, against the non-working employable.[183]

The poor tended to congregate in alleys, dead-end streets and court-yards, and in the northern cities in the suburbs and the urban areas nearest the walls. In 1460 24.6 per cent of the taxable households in Lübeck lived in cellars, outbuildings and passageways. There is no way to guess the number of beggars who simply slept in the streets. In the inner cities of Dresden and Görlitz nearly half the taxpayers were rent-ing lodgings, but the percentage of renters in the industrial suburbs was under 20 per cent. The central parishes of most cities had numerous cellar apartments. The poor also used the immunities of churches and cemeteries, which were not under the direct control of the city gov-ernment. As the proportion of poor inhabitants grew in the late Middle Ages, entire sectors of many cities became dilapidated havens for the poor, usually associated with bad hygiene and high crime rates. Even prosper-ous neighbourhoods contained pockets of poverty.[184]

Poor relief

Problems of poverty were severe in cities everywhere. The emirs handled poor relief on an ad hoc basis in the Muslim cities. They had no permanent offices for charity or poor relief.[185] In this respect the city governments of Europe were much more advanced. Most of the gov-ernments maintained offices for poor relief and assisted private charitable foundations. Some cities had had hospitals even in the twelfth century. Lucca had a dozen before 1200. Many early hospitals were founded by laypeople, although anything involving a cemetery or religious services required church approval. Most were on the peripheries of the twelfth-century cities, becoming more central as population grew in the suburbs. Five of the six hospitals of Bristol were outside the gates. The hospital of St John the Evangelist in Cambridge was unusual in being near the town centre.[186]

'Hospitals' were for those needing help; most of the early ones pro-vided cheap lodgings for the numerous transients who were flocking to the cities as well as health care. The transient foundations were often small and usually in the suburbs, to accommodate people who arrived after the gates were closed. The earliest hospitals in many cities were

183 This important point is emphasised by Geremek, *Margins of Society*, 35–6.
184 Brandt, 'Gesellschaftliche Struktur Lübeck', 237; Maschke, *Städte und Menschen*, 19–24; Geremek, *Margins of Society*, 84–6.
185 Lapidus, *Muslim Cities*, 55.
186 Rubin, *Charity and Community*, 100–11.

leper foundations, such as Saint-Lazare at Paris, established by 1147 in the swamps outside the city. They were especially numerous in the southern Low Countries: Saint-Omer, Bourbourg, Ghent, Tournai, Ypres and Arras had leper hospitals in the twelfth century. The first hospital at Cambridge was the leper facility in Stourbridge, two miles east of the modern town centre. As donations declined, Stourbridge stopped receiving lepers and became a 'free chapel'. Since livings in the hospitals were expensive, poor lepers lived as 'field sick' in huts outside the walls.[187]

General hospitals to care for the sick were still unusual before 1200, although most large cities had at least one. That of Saint-Omer, the Maladrerie, was founded about 1100.[188] Hospices that provided more general care were added in the thirteenth century. Most of the larger medieval hospitals had been founded by 1300; smaller foundations specialising in particular types of patient followed later. Bristol had six hospitals by 1230, two of them for lepers, all on the outskirts of town and founded by members of the Berkeley family. An almshouse was founded in 1292 by the merchant Simon Burton, who was five times mayor. Ypres had a single leper sanitorium before 1200, but four other hospitals were added during the thirteenth century. Bruges had several, the largest of which, St John, had about seventy-five beds. The Potterie hospital cared for the incurably ill, and there were separate hostels for the blind and the insane.[189] The hospitals increasingly became points of contention over patronage between city governments and churches. Except for the tiniest hospices, even those that were originally church foundations were coming under lay control in the thirteenth century.[190]

Charity was largely private, although city governments assisted some foundations that they did not administer directly, such as guild charities and almshouses founded by wealthy citizens. The wealthy were expected to found or donate to hospitals or almshouses, although most known cases of this are from persons who had no living heirs. The hospitals were supported by their founders' endowments, supplemented by donations from the community and the city treasury. Many hospitals sold prebends, lifetime lodgings given in a section of the hospital, in return either for a lump sum or for a guarantee that the prebendary's estate

187 Boussard, *Paris*, 265; Marechal, 'Ziekenzorg', 269–71; Rubin, *Cambridge*, 111.
188 Wolff, *Histoire de Toulouse*, 68–70; Marechal, *Brugse Hospitaalwezen*, 30–1; Marechal, 'Ziekenzorg', 272; Derville, *Histoire de Saint-Omer*, 56; Schmugge, 'Pilgerverkehrs', 42.
189 Waley, *Siena*, 136; Nicholas, *Medieval Flanders*, 138–9, 272–3, summarising a vast literature; Lobel, *Atlas* 2: 8–9; Lestocquoy, *Dynasties bourgeoises d'Arras*, 74–5.
190 Uitz, 'Kommunale Autonomie in Magdeburg', 306–7; Falck, *Mainz in seiner Blütezeit*, 51–4.

would go to the foundation. From 1445 the names of poor and honest citizens who wanted prebends in the hospitals in Lille were to be kept in a register, and the city government would chose the beneficiary when a vacancy occurred. Some wealthy prebendaries were not required to work and would even take their meals separately with the priests, although the poorer ones were expected to labour.[191]

Most guilds had almshouses to support poor masters, orphans and, in most cases, journeymen. They depended on endowments of rents and real property with minimal support from the guild treasuries, although some trades earmarked specific incomes for them, such as apprenticeship fees and surcharges. The butchers of Constance left substantial properties to their guild, with the result that their widows and orphans were well cared for, but this is much less true of the poorer trades.[192] Virtually all guild statutes of Venice provided relief for those who were physically unable to work.[193] The Weavers' Hall at Ghent originated around 1302, but it housed only sixteen prebendaries in 1375 and thus cannot have had much impact on poverty among the weavers. The Fullers' Hall was maintained even after the fullers were excluded from political participation, but with an endowment much smaller than that of the Weavers' Hall. The shippers, brewers, bakers and tailors of Ghent all had almshouses by 1400.[194]

Even the merchant guilds dispensed charity. Coventry's provided relief and short-term loans to impoverished brothers and sisters of the guild. Incapacitated members who were unable to work were maintained at the guild's expense. The English charitable fraternities, however, were much smaller than their continental counterparts. The English hospitals decayed in part because their endowments were inadequate, in part because most of them had been founded for pilgrims and lepers and thus lost business. The almshouses that were founded after 1349 catered to the poor, sometimes giving them separate rooms and generally a good diet. Many were connected to occupational guilds; but not all guilds dispensed charity, and they usually limited their concern to poor members of their own trade.[195]

In addition to the guild houses and the charity distributed by the churches and mendicant orders, smaller privately founded hospices proliferated after 1300. Most cared for special categories of the sick or

---

191 Kowaleski, 'Commercial dominance', 199; Geremek, *Margins of Society*, 190; Trenard, *Histoire de Lille*, 232; Kossmann-Putto, 'Armen- en ziekenzorg', 260–1.
192 Bechtold, *Zunftbürgerschaft und Patriziat*, 74.
193 Mackenney, *Tradesmen and Traders*, 64.
194 Nicholas, *Metamorphosis*, 44–6.
195 Clune, *Medieval Gild System*, 37–9; Dyer, *Standards of Living*, 244.

unfortunate, most often the blind, insane and orphans. In 1292 Renaud Barbou established the hospital of the blind, the Twenty-Six, at one of the gates of Chartres. Paris had several dozen hospices by 1400. In 1334 Jehan Roussel built twenty-four lodgings for 'respectable people' under one roof near the Porte Barbette. In 1415 his daughter gave the property to the Grand Prior on condition that he rent it to forty-eight persons (the rooms having been subdivided) for a penny per week. In Bordeaux the hospital of Saint-André was established in 1390 by the will of a canon who left two houses with twenty-six beds for the sick, pilgrims and other poor travellers provided that they did not stay for more than two days. In Germany most of the small foundations were earmarked for 'house poor', a term designating the working poor who had fallen into poverty through no personal fault and lacked money for decent housing but were too proud to beg. Tiny foundations that provided free meals to a handful of indigents at a time were often attached to a chapel or a city gate. In 1377 Brother Jan van Zottegem of Ghent willed a hospice with four apartments on the city wall to his next of kin, who were to rent out two of the apartments and keep the other two for 'house poor'. This was evidently an expansion of a property already used for the poor, for Brother Jan 'had succeeded in getting the good people of Ghent and elsewhere to situate the poor people in the hospice'.[196]

Parish organisations also extended poor relief. The major cities of the southern Low Countries had 'Holy Ghost' houses or 'Poor Tables' even before 1200, and the number multiplied after 1250. Ghent had a Holy Ghost table in each parish by 1260. They were administered by laymen who distributed food and occasionally clothing to the needy from endowments that more often consisted of money rents and cash income than land. Thus when food prices were high, the tables might give money rather than food to the poor. Tokens issued by the Holy Ghost masters sometimes gave admission to the hostels, as at Leiden and Middelburg.[197] English parishes had no equivalent of the Poor Tables, but most urban parishes in Spain and northern France kept lists of eligible recipients and gave them tokens that could be presented to get assistance in kind. This had the effect of distinguishing poor workers who were occasionally employed, many of them masters who did not own their shops, from professional beggars.[198]

196 Rubin, *Charity and Community*, 124; Chédeville, *Histoire de Chartres*, 169; Geremek, *Margins of Society*, 170–1, 83–4; Renouard, *Bordeaux sous les rois d'Angleterre*, 316; Maschke, 'Unterschichten', 437–8; Nicholas, *Metamorphosis*, 41–3.
197 Marechal, 'Armen- en ziekenzorg', 274–5; Kossman-Putto, 'Armen- en ziekenzorg', 258.
198 Dyer, *Standards of Living*, 246–7; Mollat, *Poor*, 140–4, 162.

Some donors willed small amounts of money or food to the poor of their parishes on the anniversaries of their deaths or a saint's day. These bequests were administered by the parish organisations or guildhalls. The larger ones provided bread or other food for several hundred persons on specific days. At Bruges when a great burgess died, his family distributed tokens of iron or pewter struck with their coats of arms; presentation of these tokens gave alms to the poor, but usually in a charitable institution; they were not negotiable or acceptable in markets. A Parisian will of 1407 gave assistance to 960 persons, one of 1412 to 2,400, and in 1411 a royal official at the parlement left charity to 3,800.[199] So numerous were the potential recipients that on 3 July 1322 fifty-two persons died in a riot to get food that had been provided in the testament of a London fishmonger.[200]

The combined charities of late medieval Lübeck could handle about 600 persons at a time. Thirty hospitals in Florence in 1339 could house 1,000. Borgo Santo Spirito at Rome had a capacity of 300, the hospices of Nuremberg and Regensburg 200–250. The Hôtel-Dieu, the chief hospital of Paris, had four rooms and 279 beds and a lying-in room of twenty-four beds. Three people often occupied each bed. The hospital usually accommodated 400–500 persons per day, although during plague years the number might reach 5,000. The Hôtel-Dieu accepted poor cripples, foundlings and pregnant women, but not pilgrims and other transients, for whom other shelters existed.[201]

In the late Middle Ages city fathers became concerned with revolutionary tendencies among the able-bodied poor, who were physically able to work but could not find employment. Mobs fuelled riots and attempted revolutions, although they were rarely if ever instigated by the indigent. The Ciompi rebellion of Florence was influenced by Taddeo Dini, who preached temporal as well as spiritual advancement for the poor. The tendency of the poor to fall into heresy troubled even those favourably disposed to them.[202] The most pitifully unfortunate gathered around churches begging alms from the pious. The council of Cologne threatened with expulsion from the city 'all who sit before the churches with sickness or go on the street with open wounds and fractures. [They] must cover their wounds and fractures and not let them be seen, so that good people will suffer no stink nor unpleasantness'. A Morningspeech declared that

199 Nicholas, *Metamorphosis*, 56; Geremek, *Margins of Society*, 185–6.
200 Hanawalt, *Growing Up in Medieval London*, 18.
201 Brandt, 'Gesellschaftliche Struktur Lübeck', 237; Mollat, *Poor*, 150–5; Geremek, *Margins of Society*, 171–5.
202 Mollat, *Poor*, 226–7, 231.

our lords have also understood that many persons, both women and men, who circulate begging in the city are strong and healthy enough to work for their bread. . . . Thus our lords decree that these healthy people must work and serve for their bread, and whoever refuses to do so will be expelled from the city. Any who refuse to leave and remain in the city anyway will be seized by the police and put in the city jail for a year on bread and water and then will be expelled physically from town.[203]

Some city governments put vagrants to work. In 1351 a royal ordinance, complaining that many beggars were frequenting taverns and brothels and refusing work when it was offered, ordered them to take a job or leave Paris. The first offence meant four days in prison, the third banishment and branding. In 1367 and 1371 the provost of Paris ordered all who were able to work but had no job to dredge the moats and repair the fortifications at whatever wage the city government thought reasonable. The seneschal of Toulouse did the same in 1395. By a royal ordinance of 1382 Paris and other 'good towns' were to send their unemployed into the rural areas, where labour was scarce. Vagabonds were frequently commandeered for labour in the fifteenth century, and in France they were already being sent to the galleys.[204]

Thus many city governments cut back severely on poor relief in the fifteenth century, particularly for transients. The government of Ghent had spent between 2 and 4 per cent of its income on alms in most years in the fourteenth century. The city donated peat bricks for fuel to thirty-two foundations, but most of them were forced entirely onto their own resources after 1390. The Holy Ghost tables stockpiled food and at least in the mid-fifteenth century were generally able to maintain their levels of assistance, but this diminished markedly after 1450 and was accompanied by a preference for distributing coins rather than food and clothing to the poor. Begging was limited to citizens. In 1491 the aldermen of Ghent, fearful of revolutionary sentiments among the beggars, cautioned the masters of the Holy Ghost tables not to give assistance to able-bodied persons, but only to 'incapacitated, poor, crippled people or blind, who have such defect in their members or senses that they cannot earn their living'.[205]

The occupational guilds of the late medieval cities were political and economic entities that controlled most of the industrial and service

203 Both sources in Keutgen, *Urkunden*, 302.
204 Geremek, *Margins of Society*, 31–4; Mollat, *Poor*, 291.
205 Rossiaud, 'Crises', 482; Nicholas, *Metamorphosis*, 58–65; Nicholas, *Medieval Flanders*, 370.

sectors of the urban economy. They included a wide range of wealth and economic orientation, but an elite of merchants or shippers with access to distant markets dominated virtually all of them. The increasing rigidity with which the guilds gave priority in admissions to children of incumbent masters placed limits on the economic potential of most apprentices and journeymen. These were beginning to constitute an underclass of the craft world in the late Middle Ages, but they had a more structured access to the workplace than did the truly marginal groups. As the incidence of structural poverty increased, public and private charity was expanded; but particularly after the mid-fifteenth century the cities adopted a more organised approach to poor relief than the essentially voluntary system that had preceded it.

CHAPTER EIGHT

The Legal Marginals of Urban Society: Women, Children and Religious Minorities in the Later Medieval Cities

The social groups that we are discussing in this chapter consist of persons who were under the legal protection of another person or corporate body. Unless formally emancipated, a woman was the ward of her husband or a male relative. Children were the wards of their parents, of other family members if the parents or, in some legal regimes, either parent had died. In extreme cases they might come under the jurisdiction of the city government. The Jews and Muslims were 'protected' in a dubious euphemism by the Christian governments. In all cases, however, much depended in practice on individual circumstances and cases and particularly on the social rank of the person concerned. Women and children of the lower and middle social orders had fewer legal constraints on their activity than did their aristocratic counterparts, but in many cases this amounted to a freedom to be indigent. Poor women and children are an important part of the growing problem of poverty that we have discussed in Chapter 7. After the Jews were expelled by the English and French monarchies in 1290 and 1306 respectively, most went to Germany, where their situation became increasingly difficult after 1300. Most then went to eastern Europe, where they enjoyed some peace if not prosperity. Even until the end of our period many Jews were wealthy and occupied high positions of state in Castile.

URBAN WOMEN IN THE LATER MIDDLE AGES

Most cities contained many single-person households, the natural results of high mortality rates and heavy immigration. Most were headed by males, but in the late Middle Ages many more households than previously were headed by single women, particularly widows. The problem may have been most serious in Italy, for the age gap between spouses was greater there than in the north, and widowhood was correspondingly prolonged. Widows' property rights were often less secure than in the northern cities. In Perugia the proportion of female heads of households was stable at around 5 per cent between 1260 and 1285 but had grown to 15 per cent by 1320. Widows were not remarrying as frequently or were living with their children. Women were 13 per cent of the heads of households in Arles in 1319. The number of households in Goslar headed by women, most of them widows, was relatively constant from about 1450 at between 12 and 14 per cent of the total.[1] The problem was compounded by the fact that most cities had more women than men, often an excess of 10 per cent. Many women thus had to remain single and could not obtain the advantages of the male-dominated occupational guilds through their husbands.[2] They tended to live in small apartments either in the workers' quarters near the walls or in the poorer parts of the city centre, usually in streets with large numbers of other women.[3] An alley behind the Friday Market in Ghent had a large concentration of single female householders who rented garrets from the church of St Nicholas.[4]

Thus, outside the guilds that dominated both the political life and, in the north, the employment market of most cities, women were vulnerable. They were the overwhelming majority of recipients of charity from the Holy Ghost table of St Nicholas of Ghent. In Frankfurt am Main in 1410 7.8 per cent of male taxpayers were 'poor', 33.6 per cent of the women. Bologna in 1395 had relatively few women workers but many beggars. Only half the poor households in the Rota district of Florence in 1378 were headed by males, and this omits those who were too poor to pay the tax.[5] Women had less identity apart from their husbands' families in Italy than in the north. The Florentine *catasto* shows only seventy unmarried women among 1,536 heads of households in 1427. Women constituted 51 per cent of the lower economic strata in Trier in 1364, 65–70 per cent in Frankfurt and Basel in the fifteenth century.[6]

---

1 Blanshei, *Perugia*, 29–30; Stouff, *Arles*, 94; Schuler, 'Goslar', 450.
2 Kowaleski, 'Urban families', 55.
3 Goldberg, 'Women in town life', 108.
4 Nicholas, *Metamorphosis*, 79.
5 Maschke, 'Unterschichten', 441; Herlihy, *Opera Muliebria*, 156–7; Brucker, 'Florentine *popolo minuto*', 157; Klapisch-Zuber, *Women*, 118.
6 Uitz, *Women*, 64.

Women in law

Women normally enjoyed full rights of citizenship along with their husbands in the cities of the continent, although the position of unattached women was less clear. Some Spanish and German cities explicitly included women as citizens. In most years between 5 and 10 per cent of the new citizens enrolling in the German cities were women. Given the problems with unattached women lacking professional training, some laws required female immigrants either to apply for citizenship and pay the fee or marry if they wished to enjoy the privileges of the city.[7] By contrast, women were rarely admitted to the franchise in an English city: only four were admitted at Norwich before 1500. York, where they accounted for about 1 per cent of new admissions, was unusually open, and even there most of the women were widows. The freedom became the equivalent of emancipation under the Roman law of the continent; for married women in York could not practise a trade apart from their husbands unless they had entered the freedom. The fact that the English cities were so closely tied to the crown strengthened the husband's guardian role under the common law, and individual cities had to give the independent women separate standing.[8]

Unless formally emancipated, women were legal wards of a male, either the husband, father or, occasionally, brother. Most cities limited the amount of money that a woman could spend without the seller risking having her husband nullify the sale on grounds that he had not consented to it. At Ghent the amount was so small that wives could barely have paid the foodmongers, but in fact the law was rarely enforced.[9] Woman who had been emancipated by their guardians became 'independent merchant women', legally able to pursue careers and enrol in some guilds. Emancipation by formal enactment was unusual for adult women, however, even in cases of women who acted on their own in business, for the consent of the responsible male seems to have been assumed in most cases.[10]

The husband as his wife's legal guardian could dispose of the income from her dowry and inherited property, but he could not alienate the title to it. Dowries in Italy gave substantial assets to the husband from the wife's family, although at his death she could recover anything that was left by the numerous retrieval mechanisms possible under Roman

7 Uitz, *Women*, 20, 114–16.
8 Goldberg, 'Women in town life', 122 n. 4; Kowaleski, 'Women's work in Exeter', 146 and 159 n. 5.
9 Schultheiss, *Satzungen*, 277; Nicholas, *Domestic Life*, 78.
10 Kuehn, *Emancipation*; Nicholas, *Domestic Life*, 24–5, 136–40; Uitz, *Women*, 10.

law. Marriage endowments in the north also gave security to the wife during the marriage, permitting the husband to use the income from her property but forbidding him to alienate the principal. Unless accompanied by a prenuptial agreement, remarriage often caused a widow to lose some property and/or her dower rights on her previous husband's estate. In some reciprocal regimes, such as in Flanders and parts of Alsace, such limitations also applied to widowers.[11]

In northern Europe, although generally not in Italy, most women enjoyed rights of common property with their husbands, and widows could take their share of it into second marriages. Most widows also had dower rights (life use, after which it reverted to the blood heirs) of one-quarter to one-third of their husbands' property. From 1302 the English courts required spouses to consent separately to the alienation of common property to determine whether the woman was acting freely or under coercion from her husband, thus giving security against later claims of dower by a widow. By the late fourteenth century spouses normally had joint tenancy in addition to common property, so that the survivor kept full possession; but property could also be entailed, especially with remarriages.[12]

Inheritance regimes were complex, and except in Italy most had considerable reciprocity. There was a broad similarity among the south German cities in granting the survivor of a childless marriage all that he/she had brought into it and two-thirds of the spouse's property. If there were children, they and the surviving parent each received half. Sons and daughters inherited equally. The survivor of a childless marriage kept the entire estate for life, but it reverted ultimately to the blood relatives. If there were children, the survivor kept the estate and used it to raise the children on the advice of their 'friends'. A widow had to have the friends' consent for alienations, but a widower did not. If the surviving parent remarried, he/she kept the house and its land, but the rest went to the children.[13] The stipulation about the house was important for the trade that it conveyed. Brewing, for example, was permitted in most German cities only in houses that had brewing privileges. Some wills left the brewing implements to the widow, excluding the children, since she would need the income to raise them.[14]

11 Keene, *Medieval Winchester*, 14–15; Uitz, *Women in the Medieval Town*, 110–14.
12 Martin, *Ipswich Recognizance Rolls*, 10, 27–8. This secured the buyer's title, but how much protection it gave against forced alienation is problematical; the wife could hardly come into court with her husband to sell property, then when alone with the judges say that she had been coerced, and afterwards go home with the husband. Keene, *Medieval Winchester*, 190.
13 Köbler, 'Familienrecht', 141, 147–50.
14 Uitz, *Women*, 58.

Women always benefited by partible inheritance, which was the norm except in Italy and parts of the French Midi. A Visigothic custom that passed into Spanish urban law and evidently from there to the north gave priority to a woman who was a closer relation to the deceased than to males who were more distantly related. Furthermore, the Spanish cities did not recognise dowries as a way of excluding women from the eventual inheritance.[15] Inheritances were partible in Germanic Flanders, with no age or gender preferences. The surviving spouse retained his/her own property, half the common property, and had dower rights on the other half, which passed in principle to the children. The children's share was placed under the separate administration of a legal guardian, who usually came from the family of the deceased parent. In Flanders and northern Germany the surviving spouse, particularly if it was the mother, usually raised the minor children while the guardian managed their property.[16]

Some urban inheritance regimes, notably in the Amienois, Boulonnais, Artois and Walloon Flanders, gave the oldest son most of the property at the expense of daughters and younger sons, but even there women were never excluded completely from inheritances. Partible inheritance, division with the surviving spouse and the universality of dower produced considerable mobility of fortunes, since it was almost impossible to keep property within families. Fortune hunters abounded: Gilles Canivet of Douai married a widow who was much older than he and promptly sold much of her property. He eventually reformed and entered public life, then remarried after his first wife's death and left much of her property to his second.[17]

Women in marriage

Although the percentage of single persons was higher in the late medieval cities than now, most persons married. Young people of the urban upper class, whose families might lose property through a bad marriage, were generally expected to obtain their parents' consent, although the parents' only legal recourse – since only the consent of the couple was required for a legal marriage if both had reached their majority – was to deny them property. Women's freedom to choose their spouses was much greater on the middle and lower social levels than among the upper orders.

Some urban customs permitted the husband absolute disposal over his wife's person, including physical chastisement. Violence within the

15 Dillard, *Daughters*, 26–7.
16 Nicholas, *Domestic Life*, 109–11; Nicholas, 'Poverty and primacy', 39.
17 Jacob, *Epoux*, 32, 51, 87–95, esp. 94–5.

family is rarely found in court actions, probably because it generally had to be life-threatening before it was illegal. There is considerable evidence of domestic violence in Venice, rather less in Ghent. Most courts intervened when permanent injury was threatened, but how much casual violence may have preceded such actions can only be surmised. Most wives were reluctant to press charges, since they had no recourse other than to continue to live with the abusive husbands.[18]

Marriages were much more stable in law than now, although the high death rates meant that many and perhaps most persons who survived into their forties were married more than once. Church law forbade divorce, and annulments and separations were uncommon. They had to be handled at church courts, but the civil magistrates of the city generally divided the property between the spouses. Many of the persons who were streaming into the cities to find jobs in the late Middle Ages were leaving spouse and children at home, and memories became dim. Some separations were thus done informally and by mutual consent. The Ghent shipper Jan Bollin was married in 1359 but by 1372 had two children by his mistress, who was living in an apartment in his family complex. When Bollin died in 1382, persons purporting to be his wife's heirs disputed his bequests to his bastards, only to find that the wife was alive, residing so inconspicuously at Bruges that even her closest kin thought she was dead. Since her long separation from Bollin had not been formalised by a church court, she and her heirs received half the common property left in his estate. A striking feature of most marital separations is the degree of knowledge possessed by the wives about their husbands' business matters and assets; lengthy finagling and consolidation of property on both sides preceded most final decrees of separation. Several cases involve spouses who were each other's business partners.[19]

Women as merchants

Women were active as merchants, either independently or as the husband's helper in a business that was titularly his. Notarial registers show numerous independent female merchants in Italy at the beginning of the thirteenth century, slightly earlier than in the French Midi. Some Italian women were involved in partnerships and other merchant ventures. One-fifth of the Genoese *commenda* contracts in the first half of the thirteenth century involved women, who provided 14.4 per cent of the capital invested. Venice and Marseilles show similar patterns. There

---

18 Chojnacki, 'Crime, punishment', 212–13; Nicholas, *Domestic Life*, 45–50; Burghartz, *Leib, Ehre und Gut*, 140–6.
19 Nicholas, *Domestic Life*, 33–52.

is some evidence of women in partnerships in Germany in the thirteenth century but more in the fourteenth and fifteenth. Women were especially likely to be their husbands' trading partners in second marriages, by which time they were more likely to have had practical business experience and capital from previous marriages to invest. Many wives kept the accounts for the family business.[20]

Aristocratic women of Ghent were active in business on their own, in partnership with their husbands, and in partnership with men to whom they were not related. Most references to them are in the wine and cloth trades and as mercers. The wives of Cologne merchants commonly handled the home office when their husbands were away. Others were prominent in the import–export trade, but mainly in the small, specialised sectors, and few were among the biggest operators. Between 1460 and 1468 a woman handled 24 per cent of the city's sugar imports, and females controlled 10 per cent of the wine trade in 1468–9. Karyssa unter Halmslegern handled 5.8 per cent of Cologne's sheet metal trade and 1.4 per cent of the copper market between 1452 and 1459. Women controlled nearly one-third of the cloth trade between 1419 and 1428.[21] Numerous cases from Flanders and England also show women as their husbands' business partners. The wife of Jan Bryselays of Bruges managed his business while he was in England, engaging in complex negotiations when property that he had sold to English merchants was seized at Sluis.[22] At Montpellier women occasionally sold silks or luxury woollen cloth, but the total number of transactions involving them is tiny in proportion to men, and many of the women were the wives or widows of the men who had established the business. No woman was in the spice trade, which required overseas contacts. Exeter, with a much less diverse and overseas-oriented economy than Montpellier, confirms this for women's involvement in large-scale merchant activity. Of 435 working women of Exeter identified by Maryanne Kowaleski, ninety-nine were merchants rather than artisans, but most were widows and were petty retailers; few were wholesale merchants or overseas traders.[23]

Although women were not involved in foreign exchange contracts at Montpellier, some were local moneylenders. Casual moneylending was not a high-status occupation, even among males, and most women who practised it were from artisan or service backgrounds. Single women and widows were the bulk of female moneylenders, since the assets of

---

20   Uitz, *Women*, 24–31, 38–9, 41.
21   Uitz, *Women*, 39.
22   Nicholas, 'English trade', 45; for evidence from York, see Goldberg, *Women, Work and Life Cycle*, 124–5.
23   Reyerson, 'Women in business', 121–3; Kowaleski, 'Women's work in Exeter', 147.

married women were controlled by their husbands. Before the 1340s women were around one-tenth of those who paid the fee taken from moneylenders at Ghent. The figure rose to 20–24 per cent during the wars between 1343 and 1348, declining thereafter until 1361, then rising steadily until 1382. Only one was a major operator, and she took over her husband's business when their marriage was dissolved. Most were casual operators, paying the fee intermittently over a few years.[24]

Although moneychanging, as opposed to casual moneylending, was unusual for women, the exchange of Willem Ruweel of Bruges linked his family's enterprise with an exchange that his wife had inherited from her father. She worked with him and continued the business after he died.[25] The most colourful businesswoman of fourteenth-century Ghent was Celie Rebbe, who came from a family of fishmongers but had become a moneychanger even before she married the money-changer Godevert Amelaken. Taking his name, she continued in business and took over his exchange on behalf of their children when he died. The Amelaken establishment was on the Fish Market, the financial centre of Ghent. Celie was one of only two women who leased tax farms from the city in the fourteenth century and twice posted bond as an innkeeper. Her eldest son Jan became a wine merchant, while the second, Jacob, became his mother's business partner. Celie broke with Jacob in 1377 in mutual suits and recriminations; even a generous reading of the documents would concede that she was trying to defraud him. She remained active at the exchange until her death. Settling her estate caused conflict between her sons, for she had given extra property to Jan and his wife, who had been Celie's maid before her marriage.[26]

Women were also innkeepers. In 1301 forty-five hostellers of York, eleven of them women, were accused of overcharging.[27] In such cases the innkeeper's principal business was lodging and feeding transients, activities in which the wife would clearly be involved. However, on the continent more than in England innkeeping often involved doing brokerage at the halls for one's guests. Although women rarely posted bond as hostellers in their own right, many were their husbands' agents. In Ghent many widows succeeded their husbands as innkeepers. This trade was unusually endogamous, with daughters of hostellers marrying their father's colleagues or competitors and thus coming to the business with professional experience.[28]

24 Reyerson, 'Women in business', 132–3; Nicholas, *Domestic Life*, 85–9.
25 Murray, 'Family, marriage and moneychanging', 117.
26 Nicholas, *Domestic Life*, 91–4.
27 Swanson, 'Artisans in the urban economy', 50–1.
28 Nicholas, *Domestic Life*, 87–9.

Women in the crafts

Most industry was conducted in the household. The husband typically made the goods in a back room that his wife sold from a shop on the street frontage of the family home. The very nature of the household productive unit thus involved women intimately in the economic life of the cities. In the physically demanding trades most of the small number of women enrolled were wives or widows of masters, but this is not true in all cases. Even in leatherworking and metalworking many women of Cologne and York helped their husbands. Matilda Penne became one of the most prominent skinners of London after her husband died in 1379. Women were employed as casual, unskilled labourers on construction sites at Würzburg in the fifteenth century, generally drawing about two-thirds the wage of a man doing the same job. A woman from Toriano was employed with a work gang of fifty-seven other women to secure the roof tiles of the Charterhouse of Parma in 1396. They were paid less than half the rate of male labourers.[29]

Women initially had a strong role in textile manufacturing, but it diminished sharply when woollen clothmaking became a primarily urban and guild-based industry. In Paris at the turn of the fourteenth century they were relatively more prominent in linen production than in woollens, where, depending on the trade, males outnumbered them by 7:1 to 25:1. They were most numerous as dyers. Women were active as cloth producers, dyers, merchants and finishers at Douai in the thirteenth century.[30] Women remained active longer in cities with newer textile industries that were not geared for export. They were masters in the nascent textile industry of Barcelona in 1304, and throughout the first half of the fourteenth century they continued to own shops and train apprentices. Five of the nineteen guilds of Toulouse admitted women in 1325, but this is not a complete list of the trades; women were doubtless involved in other occupations.[31]

The *taille* rolls of 1292–1313 permit a statistical reconstruction of the situation of women in the workforce of Paris at that time. In 1292, 15.4 per cent of households were headed by women, comparable to the 14.3 per cent in Florence in 1427. Women were in 172 occupations that year, declining to 130 in 1313; men declined from 325 to 276. Women were drapers, moneychangers, jewellers and mercers, which were wealthy

29 Wensky, 'Stellung der Frau', 293; Goldberg, *Women, Work and Life Cycle*, 127–30; Veale, 'Matilda Penne', 47–8; Uitz, *Women in the Medieval Town*, 61–4; Braunstein, 'Salaires', 130.
30 Herlihy, *Opera Muliebria*, 148; Howell, *Women, Production, and Patriarchy*, 164–7.
31 Mulholland, *Toulouse*, xxiv.

professions involving high status. They were also tavernkeepers, shoe-makers, girdlemakers, and they were in some occupations requiring physical strength, working as masons, millers, smiths and shield-makers. They trained apprentices, including some males. They were most numerous as household servants in 1292, but this group is not included in the survey of 1313. Peddlers are second in frequency in both, and women were also in various branches of the cloth industry and in food and drink preparation and sales. Several were midwives and medical doctors. They were well represented in wax and candlemaking, and women dominated all branches of silk making and linens.

The silk weavers and purse makers were exclusively female guilds at Paris in 1292. Widows could be master butchers, pancake makers, fish-mongers, bakers, rosary makers, bag-, hat- and belt makers, cordwainers, cutlers, glass grinders, tailors and dyers. Paris, however, was unusual in having a big market for luxury goods whose manufacture required manual dexterity. Yet the registers already show signs of the declining position of women in the labour market as the crafts gained control in the early fourteenth century. Most women were assessed as having far lower wealth than males in the same profession. Women also declined in wealth from 9 per cent of the total in 1292 to 5 per cent in 1313.[32]

Most guilds permitted widows to carry on their husbands' trades, if only to close down the business, but few allowed them to become masters. No woman ever held a guild office, and their rights in the trade ceased when they remarried. Daughters only occasionally inherited even these minimal privileges. Even when they did, many guilds prevented them from passing their rights to their husbands. Women could be master barbers on the same basis as men at Ghent, but their husbands could not: in 1360 the barbers' guild emancipated the wife of Clais de Ruddere as a master barber's daughter but ruled that her husband could not be recognised as a free journeyman until he had been her apprentice for four years.[33] The English cities were even more restrictive. As a rule English women could not join guilds. Although a widow might continue her husband's trade and enjoy his freedom in the guild, this does not mean that she possessed the freedom itself. Women had few formal trade organisations. There was a 'brewsterguild' at Beverley in 1364, and the wool-packers of Southampton in 1503 were exclusively female. There were bequests to 'the wives' in Winchester and Chester.[34]

Women were, however, master barber-surgeons at York, bakers at

32 Herlihy, *Opera Muliebria*, 127–8, 143–9.
33 Trenard, *Histoire de Lille*, 301; Nicholas, *Domestic Life*, 99.
34 Maschke, 'Unterschichten', 384; Kowaleski, 'Women's work in Exeter', 148; Keene, *Medieval Winchester*, 262; Goldberg, 'Women in town life', 108.

Coventry, spinners and dyers at Bristol, wool-wrappers at Leicester, knitters, candle makers and fish cutters at Coventry and weavers at York. Chaucer's Wife of Bath knew clothmaking, and the visionary Margery Kempe at various times was a brewer and miller.[35] Many trades even forbade masters to hire female labourers unless they were wives of other masters, their own wives or their wives' maids. Yet women were also apprenticed, especially in silks and other clothing trades.[36] London tanners commonly trained their daughters, and the extent of intermarriage among leatherworking families, perhaps fostered by their occupational grouping in the suburbs, suggests a cohesive work group in which the females were a bonding element. The tanners characteristically willed the tools of their trade to their children, rather than their widows, although the widow could continue to operate the family shop. Many tanners' wives sold leather goods from booths in the Tanners' Seld in Cheapside, near the shops of saddlers and shoemakers.[37]

The wives of bakers, brewers and innkeepers were essential to the success of their husbands' businesses. They generally did not enjoy guild rights but could transmit them to their sons. Brewing was more professional on the continent than in England. Wives tapped beer in taverns, and some participated in the actual manufacture, but only the husband was a master in the guild. Brewers tended to marry one another's daughters, thus gaining wives with professional competence and sometimes an inherited share in brewing vats. When Jan van den Driessche's wife died in 1377 at Ghent, leaving her common property share of the brewing business to their adult sons and daughter, the siblings agreed that the daughter would 'continue to live with her father and practice the brewing trade with him, as they have done heretofore', but she was never listed as a master in the guild book.[38]

Males resented competition from the labour even of masters' wives and daughters. The London girdlers prohibited other women from practising the trade. In 1461 a complaint was raised at Bristol that 'weavers hired or set to work for themselves their wives and daughters, thus depriving loyal men-weavers of work, and as a consequence weavers were forbidden to employ women except those who were at the time getting their living from the exercise of the craft'.[39] The blue dyers of Ghent tried to keep women out of their guild, which was one of the most highly

---

35 Herlihy, *Opera Muliebria*, 172; Kowaleski, 'Women's work in Exeter', 146 and 159 n. 5; Swanson, *Medieval Artisans*, 107.

36 Uitz, *Women in the Medieval Town*, 52–3.

37 Keene, 'Tanners' widows', 8–12, 19.

38 Nicholas, *Domestic Life*, 97–8.

39 Clune, *Medieval Gild System*, 109–10.

skilled trades practised in the city. Widows and daughters could practise the trade and transmit it to sons and were allowed to continue running the shops even if adult male descendants were acting as their business partners. Wives were permitted to work beside their husbands at the vats, despite the claim of journeymen that 'certain women who are emancipated in the guild are diminishing and destroying the free journeymen'.[40]

Women were most conspicuous in low-status positions in the victualling trades, especially as vendors of ale, bread, fish, poultry and dairy goods, all of which could be made in their back yards. The impoverished female huckster was conspicuous everywhere. The Nottingham poultry market was called the Womanmarket. A list of fifty-two petty food retailers at Strasbourg in the fifteenth century includes twenty-seven women. Women completely monopolised the trade in cheese, eggs and butter at Exeter and dominated sales of chickens and geese, while men controlled the expensive goods. Many women operated sale booths and tables on the markets and halls except in the Meat Hall; butchering was a male preserve after 1300. Women operated sale booths in the Cloth Hall in most cities, and at Ghent they could pass on to their daughters the right to lease them. Apart from the 'female occupations' women were active only as cloth sellers at Winchester: eleven of the 159 persons listed in 1394–5 as selling cloth were women. Some widows continued active in the cloth business even when a son or stepson was available. Women were in all branches of the textile industry at York but were most numerous in spinning and carding. Most were poor, particularly single women and often wives who practised it as a second family occupation.[41]

The female labour market in Cologne

Apart from Paris, Cologne was virtually the only medieval city with separate women's guilds: for yarn makers, spinners of gold thread, silk throwers and silk weavers. Only three guilds limited women's employment in the fourteenth century, and even they did not enforce the rules strictly. Women did not occupy places of prestige in clothmaking; many were spinners, combers and bleachers of linen, but few were weavers. Records of nine of the other forty-one guilds of Cologne have no reference to women in the fifteenth century, and three others prohibited women to do certain types of work. Six others severely limited widows'

---

40 Nicholas, *Domestic Life*, 101.
41 Reyerson, 'Women in business', 135; Nicholas, *Domestic Life*, 102–3; Keene, *Medieval Winchester*, 389–90; Goldberg, *Women, Work and Life Cycle*, 1–22, 86–118, 268–90.

rights, and eighteen of the remaining twenty-four limited women less strictly. The tailors admitted women only as widows, wives and daughters of masters.[42]

Large numbers of women were belt makers and goldsmiths; the spinners of gold thread and some gold beaters formed a guild in 1397 with membership obligatory for all who wished to practise the trade. It was often practised jointly by a couple, the woman spinning and the man beating. Although women provided much of the labour force, males dominated these guilds politically except in the case of the silkworkers. Cologne yarn was famed in the international market. Between 1370 and 1397 the women who made it organised a guild, with a four-year apprenticeship for girls. 'Widower's right' in this guild corresponded to 'widow's right' in male-dominated guilds. Characteristically, the husbands of the women who made yarn were generally responsible for selling it; thus they were business partners of their wives and handled the more prestigious and lucrative side of the family enterprise.[43]

Women were silk entrepreneurs at Cologne, giving work to other women. They organised a guild in 1437, from which the silk spinners split in 1456. Mistresses could work in their own homes and train their daughters and up to four apprentices. The guild had four officers, two males and two females, but only the husbands of silkmakers could be chosen. Husband and wife could not be officers simultaneously. Although silk making was a domestic, household industry, most workers came from middle- and upper-class families: of 116 silkmakers and 765 female apprentices who are known by name during the period 1437–1504, nearly 30 per cent came from families that furnished members of the city council. Most women in the silk trades were married and practised the trade in the home for long periods. As with the yarn workers, the husbands of the more successful silkmakers were long-distance traders, who could market their products. Once again we see that prosperity resulted from linking craft production with merchant activity, but prestige and wealth came only from the latter.

The fourteenth and fifteenth centuries: a contrast

Women's status and independence in the labour market declined in the late Middle Ages. They are mentioned in fewer crafts in Paris in 1313

42 Howell, *Women, Production, and Patriarchy*, 133; Uitz, *Women in the Medieval Town*, 55–6.
43 Wensky, 'Stellung der Frau', 299–300, 290–3; Irsigler, 'Industrial production', 281; Wensky, 'Women's guilds in Cologne', 631–8; Howell, *Women, Production, and Patriarchy*, 124–8; Irsigler, *Wirtschaftliche Stellung Köln*, 49.

than 1292 and were heads of proportionally fewer households. The number of occupations practised by women falls from 121 in the combined surveys of 1292–1313 to nineteen in 1421–38, while those for men increase.[44] More women worked outside the home in the fifteenth century than before, but generally in low-status occupations outside the guilds. Between 1380 and 1500 women were taverners, hotelkeepers, mercers, seamstresses, silk weavers, hairdressers, women's tailors and needlemakers. There is occasional evidence for women as tinsmiths and fishmongers. In 1371 the barbers tried to restrict women, and by 1438 they would admit only daughters and wives of barbers.[45] Women's situation even declined in Cologne, as the political guilds consolidated their control over the city government, a development that came later to Cologne than to other large cities and may explain the earlier decline of women's work elsewhere. By the late fifteenth century all but six of Cologne's guilds – the bakers, linen weavers, brewers, silk embroiderers, needlemakers and belt makers – had no more than a handful of women.[46]

Although statistically insignificant, women were still more important in the workforce in Paris than in the Italian cities. Of almost 7,000 female heads of households in Florence in 1427, only 270 listed an occupation, and 103 of those were servants. A few women were food producers and retailers and wax workers. They had completely gone from the woollen industry, but some still made silks. Although women had been important when Barcelona's woollen industry began in the early fourteenth century, they were largely confined to spinning by the fifteenth century.[47] Of 208 apprenticeship contracts in the notarial registers of Montpellier before 1350, only thirty concern women, fourteen of them recent immigrants from nearby villages. Most were in textiles, victualling and precious metal work. No woman was in a high-status occupation.[48]

The fact that women rarely received licensed professional training, however much they may have learned from their parents, relegated them to low-status work and to menial jobs within trades. Marital status and position within the household often determined the kind of work women did; it was often part-time, helping in the family business rather than acting independently. Far more widows than wives worked outside

44 Herlihy, *Opera muliebria*, 175–6.
45 Favier, *Paris 1380–1500*, 164–5.
46 Wensky, 'Stellung der Frau', 290–3; Wensky, 'Women's guilds in Cologne', 639–41, 643–5, 648–9; Howell, *Women, Production, and Patriarchy*, 133–7. Silk also became Zürich's chief export at the turn of the fourteenth century, but women who worked it there did not enjoy the social prestige of their Cologne counterparts. Burghartz, *Leib, Ehre und Gut*, 31.
47 Herlihy, *Opera Muliebria*, 159–61, 169.
48 Reyerson, 'Women in business', 120.

the home; but this reflects not only their greater legal freedom than wives, but also the fact that, deprived of their husbands' earning power, they were more likely to have to do so. Female employment tended to be even more intermittent than male, and more women than men had employment in more than one job.[49]

The decline of women in the labour market has occasioned considerable comment and search for villains. Some have argued that the patriarchal guilds diminished the role of women by replacing the household unit of production, where women's work was highly valued, by a capitalist orientation that emphasised putting out raw materials.[50] In Languedoc, where the guilds were weaker than in the north, some trades admitted women in the fourteenth century, but the sworn guilds of the fifteenth and sixteenth excluded all but widows.[51] Yet this argument ignores the considerations that households were dominated by males and that the guilds, far from being antithetical to household production, were in fact based upon it. The decline of women in the work place thus seems to have paralleled the tightening of guild control and not been caused by it.

Other arguments have stressed demographic forces. Only in the most strongly industrial cities did males outnumber females. The predominance of females was generally due to immigration, not higher male mortality, as women came to the cities because jobs were there for them.[52] Population decline at York from 1349 provoked a shortage of labour and thus a wage rise and stimulated demand for females in low-status jobs. The labour shortage at York was so severe that in 1381 the city had to allow women to work as smiths and carpenters, which were traditionally male preserves. As increasing numbers of women worked outside the home, more remained single and birth rates dropped, prolonging the population decline. Economic recession had diminished the market for female labour by 1425. By 1450 the earlier model had been reversed: men tried to secure their own jobs by excluding women.[53]

Domestic service

Domestic servants represented a high percentage of the workforce of most late medieval cities. The larger and more industrial the city, the higher the percentage of servants of both sexes was likely to be. In cities

49   Analysis of Kowaleski, 'Women's work in Exeter', 155–7.
50   Howell, *Women, Production, and Patriarchy*.
51   Gouron, *Métiers en Languedoc*, 245.
52   Mitterauer, 'Familie und Arbeitsorganisation', 14–18.
53   Dyer, *Decline and Growth*, 17; Blair and Ramsey, *English Medieval Industries*, 186–8; Goldberg, *Women, Work and Life Cycle*, 1–22, 86–118, 199–200, 268–90.

with many wholesale and long-distance traders, most servants were girls who worked in menial tasks around the house. Boys dominated the servant population in the manufacturing cities, where they are sometimes hard to distinguish from journeymen.[54]

Florentine girls were put into service as early as age 8 and remained until about 18, the normal age for marriage. They saved their wages for dowries, which might also be provided by their employers at the conclusion of the term. Orphans and poor relations of the master and mistress were frequently hired, but between 1300 and 1500 86 per cent of the domestic servants mentioned in Florentine family records were non-Tuscan girls who had come a considerable distance to take advantage of the job market; for supply was exceeded by demand, and some women negotiated favourable contracts. While in the fourteenth century two-thirds of the documented servants in Florence were males, this was reversed in the next half-century, as the job market for males became saturated while that for females grew.[55]

York generally confirms the Tuscan pattern for female servants, but the terms started and ended at later ages than in Italy. Between 20 and 30 per cent of the population were servants, the percentage being highest in the commercial and industrial quarters. In further contrast to Italy, most servants did not generally stay in one household until they married, but rather moved every year or two. A 'hiring fair' was held at Pavement, the chief marketplace of York. Urban domestic service was often sex-specific – females were most often in victualling (especially in the inns, where they were chambermaids and tapsters) and mercantile occupations, least frequently in metal- and leatherworking. There were fewer servants in clothing and dressmaking than one would expect; as in textiles, there is more evidence of women professionally involved than as servants.[56] At Ghent and Paris, by contrast, the tendency was to hire young adult women rather than children and to keep them for long terms. Many masters of Ghent willed their servants substantial sums of money, often amounting to repayment of unpaid wages going back many years. In 1373 a priest willed his house to a maid who had served him for thirty years without pay. Continued service was guaranteed in some cases by the master making a substantial bequest that would be nullified if the maid left his service.[57]

---

54 Uitz, *Women*, 64.
55 Klapisch-Zuber, 'Women servants in Florence', 59–61; Herlihy, *Medieval Households*, 153–5; Herlihy, *Opera muliebria*, 145.
56 Goldberg, *Women, Work and Life Cycle*, 158–63, 176–8, 186, 191–2; Goldberg, 'Female labour', 21–3.
57 Nicholas, *Domestic Life*, 67–8, 104–6.

Standards of sexual behaviour

Women's problems were exacerbated by a double standard of sexual conduct in which males were considered less reprehensible than females for committing a given offence, and by a casual attitude toward extramarital sexual activity. Some but not all cities had laws punishing adultery severely. The fact that adultery was actionable in church courts explains some of this silence. No specific statute of Zürich in the fourteenth century forbade adultery; sexual matters only came to the court when other issues were involved, such as honour and property, including the fiscal losses from broken marriage promises. Thus the city did not regulate sexual conduct *per se*, but only its consequences under particular circumstances.[58]

While adultery was a crime, fornication was generally not actionable except as a private matter by the families. Females from some of the most distinguished lineages of Ghent had illegitimate children, and their parents and sometimes grandparents treated them as family members. Illegitimacy involved legal disadvantages but carried little social stigma in some northern cities, although this is not true of Italy. Fathers of Ghent frequently remembered their bastards in their wills, often with genuine affection. Some cities punished marriage without parental consent; Zürich imposed fines for this and for breaking a marriage promise that were comparable to that for homicide.[59] Ghent's constitutions of 1191 and 1297 provided severe corporal penalties for seduction and rape and loss of property for the woman if she chose to remain with her abductor. Yet seduction and elopement were common, and not a single man is known to have been mutilated or executed for it in the city in the fourteenth century. Most of the girls involved had clearly had enough contact with the seducer to want to go with him. In most cases the offending couple threw themselves on the mercy of the woman's parents, who at worst would send them on pilgrimages or sequester her property for a time. Many women of the lower orders frequented taverns and other disreputable places, and sexual misconduct toward them was rarely punished with more than a pilgrimage to a nearby shrine.[60]

Prostitution

A regrettable outgrowth of the problems of females, mainly but not entirely of the lower economic levels, is that many of them were forced

58 Burghartz, *Leib, Ehre und Gut*, 179–81.
59 Burghartz, *Leib, Ehre und Gut*, 172–8.
60 Nicholas, *Domestic Life*, 154–72, 53–69.

into prostitution. 'In terms of numbers involved and capital invested, the two major industries of the Florentine underworld were gambling and prostitution'.[61] It was a career choice for some; many prostitutes were married. Most of those who were fined at Winchester also had other professions, particularly dressmakers, spinners and dairy workers. Some cities required them to wear badges, and in virtually all they were forbidden to wear certain articles of clothing and jewellery and to harass passers-by who spurned their charms.[62] Even apart from casual prostitution, many city governments maintained public brothels in the fifteenth century. Although this was justified on grounds that it was best to get prostitutes off the streets and regulate them, the houses were always comfortable, and the trade was considered a 'public service'. The 'abbess of easy women' received a wage from the city of Nîmes, and Geneva had a 'queen of the brothel' in the fourteenth century.[63] Most admittedly anecdotal evidence suggests that the brothels were frequented by citizens of standing who went there openly. University cities were notorious for prostitutes. Experience with prostitutes was considered a rite of passage for many urban youths, although authorities were sometimes criticised for placing the brothel close to a school.[64]

In 1443 Palermo confined its prostitutes into a single *cortile*, with the gates locked and supervised by the tax collector, who also kept visitors' weapons during the encounters.[65] Florence in 1403 established an 'Office of Decency' to build a municipal brothel and recruit women to work in it; the excuse was to give males an alternative to homosexuality. The main brothel was centrally located between the Old Market and the archepiscopal palace, while privately employed prostitutes were congregated nearby in the Alley of the Cows. Florence recruited many prostitutes initially from other parts of northern Italy and Germany and the Low Countries, but the foreign element had declined to insignificance in favour of north Italians by the end of the fifteenth century.[66] Dijon had many Flemish prostitutes in the 1470s who were thought to be spying for the duke of Burgundy against the French.[67]

Most brothels that were not regulated by the cities were on or near church property or in the city gates. Ghent had a Prostitutes' Street off

61 Brucker, 'Florentine *popolo minuto*', 167.
62 Keene, *Medieval Winchester*, 390–2; Geremek, *Margins of Society*, 222–3.
63 Barel, *Ville médiévale*, 240–1; Geremek, *Margins of Society*, 87.
64 Rossiaud, 'Crises', 533–4; Herlihy, *Opera Muliebria*, 157–8; Rossiaud, *Medieval prostitution*, 44.
65 Bresc, 'Rues de Palerme', 177.
66 Trexler, 'Florentine prostitution', 373–9, 385–6.
67 Rossiaud, *Medieval Prostitution*, 34, 45.

the square of the church of St Michael, but no brothels are known to have been there. Prostitutes plied their trade and solicited customers in the recesses of the city walls. At Dijon they were initially in one central street, then moved outside the town at the end of the fourteenth century. At Amiens they were originally confined to a Girls Street, but this became too small and had to be enlarged as their trade expanded.[68] The immunity district of the provost of the church of St Donatian at Bruges, which was scattered throughout the city, was notorious for criminals and prostitutes. The bailiff took fines from prostitutes, evidently amounting to a licence fee. In 1351 he collected from 131 prostitutes, but the number had declined to nine by 1402, as larger establishments developed under madams who employed girls. Venice kept lists of its prostitutes who, evidently like those of Bruges, were considered a tourist attraction. They were restricted to the Castellato, near the Rialto, where the foreign merchants were most numerous.[69] Several cities had 'Kings of the Ribalds' who performed various unpleasant duties with marginal persons, including supervising brothels and gambling houses.[70]

Prostitution was a predictably serious problem in Paris. Most were poor girls, migrants and widows of artisans. As in most cities the prostitutes were concentrated in areas of potential customers. There were fewer than one might expect on the Left Bank except around the Place Maubert, but a large group was on the Right Bank of the Île de la Cité, across from the Place de Grève, the main market. Glatigny, in the poor parish of St Landry on the Île de la Cité, was notorious. The biggest concentrations of prostitutes were along the rue Saint-Honoré and its side streets and the rue Saint-Martin, with some in the east end. Many also congregated around the public latrines on the Seine.[71]

Until the end of the fifteenth century there was less regulation of prostitution in England than on the continent. Some cities fined prostitutes but allowed them to keep up their trade. They were always found in cottages and garrets in the rougher neighbourhoods, often renting this accommodation from churches. They also moved around often. Some street names, most of them near religious houses, suggest prostitution: Love's Lane and Cock's Lane are common names in England, and several cities in Languedoc had Hot Streets. Cheapside in London had a Popkirtle Lane. London has more evidence of professional prostitution than the other English cities. John of Northampton as mayor in 1381–2 issued statutes against prostitutes and scolds. The authorities tried to

68 Nicholas, *Domestic Life*, 60; Geremek, *Margins of Society*, 87–94.
69 Nicholas, *Medieval Flanders*, 296–7.
70 Trenard, *Histoire de Lille*, 232.
71 Favier, *Paris 1380–1500*, 80–1; Geremek, *Margins of Society*, 88–94.

confine prostitutes to Cock Lane, threatening them with punishment if they were found elsewhere.[72]

Taverns, which were often run by women, and bathhouses were notorious for prostitution. The stews of Southwark outside London on the property of the bishop of Winchester were infamous. The *Cheval Blanc*, the largest inn in Aix-en-Provence in 1445, was owned by the undervicar (deputy sheriff) of the city, who fronted a pimping business through it.[73] In 1381

> it was agreed by the masters, *jurés* and common council [of Utrecht] and publicly cried and decreed from the windows [of the city hall] that no common woman who sells her body for money may sit in any other bath or brothel inside the freedom of the city than in the two baths behind Our Lady, on pain of expulsion from the town for one year and a fine of one pound as often as she is found or caught; and the owner of the house in which they are practising will be fined 3 pounds.[74]

URBAN CHILDREN

In most preindustrial societies children and servants combined, which includes most persons under age 25, constitute about half the total population. Virtually all medieval cities where statistical reconstructions are possible corroborate this. Nearly two-fifths of the population of Florence in 1427 were 14 or under, although the age pyramid was artifically skewed by recent plagues and normalised later.[75] Although in some larger cities children far outnumbered servants, they were nearly equal in two parishes of Reims in 1422 and in Coventry in 1523. Richer wards had both more children and more servants than the poorer, where the percentages of childless couples and of single heads of households were higher. These figures were minima, for children were often underreported in surveys to avoid having to pay taxes on them.[76]

Urban populations were thus considerably younger in the late Middle Ages than now. Older children of the family, who were frequently being trained at home, apprentices and journeymen constituted a peer

---

72 Goldberg, *Women, Work and Life Cycle*, 149–55; Robertson, *Chaucer's London*, 101–3; see also Keene, *Medieval Winchester*, 390–2.

73 Goldberg, 'Women in town life', 118; Coulet, 'Proprietaires et exploitants d'auberges', 135.

74 Quoted in Alberts, *Middeleeuwse stad*, 24.

75 Herlihy and Klapisch-Zuber, *Tuscans*, 192–5.

76 Phythian-Adams, *Coventry*, ch. 21.

group of young persons who had considerable free time on their hands and undoubtedly contributed to the high rates of violence in the cities. Suffixes to names denoting 'child', such as *kin*, were frequently applied to persons who from other sources appear to be unemancipated young adults. A Morningspeech of Cologne in 1408 prohibited anyone from doing business in goods or money with children without the knowledge of their parents, or to act as broker in transactions with them, or to guarantee children of burgesses for debts of more than one Rhenish gulden in the taverns.[77] Young persons had considerable latitude unless their parents or guardians exercised unusual vigilance. When rates of violent crime can be distinguished by the age of the principal perpetrator, it is apparent that many young persons were involved. Since propertied orphans had their own funds, the council of Ghent held them personally responsible for their own violence, vandalism and debauchery and usually ordered their guardians to reimburse their victims from the wards' property.[78]

The problems of the age pyramid were most severe in Italy. Contemporaries identified the most disorderly elements as the very rich and very poor, but also the young and the unmarried. Youth gangs were involved in the outbreak of the Black–White feuds in Florence and Pistoia in the late thirteenth century. Half the citizens of Florence were under the age of 22, and the average age of males was only 26 in 1427. The ratio of males to females was very high in Florence, 132:100 between the ages of 18 and 32, but in the wealthiest households the ratio was 150:100 for this age group.[79]

The large numbers of women in the cities meant that fathers had to begin early to save enough for an acceptable dowry. If a Florentine father wanted to use the *Monte delle Doti* to accumulate a dowry, he had to make the first deposit when his daughter was 6 to marry her at 16. There was often a significant age gap between spouses, particularly in Mediterranean Europe, where 'dowry wars' depleted upper-order family income and kept young males out of the marriage market in favour of older males, who married young women. The household might contain the father's bastards and numerous servants, especially from poorer branches of the family. These family alliances were important for wealth, patronage and political alliances.[80]

77 Huiskes, *Beschlüsse Köln*, 68.
78 Nicholas, *Domestic Life*, 144–8.
79 Herlihy, 'Psychological and social roots', 140–6.
80 Klapisch-Zuber, *Women*, 81–5, 189, 213–46; Herlihy and Klapisch-Zuber, *Tuscans*, 202–6; Herlihy, *Medieval Households*, 142–59. Herlihy's argument about dowries seems to hold for Valencia; Guiral-Hadziiossif, *Valence*, 450–7.

Given short life expectancies, many people were raised by step-parents, particularly in the north, where widowed persons were more likely to remarry than in Italy. In parts of Italy widowers were more likely than widows to remarry, for a woman who left her late husband's family had to abandon her children to them. In the north the stepfather's attitude was critical. If he accepted his wife's children, she could raise them; if he did not, he could forbid her to keep them, and in that event the kin of their late father brought them up.[81] The bonds of the extended family were strong, but distant relatives only intervened directly in childrearing when death or incapacity fractured the nuclear family.

But the step-parent could not touch the child's property. At Siena, as in most cities, the property of orphans (defined as minors bereft of even one parent) was placed under municipal guardianship. Separate judges heard wardship cases, validated contracts concerning minors and appointed guardians. Constance kept lists of children's guardians, managed by a city official assisted by the children's kin. The office rendered detailed annual accounts to the entire council.[82] Florence had Magistrates of the Wards who acted as guardians of all children whose mothers and close male relatives had died or absconded, or who had not been given guardians in the father's will. The Magistrates sometimes took over when such designated guardians, who were often distant relations, refused the responsibility. The position was onerous; the Magistrates, far from being professional civil servants, were chosen by lot and rotated every six months.[83] The Flemish cities administered orphans' property directly before 1302. Thereafter they detached the children's share of the deceased parent's estate from that of the surviving parent and kept a 'status of property' on file with the city council. A legal guardian was appointed, generally from the side of the deceased parent, to manage the property and invest the money. When the surviving parent was trusted by the in-laws, the guardian might yield to him/her after filing the status of property, but in most cases guardianship lasted until adulthood. As the children matured, they were expected to work, either in the family business or apprenticed in some other line of work, or in domestic service. Some were given allowances from their property, in effect testing their discretion before formal emancipation.[84]

81 Klapisch-Zuber, *Women*, 117–31; Nicholas, *Domestic Life*, 114–22.
82 Waley, *Siena*, 62; Bechtold, *Zunftbürgerschaft und Patriziat*, 32.
83 Kuehn, 'Social processes and legal processes', 374–5.
84 Nicholas, *Domestic Life*, 110–40; Nicholas, *Medieval Flanders*, 185. The mayor and council of Provins, too, managed orphans' property directly until 1319 but thereafter were required to turn it over to the nearest relative or a reliable person, who presented accounts twice yearly. Chapin, *Villes de foires*, 219.

London's laws concerning guardianship and security of property only applied to children of freemen, and their situation was strikingly different from the Flemish. The guardian was frequently the surviving parent; for while in Flanders the concern was to preserve the family's property in a partible inheritance regime, English law emphasised primogeniture and prohibited blood relations who stood to inherit from the child to be guardians. A Common Pleader or Sergeant in the mayor's court took an inventory of each child's inheritance.[85]

The situation of orphans who were totally deprived of kin who could or would raise them was of course much worse. There were obviously more of these unfortunates than surviving records show. Some children were abandoned even by living parents and had to live on the charity of neighbours. Ghent had only two orphanages, and few children were in them at any one time. Between 60 and 140 orphans were abandoned yearly at the Hôtel-Dieu of Paris.[86] The children's hospital at Montpellier, founded by James of Rome in 1309 and under city control by 1328, was the earliest in France. Toulouse had an orphanage by 1342, Aix-en-Provence in 1348. Paris had its first orphanage in 1363, and in 1421 the city bought three houses for abandoned children who were starving in the streets. The government of Montpellier even paid professional wet nurses to feed abandoned children in their homes. The Italian cities had more foundling hospitals, perhaps reflecting greater need, but the first hospital solely for foundlings in Italy was the Innocenti of Florence, which opened in 1445. Around 1450 the hospital of Santo Spirito in Rome was re-formed as a foundling hospital.[87]

THE JEWS AND THE MUSLIMS IN THE LATER MEDIEVAL CITIES

The thirteenth century

The Jews had been important in the capital formation phase of the early medieval cities. Jewish moneylenders and merchants, evidently migrants from the Black and Caspian Sea regions rather than refugees from the west as would be the case later, were numerous enough at Kiev to have their own ghetto by 1113. By 1146 a Jewish Gate, called the L'vov Gate

85 Hanawalt, *Growing Up*, 91–5.
86 Hanawalt, *Growing Up*, 62–3; Nicholas, *Domestic Life*, 115; Favier, *Paris 1380–1500*, 90.
87 Nicholas, 'Childhood', 38–9 and literature cited; Favier, *Paris 1380–1500*, 91; Herlihy and Klapisch-Zuber, *Tuscans*, 145; Otis, 'Municipal wet-nurses', 83; Otis-Cour, 'Pauvres enfants', 310–14.

by the late thirteenth century, connected Prince Yaroslav's town, which had been planned during the city's primary expansion phase, with the city's commercial district. There is little evidence of Jews at Novgorod, perhaps because it had such a thriving western commerce that their function was taken over by Christians.[88]

But the Jews became a marginal group in the thirteenth century. As Christian merchants and moneylenders became active in most cities of northern Italy, the Jewish presence declined even in the ports.[89] Philip II of France began a persecution of the Jews in 1180 that significantly altered the social geography of Paris and other cities. As the royal domain expanded, the Jews' situation became increasingly dangerous, but some local princes defied the king and protected the Jews in their cities. The predominantly Jewish quarters of Montpellier were near the major markets and included Christian residents. The Jews only declined there after the city was annexed by the crown in 1349.[90] The Jewish community of Perpignan developed late, but it was prosperous by the mid-thirteenth century. With a population of about one hundred families by 1287, it was probably second among the large Jewish communities north of the Pyrenees. Only that of Narbonne was bigger, with 140 adult males in 1305. The Jews of Perpignan were less engaged in foreign than in local trade, where their credit was more in demand. They were almost totally absent from the crafts, and there is little evidence of them as pawn-brokers at Perpignan, but 80 per cent were moneylenders, including some women. Most loans were to great merchants and to some Christian financiers, who kept a small cash reserve and borrowed from Jews to cover short-term obligations.[91]

The Jews had prospered in England in the twelfth century, but a pogrom in 1190 began their decline. As elsewhere, they tended to be most numerous in cities with big churches, especially those without many native moneylenders. The Jews of Bristol had their first synagogue in Wynch Street, and they held considerable property around the castle. Lincoln, York and London had the largest Jewries in England. Aaron of Lincoln became prosperous by loaning money to Henry II but fell from favour, and his property and outstanding debts passed to the king when he died.[92] The baronial movement against King John had an anti-Semitic element; Magna Carta had two clauses regulating the repayment of Jewish loans. The Jews' situation worsened considerably under Henry

88   Birnbaum, 'Kiev, Novgorod, Moscow', 39–40, 45–6.
89   Brentano, *Rome Before Avignon*, 46–8.
90   Faber and Lochard, *Montpellier*, 138–9.
91   This summarises the arguments of Emery, *Jews of Perpignan*.
92   Lobel, *Atlas* 2: 8; Hill, *Medieval Lincoln*, 217–20.

III. Aaron of York, the greatest Anglo-Jewish financier of the thirteenth century, had houses at York and London and loaned to men in at least fourteen counties, often in association with other Jews. But from 1243 Aaron was systematically ruined by Henry III and died in poverty. The baronial agitation of Henry's last years harmed the Jews. They were slaughtered in London in April 1263. After 1264 the Jews at Winchester were placed under guardians who became identified with the royal party, while the community, in league with the barons, attacked them. Disturbances in 1273–4 led to the expulsion of the mayor Simon le Drapir, who had protected the Jews during his seven years in office.[93]

The Jews were less persecuted in central and particularly eastern Europe. As they emigrated eastward to escape persecution in England and France, they were given privileges by the Polish, Hungarian and Austrian princes, including security of debt, enforceable by law, and the right to live under Jewish law. Buda had an exceptionally large Jewish community with its own synagogue after 1251. Although the Jews were required to wear a special costume and were not allowed to sell their goods on market days, they were generally left alone until the modern period. Although the Jews in Poland were not as urban a group as in the west, most Polish cities had large Jewish settlements. They had their own courts and several population concentrations in Kraków, where they seem to have been most active in shopkeeping within their own community and in moneylending. The Jews typically lived on the peripheries of the cities in the thirteenth century, which became more central with expansion; the original ghetto of Kraków became the university quarter in the fifteenth century.[94]

The Jews of Germany, too, were relatively better off than those in the western monarchies. Although the kings were not well disposed to them, they were too weak to do them much harm and generally contented themselves with declaring the Jews royal serfs, as the Capetians of France had done. As in France, territorial princes protected them and used their capital. There were Talmudic schools at Speyer, Worms, Mainz, Würzburg, Regensburg, and, somewhat later, Vienna.[95] The Jews' position at Mainz in the 1280s is typical. There were uprisings against them in 1281, 1283 and 1286–7, and many Jews left Mainz and the other Rhine cities. In 1293 the king demanded that the town pay the archbishop an indemnity to release confiscated Jewish property, which he needed to pay his debts to the pope. At issue was the 200

93 Tillott, *City of York*, 47–8; Keene, *Winchester*, 76–8.
94 Knoll, 'Urban development of medieval Poland', 76, 89, 92–4; Birnbaum, 'Buda', 145; Carter, *Trade and Urban Development in Poland*, 71.
95 Bosl, *Augsburger Bürgertum*, 26; Haverkamp, *Medieval Germany*, 346.

marks yearly that the Jews paid to the archbishop in recognition of his lordship, but from 1294 this was to be collected by the townspeople.[96]

The fourteenth and fifteenth centuries

The Jews were expelled from England in 1290 and from the French royal domain in 1306. They were readmitted to France by 1315 but were expelled again in 1322 and fined. Realising that matters would not improve, most did not return. Before 1348 Jewish communities were found in parts of France outside the control of the Capetian monarchy, in the Slavic east and in German cities that had not known them before. The Valois monarchs were less obdurate toward the Jews than the Capetians had been, but the French Jewish communities remained small. In 1361 Charles V permitted them to live in Paris, confined to two Jewries near the Hôtel Saint-Pol, his preferred residence, in return for a large yearly tax. He permitted interest on loans up to 4d. per livre per week. A new expulsion in 1394 ended even this modest prosperity.[97] Arles had a more active Jewish community than was usual in royal France, with a ghetto of sixty households in 1440. The Jews did most of the petty moneylending. Between 1436 and 1440, 63 Christians and 43 Jews loaned money, although the Jews were only 7 per cent of the population, and the Jews accounted for three-quarters of the surviving money loans. Most in both groups were casual moneylenders, not doing it as a real profession. Most Jewish loans were for small amounts; Christians dominated large-scale moneylending. The Jews also were responsible for nearly three-fifths of the grain loans.[98]

The Jewish quarters in most cities were walled by 1300; whether this was done at the instigation of Christians or of Jews themselves to help them enforce ritual obligations and prevent intermarriage with Gentiles seems to vary with the locality. In the Mediterranean areas it was usually the result of Jews wanting to live together, rather than force. At Marseilles both the upper and lower town had Jewries with their own officials, bathhouses and butcheries. Jews and Christians were still mixed in some cities.[99]

Jews and also Muslims were especially numerous in the cities of Navarre and Castile, absorbing many of those exiled from France and England. They constituted 33 per cent of the inhabitants at Avila in the

---

96 Falck, *Mainz in seiner Blütezeit*, 119–24.
97 Cazelles, *Paris*, 128–9; Favier, *Paris 1380–1500*, 79–80.
98 Stouff, *Arles*, 305–11.
99 Abulafia, 'Privilege to persecution', 111; Baratier, *Marseille*, 86.

thirteenth century.[100] At Tudela most of them chose to live in proximity to one another, but they were not confined to a separate quarter. They had three synagogues and used their own butchers, but many circulated among the Christians and were textile artisans. Some owned land and were moneychangers. They paid a heavy fine to the king for permission to use a collective seal. The community had 500 adults in the early fourteenth century but declined to 250 by 1400.[101]

The Jews continued to thrive in Iberia until after 1350. After Majorca was taken from the Muslims, the Jews were invited to settle but were confined within specific territory. Their privileged position, which was evidently the result of need for their capital for investment, is similar to the rights given to Genoese, Pisan and other foreign merchant communities overseas. They handled civil actions and minor violence in their own courts, but capital crimes went to the royal court. The Jews also controlled their own weights and measures and could tax sales within the quarter and goods entering or leaving it. The Jewish community collected its own taxes and was governed by four Jewish syndics. Taxes were assessed separately on the Jewish community by the king, not by the town government.[102]

In Germany Duderstadt had a synagogue by 1338. Jews are first mentioned at Tübingen in 1335, but a Jew Street suggests that they go back to the earliest period of the town. As at Kiev and elsewhere, it was in the classical location: on the edge of the old quarter, between two major streets. Despite some growth from emigrés, the German Jewish communities remained small. Regensburg's was probably the largest, with over 500 taxpayers or a total Jewish population of 2,000–2,500. Nuremberg and Frankfurt, with about 1,000 Jews, were followed by Cologne with perhaps 750, and the others were smaller.[103]

Nuremberg's Jewish community was initially prosperous, but troubles began in 1298 with anti-Jewish riots in at least forty-four cities and towns in Bavaria, the so-called Rindfleisch massacres. In 1313 the emperor gave the *Schultheiss* the duty of protecting the Jews and collecting taxes from them, but in fact the city council assumed this function. Although the decree of 1313 placed the Jews under the protection of the city without giving them citizenship, they appear from 1321 in registrations of new citizens along with Christians. But the authorities exploited them, and they did not play a significant part in moneylending in the city.

---

100 Gonthier, *Cris de haine*, 71–4.
101 Leroy, 'Tudela', 196–7.
102 Abulafia, 'Privilege to persecution', 112–18.
103 Fahlbusch, 'Duderstadt', 194–212; Sydow, *Tübingen*, 79–81; Isenmann, *Deutsche Stadt*, 101.

The Jews occasionally turned to the Christian courts to help them handle internal matters but found little sympathy. In 1314 the council of Nuremberg refused a request from the Jews to exclude one Zalkind, who led a gang of Jewish brawlers.[104]

1348 and after

The Jews received a sharp setback when they were accused of causing the epidemic of 1348–9 by poisoning the wells. Rulers used the pogroms and emotion cynically to exploit the Jews still further. In some places the disaster was only temporary. The Jewish quarter of Avignon suffered a pogrom in 1348, but it still contained 209 households in 1358–60. By 1374 there were 128 Jewish brokers. The papal capital had a large transient and international element to which they catered.[105] The larger cities of Provence in the mid-fifteenth century had Jewish communities; they constituted one-tenth of the population at Carpentras and Aix-la-Chapelle. The Jewry of Carpentras grew by half in the fifteenth century, mainly by immigration from places with less security.[106]

The persecutions were worst in Germany and Spain, the only places left with large numbers of Jews. On 16 November 1349 the emperor Charles IV permitted the council of Nuremberg to tear down the Jewish quarter for space to extend the market and pardoned the town in advance for any damage to the Jews who were under his protection. Armed with this licence to riot, mobs pillaged the ghetto on 5 December, burning 562 Jews. The Jews were readmitted in 1352, but as late as 1381 only eighteen Jewish families were living in Jew Street.[107] The Jews of Frankfurt were expelled in 1349 but were readmitted in 1360 and given freedom of religion and to loan money.[108] The Jewish community in Zürich was destroyed in 1348, but in 1354 the council readmitted them and confirmed their earlier privileges. They received tax remission for four years from 1357, but they only returned slowly. There were no more than fifty Jews in Zürich by 1400.[109]

Charles IV's reign thus witnessed a change of imperial policy toward the German Jews. A privilege of 1236 had placed them under imperial protection, but by the fourteenth century most emperors pawned or sold

104 Bischoff, 'Stadtherrschaft im ostfränkischen Städtedreieck', 99; Pfeiffer, *Nürnberg*, 38; Stow, *Alienated Minority*, 172, 231.
105 Guillemain, *Cour pontificale d'Avignon*, 642–53.
106 Rossiaud, 'Crises', 539.
107 Pfeiffer, *Nürnberg*, 74–5; Bischoff, 'Stadtherrschaft im ostfränkischen Städtedreieck', 103.
108 Dilcher, 'Bürgerbegriff', 80.
109 Burghartz, *Leib, Ehre und Gut*, 184.

to individual communities or lords the right to collect taxes and serve as 'protectors'. When the emperor gave the Jews of Worms to the city government in 1348, it unleashed a pogrom. In 1385 the thirty-seven members of the Swabian Urban League agreed to give King Wenceslaus half the Jewish tax, but in return they were granted the right to receive Jews at will. From this time the Jews of such cities as Worms, Frankfurt and Nuremberg had citizenship on the same basis as Christians, but this did not mean political rights. Most cities reserved the right to expel them at any time. The Jews continued to live apart and choose their own magistrates. Curiously, Charles's capital, Prague, was an exception to the general deterioration of the situation of the Jews in the Empire. Although most Jewish ghettoes in central and eastern Europe were poor even if unmolested, the Jews of Prague had their own 'city' with four guildhalls and several synagogues.[110]

Although the cities of Muslim Spain were among the largest of medieval Europe, the conquest of the Iberian peninsula by Christian princes was generally accompanied by the ejection of the Muslims from the captured cities, which became predominantly Christian within a generation of the Conquest. Some Muslims, called Mudejars, did return to the cities, usually living in distinct quarters. They were permitted their own law, subject to payment of tribute. The Mudejars became an important element in urban craft production by the second half of the fourteenth century, particularly in tilemaking and pottery, where their distinctive artistic styles were renowned, and in leatherworking, which had been an important Spanish export since the early Middle Ages. But with inevitable intermarriage, the Mudejar element in the cities was declining by the early fifteenth century. The Mudejar specialities were not prestigious crafts, as we have seen; and the fact that they lived so inconspicuously may explain why they were left in peace for much longer than the Jews and *conversos* (converts to Christianity).[111]

But while the Muslims became a largely dependent group in the Castilian countryside, with small numbers in the cities, the Jews were a mainly urban group. Virulent anti-Semitism struck Spain in the 1360s, when King Peter the Cruel was accused by his rival for the Castilian throne of being pro-Jewish. A small group of Jewish financiers was involved in urban and royal government, particularly finance, but this was no more typical of Jews than of Christians. Most Iberian Jews were artisans and shopkeepers, excluded like Christians of that social level from urban oligarchies and royal offices. This did not stop complaints from

110 Isenmann, *Deutsche Stadt*, 100; Pfeiffer, *Nürnberg*, 81–2; Möncke, *Quellen*, 241–4.
111 MacKay, *Spain*, 60–6, 200–2; O'Callahan, *Medieval Spain*, 461–6, 605–9.

Christians. Most large cities in Spain had anti-Jewish riots in 1391, when a pogrom incited by Franciscan preachers erupted at Seville and spread to the other cities of Castile and Aragon. Thousands of Jews were killed in each of the major cities in an orgy of bloodshed that lasted three months. Many converted to Christianity to escape.

After order was restored, so many Jews became *conversos* that many formerly Jewish families intermarried with Christians and entered urban government. The Jews themselves regained some prosperity. Although they may not have been wealthier per capita than the Christians, their 'strangeness' and obvious ties with the Muslims who were so disliked in Spain fuelled Christian hatred. Yields from special taxes on them undoubtedly exaggerate our impressions of their wealth: Jewish taxes accounted for 14 per cent of the municipal receipt of Zaragoza in 1440.[112] Thus anti-*converso* factions developed in the Spanish cities in the fifteenth century on the pretext that their conversions had been insincere. A new wave of pogroms began in 1449, when riots at Toledo were set off because a royal tax was farmed to a *converso* who was a prominent merchant and treasurer of the city council. Toledo had two Christian civic confraternities, one for *conversos* and another dedicated to Mary for the old Christian families. During a procession organised by the Marian fraternity in 1473, a blacksmith yelled that wine had been thrown at Mary's image from a house owned by a *converso*. He then put himself at the head of a mob that sacked the city for several days. The crown initially tried to protect the Jews and *conversos*, which only deepened its problems. The monarchy only regained popularity in the Spanish cities after Ferdinand and Isabella established the Inquisition in 1478.[113]

The cities of late medieval Europe were thus diverse communities that housed sophisticated political institutions, the leading schools of their age, a wealthy and prosperous commerce, and a productive industrial plant, but they were also plagued by social, family and ethnic conflict. We now turn to more general questions of the quality of life in the human microcosm of late medieval urban civilisation.

---

112 Lacarra, 'Budget de la ville de Saragosse', 382–3.
113 MacKay, *Spain*, 183–7, 194–5; for a general overview see Sachar, *Jews*, 184–213.

CHAPTER NINE

Education, Culture and Community in the Later Medieval City

Education in the cities

Lay literacy was widespread in most cities, particularly among the wealthier burgesses. Commerce relied everywhere on written instruments to such an extent that anyone whose career involved more than working for a wage in a single locality required at least basic literacy. Although social status was a great divide, literacy cut across gender lines. In the late medieval cities as in the rural areas, educational levels were at least as high among women as among men. The urban bureaucracies generated massive written records. Daniel Waley has spoken of an 'intensely literate mode of government characterized by a spectacular consumption of paper, parchment and ink' at Siena even in the thirteenth century. The municipal chancery kept copies of all correspondence and property transactions and inserted copies of those with particular legal significance in 'cartularies of privileges'. Every transaction of the chamberlain and the four provisors had to be in writing. All accounts of the Biccherna were kept in duplicate. At the end of each six-month term of office the rough drafts of correspondence were recopied into finished versions.[1] The government of Pisa kept such detailed records that its needs occupied nearly half the professional time of the city's notaries in the early fourteenth century.[2]

Formal schools played a lesser role in developing literacy in the medieval cities than now, for private tutors, and licenciates in arts from the cathedral schools and universities that were found in all major cities, were easily available to teach the children of the merchant elite.[3] Most

1 Waley, *Siena*, 155–6.
2 Herlihy, *Pisa*, 32–3.
3 Wriedt, 'Schulen und bürgerliches Bildungswesen', 164.

large cities had 'song' or elementary schools by the thirteenth century, teaching a mainly Latin curriculum before 1250. The course was essentially the same in both urban/municipal and church schools, but the secular schools were more likely to take boys and girls together, and a few employed women as teachers. The memoir of Jan Sloesgin shows that children were expected to attend school in late-fourteenth-century Cologne. They changed schools when the family moved to a new parish. School began at the age of 6; boys stayed for eight years, girls four. Sloesgin sent his 6-year-old daughter to school at Klein St Martins, then characteristically in 1432 brought her home so that she could learn how to be a merchant. The school term always began on 12 March.[4] Some pupils continued after elementary school in 'schools of commerce', where they learned arithmetic, book-keeping, commercial correspondence and sometimes foreign languages and geography. Most attended these schools only briefly, then gained practical experience through apprenticeship or work in the family shop. Although schooling might precede apprenticeship, some contracts, especially of younger apprentices, required the master to send the young person to school for one or two years. Children of craftsmen who were trained at home by working in the family shop were less likely to be sent to school than those who were sent outside the home.[5]

The mendicant orders also established schools in the major cities. A procession at Paris on 13 October 1449 included 'the children of the four mendicant orders and of all the schools in Paris, both boys and girls. There were reckoned to be twelve thousand five hundred children or more'.[6] The smaller French cities were less advanced. Fewer than one hundred families of Tours sent their children to school in 1429. Although merchants' sons could learn privately, education was at a generally low level.[7]

Education was initially a monopoly of the church. The pope confirmed the exclusive educational rights of selected urban churches in Flanders in the 1190s, but his mandate was a dead letter by the 1250s. The citizens of Ypres were guaranteed the right in 1253 to employ private tutors in the home for their children, and anyone who wished could run an elementary school. Most cities had parish schools within a few years of the first reference to a city council. The older cities had bigger and older churches with established schools; the clerical monopoly

4 Wriedt, 'Schulen und bürgerliches Bildungswesen', 172; Herborn, 'Bürgerliches Selbstverständnis', 507–8.
5 Shahar, *Childhood*, 225–6, 231.
6 *Journal Paris*, 371.
7 Chevalier, *Tours*, 196–210.

over education here thus took longer to break than in the smaller places and the founded towns.[8]

New schools were founded in the urban parishes as population grew. Establishing a parish school required long negotiations with the clergy. In some cities, such as Lübeck and Brunswick, the new schools were only founded with papal authorisation and over the objection of the local cathedral. Lübeck had a Latin school in the St Jacob church by 1262, but some cities only had municipal parish schools after 1400. In cases where the council obtained patronage of the schools, 'presented' the schoolmaster, provided buildings and paid him, it had determining influence on curriculum and discipline. The schoolmaster could appoint the subordinate personnel of the school. Sometimes the municipal clerk would be rector of the school, particularly in small cities.[9]

The newer parish schools in the large cities were usually confined to the elementary curriculum in the beginning, while the cathedral school handled advanced subjects; the disputes were more over patronage and appointment of schoolmasters than over the curriculum. By 1300 the issue in most cities was not schooling *per se*, but the right of the church schools to control training in the more advanced subjects of the liberal arts. The papal legate in 1267 gave permission to the council and citizens of Breslau to open an elementary school. He noted that boys were being endangered and harassed physically by having to attend the cathedral school outside the town walls and across the river. Thus he permitted a sing school for 'small boys' at the church of St Mary Magdalene, where they could learn grammar and chanting. Only boys who wanted more advanced subjects, specifically concerning doctrine, had to transfer to the church school at St John in the castle.[10]

The Latin education of the earlier period changed to a mainly vernacular culture in the late Middle Ages. The language used in municipal chanceries shows the advance of the vernacular language everywhere. Many French urban charters exist first in a Latin version, then in French, perhaps with a third in the regional dialect. The *échevins* of Reims in 1351 asked the archbishop to write to them in French because 'they are simple people who understand no Latin'.[11] In Flanders, which had a substantial French-speaking element and always depended on foreign trade, virtually all businessmen were bilingual in Flemish and French. The language of municipal record-keeping shifted abruptly from Latin

8 Nicholas, *Medieval Flanders*, 144–5; Wriedt, 'Schulen und bürgerliches Bildungs-wesen', 155–9, 169.
9 Isenmann, *Deutsche Stadt*, 181–2; Peters, *Literatur in der Stadt*, 277.
10 Möncke, *Quellen*, 90–3.
11 Le Goff, 'L'Apogée', 375.

to French (the preferred language of the Francophile party among the city patricians) in the 1260s at Douai and Ypres, from Latin to Flemish at Ghent by 1280 and at Bruges in 1300. In the fourteenth century Flemish was used everywhere except at Ypres, where the older lineages held sway and used French as a form of cultural snobbery.[12] Understanding of Latin was declining even in Italy. Minutes of testimony in the courts of Siena were taken in Latin, then read back to the witness in Tuscan.[13]

Education in the vernacular languages, however, remained unusual in formal schools until after 1350, particularly in Germany. Only in 1418 did Lübeck establish exclusively German instruction in any school, and other cities quickly followed. A few of them also taught elementary Latin, but this usually remained with the cathedral and parish schools. The most significant difference in curriculum between lay and church schools came less in the parish schools than in the vernacular writing schools, which are attested frequently from the early fifteenth century but were clearly present earlier. They taught letter-writing, which was so important for merchant correspondence. Surviving wax tablets from the St Jacob school of Lübeck show that writing and style were being taught through examples from business correspondence and commercial papers and the city chancery. Most of these schools were founded by private citizens and eventually taken over by the city. The council of Hamburg founded several in 1402.[14]

Curiously, in view of the commercial pre-eminence of Flanders and the large number of foreigners at Bruges, educational opportunities for students who desired a professional education without going to a university were limited in the Low Countries, although the larger cities had Latin schools that taught the seven liberal arts in preparation for university studies. Until the fourteenth century the few commercial manuals available were elementary; there was nothing of the sort of pre-merchant-career training that was available in Italy. In the fifteenth century some works on the art of letter-writing, accounting and foreign language instruction became available in the Low Country cities. Bruges had a 'school of administration', a school for minstrels even in the thirteenth century, and a school for rhetoricians is mentioned in 1428. Vocational training was definitely at a lower level. Mons at the end of the fourteenth century had 'schools in the mechanical arts', and a

---

12 Nicholas, *Medieval Flanders*, 144. The switch in the Brabant cities took place only in the mid-fourteenth century. van Uytven, 'Stadsgeschiedenis', 241.

13 Waley, *Siena*, 54, 156–9.

14 Wriedt, 'Schulen und bürgerliches Bildungswesen', 164–7; Peters, *Literatur in der Stadt*, 275–7.

police regulation of 1417 shows that girls were being taught to sew in schools.[15]

Lay education was more advanced in the south. Instruction was largely lay except for students who were preparing for a clerical vocation. Even in the thirteenth century most Italian cities had grammar masters who received some pay from the city governments but derived most of their income from student fees. The government of Siena recruited teachers for arithmetic, law, and Latin and set their salaries. Some gave incentives to attract masters, such as promising them a monopoly of instruction, tax advantages or a rent-free house. By the fourteenth century most cities were hiring and paying the main salary of grammar teachers, although the students still paid fees.[16] Giovanni Villani claimed that by 1338 8,000–10,000 children were in school in Florence, a figure that suggests that most established citizens sent their children to school, including their daughters, although girls more often went to convents than to parish or mendicant schools.[17] Villani's figures have been criticised as inflated, for they suggest that some 37–45 per cent of the school-age (6–15) population of the city attended school; and since more boys would attend than girls, the rate among boys would must have been nine-tenths, which is higher than most modern cities before the twentieth century. The *catasto* of 1480, by which time lay literacy was undoubtedly more generalised than in Villani's time, suggests that only about 28 per cent of Florentine boys aged 10–13 were attending school. The rates ranged from the almost universal among boys from propertied families to much lower among the artisans, but many workers' children also received an education.[18]

Lay schools dominated at Florence. The merchants understood the need to be educated, and their family records (*ricordanze*) show a concern with education – especially that of boys – from the earliest years. Parents followed their children's education carefully. Youngsters usually began school at age 5–7, with the range tending to lower in the fifteenth century. Although girls were less invariably sent to school than boys, upper-class girls generally went at least long enough to learn to read and write. Primary education usually lasted between two and four years, depending on the pupil's aptitude and how old he was when he began. Boys learned to read notarial acts and do elementary arithmetic in the primary school years in preparation for business careers.

Secondary education was a mixture of technical and literary subjects.

15 De Ridder-Symoens, 'Sécularisation de l'enseignement', 727–9.
16 Denley, 'Governments and schools', 94–8.
17 Klapisch-Zuber, *Women, Family, and Ritual*, 109.
18 Grendler, *Schooling in Renaissance Italy*, 71–7, 102.

It began with traditional works such as Aesop's Fables, then passed to a generally classical curriculum, although it also included Italian vernacular works such as Dante Alighieri's *Divine Comedy* and Boccaccio's *Decameron*. The pupils also studied chivalric literature. Cicero was studied intensively, and the course culminated in Aristotle's *Politics* and *Nichomachean Ethics*. Instruction also included calculation. The basis of mathematical instruction was the 'Book of the Abacus' of Leonardo Fibonacci of Pisa (c. 1170–1240). Fibonacci's *abbaco* was actually a complex system of practical mathematics that was illustrated by problems peculiar to merchants. It did not even use an abacus – the treatise assumed that mathematical problems would be solved on paper or parchment – and it included arithmetic, algorism, algebra and geometry. The original or one of numerous abridgements was taught in virtually all Italian schools, even those of a basically literary bent. The schools also taught double-entry book-keeping occasionally in the fourteenth century and often in the fifteenth, and Francesco Pegolotti's *Practice of Commerce*, which concentrated on practical problems such as finances, exchange and transporting merchandise, was an important text.[19]

There is more evidence in Italy than in the north that merchants read literature for enjoyment and personal edification. Many merchants of Florence owned law books and the *Divine Comedy*, and some had medical books. Many had works in the vernacular, such as the *Cent Nouvelles Nouvelles*. Although the Latin works of Petrarch and Boccaccio were found in only the biggest libraries and in those of the greatest merchants, most merchants' libraries contained 'vulgar' (vernacular) histories.[20]

The universities added a new element to the cultural life of the cities. Oxford and Cambridge were unusual among universities in being in places that did not develop into major cities. Most of the sixty-five new universities of the period 1200–1500 were established places that were already major population centres, including Bologna, Padua, Naples, Toulouse, Salamanca, Huesca and Lisbon before 1300. Toulouse was established when the pope forbade the arts faculty at Paris to teach the works of Aristotle. In 1229 the city government openly advertised the attractions of the forbidden learning for the young, adding that 'plentiful food and cheap wine' were also available. These university cities were joined in the fourteenth century by Prague, Vienna, Cologne, Erfurt, Heidelberg, Kraków and Buda. The schools of Paris probably accounted for some 10 per cent of the population of the city in the late thirteenth century. Town–gown conflicts were serious and often violent

19   Bec, *Marchands écrivains*, 286–7, 385–7; Grendler, *Schooling in Renaissance Italy*, 307, 319.
20   Bec, *Marchands écrivains*, 384–400, 408–11.

in the university centres of northern Europe. The hostility of students to townspeople was a serious problem in English cities and may have stifled urban growth in both Oxford and Cambridge. Bologna, where the students were in a guild of foreigners, was the only Italian university city to experience much conflict between students and townspeople. At Siena and Padua the *popolo* regimes permitted the students to have the privileges but not the obligations of citizenship.[21]

The universities brought a mobile population into the cities, and many scions of the municipal aristocracy attended, mainly in the arts faculties unless they intended to take holy orders. Not until the fifteenth century is there significant evidence that university training, even in law, was obtained by many city councillors. After 1450 several conciliar families of Trier sent members to the universities, especially to study law. The city founded its own university in 1479. Virtually all preceded this with study in local schools, as the universities became more regional and less international. But magistrates' political careers were made by their family and occupational bonds, not by their education. The technical personnel – clerks, attorneys and accountants – who worked for a salary were another matter; many had university training by 1350, and these positions carried high prestige.[22]

The cities became increasingly involved in founding and endowing universities. The university of Florence was founded by the city in 1349, then refounded in 1385 under the patronage of the municipal chancellor, Coluccio Salutati. From 1386 medicine, arts and both canon and civil law were taught there. Florence remained faithful to the Aristotelian tradition until the arrival of Chrysoloros in 1396, then became a centre of humanist culture and the leading centre in the west for the study of Greek. Merchant families donated property to the university and were involved in its financial administration.[23] Townsmen participated in the creation of the university of Louvain in 1425. The government of Cologne founded its university in 1388, and Basel did so in 1459.[24]

The cities as cultural centres in the thirteenth century

Except for the university cities of Paris and Bologna, most cities were not great cultural centres in the thirteenth century. Their patriciates, many of them still of ministerial origin or in process of intermarrying

21   Hyde, 'Universities and cities in medieval Italy', 19; Ferruolo, *'Parisius-Paradisus'*, 35.
22   Matheus, *Trier*, 266–74, 291, 311.
23   Bec, *Marchands écrivains*, 362–3.
24   Maschke, *Städte und Menschen*, 79.

with ministerial families, patronised 'courtly' literature. In an age when the landed magnate element in most urban patriciates was losing power, the authors who were patronised by nobles, clergy and those who sought their approbation considered the merchant a vile moneygrubber who, concerned only with gain, could not comprehend virtue. The hero of the epic *Vivien's Youth* was the nephew of a nobleman, but he grew up, with his identity unknown, in a rich merchant household of Pamplona. His adoptive father wanted to train him as a merchant; but the virtuous Vivien rejected business in favour of horses and hunting, deplored his father's thriftiness and called his acquisitions usury. He exchanged the poor man's entire merchant inventory on the local market for hunting dogs and a falcon, then abandoned a merchant caravan to go off to fight the Saracens. The German *Hervis von Metz* has a similar theme: the father says that for his son Hervis to become a knight would be a waste. The son was sent to the Provins fair, where like Vivien he spent the proceeds of his father's cargo on horses and dogs.[25]

Arras, the banking capital of northern Europe and the centre of the court of Artois in the thirteenth century, is a conspicuous exception to the general situation of cultural backwardness in the northern cities before 1300. The plays composed there are especially interesting. The best known poet-dramatist was Adam de la Halle, whose *Jeu de la Feuillée* [*Play of the Bower*] begins with master Adam's decision to recommence his studies at Paris, which his marriage had interrupted. The last in the series is *Robin et Marion*, perhaps written by de la Halle but first performed at Arras in 1287 after his death. Arras had two literary societies: the Confraternity of the Ardents, probably founded in 1194, and the Peak (*Pui*), which sponsored literary competitions much earlier than they are found elsewhere. The great families of the city are often mentioned in records of the competitions, especially as judges or dedicatees.[26]

Most of the poetic output at Arras was courtly, for a patrician audience, but the plays and satires also appealed to the upwardly mobile burgesses. *Jeu de la Feuillée* included a satire of crookedness in city government, a fact that suggests that it may not have been written by de la Halle, who enjoyed the patronage of the banking families.

'Arras, Arras, city of chicanery
And of hatred and degeneracy,
You could hardly be so noble.

25 Peters, *Literatur in der Stadt*, 56.
26 Peters, *Literatur in der Stadt*, 63–6. London had a Peak with a chapel by 1273. It held a festival each year, at which a Prince was selected and compositions submitted by members competed for prizes. It is uncertain whether the Peak of London still existed in the late fourteenth century; Robertson, *Chaucer's London*, 87–8.

Everywhere they say that you ruin us,
And if God doesn't restore virtue
I don't know who will reestablish peace;
They love money too much.
Everyone is stupid in that town.
They're really in a mess there.
Good bye, more than 100,000 times,
Otherwise I'm going to hear the Evangel,
Because there they only know how to lie.'[27]

The Italian cities were more noteworthy for the decorative arts than for literature in the thirteenth century, but the level of lay literacy was already producing a consciousness of history there considerably earlier than in the north. The merchant Dino Compagni, author of a chronicle in the Tuscan vernacular of the party struggles in Florence at the turn of the fourteenth century, was several times consul of the guild of Por Santa Maria, prior and standard-bearer of justice. He began writing in 1310 of events that had commenced more than two decades earlier, and this distance explains some inaccuracies of detail. For a variety of reasons, notably the vicissitudes of his political career, his chronicle did not achieve the success or popularity that Villani's did later, but nothing of the type was produced in a city of northern Europe this early.[28] The example of Dante Alighieri (1265–1321), scion of a Guelf family of Florence and perhaps the greatest literary figure of medieval Europe, shows the level of learning in theology, cosmology, and vernacular and classical literature that could be attained in the schools of Florence, granted that this was no ordinary layman.

Lay culture in the fourteenth and fifteenth centuries

There is much more evidence after 1300 of northern cities as genuine literary centres, but as a continuation of the thirteenth-century tradition rather than as forerunners of what developed for example in the Italian cities during the Renaissance, and at Nuremberg and the national capitals in the fifteenth and sixteenth centuries. In the fourteenth century most literary activity was connected to the princely courts that happened to be in the cities, rather than being specifically urban.[29] This is true both of the royal and ducal residences of the north and of the cultural life fostered by the humanist princes of Italy; Italian humanism was more

27 Text quoted Lestocquoy, *Dynasties bourgeoises d'Arras*, 39.
28 Introduction by Bornstein to Compagni, *Chronicle*, xx–xxvii.
29 Peters, *Literatur in der Stadt*, 138.

a court culture and in Lauro Martines' words 'a program for the ruling classes' than has generally been admitted.[30]

The story of humanism in Italy and its expansion to the north is more a feature of the next period than of the Middle Ages, and an aspect of broader cultural currents than specifically of urban society. There was a booming art market among the middle economic echelons in Italy in the fifteenth century, a development that only spread to the north a century later.[31] The northern and Italian cities shared a common interest in linking their histories to classical themes. The humanists saw around them the physical ruins of an ancient civilisation and gloried in its literary traditions. Their attitude toward the classics was literary and limitative, but they did heighten the consciousness of their readers in history and promoted the search for a more realistic exploration of their cities' cultural origins. The 'civic humanists' patronised intellectuals who sought to link the city's past to the glories of Rome: republican Rome in the case of the Florence of the Medici, imperial Rome with the Sforza dukes of Milan. Civic humanism in the chancery of Coluccio Salutati, chancellor of Florence, was associated with the university there and a conscious cultivation of ancient Latin models of style in chancery practice. Soon thereafter the threat to Florence of Giangaleazzo Visconti of Milan led to a concentration on the works of Cicero, both for his Latin style and his self-conscious urban patriotism. The municipal bureaucracies hired large numbers of intellectuals who were steeped in the classics of antiquity. Humanist education generally began only in the late teens, after the young person had basic schooling and some business training. It was a classical Latin and Greek curriculum. Most humanists disdained anything in the vernacular language or particularly in medieval Latin as it had evolved; Salutati considered even Dante Alighieri a 'poet for shopkeepers' because of his use of the Tuscan vernacular. Humanism barely affected the lower orders or indeed most merchants, who read the vernacular but not Latin or Greek. Some of them mocked the humanists as *poseurs*.

Civic patriotism was important in the cities of the north as well. Until the mid-fourteenth century only Italian cities and a few in the French Midi tried seriously to develop a civic historiography. Around 1300 the legend was developed locally, perhaps inspired by its enormous wall, that ancient Toulouse had been a capital on the scale of Rome or Constantinople. Charlemagne was alleged to have built the wall of both City and bourg at Bourges.[32] The myth was spread that

---

30 Martines, *Power and Imagination*, 191.
31 Goldthwaite, *Wealth and the Demand for Art in Italy*, 47.
32 Le Goff, 'L'Apogée', 394.

Remus had founded Reims, and the city fathers also played on the fact of royal consecration in the city and the baptism of Clovis by Saint Rémi. Reims was one of the centres where the cult of St Louis originated. The royal coronation was the occasion of elaborate processions with civic corporations attired in uniforms replete with symbolism.[33] Tours tried to attach itself to Vergil's hero Turnus and even claimed to show his tomb.[34] When King Henry VII visited Bristol in 1486, he was greeted by a procession led by King Bremius, who according to Geoffrey of Monmouth was a Trojan; another legend has him as founder of Bristol. Since Henry claimed descent from Celtic kings, Bremius symbolised Bristol's earlier tie with the monarchy.[35]

Particularly in the German cities municipal chronicles were being kept in the city hall. They served to heighten civic pride and coincidentally to give an official version of controversial events. Some have multiple authors. Eighteen chronicles survive from the Hanse cities, about half each by clergy and laymen. A few family chronicles also survive, such as that of Jacob Lubbe of Dortmund and the Cologne chronicles that we have discussed.[36] The oldest surviving municipal chronicle in the German vernacular is the *Boich van der stede Colne* [*Book of the City of Cologne*], a rhymed history of Cologne written about 1270 by the city clerk Gottfried Hagen and intended to be read publicly. Rarely if ever were such municipal histories critical of the regimes. The patrician Circle Society of Lübeck had a chapel in the Franciscan convent; the Franciscan Detmar wrote a history of the city in 1385, after a conspiracy against the regime was discovered. His task was a revival of patrician consciousness of their own valour. The city clerk of Lübeck, Johann Rode, in 1347 began on assignment from the city government a chronicle going back to the origins of the city. Shortly after 1360 the clerk of the *Schöffen* of Magdeburg, Heinrich von Lammespringe, wrote his *Schöppenchronik*, also on their orders; in his introduction he asked them to have his successors as clerks continue the chronicle, and they did.[37]

Some city clerks contributed to the general intellectual life of their cities not just by writing chronicles, but also by didactic works. The best example is Jan Boendale, city clerk of Antwerp. Boendale died in 1351, evidently elderly, for he was already city clerk by 1312. His most important literary patron was Rogier van Leefdale, a Brabant noble. His

33 Desportes, *Reims*, 530–4.
34 Chevalier, 'Paysage urbain', 20 n. 17.
35 Sachs, 'Celebrating authority in Bristol', 195.
36 Sprandel, *Quellen zur Hanse-Geschichte*, 126–7.
37 Schmidt, 'Geschichtsschreibung', 627–31.

major work, *Brabantsche Yeesten* [Deeds of Brabant], is a history of the duchy based principally on the work of Jacob van Maerlant. It was begun in 1318 on commission from the alderman Willem Bornecalve of Antwerp. Other scholarly works are attributed to Boendale with less certainty. The *Yeesten* were not written on commission from the city; the work is a chronicle of the duchy, and nothing in it betrays urban outlook or information about city politics or conflicts. Curiously, Boendale's didactic poetry shows a more urban orientation, especially the religious encyclopedia entitled *Lekenspieghel* [Layman's Mirror], than do his historical works. *Lekenspieghel* has sections on 'town government' and discusses the behaviour of the city councillors. Boendale used Rome for lessons about the rise and fall of cities, then applied them to the Flemish cities, whose rulers he thought cared only for personal gain, forgetting the 'common good'.[38]

The family records (*ricordanze*) kept by the Italian merchants are justly famous. While the humanists emphasised the civic context of ancient Greece and Rome in language borrowed from the stylistic models of antiquity, the *ricordanze*, like the German civic chronicles, were written in the vernacular. Their theme was family, discussing in great detail their ancestors, marriage alliances, and in many cases business deals. Different styles are observable even within the same record, depending on whether the author was writing of family, morals, advice, business practice or the city. The style in some is clumsy, but in virtually all the sense of the past is more immediate than with the humanists; even their classical allusions seem less forced.[39]

The merchants' cultural interests were reflected in literary societies. The city governments patronised cultural activity. Most paid students from the cathedral and parish schools who gave dramatic presentations, usually after choosing a 'bishop' or 'king'. They also fostered chambers of rhetoric, which are found in the Flemish cities and many in France by the fifteenth century. Their members debated questions of public policy, theology and literary form and had competitions. The 'Company of the Jolly Sabre' of Toulouse, founded in 1323 by seven Toulouse troubadours, had yearly competitions starting on 1 May 1324. It took in new members in a format resembling the university course, with doctors, bachelors and a chancellor. Doctoral examinations included a poetry reading and a public lecture or disputation on a problem of poetic form. The new statutes of the Company, issued in 1356, became a model of chambers of rhetoric elsewhere. The city government contributed to

38 Peters, *Literatur in der Stadt*, 254–61.
39 Bec, *Marchands écrivains*, 50–4, 58, 72–3.

the grand prize, the golden violet, and provided a meeting place. Both the Toulouse society and the later German examples expressly considered themselves to be a rebirth of old courtly poetic tradition, not a new or specifically urban form.[40]

Some city fathers liked the jousting societies and tourneys that were favoured by the elite in imitation of the nobles. As early as 1292 the aldermen of Bruges sent several orators (*histriones*) to Arras to the candle ceremony of the jugglers' confraternity. Jousting societies were an important means of cementing group consciousness among the municipal elites, and most of them sponsored poetry or vocal competitions. Some German cities, where there was still open antagonism between ministerial nobles in the town and the burgesses, strictly prohibited jousting in the city. A Nuremberg statute of 1362 forbade citizens and their dependents from participating in tourneys.[41] But urban tourneys revived in Germany in the late Middle Ages as an aspect of the rapprochement of the rural nobility with the urban upper orders. It was probably more important in this respect than intermarriage, which cannot be documented in many cases. Duke Otto of Brunswick held five tournaments in Göttingen between 1368 and 1376.[42]

The fact that frequent jousts were held in the cities of Flanders and northern France shows the growing connection between the nobles and the urban upper strata. The burgesses imitated noble manners and customs as they tried to gain noble status through purchase and marriage. In 1284, when jousters of Lille and other cities were in Douai for the annual festival of the Rose, an altercation that began when Douai refused to provide opponents for the two Lille jousters escalated into war between the two cities. In 1331 Tournai held a festival of King Galahad. The magistrates invited other cities to send their jousters. The lower orders imitated the nobles, using sticks and barrels as swords and armour. The Epinette festival on Shrove Tuesday at Lille began with a king chosen from the patricians of the city, many of them of knightly rank. An investiture banquet was followed by a tournament at which contestants from throughout Flanders jousted.[43]

City governments often gave gratuities to players and other entertainers who accompanied a princely festival in the city, and some had their own pipers and trumpeters in uniform. A wandering piper was paid to hold a 'school' in Deventer in 1364, and Ypres in 1313 paid 'master Simon, master of the minstrels of the town, who keeps a school at Ypres

40   Peters, *Literatur in der Stadt*, 219–22.
41   Schultheiss, *Satzungen*, 211.
42   Rösener, 'Aspekte der Stadt-Land-Beziehungen', 677–9.
43   Vale, *Chivalric Society*, 26–33; Fouret, 'Epinette', 377–83.

at the fair'.[44] The musicians formed brotherhoods in some cities. Church choirs and city minstrels were the chief musical sources. Most cities had their own bands, generally with three or four members. At Arras they played in the belfry daily when the gates were opened and closed. Trumpeters performed at processions, proclamations and important or ritual occasions, such as the 'crying' of the excises. There were some guilds of master singers, but most musicians were amateurs, persons with other professions who had musical talent and might perform for the city. A carpenter was the town piper in Frankfurt am Main in 1425, a cobbler in 1440.[45] In 1321 a confraternity of St Julian of the Minstrels gave craft guild status to the Paris minstrels. Statutes forbade contracts through middlemen, sending substitutes to perform, cancelling engagements to accept jobs that were more lucrative and bargaining competitively against guild brothers. Apprentices could play only in taverns, not for weddings 'and other honest assemblies'. By the time a new set of statutes was issued in 1407, the guild had a hospice and more internal organisation, led by a 'king of the minstrels'. The king of France appointed the king; he was not elected from the membership. In turn, the king of the minstrels of Paris appointed kings of the guild in other cities.[46]

The guilds sponsored festivals on the days of their patron saints and are particularly notable for performing plays. Students participated in dramas, beginning with biblical stories and moving toward more secular topics. The 'Feasts of Fools' in many cities, in addition to providing a carnival atmosphere, became the occasions of dramatic presentations. Virtually all cities had at least one youth confraternity, called 'principality', 'realm' or more often 'abbey'. These organisations had an abbot, with priors representing the nobles, artisans and labourers and/or quarters of the city. The 'abbeys' included parish, street and quarter captaincies whose chiefs took fantastic titles. These youth societies united most single young men and some married men between the ages of 18 and 36.[47]

Developments in theatre were especially original in Paris. Before 1380 there was an annual *Mystery of the Passion* that used elaborate sets and machines, including a cannon that killed the man firing it in 1380. Different versions of the Passion were written in Paris. Arnoul Gréban, master of the chapel of Notre-Dame, wrote one on commission from a burgess of Abbeville that was widely performed after 1450. In 1402 a 'Confraternity of the Passion' received a royal charter. At about the

44 Peters, *Literatur in der Stadt*, 190–8, 212–14.
45 Salmen, 'Musizieren', 79.
46 Brown, 'Minstrels', 144.
47 Rossiaud, 'Crises', 532; Gonthier, *Cris de haine*, 174.

same time the clerks of the royal courts created a sort of theatrical company that performed widely. Secular plays were added, especially after 1450.[48] Theatrical presentations became a commonplace of city life in the late Middle Ages. Streets and squares were filled with entertainers much of the time. The more formal ones were the mystery plays, the Peaks or Chambers of Rhetoric, and the youth abbeys.

Not all entertainments in the cities were of this elevated type. Charivaris were common against people who remarried. Cuckolded husbands were paraded backward on an ass. Phallic corteges grossly insulted all girls of less than irreproachable behaviour. Valenciennes and the cities of Provence elected a Plain Jane annually, in ceremonies without bloodshed but replete with emotional cruelty.[49] Hangings and mutilations provided titillation for the masses. Amusements that were banned in the city of London were available at nearby Westminster, which had archery butts from the 1460s and bowling alleys by 1500.[50] By 1300 all bulls that were to be slaughtered by the butchers of Winchester had to be baited first to provide entertainment.[51] The anonymous Parisian diarist describes a spectacle in 1425:

> On the last Sunday in August an entertainment was given in the Hôtel known as the Hôtel d'Armagnac in the Rue St Honoré. Four blind men wearing armour and each carrying a club were put into an enclosure in which there was also a strong pig. They were to have it if they could kill it. They fought this strange battle, giving each other tremendous blows with the clubs – whenever they tried to get a good clout at the pig, they would hit each other, so that if they had not been wearing armour they would certainly have killed each other. On the Saturday before this Sunday the blind men were led through Paris wearing their armour, with a great banner in front of them with a picture of a pig on it. In front of this went a man bearing a drum.[52]

THE RENDING OF COMMUNITY: VIOLENCE IN THE LATER MEDIEVAL CITY

The coarse entertainments that were such a prominent part of the social environment in the late medieval city show that emotions were raw

48   Favier, *Paris 1380–1500*, 397–9.
49   Rossiaud, 'Crises', 557–68.
50   Rosser, 'London and Westminster', 54–5.
51   Keene, *Winchester*, 257.
52   *Journal Paris*, 205–6.

and close to the surface. More sophisticated government and elevated cultural expression in the cities was paradoxically accompanied by public grossness and by the mushrooming of endemic violence. Most people carried at the very least a small knife. The fact that the townsmen jousted and had archery contests and in England were required by the Assize of Arms to keep themselves in a state of readiness meant that they usually had weapons at hand. Citizens were expected to help themselves. Statutes of Cologne in the 1340s provided that 'if anyone by night or day, whether local or stranger, takes it upon himself to seize or strike anyone or get surety from anyone or to commit rape or force in the city of Cologne, whoever becomes aware of it is to run quickly with loud noise, break open his door and enter and hold the person who has done these deeds there'.[53] The statutes concerning illicit weapons were more honoured in the breach than in practice. Not a single court case in late medieval Zürich made an issue of violation of the municipal statutes forbidding bearing weapons.[54]

The problem was compounded by the presence of many transients in the cities, who had to have the means to defend themselves on the unpoliced roads while en route. A Nuremberg ordinance forbade sharp knives that could be concealed. Swords were forbidden to all except the prince's officials and the city *Schultheiss*, and those 'who eat their bread'. Other laws forbade citizens to conceal weapons in leggings or shoes.[55] The inns were disorderly. In many cities the hostellers took oaths and posted bond. A Lübeck *Bursprake* of 1350–1 required guests to leave their weapons in their inns. When guests arrived, the landlord, his housekeeper or personnel were to take possession of their knives and swords. Enforcement was by the innkeeper, not city police: if the guests refused to surrender their weapons, the hostellers were to refuse to provide food and drink to them or their horses until they complied. The innkeepers of Paris were required in 1407 to furnish the provost with the names of all guests.[56]

Given the amount of leisure that irregular employment imposed on so many, taverns did a thriving business and were a problem for public order. Since the water was polluted and unrefrigerated milk spoiled rapidly – most milk was consumed as cheese – much of the population of the medieval cities drank low-grade fermented beverages most of the time. In virtually all cities the amount of beer that was charged the

303

excise suggests a high level of consumption.[57] Per capita consumption of wine rose sharply at Ghent in the late fourteenth century; figures for imported wine suggest an adult consumption of 102 litres per capita, although the amount of the drink that was re-exported cannot be measured and would have lowered this figure.[58] The tavernkeepers were strictly regulated in principle, although this was hard in the case of those on church immunities. Most meetings and many entertainments, insofar as they were not in the open air or in guildhalls, were held in taverns and the homes of innkeepers. Avignon had sixty-six taverns in the fourteenth century, Bruges fifty-four in 1441, Rouen and Ypres about sixty each. Paris had at least 200 professional taverners and many others for whom tavernkeeping was part-time. Even Winchester, which had a population of no more than 5,000, had eighty-two drinking places in 1417: ten wine taverns, nine inns, twenty-seven alehouses and thirty-six establishments run by brewers. By contrast, Nottingham in the 1370s had at least 116 winesellers. London in 1309 had 354 taverns and 1,334 brewers.[59]

Gambling also seems to have been ubiquitous, much of it in taverns. Nuremberg fined any innkeeper 'who has games in his house after bells, whether with wine or not, and whoever serves wine in his house or before his gate after bells must provide light'. Burgesses were forbidden to gamble 'either in the countryside or in the city' for more than 60 Heller for one day and night but could start again the next day.[60] Florence had so many gambling dens that in some places the tables blocked street access. In the early fifteenth century the authorities broke a neighbourhood gambling ring organised by private persons in wine shops and homes. One priest who was a compulsive gambler tried to bribe the police, then was subjected to extortion. Ypres forbade gambling houses, but the count's bailiff refused to enforce the ban and even became the partner of several aldermen who operated a casino on the town square. In 1408 the council, *Schöffen* and chief court of Cologne confirmed a prior Morningspeech forbidding 'nocturnal activity' at a city gate and at other cabarets. An innkeeper who violated this by arranging dice games at night at the gate was exiled along with the gamblers.[61]

Although the magistrates in some cities forbade gambling outright, others made income from it. Mainz had a municipal casino, the 'Hot

57 Dyer, *Standards of living*, 197.
58 Nicholas, *Metamorphosis*, 228.
59 Gonthier, *Cris de haine*, 98; Rossiaud, 'Crises', 551; Favier, *Paris 1380–1500*, 310; Keene, *Medieval Winchester*, 273–7; Schofield, *Medieval London Houses*, 54.
60 Gonthier, *Cris de haine*, 98; Rossiaud, 'Crises', 551; Favier, *Paris 1380–1500*, 310; Schultheiss, *Satzungen*, 66–7, 117.
61 Brucker, 'Florentine *popolo minuto*', 168–9; Brucker, *Society of Renaissance Florence*, 183–9; Nicholas, *Medieval Flanders*, 343; Huiskes, *Beschlüsse Köln*, 79.

Stone' [Heisse Stein], which it leased to a five-person syndicate. The name was used elsewhere, for the Rhineland cities seem to have had a common standard of vice similar to that found in statutes and guild regulations: a clause in a regulation of 1425 cautioned the magistrates about disorder, forbade loaded dice and specified that the standard weight and sized dice were those used at the Hot Stone at Frankfurt. Gambling in the city and ban mile was limited to the official Hot Stone except at private parties in the home for the owner and his friends and guests and at wedding parties. The leaseholder was to stand at the entrance of the Hot Stone to make sure that no long knives or other dangerous weapons were brought in. Interestingly, ecclesiastical immunities were also exempt from the city monopoly on gambling.[62]

Weddings, funerals and even baptisms gave rise to disorder. Families spent immense sums on weddings. Although authorities in many cities tried to limit the size of the parties, those of Nuremberg were especially strict. Statutes forbade more than eight people in addition to the parents to attend baptisms. Around 1340 the magistrates declared that 'no one may have a public wedding in the future, and furthermore there is to be no more eating or dancing, morning or night. A man or woman may invite his or her friends two weeks later, if he or she wishes'. The actual wedding party was limited to six men and six women, including those accompanying the bride and groom to the church.[63] Zürich allowed a maximum of ten female servants at weddings. In 1381 the city council condemned Heinric Hagnouwer, dean of the saffron importers' guild and a member of the council itself that year, because he and his bride had invited more than twice this number of guests to their wedding.[64] Italian weddings were also disorderly, although evidently less so than French. City statutes prohibited nocturnal noise and music at marriages, perhaps not only to avoid disorder but also to hinder lineage-imperilling liaisons. This was apparently directed initially at all brides, although in the fifteenth century it was limited to widows. In Piedmont and France young people led charivaris, but there is no indication of this in central Italy.[65]

City governments tried to keep people from going about unnecessarily at night, when most crime seems to have occurred. The bell sounded a curfew, usually at sunset, and the gates and taverns were closed.[66] Guild or ward patrols provided a night watch and stopped persons who were out without authorisation, but the numbers of peacekeepers were

---

62 Keutgen, *Urkunden*, 459–61.
63 Schultheiss, *Satzungen*, 148, 220.
64 Burghartz, *Leib, Ehre und Gut*, 109, 254.
65 Klapisch-Zuber, *Women, Family, and Ritual*, 262–77.
66 Hanawalt, *Growing Up in Medieval London*, 30.

hopelessly inadequate to keep order. Except during wartime and periods of political strife, Ghent usually had about forty sergeants and 'fellows', together with a guild watch of seventeen and two night watchmen stationed in the centrally located church tower of St Nicholas to watch for illicit lights. The police force dropped to about twenty-five after 1360 as conditions became more peaceful.[67] Paris had two hundred sergeants attached to the Chatelet in the early fourteenth century, rising to four hundred foot and horse by 1400. The night watch was the responsibility of the crafts. Sixty guards went around each night, on a rotating basis, supplemented by a royal guard and foot soldiers. Given the differences in size between Ghent and Paris, the two were probably policed with comparable effectiveness.[68]

Patterns and extent of urban violence

Enforcement and court records survive for the last two medieval centuries that can give some approximation of the nature and incidence of crime. Most violence was committed by males against males. Female criminality in the cities was very low. At Zürich 97 per cent of the perpetrators and 86 per cent of the victims of crime were males, and both parties were male in 83 per cent of the cases. Although tax lists show twice as many maids as male servants at Zürich in the late fourteenth century, only thirty-two of the 353 servants who appeared before the city court were maids. The women of Ghent were somewhat less retiring, but there too male criminality dominated. Between 1350 and 1380, 699 men were killed in Ghent but only twenty-six women. Women were much more involved as both victims and perpetrators in deeds of petty violence and the use of foul language from which violence might escalate. Women were involved in nearly one-third of the cases, but nearly three-fifths of these involve women as victims of aggression by males or other women. Women rarely attacked men except verbally; but while 158 females were punished for actionable language about a man, only sixty men slandered a woman. At Zürich insults were a factor in 14 per cent of the cases involving men, 38 per cent with women. With men, the most common insults were against their honesty; with women they usually concerned sexual behaviour. When men were accused of sexual offences, it was rarely adultery or fornication but more often sodomy or sometimes incest.[69]

67 Nicholas, 'Crime and punishment', 308–9; Nicholas, 'Governance', 254–5.
68 Geremek, *Margins of Society*, 23–8.
69 Burghartz, *Leib, Ehre und Gut*, 69–71, 82, 126–34, 99–100; Nicholas, *Domestic Life*, 18–21.

Insult was much more significant in the honour-driven society of the Middle Ages than now. It included words, gestures and even attitudes. More than with deeds of violence, the punishment often hinged on the situations and status of the persons involved; what was actionable in one case might not be in another.[70] An insult often preceded actual violence. There was often a theatrical element, with the intent to defame one's antagonist before an audience, which was exaggerated by the fact that most buildings were open, and many activities that are now done indoors had to be conducted outside.[71] At Nuremberg if a city official was present at a fight and ruled that the victim had brought it upon himself with bad language, the fine went to the city rather than to the injured party. Actionable foul language included blasphemy. Nuremberg forbade swearing and cursing.

> People should leave off all loose practice with words. And specifically, they [the magistrates] forbid that in the future anyone swear by God's body, by his head, his heart, his blood, and also by his other body parts, or by other creatures whom people call 'God' mockingly, nor by the new oaths that are now common in this world.

Citizens were required to report cursing to the magistrates, and the 'sworn innkeepers' were to report on their guests.[72]

The city councils had time only for the most important or politically sensitive actions. All cities had lower jurisdictions that handled less serious infractions, and most of their records have not survived. Most subordinate jurisdictions were market-, neighbourhood- or parish-based, as in the English frankpledge system, which bound neighbours to vouch for one another. At Florence each parish council chose four headmen from the *popolo* for six-month terms. Two-thirds of the assaults and one-third of the murders judged by the *podestà*'s court between 1343 and 1345 were brought there by the headmen, whose role declined thereafter.[73] Much violence was unreported. In 1353 Mattheus de Mets of Ghent threw a goblet of wine in the face of another man, then agreed to make whatever atonement the bystanders suggested. The case only reached the aldermen's court because, disregarding their ruling, he had pursued the other man and stabbed him.[74]

The records are also distorted downward in cities where guild courts,

70 Burghartz, *Leib, Ehre und Gut*, 125–6.
71 Gonthier, *Cris de haine*, 132; Gauvard, 'Criminalité parisienne', 362.
72 Schultheiss, *Satzungen*, 43–4, 161.
73 Gonthier *Cris de haine*, 164.
74 Nicholas, 'Crime and punishment', 1166–7.

few of whose records survive, were strong enough to judge property and personal crimes involving their own members. The guild courts of Zürich were probably more important in the daily life of the citizens than those of the city. A text of 1382 required

> that in their guild they swear to the saints when they choose a master that in all quarrels that they have among themselves they will only seek justice from the master, except in serious cases in which the guild does not have the right to judge, and when a complaint is not judged by the master within a week of being filed, the plaintiff can complain where he wishes.[75]

Venice was exceptional. The Council of Ten controlled the city with vague powers over everything from violence to potentially seditious speech, confraternities (which might be revolutionary) and meetings. The patrols of the Ten amounted to a secret police. They could apprehend, try and execute immediately. Between the patrols in the Sixths, the Five of the Peace and the Lords of the Night there were about 310 on patrol, about one per 250 citizens. This seems to have been sufficient to stop most violence, for in 1382 the numbers were reduced.[76]

Punishments

Most felonies were punishable by execution or mutilation. Actual punishments for crime ranged from the gruesome and symbolic to the relatively mild. Pardons or remission of penalty were common, usually for a fee, and modern students are struck by the lack of consistency in the application of the law; for brutal crimes often received little punishment, while less violent deeds were sometimes corrected gruesomely.

Except at Venice, imprisonment was generally not used except for detention awaiting trial. Prisoners in many cities paid their own expenses directly to the jailor or his wife, who was a virtual innkeeper. In Paris those who could not pay or who had no family to pay for them went to the dungeon, and even that cost a small amount.[77] Prisoners of high birth were not forced to mingle with commoners at Siena and had even servants and guests for overnight visits. It was common during religious festivals at Siena to issue wholesale pardons. Most prisoners were debtors, persons awaiting trial and persons sentenced to fines but unable to raise

---

75 Burghartz, *Leib, Ehre und Gut*, 37, 231.
76 Ruggiero, *Violence*, 7–17.
77 Nicholas, 'Crime and punishment', 324–5; Ruggiero, *Violence*, 49; Geremek, *Margins of Society*, 17–18.

the money. Exile/outlawry was used both for contumacy (failure to appear for trial) and as punishment for violent deeds, but the cities realised substantial incomes from remitting banishment for a fee; there were six thousand such cases between 1243 and 1256 at Siena alone. By the early fourteenth century such remissions generally took effect only if the exile had made peace with the injured party or his heirs. Ghent lost significant revenues in 1415 when the magistrates stopped remitting banishments.[78]

Petty violence did not present much of a threat to social norms and accordingly was handled summarily. When a trial resulted in conviction for a serious offence, however, punishment was often symbolic and exemplary. The gates and public squares of most cities were festooned with the amputated body parts of convicted miscreants, most often their heads. Hangings and gruesome mutilations were public spectacles, often accompanied by processions to the place of execution. Political executions usually included the condemned person wearing his family or party insignia to his fate.[79] The authorities also used exemplary punishments, but of a less bloody nature, for commercial fraud. Bakers who sold bread that was too light were dragged through the streets on a hurdle behind a horse. Butchers who sold spoiled meat and others who made substandard goods or falsified weights or measures were put in the stocks.[80]

Apprehending and punishing criminals continued to be complicated by overlapping jurisdictions in the city. The town lord or territorial prince usually had gendarmes and sometimes a court in addition to the city officials. Although relations between the two were generally correct, particularly when the city did not have the right of blood justice, there was sometimes competition. In Ghent the Law Aldermen were a criminal tribunal, trying some cases and ordering arbitration in others, while the lower bench handled misdemeanours and breaches of the peace in massive trial days several times a year. The bailiff of the count of Flanders had the unfortunate habit of imprisoning persons on charges that would not stand up in court, then holding them until they paid a monetary 'composition'. Composition was also used by accused persons who wanted to avoid a trial in which they would presumably be convicted. The punishments were most often pilgrimages for those who started fights, but everyone had to pay monetary compensation to their antagonists for physical injury.[81]

78 Waley, *Siena*, 68–70; Boone, *Geld en Macht*, 195.
79 Cohen, 'Execution ritual', 285–96.
80 Robertson, *Chaucer's London*, 105.
81 Nicholas, 'Crime and punishment', 289–334. Valenciennes had separate justices of the peace to hear lesser cases; Platelle, *Histoire de Valenciennes*, 64.

Arbitration

Given the severity of punishment if convicted in court, most persons whose misdeeds were not political but rather concerned other individuals either resorted to feuds, which escalated the violence, or accepted arbitration. Cases handled by arbitration, the vast majority in many cities, were civil in nature.[82] Thus a homicide that came to trial before the bailiff of Ghent was a criminal action for which the punishment was death; but the 751 homicides handled by arbitration between 1351 and 1379 were private offences in which the guilty party paid a blood price to the deceased's family but nothing to the city government. When feuding parties at Nuremberg would not make peace, two councillors or *Schöffen* had the right to impose peace, taking bond from the principals; if the bond was forfeited through renewed violence, the city had jurisdiction.[83]

Since arbitration generally imposed less severe penalties than court trials, the magistrates encouraged it, and most accused parties were willing. While Ghent may represent an extreme case, only after 1381 did more than a slight majority of cases coming before the city council at Zürich result even in a full inquiry. The number of cases that the city prosecuted as offences against public order without a private complaint being raised was rising after the 1380s. The effacement of private complaint by state prosecution becomes much clearer in the fifteenth century, and the proportion of cases in which the city ordered punishment as opposed to recommending arbitration had risen to nearly four-fifths at Zürich by the 1480s.[84]

Most reported crimes appear to have been against persons rather than property, although the record is distorted by some property crimes being subsumed in the records by their accompanying violence, such as armed robbery. This is especially striking in view of the fact that clothing had no pockets. People carried money in a bag hanging from the belt or occasionally around the neck, making the work of 'cutpurses' easy. Itinerant peddlers and second-hand dealers were especially good fronts for stolen property. The used clothing dealers of Paris, many of them wandering peddlars, were enjoined from buying from thieves and lepers or buying ecclesiastical vestments or ornaments.[85]

82 Burghartz, *Leib, Ehre und Gut*, 9, 75.
83 Nicholas, *Domestic Life*, 18–19; Nicholas, 'Crime and punishment', 289–90; Schultheiss, *Satzungen*, 50–1. Whether this makes it appropriate to speak of a 'conflict culture' in which the municipal courts were caught between punishment and conflict resolution is problematical. For this view see Burghartz, *Leib, Ehre und Gut*, 9–16.
84 Burghartz, *Leib, Ehre und Gut*, 61–8.
85 Geremek, *Margins of Society*, 107–8, 264–7.

Education, Culture and Community

The Châtelet of Paris, where property crimes were two-thirds of the criminal cases in the late 1380s, is the only significant exception to the rule that the incidence of violence against persons was higher than that of property crime. Letters of pardon given by Charles VI's government provide a different perspective, for fights and homicides account for over half the pardons and theft one-quarter. Records from seigniorial jurisdictions in and around Paris make the city conform more closely to the pattern found elsewhere, with brawls and petty fighting involved in most actions and theft relatively unimportant. The two-decade total for 1401–20 from the Temple shows 197 brawls among 257 cases, against only eighteen robberies. The register of 1404–6 of the Chapel of Notre-Dame, on the Île de la Cité, has many cases involving Seine boatmen and workers in the port: fighting accounted for over half the cases, games of chance one-fifth, and theft only one-twentieth.[86] Property crimes and fraud made up no more than 18 per cent of the cases in the courts of Zürich in any given year, even if breaking and entering and arson are counted as property crimes, as compared with two-thirds in the modern city.[87]

The social pattern of urban violence

Information about the profession or economic standing of perpetrators of violence is too sketchy to permit statistically valid conclusions for most cities. University students were disorderly, and the problems of local authorities in dealing with them were compounded by the fact that they were entitled to judgement as clerks by the ecclesiastical arm. University closes were the scenes of pitched battles. Some streets such as the Grand-Pré-aux-Clercs at Paris were virtually abandoned to student violence by the city government. In 1435 the rumour spread in Heidelberg that the students were going to burn the town.[88] The homicide rate in late medieval Oxford was quintuple that of most modern American cities, and the killings occurred mainly in student-dominated areas. Virtually all victims were adult males of low social standing. The incidence of violent crime in other English cities was less than half that of Oxford. Interestingly, however, only eleven of the thirty-six persons convicted for homicide in the fourteenth century were in holy orders. Thus, although crime rates were high overall, the university population may not have

86 Gauvard, 'Criminalité parisienne', 361; Geremek, Margins of Society, 56–62.
87 Burghartz, Leib, Ehre und Gut, 73–5, 155–63; Cohn, 'Criminality', 211–33.
88 Gonthier, Cris de haine, 101; Geremek, Margins of Society, 35–6; Moraw, 'Heidelberg Universität', 543.

been responsible for a statistically unreasonable amount of homicide. 'Strangers' were more often accused.[89]

Ports as well as university cities were notorious for violence. More than one-third of the defendants in homicide cases in Venice in the 1360s and more than half those in thefts were foreigners and marginals such as prostitutes and dockworkers.[90] The city fathers feared immigrants. Most crime recorded at the Châtelet in Paris was committed by migrants and marginals, and the same appears to have been true in Brescia in the early fifteenth century. Since exiles from one city were usually not received in others, they were condemned to perpetual vagabondage, increasing the already large floating population, unless they could slip into a city, as many undoubtedly did.[91] In Ghent most violence was family-based and thus between persons who knew one another. Antagonism between persons of different trades is rarely recorded unless there was a political dimension, such as between weavers and fullers. Fights between members of the same guild are at least as frequent as those between persons of demonstrably different economic or political ranks.

The question naturally arises of whether there was a link between urban poverty and violent crime. In both the north and Italy most violent crime seems to have been perpetrated by the magnates and the poorest inhabitants. The middle classes, the merchants and the more substantial craftspeople, were more placid.[92] Comparing lists of taxpayers and office-holders of Zürich with persons appearing in court between 1376 and 1385 confirms this: except for numerous references to the young, there is no clear link of social standing, profession or property with propensity to crime. The two-thirds of the taxpayers paying the lowest taxes accounted for only 38 per cent of persons appearing before the court. The richest payers are thus much over-represented, which is especially notable since most actions concerned violence, not crimes against property.[93]

Thus, granted that violence by the lower orders often did not reach the courts whose records have survived, there are serious problems with a social 'class' interpretation of violence. Not all labourers took the same side even in political conflicts; and while the middle class was divided, the rich and their clients, the poor, had some community of political interest. Although 'class' divisions become clearer in the fifteenth and sixteenth centuries, they are not enough to explain violence. Except for the vendettas of the upper orders, most violence was between persons

89   Hammer, 'Patterns of homicide', 3–23.
90   Chojnacki, 'Crime in Venetian state', 203–5, 215–16.
91   Burghartz, *Leib, Ehre und Gut*, 19; Geremek, *Margins of Society*, 21.
92   Brucker, 'Florentine *popolo minuto*', 16.
93   Burghartz, *Leib, Ehre und Gut*, 101–7.

of the same social level, occurring spontaneously in chance encounters and without premeditation. Participants simply explained it by 'choler' that had deprived them temporarily of their senses.[94]

Vendettas and the crisis of public order

Aristocratic party conflicts including extended clienteles probably occasioned more disorder in the larger cities than economic violence. The Venetian nobles had little respect for the laws and often mauled bailiffs and other law enforcement officials and flouted judicial verdicts, but they were punished for their crimes. Yet, although the wealthy paid higher fines than the poor for some misdeeds, the authorities saw greater danger in attacks on prominent persons by those outside the elite than when those of the same group fought. When the Venetian nobles attacked officers of the city, they were punished less severely than artisans for the same crime. A commoner went to prison for attacking a guard of the night watch, while a noble paid a small fine; for it was a revolutionary act for the former, defence of honour and style of life for the latter. The Venetian nobles were involved in numerous speech crimes; for insults were more threatening to the upper orders than to the lower. They were also implicated in many rapes. Given that the courts were staffed by nobles, murder and rape cases were almost certainly underreported. But under-reporting worked both ways; since speech crimes involving the lower orders were considered unthreatening, the authorities generally did not bother with them.[95]

Defence of family honour was the motive in vendettas, not economic rivalry. Most involved assassinations and stealth. At Ghent a contract to commit premeditated murder was legally enforceable in the courts.[96] Party members often wore badges or distinctive clothing so that members could identify one another, particularly in periods of stress.[97] The blood feud was legally recognised in many city law codes, which required the parties to declare the feud formally. The statutes of the *podestà* of Florence prohibited applying the Ordinances of Justice against men pursuing a 'lawful' vendetta, which meant limiting vengeance to the offender as long as he was alive and thereafter to relatives not more distant than fourth cousins. Similar laws are found in most Italian cities. Some city governments did take feeble action against feuds. A statute

---

94 Chojnacki, 'Crime, punishment', 214; Gonthier, *Cris de haine*, 18, 111.

95 Gonthier, *Cris de haine*, 200, 212; Chojnacki, 'Crime in Venetian state', 194–5, 201; Ruggiero, *Violence*, 66–75, 96.

96 Nicholas, 'Crime and punishment', 1168–73.

97 Thompson, *Paris Under English Rule*, 172; Nicholas, *van Arteveldes*, 165.

of Siena in 1238 made the penalty for a retaliatory deed against someone other than the actual perpetrator of the first act triple what the punishment would have been otherwise. Yet in Siena vendettas were encouraged by the fact that anyone known to have 'capital enemies' could get permission from the city to bear 'defensive' weapons.[98]

The blood feuds of leading families had always been a concern for Italian urban magistrates, and perhaps for those of the north, but we have much more evidence for this in the northern cities in the fourteenth and fifteenth centuries than before. The feuds might last for several generations and involve collateral kin and retainers of the principal parties. Occasionally the city government intervened, usually to order a truce followed by arbitration and rarely to bring a miscreant to trial. Every homicide had to be atoned to the deceased's family or lord. The murder of a retainer or even a tenant of a prominent burgess might unleash a feud. Personal injuries were compensated by money, and the amounts on each side might cancel out and a balance be drawn at the end, payable by the chief of the extended family. The blood price for the dead victim was fixed by arbitration, with persons of high standing commanding a higher price than their retainers. It was divided by fixed principles among the deceased's male kin. Innocent relatives of a murderer were expected to help him pay for his deeds. Persons seeking vengeance might mistakenly attack persons who shared a name but no blood relation with their antagonist; but in such cases the burden of proof was on the person claiming his innocence – he not only had to prove his lack of involvement in the deed, but also that he was no blood relation to the principal. Failure to do this opened him both to personal sanctions by the kindred and in some cases criminal prosecution by the city government.[99]

The lineages maintained armies of retainers. Violence often had its roots in rural environments, then spilled over into the city, where it was continued in an environment familiar to the perpetrators. But the traffic in criminals was two-way: exiles from the cities turned their suburbs into war zones.[100] In 1373 a brawl erupted between gangs led by wealthy rival butcher, brewer and dyer families of Ghent at a wedding in the nearby village of Eeklo, where the Ghent aristocrats had property interests and family branches.[101] The feuds were not limited to the upper orders. Two coopers of Cologne who swore a vendetta against a shoemaker were forbidden to involve the council or other officials of the

98 Larner, *Age of Dante and Petrarch*, 123; Waley, *Siena*, 66.
99 Nicholas, 'Crime and punishment', 1141–76.
100 Gauvard, 'Violence citadine', 1115–17.
101 Nicholas, 'Marriage and the meat hall', 27–48.

city in their hostilities and had to stay beyond 25 miles of the city or be executed without trial.[102]

The children, other blood heirs, widows and even the heirs of a late wife were bound to help pay blood prices or suffer the vendetta. The most famous of these is the case of the van Artevelde family of Ghent (see Chapter 4). James van Artevelde was killed in a riot in 1345, evidently lured to his death by personal enemies in the city government. When his sons were repatriated in 1361 after a twelve-year exile, the eldest immediately murdered the aldermen of 1345 whom he held responsible. Their kinsmen evidently agreed, for they demanded no blood price. The scene then shifted to van Artevelde properties in the polder village of Weert, where they crossed swords with other families of Ghent who had holdings there and had been involved in the deed of 1345 at Ghent. James van Artevelde the younger was killed in 1370 at Weert. But when Philip van Artevelde, the youngest son, became captain of Ghent in late 1381, he gained access to city records from 1345 that showed him that the conspiracy against his father had been much broader than he and his brothers had realised. Although the principals of 1345 were long dead, Philip van Artevelde hunted down and killed those of their eldest sons who had not left Ghent immediately when he took power. Only after his family's honour had been redeemed did he turn his attention to public policy.[103]

The argument has been made that homicide rates in England were lower in the cities than the rural areas because so much rural violence was kin-based, while immigrants to the cities were living apart from their relatives. Yet the largest cities at least fit the continental pattern of vendetta. London factions in 1228 pitted the Bukerel, Bat and Tovy families against the Juvenal, Lambert and FitzMary. A feud between Ralph Crepyn, the first Common Clerk of London and a sometime alderman, and the goldsmith Laurence Duket is perhaps indicative, if with unusual ramifications. Duket had killed a man and turned to Crepyn for aid; Crepyn had obtained a pardon for him but had allegedly cheated him of some money. Part of the problem may have been that Duket's sister had sold buildings to Crepyn in 1273. In 1284 Duket seriously wounded Crepyn, then sought sanctuary in the church of St Mary le Bow. Crepyn's supporters violated the sanctuary and tortured and hanged Duket there. In turn seven of them were drawn and hanged. Others saved themselves from execution by pleading benefit of clergy.[104]

102 Huiskes, *Beschlüsse Köln*, 110.
103 Nicholas, *Domestic Life*, 198–206 and particularly Nicholas, *van Arteveldes*.
104 Given, *Society and Homicide*, 175–7, 184–5. This incident has been the subject of a historical novel: P. C. Doherty, *Satan in St Mary's* (New York: St. Martin's Press, 1986).

THE RESTORATION OF COMMUNITY: PROCESSIONS, DISPLAY AND CIVIC PATRIOTISM IN THE LATER MIDDLE AGES

If violence rent the civic fabric apart, civic ceremony helped to restore it. All cities had numerous festivals and processions in the late Middle Ages. Venice's famous patriotic celebrations were conducted throughout the year. The visit of Pope Alexander III to Venice in 1177, in which he is supposed to have bestowed symbols of Venice's autonomy on the doge, was a major civic occurrence. Saints' days, particularly that of St Mark, the patron of the city, were always observed with highly symbolic festivals. The two high points of the year were the celebration on 25 June of the translation of the relics of St Mark to Venice, which was claimed to have occurred in the ninth century; and the famous marriage of Venice with the sea. This ceremony, on Ascension Day, may go back to a blessing of the Adriatic around 1000 and definitely existed by 1267. It began with Mass chanted in St Mark's; then the high civic officials, led by the doge, were rowed onto the lagoon, accompanied by bannered companies, choirs and the pealing of church and monastery bells. At the point where the lagoon emptied into the Adriatic the patriarch of Castello emptied a large vessel of holy water into the lagoon, and the doge dropped his gold ring into the sea and repeated 'We espouse thee, O sea, as a sign of true and perpetual dominion'. Prayers and banqueting then continued into the evening.[105]

Although many civic ceremonies were observances of religious holidays, others were locally based and essentially secular. Even religious ceremonies took on secular overtones, inculcating notions of hierarchy and fostering the preservation of the existing political order. The festival of the patron saint of the city was celebrated with great pomp, and in Tuscany and Umbria residents of the *contado* were often required to attend. The requirement to participate in the city's ceremonies was sometimes included in acts of submission of the nobles, and *contado* communities had to send offerings and delegations of marchers. The civic cult thus became an aspect of the domination of the *contado* by the city. References to resistance by *contadini* to the city cults become more frequent in the fifteenth century.[106]

Most cities had Corpus Christi Day processions. The body in the form of the Host at the Mass was carried through the town in processions attended by various groups, including guildsmen dressed in their

105 Muir, *Civic Ritual*, 77–8, 119–34, with quotation 122.
106 Chittolini, 'Civic religion and the countryside', 69–78.

uniforms, but symbols transferred the specific identity from Christ to the body social of the community. Whatever differences of personality, family rivalry, economic situation or guild affiliation might divide members of the community, they came together as one body in the procession honouring Christ's body.[107]

The 'community' that was being affirmed in these processions consisted of persons with some financial stake in civic life, who had paid fees and registrations for a corporate identity, notably members of the guilds, both occupational and civic. Since craft membership was the prerequisite of the freedom in England, the Corpus Christi processions took in the entire citizenry. Women were thus excluded from the community unless married to a freeman (hence marriages of guildsmen had to be attended by the entire membership) or the widow of one (hence the importance of funerals as a symbolic transfer of community identity). The order of precedence of the guilds in the Corpus Christi and Midsummer processions at Coventry was fixed in 1445, not according to economic criteria but rather on the basis of the extent of their participation in civil officeholding. Since a parliamentary statute banned the foodmongers from holding public office unless they gave up their occupation, they were last in order of precedence, despite their wealth. Accordingly, they began the procession, which culminated in the more elaborate tableaux and presentations of the prestigious guilds, the dyers, drapers, and finally the mercers. Yet the hierarchy that was reified in the Corpus Christi order was bridged by other ceremonies that emphasised social integration: most parish celebrations were without social barriers, and Coventry celebrated a Hock Tuesday play in which the sexes reversed their stereotypical roles.[108]

The guild processions were often accompanied by pageants and plays that were performed as the wagons moved through the city. The first detailed account of the fifty-one Corpus Christi plays at York is from 1415, but they were being given by 1376 and probably much earlier. Staging them was burdensome, and some crafts featured joint productions. Old and New Testament tableaux were featured. The cities used plays to entertain visitors. Richard II attended the Corpus Christi procession at York in 1397, and Richard III the Creed cycle in 1483. The plays brought tourists, pilgrims and considerable business for local merchants.[109] Recent work has attributed details of the English urban theatrical tradition of the late Middle Ages to the contacts of English merchants with the Burgundian Netherlands. Members of the York

107 James, 'Ritual, drama and social body', 4–5, 10–11.
108 Phythian-Adams, 'Ceremony and the citizen', 57–85.
109 Kermode, 'Merchants', 35.

mercers' guild who are known from commercial records to have been active in trade at Bruges and other cities and at the Low Country fairs were also involved in staging the plays. The city government, which was dominated by the mercers, controlled the processions and decided on what scenes would be handled by which guilds. The English cycles borrowed Dutch phraseology and *topoi*, sometimes out of context. Several English cities had processions similar to the *ommegange* (circuits) of the Low Countries, and the English Everyman appears only in the sixteenth century, considerably later than the Dutch *Elckerlijc*. The urban cultural symbiosis that was developing in the late Middle Ages can hardly be demonstrated more convincingly.[110]

But the Corpus Christi plays, in addition to inculcating notions of community, also spawned conflict and lawsuits over orders of precedence and the question of which guild would stage which scene in plays that were performed jointly. Many guilds required members to pay a special fee to defray costs of the guild's play, and they had to attend the procession attired in the guild's elaborate livery. This caused complaints from the poorer elements, but their grumbling took second place in the eyes of the corporate fathers to a question of the honour of the guild in relation to the entire social body. The York cycle was associated at first with processions of city officials and some crafts to the minster and St Leonard's hospital; but after fights erupted between carpenters and cordwainers in 1419, the plays were confined to Corpus Christi Day followed by the procession the next day.[111] The processions of the confraternity of St George at Norwich assumed political symbolism that divided the community in the 1430s and 1440s over Thomas Wetherby, a controversial mayor who was a member of the guild. In 1452 Wetherby's opponents gained the upper hand with a regulation that made the outgoing mayor *ex officio* alderman of the guild. A dragon figure that had been associated with the Wetherby faction was removed from the procession for some years and only restored in conjunction with a St George figure who slew it.[112]

The university and the churches of Paris had many civic processions to pray for the deliverance of the city during its troubles and during the years of English occupation. They were very important to the anonymous author of the Journal of Paris. For 1412 he describes daily processions in each of the parishes from Sunday, 5 June, praying for peace between the king and the great lords. On Thursday the faithful from several parishes made a joint procession to Boulogne-la-Petite, 'accompanied

---

110 Johnston, 'Traders and playmakers', 100–5.
111 Tillott, *City of York*, 96; James, 'Ritual, drama and social body', 5, 15–18.
112 McRee, 'Guild ceremony', 192–201.

by a great many people, both clergy and ordinary folk, all barefoot, carrying many lights and relics; there they made their devotions, said high mass, and then came back again'. A city-wide procession followed on Friday,

one of the finest ever seen. Every church, college, and parish was there, barefoot, and people past reckoning (an order had been announced the day before, every house to send one person). Many contingents came in from parishes outside Paris. . . . They brought all the relics they could get hold of and all came barefoot, very old men, pregnant women, little children, and all with tapers or candles.

The processions continued through Thursday 16 June despite torrential rainfall.[113]

While cities used processions to affirm their corporate identity and honour, princes used them to reinforce the symbolic subjection of their cities when they were in a position to do so. Formal Entries of the local prince into the city were accompanied by sumptuous display involving music, dancing, tableaux, jousting, processions in symbolic costumes, readings of the city liberties, and liberal dispensation of food and wine. At the arrival of King Henry V on 1 December 1420

they made a magnificent entry into Paris. The whole of the Grand Rue St Denis, by which they entered, was hung and decorated most nobly from the second gate to Notre-Dame, and most of the people in Paris who could manage it were wearing red. In the rue de la Calandre in front of the Palais there was a touching mystery, a living tableau of the Passion of Our Lord, just as it is depicted around the choir of Notre-Dame. The staging was about a hundred paces long, reaching from the rue de la Calandre to the walls of the palace; no one could see this mystery and not be moved. No princes were ever welcomed more joyfully than these; in every street they met processions of priests in copes and surplices carrying reliquaries and singing *Te Deum laudamus* and *Benedictus qui venit*. It was between five and six in the afternoon and quite dark by the time they got back to their churches, yet how happy, how delighted they were to do all this! And so were the common people.[114]

Henry V and VI both used processions and particularly Entries to reinforce their legitimacy among the Parisians, frequently forcing the entire population to take an oath of loyalty to their regime. In 1431 the

---

113 *Parisian Journal*, 63–9.
114 *Parisian Journal*, 153–4.

guilds of Paris took the initiative and insisted on the right to participate in Henry VI's coronation Entry with tableaux stressing the dual nature of the monarchy and the legitimacy of Paris' ancient liberties. In the Flemish cities the greatest civic processions in the late Middle Ages were linked to the prince's presence, particularly his formal Entries; Ghent, which was usually hostile to the new Burgundian dynasty in Flanders, actually witnessed fewer processions after their accession in 1384 than previously. When Count Philip the Good finally conquered Ghent, he staged a grand Entry in 1458 that emphasised his nobility and grace in pardoning the rebels, who were perhaps too numbed by the indemnities that he levied to be truly appreciative. The Entries used by the counts at Bruges, in a ceremony whose essential format may go back to the twelfth century, laid emphasis on reconciliation along with subjection. Even more than civic processions the Entries were 'an over-whelming sensory experience: the sight of the magnificent silk robes worn by the canons and choir, the smell of incense, but above all the sounds of music and bells'. Just as the Corpus Christi pageants linked the urban community and its component corporations with the body of Christ, so the Entries assimilated the city's prince to Him.[115]

City-wide celebrations also accompanied the rotation of the city government. Beginning in 1350 Exeter incurred large expenses, mainly for wine, on election day.[116] Ghent had a two-day celebration, including performances by trumpeters and banquets for electors, guild deans and other dignitaries, culminating in the new aldermen taking the oath of office.[117] Locally observed secular holidays took place throughout the year. After 1383 Ypres observed 'Garden Day' on the first Sunday of August to celebrate the end of the English siege of the city in that year.[118] London had parades and festivities throughout the Christmas season, Shrove Tuesday, Easter, St John's Eve, Midsummer Watch, the change of magistracy and inauguration of the Lord Mayor, guild festivals on their patron saints' days, funerals, weddings and christenings. This meant that somebody was celebrating something in public most of the time. Most of these festivities required considerable expenditure on fine clothing and wine, giving business to local merchants and craftsmen.[119]

The civic festivals were usually disorderly. Saint-Omer banned nocturnal mummeries as early as 1320. Ghent sent a delegation to the annual

---

115 Bryant, 'Paris and London', 13–17; Murray, 'Liturgy of the Count's advent in Bruges', 137–44, with quotation 143; Nicholas, 'In the pit', 272, 290–1.
116 Rowe and Draisey, *Exeter Receivers' Accounts*, 58, 78.
117 Nicholas, 'In the pit', 280–1.
118 Nicholas, *Medieval Flanders*, 353.
119 Hanawalt, *Growing Up in Medieval London*, 16–17.

procession from St Bavo's abbey, which housed the relics of St Lievin, to the village of St Lievins Houtem. The procession included mummers, and returning revellers were a serious problem for public order. Ghent was the only Flemish city that sent a delegation to the annual procession of Our Lady at Tournai on 14 September. Most of the aldermen and the overdeans of the three political members attended, clad in fine uniforms and riding horses provided for the occasion by the city government. The other participants – at least five hundred normally attended in the 1330s – paid their own expenses. Expenses for Our Lady's Cap and for adorning pennants – whether for guild contingents is unclear but likely – are mentioned, as well as payments to trumpeters and pipers.[120]

Ghent celebrated Shrove Tuesday with a procession accompanied by wholesale debauchery and evidently a candlelit ceremony, although whether the guilds marched in procession is unclear. Shrove Tuesday celebrations elsewhere were so riotous that the authorities had to limit them. Nuremberg forbade the lower orders ('whether artisan, journeyman or servant') to run through the city or go about with pipers except on the three days of Shrovetide. Dancing was forbidden after vespers were sounded. From 1431 the council of Cologne issued an annual Morningspeech forbidding mummeries and parades on Shrove Tuesday and dancing in the meetings of the *Gaffeln* and 'offices'.[121] Although elements of the festivities, such as the Feast of Fools and the youth abbeys, appear to have been directed against the social order, the authorities controlled them carefully. Although they were disorderly, they never degenerated into riots against the city government. Indeed, the Feasts and youth affairs soon became hierarchical themselves, with the wealthiest burgesses chosen as kings.[122]

Profound changes occurred in the intellectual climate of the cities in the late Middle Ages. While in 1200 cultural activity was centred on princely courts, western Europe by 1500 had a culture that was principally urban, through the development of the universities, the burgeoning network of schools, and the fact that the princes and nobles who had traditionally been the patrons of literature and the arts more often resided in the cities than before. Merchants and some craftsmen were developing cultural interests that gave rise to an urban art and particularly drama and literature.

120 Nicholas, 'In the pit', 281–9.
121 Derville, *Saint-Omer*, 62; Schultheiss, *Satzungen*, 275; Huiskes, *Beschlüsse Köln*, 141.
122 Hilton, *English and French Towns*, 117–21.

CHAPTER TEN

The Tenor of Daily Life in the Later Medieval City

MATERIAL LIFE IN THE LATER MEDIEVAL CITY

Information about conditions of material life is fragmentary for the thirteenth century but becomes fuller thereafter. In this chapter we shall use diverse examples from a wide time frame to build a composite picture of city life in the late Middle Ages.

Domestic architecture

Land plots in the cities were initially large. The most common form of urban tenement in northern Germany in the twelfth and thirteenth centuries was a gabled house on one side of a 14–15-metre-wide parcel, beside which a vacant area of 3–4 metres was left between the houses for a path to an inner courtyard; sometimes the yard went through to the back street. Florentine plots in the thirteenth century were typically 4–6 metres wide and 10–15 metres deep.[1] Thus many cities had entire streets, even in the centre, without residential frontage.

The increased activity in the land market during the population expansion of the central Middle Ages forced subdivision. Typically, the early medieval houses at Winchester were not larger than the later ones, but they were on larger pieces of land, which were then subdivided as population rose. Larger houses were often subdivided as well. The 'right angle' type was most common, with a narrow front; the plot then widened as the building extended back from the street, sometimes with gates on the front for horses and carts. Some properties had an L shape,

---

1 Balestracci, 'Immigrazione e morfologia urbana', 101.

with the street frontage used for shops and rental properties, then the hall situated at a right angle and opening onto the courtyard.[2]

In the shipping cities of the coast, merchants still needed both front and rear access; but in the interior the area between the houses was also being built up with small outbuildings in the fourteenth and fifteenth centuries. In many cities the façades and side walls of adjacent houses actually touched, a fact that allowed greater height even of wooden buildings without danger of collapse. The houses were built to a height of up to three storeys for modest residences, even higher for patrician palaces. The storeys, however, were rarely more than seven feet high.[3] As pressure on urban space was relieved after the plagues, new houses in the suburbs often contained only one or two storeys; in the older parts they continued to be much higher, but with greater variation in height and style between buildings except in cities with strict building codes.[4]

A house type common in England and Flanders was spreading to northern Germany by the 1220s, with a ground floor, merchant cellar, a great hall on the first upper storey and smaller rooms on the second and third storeys. Most London houses of the thirteenth century had the hall at the rear of the courtyard but sometimes on its side. This remained common for structures that doubled as businesses and family residences. Some cellars were freehold tenements, and accordingly they had to be accessible without crossing another's freehold; thus steps led from the street into the cellar.[5] More commonly after 1250, in Lübeck and the Hanse cities, as land plots were subdivided into their modern sizes, merchants built hall houses adjacent to each other. About 1250, as Baltic merchants expanded increasingly into large-scale grain trading, a different type appeared with a great hall on the ground floor, used as a warehouse or work place, but its domestic amenities were confined to a kitchen and small sleeping quarters for employees; the owner and his family lived elsewhere.[6]

Private houses on the northern continent tended to be higher than in England (even up to 7–9 storeys), but in both 'living space' was usually confined to a room or two, with the rest given over to craft work, sales, storage and quarters for apprentices and journeymen. At Arles,

2 Keene, *Medieval Winchester*, 156; Hanawalt, *Growing Up in Medieval London*, 24.
3 Vance, *Continuing City*, 152–5.
4 Faber and Lochard, *Montpellier*, 241.
5 As population pressure eased after 1348, the undercrofts were generally used for storage only. Schofield and Vince, *Medieval Towns*, 71, 90; Salter, *Medieval Oxford*, 82–3.
6 Erdmann, 'Typenentwicklung des lübeckischen Kaufmannshauses', 105–6; Terlau and Kaspar, 'Städtische Bauen', 470–3.

where houses rarely had more than one storey above street level, the number of individually partitioned living rooms was the key difference between the houses of the wealthy and of the poor.[7]

Northern Germany generally conformed to the pattern of living quarters with the workshop or office and an anteroom on the ground floor, and the upper storeys used for storage, particularly of grain. Further south the family lived on the first upper storey, while the ground floor space had two rooms, with the family business on one side, the stairs and access to the courtyard on the other. The upper storey was divided lengthwise into rooms. The hearth was on the street side, with the kitchen behind it, often without lighting. The bedrooms were behind this on the side away from the street. The richer burgesses had a formal parlour on this second floor. The outbuildings could include privies, a well or fountain, stall, barns, washrooms, occasionally a private chapel, and in the larger courtyards a garden. Most private houses – in some cities even the smaller ones – had wells, although this was less easy to maintain in the more densely populated larger cities.[8]

Excavations since World War II have revealed that most north European city buildings except palaces and churches were timber throughout the twelfth century. 'King John's House' and 'Canute's Palace', from late twelfth-century Southampton, were of the 'house over warehouse' type. Each had a hall and at least one other private room. King John's house had a side-wall fireplace. The roofs of the lower storey supported the floor of the upper rooms, which contained the living quarters, with pillars and beams. Arches contained the windows. Families usually owned these houses for several generations, even more than a century. Just before 1200, however, a change to stone building began, evidently nationwide. The records of substantial houses built at Southampton in the thirteenth century indicate that they were all of stone. Central Canterbury had at least twenty-seven stone houses before 1200. London had some stone domestic building even by 1100 in the Cheapside and waterfront areas. An ordinance of 1189 required stone building instead of wood and tile rather than thatched roofs.[9]

Italian urban tenements during the thirteenth century generally had the short side to the front. Shops were on the ground floor, sometimes divided horizontally by a raised area on a wooden floor on one side. The higher part was a mezzanine for storage. In the larger shops there were sometimes separate cubicles for the workers. The rear exit led into the garden, where the well, oven and privy were located. Small apartments

---

7 Stouff, *Arles*, 334–6; Vance, *Continuing City*, 152–5.
8 Isenmann, *Deutsche Stadt*, 51; Keene, *Medieval Winchester*, 65.
9 Platt, *Medieval Southampton*, 39–43; Schofield, *Medieval London Houses*, 31–2.

also divided the larger interior courtyards. The upper storeys had two long rooms, the *sala* and the *camera*, that were divided laterally into apartments or rooms.

By the late thirteenth century, however, the earlier partitions within the houses had often been enclosed into separate apartments, each of them rented. Tenures and houses were often divided up as population grew in the thirteenth century, and this was accompanied by a rise in absentee landlordship. Particularly in the peripheral artisan quarters there are fewer references in property transfers to the properties having gardens or courts, while mentions of common walls, little paths and wooden enclosures abound. There was considerable 'doubling up' of habitation: persons who had to live in the city for a certain number of months per year or lose their citizenship would often take small apartments in the establishments of their relatives who stayed permanently in the city or with persons from the same natal village who were personal acquaintances. Tenements were frequently sublet, although a Florentine statute of 1325 forbade the practice without the owner's consent.[10]

Aristocratic residences on the continent were often of brick by 1300, while in England the number of stone houses of wealthy townspeople was increasing. Jewish merchants were associated with stone houses, perhaps both for protection and because they could afford them. Façades became more elaborate in some cities during the late Middle Ages, although at York even the palace of the aristocratic de la Poles had little ornamentation.[11] Some Italian cities required a standard height for windows and specified architectural styles for private buildings around the markets and public buildings even in the thirteenth century. Of the northern cities, Nuremberg has the most precise building ordinances from the Middle Ages, requiring consistency in style of the façades and an even line with the street, and specifying kinds of ornamentation and number of bay and oriel windows allowed.[12]

Although Flemish urban aristocrats had stone towers even in the twelfth century (some from the thirteenth are still standing), stone buildings were unusual in the French cities even as late as the fourteenth century, although most wooden houses had stone floors to keep the timbers from coming into contact with the ground. Most lacked exterior ornamentation until the late fifteenth century. Besançon had only thirteen stone houses in 1350. Only in Provence and Bas-Languedoc did many non-nobles have them. Artisan houses were wood, bricks or rubble. Some were constructed from prefabricated materials. Carpentry

10 Sznura, *Espansione urbana di Firenze*, 26, 36–9, 103, 137–41.
11 Keene, *Medieval Winchester*, 172; Kermode, 'Merchants', 33.
12 Braunfels, *Urban Design*, 130.

was 70 per cent of the cost, and maintaining them, given the flimsiness of construction, required constant attention.[13]

The gabled terraced house became more common in the thirteenth and fourteenth centuries. It was only completely possible in stone or brick buildings; when wood was used, there was usually a narrow conduit between the houses for drainage, a well and a privy, built when a common fire-wall was erected between the houses. London required gables to extend toward the street frontage. Half-timbering goes back at least to the twelfth century and gradually replaced board structures, though houses exclusively of wood continued to be built in some cities into the sixteenth century. Façades might be built in wood or stone, the rest in wattle and daub or brick.[14] The first floor above ground had large apartments, often the residence of the owners; then the upper storeys had progressively smaller apartments as one ascended the stairs. Some houses had external rather than, or in addition to, internal stairs between floors. Shacks in the back yards served as kitchens and privies, but some were also rented out. The land speculation by patricians to build big residences in the late Middle Ages involved pulling down the outbuildings and replacing them with more substantial structures. This created a sort of segregation or 'zoning', especially from the second half of the fifteenth century.[15]

The cellar was used to store food and merchandise, but some prosperous merchants used outbuildings instead. Francesco Datini of Prato, who spent much of his time and centred his business in Florence, built a new home in the late fourteenth century, with a warehouse at the end of the yard, separated from the living space. Unike the Venetian palace, the Florentine was not a place of business or warehouse. There were no shops, although a banker might work from a study in his home. The Medici used the ground floor of their sumptuous palace for business, but the upper storeys were decorated. Formidable façades separated the interior from the outside. The ceilings were high; buildings that now would have six storeys usually had no more than three in the fifteenth century. Even the biggest Florentine palaces might have no more than twelve rooms. The inner court was a private yard, cut off from the outside. Most were designed to accommodate only one household, contrary to the Venetian custom.[16]

---

13   Rossiaud, 'Crises', 436; Lavedan, *French Architecture*, 191–2.
14   Schofield and Vince, *Medieval Towns*, 68; Hanawalt, *Growing Up in Medieval London*, 25.
15   Gonthier, *Cris de haine*, 24–5.
16   Goldthwaite, *Building of Renaissance Florence*, 103–5; Anderson and Zinsser, *Women*, 356.

Jacques Coeur's palace in Bourges had a fortress quality. A street doorway opened onto an inner courtyard where goods were received and stored in warehouses, and visitors were received. Thus business was transacted on the ground floor; the second level was opulently furnished for Coeur and his family, and the attics were used for storage. In the 1370s the Runtinger of Regensburg acquired three adjacent buildings and redesigned them, leaving the office and kitchen on the ground floor, the public reception rooms on the second, and the family quarters on the third. Instead of warehouses behind the main building, however, they built two additional upper storeys that they used for merchandise, which was brought in by crane. This feature is found increasingly in German patrician houses at the end of the Middle Ages.[17]

Since roofs were originally of straw or wood tiles, few cities escaped major fires. Ventilation was also a problem, since smoke had to leave the house through the roof. Only in the late thirteenth century were tiled stoves attached to stone or brick chimneys starting to replace the open hearth with smoke escaping through the roof. The hall had been the most important room in the thirteenth century, often the only heated room, but by the fifteenth it was usually much smaller and was sometimes used as a smoke bay except in houses with brick chimneys. Many houses in Constance had heating on all storeys. Even humble houses might have a 'fire-back' of masonry or tile, sometimes of iron, as a hearth, but permitting smoke to escape was still a problem. Some small houses had wooden louvres consisting of slats mounted in runners in the ceiling, adjustable according to the wind and accordingly usable for ventilation in warm weather.[18]

Most houses had few conveniences or amenities indoors. Many buildings, particularly in the city centres, had upper storeys extending beyond those below. This gave extra space for the family's living quarters, made cross street access easy and facilitated dumping wastes from the upper floors into the street (a practice forbidden everywhere by the fourteenth century), but the outcroppings obscured the natural light. Statutes prohibited this without the authorisation of the council, with varying success, but at least this was easier to enforce than the requirement of tiled roofs.[19]

There was little furniture except for beds and tables. Oak was the preferred wood, for it was widely available and very durable, but while

17 Lavedan, *French Architecture*, 194; Vance, *Continuing City*, 140–1; Anderson and Zinsser, *Women*, 356.
18 Schultheiss, *Satzungen*, 55; Bechtold, *Zunftbürgerschaft und Patriziat*, 102; Keene, *Medieval Winchester*, 158–9, 175–8; Isenmann, *Deutsche Stadt*, 34.
19 Kühnel, 'Alltagsleben', 43; Anderson and Zinsser, *Women*, 355.

the furnishings of the wealthy were elaborately carved and sometimes painted, with wrought iron decorations added, those of the poorer citizens were plain and rectangular. Most wealthy homes had an oak armoir of varying size, while a buffet or cupboard was a mark of the elite. The 'throne', an individual raised seat, was also mainly found in wealthy homes. The middle and lower classes contented themselves with benches that accommodated several persons simultaneously. Tables were ubiquitous but varied in size and elegance.[20] Beds were normally shared by several persons and usually did not have sheets.

Although the urban rich of Italy built imposing palaces during the Renaissance, they did not furnish them much if any more opulently than the northerners did. Only for Florence do we have much information. Most rooms had beds, but apart from that little is mentioned. The master's chamber was the centre from which the other rooms radiated, and his was the best furnished. The central chamber usually contained a large bed and sometimes a high raised bench, the top of which could be used as a bed with storage space below. These were sometimes ornately carved in the houses of the wealthy. Such works of art as the family owned, even the Medici, were in the chambers and antechambers of the master and his sons. The chambers became more lavishly decorated in the fifteenth century, and furnishings, albeit utilitarian, are found in greater quantity elsewhere in the house. Yet even in the fifteenth century chairs were still unusual, for benches were preferred. The entire Medici palace in Florence in 1418 had only six chairs.[21]

The homes were also dark, partly because the narrow streets and overhanging buildings obscured the light, partly because they were so flimsy that much window space would weaken them structurally. The windows were kept closed for fear of vapours, the stink that pervaded all cities and the received opinion that diseases were in the air. Few city houses had glass windows in the thirteenth century; although glass became increasingly popular, many were still made of linen, hides or oiled parchment as late as the fifteenth century. With so little to keep them indoors except the family workshop, people spent much time, and virtually all of their leisure time, in the streets and markets.[22] The Islamic urban home was even more sparely furnished, with tapestries and cushions instead of chairs.[23]

Most houses continued to be for nuclear families, although in the late

20   Eames, *Furniture*, 234–44.
21   Goldthwaite, *Wealth and the Demand for Art in Italy*, 225–9.
22   Waley, *Siena*, 1–2; Kühnel, 'Alltagsleben', 49.
23   Hourani, *History of the Arab Peoples*, 127.

Middle Ages, as wealthy families expanded their town houses, enormous complexes housed the numerous nuclear families that made up the lineage. In the wealthier parishes of Reims the number of taxpayers was 20–25 per cent higher than the number of houses, resulting from several nuclear families living under one roof among the rich, while the reverse was true in parishes with a strong clerical element. Constance had about 750 houses but some 2,000 taxpayers; most houses must have had multiple occupancy, but of a nuclear family and renters, not extended families.[24] Most houses at Genoa, which were famed for their height, contained more than a single taxable household, with some having as many as six, suggesting a minimum average of fifteen inhabitants per house.[25] These multitudes occupied an area opening onto a common interior courtyard, with only one exit to the street. Proximity to neighbours fostered neighbourhood associations and militia organisations, but problems of access, waste disposal, drainage, drinking water and common wells gave sources for discord among neighbours.[26]

Some entire houses were rented as apartments in the largest cities, although evidently to a greater extent in the north than in the more crowded Italian cities. The apartment house was rare in Florence before the fifteenth century. By the early fifteenth century there was some speculation in noble palaces, with the new owners usually converting the ground floor to shops and the upper storeys to single-room flats that occupied the entire level. Most artisans of Florence lived in such dwellings. The ground levels, which were business property, always paid higher rent than the upper. London and Paris as court centres and places such as Constance, whose famous council gave a great impulse to inn-keeping for four years, did a thriving trade with persons of property needing temporary accommodation.[27]

The styles of private homes in the Muslim cities changed little in the late Middle Ages. Entryways were still on alleys that were off the main street. Portals could be elaborate, depending on the wealth and status of the owner. Once inside, the visitor entered a corridor that was turned so that nothing that went on inside could be seen from the street. This led to a central courtyard, onto which numerous rooms had individual entrances. These rooms included a main hall or reception area. The living quarters were off the main hall and might be separated from it by a second courtyard. Some houses had bathhouses.[28]

24 Desportes, *Reims*, 462–7; Bechtold, *Zunftbürgerschaft und Patriziat*, 101–2.
25 Heers, *Gênes. Civilisation*, 55–9.
26 Gonthier, *Cris de haine*, 89–92.
27 Vance, *Continuing City*, 138–41; Geremek, *Margins of Society*, 78–81.
28 Hourani, *History of the Arab Peoples*, 126–7.

Amenities in the late medieval city

Late medieval urban governments were much more concerned with sanitation, cleanliness and general quality of life than their predecessors had been. The Muslim cities continued to have more sophisticated physical plants than did those of the west. While streets, water supply, and sanitation were handled by separate offices in the western cities, the emirs appointed governors of their cities who centralised these operations.[29]

Western urban approaches to these problems reflect the often poly-nuclear and always multijurisdictional nature of the cities of Europe. Much of this was simply a matter of public safety. Fires were a notorious hazard. Rouen had at least thirteen in the first half of the thirteenth century. Valenciennes in 1435 was the first medieval city with a salaried fire brigade.[30] Elsewhere service in the fire brigade was organised by guild or parish and was incumbent on all citizens. In England some cities required newcomers to donate a leather water-bucket upon their admission to the freedom. Cologne fined any able-bodied person who failed to come when summoned. A second offence meant banishment for a year and loss of his trade. The city furnished buckets and ladders that evidently remained in the possession of the person to whom they were assigned; for he, not the city, paid for replacement in the event of loss or damage. The burgomaster and council could require the nearest bathhouses, bakeries and breweries to open their wells to firefighters and assign their employees to carry water. A Morningspeech of 1400 established a continuous fire guard of forty-four persons, including four magistrates and one or two from every office and *Gaffel*. Everyone was ordered to keep enough water in his house to extinguish a fire that could be confined to that place.[31]

The authorities tried to insist on non-combustible roofs, but this was impossible because earth tiles and slate were so expensive. Munich, Göttingen, Bern and Bruges provided subsidies to help burgesses re-roof with tiles. Much of the problem was that the exterior walls could not support the extra weight of the heavier roof. Most references to tile roofs come when the entire house is being rebuilt, or in new constructions, when a house on pillars was changed to a stone foundation with cellar and with half-timbering above.[32] The dilapidation of houses gave an opportunity for urban renewal through higher standards. Although most Italian cities did not forbid rebuilding ruined houses,

29 Hourani, *History of the Arab Peoples*, 134.
30 Mollat, *Histoire de Rouen*, 80; Platelle, *Histoire de Valenciennes*, 63.
31 Keutgen, *Urkunden*, no. 337–8, pp. 435–7.
32 Kühnel, 'Alltagsleben', 47–9, 56; van Uytven, 'Stadsgeschiedenis', 203.

most required stone building and tile roofs and regulated the thickness of walls.[33]

As populations grew and opportunities for irritation multiplied, detailed regulations specified access facilities and the space to be left between buildings. They also forbade diverting drainage or sewage in a way that would inconvenience one's neighbours. While adjacent tenements were supposed to be separated by walls, and a right of privacy was respected, they often had common rights and obligations concerning drainage. At London the Husting court and the court of the mayor and aldermen heard cases under the royal Assize of Nuisance. Most actions were between neighbours. Surprisingly few resulted from craft practices, such as the effluents of the dyeing and tanning processes, damages to walls from tentering frames and the like.[34]

While urban environmental pollution is mainly industrial today, it was organic in the late Middle Ages. Enclosing the moats and keeping the city's water within, in effect recycling it through drainage canals and conduits, created problems. Streets sloped from both sides toward the centre, where there was an open drain.[35] As woollens gave way to flax working in the late Middle Ages, as dyers' wastes remained in the city, as tanning and smithing occupied more of the workforce, and as more meat entered the diet, the result was some industrial and considerable animal pollution.[36] Butchers generally did not slaughter their animals outside the city; they drove the beasts through the streets, killed them at the Meat Hall and immediately offered the flesh for sale. Once the beasts were slaughtered, their wastes became the next problem. As early as 1250 the butchers of Bologna and Verona were being required to take the offal outside the city. Ferrara required the butchers to establish themselves along the city streams, which may simply have substituted one pollution problem for another, and to have pits next to their shops to collect the blood. Many private citizens kept chickens or goats, and rare is the city whose statutes do not include periodic admonitions against permitting pigs to run loose. A Nuremberg law prohibited bringing three pigs at a time into the city except for hospices and cloisters, which could have more if they had a herdsman to keep them from running in the streets. Anybody keeping pigs had to have a sty for them in his yard.[37]

33 Balestracci, 'Immigrazione e morfologia urbana', 99–101.
34 Schofield and Vince, *Medieval Town*, 68; Chew and Kellaway, *London Assize of Nuisance*, vii, xxxi, 13, 26.
35 Salter, *Medieval Oxford*, 85.
36 Guillerme, *Age of Water*, 138–58.
37 Zupko and Laures, *Straws in the Wind*, 35–7; Keutgen, *Urkunden*, no. 303; De Pauw, *Voorgeboden*, 23; Schultheiss, *Satzungen*, 297.

London was an exception. Animals were initially slaughtered at the Shambles, a row of butchers' stalls between West and East Cheap rather than at a municipal Meat Hall. Waste was carried to the Fleet, but the droppings from the carts became so malodorous that royal ordinances between 1369 and 1381 moved slaughtering outside the city, resulting in a concentration of butchers at suburban Westminster. Winchester in 1409 required butchers to chop mess into pieces four inches or less before dumping it into the river, which ran through the cathedral precinct.[38]

The horse, whose manure fertilised the fields, fouled the city streets constantly in its capacity as the medieval automobile and lorry. Dogs and cats were kept as pets, but many ran loose. The butchers of Winchester kept dogs to herd animals and bait bulls. Many were fined for letting the dogs, which were hardly of a playful disposition, run loose. Douai and Dijon maintained uniformed 'dog bashers'; those of Bruges beat 1,121 animals to death in 1455. So far had Arles declined that by the fourteenth century the ruins of the Roman baths were used as a pound for stray animals![39]

The few public latrines were concentrated in specific areas, such as the ring street inside the walls and around the markets, rather than scattered throughout the city. Most cities had a dead-end 'Easement Alley', 'Ordure Street', or something similar near the main market. Few houses had latrines. Privies and cesspits were in the walls that marked property boundaries. By the fourteenth century a few large houses, particularly those in stone, had privies with waste channelled down a chute to the pit in the wall. The chamber pot was ubiquitous. Statutes forbade leaving waste at neighbours' doors or dumping liquids into the streets from upper storeys.[40] Wealthy citizens who had their own privies risked contaminating the water supply when they tried to link them by subterranean channels to drainage ditches. Paris paid 'fify masters', to remove wastes from cesspits, while Buda had a garbage collector called the Manure Count.[41] Many cities made inhabitants responsible for their own waste disposal, even requiring them to take it beyond the walls. Noyon forbade residents to pile ordure before their doors for more than three days or dump it in abandoned houses or in the ditches and towers of the city itself. Nuremberg required every homeowner to provide a

---

38 Robertson, *Chaucer's London*, 23–4; Keene, *Medieval Winchester*, 64.
39 Keene, *Medieval Winchester*, 257; Isenmann, *Deutsche Stadt*, 34; Nicholas, *Medieval Flanders*, 297; Stouff, *Arles*, 66.
40 Schofield, *Medieval London Houses*, 33; Guillerme, *Age of Water*, 165.
41 The origin of the name is unknown. Favier, *Paris 1380–1500*, 331; Birnbaum, 'Buda', 142.

privy for his household and those living in his outbuildings and forbade throwing waste into the street.[42]

The practical impact of this on reducing the pervasive miasma is questionable: the houses of the Tucher and Behain, prominent merchants of Nuremberg, had cesspits of 30 metres, but they were only cleaned every thirty years.[43] The house of a merchant of Rodez in 1370 was supposed to have a subterranean stone pipe to carry sewage to the main drain of the Bourg of Rodez, which ran downhill; instead, this one was built east-west, and accordingly the waste was not running off. The owner evidently thought that the city was responsible for clearing the drain, but local custom clearly made that the responsibility of the home-owner.[44] At Lübeck drainage conduits led from streets to the river, which was also the source of fresh water. Human waste was sometimes dumped along the streets but more often in cesspits, usually about 4 metres wide and up to 12 metres deep. As with fountains, the first cesspits were of wood, but from the late Middle Ages they were made increasingly of stone.[45] London was somewhat cleaner. City ordinances required that privies be lined with stone, and they might be in cellars or in the yards. Cesspit crews cleaned them for a fee; this was usually required at intervals of about two years. London had public latrines, always near water currents that could flush them out naturally. Despite this, people regularly relieved themselves from the upper storeys or in the streets, and the city had 'rakers' to remove the refuse.[46]

Just as now, some cities were cleaner than others. Many began paying cleanup crews to work on the markets, particularly after the plagues heightened concern about sanitation. Street cleaners and garbage removers made weekly circuits at Dijon, Strasbourg, and Compiègne.[47] The *échevins* were careless by modern standards but well ahead of their fellow citizens; in 1370 the archbishop of Reims had to prohibit urinating inside the Bread Hall. Some cities owned ditches for sewage in the ban mile. Chirurgien/barbers had to keep blood inside their own houses 'so that pigs won't eat it'. They used a 'blood trench' at Noyon, a blood pit at Ghent.[48]

---

42 F. Desportes, 'Police des métiers', 329; Billot, *Chartres*, 36; Schultheiss, *Satzungen*, 152.

43 Diermeier, 'Condizioni materiali', 90.

44 The owner had buried a jug of gold coins in the drain to hide it from the English. When the waste backed up, his son-in-law gave permission for the excavation but removed the money to his own house before the old man knew what was happening. Thus the matter eventuated in a suit. Wroe, *A Fool and His Money*, 48–9, 78–9, 147–8.

45 Fehring, 'Beitrag der Archäologie', 14.

46 Hanawalt, *Growing Up in Medieval London*, 28–9.

47 Rossiaud, 'Crises', 572.

48 F. Desportes, 'Police des métiers', 329; Desportes, *Reims*, 490–1.

Streets

The city streets were initially little more than mud tracks, for whatever paving the Romans had left had long since worn away. But some central areas were already being paved with timbers or crushed stones even in the twelfth century. Most cities began paving their major streets with gravel and their markets with cobblestones in the thirteenth century, and cobblestones became general in the fourteenth. Maintaining the roads, bridges, canals and conduits that laced the city became a major item in city budgets. Although Philip Augustus ordered Paris to be paved in 1184, London was not paved until the time of Edward I.[49] Each wardmoot thereafter elected four street inspectors, and from 1303 pavers operated city-wide. The street repairs that they required were paid for by the householders before whose properties the repaired route would pass. The Italian cities were more advanced. Florence had some paved streets by 1235 and was completely paved by 1339. Street paving at Perugia began characteristically with the main square in 1253. In 1268 the chief streets were paved, and in 1294 the government undertook to pave all public thoroughfares. All householders were responsible for cleaning the streets outside their own buildings and maintaining the pavement.[50]

The first municipally paved streets at Brussels are recorded in 1265. The side streets remained unpaved tracks until later. Before 1300 Brussels and Louvain had municipal offices for street maintenance, called *Chaussées*, directed by 'masters' chosen by the *échevins* and rendering accounts to them, and with their own incomes by 1326. The *Chaussée* had a corps of pavers directed by a *chef-de-chantier* who was usually a contractor, often a mason.[51] Depending on how much had to be spent on police and defence, the share of public works in the budget of Ghent, including street paving and bridge repair, ranged from less than 5 per cent in wartime to nearly one-quarter of the receipt in quiet years. Street maintenance took 9 per cent of Nantes' budget in 1467, 18 per cent at Rennes in 1483.[52]

As city governments used confiscated property to alleviate congestion and construct public buildings, they also concerned themselves with

49   Zupko and Laures, *Straws in the Wind*, 49; Leguay, 'La rue', 40; Le Goff, 'Town as an agent of civilisation', 89.

50   Williams, *Medieval London*, 86; Blanshei, *Perugia*, 25; Waley, *Siena*, 10; Morris, *Urban Form*, 70.

51   There was no equivalent of this level of municipal control elsewhere in Brabant or the Flemish cities, where public works were leased to 'city masters' on a per task basis. Martens, *Histoire de Bruxelles*, 81, 103–4.

52   Nicholas, 'Governance', 253; Leguay, *Réseau urbain Bretagne*, 221.

street widths, building heights and overhangs that impinged on relations among neighbours. The cities were regulating overhangs on the main streets by the twelfth and thirteenth centuries. London forbade such 'penthouses' lower than nine feet from street level, so that mounted riders could clear them.[53] Ghent in 1365 fined Hugh de Buc the substantial sum of 200 pounds for having 'built over the street without permission'.[54] The mercers of Rennes were repairing their share of the roof of the city hall in 1475 but threatened to stop work if the drunks from a nearby tavern were not stopped from 'pissing and throwing ordure and pollution on the workers' from the upper storey windows.[55] Streets were more than means of access. Given that so little could be done inside except one's craft, most persons spent a considerable amount of time in the street buying, selling, talking and fighting. The street was a market and an entertainment centre. The widened streets that had sufficed for markets in the cities' early days were hopelessly congested by this time. Oxford's two main streets were markets with specific locales for given products. Although the High was so wide that the university students used it as a sports field, the road was blocked by sale booths in the middle and at both ends.[56]

Some streets had arcades, especially in Italy. The central area of Montpellier had numerous covered passageways with residences over the street, linking the establishments of wealthy citizens on opposite sides of the street.[57] In addition to penthouses, jutting walls and towers, galleries and external staircases impeded access. So did sale booths for displaying merchandise, but the authorities were generally more tolerant of these. Particularly during the fairs the merchant halls were inadequate, and shops spilled over into the streets. Peddlers, jugglers, street poets and animal trainers complicated the street scene even more.[58]

The Italian cities had street inspectors and building codes by the early thirteenth century. Bologna had statutes concerning street widths and requiring paving from 1211. From 1265 Siena chose six Masters of the Streets annually. From 1224 Venice had two overseers of embankments, public streets and waterways, reorganised in 1282 as a body of judges. In 1208 103 property owners at Vicenza were required to demolish walls, columns, porticoes, stairways and other buildings obstructing the streets.[59] Similar regulations proliferate in northern Europe after 1300.

---

53 Hanawalt, *Growing Up in Medieval London*, 25.
54 Municipal Archive of Ghent, ser. 400, ix, fo. 236r.
55 Leguay, *Réseau urbain Bretagne*, 221.
56 Leguay, 'La rue', 28–9; Salter, *Medieval Oxford*, 77–81.
57 Faber and Lochard, *Montpellier*, 242.
58 Leguay, 'La rue', 23–7, 31–4.
59 Schulz, 'Urbanism in medieval Venice', 422–5.

In 1315 Speyer prohibited overhanging buildings and arches that blocked the streets. Avignon in 1243 ordered that streets and bridges should be at least two *cannes* wide (about 3.75 metres). From 1331 Prague required all building to have the prior authorisation of the city council.[60] Most cities maintained municipal surveyors to handle boundary disputes between citizens, but some also sent them through the streets with a measuring rod. Anything that the rod touched had to be removed as impeding access.

The city fathers' concern was not misplaced. Relatively few streets were as wide as 6–12 metres, the minimum that would permit two vehicles to pass in opposite directions without difficulty. Such thoroughfares were often named something like Grande Rue [Great Street] and might extend into the suburbs. They were often the only streets on which houses were more or less aligned regularly with the street, and they were the most likely to be paved. Secondary streets were usually crooked and might be as little as two metres across, with vehicular traffic impossible. At Rennes, even the street linking the old City to the nearest gate, one of the busiest of the city, was only just over 2 metres wide.[61]

Paris was a notorious bottleneck. Its main streets were 5–8 metres across, the alleys 2–3 metres. Many were still unpaved in the fifteenth century. Some had gates at the ends, and others could be blocked by chains during disorder. The Grand-Pont was a natural extension of the rue Saint-Denis but was separated from it by the Grand Châtelet, which created a cul-de-sac that became a haven for cutpurses. Slightly downstream, the wooden Millers' Bridge [Pont aux Meuniers] was used by many, but it was too small to accommodate horses. Another footpath, called the Pont-Notre-Dame from 1413, was an extension of the rue Saint-Martin, closer to the place de Grève than to the Grand-Pont. The narrow streets and difficulties of access explain why most goods came to Paris by river.[62]

The emirs could, as general controllers of property in the Muslim cities, exercise their authority to clear public spaces and widen markets or streets as needed. The regime could also requisition labour on public works and buildings and even commandeer the services of craftsmen. They could impose 'liturgies', such as requiring shopkeepers to clean and even repair streets in front of their houses. Private owners who were removed from their properties to make room for a public structure were

60   Keutgen, *Urkunden*, no. 332, pp. 429–30; Le Goff, 'Town as an agent of civilisation', 89.
61   Leguay, *Réseau urbain Bretagne*, 221.
62   Leguay, 'La rue', 24–5; Favier, *Paris 1380–1500*, 15, 22–6.

not always compensated, in contrast to the west, where private owner-ship was stronger in law.[63] In the west the cities' problems in maintain-ing the streets and guaranteeing the free flow of traffic were exacerbated by the persistence of private ownership of some streets, particularly culs-de-sac, and even substantial parts of markets. In Italy the right of units of the city government to use private land for the community developed earlier and was facilitated by the massive confiscations and resultant city planning of the thirteenth century. But the city councils ratified control of entire quarters by *consorterie*. In 1179 an association of families living around the Old Market of Florence required all members who bought property in a specified zone to share it with other members. Although new residential streets were breaking down these family enclaves, a municipal statute of the fourteenth century required members of *consorterie* to offer property for sale to other members before selling to an out-sider.[64] By contrast, by the thirteenth century the Venetian courts often overrode nobles' claims to own and block streets on grounds of use and declared them public space. In 1328 the judges decreed that all land and facilities were publicly owned unless written evidence proved the contrary.[65]

The notion of 'public space' took longer to reach the north. The Bonami family of Montpellier claimed ownership of an entire square on which they held several houses, near the busy fruit and vegetable market and adjacent to the city hall. Persons operating sale booths and tables paid rent to the Bonami or to others who rented houses on the square from them. When the king erected a barrier on the square to protect the private interests of the Bonami, the city sued to have it removed on grounds that the square was public space. Most sellers who used the square and testified at the hearing favoured the Bonami. The consuls used the fact that the flow of traffic was being impeded – most of their witnesses were craftsmen whose business forced them to cross the square – to argue that it was public, but the issue of hiring labour and renting tables had elements favouring both sides. The Bonami had made an important improvement to the square by raising the centre and sloping it outward to facilitate drainage of rainwater. The suit was resolved by allowing the Bonami private possession of the frontages under the awn-ings, which they could have raised. The rest of the square was to be flattened and be considered public.[66]

---

63 Lapidus, *Muslim Cities*, 61–6.
64 Friedman, *Florentine New Towns*, 211–16.
65 Romano, *Patricians*, 22–5.
66 Reyerson, 'Public vs. private space'. Used with the author's permission.

Waterways

Cities depended on streams for drinking water, for access and to power mills. Most were on a navigable waterway, which was then channelled for fish, fresh water and drainage. At Provins the Count of Champagne and the city government jointly built conduits linking private properties to streams and canals.[67] Lords who founded towns in the twelfth and thirteenth centuries were more careful about the water supply than their ancestors had been. New Salisbury had a system of open water-channels flowing down the middle of its streets, many of them crossed by bridges. This is found in no other English city.[68]

Virtually all cities near the coast used rivers and canals as thoroughfares. Venice is the most famous example. The Grand Canal running through the city was the main street, just as single overland routes sometimes were in the north, and determined social geography. The prime residential district was along its banks. Mainland boats met overseas boats at the Rialto bridge, while the municipal granary was downstream. Other food trades and warehouses, originally on the Grand Canal, were moved away in the thirteenth century to make room for financial offices. The cloth industry was around a bend in the Grand Canal from the Rialto, on the west side toward the mainland. Shipyards were initally further downstream; but after the Arsenal was founded at the western edge of the Grand Canal, shipbuilding was moved there, and earlier shipbuilding areas were given over to the sale of grain. Neighbourhood rivalries developed between districts north and south of the Grand Canal. Since most crafts except shipbuilding were dispersed, some guilds required that officials come from opposite sides of the Canal in alternate years.[69] The northern cities also used the waterways for transport. Ghent and particularly Bruges had numerous canals crossed by bridges. At Paris an advisory board of carpenters and masons appointed by the city advised the provost of the merchants on navigation questions. The city required boatmen to be attached to one of the six ports; since overland transport was so hard, boats became virtual 'taxis'.[70]

The drinking water supply was also critical and drew increased public attention. Pipes carrying running water came earliest to the monasteries, then spread to the cities. They usually ran along the edge of the streets, then had side channels going to canals that were linked to the natural streams of the city; examples are found at Basel, Strasbourg, Speyer,

67   Chapin, *Villes de foires*, 194.
68   Lobel, *Historic Towns*, 4–5.
69   Lane, *Venice*, 14–17; Romano, *Patricians*, 20–1.
70   Cazelles, *Paris*, 212.

Erfurt, Goslar and Quedlinburg. Basel, Stralsund and Goslar used hollowed tree trunks as water pipes.[71] Most large houses had wells in the rear courtyard, but seepage from the privies contaminated them. More public wells were dug as population grew. The government of London, realising that the Thames was hopelessly polluted, in 1237 bought out a private owner and converted his wells at Tyburn into a reservoir, from where water was piped to a conduit in Cheap. The city assigned specific revenues to maintain the reservoir. This was the first documented fresh-water facility in a medieval city, followed by Breslau in 1272, Lübeck in 1294, Brunswick in 1332, Nuremberg in 1331, Bern in 1393, Bremen in 1394, and others in the fifteenth century.[72] Bristol had a well in Pitney Street and conduits from sources outside the city that led to public cisterns and fountains. Brussels, located at the base of a hill, obtained fresh water by drainage and from the Senne. The city had a large reservoir by 1300, and a smaller one was added in the fifteenth century. The reservoirs served numerous fountains, administered by a fountain master by 1359.[73] Provins built four new fountains in 1281 to take care of the problem of insufficient fresh water.[74] Fountains of the twelfth and thirteenth centuries were generally small, between 6 and 9 metres deep and lined with wood. But by 1294 Lübeck had wooden channels with joints of copper or tin leading into the city from water towers on the river. The city had no brick reservoirs until the mid-sixteenth century.[75]

The Italian and Polish cities also maintained aqueducts and canals. Kraków in 1399 built an aqueduct from the Rudawa river and channelled it by pipes to the royal palace and various locations in the city.[76] In the 1330s Siena built the *bottino*, an underground aqueduct 25 kilometres long, linking the central city to fresh water sources in the *contado*. Siena's hill site exacerbated the problem of water supply; the government rebuilt one fountain and built three new ones in the thirteenth century. Public fountains were especially numerous there, becoming social centres of quarters in the late Middle Ages.[77] Bologna required each *contrada* of the city and suburbs to maintain at least one public well, but citizens who had wells outside their homes were exempt from

71 Mollat, *Rouen*, 56; Steuer, 'Urban archaeology', 87–8; Platt, 'Evolution', 53.
72 Williams, *Medieval London*, 84–5; Busch, 'Wasserversorgung', 302–3.
73 Lobel, *Atlas* 2: 9; Martens, *Histoire de Bruxelles*, 104; Diermeier, 'Condizioni materiali', 87; Lesage, *Marseille angevine*, 112–13.
74 Chapin, *Villes de foires*, 194.
75 Fehring, 'Beitrag der Archäologie', 14.
76 Carter, *Trade and Urban Development in Poland*, 69.
77 Balestracci, 'Development to crisis', 204–5; Waley, *Siena*, 2, 14–15; Heers, 'En Italie centrale', 293–5.

the use fee. From 1254 the government of Perugia was trying to build an aqueduct from the mountains, finally succeeding in 1278. In the 1260s the city built five new fountains, one per district at its extreme outer limits and thus in the suburbs outside the medieval walls.[78]

Bridges

Given the ubiquity of interior canals, bridges were critical for the free movement of people and goods. Until the thirteenth century the Ponte Vecchio was the only bridge across the Arno at Florence, but three more were added between 1218 and 1252.[79] Urban bridges not only gave access across streams but also were commonly lined with shops. 'London Bridge in the fourteenth century was a village in itself', with a tavern at each end, a chapel dedicated to St Thomas Becket in the centre and 138 shops in 1358.[80] Public buildings and squares were often at the end of a bridge. The older wooden Ouse Bridge at York was rebuilt in stone between 1189 and 1200. Houses and shops lined it on both sides. At one end was St William's Chapel, the Council Chamber and the Exchequer; at the other, a hospital, the Tollbooth and public latrines. A wooden bridge across the Foss had twenty-three tenements and two shops in 1376; rebuilt in stone soon afterwards, the new bridge had twenty-five tenements and two shops in 1417. By the mid-fifteenth century there were nineteen tenements on the southwest side, twenty-three on the northeast, and ten in Fish Shambles.[81]

In Paris the Petit-Pont, across the smaller branch of the Seine between the Châtelet and the Hôtel-Dieu, was for long the only link between the Île de la Cité and the left bank. It was still wood in the early fifteenth century. The Grand-Pont was the major link across the larger branch, to the right bank. The Pont-Saint-Michel was built in 1378. It had sixteen shops on each side, the Petit-Pont eleven and nine. After a flood in 1408 inundated both and isolated the left bank, the bridges were rebuilt with royal aid, the Petit-Pont in stone, Saint-Michel in wood. The stone Grand-Pont was not damaged in 1408. Around 1434 it had sixty-eight buildings on one side and sixty-two on the other, and by 1440–50 at least 112 small shops.[82]

78 Blanshei, *Perugia*, 25–7.
79 Braunfels, *Urban Design*, 50.
80 Robertson, *Chaucer's London*, 57–8.
81 Tillott, *City of York*, 515, 518.
82 Favier, *Paris 1380–1500*, 14.

Transients and inns

Although most transients in the cities seem to have been poor, the nature of business meant that merchants or their agents had to spend a considerable amount of time on the road. Thus all major cities had several inns. London, with an enormous transient population, had 197 'commercial inns' in 1397 in addition to the town houses of major ecclesiastics and nobles and foundations for the poor. The Tabard Inn of Chaucer's time was part of the inn of the abbot of Hyde in London's notorious suburb of Southwark.[83] Most cities in southern France had between twenty and thirty inns, but Avignon during the residence of the popes had about sixty.[84] These figures are minima. The sources do not always distinguish clearly between innkeepers who simply gave lodging and those who did brokerage for their customers for a fee, usually calculated on the value of the item sold. The innkeeper vouched for the legitimacy of transactions on his premises. At Piacenza a statute of 1321 permitted innkeepers to sequester their guests' property until they were satisfied that they had fulfilled all obligations to their business partners. The brokerage inns in Italy were called *fondachi* (from the Arabic *funduq*) and paid toll to the city. One of the earliest was the *Fondaco dei Tedeschi* [German Inn] of Venice, which was established in 1228. There were so many *fondachi* in Pisa in the thirteenth century that their leaders, the *fondacarii*, had their own statute.

The innkeepers who simply gave lodging were a much more modest group than the brokers. Florence had 235 registered innkeepers in 1353. By 1394 there were 622, but this included 244 in the suburbs and dependent communities of the *contado*. Siena in 1355 had 100 in the city alone. No other Italian figures exist before the sixteenth century. Florence had three categories, depending on the sophistication of the accommodation they offered. Some Italian cities had separate guilds for 'major' and 'minor' innkeepers, but most had a single organisation. Naturally the innkeepers had some conflicts with the butchers and bakers. Inns had to have signs with their escutcheons and names outside to avoid confusion with guildhalls. In Florence they also had to display a red, octagonal star to prove that they had paid the wine tax and belonged to the innkeepers' guild.[85]

Most inns provided spartan accommodation. The single bed was virtually unheard of. Toulouse in the fourteenth century had seventy inns

83 Robertson, *Chaucer's London*, 12–13; Schofield, *Medieval London Houses*, 41.
84 Coulet, 'Proprietaires et exploitants d'auberges', 121.
85 Szabó, 'Hospitäler und Herbergen', 82–3, 88–9.

with about 600 beds, each for two or three people. Aix-en-Provence had twenty-seven establishments in the mid-fifteenth century and 200–250 beds. Confiscation lists at Bruges show up to eight beds in one room in an unnamed inn in 1383. The hospices of St Julien, with fifty beds, and of St Nicholas, founded in 1394 to cater for merchants and especially those visiting the Bruges fairs, with twenty-three beds, between them could accommodate over 200 persons at a time. Since they charged nothing, it is clear that many visitors to the fairs were poor vagabonds. Guests were usually given a bed, free bread, and pottage.[86] There were many semi-permanent guests at these places, particularly those catering for the poor, who might also circulate among several houses.[87]

The rhythm of market life

Although the guilds tried to centralise industrial and merchant operations, there were gaps in their monopolies. Although the cities had designated markets, trade and production occurred throughout the city. The streets were crowded with hucksters wandering about, calling and selling a variety of cheap goods from packs carried on their backs. Lübeck, a city of 15,000 around 1290, had at that time nearly 1,100 places where goods could be bought, from great markets and halls to tiny shops.[88] On market days the farmers from the surrounding country came to town; for the cities, faced with the loss of their central market functions in the central Middle Ages, had turned themselves into staples. The most active market day varied between cities, but goods were sold throughout the week, including Sundays. Given the perishability of food, the meat, fish and bread halls operated every day, and the Exchange was open to accommodate those needing its services to buy at the markets. From 1428 most merchants of Winchester and York were ordered to close their shops on Sunday, but butchers and other foodmongers were allowed to remain open for restricted hours.[89]

The market squares were the scenes of frenetic activity. Many market buildings were prefabricated shacks that could be carried by itinerant pedlars from place to place. Although typically the family shop was in the home, some non-resident owners leased entire blocks of shops either on the street in front of a larger house or sometimes in the alley behind it to craftsmen. By the early fourteenth century 'row' was used

86 Hilton, *English and French Towns*, 61; van Houtte, 'Herbergswesen', 177–8, 181.
87 Szabó, 'Hospitäler und Herbergen', 90.
88 Morris, *Urban Form*, 70; Irsigler, 'Kaufmannstypen', 393.
89 Desportes, *Reims*, 375–8; Keene, *Medieval Winchester*, 333; Swanson, *Medieval Artisans*, 14.

for blocks of shops for the same trade, and before 1400 sections of streets were planned as rows. The Cheapside area of London had 'selds', covered arcades with small booths at right angles to the main street. Cheapside amounted to an enlarged street market just off the city centre. West Cheap had luxury goods and shops, East Cheap more mundane items. Various markets for specialised goods were nearby, such as Bread Street, Milk, Wood and Friday Streets, Shambles for the butchers' stalls, Poultry, Ironmonger Lane and Fishmarket.[90]

In places where several trades competed for places on the market, guilds rotated the sections of the square, or the space would be reserved for different products on separate days.[91] At the Rialto in Venice the stalls had numbers, and the places were rotated among the guilds so that all would have a chance at the choice spots.[92] At Ghent the main square, the Grain Market, extended northwards into the Short Mint and onward to the Fish Market, which in turn gave access to aristocratic streets leading east and to the bridge to the count's castle on the west. The magistrates had barriers erected between these markets. Most moneychangers were on the Fish Market, but some were in the Short Mint. In 1366 the council prohibited sellers of spices, dairy products and fruit from setting up their stalls beyond this barrier, thus in the Grain Market rather than in the Short Mint. The hucksters who had until then sold onions, mercery and other goods in the Short Mint were ordered to take up position in front of the city jail, on the south end of the Grain Market, while those who had sold foods at the count's bridge and the Short Mint were to move to the Grain Market. In 1371 the aldermen forbade sellers of poultry, vegetables and French cheese to block the sides of the street between the count's bridge and the streets on the east side of the Fish Market. The Fish Market was sectioned off for sales of particular fish, and peas were sold at the corner of the Short Mint and the Long Mint. The city police – ten officers in that year – patrolled the area and tried to keep confusion to a minimum.[93]

From the planning and order of Roman urbanisation we have moved to the overregulated chaos of the late medieval city. The consumer city had yielded to a network of industrial centres and vibrant farm markets. The movement of diverse goods and services through the cities was so intense that late medieval urbanism seems to have little relationship to

90 Keene, 'Property market in English towns', 222–3; Schofield, *Medieval London Houses*, 55–6.
91 Schofield and Vince, *Medieval Town*, 49.
92 Mackenney, *Tradesmen and Traders*, 17.
93 Nicholas, *Metamorphosis*, 77–8.

its distant ancestor. The Roman city when it survived at all was only a central core of a settlement that was far more complex socially, economically and topographically than its ancient predecessor had been. Yet there are similarities, notably in the ethical and economic orientations of the elites, concentrating on wholesale commerce and landowning. The urban pattern of the modern period was clearly recognisable by 1450.

Glossary

aides	[French]. Indirect taxes, most often on sales.
albergo	plural *alberghi* [Italian]. Unions of lineages and nuclear families, creating a family in law.
amman	[German]. Representative of town lord, often functioning alongside the city government.
balia	plural *balie* [Italian]. Commission given extraordinary power to override normal governing bodies and legal procedures in the Italian cities.
bayles	[French]. Guild leaders appointed by city governments in French Languedoc.
blood justice	Justice in which blood can be shed, either through capital sentence or mutilation.
burgomaster	mayor.
Burspraken	[Latin *colloquia*]. Assemblies held to conduct police matters and issue statutes in most cities of the Baltic and Scandinavia that used the law of Lübeck.
catasto	[Italian]. Form of direct tax assessment based on ability to pay, levied on both moveable and immovable property as listed in a written declaration by the head of the household of his/her family's assets.
consorteria	Unions of nuclear families into an extended group. The term is also used for businesses that originated in family partnerships.
consul	Member of early city council in Italy and southern France; the term is occasionally used elsewhere for members of city councils and for leaders of guilds or merchant associations.
contado	plural *contadi* [Italian]. Countryside, specifically the area

345

around the city that was initially subject to the count but was gradually subordinated to the city.

dazio   plural *dazi* [Italian]. Direct tax.

dean   Chief official of a guild.

échevins   [French]. Judges and assessors in the court of a town lord. In Flanders and some cities of northern France, the *échevins* became the city council. The term is the same as *schepenen* [Flemish], *Schöffen* [German] and *scabini* [Latin]. In cases where the *échevins* became the city council, the term may be translated 'aldermen'.

estimo   [Italian]. Sworn estimate by the taxpayer of his/her taxable property, initially given orally, but eventually put into writing in most Italian cities. The same principle of self-assessment is also found in the north, particularly in Germany, but oral rather than written declarations were used longer there than it Italy.

gabelle   Indirect taxes in cities of northern Europe; *gabella* in the Italian cities included both direct and indirect taxes.

gonfaloniere   [Italian]. Standard-bearer, military leader of the *popolo* or a sector of it. His district was the *gonfalone*.

high justice   Justice in which the verdict can involve a capital sentence.

jurés   [French]. Officials of the sworn association of inhabitants of the town, to be distinguished from the *échevins*, who were officials of the town lord. In most cities of northern France and some in the eastern Low Countries, the *jurés* became a city council, sometimes replacing the older board of *échevins* but more often leaving it in existence while depriving it of its most important functions. The *jurés* are the equivalent of the German *Räte*. The council members of occupational guilds, whose function was to advise the guild dean, and of parishes also were often called *jurés* or the equivalent word meaning 'sworn person' in another language.

lira   plural *lire* [Italian]. Tax assessment based on the principle of the pound or 100 units.

loge   Hall used by merchants.

member   Groups of guilds or other units that acted together in choosing members of city councils and in some cases performing other municipal functions. Different terms for this principle are sometimes used, such as 'scale', *Gaffel* (Cologne), 'ladder', 'tribe', 'estate' or 'hand'.

mercanzia	[Italian]. Office of the merchants' guild.
ministerials	Serfs, mainly in the cities of Germany and the Low Countries, who performed honourable services such as castle guard for their lord or had responsibilities in his household or bureaucracy, such as in his mint. Some ministerial families held fiefs and achieved knighthood. During the late Middle Ages, many of the leading families of the west German cities were descendants of ministerials.
mistery	Craft organisation.
monte	[Italian]. Public debt.
Morgensprachen	[German]. 'Morning speeches', revisions of statutes issued every six months by Cologne.
podestà	[Italian]. Administrative, police and judicial official of the commune in some Italian cities.
popolo	plural *popoli* [Italian]. Organisation, mainly of prosperous merchants, but with some craftspeople and magnates, that formed a political pressure group in many Italian cities in the thirteenth century. Originally all-inclusive and intended as a militia organisation, it became directed chiefly against the magnates after 1250 and particularly 1270. In some cities the *popolo* became a separate government for its members. Members of the *popolo* were *popolani*. The *popolo* is often divided into an upper group, the 'fat *popolo*' (*popolo grosso*), a middle group (*popolo mediano*), and a 'little *popolo*' (*popolo minuto*).
Rat	[German]. City council. Plural form *Räte* means councillors.
receiver	Chief financial officer of a city.
scabini	[Latin]. See *échevins*.
schepenen	[Flemish]. See *échevins*.
Schöffen	[German]. See *échevins*.
scrutiny	Procedure by which officials were chosen in the Italian cities from among those whose wealth and family connections made them eligible.
Signoria	[Italian]. Chief governing body of an Italian city, usually a rotating council.
staple	Privilege of having the sole right to manufacture, sell, transport or provide a given commodity or service.
taille	[French]. Direct tax assessed on the wealth of the hearth.

Suggestions for Further Reading

This book represents the distillation of some thirty-five years of professional preoccupation with urban development in medieval Europe. The subject is immense, and no single volume can hope to capture every nuance or exception. Although I have used some original documents in translation for purposes of illustration, the book is intended principally as a synthesis and comparison of scholarly literature. It is thus based essentially on urban monographs, relatively few of which are in English except for cities in the British Isles, and on scholarly articles. These suggestions to aid the student who wishes to explore particular topics in greater depth will concentrate on the limited literature in English, but the complexity of the topic precludes limiting it to that. This essay includes only authors and titles; complete citations can be found in the bibliography.

1. GENERAL TREATMENTS

The history of the medieval city is a chapter in the broader history of urban development. The series that includes the present volume will provide a general survey of urbanisation in five volumes from classical antiquity to the present. Two companion volumes, Christopher Friedrichs, *The Early Modern City*, and David Nicholas, *The Growth of the Medieval City. From Late Antiquity to the Early Fourteenth Century* have already appeared; the latter is especially important for background to the present study. The synthesis provided by Max Weber, *The City* remains extremely provocative. Paul Bairoch, *Cities and Economic Development*, takes a suggestive and global approach to urbanisation from the beginning of

348

history to the present. Aspects of city planning and of the role of the city in a larger social environment are given in Lewis Mumford, *The City in History*. City planning and architecture are also emphasised in Wolfgang Braunfels, *Urban Design in Western Europe*; Marc Girouard, *Cities and People*; James E. Vance, *The Continuing City*; and Josef W. Konvitz, *The Urban Millennium*. All are stronger on the modern period than on the Middle Ages. The eight-volume *International History of City Development* edited by E. A. Gutkind has much of interest to the medievalist, particularly on city plans. In *The Making of Urban Europe* Paul Hohenberg and Lynn Hollen Lees have provided an analysis of urbanisation that is of interest to medievalists but concentrates on the period since 1500. They analyse the impact of politics and nationality on two urban models: the city as the central place of an economic, administrative and cultural region, and cities in networks, providing links between their own regions and the outside world. Within the regions a hierarchy of cities develops, in a generally discernible rank–size pattern that some geographers, followed too rigidly by the historian and demographer Josiah Cox Russell in *Medieval Regions and Their Cities*, have suggested can be determined by formulas based on population and population rank within the region. Philip Abrams and E. A. Wrigley's edited work *Towns in Societies* has important articles.

Of general works dealing specifically with the Middle Ages, Henri Pirenne's classics, *Medieval Cities. Their Origins and the Revival of Trade* and *Early Democracies in the Low Countries: Urban Society and Political Conflict in the Middle Ages and the Renaissance*, were the first significant summaries of their topics to appear in English and can still be read with profit, although their interpretations are outdated. Edith Ennen's *The Medieval Town*, a translation of a book originally published in German, is a distinguished work by the doyenne of modern German historians of medieval urban life. It shows the author's intimate familiarity with the scholarly literature, particularly in German, and her interests in urban origins and medieval women. Unfortunately, it shares with most German work a hypersensitivity to juridical questions. Rodney Hilton's *English and French Towns* compares French and English urban life in general terms, focusing on the smaller centres and placing them into a Marxist framework of feudalism. Although it must be used with care and conflates the city with the town, it is a useful survey of the literature. Of general works not in English, Jacques Heers's *La ville au moyen age en occident: paysages, pouvoirs et conflits* reflects Heers's interest in questions of space utilisation and urban topography as well as his scholarly preoccupation with Italy. Yves Barel's Marxist analysis *La ville médiévale* has some useful insights.

Studies on particular topics in a Europe-wide context have value for comparative questions. For founded towns, some of which developed into genuine cities, the best English work is Maurice Beresford, *New Towns of the Middle Ages*. Two general treatments of guilds have been published recently. Antony Black, *Guilds and Civil Society in European Political Thought from the Twelfth Century to the Present*, is theoretical, while Steven A. Epstein's *Wage Labor and Guilds in Medieval Europe* is an ambitious effort that is marred by questionable readings of documents and an uncertain focus. The best comprehensive work on the occupational guilds remains Sylvia L. Thrupp, 'The Gilds'.

2. FRANCE

The only survey of even a single aspect of French urbanisation in English is Charles Petit-Dutaillis's classic *The French Communes*. A fine survey of urbanisation in France is Georges Duby (ed.), *Histoire de la France urbaine*, whose first two volumes concern late antiquity and the Middle Ages. For the French cities of the late Middle Ages the best general work is Bernard Chevalier, *Les bonnes villes de France*. Irving Agus' *Urban Civilization in Pre-Crusade Europe* studies city life in the early Middle Ages from the perspective of the Jewish *responsa* literature. André E. Guillerme, *The Age of Water* gives a provocative thesis concerning hydrographic problems in the cities of northern France. André Gouron, *La Réglementation des Métiers en Languedoc au Moyen Age* is the only general study of the French crafts and occupational guilds for the Middle Ages. Michel Mollat, *The Poor in the Middle Ages* contains considerable material on urban poverty, particularly in but not confined to France.

Most urban monographs on individual French cities in the late Middle Ages are in French. Some work in English concerns specific topics of urban history rather than providing a comprehensive treatment of one city, for example Jacques Rossiaud, *Medieval Prostitution*. The studies in French that are most important for English readers are the second and third volumes of the New History of Paris: Raymond Cazelles, *Paris de la fin du règne de Philippe Auguste à la mort de Charles V, 1223–1380*; and Jean Favier, *Paris au XVe siècle, 1380–1500*. Bronislaw Geremek, *The Margins of Society in Late Medieval Paris* and *Le salariat dans l'artisanat parisien aux XIIIe–XVe siècles* deal with the labourers and unemployed in the French capital. The cities of Brittany have received treatment in Jean-Pierre Leguay, *Un Réseau urbain au Moyen Age*.

Other monographs on the French cities are also useful. Some are edited works, such as Alain Derville, *Histoire de Saint-Omer* and Louis Trenard,

Histoire de Lille. A series of popular and nicely illustrated studies of individual cities has been published by the Privat firm of Toulouse. Important works include Bernard Chevalier, *Tours, ville royale (1356–1520)*; Ghislaine Faber and Thierry Lochard, *Montpellier*; Kathryn L. Reyerson, *Business, Banking and Finance in Medieval Montpellier*; Yves Renouard, *Bordeaux sous les rois d'Angleterre*; and Louis Stouff, *Arles à la fin du Moyen Age.* Jean Schneider, *La Ville de Metz* is of fundamental importance.

3. ITALY

There is considerable material in English on the Italian cities after 1300. J. K. Hyde, *Society and Politics in Medieval Italy. The Evolution of the Civic Life, 1000–1350* and John Larner, *Italy in the Age of Dante and Petrarch, 1216–1380* are useful summaries. The early monographs of David Herlihy, *Pisa in the Early Renaissance* and *Medieval and Early Renaissance Pistoia*, deepened our understanding of the urban economy its symbiotic relation with the countryside; his later works, *Medieval Households, Opera Muliebria*, and particularly his collaborative work with Christiane Klapisch-Zuber, *Tuscans and their Families* revolutionised the study of the medieval women and propounded theses that will be debated for generations. Most of Jacques Heers' many studies remain in French, unfortunately including his monographs on Genoa. Two dealing with the nature of the extended family and with the composition of urban factions and their political role in the cities are available in English: *Parties and Political Life in the Medieval West* and *Family Clans in the Middle Ages.*

Venice has been studied by Frederic C. Lane in a survey monograph, *Venice. A Maritime Republic*, but readers should also see Lane's collected papers, *Venice and History* and Donald E. Queller, *The Venetian Patriciate.* Richard MacKenney, *Tradesmen and Traders* deals with an often-neglected aspect of Venetian history, those outside the elite. Lauro Martines's edition of studies relating to urban violence in Italy, *Violence and Civil Disorder in Italian Cities* can be supplemented by Guido Ruggiero, *Violence in Early Renaissance Venice.*

David Friedman, *Florentine New Towns*, studies the effort of a major city to export its principles of urban planning to communities that it founded. Richard A. Goldthwaite, *The Building of Renaissance Florence* has considerable material on urban architecture, the construction trades and the labour market. An unusual comparative treatment is George Holmes, *Florence, Rome and the Origins of the Renaissance.* Renaissance Florence has received treatments far too numerous to be listed here. An older but still useful account is Ferdinand Schevill, *Medieval and Renaissance Florence.*

Among the most stimulating are three books by Gene A. Brucker: *The Civic World of Early Renaissance Florence, Florentine Politics and Society, 1343–1378* and *Renaissance Florence*. Also important are Dale Kent, *The Rise of the Medici* and Anthony Molho, *Florentine Public Finances in the Early Renaissance*; and Nicolai Rubinstein, *The Government of Florence Under the Medici (1434 to 1494)*. John M. Najemy, *Corporatism and Consensus in Florentine Electoral Politics, 1280–1400* is an important prosopographical examination of the interaction of parties, guilds and lineages in staffing the city government. The continued importance of neighbourhood bonds is emphasised by D. V. and F. W. Kent, *Neighbours and Neighbourhood in Renaissance Florence*. Readers conversant with Italian should see Francesca Bocchi, *Attraverso le città italiane nel medioevo*, a statistical summary of the vicissitudes of the late medieval Italian cities, and Maria Ginatempo and Lucia Sandri, *L'Italia della città*; and Gioacchino *Volpe, Medio Evo Italiano*.

On the smaller Italian cities, many of which were quite large by north European standards, a model work is Sarah R. Blanshei, *Perugia 1260–1340: Conflict and Change in a Medieval Italian Urban Society*. Siena is well served by William Bowsky's two books: *The Finances of the Commune of Siena, 1287–1355* and *A Medieval Italian Commune. Siena Under the Nine, 1287–1355*. Christine Meek's two volumes on fourteenth-century Lucca, *The Commune of Lucca Under Pisan Rule, 1342–1369* and *Lucca 1369–1400. Politics and Society in an Early Renaissance City-State* are excellent. J. K. Hyde, *Padua in the Age of Dante*, is an important study of a large city that escaped much of the turmoil of the Tuscan centres. Daniel Waley's older study of *Mediaeval Orvieto. The Political History of an Italian City-State, 1157–1334* can be read with profit. Elisabeth Carpentier, *Une ville devant la peste. Orvieto et la Peste Noire de 1348* is invaluable as a test of one community's reaction to the plagues.

4. SPAIN

Little exists in English on the Spanish cities, most of which were small into the thirteenth century. Heath Dillard, *Daughters of the Reconquest*, uses urban charters to eludicate the situation of women in the frontier towns. Claude Carrère, *Barcelone. Centre économique à l'époque des difficultés, 1380–1462* is a fine treatment of the declining fortunes of Aragon's major city in the fifteenth century. Jacqueline Guiral-Hadziiossif, *Valence, port méditerranéen au XVe siècle* surveys the rise of Valencia into a major centre. John Edwards, *Christian Córdoba*, deals with the city after the Christian conquest from a regional perspective. Miguel Angel Ladero-

Quesnada, *La ciudad medieval* is part of Francisco Morales Padron's multivolume edited *Historia de Sevilla*.

5. GERMANY, AUSTRIA AND SWITZERLAND

Little on the German cities exists in English. Martha C. Howell, *Women, Production, and Patriarchy in Late Medieval Cities* approached late medieval Cologne from a Marxist and feminist perspective. Readers conversant with German can benefit from an immense literature. Several collected works in the series *Vorträge und Forschungen* of the Konstanzer Arbeitskreis für Mittelalterliche Geschichte are useful, particularly *Untersuchungen zur gesellschaftlichen Struktur der mittelalterlichen Städte in Europa*. Several monographs in the Städteforschung series A published by the University of Münster have been of critical importance for this book. Carl Haase has published numerous scholarly articles in a three-volume collection, *Die Stadt des Mittelalters*.

Scholars now recognise that city lords played a much more important role in urban development, both in generating demand for goods and services and in intervening in government, than was once thought. On this subject, a useful collection is Wilhelm Rausch, *Stadt und Stadtherr im 14. Jahrhundert*. Of urban monographs in German, readers should see especially Ludwig Falck's two-volume *Geschichte der Stadt Mainz*, which takes the story of the city to 1328 and Michael Matheus, *Trier am Ende des Mittelalters*. The guilds and labourers have been given superb treatment in Klaus D. Bechtold, *Zunftbürgerschaft und Patriziat* and Knut Schulz, *Handwerksgesellen und Lohnarbeiter*.

6. LOW COUNTRIES

Given the importance of this region in the urban development of Europe, it is especially unfortunate that until recently little has been available in English except for Pirenne's works. There is a substantial literature in French, but most remains in Dutch. Considerable recent work has been published in English on Ghent, Flanders' largest city, by David Nicholas: *The Domestic Life of a Medieval City* studies women and the family in Ghent; *The Metamorphosis of a Medieval City: Ghent in the Age of the Arteveldes, 1302–1390* is an economic history of the fourteenth-century city; *Town and Countryside: Social, Economic, and Political Tensions in Fourteenth-Century Flanders* discusses the efforts of the larger centres to dominate rural Flanders; *The van Arteveldes of Ghent: the Varieties of*

Vendetta and the Hero in History discusses a Flemish political family and the role that blood feuds continued to play in urban culture in the late Middle Ages. Nicholas's *Medieval Flanders* summarises Dutch work on other Flemish cities. The best book on Bruges in English remains Raymond de Roover, *Money, Banking, and Credit in Mediaeval Bruges*; and in French J. A. van Houtte, *Bruges. Essai d'histoire urbaine*. A promising new series that links history with urban planning is the *Historische Stedenatlas van België* [Urban Historical Atlas of Belgium].

7. ENGLAND

Several syntheses of early city life in the British Isles are useful: R. A. Butlin, *The Development of the Irish Town*; for early constitutional developments, James Tait, *The Medieval English Borough*; Susan Reynolds, *An Introduction to the History of English Medieval Towns*; John Schofield and Alan Vince, *Medieval Towns* and Colin Platt, *The English Mediaeval Town* both discuss urban development from the archaeologist's perspective, an orientation conspicuous also in Platt's *Medieval Southampton*. R. H. Britnell's recent synthesis *The Commercialisation of English Society, 1000–1500* has much of value for urban history. Edward Miller and John Hatcher, *Medieval England. Towns, Commerce and Crafts* is useful for background.

A work of fundamental importance is the ongoing series edited by M. D. Lobel, *Historic Towns. Maps and Plans of Towns and Cities in the British Isles*. Heather Swanson, *Medieval Artisans* has a wealth of information on the craftspeople, particularly of York. Two edited collections of articles useful for the urban historian are Richard Holt and Gervase Rosser, *The Medieval Town* and John A. F. Thomson, *Towns and Townspeople in the Fifteenth Century*. An important collection of articles on city-sponsored pageantry in the late Middle Ages, mainly in England, France and the Low Countries is edited by Barbara A. Hanawalt and Kathryn L. Reyerson, *City and Spectacle in Medieval Europe*.

Several fine monographs on English cities have appeared within the past several decades: Margaret Bonney, *Lordship and the Urban Community. Durham and Its Overlords, 1250–1540*; R. H. Britnell, *Growth and Decline in Colchester, 1300–1525*; A. E. Brown, *The Growth of Leicester*; Robert S. Gottfried, *Bury St. Edmunds and the Urban Crisis*; and Gervase Rosser, *Medieval Westminster*. P. J. P. Goldberg, *Women, Work, and Life Cycle in a Medieval Economy* offers a fascinating thesis on the situation of working women in a late medieval city. Francis Hill, *Medieval Lincoln* can still be read with profit. Derek Keene's monumental *Survey of Medieval Winchester* is important both for its methodology and its conclusions.

The same is true of Charles Phythian-Adams, *Coventry*, although its focus is the early sixteenth century.

London's growth so outstripped the other English cities that it became a depressant on them. The capital has been the subject of a vast literature. Gwyn A. Williams, *Medieval London. From Commune to Capital*, is a riveting account of social change and political rivalries during the thirteenth and early centuries. A particularly important recent book is Pamela Nightingale, *A Medieval Mercantile Community. The Grocers' Company and the Politics and Trade of London*. Fourteenth- and fifteenth-century London still has not received a definitive survey treatment, but the period of Richard II has been examined by Ruth Bird, *The Turbulent London of Richard II*. A wealth of detail on late fourteenth-century London in a popular format is given in D. W. Robertson, *Chaucer's London*. Although its focus is the history of youth rather than of the city as such, Barbara Hanawalt, *Growing Up in Medieval London* provides considerable information about the physical environment of the city.

Abbreviations

AESC	*Annales. Economies. Sociétés. Civilisations.*
AGN	*Algemene Geschiedenis der Nederlanden.* Utrecht: Fibula-Van Dishoeck, 1982.
AHR	*American Historical Review.*
BSL	Josef Fleckenstein and Karl Stackmann (eds). *Über Bürger, Stadt und städtische Literatur im Spätmittelalter.* Bericht über Kolloquium der Kommission zur Erforschung der Kultur des Spätmittelalters, 1975–1977. Abhandlungen der Akademie der Wissenschaften in Göttingen, Phil.-Hist. Klasse, ser. 3, no. 121. Göttingen: Vandenhoeck and Ruprecht, 1980.
BSS	Bernhard Diestelkamp (ed.). *Beiträge zum spätmittelalterlichen Städtewesen.* Cologne and Vienna: Böhlau, 1982. Stadtforschungen A/12.
CC	Trevor Dean and Chris Wickham (eds). *City and Countryside in Late Medieval and Renaissance Italy. Essays Presented to Philip Jones.* London: Hambledon Press, 1990.
CHUO	H. B. Clarke and Anngret Simms (eds). *The Comparative History of Urban Origins in Non-Roman Europe. Ireland, Wales, Denmark, Germany, Poland and Russia from the Ninth to the Thirteenth Century.* 2 vols continuously paginated. BAR International Series 255. Oxford: British Archaeological Reports, 1985.
CS	Barbara A. Hanawalt and Kathryn L. Reyerson (eds). *City and Spectacle in Medieval Europe.* Minneapolis: University of Minnesota Press, 1994.
EcHR	*Economic History Review.*
EHR	*English Historical Review.*

FC   *Finances et comptabilités urbaines du XIIIe au XVIe siècle. Financiën en boekhouding der steden van de XIIIe tot de XIVe eeuw.* Brussels: Pro Civitate, 1964.

FSE   Werner Besch *et al.* (eds). *Die Stadt in der europäischen Geschichte. Festschrift Edith Ennen.* Bonn: Ludwig Rohrscheid, 1972.

GTG   Hans Conrad Peyer (ed.). *Gastfreundschaft, Taverne und Gasthaus im Mittelalter.* Munich and Vienna: Oldenbourg, 1983.

HFU   Georges Duby (ed.). *Histoire de la France urbaine.* I. *La ville antique. Des origines au IXe siècle.* II. *La ville médiévale. Des Carolingiens à la Renaissance.* Paris: Editions du Seuil, 1980.

IC   A. H. Hourani and S. M. Stern (eds). *The Islamic City. A Colloquium.* Papers on Islamic History, 1. Philadelphia: University of Pennsylvania Press, 1970.

JMH   *The Journal of Medieval History.*

LCS   *Law, Custom, and the Social Fabric in Medieval Europe. Essays in Honor of Bryce Lyon.* Edited by Bernard S. Bachrach and David Nicholas. Kalamazoo, Michigan: Medieval Institute Publications, 1990.

LS   *Das Leben in der Stadt des Spätmittelalters.* Internationaler Kongress Krems an der Donau 20. bis 23. September 1976. Veröffentlichungen des Instituts für mittelalterlichen Realienkunde Österreichs, no. 2. Österreichsche Akademie der Wissenschaften, Phil.-Hist. Klasse, Sitzungsberichte, 325. Vienna: Verlag der österreichischen Akademie der Wissenschaften, 1977.

LUR   *Les Libertés urbaines et rurales du XIe au XIVe siècle. Vrijheden in de stad en op het platteland van de XIe tot de XIVe eeuw.* Colloque International, Spa 5–8 IX 1966. *Actes. Handelingen.* Brussels: Pro Civitate, 1968.

MT   Richard Holt and Gervase Rosser (eds). *The Medieval Town. A Reader in English Urban History, 1200–1540.* London: Longman, 1990.

OT   Thomas W. Blomquist and Maureen F. Mazzaoui (eds). *The "Other Tuscany." Essays in the History of Lucca, Pisa, and Siena during the Thirteenth, Fourteenth, and Fifteenth Centuries.* Kalamazoo, Michigan: Medieval Institute Publications, 1994.

PP   *Past and Present.*

PS   Nicolai Rubinstein (ed.). *Florentine Studies. Politics and Society*

	in Renaissance Florence. Evanston: Northwestern University Press, 1968.
PT	M. W. Barley (ed.). *The Plans and Topography of Medieval Towns in England and Wales.* CBA Research Report #14. N.P.: Council for British Archaeology, 1976.
PTME	Jean-Marie Duvosquel and Erik Thoen (eds). *Peasants and Townsmen in Medieval Europe. Studia in honorem Adriaan Verhulst.* Ghent: Snoeck-Ducaju en Zoon, 1995.
PU	*Le Paysage urbain au Moyen Age.* Actes du XIe Congrès des historiens médiévistes de l'enseignement supérieur. Lyon: Presses Universitaires de Lyon, 1981.
RBPH	*Revue Belge de Philologie et d'Histoire*
RN	*Revue du Nord.*
SAES	*Studien zu den Anfängen des europäischen Städtewesens.* Vorträge und Forschungen herausgegeben vom Konstanzer Arbeitskreis für mittelalterliche Geschichte, 4. Constance and Lindau: Jan Thorbecke, 1958.
SB	Bernd Moeller, Hans Patze and Karl Stackmann (eds). *Studien zum städischen Bildungswesen des späten Mittelalters und der frühen Neuzeit.* Abhandlungen der Akademie der Wissenschaften in Göttingen, Phil.-Hist. Klasse, ser. 3, no. 137. Göttingen: Vandenhoeck und Ruprecht, 1983.
SMOE	Jean-Claude Maire Vigueur (ed.). *D'une ville à l'autre: Structures matérielles et organisation de l'espace dans les villes européennes (XIIIe–XVIe siècle).* Actes du Colloque organisé par l'Ecole française de Rome avec le concours de l'Université de Rome (Rome 1er–4 décembre 1986). Rome: Ecole Française de Rome, 1989.
SS	Bernhard Töpfer (ed.). *Stadt und Städtebürgertum in der deutschen Geschichte des 13. Jahrhunderts.* Berlin: Akademie Verlag, 1976.
SSt	Bernhard Töpfer (ed.). *Städte und Ständestaat. Zur Rolle der Städte bei der Entwicklung der Ständesverfassung in europäischen Staaten vom 13. bis zum 15. Jahrhundert.* Berlin: Akademie-Verlag, 1980.
Stoob FS	Helmut Jäger, Franz Petri and Heinz Quirin (eds). *Civitatum Communitas. Studien zum europäischen Städtewesen. Festschrift Heinz Stoob zum 65. Geburtstag.* Cologne and Vienna: Böhlau, 1984. 2 vols Städteforschung 19, 21.
Strayer FS	*Order and Innovation in the Middle Ages: Essays in Honor of Joseph R. Strayer.* Princeton: Princeton University Press, 1976.

TRHS	Royal Historical Society, London. *Transactions.*
TT	John A. F. Thomson (ed.). *Towns and Townspeople in the Fifteenth Century.* Gloucester: Alan Sutton, 1988.
UGS	*Untersuchungen zur gesellschaftlichen Struktur der mittelalterlichen Städte in Europa.* Reichenau-Vorträge 1963–1964. Vorträge und Forschungen herausgegeben vom Konstanzer Arbeitskreis für mittelalterliche Geschichte, 11. Constance and Stuttgart: Jan Thorbecke, 1966.
USEE	Barisa Krekic (ed.). *Urban Society of Eastern Europe in Premodern Times.* Berkeley and Los Angeles: University of California Press, 1987.

Bibliography

Abrams, Philip, and E. A. Wrigley (eds). *Towns in Societies. Essays in Economic History and Historical Sociology.* Cambridge: Cambridge University Press, 1978.

Abulafia, David, Michael Franklin and Miri Rubin (eds). *Church and City 1000–1500. Essays in honour of Christopher Brooke.* Cambridge: Cambridge University Press, 1992.

Abulafia, David. 'From privilege to persecution: crown, church and synagogue in the city of Majorca, 1229–1343'. In Abulafia, *Church and City*, 111–26.

Ackerman, James S., and Myra Nan Rosenfeld. 'Social stratification in Renaissance urban planning'. In Zimmerman and Weissman, *Urban Life in the Renaissance*, 21–49.

Alberts, W. Jappe. *De middeleeuwse stad.* Bussum: Fibula-Van Dishoeck, 1968.

Algemene Geschiedenis der Nederlanden. 2nd ed. Utrecht: Fibula-Van Dishoeck, 1982.

Allmand, Christopher. 'Taxation in medieval England: the example of murage'. In Bourin, *Villes*, 223–30.

Anderson, Bonnie S., and Judith P. Zinsser. *A History of Their Own. Women in Europe from Prehistory to the Present.* 1. New York: Harper and Row, 1988.

Ascheri, Mario. 'Siena in the fourteenth century: state, territory, and culture'. *OT*, 163–97.

Aston, Michael, and James Bond. *The Landscape of Towns.* Gloucester: Alan Sutton, 1987.

Attreed, Lorraine. 'Arbitration and the growth of urban liberties in late medieval England'. *Journal of British Studies* 31 (1992): 205–35.

Bachrach, Bernard S., and David Nicholas (eds). *Law, Custom, and the*

Social Fabric in Medieval Europe. Essays in Honor of Bryce Lyon. Kalamazoo, Michigan: Medieval Institute Publications, 1990.

Bairoch, Paul. *Cities and Economic Development. From the Dawn of History to the Present.* Translated by Christopher Braider. Chicago: University of Chicago Press, 1988.

Bairoch, Paul, Jean Batou and Pierre Chèvre. *La Population des villes européennes. Banque de données et analyse sommaire des resultats. 800–1850. The Population of European Cities. Data Bank and Short Summary of Results.* Geneva: Droz, 1988.

Baker, Robert L. 'The government of Calais in 1363'. *Strayer FS*, 207–14.

Baldwin, John W. *The Scholastic Culture of the Middle Ages, 1000–1300.* Lexington, Mass.: D. C. Heath, 1971.

Balestracci, Duccio. 'From development to crisis: changing urban structures in Siena between the thirteenth and fifteenth centuries'. *OT*, 199–213.

Balestracci, Duccio. 'Immigrazione e morfologia urbana nella Toscana bassomedievale'. *SMOE*, 87–105.

Baratier, Edouard (ed.). *Histoire de Marseille.* Toulouse: Privat, 1973.

Barel, Yves. *La ville médiévale. Système sociale. Système urbain.* Grenoble: Presses Universitaires de Grenoble, 1977.

Barral I Altet, Xavier (ed.). *Artistes, Artisans et Production artistique au Moyen Age. Colloque international.* Paris: Picard, 1986.

Barron, Caroline M. 'London and the Crown, 1451–61'. In Highfield and Jeffs, *Crown and Local Communities*, 88–109.

Barron, Caroline M. and Anne F. Sutton (eds). *Medieval London Widows, 1300–1500.* London: Hambledon Press, 1994.

Barron, Caroline M. 'Ralph Holland and the London radicals, 1438–1444'. Originally in *A History of the North London Branch of the Historical Association, Together with Essays in Honour of its Golden Jubilee* (London, 1970), reprinted *MT*, 160–83.

Barron, Caroline M. 'Richard Whittington: the man behind the myth'. In Hollaender and Kellaway, *Studies in London History*, 195–248.

Bartel, Wojciech M. 'Stadt und Staat in Polen im 14. Jahrhundert'. In Rausch, *Stadt und Stadtherr*, 129–62.

Bassett, Steven (ed.). *Death in Towns. Urban Responses to the Dying and the Dead, 1000–1600.* Leicester: Leicester University Press, 1992.

Beaumanoir, Philippe de. *The Coutumes de Beauvaisis of Philippe de Beaumanoir.* Translated by F. R. P. Akehurst. Philadelphia: University of Pennsylvania Press, 1992.

Bec, Christian. *Les marchands écrivains. Affairs et humanisme à Florence, 1375–1434.* Paris and The Hague: Mouton, 1977.

Bechtold, Klaus D. *Zunftbürgerschaft und Patriziat. Studien zur Sozialgeschichte der Stadt Konstanz im 14. und 15. Jahrhundert*. Sigmaringen: Jan Thorbecke, 1981.

Becker, Marvin B. 'The Florentine territorial state and civic Humanism in the early Renaissance'. *PS*, 109–39.

Bender, Thomas (ed.). *The University and the City. From Medieval Origins to the Present*. New York: Oxford University Press, 1988.

Benevolo, Leonardo. *The History of the City*. Translated by Geoffrey Culverwell. Cambridge, Mass.: MIT Press, 1980.

Berghans, H. P. 'Die Münzpolitik der deutschen Städte im Mittelalter'. *FC*, 75–84.

Berthold, Brigitte. 'Städte und Reichsreform in der ersten Hälfte des 15. Jahrhunderts'. *SSt*, 59–111.

Billot, Claudine. *Chartres à la fin du Moyen Age*. Paris: Editions de l'Ecole des Hautes Etudes en Sciences Sociales, 1987.

Bird, Ruth. *The Turbulent London of Richard II*. London: Longman, Green and Company, 1949.

Birnbaum, Henrik. 'Kiev, Novgorod, Moscow: three varieties of urban society in east Slavic territory'. *USEE*, 1–62.

Birnbaum, Henrik. *Studies in Early Slavic Civilization*. Munich: Wilhelm Fink, 1981.

Birnbaum, Marianna D. 'Buda between Tatars and Turks'. *USEE*, 137–57.

Bischoff, Johannes. 'Die Stadtherrschaft des 14. Jahrhunderts im ostfränkischen Städtedreieck Nürnberg-Bamberg-Coburg-Bayreuth'. In Rausch, *Stadt und Stadtherr*, 97–124.

Biskup, Marian. 'Die Rolle der Städte in der Ständesvertretung des Königsreiches Polen, einschliesslich des Ordensstaates Preussen im 14./15. Jahrhundert'. *SSt*, 163–93.

Bisson, T. N. *The Medieval Crown of Aragon. A Short History*. Oxford: Clarendon Press, 1986.

Black, Antony. *Guilds and Civil Society in European Political Thought from the Twelfth Century to the Present*. Ithaca: Cornell University Press, 1984.

Blair, John, and Nigel Ramsey (eds). *English Medieval Industries. Craftsmen, Techniques, Products*. London: Hambledon Press, 1991.

Bland, A. F., P. A. Brown and R. H. Tawney (eds). *English Economic History. Select Documents*. London: G. Bell and Sons, 1914.

Blaschke, Karlheinz. 'Sonderbereiche in sächsischen Städten an der Wende vom Mittelalter zur Neuzeit'. *Stoob FS*, 254–65.

Blaschke, Karlheinz. 'Städte und Stadtherren im meissnisch-lausitzischen Raum während des 14. Jahrhunderts'. In Rausch, *Stadt und Stadtherr*, 55–72.

Blanshei, Sarah Rubin. *Perugia 1260–1340: Conflict and Change in a Medieval Italian Urban Society*. Transactions of the American Philosophical Society, n.s. 66, part 2. Philadelphia: American Philosophical Society, 1976.

Blockmans, F. 'Le contrôle par le prince des comptes urbains en Flandre et en Brabant au Moyen Age'. In *Finances et comptabilités urbaines du XIIIe au XVIe siècle*, 287–338.

Blockmans, W. 'Vers une société urbanisée'. In Els Witte (ed.), *Histoire de Flandre des origines à nos jours*. Brussels: La Renaissance du Livre, 1983.

Blom, Grethe Anthen. 'Der Ursprung der Gilden in Norwegen und ihre Entwicklung in den Städten während des Mittelalters'. In Friedland, *Gilde*, 5–27.

Blomquist, Thomas W., and Maureen F. Mazzaoui (eds). *The "Other Tuscany". Essays in the History of Lucca, Pisa, and Siena during the Thirteenth, Fourteenth, and Fifteenth Centuries*. Kalamazoo, Michigan: Medieval Institute Publications, 1994.

Bocchi, Francesca. *Attraverso le città italiane nel medioevo*. Casalecchio di Reno: Grafis Edizioni, 1987.

Bonney, Margaret. *Lordship and the Urban Community. Durham and Its Overlords, 1250–1540*. Cambridge: Cambridge University Press, 1990.

Boone, Marc. *Geld en Macht. De Gentse stadsfinanciën en de Bourgondische staatsvorming (1384–1453)*. Ghent: Maatschappij voor Geschiedenis en Oudheidkunde te Gent, 1990.

Boone, Marc. *Gent en de Bourgondische hertogen, ca. 1384–ca. 1453. Een sociaal-politieke studie van een staatsvormingproces*. Brussels: Paleis der Academiën, 1990.

Boone, Marc, Machteld Dumon and Birgit Reusens. *Immobiliënmarkt, Fiscaliteit en Sociale Ongelijkheid te Gent, 1483–1503*. Courtrai-Heule: UGA, 1981. Standen en Landen 78.

Booton, Harold W. 'Inland trade: a study of Aberdeen in the later Middle Ages'. In Lynch *et al.*, *Scottish Medieval Town*, 148–60.

Bosl, Karl (ed.). *Die mittelalterliche Stadt in Bayern*. Munich: C. H. Beck, 1974.

Bosl, Karl. 'Die Sozialstruktur der mittelalterlichen Residenz- und Fernhandelsstadt Regensburg. Die Entwicklung ihres Bürgertums vom 9.–14. Jahrhundert'. *UGS*, 93–213.

Bosl, Karl. *Die wirtschaftliche und gesellschaftliche Entwicklung des Augsburger Bürgertums vom 10. bis zum 14. Jahrhundert*. Munich: Bayerische Akademie der Wissenschaften, 1969.

Bourin, Monique (ed.). *Villes, bonnes villes, cités et capitales. Etudes d'histoire urbaine (XIIe–XVIIIe siècle) offertes à Bernard Chevalier*. Tours: Université de Tours, 1989.

Boussard, Jacques. *Nouvelle Histoire de Paris. De la fin du siège de 885–886 à la mort de Philippe Auguste.* Paris: Hachette, 1976.

Bowsky, William M. *The Finances of the Commune of Siena, 1287–1355.* Oxford: Clarendon Press, 1970.

Bowsky, William F. 'The impact of the Black Death upon Sienese government and society'. *Speculum* 39 (1964): 1–34.

Bowsky, William M. *A Medieval Italian Commune. Siena Under the Nine, 1287–1355.* Berkeley: University of California Press, 1981.

Boyer, Marjorie N. 'Working at the bridge site in late medieval France'. In Barral I Altet, *Artistes*, 217–27.

Brandt, Ahasver von. 'Die gesellschaftliche Struktur des spätmittelalterlichen Lübeck'. *UGS*, 215–39.

Bratschel, Michael E. 'Lucca 1430–94: the politics of the restored republic'. *OT*, 19–39.

Braunfels, Wolfgang. *Urban Design in Western Europe. Regime and Architecture, 900–1900.* Translated by Kenneth J. Northcott. Chicago: University of Chicago Press, 1988.

Braunstein, Philippe. 'Les salaires sur les chantiers monumentaux du Milanais à la fin du XIVe siècle'. In Barral I Altet, *Artistes*, 123–32.

Brentano, Robert. *Rome Before Avignon. A Social History of Thirteenth-Century Rome.* New York: Basic Books, 1974.

Bresc, Henri, ' "In ruga que arabice dicitur zucac" . . .!' les rues de Palerme (1070–1460)'. *PU*, 155–86.

Bridbury, A. R. *Medieval English Clothmaking: an Economic Survey.* London: Heinemann, 1982.

Britnell, R. H. *The Commercialisation of English Society, 1000–1500.* Cambridge: Cambridge University Press, 1993.

Britnell, R. H. 'England and northern Italy in the early fourteenth century: the economic contrasts'. *TRHS*, ser. 5, 39 (1989): 167–83.

Britnell, R. H. *Growth and Decline in Colchester, 1300–1525.* Cambridge: Cambridge University Press, 1986.

Brown, A. E. (ed.). *The Growth of Leicester.* Leicester: Leicester University Press, 1970.

Brown, Howard Mayer. 'Minstrels and their repertory in fifteenth-century France: music in an urban environment'. In Zimmerman and Weissman, *Urban Life in the Renaissance*, 142–64.

Brucker, Gene A. 'The Ciompi revolution'. *PS*, 314–45.

Brucker, Gene A. *The Civic World of Early Renaissance Florence.* Princeton: Princeton University Press, 1977.

Brucker, Gene A. *Florentine Politics and Society, 1343–1378.* Princeton: Princeton University Press, 1963.

Brucker, Gene A. 'The Florentine *popolo minuto* and its political role, 1340–1450'. In Martines, *Violence and Civil Disorder*, 155–83.

Brucker, Gene A. (ed.). *The Society of Renaissance Florence. A Documentary Study*. New York: Harper and Row, 1971.

Brucker, Gene A. *Renaissance Florence*. New York: John Wiley & Sons, 1969.

Bryant, Lawrence M. 'Configurations of community in late medieval spectacles: Paris and London during the Dual Monarchy'. *CS*, 3–33.

Bueno da Mesquita, D. M. *Giangaleazzo Visconti, Duke of Milan (1351–1402). A Study in the Political Career of an Italian Despot*. Cambridge: Cambridge University Press, 1941.

Bulst, Neithard, and Jean-Philippe Genet (eds). *Medieval Lives and the Historian. Studies in Medieval Prosopography*. Kalamazoo: Medieval Institute Publications, 1986.

Bulst, Neithard. 'Vier Jahrhunderte Pest in niedersächsischen Städten. Vom Schwarzen Tode (1349–1351) bis in die erste Hälfte des 18. Jahrhunderts'. In *Stadt im Wandel* 4: 251–70.

Bunge, F. G. von. *Die Stadt Riga im dreizehnten und vierzehnten Jahrhundert. Geschichte, Verfassung und Rechtszustand*. Leipzig, 1878, reprinted Amsterdam, E. J. Bonset, 1968.

Bur, Michel (ed.). *Histoire de Laon et du Laonnais*. Toulouse: Privat, 1987.

Burghartz, Susanna. *Leib, Ehre und Gut. Delinquenz in Zürich Ende des 14. Jahrhunderts*. Zürich: Chronos Verlag, 1990.

Busch, Ralf. 'Die Wasserversorgung des Mittelalters und der frühen Neuzeit in norddeutschen Städten'. In *Stadt im Wandel* 4: 301–15.

Butcher, A. F. 'English urban society and the revolt of 1381'. In Hilton and Aston, *English Rising of 1381*, 84–111.

Butlin, R. A. (ed.). *The Development of the Irish Town*. Totowa, N. J.: Rowman and Littlefield, 1977.

Caenegem, R. C. van. *Law, History, the Low Countries and Europe*. Edited by Ludo Milis, Daniel Lambrecht, Hilde De Ridder-Symoens, and Monique Vleeschouwers-Van Melkebeek. London and Rio Grande: Hambledon Press, 1994.

Carpentier, Elisabeth. *Une ville devant la peste. Orvieto et la Peste Noire de 1348*. Paris: SEVPEN, 1962.

Carr, David R. 'The problem of urban patriciates: office holders in fifteenth century Salisbury'. *The Wiltshire Archaeological and Natural History Magazine* 83 (1990): 118–35.

Carrère, Claude. *Barcelone. Centre économique à l'époque des difficultés, 1380–1462*. 2 vols. Paris and The Hague: Mouton, 1967.

Carter, F. W. *Trade and Urban Development in Poland: An Economic*

Geography of Cracow, from Its Origins to 1795. Cambridge: Cambridge University Press, 1994.

Castagnetti, Andrea. 'Appunti per una storia sociale e politica delle città della Marca Veronese-Trevigiano (secoli XI–XIV)'. In Elze and Fasoli, *Aristocrazia cittadina*, 41–77.

Castaldo, André. *Seigneur, villes et pouvoir royal en Languedoc: le consulat médiéval d'Agde (XIIIe–XIVe siècles)*. Paris: A. and J. Picard, 1974.

Cazelles, Raymond. 'The Jacquerie'. In Hilton and Aston, *The English Rising of 1381*, 74–83.

Cazelles, Raymond. *Paris de la fin du règne de Philippe Auguste à la mort de Charles V, 1223–1380*. Paris: Hachette, 1972.

Chapin, Elisabeth. *Les villes de foires de Champagne des origines au début du XIVe siècle*. Paris: Honoré Champion, 1937.

Charles, J. L. *La ville de Saint-Trond au Moyen Age. Des origines à la fin du XIVe siècle*. Bibliothèque de la Faculté de Philosophie et Lettres de l'Université de Liège, fasc. 173. Paris: Société d'Edition 'Les Belles Lettres', 1965.

Chédeville, André (ed.). *Histoire de Chartres et du pays chartrain*. Toulouse: Privat, 1983.

Chevalier, Bernard. 'The *bonnes villes* and the King's Council in fifteenth-century France'. In Highfield and Jeffs, *Crown and Local Communities*, 110–28.

Chevalier, Bernard. *Les bonnes villes de France, du XIVe au XVIe siècle*. Paris: Aubier Montaigne, 1982.

Chevalier, Bernard. 'Le paysage urbain à la fin du Moyen Age: imaginations et réalités'. *PU*, 7–21.

Chevalier, Bernard. *Tours, ville royale (1356–1520)*. Paris: Nauwelaerts, n.d.

Chew, Helena M., and William Kellaway (eds). *London Assize of Nuisance 1301–1431*. London: London Record Society, 1973.

Chittolini, Giorgio. 'Civic religion and the countryside in late medieval Italy'. *CC*, 69–80.

Chittolini, Giorgio. 'The Italian city-state and its territory'. In Molho *et al.*, *City States*, 589–602.

Chojnacki, Stanley. 'Crime, punishment, and the Trecento Venetian state'. In Martines, *Violence and Civil Disorder*, 184–228.

Chojnacki, Stanley. 'Marriage legislation and patrician society in fifteenth-century Venice'. *LCS*, 163–84.

Cipolla, Carlo M. *Before the Industrial Revolution. European Society and Economy, 1000–1700*. 2nd ed. New York: Norton, 1980.

Clune, George. *The Medieval Gild System*. Dublin: Browne and Nolan, 1943.

Cohen, Esther. 'Patterns of crime in fourteenth-century Paris'. *French Historical Studies* 11 (1980): 307–27.

Cohen, Esther. '"To die a criminal for the public good": the execution ritual in late medieval Paris'. *LCS*, 285–304.

Cohen, Mark R. *Under Crescent and Cross. The Jews in the Middle Ages.* Princeton: Princeton University Press, 1994.

Cohn, Samuel, Jr. 'Criminality and the state in Renaissance Florence, 1344–1466'. *Journal of Social History* 16 (1981): 211–33.

Cohn, Samuel, Jr. 'Florentine insurrections, 1342–1385, in comparative perspective'. In Hilton and Aston, *English Rising of 1381*, 143–64.

Coleman, Olive. 'The collectors of customs in London under Richard II'. In Hollaender and Kellaway, *Studies in London History*, 179–94.

Compagni, Dino. *Chronicle of Florence.* Translated, with an introduction and notes, by Daniel E. Bornstein. Philadelphia: University of Pennsylvania Press, 1986.

Corfield, Penelope J., and Derek Keene (eds). *Work in Towns 850–1850.* Leicester: Leicester University Press, 1990.

Coulet, Noël. 'Proprietaires et exploitants d'auberges dans la France du Midi au bas Moyen Age'. *GTG*, 119–36.

Coulet, Noël. 'Quartiers et communauté urbaine en Provence (XIIIe–XVe siècles)'. In Bourin, *Villes*, 351–9.

Csendes, Paul. 'Stadtherr und bürgerliches Führungsschicht in Wien des 14. Jahrhunderts'. In Rausch, *Stadt und Stadtherr*, 251–6.

Cunliffe, Barry. *The City of Bath.* New Haven: Yale University Press, 1986.

Curry, Anne E. 'Towns at war: relations between the towns of Normandy and their English rulers'. *TT*, 148–72.

Czacharowski, Antoni. 'Forschungen über die soziale Schichten in den Städten des deutschen Ordenslandes im 13. und 14. Jahrhundert'. *BSS*, 119–29.

Czok, Karl. 'Die Bürgerkämpfe in Süd- und Westdeutschland im 14. Jahrhundert'. In Haase, *Stadt des Mittelalters* 3: 303–44.

Dean, Trevor, and Chris Wickham (eds). *City and Countryside in Late Medieval and Renaissance Italy. Essays Presented to Philip Jones.* London: Hambledon Press, 1990.

Dean, Trevor. 'Commune and despot: the commune of Ferrara under Este Rule, 1300–1450'. *CC*, 183–97.

Dejevsky, N. J. 'Novgorod: the origins of a Russian town'. In Barley, *European Towns*, 391–403.

De la Roncière, Charles. 'Indirect taxes or "Gabelles" at Florence in the fourteenth century'. *PS*, 140–92.

Denecke, Dietrich. 'Sozialtopographie und sozialräumliche Gliederung der spätmittelalterlichen Stadt. Problemstellungen, Methoden und

Betrachtungsweisen der historischen Wirtschafts- und Sozialgeographie'. *BSL*, 161–202.

Denley, Peter. 'Governments and schools in late medieval Italy'. *CC*, 93–107.

De Pauw, Napoléon (ed.). *De Voorgeboden der stad Gent in de XIVe eeuw (1337–1382)*. Ghent: C. Annoot-Braeckman, 1885.

De Roover, Raymond. 'Labour conditions in Florence around 1400: theory, policy and reality'. *PS*, 277–313.

De Roover, Raymond. 'Les comptes communaux et la comptabilité communale de la ville de Bruges au XIVe siècle'. *FC*, 86–102.

De Roover, Raymond. *Money, Banking, and Credit in Mediaeval Bruges. Italian Merchant-Bankers, Lombards, and Money-Changers. A Study in the Origins of Banking*. Cambridge, Mass.: Mediaeval Academy of America, 1948.

Derville, Alain (ed.). *Histoire de Saint-Omer*. Lille: Presses Universitaires de Lille, 1981.

De Soignie, Raphael R. 'The fairs of Nîmes: evidence on their function, importance, and demise'. *Strayer FS*, 195–205.

Desportes, Françoise. 'Droit économique et police des métiers en France du Nord (milieu du XIIIe–début du XVe siècle'. *RN* 63 (1981): 321–36.

Desportes, Pierre. 'Nouveaux bourgeois et métiers à Amiens au XVe siècle. *RN* 64 (1982): 27–50.

Desportes, Pierre. 'Réceptions et inscriptions à la bourgeoisie de Lille aux XIVème et XVème siècles'. *RN* 62 (1980): 541–71.

Desportes, Pierre. *Reims et les Rémois aux XIIIe et XIVe siècles*. Paris: A. and J. Picard, 1979.

Dez, Gaston. *Histoire de Poitiers*. Poitiers: Société des Antiquaires de l'Ouest, 1969.

Dickinson, Robert E. *The West European City. A Geographical Interpretation*. 2nd ed. London: Routledge and Kegan Paul, 1961.

Dickstein-Bernard, C. 'Activité économique et développement urbain à Bruxelles (XIIIe–XVe siècles)'. *Cahiers Bruxellois* 24 (1979): 52–62.

Diermeier, Ulf. 'Le condizioni materiali dell'esistenza nelle città tedesche del Basso Medioevo: ambiente esterno, reddito, consumi'. In Elze and Fasoli, *Aristocrazia cittadina*, 79–122.

Diermeier, Ulf, and Gerhard Fouquet. 'Eigenbetriebe niedersächsischer Städte im Spätmittelalter'. In *Stadt im Wandel* 3: 257–79.

Diestelkamp, Bernhard (ed.). *Beiträge zum spätmittelalterlichen Städtewesen*. Cologne and Vienna: Böhlau, 1982. Stadtforschungen A/12.

Dilcher, Gerhard. 'Zum Bürgerbegriff im späteren Mittelalter. Versuch einer Typologie am Beispiel von Frankfurt am Main'. *BSL*, 59–105.

Dillard, Heath. *Daughters of the Reconquest. Women in Castilian Town Society, 1100–1300*. Cambridge: Cambridge University Press, 1984.

Dobson, Barrie. 'Cities and chantries in late medieval York'. In Abulafia, *Church and City*, 311–32.

Dobson, R. B. 'The risings in York, Beverley and Scarborough, 1380–1381'. In Hilton and Aston, *English Rising of 1381*, 112–42.

Dobson, R. B. 'Urban decline in late medieval England'. *TRHS* 27 (1977), reprinted *MT*, 265–86.

Dollinger, Philippe. *The German Hansa*. Stanford: Stanford University Press, 1970.

Dollinger, Philippe (ed.). *Histoire de l'Alsace*. Toulouse: Privat, 1970.

Dollinger, Philippe. 'La population de Strasbourg et sa répartition aux XVe et XVIe siècles'. *FSE*, 521–8.

Doren, Alfredo. *Le Arti Fiorentine*. 2 vols. Florence: Felice Le Monnier, 1918.

Dubois, Henri. 'Démographie urbaine médiévale: trois modelles de mortalité à Dijon (1385–1407)'. In Bourin, *Villes*, 333–41.

Du Boulay, F. R. H. *Germany in the Later Middle Ages*. London: Athlone Press, 1983.

Duby, Georges (ed.). *Histoire de la France urbaine. II. La ville médiévale. Des Carolingiens à la Renaissance*. Paris: Editions du Seuil, 1980.

Duvosquel, Jean-Marie, and Erik Thoen (eds). *Peasants and Townsmen in Medieval Europe. Studia in honorem Adriaan Verhulst*. Ghent: Snoeck-Ducaju en Zoon, 1995.

Dyer, Alan. *Decline and Growth in English Towns, 1400–1600*. London: Macmillan, 1991.

Dyer, Christopher. *Standards of Living in the Later Middle Ages. Social Change in England, c. 1200–1520*. Cambridge: Cambridge University Press, 1989.

Eames, Penelope. *Furniture in England, France and the Netherlands from the Twelfth to the Fifteenth Century*. London: Furniture Society, 1977.

Ebel, Wilhelm. 'Lübisches Recht im Ostseeraum'. In Haase, *Stadt des Mittelalters* 2: 255–80.

Edwards, John. *Christian Cordoba. The City and its Region in the Late Middle Ages*. Cambridge: Cambridge University Press, 1982.

Eggert, Wolfgang. 'Städtenetz und Stadtherrenpolitik. Ihre Herausbildung im Bereich des späteren Württenberg während des 13. Jahrhunderts'. *SS*, 108–228.

Eitel, Peter. *Die oberschwäbischen Reichsstädte im Zeitalter der Zunftherrschaft. Untersuchungen zu ihrer politischen und sozialen Struktur unter besonderer Berücksichtigung der Städte Lindau, Memmingen, Ravensburg und Überlingen*. Stuttgart: Müller and Gräff, 1970. Schriften zur südwestdeutschen Landeskunde 8.

Elze, Reinhard, and Gina Fasoli (eds). *Aristocrazia cittadina e ceti popolari nel tardo Medioevo in Italia e in Germania*. Bologna: Il Mulino, 1984.

Emery, Richard W. *The Jews of Perpignan in the Thirteenth Century. An Economic Study Based on Notarial Records*. New York: Columbia University Press, 1959.

Engel, Evamaria. 'Frühe ständische Aktivitäten des Städtebürgertums im Reich und in der Territorien bis zur Mitte des 14. Jahrhunderts'. *SSt*, 13–58.

Ennen, Edith. *The Medieval Town*. Amsterdam: North Holland, 1979, translated from her *Die europäische Stadt des Mittelalters*. Göttingen: Vandenhoeck and Ruprecht, 1972.

Ennen, Edith and Dietrich Höroldt. *Kleine Geschichte der Stadt Bonn*. Bonn: Wilhelm Stollfuss, 1967.

Epstein, S. R. 'Cities, regions and the late medieval crisis: Sicily and Tuscany compared'. *PP* 130 (1991): 3–50.

Epstein, Steven A. *Wage Labor and Guilds in Medieval Europe*. Chapel Hill: University of North Carolina Press, 1991.

Erdmann, Wolfgang. 'Forschungen zur Typenentwicklung des lübischen Kaufmannshauses im Mittelalter'. In Friedland, *Gilde*, 105–6 [sic].

Erler, Adalbert. *Bürgerrecht und Steuerpflicht im mittelalterlichen Städtewesen, mit besonderer Untersuchung des Steuereides*. 2nd ed. Frankfurt am Main: Vittorio Klostermann, 1963.

Esch, Arnold. 'Zur Prosopographie von Führungsgruppen im spätmittelalterlichen Rom'. In Bulst and Genet, *Medieval Lives*, 219–302.

Ewan, Elizabeth L. 'The community of the burgh in the fourteenth century'. In Lynch *et al.*, *Scottish Medieval Town*, 228–44.

Faber, Ghislaine, and Thierry Lochard. *Montpellier. La Ville médiévale*. Paris: Imprimerie Nationale, 1992.

Faith, Rosamond. 'The "great rumour" of 1377 and peasant ideology'. In Hilton and Aston, *English Rising of 1381*, 43–73.

Fagniez, Gustave (ed.). *Documents relatifs à l'histoire de l'industrie et du commerce en France*. 1: *Depuis le Ier siècle avant J.-C. jusqu'à la fin du XIIIe siècle*. 2: *XIVe et XVe siècles*. Paris: Alphonse Picard et fils, 1899, 1900.

Fahlbusch, F. B. 'Die Wachstumsphasen von Duderstadt bis zum Übergang an Mainz 1334/66'. *Stoob FS*, 194–212.

Falck, Ludwig. *Mainz in seiner Blütezeit als freie Stadt (1244 bis 1328)*. Düsseldorf: Walter Rau, 1973.

Fasoli, Gina. 'Oligarchia e ceti popolari nelle città padane fra il XIIIe e il XIV secolo'. In Elze and Fasoli, *Aristocrazia cittadina*, 11–39.

Favier, Jean, *De l'or et des épices. Naissance de l'homme d'affaires au Moyen Age*. Paris: Fayard, 1987.

Favier, Jean (ed.). *Paris au XVe siècle, 1380–1500.* Paris: Hachette, 1974.

Favresse, Félicien. *L'Avènement du régime démocratique à Bruxelles pendant le Moyen Age (1306–1423).* Brussels: Marcel Hayez, 1932.

Feger, Otto. 'Vergleichende Betrachtungen zur Finanzgeschichte von Konstanz und Basel'. *FC,* 222–35.

Fehring, Günter P. 'Der Beitrag der Archäologie zum Leben in der Stadt des späten Mittelalters'. *LS,* 9–35.

Fehring, Günter P., and Rolf Hammel. 'Die Topographie der Stadt Lübeck bis zum 14. Jahrhundert'. In Meckseper, *Stadt im Wandel* 3: 167–90.

Ferruolo, Steven. '*Parisius-Paradisus*: The city, its schools, and the origins of the university of Paris'. In Bender, *University,* 22–43.

Finances et comptabilités urbaines du XIIIe au XVIe siècle. Financiën en boekhouding der steden van de XIIIe tot de XIVe eeuw. Brussels: Pro Civitate, 1964.

Fleckenstein, Josef, and Karl Stackmann (eds). *Über Bürger, Stadt und städtische Literatur im Spätmittelalter.* Bericht über Kolloquium der Kommission zur Erforschung der Kultur des Spätmittelalters, 1975–1977. Abhandlungen der Akademie der Wissenschaften in Göttingen, Phil.-Hist. Klasse, ser. 3, no. 121. Göttingen: Vandenhoeck and Ruprecht, 1980.

Fohlen, Claude. *Histoire de Besançon. Des origines à la fin du XVIe siècle.* 2nd ed. Besançon: Cêtre, 1964.

Font-Rius, J. M. 'Organos y funcionarios de la administración económica en la principales localidades de Cataluña. *FC,* 257–75.

Fouret, Claude. 'La violence en fête: la course de l'Epinette à Lille à la fin du Moyen Age'. *RN* 63 (1981): 337–90.

Fradenburg, Louise Olga. *City, Marriage, Tournament. Arts of Rule in Late Medieval Scotland.* Madison: University of Wisconsin Press, 1991.

Friedland, Klaus (ed.). *Gilde und Korporation in den nordeuropäischen Städte des späten Mittelalters.* Cologne and Vienna: Böhlau, 1984. Quellen und Darstellungen zur hansischen Geschichte, ed. Hansisches Geschichtsverein, n.s. 29.

Friedman, David. *Florentine New Towns. Urban Design in the Late Middle Ages.* Architectural History Foundation Books, 12. Cambridge, Mass.: MIT Press, 1988.

Friedrichs, Christopher R. *The Early Modern City.* London: Longman, 1994.

Frugoni, Chiara. *A Distant City. Images of Urban Experience in the Medieval World.* Translated by William McCuaig. Princeton: Princeton University Press, 1991.

Gauvard, Claude. 'La criminalité parisienne à la fin du moyen âge: une criminalité ordinaire'. In Bourin, *Villes,* 361–70.

Gauvard, Claude. 'Violence citadine et réseaux de solidarité. L'exemple français aux XIVe et XVe siècles'. *AESC* 48 (1993): 1113–26.

Genecke, Dietrich, and Gareth Shaw (eds). *Urban Historical Geography. Recent Progress in Britain and Germany*. Cambridge: Cambridge University Press, 1988.

Geremek, Bronislaw. *The Margins of Society in Late Medieval Paris*. Translated from the French by Jean Birrell. Cambridge: Cambridge University Press, 1987.

Geremek, Bronislaw. *Le salariat dans l'artisanat parisien aux XIIIe–XVe siècles. Etude sur le marché de la main d'oeuvre au Moyen Age*. Paris and The Hague: Mouton, 1968.

Ginatempo, Maria, and Lucia Sandri. *L'Italia della città. Il popolamento urbano tra Medioevo e Rinascimento (secoli XIII–XVI)*. Florence: Le Lettere, 1990.

Girouard, Mark. *Cities and People. A Social and Architectural History*. New Haven and London: Yale University Press, 1985.

Given, James Buchanan, *Society and Homicide in Thirteenth-Century England*. Stanford: Stanford University Press, 1977.

Gleba, Gudrun. *Die Gemeinde als alternatives Ordnungesmodell: zur sozialen und politischen Differenzierung des Gemeindebegriffs in den innerstädtischen Auseinandersetzungen des 14. und 15. Jahrhunderts. Mainz, Magdeburg, München, Lübeck*. Cologne and Vienna: Böhlau, 1989.

Glénissen, Jean, and Charles Higounet. 'Remarques sur les comptes et sur l'administration financière des villes françaises entre Loire et Pyrénées (XIV–XVIe siècle)'. *FC*, 31–67.

Godding, Philippe. *Le droit privé dans les Pays-Bas méridionaux du 12e au 18e siècle*. Académie royale de Belgique. Mémoires de la Classe des Lettres 14, fasc. 1. Brussels: Palais des Académies, 1987.

Goehrke, Carsten. 'Die Sozialstruktur des mittelalterlichen Novgorod'. *UGS*, 357–78.

Goldberg, P. J. P. 'Female labour, service and marriage in the late medieval urban north'. *Northern History* 22 (1986): 19–38.

Goldberg, P. J. P. 'Urban identity and the poll taxes of 1377, 1379 and 1381'. *EcHR* 43 (1990): 194–216.

Goldberg, P. J. P. 'Women in fifteenth-century town life'. *TT*, 107–28.

Goldberg, P. J. P. *Women, Work, and Life Cycle in a Medieval Economy. Women in York and Yorkshire, c. 1300–1520*. Oxford: Clarendon Press, 1992.

Goldthwaite, Richard A. *The Building of Renaissance Florence. A Social and Economic History*. Baltimore: The Johns Hopkins University Press, 1980.

Goldthwaite, Richard A. *Wealth and the Demand for Art in Italy, 1300–1600*. Baltimore: The Johns Hopkins University Press, 1993.

Gonthier, Nicole. *Cris de haine et rites d'unité. La violence dans les villes, XIII–XVIe siècle.* Turnhout: Brepols, 1992.

Gonthier, Nicole. 'Une esquisse du paysage urbain lyonnais aux XIVe et XVe siècles'. *PU*, 253–77.

Gottfried, Robert S. *Bury St. Edmunds and the Urban Crisis: 1290–1539.* Princeton: Princeton University Press, 1982.

Gouron, André. *La Réglementation des Métiers en Languedoc au Moyen Age.* Etudes d'histoire économique, politique et sociale, 22. Geneva: E. Droz, 1958.

Gouron, André. *La science du droit dans le Midi de la France au Moyen Age.* London: Variorum Reprints, 1984. Articles are reprinted with pagination of original publication.

Grant, Alexander. *Independence and Nationhood. Scotland 1306–1469.* London: Edward Arnold, 1984.

Grendler, Paul F. *Schooling in Renaissance Italy. Literacy and Learning, 1300–1600.* Baltimore: The Johns Hopkins University Press, 1989.

Guillemain, Bernard. *La cour pontificale d'Avignon (1309–1376). Etude d'une société.* Paris: E. de Boccard, 1962.

Guillerme, André E. *The Age of Water. The Urban Environment in the North of France, A.D. 300–1800.* College Station, Texas: Texas A & M University Press, 1988.

Guiral-Hadziiossif, Jacqueline. *Valence, port méditerranéen au XVe siècle.* Paris: Sorbonne, 1986.

Gundesheimer, Werner L. 'Crime and punishment in Ferrara, 1440–1500'. In Martines, *Violence and Civil Disorder*, 104–28.

Gutkas, Karl. 'Das Städtewesen der österreichischen Donauländer und der Steiermark im 14. Jahrhundert'. In Rausch, *Stadt und Stadtherr*, 229–45.

Gutkind, E. A. (ed.). *International History of City Development*, 8 vols. New York: Free Press of Glencoe, 1964–72.

Haas, Walter, and Johannes Cramer. 'Klosterhöfe in norddeutschen Städten'. In *Stadt im Wandel* 3: 399–440.

Haase, Carl (ed.). *Die Stadt des Mittelalters.* 3 vols. 1: *Begriff, Entstehung und Ausbreitung.* Darmstadt: Wissenschaftliche Buchgesellschaft, 1969. 2: *Recht und Verfassung.* Darmstadt: Wissenschaftliche Buchgesellschaft, 1972. 3: *Wirtschaft und Gesellschaft.* Darmstadt: Wissenschaftliche Buchgesellschaft, 1984.

Hallam, Elizabeth M. *Capetian France, 987–1328.* London: Longman, 1980.

Hammer, Carl I. 'Patterns of homicide in fourteenth-century Oxford'. *PP* 78 (1978): 3–23.

Hanawalt, Barbara A. *Growing Up in Medieval London. The Experience of Childhood in History.* Oxford: Oxford University Press, 1993.

Hanawalt, Barbara A. (ed.). *Women and Work in Preindustrial Europe.* Bloomington: Indiana University Press, 1986.

Hanawalt, Barbara A., and Kathryn L. Reyerson (eds). *City and Spectacle in Medieval Europe.* Minneapolis: University of Minnesota Press, 1994.

Haverkamp, Alfred. ' "Conflitti interni" e collegamenti sovralocali nelle città tedesche durante la prima metà del XIV secolo'. In Elze and Fasoli, *Aristocrazia cittadina,* 123–76.

Haverkamp, Alfred. *Haus und Familie in der spätmittelalterlichen Stadt.* Cologne and Vienna: Böhlau, 1984. Städteforschung A/18.

Haverkamp, Alfred. *Medieval Germany, 1056–1273.* Oxford: Oxford University Press, 1988.

Haverkamp, Alfred. 'Topografia e relazioni sociali nelle città tedesche del tardo medioevo'. *CMOE,* 25–54.

Heers, Jacques. 'En Italie centrale: les paysages construits, reflets d'une politique urbaine'. *CMOE,* 279–322.

Heers, Jacques. *Fêtes, joux et joutes dans les sociétés d'occident à la fin du Moyen Age.* Montreal: University of Montreal, 1971.

Heers, Jacques. *Esclaves et domestiques au Moyen Age dans le monde méditerranéen.* Paris: Fayard, 1981.

Heers, Jacques. *Family Clans in the Middle Ages. A Study of Political and Social Structures in Urban Areas.* Amsterdam: North Holland, 1977.

Heers, Jacques (ed.). *Fortifications, portes de villes, places publiques dans le monde méditerranéen.* Paris: Université de Paris – Sorbonne, 1985.

Heers, Jacques. *Gênes au XVe siècle. Activité économique et problèmes sociaux.* Paris: Ecole pratique des Hautes Etudes, 1961.

Heers, Jacques. *Gênes au XVe siècle. Civilisation méditerranéenne, grand capitalisme, et capitalisme populaire.* Paris: Flammarion, 1971.

Heers, Jacques. *Parties and Political Life in the Medieval West.* Amsterdam: North Holland, 1977.

Heers, Jacques. *La ville au moyen-age en occident: paysages, pouvoirs et conflits.* Paris: Fayard, 1990.

Herborn, Wolfgang. 'Bürgerliches Selbstverständnis im spätmittelalterlichen Köln. Bemerkungen zu zwei Hausbüchern aus der ersten Hälfte des 15. Jahrhunderts'. *FSE,* 490–520.

Herlihy, David. 'Direct and indirect taxation in Tuscan urban finance, ca. 1200–1400'. *FC,* 385–405.

Herlihy, David. 'The distribution of wealth in a Renaissance community: Florence 1427'. In Abrams and Wrigley, *Towns in Societies,* 131–7.

Herlihy, David. *Medieval and Renaissance Pistoia.* New Haven: Yale University Press, 1967.

Herlihy, David. *Medieval Households.* Cambridge, Mass.: Harvard University Press, 1985.

Herlihy, David. *Opera Muliebria. Women and Work in Medieval Europe.* Philadelphia: Temple University Press, 1990.

Herlihy, David. *Pisa in the Early Renaissance. A Study of Urban Growth.* New Haven: Yale University Press, 1958.

Herlihy, David. 'The rulers of Florence, 1282–1530'. In Molho, Raaflanb and Emden, *City States,* 197–221.

Herlihy, David. 'Some psychological and social roots of violence in the Tuscan cities'. In Martines, *Violence and Civil Disorder,* 129–54.

Herlihy, David. *Women, Family and Society in Medieval Europe. Historical Essays, 1978–1991.* Providence, R. I.: Berghahn Books, 1995.

Herlihy, David, and Christiane Klapisch-Zuber. *Tuscans and Their Families. A Study of the Florentine Catasto of 1427.* London and New Haven: Yale University Press, 1985.

Highfield, J. R. L., and Robin Jeffs (eds). *The Crown and Local Communities in England and France in the Fifteenth Century.* Gloucester: Allan Sutton, 1981.

Hill, Francis. *Medieval Lincoln.* Cambridge: Cambridge University Press, 1965.

Hilton, R. H. *English and French Towns in Feudal Society. A Comparative Study.* Cambridge: Cambridge University Press, 1992.

Hilton, R. H., and T. H. Aston (eds). *The English Rising of 1381.* Cambridge: Cambridge University Press, 1984.

Hirschfelder, Gunther. *Die Kölner Handelsbeziehungen im Spätmittelalter.* Cologne: Veröffentlichungen des Kölnischen Stadtmuseums, 1994.

Historische Stedenatlas van België. Lier. Brussels: Gemeentekrediet van België, 1990.

Hoffmann, Erich. 'Die Schleswiger Knustgilde als mögliches Bindeglied zwischen west- und mitteleuropäischen und nordischen Gildewesen'. In Friedland, *Gilde,* 51–63.

Hofmann, Hanns Hubert. '*Nobiles Norimbergenses.* Beobachtungen zur Struktur der reichsstädtischen Oberschicht'. *UGS,* 53–92.

Hohenberg, Paul M., and Lynn Hollen Lees. *The Making of Urban Europe, 1000–1950.* Cambridge: Harvard University Press, 1985.

Hollaender, A. E. J., and William Kellaway (eds). *Studies in London History Presented to Philip Edmund Jones.* London: Hodder and Stoughton, 1969.

Holmes, George. *Florence, Rome and the Origins of the Renaissance,* Oxford: Clarendon Press, 1986.

Holt, Richard. 'Gloucester in the century after the Black Death'. Originally in *Transactions of the Bristol and Gloucestershire Archaeological Society* 103 (1985), reprinted *MT,* 141–59.

Holt, Richard, and Gervase Rosser (eds). *The Medieval Town. A Reader in English Urban History, 1200–1540.* London: Longman, 1990.

Horrox, Rosemary. 'The urban gentry in the fifteenth century'. *TT*, 22–44.

Hourani, Albert. *A History of the Arab Peoples*. Cambridge, Mass.: Harvard University Press, 1991.

Hourani, A. H., and S. M. Stern (eds). *The Islamic City. A Colloquium*. Papers on Islamic History, 1. Philadelphia: University of Pennsylvania Press, 1970.

Hourani, A. H. 'The Islamic city in the light of recent research'. *IC*, 10–24.

Houtte, J. A. van. *Bruges. Essai d'histoire urbaine*. Brussels: La Renaissance du Livre, 1967.

Houtte, J. A. van. *An Economic History of the Low Countries, 800–1800*. New York: St. Martin's Press, 1977.

Houtte, J. A. van. 'Herbergswesen und Gastlichkeit im mittelalterlichen Brügge'. *GTG*, 177–87.

Houtte, J. A. van and R. van Uytven. 'Nijverheid en handel'. *AGN* 4: 87–111.

Howard, Donald R. *Chaucer. His Life. His Works. His World*. New York: E. P. Dutton, 1987.

Howell, Martha C. *Women, Production, and Patriarchy in Late Medieval Cities*. Chicago: University of Chicago Press, 1986.

Hubert, Etienne. *Espace urbain et habitat à Rome du Xe siècle à la fin du XIIIe siècle*. Collection de l'Ecole française de Rome, 135. Rome: Palais Farnese, 1990.

Hughes, Diane Owen. 'Urban growth and family structure in medieval Genoa'. *PP* 66 (1975): 3–28.

Huiskes, Manfred (ed.). *Beschlüsse des Rates der Stadt Köln, 1320–1550. 1: Die Ratsmemoriale und ergänzende Überlieferung, 1320–1543*. Düsseldorf: Droste, 1990. Publikationen der Gesellschaft für Rheinische Geschichtskunde, 65.

Hummelberger, Walter. 'Die Bewaffnung der Bürgerschaft im Spätmittelalter am Beispiel Wiens'. *LS*, 191–206.

Hundsbichler, Helmut. 'Stadtbegriff, Stadtbild und Stadtleben des 15. Jahrhunderts nach ausländischen Berichterstattern über Österreich'. *LS*, 89–131.

Hyde, J. K. *Padua in the Age of Dante*. Manchester: Manchester University Press, 1966.

Hyde, J. K. *Society and Politics in Medieval Italy. The Evolution of the Civic Life, 1000–1350*. New York: St. Martin's Press, 1973.

Hyde, J. K. 'Universities and cities in medieval Italy'. In Bender, *University*, 13–21.

Imray, Jean M. ' "Les Bones Gentes de la Mercerye de Londres":

a study of the membership of the medieval Mercers' Company'. In Hollaender and Kellaway, *Studies in London History*, 155–78.

Irsigler, Franz. 'Getreidepreise, Getreidehandel und städtische Versorgungspolitik in Köln vornehmlich im 15. und 16. Jahrhundert'. *FSE*, 571–610.

Irsigler, Franz. 'Industrial production, international trade and public finance in Cologne (XIVth and XVth Century)'. *Journal of European Economic History* 6 (1977): 269–306.

Irsigler, Franz. 'Kaufmannstypen im Mittelalter'. In *Stadt im Wandel* 3: 385–97.

Irsigler, Franz. *Die wirtschaftliche Stellung der Stadt Köln im 14. und 15. Jahrhundert. Strukturanalyse einer spätmittelalterlichen Exportgewerbe und Fernhandelsstadt.* Wiesbaden: Franz Steiner, 1979.

Isenmann, Eberhard. *Die deutsche Stadt im Spätmittelalter, 1250–1500. Stadtgestalt, Recht, Stadtregiment, Kirche, Gesellschaft, Wirtschaft.* Stuttgart: Eugen Ulmer, 1988.

Jacob, Robert. *Les époux, le seigneur et la cité. Coutume et pratiques matrimoniales des bourgeois et paysans de France du Nord au moyen âge.* Brussels: Facultés Universitaires de Saint-Louis, 1990.

Jäger, Helmut, Franz Petri and Heinz Quirin (eds). *Civitatum Communitas. Studien zum europäischen Städtewesen. Festschrift Heinz Stoob zum 65. Geburtstag.* Cologne and Vienna: Böhlau, 1984. 2 vols. Städteforschung 19, 21.

Jakob, Volker, and Gerhard Köhn. 'Wege zum Modell einer mittelalterlichen Stadtsozialtopographische Ermittlungen am Beispiel Soest'. *Stoob FS*, 296–308.

James, Mervyn. 'Ritual, drama and social body in the late medieval English town'. *PP* 98 (1983): 3–29.

Jansen, Henrik. 'Early urbanization in Denmark'. *CHUO*, 183–216.

Jansen, H. P. H. 'Handel en Nijverheid 1000–1300'. *AGN*, 148–86.

Johnston, Alexandra F. 'Traders and playmakers: English guildsmen and the Low Countries'. In Caroline Barron and Nigel Saul (eds), *England and the Low Countries in the Late Middle Ages.* New York: St. Martin's Press, 1995, 99–114.

Joris, André. *Huy, ville médiévale.* Brussels: La Renaissance du Livre, 1965.

Joris, André. *La ville de Huy au Moyen Age, des origines à la fin du XIVe siècle.* Paris: Université de Liège, 1959.

Keene, Derek. 'Continuity and development in urban trades: problems of concepts and the evidence'. In Corfield and Keene, *Work in Towns*, 1–16.

Keene, Derek. 'The property market in English towns, A.D. 1100–1600'. *SMOE*, 201–26.

Keene, Derek. 'Small towns and the metropolis: the experience of medieval England'. *PTME*, 223–38.

Keene, Derek. 'Suburban growth'. *PT*, 71–82.

Keene, Derek. *Survey of Medieval Winchester*. 2 vols. Oxford: Clarendon Press, 1985. Winchester Studies, 2.

Keene, Derek. 'Tanners' widows, 1300–1350'. In Barron and Sutton, *Medieval London Widows*, 1–27.

Kejr, Jiri. 'Les privilèges des villes de Bohême depuis les origines jusqu'aux guerres hussites (1419)'. *LUR*, 126–60.

Kejr, Jiri. 'Organisation und Verwaltung des Köninglichen Städtewesens in Böhmen zur Zeit der Luxemburger'. In Rausch, *Stadt und Stadtherr*, 79–97.

Kejr, Jiri. 'Zur Entstehung des städtischen Stände im hussitischen Böhmen'. *SSt*, 195–213.

Keller, Hagen. 'Über den Charakter Freiburgs in der Frühzeit der Stadt. *Festschrift für Berent Schwineköper* (Signaringen: Jan Thorbecke, 1982), 249–82.

Kent, Dale. *The Rise of the Medici. Faction in Florence, 1426–1434*. Oxford: Oxford University Press, 1978.

Kent, D. V. and F. W. *Neighbours and Neighbourhood in Renaissance Florence: The District of the Red Lion in the Fifteenth Century*. Locust Valley, New York: J. J. Augustin, 1982.

Kermode, Jennifer I. 'The merchants of three northern English towns'. In Cecil H. Clough (ed.), *Profession, Vocation, and Culture in Later Medieval England. Essays Dedicated to the Memory of A. R. Myers*. Liverpool: Liverpool University Press, 1982.

Kermode, Jennifer I. 'Obvious observations on the formation of oligarchies in late medieval English towns'. *TT*, 87–106.

Keutgen, Friedrich (ed.). *Urkunden zur städtischen Verfassungsgeschichte*. Berlin: Emil Felber, 1901.

Kiessling, Rolf. 'Das Augsburger Bürgertum im 15. Jahrhundert. Ein Versuch zur Bestimmung spezifischer Verhaltensweisen gegenüber der Kirche und ihrem Wertsystem'. In Bosl, *Mittelalterliche Stadt in Bayern*, 163–86.

Kirchgässner, B. 'Studien zur Geschichte des kommunalen Rechnungswesens der Reichsstädte Südwestdeutschlands vom 13. bis zum 16. Jahrhundert'. *FC*, 237–52.

Klapisch-Zuber, Christiane. *Women, Family, and Ritual in Renaissance Italy*. Chicago: University of Chicago Press, 1985.

Klapisch-Zuber, Christiane. 'Women servants in Florence during the fourteenth and fifteenth centuries'. In Hanawalt, *Women and Work*, 56–80.

Klebel, Ernst. 'Regensburg'. *SAES*, 84–104.

Klep, P. M. M. 'Urban decline in Brabant: the traditionalization of investments and labour (1374–1806)'. In van der Wee, *Rise and Decline of Urban Industries*, 261–86.

Knoll, Paul W. 'The urban development of medieval Poland, with particular reference to Krakow'. *USEE*, 63–137.

Köbler, Gerhard. 'Das Familienrecht in der spätmittelalterlichen Stadt'. In Haverkamp, *Haus und Familie*, 136–60.

Köln, das Reich und Europa. Abhandlungen über weiträumige Verflechtungen der Stadt Köln in Politik, Recht und Wirtschaft im Mittelalter. Mitteilungen aus dem Stadtarchiv von Köln, 60. Cologne: Paul Neubner, 1971.

Koller, Heinrich. 'Der Ausbau der Stadt Hallein im hohen und späten Mittelalter'. *Stoob FS*, 181–93.

Konvitz, Josef W. *The Urban Millennium. The City-Building Process from the Early Middle Ages to the Present*. Carbondale: Southern Illinois University Press, 1986.

Kossmann-Putto, J. A. 'Armen- en ziekenzorg in de Noordelijke Nederlanden'. *AGN* 2: 254–67.

Kowaleski, Maryanne. 'The commercial dominance of a medieval provincial oligarchy: Exeter in the late fourteenth century'. Originally *Medieval Studies* 46 (1984), reprinted *MT*, 184–215.

Kowaleski, Maryanne. 'The history of urban families in medieval England'. *JMH* 14 (1988): 47–63.

Kowaleski, Maryanne. 'Town and country in late medieval England: the hide and leather trade'. In Corfield and Keene, *Work in Towns*, 57–73.

Kowaleski, Maryanne. 'Women's work in a market town: Exeter in the late fourteenth century'. In Hanawalt, *Women and Work*, 145–64.

Krekic, Barisa. 'Developed autonomy: the patricians in Dubrovnik and Dalmatian cities'. *USEE*, 185–215.

Krekic, Barisa (ed.). *Urban Society of Eastern Europe in Premodern Times*. Berkeley and Los Angeles: University of California Press, 1987.

Kuehn, Thomas J. *Emancipation in Late Medieval Florence*. New Brunswick, N. J.: Rutgers University Press, 1982.

Kuehn, Thomas J. 'Social processes and legal processes in the Renaissance: a Florentine inheritance case from 1452'. *Quaderni Fiorentini* 23 (1994), 365–96.

Kühnel, Harry. 'Das Alltagsleben im Hause der spätmittelalterlichen Stadt'. In Haverkamp, *Haus und Familie*, 37–65.

Kümmell, Juliana. *Bäuerliche Gesellschaft und städtische Herrschaft im Spätmittelalter. Zum Verhältnis von Stadt und Land im Fall Basel/Waldenburg 1300–1535*. Constance: Wolfgang Hartung-Gorre, 1983.

Lacarra, José M. 'Le budget de la ville de Saragosse au XVe siècle: dépenses et récettes'. *FC*, 381–4.

Ladero Quesnada, Miguel Angel. *La Ciudad medieval (1248–1492)*. 2nd ed. In Francisco Morales Padron (ed.), *Historia de Sevilla*. Seville: University, 1980.

Ladero Quesnada, Miguel Angel. 'Les fortifications urbaines en Castille aux XIe–XVe siècles: Problématique, financement, aspects sociaux'. In Heers, *Fortifications*, 145–76.

Lane, Frederic C. *Venice. A Maritime Republic*. Baltimore: The Johns Hopkins University Press, 1973.

Lane, Frederic C. *Venice and History. The Collected Papers of Frederic C. Lane*. Baltimore: The Johns Hopkins University Press, 1966.

Langer, Lawrence M. 'The medieval Russian town'. In Michael F. Hamm (ed.), *The City in Russian History*. Lexington: University Press of Kentucky, 1976, 11–33.

Lapidus, Ira M. *Muslim Cities in the Later Middle Ages*. Cambridge: Cambridge University Press, 1984.

Lapidus, Ira M. 'Muslim urban society in Mamluk Syria'. In Hourani and Stern, *The Islamic City*, 195–205.

Larner, John. *Italy in the Age of Dante and Petrarch, 1216–1380*. London: Longman, 1980.

Latreille, André (ed.). *Histoire de Lyon et du Lyonnais*. Toulouse: Privat, 1975.

Lavedan, Pierre. *French Architecture*. London: Scolar Press, 1979.

Lavedan, Pierre, and Jeanne Hugueney. *L'Urbanisme au Moyen Age*. Geneva: Droz, 1974. Bibliothèque de la Société française d'archéologie, 5.

Law, John D. 'The Venetian mainland state in the fifteenth century'. *TRHS*, ser. 6, 2 (1992): 153–74.

Law, Custom, and the Social Fabric in Medieval Europe. Essays in Honor of Bryce Lyon. Edited by Bernard S. Bachrach and David Nicholas. Kalamazoo, Michigan: Medieval Institute Publications, 1990.

Das Leben in der Stadt des Spätmittelalters. Internationaler Kongress Krems an der Donau 20. bis 23. September 1976. Veröffentlichungen des Instituts für mittelalterlichen Realienkunde Osterreichs, no. 2. Österreichische Akademie der Wissenschaften, Phil.-Hist. Klasse, Sitzungsberichte, 325. Vienna: Verlag der österreichischen Akademie der Wissenschaften, 1977.

Le Goff, Jacques. 'L'apogée de la France urbaine médiévale'. *HFU* 2: 183–405.

Le Goff, Jacques. 'The town as an agent of civilisation'. *Fontana Economic History of Europe* 1. London: Fontana, 1972: 71–106.

Leguai, André. 'Relations between the towns of Burgundy and the French Crown in the fifteenth century'. In Highfield and Jeffs, *Crown and Local Communities*, 129–45.

Leguay, Jean-Pierre. 'La propriété et le marché de l'immobilier à la fin du Moyen Age dans le royaume de France et dans les grands fiefs périphériques'. *SMOE*, 135–99.

Leguay, Jean-Pierre. *Un réseau urbain au Moyen Age: les villes du duché de Bretagne aux XIVème & XVème siècles*. Paris: Librairie Maloine, 1981.

Leguay, Jean-Pierre. 'La rue: élément du paysage urbain et cadre de vie dans les villes du Royaume de France et des grands fiefs aux XIVe et XVe siècles'. *PU*, 23–60.

Leroy, Béatrice. 'Tudela, une ville de la vallée de l'Ebre, aux XIIIe–XIVe siècles'. *PU*, 187–212.

Lesage, Georges. *Marseille angevine. Recherches sur son évolution administrative, économique et urbaine, de la victoire de Charles d'Anjou et l'arrivée de Jeanne Ire (1264–1348)*. Paris: E. de Boccard, 1950.

Lestocquoy, Jean. *Aux Origines de la Bourgeoisie: les villes de Flandre et d'Italie sous le government des patriciens*. Paris: Presses Universitaires de France, 1952.

Lestocquoy, Jean. *Patriciens du Moyen-Age. Les Dynasties bourgeoises d'Arras du XIe au XVe siècle*. Arras: Mémoires de la Commission Départementale des Monuments Historiques du Pas-de-Calais, V, 1. 1945.

Leuschner, Joachim. *Germany in the Late Middle Ages*. Amsterdam: North Holland, 1980.

Les Libertés urbaines et rurales du XIe au XIVe siècle. Vrijheden in de stad en op het platteland van de XIe tot de XIVe eeuw. Colloque International, Spa 5–8 IX 1966. *Actes. Handelingen*. Brussels: Pro Civitate, 1968.

Lloyd, T. H. *England and the German Hanse, 1157–1611. A Study of Their Trade and Commercial Diplomacy*. Cambridge: Cambridge University Press, 1991.

Lobel, M. D. (ed.). *The Atlas of Historic Towns. 2: Bristol: Cambridge: Coventry: Norwich*. Baltimore: The Johns Hopkins University Press, 1975.

Lobel, M. D. (ed.). *Historic Towns. Maps and Plans of Towns and Cities in the British Isles, with Historical Commentaries, from Earliest Times to 1800*. Baltimore: The Johns Hopkins University Press, 1969.

Lodge, Eleanor C. *Gascony Under English Rule*. London: Kennikat Press, 1926, 1971.

Lopez, Robert S., and Irving W. Raymond (eds). *Medieval Trade in the Mediterranean World*. New York: W. W. Norton, 1955.

Luzzatto, Gino. *An Economic History of Italy from the Fall of the Roman*

Empire to the Beginning of the Sixteenth Century. Translated by Philip
   Jones. London: Routledge and Kegan Paul, 1961.
Lynch, Michael, Michael Spearman and Geoffrey Stell (eds). *The Scot-
   tish Medieval Town.* Edinburgh: John Donald, 1988.
Lynch, Michael. 'Towns and townspeople in fifteenth-century Scot-
   land'. *TT*, 173–89.
Lyon, Bryce. 'What role did communes have in the feudal system?'
   RBPH 72 (1994): 241–53.
MacKay, Angus. *Spain in the Middle Ages. From Frontier to Empire, 1000–
   1500.* London: Macmillan, 1977.
MacKenney, Richard. *Tradesmen and Traders. The World of the Guilds in
   Venice and Europe, c. 1250–c. 1650.* Totowa, N. J.: Barnes and Noble,
   1987.
McRee, Benjamin R. 'Peacemaking and its limits in late medieval
   Norwich'. *EHR* 109 (1994): 831–66.
McRee, Benjamin R. 'Unity or division? The social meaning of guild
   ceremony in urban communities'. *CS*, 189–207.
Mägdefrau, Werner. 'Patrizische Ratsherrschaft, Bürgeropposition und
   städtische Volksbewegungen in Erfurt. Von der Herausbildung des
   ersten bürgerlichen Rates um die Mitte des 13. Jahrhunderts bis zu
   den innerstädtischen Auseinandersetzungen von 1309 bis 1310'. *SS*,
   324–71.
Malowist, Marian. 'The trade of Eastern Europe in the later Middle
   Ages'. In *The Cambridge Economic History of Europe*, II. *Trade and Industry in the Middle Ages*. 2nd ed. Cambridge: Cambridge University Press,
   1987, 525–612.
Maire Vigueur, Jean-Claude (ed.). *D'une ville à l'autre: Structures matérielles
   et organisation de l'espace dans les villes européennes (XIIIe–XVIe siècle).*
   Actes du Colloque organisé par l'Ecole française de Rome avec le
   concours de l'Université de Rome (Rome 1er–4 décembre 1986).
   Rome: Ecole Française de Rome, 1989.
Mallett, Michael. 'Pisa and Florence in the fifteenth century: aspects of
   the period of the first Florentine Domination'. *PS*, 403–41.
Marechal, Griet. 'Armen- en ziekenzorg in de Zuidelijke Nederlanden'.
   AGN, 268–80.
Marechal, Griet. *De sociale en politieke gebondenheid van het Brugse
   hospitaalwezen in de Middeleeuwen.* Standen en Landen 73. Kortrijk-
   Heule: UGS, 1978.
Marsilje, J. W. *Het financiële beleid van Leiden in de laat-Beierse en Bourgon-
   dische periode, c. 1390–1477.* Hilversum: Verloren, 1985.
Martens, Mina (ed.). *Histoire de Bruxelles.* Toulouse: Privat, 1976.

Martin, G. H. (ed.). *The Ipswich Recognizance Rolls, 1294–1327. A Calendar.* Ipswich: Suffolk Record Society, 1973.

Martines, Lauro. *Power and Imagination. City-States in Renaissance Italy.* New York: Random House, 1979.

Martines, Lauro (ed.). *Violence and Civil Disorder in Italian Cities, 1200– 1500.* Berkeley and Los Angeles: University of California Press, 1972.

Maschke, Erich. 'Soziale Gruppen in der deutschen Stadt des späten Mittelalters'. *BSL*, 127–45.

Maschke, Erich. *Städte und Menschen. Beiträge zur Geschichte der Stadt, der Wirtschaft und Gesellschaft 1959–1977.* Vierteljahrschrift für Sozial- und Wirtschaftsgeschichte, Beiheft 68. Wiesbaden: Franz Steiner, 1980.

Maschke, Erich. 'Die Unterschichten der mittelalterlichen Städte Deutschlands'. In Haase, *Stadt des Mittelalters* 3: 345–454.

Matheus, Michael. *Trier am Ende des Mittelalters. Studien zur Sozial-, Wirtschafts- und Verfassungsgeschichte der Stadt Trier vom 14. bis 16. Jahrhunderte.* Trierer Historische Forschungen, 5. Trier: Verlag Trierer Historische Forschungen, 1984.

Maurer, Helmut, and Hans Patze (eds). *Festschrift für Berent Schwineköper zu seinem siebzigsten Geburtstag.* Sigmaringen: Jan Thorbecke, 1982.

Meckseper, Cord (ed.). *Stadt im Wandel. Kunst und Kultur des Bürgertums in Norddeutschland, 1150–1650.* 4 vols. Stuttgart-Bad Cannstadt: Edition Cantz, 1985.

Meek, Christine. *The Commune of Lucca Under Pisan Rule, 1342–1369.* Cambridge, Mass.: Mediaeval Academy of America, 1980.

Meek, Christine. *Lucca 1369–1400. Politics and Society in an Early Renaissance City-State.* Oxford: Oxford University Press, 1978.

Meek, Christine. 'Public policy and private profit: tax farming in fourteenth-century Lucca.' *OT*, 41–82.

Mickwitz, Gunnar. *Die Kartellfunktionen der Zünfte und ihre Bedeutung bei der Entstehung des Zunftwesens. Eine Studie in spätantiker und mittelalterlicher Wirtschaftsgeschichte.* Helsinki: Societas Scientiarum Fennica. Commentationes Humanarum Litterarum, VIII, 8. 1936.

Miller, Edward, and John Hatcher. *Medieval England. Towns, Commerce and Crafts.* London: Longman, 1995.

Mirot, Léon. *Les insurrections urbaines au début du règne de Charles VI (1380–1383). Leurs causes, leurs conséquences.* Paris: Albert Fontemoing, 1905.

Mitterauer, Michael. 'Familie und Arbeitsorganisation in städtischen Gesellschaften des späten Mittelalters und der frühen Neuzeit'. In Haverkamp, *Haus und Familie,* 1–36.

Bibliography

Mitterauer, Michael. *Markt und Stadt im Mittelalter. Beiträge zur historischen Zentralitätsforschung.* Stuttgart: Anton Hiersemann, 1980.

Moeller, Bernd. 'Die Anfänge kommunaler Bibliotheken in Deutschland'. *SB*, 136–52.

Moeller, Bernd, Hans Patze and Karl Stackmann (eds). *Studien zum städtischen Bildungswesen des späten Mittelalters und der frühen Neuzeit.* Abhandlungen der Akademie der Wissenschaften in Göttingen, Phil.-Hist. Klasse, ser. 3, no. 137. Göttingen: Vandenhoeck und Ruprecht, 1983.

Molenat, Jean-Pierre. 'Deux éléments du paysage urbain: *adarves* et *alcaicerias* de Tolède à la fin du Moyen Age'. *PU*, 213–24.

Molho, Anthony. *Florentine Public Finances in the Early Renaissance, 1400–1433.* Cambridge, Mass.: Harvard University Press, 1971.

Molho, Anthony, Kurt Raaflaub and Julia Emden (eds). *City States in Classical Antiquity and Medieval Italy.* Ann Arbor: University of Michigan Press, 1991.

Mollat, Michel (ed.). *Histoire de Rouen.* Toulouse: Privat, 1979.

Mollat, Michel. *The Poor in the Middle Ages. An Essay in Social History.* Translated by Arthur Goldhammer. New Haven and London: Yale University Press, 1986.

Mollat, Michel, and Philippe Wolff. *The Popular Revolutions of the Late Middle Ages.* London: George Allen and Unwin, 1973.

Möncke, Gisela (ed.). *Quellen zur Wirtschafts- und Sozialgeschichte Mittel- und Oberdeutscher Städte im Spätmittelalter.* Darmstadt: Wissenschaftliche Buchgesellschaft, 1982. Ausgewählte Quellen zur deutschen Geschichte des Mittelalters, 37.

Möncke, Gisela. 'Zur Problematik des Terminus "Freie Stadt" im 14. und 15. Jahrhundert'. In Petri, *Bischofs- und Kathedralstädte*, 84–94.

Moraw, Peter. 'Heidelberg: Universität, Hof und Stadt im ausgehenden Mittelalter'. *SB*, 524–52.

Mörke, Olaf. 'Der "Konflikt" als Kategorie städtischer Sozialgeschichte der Reformationszeit. Ein Diskussionsbeitrag am Beispiel der Stadt Braunschweig'. *BSS*, 144–61.

Morris, A. E. J. *History of Urban Form From Prehistory to the Renaissance.* London: George Godwin, 1972.

Muir, Edward. *Civic Ritual in Renaissance Venice.* Princeton: Princeton University Press, 1981.

Muir, Edward. 'Images of power: art and pageantry in Renaissance Venice'. *AHR* 84 (1979): 16–52.

Mulholland, Mary Ambrose (ed.). *Early Gild Records of Toulouse.* New York: Columbia University Press, 1941.

Müller, Wolfgang (ed.). *Freiburg im Mittelalter. Vorträge zum Stadtjubiläum 1970*. Bühl/Baden: Konkordia, 1970.

Mumford, Lewis. *The Culture of Cities*. New York: Harcourt, Brace and Company, 1938.

Murray, James M. 'Family, marriage and moneychanging in medieval Bruges'. *JMH* 14 (1988): 114–25.

Murray, James M. 'The liturgy of the Count's Advent in Bruges, from Galbert to Van Eyck'. *CS*, 137–52.

Najemy, John M. *Corporatism and Consensus in Florentine Electoral Politics, 1280–1400*. Chapel Hill: University of North Carolina Press, 1982.

Nicholas, David. 'Child and adolescent labour in the medieval city: a Flemish model in regional perspective'. *EHR* 110 (1995): 1103–31.

Nicholas, David. 'Crime and punishment in fourteenth-century Ghent', *RBPH* 48 (1970): 289–334, 1141–76.

Nicholas, David. *The Domestic Life of a Medieval City: Women, Children, and the Family in Fourteenth-Century Ghent*. Lincoln: University of Nebraska Press, 1985.

Nicholas, David. 'The English trade at Bruges in the last years of Edward III'. *JMH* 5 (1979): 23–61.

Nicholas, David. *The Evolution of the Medieval World. Society, Government and Thought in Europe, 312–1500*. London: Longman, 1992.

Nicholas, David. 'The governance of fourteenth-century Ghent: the theory and practice of public administration'. *LCS*, 235–60.

Nicholas, David. 'In the pit of the Burgundian theater state: urban traditions and princely ambitions in Ghent, 1360–1420'. *CS*, 271–95.

Nicholas, David. 'The marriage and the meat hall: Ghent/Eeklo 1373–75'. *Medieval Prosopography* 10 (1989): 22–53.

Nicholas, David. 'Medieval urban origins in northern continental Europe: state of research and some tentative conclusions'. *Studies in Medieval and Renaissance History* 6 (1969): 53–114.

Nicholas, David. *Medieval Flanders*. London: Longman, 1992.

Nicholas, David. *The Metamorphosis of a Medieval City: Ghent in the Age of the Arteveldes, 1302–1390*. Lincoln: University of Nebraska Press, 1987.

Nicholas, David. 'Of poverty and primacy: demand, liquidity, and the Flemish economic miracle, 1050–1200'. *AHR* 96 (1991): 17–41.

Nicholas, David. 'Patterns of social mobility'. In R. L. DeMolen (ed.), *One Thousand Years. Western Europe in the Middle Ages*. Boston: Houghton Mifflin, 1974, 45–105.

Nicholas, David. 'The Scheldt trade and the "Ghent War" of 1379–1385'. *Bulletin de la Commission Royale d'Histoire* 144 (1978): 189–359.

Nicholas, David. *Stad en Platteland in de Middeleeuwen*. Bussum (Neth.): Fibula-Van Dishoeck, 1971.

Nicholas, David. 'Structures du peuplement, fonctions urbaines et formation du capital dans la Flandre médiévale'. *AESC* 33 (1978): 501–27.
English translation, 'Settlement patterns, urban functions, and capital
formation in medieval Flanders'. In Nicholas, *Trade, Urbanisation and
the Family.*

Nicholas, David. *Town and Countryside: Social, Economic, and Political
Tensions in Fourteenth-Century Flanders.* Bruges: De Tempel, 1971.

Nicholas, David. *Trade, Urbanisation and the Family. Studies in the History
of Medieval Flanders.* Aldershot: Variorum Reprints, 1996.

Nicholas, David. *The van Arteveldes of Ghent: the Varieties of Vendetta and
the Hero in History.* Ithaca and London: Cornell University Press,
1988.

Nightingale, Pamela. 'Capitalists, crafts and constitutional change in late
fourteenth-century London'. *PP*, 3–35.

Nightingale, Pamela. *A Medieval Mercantile Community. The Grocers' Company and the Politics and Trade of London, 1000–1485.* New Haven:
Yale University Press, 1995.

Nürnberger Urkundenbuch. Herausgegeben vom Stadtrat zu Nürnberg.
Bearbeitet vom Stadtarchiv Nürnberg. Nürnberg: Selbstverlag des
Stadtrats, 1959. Quellen und Forschungen zur Geschichte der Stadt
Nürnberg, 1.

Nyberg, Tore. 'Gilden, Kalande, Brüderschaften: der skandinavische
Einfluss'. In Friedland, *Gilde,* 29–40.

Obst, Karin. *Der Wandel in den Bezeichnungen für gewerbliche Zusammen-
schlüsse des Mittelalters. Eine rechtssprach-geographische Analyse.* Frankfurt
am Main: Peter Lang, 1983.

O'Callahan, Joseph F. *A History of Medieval Spain.* Ithaca: Cornell University Press, 1975.

O'Connor, S. J. 'Finance, diplomacy and politics: royal service by two
London merchants in the reign of Edward III'. *Historical Research* 67
(1994): 18–39.

*Order and Innovation in the Middle Ages: Essays in Honor of Joseph R.
Strayer.* Princeton: Princeton University Press, 1976.

Otis, Leah L. 'Municipal wet nurses in fifteenth-century Montpellier'.
In Hanawalt, *Women and Work,* 83–93.

Otis-Cour, Leah. 'Les "pauvres enfants exposés" à Montpellier aux
XIVe et XVe siècles'. *Annales du Midi* 105 (1993): 309–27.

Owen, Dorothy M. (ed.). *The Making of King's Lynn. A Documentary
Survey.* Oxford: Oxford University Press, 1984.

Palliser, D. M. 'Urban decay revisited'. *TT,* 1–21.

A Parisian Journal 1405–1449. Translated from the Anonymous *Journal
d'un Bourgeois de Paris* by James Shirley. Oxford: Clarendon Press, 1968.

Patze, Hans. 'Die Bildung der landesherrlichen Residenzen im Reich während des 14. Jahrhunderts'. In Rausch, *Stadt und Stadtherr*, 1–54.

Paul, Jürgen. 'Rathaus und Markt'. In *Stadt im Wandel* 4: 89–118.

Le Paysage urbain au Moyen Age. Actes du XIe Congrès des historiens médiévistes de l'enseignment supérior. Lyon: Presses Universitaires de Lyon, 1981.

Pérouas, Louis (ed.). *Histoire de Limoges*. Toulouse: Privat, 1989.

Peeters, J. P. 'De-industrialization in the small and medium-sized towns in Brabant at the end of the Middle Ages. A case-study: the cloth industry of Tienen'. In van der Wee, *Rise and Decline of Urban Industries*, 165–86.

Peters, Ursula, *Literatur in der Stadt. Studien zu den sozialen Voraussetzungen und kulturellen Organisationsformen städischer Literatur im 13. und 14. Jahrhundert*. Tübingen: Max Niermeyer, 1983. Studien und Texte zur Sozialgeschichte der Literatur, 7.

Petit-Dutaillis, Charles. *The French Communes in the Middle Ages*. Translated by Joan Vickers. Amsterdam: North Holland, 1978.

Petri, Franz (ed.). *Bischofs- und Kathedralstädte des Mittelalters und der frühen Neuzeit*. Cologne and Vienna: Böhlau, 1976. Städteforschung, Reihe A, v. 1.

Peyer, Hans Conrad (ed.). *Gastfreundschaft, Taverne und Gasthaus im Mittelalter*. Schriften des historischen Kollegs, 3. Munich and Vienna: Oldenbourg, 1983.

Pfeiffer, Gerhard (ed.). *Nürnberg – Geschichte einer europäischen Stadt*. Munich: C. H. Beck, 1971.

Phythian-Adams, Charles. 'Ceremony and the citizen: the communal year at Coventry, 1450–1550'. In Peter Clark and Paul Slack (eds), *Crisis and Order in English Towns, 1500–1700*. London: Routledge, 1972, 57–85.

Phythian-Adams, Charles. *Desolation of a City. Coventry and the Urban Crisis of the Late Middle Ages*. Cambridge: Cambridge University Press, 1979.

Phythian-Adams, Charles. 'Urban decay in late medieval England'. In Abrams and Wrigley, *Towns in Societies*, 159–85.

Pirenne, Henri. *Early Democracies in the Low Countries: Urban Society and Political Conflict in the Middle Ages and the Renaissance*. New York: Harper and Row, reprinted 1963.

Pirenne, Henri. *Medieval Cities. Their Origins and the Revival of Trade*. New York: Doubleday, reprinted 1956.

Pitz, Ernst. 'Wirtschaftliche und soziale Probleme der gewerblichen Entwicklung im 15./16. Jahrhundert nach hansisch-niederdeutschen Quellen'. In Haase, *Stadt des Mittelalters*, 3: 137–76.

Planitz, Hans. *Die deutsche Stadt im Mittelalter. Von der Römerzeit bis zu den Zunftkämpfen.* 2nd ed. Cologne and Graz: Böhlau, 1965.

Platelle, Henri (ed.). *Histoire de Valenciennes.* Lille: Presses Universitaires de Lille, 1982.

Platt, Colin. *The English Mediaeval Town.* London: Paladin, 1979.

Platt, Colin. 'The evolution of towns: natural growth'. *PT*, 48–56.

Platt, Colin. *Medieval Southampton. The Port and Trading Community, A.D. 1000–1600.* London: Routledge and Kegan Paul, 1973.

Plesner, Johan. *L'émigration de la campagne à la ville libre de Florence au XIIIe siècle.* Copenhagen: Gyldendal, 1934.

Portmann, Urs. *Bürgerschaft im mittelalterlichen Freiburg. Sozialtopographische Auswertungen zum ersten Bürgerbuch 1341–1416.* Freiburg (Switzerland): Universitätsverlag, 1986. Historische Schriften der Universität Freiburg, 11.

Prevenier, Walter. 'Quelques aspects des comptes communaux en Flandre au Moyen Age'. *FC*, 111–45.

Prevenier, Walter. 'Violence against women in a medieval metropolis: Paris around 1400'. *LCS*, 263–84.

Puhle, Matthias. *Die Politik der Stadt Braunschweig innerhalb des sächsischen Städtebundes und der Hanse im späten Mittelalter.* Brunswick: Waisenhaus, 1985.

Queller, Donald E. 'The Venetian family and the *Estimo* of 1379'. *LCS*, 185–210.

Queller, Donald E. *The Venetian Patriciate. Reality versus Myth.* Urbana: University of Illinois Press, 1986.

Rabe, Horst. 'Frühe Stadien der Ratsverfassung in den Reichslandstädten bzw. Reichsstädten Oberdeutschlands'. *BSS*, 1–17.

Rabe, Horst. 'Stadt und Stadtherrschaft im 14. Jahrhundert. Die schwäbischen Reichsstädte'. In Rausch, *Stadt und Stadtherr*, 301–18.

Raiser, Elisabeth. *Städtische Territorialpolitik im Mittelalter. Eine vergleichende Untersuchung ihrer verschiedenen Formen am Beispiel Lübecks und Zürichs.* Historische Studien 406. Lübeck and Hamburg: Matthiesen, 1969.

Rapp, Francis. 'Sozialpolitische Entwicklung und volkssprachlichten Wortschatz in spätmittelalterlicher Strassburg'. *BSL*, 146–60.

Rausch, Wilhelm. 'Das Rechnungswesen der österreichischen Städte im ausgehenden Mittelalter under besonderer Berücksichtigung der Städten in den österreichischen Stammlanden Nieder- und Oberösterreich'. *FC*, 180–204.

Rausch, Wilhelm (ed.). *Stadt und Stadtherr im 14. Jahrhundert. Entwicklungen und Funktionen.* Linz: Osterreichischer Arbeitskreis für Stadtgeschichtsforschung, 1972.

Raveggi, Sergio. 'Gli aristocratici in città: considerazioni sul caso di Firenze'. *SMOE*, 69–86.

Reinecke, Heinrich. 'Bevölkerungsprobleme der Hansestädte'. In Haase, *Stadt des Mittelalters* 3: 256–302.

Renkhoff, Otto. *Wiesbaden im Mittelalter*. Wiesbaden: Franz Steiner, 1980.

Renouard, Yves (ed.). *Bordeaux sous les rois d'Angleterre*. Bordeaux: Fédération historique du Sud-Ouest, 1965.

Reyerson, Kathryn L. 'The adolescent apprentice/worker in medieval Montpellier'. *Journal of Family History* 17 (1992): 353–70.

Reyerson, Kathryn L. *Business, Banking and Finance in Medieval Montpellier*. Toronto: Pontifical Institute of Medieval Studies, 1985.

Reyerson, Kathryn L. 'Public vs. private space in medieval Montpellier: the Bonami *Platea* in the first half of the fourteenth century'. Paper read at meeting of American Historical Association, 28 December 1992 and cited here with the author's permission.

Reyerson, Kathryn L. 'Women in business in medieval Montpellier'. In Hanawalt, *Women and Work*, 117–44.

Reynolds, Susan. *An Introduction to the History of English Medieval Towns*. Oxford: Clarendon Press, 1977.

Ridder-Symoens, Hilde de. 'Le sécularisation de l'enseignement aux anciens Pays-Bas au Moyen Age et à la Renaissance'. *PTME*, 721–37.

Riesenberg, Peter. *Citizenship in the Western Tradition. Plato to Rousseau*. Chapel Hill, N. C.: University of North Carolina Press, 1992.

Rigby, Stephen. 'Urban "oligarchy" in late medieval England'. *TT*, 62–86.

Robertson, D. W., Jr. *Chaucer's London*. New York: John Wiley & Sons, 1968.

Robertson, Joseph R., Jr. *The English Administration of Gascony, 1372–1390*. Ph.D. Dissertation, Emory University, 1963. University Microfilms, Ann Arbor.

Rogers, J. M. 'Samarra. A study in medieval town-planning'. *IC*, 119–55.

Rogozinski, Jan. *Power, Caste, and Law. Social Conflict in Fourteenth-Century Montpellier*. Cambridge, Mass.: Medieval Academy of America, 1982.

Romano, Dennis. *Patricians and Popolani. The Social Foundations of the Venetian Renaissance State*. Baltimore: The Johns Hopkins University Press, 1987.

Rösener, Werner. 'Aspekte der Stadt-Land-Beziehungen in spät-mittelalterlichen Deutschland'. *PTME*, 663–80.

Rosser, Gervase. 'London and Westminster: the suburb in the urban economy in the later Middle Ages'. *TT*, 45–61.

Rosser, Gervase. *Medieval Westminster, 1200–1540*. Oxford: Clarendon Press, 1989.

Rosser, Gervase. 'The essence of medieval urban communities: the Vill of Westminster, 1200–1540'. *Transactions of the Royal Historical Society*, ser. 5, vol. 34 (1984): 91–112.

Rossiaud, Jacques. 'Crises et consolidations'. *HFU* 2: 407–613.

Rossiaud, Jacques. *Medieval Prostitution*. Oxford: Basil Blackwell, 1988.

Rotz, Rhiman A. 'Investigating urban uprisings with examples from hanseatic towns, 1374–1416'. *Strayer FS*, 215–33.

Roux, Simone. 'Le coût du logement ordinaire à Paris au XV siècle'. *SMOE*, 243–63.

Rowe, Margery M., and John M. Draisey (eds). *The Receivers' Accounts of the City of Exeter 1304–1353*. Exeter: Devon and Cornwall Record Society, 1989. Publications no. 32.

Rubin, Miri. *Charity and Community in Medieval Cambridge*. Cambridge: Cambridge University Press, 1987.

Rubinstein, Nicolai (ed.). *Florentine Studies. Politics and Society in Renaissance Florence*. Evanston: Northwestern University Press, 1968.

Rubinstein, Nicolai. *The Government of Florence Under the Medici (1434 to 1494)*. Oxford: Clarendon Press, 1966.

Ruggiero, Guido. *Violence in Early Renaissance Venice*. New Brunswick, N. J.: Rutgers University Press, 1980.

Ruiz, Teofilo F. *The City and The Realm: Burgos and Castile 1080–1492*. Aldershot: Variorum Reprints, 1992.

Russell, Josiah Cox. *Medieval Regions and Their Cities*. Bloomington, Ind.: Indiana University Press, 1972.

Sachar, Abram Leon. *A History of the Jews*. 5th ed. New York: Knopf, 1974.

Sachs, David Harris. 'Celebrating authority in Bristol, 1475–1640'. In Zimmerman and Weissman, *Urban Life in the Renaissance*, 187–223.

Salmen, Walter. 'Vom Musizieren in der spätmittelalterlichen Stadt'. *LS*, 77–87.

Salter, H. E. *Medieval Oxford*. Oxford: Clarendon Press, 1936. Publications of the Oxford Historical Society, no. 100.

Scarlata, Marina. 'Caratterizzazione dei quartieri e rapporti di vicinato a Palermo fra XIIIe e XV secolo'. *SMOE*, 681–709.

Schevill, Ferdinand. *Medieval and Renaissance Florence*. 2 vols. Revised ed. New York: Harper and Row, 1963.

Schich, Winfried. 'Slavic proto-towns and the German colonial town in Brandenburg'. *CHUO*, 531–45.

Schmidt, Heinrich. 'Uber Geschichtsschreibung in norddeutschen Städten des späten Mittelalters und der Reformationszeit'. In *Stadt im Wandel* 3: 627–42.

Schmugge, Ludwig. 'Zu den Anfängen des organisierten Pilgerverkehrs und zur Unterbringung und Verpflegung von Pilgern im Mittelalter'. *GTG*, 37–60.

Schneider, Jean. *La ville de Metz aux XIIIe et XIVe siècles*. Nancy: Georges Thomas, 1950.

Schofield, John. *The Building of London from the Conquest to the Great Fire*. London: A Colonnade Book published by British Museum Publications Ltd in association with the Museum of London, 1984.

Schofield, John. *Medieval London Houses*. New Haven and London: Yale University Press, 1994.

Schofield, John, and Roger Leech (eds). *Urban Archaeology in Britain*. Research Report 61. London: Council for British Archaeology, 1987.

Schofield, John, and Alan Vince (eds). *Medieval Towns*. Madison: Fairleigh Dickinson University Press, 1994.

Schuler, Peter-Johannes. 'Goslar – zur Bevölkerungsgrösse einer mittelalterlichen Reichsstadt'. In *Stadt im Wandel*, 3: 443–55.

Schultheiss, Werner (ed.). *Satzungsbücher und Satzungen der Reichsstadt Nürnberg aus dem 14. Jahrhundert*. Nürnberg: Selbstverlag des Stadtrats, 1965. Quellen zur Geschichte und Kultur der Stadt Nürnberg, 3.

Schulz, Knut. *Handwerksgesellen und Lohnarbeiter. Untersuchungen zur oberrheinischen und oberdeutschen Stadtgeschichte des 14. bis 17. Jahrhunderts*. Sigmaringen: Jan Thorbecke, 1985.

Schulz, Juergen. 'Urbanism in medieval Venice'. In Molho *et al.*, *City States*, 419–45.

Schwarz, Brigide. 'Stadt und Kirche im Spätmittelalter'. In *Stadt im Wandel* 4: 53–73.

Schwineköper, Berent. 'Die Anfänge Magdeburgs'. *SAES*, 389–450.

Shahar, Shulamith. *Childhood in the Middle Ages*. London: Routledge, 1990.

Shahar, Shulamith. *The Fourth Estate. A History of Women in the Middle Ages*. London: Methuen, 1983.

Shaw, David Gary. *The Creation of a Community: The City of Wells in the Middle Ages*. Oxford: Clarendon Press, 1993.

Simmons, Jack. *Leicester, Past and Present. 1: Ancient Borough to 1860*. London: Eyre Methuen, 1974.

Sjoberg, Gideon. *The Preindustrial City. Past and Present*. New York: Free Press, 1960.

Sortor, Marci. 'Saint-Omer and its textile trades in the late Middle

Ages: a contribution to the proto-industrialization debate'. *AHR* 98 (1993): 1475–99.

Sosson, J.-P. 'Finances communales et dette publique. Le cas de Bruges à la fin du XIIIe siècle'. *PTME*, 239–57.

Sosson, J.-P. 'Die Körperschaften in den Niederländen und Nordfrankreich: neue Forschungsperspektiven'. In Friedland, *Gilde*, 79–90.

Sosson, J.-P. 'La Structure sociale de la corporation médiévale. L'exemple des tonneliers de Bruges de 1350 à 1500'. *RBPH* 44 (1966): 457–78.

Sosson, J.-P. *Les Travaux publics de la ville de Bruges, XIVe–XVe siècles. Les matériaux. Les hommes.* Brussels: Crédit Communal de Belgique, 1977. Coll. Pro Civitate, ser. in 8°, no. 48.

Sprandel, Rolf. 'Der handwerkliche Familienbetrieb des Spätmittelalters und seine Probleme'. In Haverkamp, *Haus und Familie*, 327–37.

Sprandel, Rolf (ed.). *Quellen zur Hanse-Geschichte.* Darmstadt: Wissenschaftliche Buchgesellschaft, 1982.

Stever, Heiko. 'Urban archaeology in Germany and the study of topographic, functional and social structures'. In Genecke and Shaw, *Urban Historical Geography*, 81–92.

Stoob, Heinz, Friedrich Bernhard Fahlbusch and Wolfgang Hölscher (eds.), *Urkunden zur Geschichte des Städtewesens in Mittel- und Niederdeutschland bis 1350.* Städteforschung, Reihe C: Quellen, vol. 1. Cologne and Vienna: Böhlau, 1985.

Störmer, Wilhelm. 'Stadt und Stadtherr im wittelsbachischen Altbayern des 14. Jahrhunderts'. In Rausch, *Stadt und Stadtherr*, 257–73.

Stouff, Louis. *Arles à la fin du Moyen-Age.* 2 vols. Aix-en-Provence: Université de Provence, 1986.

Stouff, Louis. 'Arles à la fin du Moyen Age: Paysage urbain et géographie sociale'. *PU*, 225–51.

Stow, Kenneth R. *Alienated Minority. The Jews of Medieval Latin Europe.* Cambridge, Mass.: Harvard University Press, 1992.

Strobel, Richard. 'Regensburg als Bischofstadt in bauhistorischer und topographischer Sicht'. In Petri, *Bischofs- und Kathedralstädte*, 60–83.

Stuard, Susan M. 'To town to serve: urban domestic slavery in medieval Ragusa'. In Hanawalt, *Women and Work*, 39–55.

Swanson, Heather. 'Artisans in the urban economy: the documentary evidence from York'. In Corfield and Keene, *Work in Towns*, 17–41.

Swanson, Heather. *Medieval Artisans. An Urban Class in Late Medieval England.* Oxford: Basil Blackwell, 1989.

Sydow, Jürgen. *Geschichte der Stadt Tübingen. I. Teil. Von den Anfängen bis zum Übergang an Württemberg 1342.* Tübingen: H. Laupp, 1974.

Sydow, Jürgen. 'Tübingen und seine Stadtherren als Beispiel der Entwicklung einer süddeutschen Territorialstadt'. In Rausch, *Stadt und Stadtherr*, 283–300.

Sydow, Jürgen. 'Zur verfassungsgeschichtlichen Stellung von Reichsstadt, freier Stadt und Territorialstadt im 13. und 14. Jahrhundert'. In *Les Libertés Urbaines et Rurales du XIe au XIVe siècle. Vrijheden in de Stad en op het Platteland van de XIe tot de XIVe eeuw*. Brussels: Pro Civitate, 1968, 281–309.

Szabo, Thomas. 'Xenodochia, Hospitäler und Herbergen – kirchliche und kommerziele Gastung im mittelalterlichen Italien (7. bis 14. Jahrhundert)'. *GTG*, 61–92.

Sznura, Franek. *L'Espansione urbana di Firenze nel Dugento*. Florence: La Nuova Italia, 1975.

Tabacco, Giovanni. *The Struggle for Power in Medieval Italy. Structures of Political Rule*. Translated by Rosalind Brown Jensen. Cambridge: Cambridge University Press, 1989.

Tait, James. *The Medieval English Borough. Studies on its Origins and Constitutional History*. Manchester: Manchester University Press, 1936.

Terlau, Karoline, and Fred Kaspar. 'Städtische Bauen im Spannungsfeld zwischen Bautechnik, Baugesetzen und Parzellenschnitt. Zur Frühzeit des Wohnhauses in Norddeutschland'. In *Stadt im Wandel* 3: 469–511.

Thompson, Guy Llewelyn. *Paris and Its People Under English Rule. The Anglo-Burgundian Regime, 1420–1436*. Oxford: Clarendon Press, 1991.

Thomson, John A. F. (ed.). *Towns and Townspeople in the Fifteenth Century*. Gloucester: Alan Sutton, 1988.

Thrupp, Sylvia L. 'Aliens in and around London in the fifteenth century'. In Hollaender and Kellaway, *Studies in London History*, 249–72.

Thrupp, Sylvia L. 'The gilds'. In *The Cambridge Economic History of Europe*, 3 (Cambridge, 1963), 230–80.

Thrupp, Sylvia L. *The Merchant Class of Medieval London*. Ann Arbor: University of Michigan Press, 1948.

Tillott, P. M. (ed.). *A History of Yorkshire. The City of York*. London: Institute of Historical Research by Oxford University Press, 1961. Victoria History of the Counties of England.

Tittler, Robert. *Architecture and Power. The Town Hall and the English Urban Community, c. 1500–1640*. Oxford: Clarendon Press, 1991.

Tittler, Robert. 'Late medieval urban prosperity'. *EcHR* n.s. 37 (1984): 551–4.

Töpfer, Bernhard (ed.). *Städte und Ständestaat. Zur Rolle der Städte bei der Entwicklung der Ständesverfassung in europäischen Staaten vom 13. bis zum 15. Jahrhundert*. Berlin: Akademie Verlag, 1980.

Trautz, Fritz. 'Zum Problem von Versorgung und Verbrauch privater Haushalte im Spätmittelalter'. In Haverkamp, *Haus und Familie*, 257–88.

Trenard, Louis (ed.). *Histoire de Lille*. 1: *Des origines à l'avènement de Charles-Quint*. Lille: Publications de la Faculté des Lettres et Sciences Humaines de Lille, 1991.

Trexler, Richard C. 'Florentine prostitution in the fifteenth century: patrons and clients'. In Trexler, *Dependence in Context in Renaissance Florence*. Binghamton, N. Y.: Center for Medieval and Early Renaissance Studies, 1994, 373–414.

Trio, Paul. *De Gentse Broederschappen (1182–1580). Ontstaan, naamgeving, materiële uitrusting, structuur, opheffing en bronnen*. Ghent: Maatschappij voor Geschiedenis en Oudheidkunde te Gent, 1990.

Trio, Paul. *Volksreligie als spiegel van een stedelijke samenleving. De Broederschappen te Gent in de late Middeleeuwen*. Louvain: Universitaire Pers Leuven, 1993.

Turner, Hilary L. *Town Defences in England and Wales. An Architectural and Documentary Study, AD 900–1500*. Hamden, Conn.: Archon Books, 1971.

Uitz, Erika. 'Der Kampf um kommunale Autonomie in Magdeburg bis zur Stadtverfassung von 1330'. *SS*, 228–323.

Uitz, Erika. *Women in the Medieval Town*. London: Barrie and Jenkins, 1990.

Untersuchungen zur gesellschaftlichen Struktur der mittelalterlichen Städte in Europa. Reichenau-Vorträge 1963–1964. Vorträge und Forschungen herausgegeben vom Konstanzer Arbeitskreis für mittelalterliche Geschichte, 11. Constance and Stuttgart: Jan Thorbecke, 1966.

Uytven, R. van. 'Stadsgeschiedenis in het Noorden en Zuiden'. *AGN* 2: 188–253.

Uytven, R. van. 'Stages of economic decline: late medieval Bruges'. *PTME*, 259–69.

Vale, Juliet. *Edward III and Chivalry. Chivalric Society and Its Context 1270–1350*. Woodbridge: Boydell Press, 1982.

Valous, Guy de. *Le patriciat Lyonnais aux XIIIe et XIVe siècles*. Paris: A. and J. Picard, 1973.

Vance, James E., Jr. *The Continuing City. Urban Morphology in Western Civilization*. Baltimore: The Johns Hopkins University Press, 1990.

Veale, Elspeth M. 'Craftsmen and the economy of London in the fourteenth century'. In Hollaender and Kellaway, *Studies in London History*, 131–51.

Veale, Elspeth M. 'Matilda Penne, Skinner (d. 1392/3)'. In Barron and Sutton, *Medieval London Widows*, 47–54.

Vercauteren, Fernand. *Luttes sociales à Liège (XIIIe et XIVe siècles)*. 2nd ed. Brussels: La Renaissance du Livre, 1946.

Vicens Vivas, Jaime. *An Economic History of Spain*. Princeton: Princeton University Press, 1969.

Villani, Giovanni. *Chronicle. Being Selections from the First Nine Books of the Croniche Fiorentine of Giovanni Villani*. Translated by Rose E. Selfe and edited by Philip H. Wicksteed. London: Archibald Constable & Co., 1906.

Vogt, Emil, Ernst Meyer, and Hans Conrad Peyer. *Zürich von der Urzeit zum Mittelalter*. Zürich: Berichthaus, 1971.

Vollenhoven, Adriaan van. *Ambachten en neringen in Dordrecht*. The Hague: M. Nijhoff, 1923.

Volpe, Gioacchino. *Medio Evo Italiano*. 3rd ed. Rome: Editori Laterza, 1992.

Waley, Daniel. *Mediaeval Orvieto. The Political History of an Italian City-State, 1157–1334*. Cambridge: Cambridge University Press, 1952.

Waley, Daniel. *Siena and the Sienese in the Thirteenth Century*. Cambridge: Cambridge University Press, 1991.

Weber, Max. *The City*. Translated and edited by Don Martindale and Gertrud Neuwirth. New York: Free Press, 1958.

Wee, Herman van der. 'Structural changes and specialization in southern Netherlands industry, 1100–1600'. *EcHR*, ser. 2, 28 (1975): 201–22.

Wee, Herman van der (ed.). *The Rise and Decline of Urban Industries in Italy and in the Low Countries (Late Middle Ages–Early Modern Times)*. Leuven: Leuven University Press, 1988.

Wensky, Margret. 'Die Osnabrücker Gilden im Spätmittelalter'. In Meckseper, *Stadt im Wandel* 3: 371–83.

Wensky, Margret. 'Die Stellung der Frau in Familie, Haushaut und Wirtschaftsbetrieb im spätmittelalterlich-frühneuzeitlichen Köln'. In Haverkamp, *Haus und Familie*, 289–303.

Wensky, Margret. 'Women's guilds in Cologne in the later Middle Ages'. *Journal of European Economic History* 11 (1982): 631–50.

Werveke, Hans van. *De Gentse Stadsfinanciën in de Middeleeuwen*. Brussels: Paleis der Academiën, 1934.

Werveke, Hans van. 'The rise of the towns'. In *The Cambridge Economic History of Europe*, III. Cambridge: Cambridge University Press, 1965, 3–41.

Williams, Gwyn A. *Medieval London. From Commune to Capital*. Second ed. London: Athlone Press, 1970.

Win, Paul de. 'The lesser nobility of the Burgundian Netherlands'. In Michael Jones (ed.), *Gentry and Lesser Nobility in Late Medieval Europe*. New York: St. Martin's Press, 1986, 95–118.

Bibliography

Wolff, Philippe (ed.). *Histoire de Toulouse*. Toulouse: Privat, 1974.

Wolff, Philippe. 'Structures sociales et morphologies urbaines dans le développement historique des villes (XIIe–XVIIIe siècles)'. *Cahiers Bruxellois* 22 (1977): 5–72.

Wriedt, Klaus. 'Amtsträger in norddeutschen Städten des Spätmittelalters'. In Bulst and Genet, *Medieval Lives*, 227–34.

Wriedt, Klaus. 'Schulen und bürgerliches Bildungswesen in Norddeutschland im Spätmittelalter'. *SB*, 152–72.

Wriedt, Klaus. 'Stadtrat-Bürgertum-Universität am Beispiel norddeutscher Hansestädte'. *SB*, 499–523.

Wroe, Ann. *A Fool and His Money: Life in a Partitioned Medieval Town*. London: Jonathan Cape, 1995.

Wyffels, Carlos. 'Hanse, grands marchands et patriciens de Saint-Omer'. *Société Académique des Antiquaires de la Morinie. Mémoires* 38 (1962). Separately paginated.

Zimmerman, Susan, and Ronald F. E. Weissman (eds). *Urban Life in the Renaissance*. Newark, Del.: University of Delaware Press, 1989.

Zupko, Ronald E., and Robert A. Laures, *Straws in the Wind. Medieval Urban Environmental Law. The Case of Northern Italy*. Boulder, Colorado: Westview Press, 1996.

Map 1   Italy

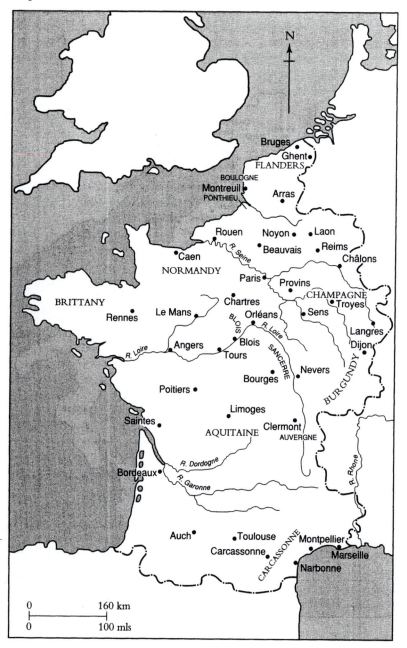

Map 2   France

Map 3   Germany

Map 4   England

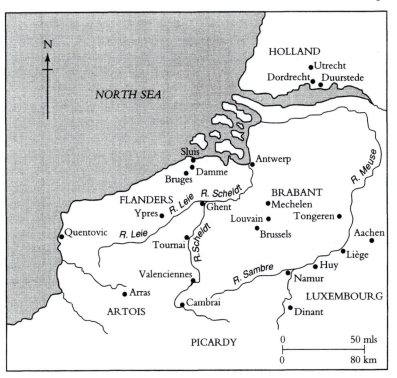

Map 5   Flanders and the Low Countries

City Plans

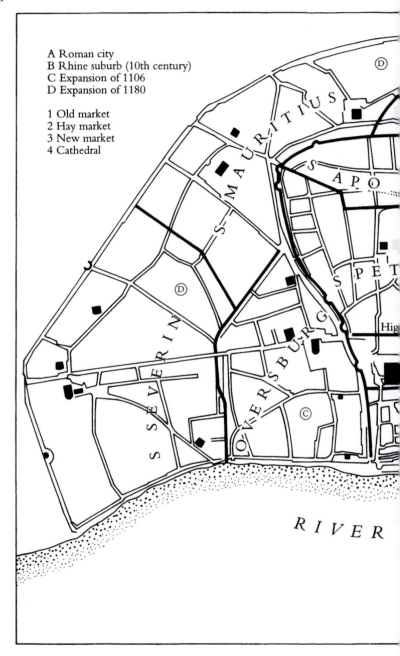

A Roman city
B Rhine suburb (10th century)
C Expansion of 1106
D Expansion of 1180

1 Old market
2 Hay market
3 New market
4 Cathedral

Plan 1 Cologne

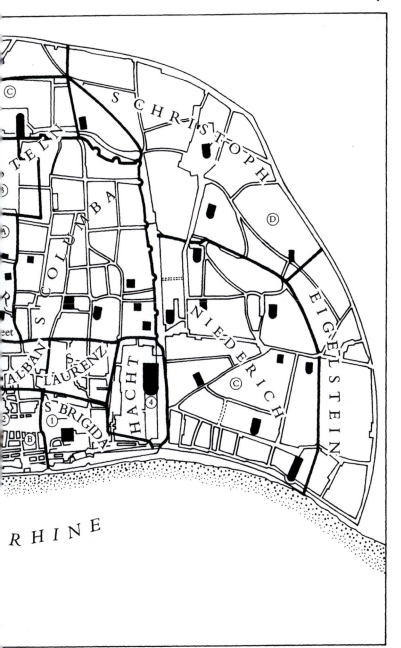

City Plans

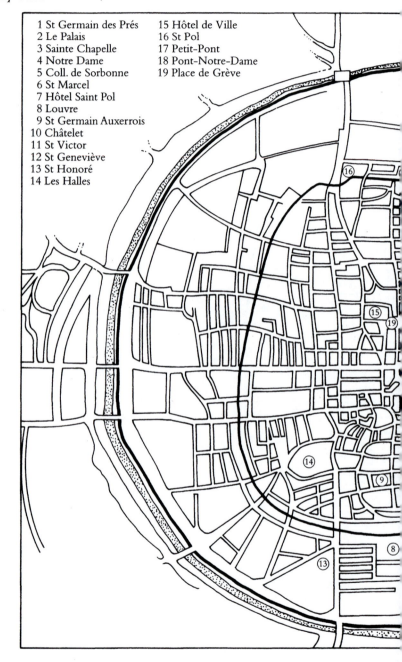

1 St Germain des Prés
2 Le Palais
3 Sainte Chapelle
4 Notre Dame
5 Coll. de Sorbonne
6 St Marcel
7 Hôtel Saint Pol
8 Louvre
9 St Germain Auxerrois
10 Châtelet
11 St Victor
12 St Geneviève
13 St Honoré
14 Les Halles

15 Hôtel de Ville
16 St Pol
17 Petit-Pont
18 Pont-Notre-Dame
19 Place de Grève

Plan 2   Paris

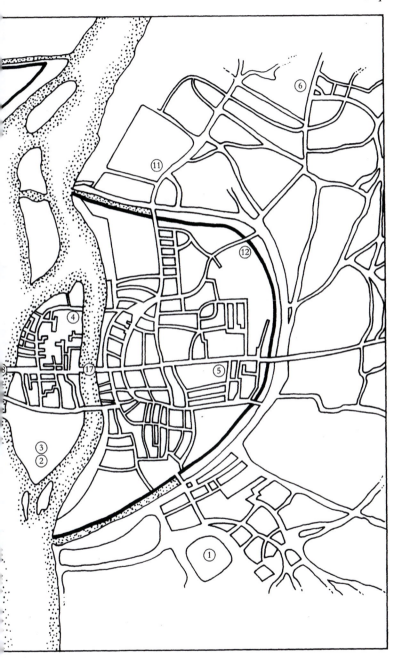

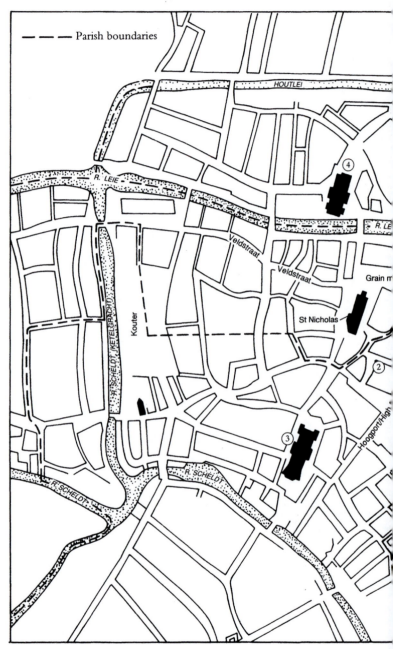

Plan 3   Ghent

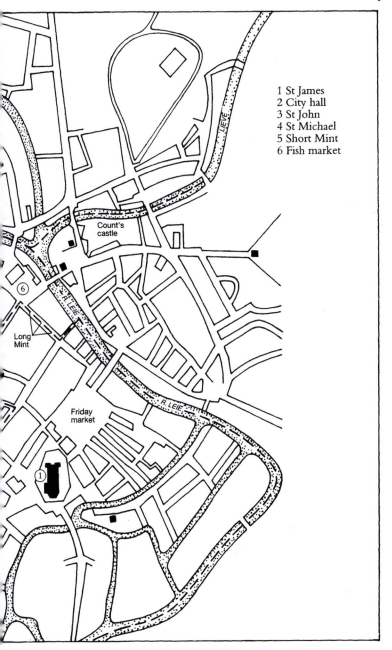

1 St James
2 City hall
3 St John
4 St Michael
5 Short Mint
6 Fish market

Count's castle

Long Mint

Friday market

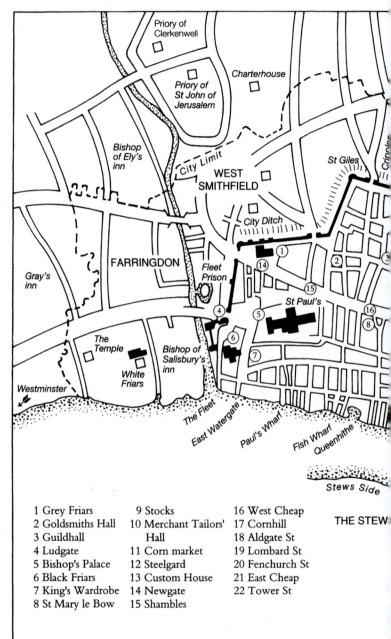

1 Grey Friars
2 Goldsmiths Hall
3 Guildhall
4 Ludgate
5 Bishop's Palace
6 Black Friars
7 King's Wardrobe
8 St Mary le Bow
9 Stocks
10 Merchant Tailors' Hall
11 Corn market
12 Steelgard
13 Custom House
14 Newgate
15 Shambles
16 West Cheap
17 Cornhill
18 Aldgate St
19 Lombard St
20 Fenchurch St
21 East Cheap
22 Tower St

Plan 4   London

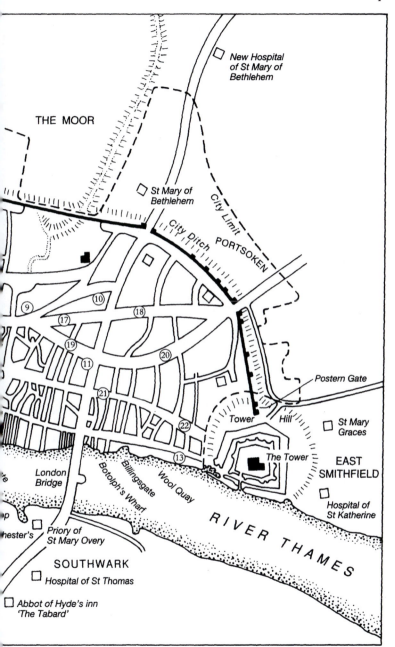

THE MOOR

New Hospital
of St Mary of
Bethlehem

St Mary of
Bethlehem

City Ditch

City Limit

PORTSOKEN

9

10

17

18

19

11

20

21

22

Postern Gate

Tower Hill

St Mary
Graces

13

EAST
SMITHFIELD

The Tower

London
Bridge

Billingsgate

Botolph's Wharf

Wool Quay

Hospital of
St Katherine

RIVER THAMES

hester's

Priory of
St Mary Overy

SOUTHWARK

Hospital of St Thomas

Abbot of Hyde's inn
'The Tabard'

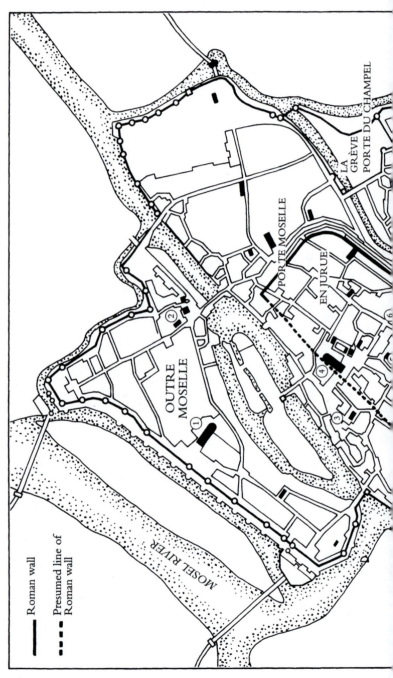

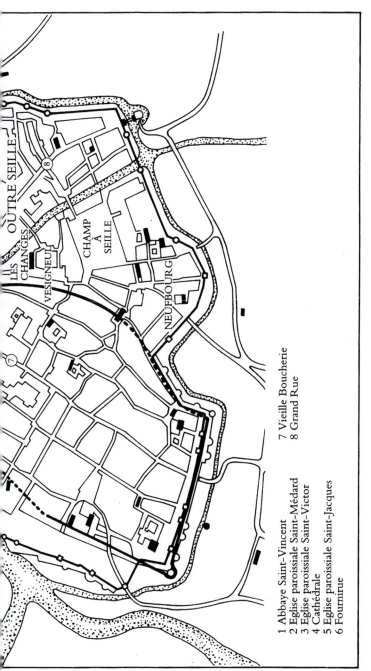

1 Abbaye Saint-Vincent
2 Eglise paroissiale Saint-Médard
3 Eglise paroissiale Saint-Victor
4 Cathédrale
5 Eglise paroissiale Saint-Jacques
6 Fournirue

7 Vieille Boucherie
8 Grand Rue

Plan 5   Metz

413

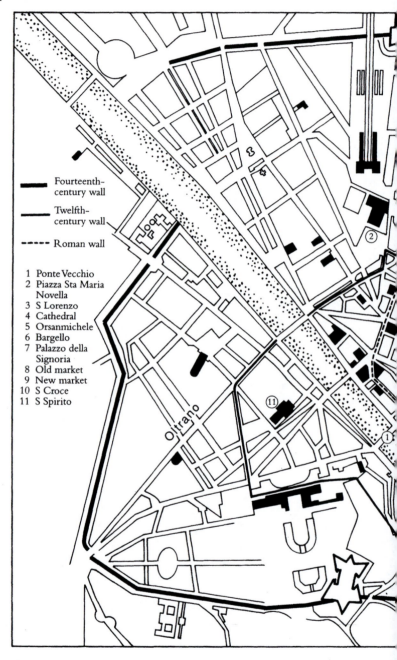

Plan 6   Florence

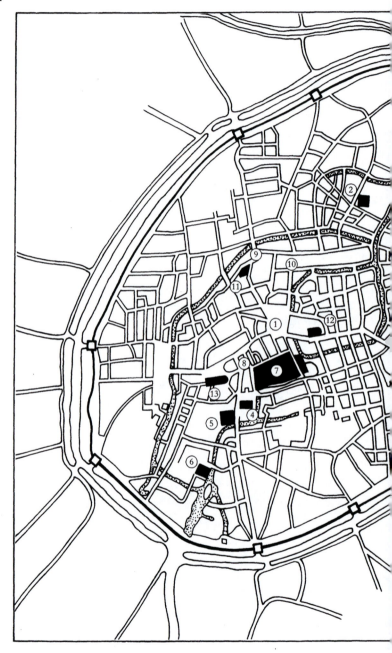

Plan 7   Bruges

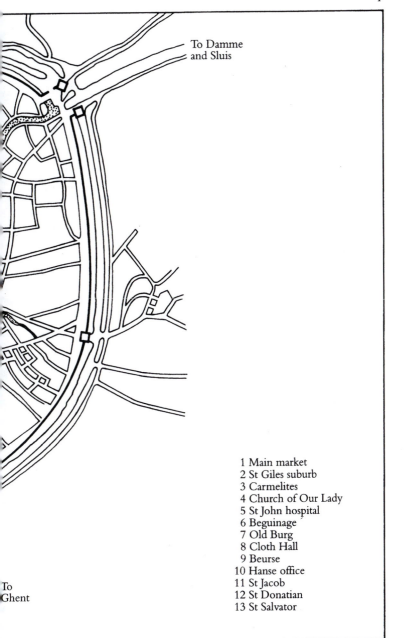

To Damme
and Sluis

To
Ghent

1 Main market
2 St Giles suburb
3 Carmelites
4 Church of Our Lady
5 St John hospital
6 Beguinage
7 Old Burg
8 Cloth Hall
9 Beurse
10 Hanse office
11 St Jacob
12 St Donatian
13 St Salvator

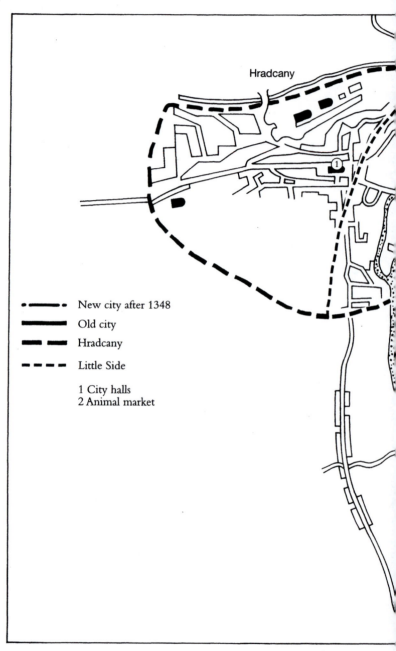

Plan 8 Prague

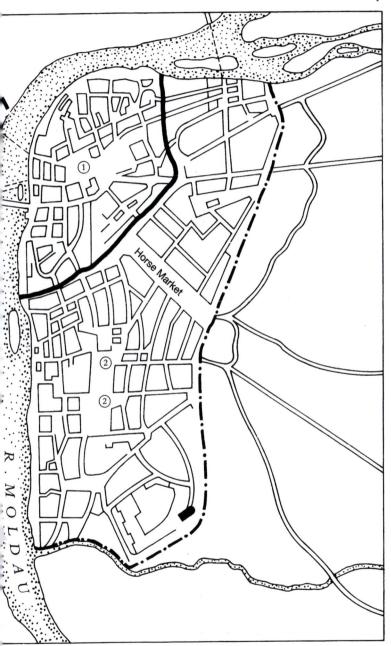

Plan 9   Nuremberg

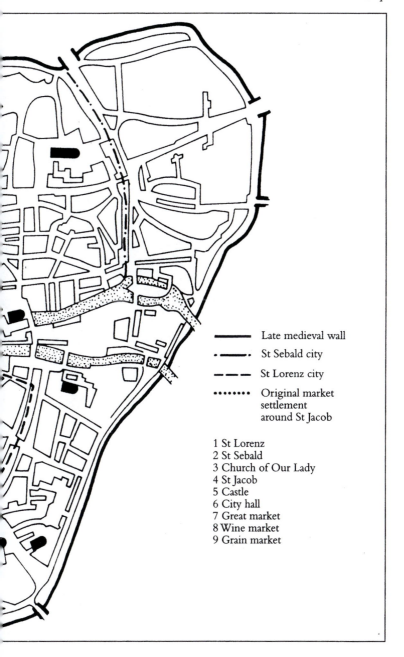

Late medieval wall

—·—·— St Sebald city

— — — St Lorenz city

•••••••• Original market
settlement
around St Jacob

1 St Lorenz
2 St Sebald
3 Church of Our Lady
4 St Jacob
5 Castle
6 City hall
7 Great market
8 Wine market
9 Grain market

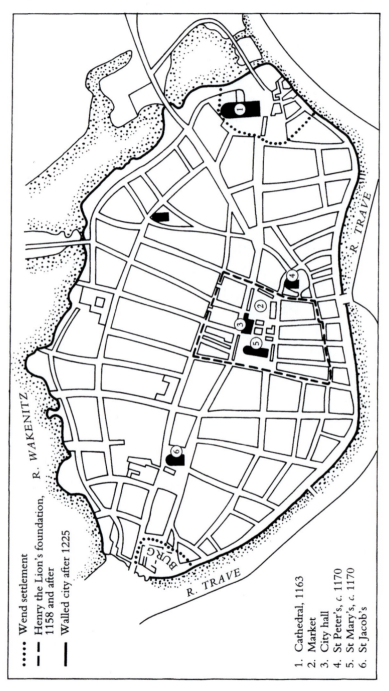

City Plans

Wend settlement

Henry the Lion's foundation, 1158 and after

Walled city after 1225

R. WAKENITZ

R. TRAVE

R. TRAVE

BURG

1. Cathedral, 1163
2. Market
3. City hall
4. St Peter's, *c.* 1170
5. St Mary's, *c.* 1170
6. St Jacob's

Plan 10 Lübeck

Index

Index

Index

Index

Index